Trial of Pedro de Z

On a Charge of Slave Trading cap. 113, on Friday the 27th, Saturday the 28th, and Monday the 30th of October, 1843, at the Central Criminal Court, Old Bailey, London

A Full Report from the Short-hand Notes of W. B. Gurney, Esq.

William Brodie Gurney

Pedro de Zulueta

Alpha Editions

This edition published in 2024

ISBN : 9789362096906

Design and Setting By
Alpha Editions
www.alphaedis.com
Email - info@alphaedis.com

TO THE MERCHANTS, MANUFACTURERS, AND TRADERS OF GREAT BRITAIN.

The case, which will be laid before you in the following pages, must be admitted to be one of an unprecedented character.

A merchant, to all practical purposes a British merchant, the junior member of a firm of unquestioned respectability, in which his father and brother are active partners with himself, which has been established for upwards of seventy years in Spain, and of twenty in the City of London, during which period they have maintained, both as merchants and as individuals in private life, the character which will be found in the following pages to have been given them upon oath by several of the most eminent of their fellow-merchants—this individual finds himself suddenly arrested, in the manner hereafter described, within the precincts of his own private office, which is situated in the most conspicuous spot in the City of London, whilst in the pursuit of his ordinary business, upon a bench-warrant, as it is said (but which was never shown to, or has been since seen by him), a true bill having been found against him by the Grand Jury of the County of Middlesex. The charge will be found in the two indictments inserted in pages 211 and 214, the former for felony, under the Act of 5 Geo. IV, cap. 113, entitled "An Act to amend and consolidate the Laws relating to the Abolition of the Slave Trade;" the latter for conspiracy, to do that which the former indictment describes as done, *viz.* "manning," &c. &c., "and shipping certain goods on board a certain vessel, called the Augusta, for the purpose of dealing in slaves;" and the penalty, amounting, in fact, to a person in the rank and station of the accused and of his family, to a forfeiture of life, and those objects which are dearer than life itself. He is carried in custody to the police-station on Garlick Hill, where shortly afterwards, a London attorney, whose name he had never before heard, appears and prefers a charge of slave dealing. The prisoner is immediately conveyed to the Central Criminal Court, then sitting at the Old Bailey; there the two indictments are read to him *pro formâ*, for they leave him in utter ignorance of who the prosecutor is, or upon what depositions the Grand Jury had found the bill, although his defence, to be effectual, must be directed against them: they remain to this moment an undisclosed mystery, and no one is answerable for the accuracy of those statements, whilst who the prosecutor was, was only disclosed by the counsel for the prosecution at the trial, before the examination of the witnesses began.

The prisoner's application to the Central Criminal Court to be admitted to bail was strenuously opposed by the prosecuting attorney in person, when the Court, yielding to the representation of the probable result of the refusal upon the members of an honourable family thus violently taken by surprise and distracted, granted the application on terms indeed which the Court itself deemed excessive, but which were the only terms to which the attorney's consent could be obtained. It was found impossible, on account of the lateness of the hour, to meet with one of the two individuals who had been approved of by the attorney; and under these circumstances the Court consented to receive one security alone for 2,000*l.*, and the prisoner's own recognizance for 6,000*l.* Thus it happened, that he who had left his home, his wife, and his children in the morning, with as assured a conscience as any of you can do, returned about ten o'clock in the evening a prisoner, with the possibility of a sentence of transportation hanging over his head, as ignorant of his accuser, or of the facts deposed to against him, as if he had fallen into the hands of the Inquisition.

The whole transaction, embracing the purchase and dispatch of the vessel Augusta, named in the indictment, had formed part of the subject of an examination, for which the house of Zulueta & Co. tendered themselves in the person of Pedro de Zulueta, before a Select Committee appointed in March, 1842, by the House of Commons, to inquire into the State of the British Possessions on the West Coast of Africa, and which was sitting in July and August, 1842, and the Report of whose proceedings had then been nearly a year before the public. Before that Committee, among several other witnesses, two officers of the navy (whose names may be seen on the back of the indictments), who had been in command of British cruisers on the African coast, and another individual, who it seems has discharged the duties of a Judge at Sierra Leone, appeared and were examined. Their examinations were published in the Report, and from thence are inserted in the following pages; but it should be observed that the last-mentioned of these three individuals did not appear in the prosecution, his evidence being inserted here only from the anxiety that a complete case should be placed before you.

As it is in the power of every reader to verify the correctness of any observations that may be made upon the merits of the evidence given by these individuals before the Committee, it cannot be improper to call attention to the temper which evidently pervades it, not for the purpose of invective, but because it is a circumstance of very great practical application to the matter in hand. It is impossible not to be struck upon its perusal with the absolute recklessness of statement, both as to fact and theory. The most formidable conclusions are built upon the most slender foundations. Facts and theories are so mixed up together, that it is only after much sifting that it turns out that what was stated as fact was no more than a theory in the speaker's mind; and these theories, too, embracing all questions, whether of commerce, of fiscal science, policy, legislation, international law, education, morals, and religion: after which, the character of individuals, or that of a commercial house, is no doubt a matter about which much circumspection cannot be expected to be exercised. The fate of Africa, the immense interests of British commerce, of the commerce of the world; the interpretation of existing laws, under which property, life, honour, may be forfeited; their modification and adjustment; public opinion with its powerful influence, so dangerous when misled, so difficult to be set right; all these awfully important matters seem to hang upon the lips of those two officers of the navy—and they do not seem to feel any hesitation in disposing of such momentous interests. Can it be expected that they would stop and consider before they make a statement regarding private individuals, even though they may happen to be, to say the least of it, accounted by the first men of this city, and in others of the first cities of the world, honourable by birth, profession, and personal character? The crime of which they would be guilty, were mere assertion to be taken as positive proof, is according to the witnesses so heinous, that it exceeds in their estimation almost every other, not only in the law of man, but in the law of God; and yet it is to be imputed upon their construction of some rumours which they themselves, it is quite possible, indeed very probable, may quite unconsciously have helped to mould into a shape by their readiness to accumulate this miscalled evidence. Whether this representation of the general character of the evidence given before the Committee by these individuals is, or is not, correct, may be seen at once by a reference to it in the following pages.

The first information, which any of the members of the house of Zulueta & Co. had of even the existence of the Committee, was the receipt of a letter (see p. 1) accompanying a copy of a lengthy Report, by a Dr. Madden, on the Coast of Africa, which called forth a reply (see p. 5) addressed by Zulueta & Co. to the Chairman of the Committee—a reply, which, in truth, contains the whole of their case, and to which they may well look back with just pride, since the keenest appetite for the discovery of guilt has not been able to detect one single circumstance contradictory of one tittle of its contents. Neither the examination before the Committee in 1842, nor the trial in 1843, circumstances which could not be foreseen or anticipated, have elicited one single fact at variance with the statements of that letter, impossible as it was to have contemplated at the time it was written, that its accuracy would be subject to so severe a test as either the examination before the Committee, which took place two months afterwards, or the trial, which did not occur till after the lapse of more than a year.

After that letter was sent, it became known to the house of Zulueta & Co. that further statements, unfavourable to their character as merchants, had been made before the Committee; and in consequence of a verbal representation of the unfairness of such mode of accusation, copies of the examinations of two of the witnesses were sent to them. The individual who now addresses you, then offered himself, at the request of his partners, to be examined, the selection of himself being made for no other reason than that he was thought more capable of making himself understood.

It was thus therefore that I, Pedro de Zulueta the younger, appeared before the Committee, and, as will be seen by the minutes of my evidence, entered into an examination of every statement which was brought before me as having been made by the witnesses concerning my house, contradicted several of them, explained others, and volunteered a description of the nature of the dealings of my firm with the two others (whose names had been flung at us) from the time of the establishment of Zulueta & Co. in London, twenty years ago. I also underwent a cross-examination, of which one very remarkable feature was, that Captain Denman himself, one of the witnesses against me both at this examination and at the trial, was sitting close to several members of the Committee, and was seen by me to whisper repeatedly into the ear of more than one member, what, it is not unnatural to suppose, may have been directions for the more effectual discovery of the truth.

I can hardly restrain the expression of my feelings when I consider now the use which has been made of the unreserved frankness, the unguarded, because unsuspecting, candour of the statements made by me before that Committee. The thought never occurred to me, that evidence, professedly taken for the benefit of the public service, required any thing more than substantive truth, and a general bearing upon the points in question; nor could I ever have conceived that it would be scanned with critical severity, in order to take advantage to my detriment of the worst construction that might be put upon this or that verbal slip, so as to place my very existence at stake upon it. I considered myself as doing nothing more than (whilst attempting to eradicate from the minds of the Committee any unfavourable impression, which might have been made upon them by incorrect statements against the character of my house) affording information for placing the legislation on the subjects before the consideration of the Committee on a more satisfactory basis—not by indulging in assertion of crude theories, or in vague declamations, but by the simple statement of a practical case—anxious to show in the instance of my house the situation in which a firm of acknowledged honour and respectability, whose private character, and the prominent political position of one of its members in another country, renders them at least very unlikely abettors of the slave trade—may yet be placed, because, living in England, they happen to have a mercantile intercourse with persons residing in places where this trade is unhappily one of the existing evils, and in which therefore those persons may be more or less implicated, inasmuch as it is well known that no trade whatever can be carried on with a country where the slave trade exists without its being, in some measure, of more or less direct assistance to this illicit traffic. And as the assertion which had been made against some of our correspondents tended, if true, to place this position of merchants in England in a very striking light, I did think that whilst the statements made *might* be true (and to disprove them could not be in my power nor in the power of any man in my situation) the proper and fair course was not to controvert the matter at all; but, taking the statements for granted, practically to direct the attention of the Committee to the position in which British merchants are left upon the very case itself, which was made out by the bitterest impugners of the character of British commerce.

I appeal to every man who reads my evidence before the Committee— without a previous determination to find out some one upon whom an experiment of the power of the Act of 5 Geo. IV may be tried, and a corroboration of the theory respecting the alleged existence of British slave trading—whether upon any other hypothesis, but that of conscious innocence or of consummate effrontery, my answers to the questions put by the Committee can be possibly reconciled with common sense or common prudence, much less be consistent with that deep skilfulness and far-seeing intelligence, which have been so lavishly attributed to me and to my partners for the purposes of my destruction.

Not for an instant, even when those outraged feelings, which have not been spared, possessed greatest sway over my mind, has the thought occurred to me, that at the time of my examination the object of any one member of the Committee, or even of Captain Denman himself (for I have alluded to the fact of his being present), could be the collecting materials for a secret accusation before a Grand Jury; and I wish very distinctly to protest against any such inference being drawn from my remarks, not for the sake of the members of the Committee, who are above being injured by insinuations, but for my own sake, who alone could be injured by the supposition. I am conscious of having appeared before several men whose names are, and have been ever since I can recollect having heard them, associated in my mind with nothing but what is honourable and high principled: I received from some of them complimentary expressions upon the apparent candour and openness, the straightforward character of the evidence given; and I cannot help believing that my statements were considered moreover valuable, as tending to show the inexpediency, the gross injustice, of encouraging on the one hand trade with countries in which slave trade prevails, and yet, on the other hand, attempting to make the natural and well-known tendency of all trade to mix itself with the general state of society of the country into which it is carried, the evidence of some peculiar criminal knowledge in the parties necessarily nearest in contact with those countries, and visiting that knowledge upon them, after the community have derived profit and advantage from the transaction, although it is well known that the parties so to be sacrificed have it not in their power to guard any but themselves from being directly instrumental to the deviation of the trade into channels rendered illegal by Act of Parliament. I venture to assert, that the prominent feature of my evidence was felt by the Committee to be its *unconnectedness* with any party or theory; and this feature stamped it with the character of truth which, if fairly and honestly stated, must at times militate against one theory or another.

This is an offence to all who thrive upon theories, and in exactly the proportion of their affected or unreasonable belief of them. An instinctive alarm takes possession of such minds, and as they themselves cannot conceive that other people may have no theory of their own to serve upon that particular subject, which to them, and therefore in their opinion to all, must be paramount, they are disposed to imagine one theory of their own, which they at once fix upon the party thus offending against the assumed mental necessity of universal theorism. If the writer is not much mistaken, the irritation which is produced by this process of the mind, still more if self-interest is at the bottom, will materially help to reveal the moving-spring of the proceedings which are recorded in the following pages.

Be this as it may, one thing is altogether unquestionable (and indeed there has been no attempt to disguise the fact, and to it I beg to call the attention of every man in Great Britain)—it is this: Pedro de Zulueta could never have been placed in the position in which he was (charged with felony under the finding of the Grand Jury), with the remotest chance of a conviction, if he had not voluntarily offered himself for examination before a Committee of the British House of Commons—the way being this—a London attorney lays hold of the printed Report of the proceedings; every part of the evidence given by Pedro de Zulueta, that was destructive of the hypothesis of his being a well-knowing and wilful abettor of an alleged slave trading speculation *in 1840*, is disconnected from those passages in which he had stated that, *in 1842, when he was speaking* (after hearing and reading a mass of evidence given for the first time before that Committee), he had heard statements about his correspondents being participators in the slave trade which might be true, which were not, he felt, material to himself, and which, as he had not the means of disproving, he *then* stated that he must *then* believe; and then using this intelligible admission, *made in 1842*, the only one that could be found at all available, as the only presumptive proof of *guilty knowledge in 1840*. Nothing could be done or attempted against the house of Zulueta & Co., much less against the individual who was attacked, without this management, this distortion of the evidence—for some knowledge of some kind must be made out *in* 1840, and although the fallacy was transparent, it might and unfortunately did serve for the purpose of the attack at the heart, and might still serve for the next, but not the sole object, of the prosecution. It is true, that the whole of the evidence given by me was read at the trial, for so the law requires it; but that same law, as was observed, also permits that those parts of a man's statements which make in his favour should not be believed or taken for any thing, whilst such admissions as might be made to appear criminatory of himself are received as evidence against him. By such a process of distortion alone could a case be made out against my house, or fixed upon myself, who was totally unknown to the so-called witnesses as they themselves admitted, and who did not personally appear in any part of the transactions excepting at my own examination before the Committee. If the facts are not so, let it be at once explained what other circumstance marked me out for prosecution. Let the reader of the following pages, after perusing the trial carefully, attempt to solve the problem for himself of how (apart from the fact of my appearing, and of the application which is made of my statements before the Committee of the House of Commons) the firm of Zulueta & Co. came to be prosecuted in my person to the exclusion of others. Let every other part of the evidence given before and at the trial, of matter of fact, by the witnesses on the transaction of the Augusta be considered, and where is one single fact that can connect Zulueta & Co. with the alleged, and only alleged, designs of the parties by whose orders they had acted in that transaction—an acting in itself admitted to be innocent? And if the reader does not find any other solution of the difficulty, it is clearly demonstrated that Pedro de Zulueta has been prosecuted upon partial statements from his own evidence, given before a Committee of the House of Commons, where he appeared voluntarily, where he was encouraged to explain transactions of business, and neither refused nor even hesitated to answer one single question that was put to him, as conducive to a great public object; but without the slightest intimation of the ulterior object to which it has been perverted.

For the purpose not certainly of clearing up the question, but of sophisticating a very plain case, it will perhaps be asked, whether, if a man should avow himself before a Committee of the House of Commons to have been guilty of a crime, or to have partaken in it, is it meant to be contended that his candour is to be the safeguard of his guilt? One short answer is, that the remark is inapplicable to the case; for no such avowal has been even contended to have been made, but on the contrary a distinct and repeated general and circumstantial disavowal was made. Whether my declarations did or did not amount to such degree of information in my mind, at the time of giving my evidence, as presumed a knowledge two years before, that would be brought under the description of the *guilty knowledge* described in legal phraseology, in an Act of Parliament, very obscure as is generally admitted, and never before put in practice, this was the utmost that the ingenuity of the prosecution could make out of my evidence—and this cannot be called an avowal of crime. The question is not, whether a crime avowed before a Committee of the House of Commons should or should not be prosecuted, using the avowal as one of the means of conviction—a question, which even so put is argued, I believe, on both sides by eminent lawyers—but whether in my case, such as it is, I have not a right to complain of the grossest and most unparalleled breach of good faith—whether the use made of my evidence is not one against which the conscience of every man revolts—whether it is likely to facilitate the public service, or to increase the respect due to the British Legislature at home and abroad, or to their proceedings—even if in other respects the course adopted is free from legal objections, which I believe is at least doubtful.

The fact itself is unquestionable, and I must repeatedly assert it—that the materials for my prosecution were collected from my own evidence as laid before the public, in the printed Report of the Committee, for whose information it was given—that in collecting these materials the statements, although formally read as they were made, were virtually vitiated—that, although the whole was read, only that part which was thought susceptible of some adverse construction was avowed to be of any necessary weight; and statements, such as they were, which had been *made in 1842*, after information that was at any rate only furnished in that year, were applied for the purpose of raising *a presumption of guilty knowledge in 1840*.

I have insisted so much upon this point, because it is very material that it should be borne in mind throughout the perusal of the following pages. I do not hesitate to believe that the unsophisticated sense of the people of this country will revolt at the fact of a Committee of the House of Commons having been turned into a trap wherein to take a man—a snare to his good faith—the more effectual, because the members who happen to compose the Committee stand high for honour and integrity in the land, and therefore their very names seemed to afford a guarantee that the fairest construction would be put upon the words of a respectable individual, who appeared voluntarily before them, without assuming from the outset that he is a self-convicted felon, who comes before them for no other purpose than to deceive, and who must be listened to only in order to see if he does not betray himself into some acknowledgment of his crimes, of which advantage is to be taken to secure the ends of justice, which he craftily endeavours to defeat. It may suit those who want such a monster of craft and subtlety in order to justify the monstrous proceedings, which have been deemed necessary to support a mischievous and unfounded theory that British capital is employed in the slave trade—it may suit them, to make me out to be this desideratum in their system; but, without laying claim to any more extended or more favourable notoriety than that which is on record, I venture to say that the attempt must fall to the ground, by the weight of its intrinsic absurdity, before the common sense of the people of this country.

But what the Committee thought of the evidence, after hearing at length the very individuals who appeared against me at the Old Bailey, and after hearing my own evidence, which formed the chief weapon against me in that Court, will be found in their own Report, printed in the following pages. Every reader may judge for himself, whether, in point of fact, it is not an anticipated condemnation of such proceedings as have been inflicted upon me—a verdict of not guilty, not only upon the transactions of the Augusta, but upon the whole of Zulueta & Co.'s agency for the houses mentioned, in my evidence, if the representation given by me of the transaction be substantially correct. In page 203 the following words will be found:—"In the first place, it is fair to state that we have no evidence, or reason to believe, that any British merchant, concerned in the trade with the West Coast of Africa, either owns or equips any vessel engaged in the slave trade, or has any share in the risk or profits of any slave trade venture"—a declaration this, the correctness of which every one conversant with the characteristic features of British commerce must acknowledge. Have any facts been elicited subsequent to this Report, and previously to the prosecution being instituted—any new evidence, which was not before the Committee of the House of Commons? This is a question which happily every reader of the following pages may settle for himself. Let him, as he peruses the evidence, at each stage of it ask himself the question—Was this before the Committee of the House of Commons? That it was, must be the answer upon every point. Not one statement was elicited from a single witness which had not been before the Committee. There was indeed an unworthy attempt to create a false impression about some casks and shackles having been left on board, even after the most unsparing of the witnesses for the prosecution had acquitted the vessel of even the shadow of a suspicion of containing the least implement available for a slaving equipment. How the attempt was foiled by their own witness afterwards will be seen; and I will not say a word more about an attempt upon which the very existence of a fellow-creature perhaps might hang, leaving it to be visited with the feeling of abhorrence which it must excite in every reader. Apart from this, there was before the Committee much more against me than there was before the Court, as may be seen by a comparison of the evidence as given before the one with that given before the other; because the nature of legal proceedings keeps the witness, even if otherwise disposed, within the limits of matter of fact—limits, which before the Court they did attempt to transgress, as may be seen very prominently in the case of the chief of them, but from which before the Committee it was in their power to wander, and they did accordingly so wander at every moment. Is it not fair to infer, that it was not to serve the purposes of justice, but at the very best that of some fancied expediency, that this prosecution was undertaken—a prosecution demonstrated to have been undertaken against the recorded sense and opinion of the Select Committee of the House of Commons? Suppose, for a moment, that by some quibble of law, by the forced interpretation of an Act of Parliament, admitted to be sufficiently obscure—not to speak of attempts to pervert evidence, or of the effort to carry off the victory, which constitutes the very essence of all legal conflict between individuals, and which of itself renders the right of private prosecution of public wrongs the destruction of civil liberty and of individual security—suppose, that by such means, what to the deliberate judgment of the Committee of the House of Commons did not appear to deserve even animadversion, might have been made out before an Old Bailey Jury to be such evidence of guilt, as to have procured an adverse verdict—is this the kind of justice which the people of this country would have approved? Impossible! I cannot believe it: the idea cannot be for a moment entertained.

But this is not all. We have seen what the Committee of the House of Commons decided. The Government—the proper, and the only proper agents, in a prosecution of this kind, upon whom, if sufficient ground existed, it was a bounden duty to have taken it in hand—seem to have treated the matter in the same manner as the Committee. All the documents which have been received in evidence, and some which were offered and were not received by the Court—that, in short, which forms all the evidence against the accused at the trial, and more, were in possession of Government before the last Administration went out (the proceedings before the Committee alone excepted)—that Administration did not take up the prosecution. The law-officers of the present Administration have had them also, and moreover the proceedings before the Committee, one of the members of which was a leading member of the preceding Government—they have not taken up the prosecution. A print in the favour and confidence, as it seems, of the parties to the late proceedings, has stated, that the actual law-officers of the Government were consulted and decided against their being undertaken; that again, when the bill was found by the Grand Jury, the prosecution was offered to them, but that they declined to be parties to it. These statements are followed up by remarks upon the apathy and indifference of the Government, which can only serve to render the testimony borne to the fact the more unexceptionable, because unwilling; for, otherwise, they afford only a lamentable specimen of how much mischief is done to a cause, the sole merit of which must consist in its being one purely of humanity, by its being used for the purposes of political warfare. This indeed is to trade with the cause of the slave.

The fact remains unshaken, that neither the Attorney-General of the present nor of the late Administration has prosecuted by himself or by others, and therefore the Queen's name was as much usurped under the cover of the forms of the Court, as that of the public, whose name is invoked in support of these proceedings. I will venture to say, that no one who has really looked into them for himself, and is possessed of all the facts from the examination before the Committee of the House of Commons, can think with other feelings than those of shame and indignation, that they can take place in England—feelings, the more strong, because such proceedings are pretended to be undertaken in order to serve a cause with which, if they are identified, they will only serve to disgrace it. I cannot but believe that all this is felt by the majority (I know it is felt by very many) of the members of a society, whose zeal may be imposed upon at times, but the majority of whom must have that real benevolence of heart and soundness of judgment, which will make them wish for no other principle of action than that contained in the well-expressed sentiments of a noble lord—"That a good, however eminent, should not be attained otherwise than by lawful means[1]:" it may be added, that by no other can it be permanently attained.

[1] Lord Aberdeen's Letter to the Lords of the Admiralty, 20th May, 1842.

The Society, to which I am alluding, was not more eager to start or to adopt the prosecution than the Committee of the House of Commons disposed to find a ground for its being undertaken, or than the last and the present Administration; indeed, the Society volunteered a disavowal of any connexion with the proceedings at their commencement, and did not express even an approval of them. In this, their organ only represented faintly the sentiments more strongly and decidedly repeated to myself by many members of that Society in a tone of unequivocal reprobation, and viewing the proceedings as calculated only to injure the cause which they had at heart. That such has been a very generally prevailing impression is fully attested by the plaintive remarks of the organs of the prosecution, and the libellous stimulants which, whilst the proceedings for the trial were in progress, they thought it necessary to apply. It is, indeed, but too true that a society, proposing to itself the accomplishment of some great moral and benevolent object, is most specially bound to confine itself to the use of such means only as are of as unexceptionable and even as benevolent a character as the end. Crime is, indeed, a just object of abhorrence; but a society, like the Anti-Slavery Society, is specially bound to guard themselves against the danger of encouraging one species of crime in their attempt to put down another; every one of the means they employ or sanction must be of as unquestionable purity as the end they profess to aim at: expediency, as distinct from justice, must be jealously guarded against, apt as it is to insinuate itself into all human proceedings, and never more subtilely than under the cloak of zeal in a good, cause: the smallest degree of evil to be done must stand as an insurmountable barrier to the accomplishment of the most undoubted good. It is in the power of man to destroy the very end in view, whilst he thinks he is advancing it; but he cannot alter the law of Providence, which dooms to certain defeat, even amidst the tokens of apparent triumph, whomsoever dares to modify for himself the moral code of the universe: the moment that violent hands are laid upon it, in order to smooth down a difficulty in the way of action, the very end itself becomes contaminated. All this is evident enough, and approves itself to the enlightened conscience. A society, as a body, taken in the abstract, may be supposed less likely to be led away by such apparently *short cuts* when presenting themselves in their path; but these societies are, in practice, managed by individuals of whom the least scrupulous are sure to appear as the most zealous and most efficient—they are the most busy and the most forward—and, hence, the additional necessity for caution on the part of the more conscientious, inasmuch as the names of the good are too often the cover of the deeds of the bad, whose power consists exclusively in the moral weight attached to the acts which the good are made to appear as having sanctioned.

It would have been well for the credit of the Anti-Slavery Society, therefore, if the London Committee had retained the position in which they placed themselves by their own act of disavowal; instead of which, after being taunted by one or two prints, which have, pending the proceedings, used every exertion in their limited power to stimulate the passions of those whose good sense it was necessary to mislead, the London Committee have passed and published the following resolution:—

"At a meeting of the Committee of the British and Foreign Anti-Slavery Society, held at No. 27, New Broad Street, London, on Friday, December 8, 1843, Josiah Forster in the Chair,—The conduct of Sir George Stephen, in the prosecution of Pedro de Zulueta, Jun., in October last, being taken into consideration, the following resolution was unanimously adopted—

"That this Committee feel it to be due alike to Sir George Stephen himself, and the public interests of justice and humanity, to express their high sense of his philanthropic and public spirited conduct, in carrying on, upon his own responsibility, the prosecution of Pedro de Zulueta, Jun., and another, for slave trading; a course in which the decision of the Grand Jury, and the declared opinion of the Judge, have fully sustained him, and by which it may be hoped a salutary check will be given to the notorious implication of British capital and commerce in that nefarious traffic. JOSIAH FORSTER, Chairman."

Here, after using that description of the charge, which is calculated to convey a false notion of what was, and could alone, even by the worst construction and perversion, be imputed, as if the charge had been dealing in slaves, they express a high sense of the philanthropic and public spirited conduct of the prosecutor—necessarily including the inquisitorial proceeding before the Grand Jury—the mode of apprehension of the accused—the resistance to his being released on even large bail, and to his having time given him to prepare his defence—the shrinking from appearing as a witness in public, and stating there what he, the prosecutor, had been ready to swear before the Grand Jury—the bringing up of a witness to raise an appearance of the existence of facts, the very contrary of which had been deposed to before the Committee of the House of Commons by the leading witness for the prosecution in Court—all this forms that conduct, which must have been taken into the consideration of a committee of a benevolent society, and which in discharge of a duty of both justice and humanity that committee have pronounced as both philanthropic and public spirited.

The resolution proceeds to state, that in the course adopted by the prosecutor he has been fully supported by the decision of the Grand Jury and the declared opinion of the Judge. It is impossible to estimate what value to attach to the finding of a Grand Jury without knowing upon what evidence their finding was based. In the present case, one fact is beyond all dispute, viz. that Sir George Stephen appeared before the Grand Jury as the first witness, his name standing as such on the back of the indictment, and that he did not present himself in the witness-box at the public trial, although in Court from the beginning to the close of it—from which it results, that the Grand Jury had before them a witness, giving to them in private, evidence which he did not think proper to give in public. Must not the inference be permitted, that the Grand Jury would have thrown out the bill, as the Petty Jury threw out the indictment, unless some evidence, which was not offered to the latter, had been given to the former by a witness, and that too, unfortunately, by a witness who seems to have preferred the secret inquisitorial form, which still remains in British law, to the open and public path which was before him, and which is the proper boast of British justice?

Regarding the support derived from the expressions of Judge Maule, when applied to by Serjeant Bompas for an order for the payment of the expenses of the prosecution, it is not for me to speak; but that it does not extend to a sanction, in point of propriety, to the part taken by the prosecutor, nor to the manner in which he has discharged it, is very obvious.

This, however, is not the point to which I wish now to refer. The object of this publication, and of the preceding and following remarks, is not any vindication of myself, nor a crimination of the motives of any one beyond what the statement of facts may carry in itself; my vindication I consider ample in the exhibition of the facts themselves—in the verdict of the Jurors, after hearing a trial of two days duration, after a long and elaborate charge delivered when a clear day had elapsed subsequent to the defence—a verdict, which was not agreed to without consideration, which was pronounced by the foreman in the emphatic manner which the crowded Court witnessed, which was received by the spectators, consisting of some of the most respectable merchants, bankers, and professional men of the City of London, who had sat daily and patient witnesses of the proceedings, in a manner which has been noticed by the public press, and echoed by the leading journals of London, of Liverpool, and of other important mercantile cities of Europe.

The chief object proposed in this publication, and in these observations, is to place before my brother-merchants, in a connected form, the whole of the facts, which form my case, or rather the case of the firm of Zulueta & Co., from the first communication which preceded my examination before the Committee of the House of Commons, to the close of the proceedings at the Old Bailey, in order that the merchants of England may judge for themselves, and reflect upon the position in which they are placed, as resulting from the principle and doctrines which the proceedings contained in the following pages have disclosed to emanate from an Act of Parliament which has been passed these twenty years, but which has been for the first time tried upon my case. It may be said, that by merchants in general it is hardly known: we all know that dealing in slaves is prohibited, under severe penalties, by the law of England—we know that it is repugnant to the prevailing tone of education, to the opinions and feelings of our people—we know that, at all events, as it is carried on and can only be carried on, it is at variance with the spirit of Christianity, and therefore no man need read an Act of Parliament to abstain from having any, the slightest, concern in or with such a traffic; but even if these considerations were not enough—which England surely will not suffer to be supposed of her own merchants—even if these considerations did not go to the extent of precluding British merchants from laying out their capital on slave adventures, whether for themselves or others' account, common prudence, in which respectable merchants in this country cannot be said to be deficient, does at once warn a man not to trust his funds to the issue of speculations which afford no security, over which he can exercise no control—so much so, that it is hardly possible to conceive in what shape, looking at all like business, British capital could be lent for the purpose or on the security of a slave trade adventure. All this has contributed to maintain merchants in utter ignorance of the provisions of this Act of Parliament, or of the use which might be made of its legal phraseology: but now, when a merchant, not at all suspected by his fellows—for that is on record—has been, to the astonishment of every one, dragged from his office to the police-station, and to the Old Bailey dock (more especially when this is done in spite of the resolution of the House of Commons' Committee, in spite of the opinion of the law officers of the Crown) by a London attorney, it is time to look at the exposition of the law and the practical application of its provisions, which so extraordinary a proceeding has elicited; the more so, as it has been stated that "higher game is in view," and that the prosecutor is still occupied in analysing the evidence given before the Committee; and when the Anti-Slavery Committee adopt and publish a resolution, in which it is stated, in reference to the late prosecution, that by it "it may be hoped a salutary check will be given to the *notorious* implication of British capital and commerce in that nefarious traffic, the slave trade." At any other time the absolute folly of the assertion would have suffered it to remain unnoticed; experience has shown, however, that there is somewhere the means, and that the will does exist, of doing mischief to an appalling degree.

As explaining the practical operation of the law, then, I shall look upon the summing up of the learned Judge, not with a critical eye, in order to decide whether the law has been well or ill administered—this is the province of a professional man, into which it would be preposterous for me to enter. Upon the propriety or impropriety of the Judge's acts and opinions, or even of his exposition of the law and its requirements, I must be understood as maintaining a complete reserve. For the present purpose, and for every practical purpose that can affect others, the law must be taken as laid down by his Lordship. As to its meaning, the evidence which is required under the Act to bring an individual to trial, the degree of evidence which will send a case to the Jury, that upon which a case in answer shall be demanded of the accused—until it is otherwise declared by competent authority—until then, those who really wish to obey the law must look upon the late administration of it as that which is to be expected, and the extent and applicability of the Act of Parliament to be that which is exhibited in the late proceedings.

The first consideration which presents itself is the nature and definition of the offence. In the outset of his summing up, the learned Judge stating the nature of the charge, alluding to the vessel which the prisoner is alleged to have employed, lays down, "that it was not necessary to be proved that the ship in question (the Augusta) was intended to be used for the conveyance of slaves from the coast of Africa. If there was a slave adventure—if there was an adventure, of which the object was that slaves should be brought from the coast of Africa, that there should be slave trading there—and if this vessel was dispatched and employed for the purpose of accomplishing that object, although it was intended to accomplish that object otherwise than by bringing home the slaves in that vessel—that is within the Act of Parliament. So, if the goods were loaded for the purpose of accomplishing the slave trade ... the crime charged in this indictment would be committed, the allegations in the indictment would be supported, and the prohibition of the Act of Parliament would be violated."

Such is the nature of the offence. If there is a slave adventure in the port of destination of the vessel and goods which you dispatch, for the purpose of accomplishing which they may be said to have been intended, the prohibition is violated; but as, in the case of the vessel and the goods in question, no attempt was even made to prove the existence of any such adventure, but only a general slaving character of the port of destination, it follows that not even the existence of such particular slave adventure is necessary to be proved in order to support an indictment under the Act, but it is enough if a general slaving character of the trade at the port of destination is proved, in order to lay the ground of an indictment. Let this general slave trading character be discovered by any one of a port in Africa, to which you may have sent goods—and of course, if a port not in Africa is (as may very well be) largely concerned in the trade, the case is not very much altered—and you stand open to a charge under the Act, for the crime has been committed. It is as when a man is found murdered in the street—the crime has been committed—the only thing is to find out the criminal. How this is done under the Act of Parliament on the slave trade is the next thing to be seen.

"The employment, the dispatch of the vessel," says the learned Judge, "is no conclusive proof of the guilt, till going further, and showing that the party doing so did it for the illegal purpose charged." But then, for the purpose of beginning the inquiry, without which there would have been no beginning of it, the foundation must be laid in the employment of the vessel by the person accused. If slave trading is intended, and the vessel be sent for the purpose, the important consideration then is, whether the person employing the vessel is cognizant of the intention. We have seen the large meaning of the terms slave trading. It is not like wine trade—dealing in wine: it is not dealing in slaves, but dealing in Manchester and Birmingham goods, adapted and purposely manufactured for the African markets, so long as it is found that slave traders, that is, as heretofore the term has been understood, dealers in slaves—resort to the port for which they are shipped. Of course the crime having been committed by some one, that is, by the person who intended that slave traders should use them for slave purposes—and no other will be supposed as possible—the existence of the law punishing such an intention demands that an inquiry should be made. For this purpose the commission-agent in England, who employed the vessel, must be laid hold of—not that in that one act there is a conclusive proof of guilt, until it be further shown that he was cognizant of and intended the illegal object, but because an inquiry is imperative under the Act. With whom the right and duty of making it rests it matters not—any one that may be so disposed from a philanthropic and public-spirited motive. It is not enough that a Parliamentary inquiry has been made already—it is not enough that the law-officers of the Crown see no reason to institute a further inquiry—it matters not, if the case has been lying in all its details before the public, the ends of public justice are never satisfied until the so-called inquiry takes the shape of a bill before the Grand Jury—*the inquisition* of the country. There certain depositions are secretly made upon oath, which you shall never see; and upon this *mild* and *fair* procedure you will have your very life, and the life of every one dear to you placed in jeopardy, for I believe that there is nothing in the mercantile profession which is likely to prepare a man, and a man's family, for his being treated as a felon. It is indeed true, that in the evidence before the Committee of the House of Commons merchants are treated by some of the witnesses in a tone and manner becoming only those times in which merchants were tolerated for the sake of the money that might be extorted from them, but otherwise were considered as a caste whose instinct was money-making by all means, right or wrong, and against whom every crime might be presumed; but, whatever may be in the heart of some, and whatever may rise to their lips, against a profession which England honours and distinguishes, a distinct avowal dare not be made such as will justify the insinuation that there is absolutely nothing in carrying a merchant, considered respectable, from his private office to a felon's den, without his knowing his accuser, or upon what he is charged, which ought to shake his mind or that of his family.

But, then, unless you are proved to have been cognizant of the intended purpose, you will be acquitted. The nature of the offence has been explained and laid down to embrace a very wide compass. If there existed a slave adventure at the port of destination of a vessel, to accomplish which that vessel carried goods, the offence has been committed. The penalty, to whomsoever committed it, is by the Act only short of the greatest imposed by the law. You employed the vessel—this is not conclusive of guilt, until it is shown further that there was slave trading intended, and that you were cognizant of the intention. Let us see how both things are to be proved and brought home to you. Heretofore the way between your office and the Old Bailey is one which there is no merchant, trading with countries wherein the slave trade is allowed to exist, may not be dragged through without risk or responsibility by any ruffian in London. Now, perhaps, though not exactly at the earliest stage that may be desirable for the safety of the innocent and the repose of honourable families—still now, perhaps, the requirements of the law in regard to proof are commensurate with the facility afforded on the outset, and with the terrible penalty which follows a conviction.

The Judge proceeds upon this part of the evidence as follows: "It appears from the evidence, that the Gallinas is a place described by some witnesses of great experience—two captains in the navy, and Colonel Nichol, who was the governor of a district in the neighbourhood" (about 1,500 miles from it, see his evidence), "whose employment was mainly to watch the slave coast, of which the Gallinas forms a part, and to contribute to the putting down the slave trade—that the Gallinas is a place of slave trading, and of no other trade at all." His Lordship continues as follows: "It is said, and I think with great probability, that the Gallinas is not generally known as a slave trading place, in fact, it seems very little known at all; it seems to be a place where any other description of felons may resort to concert their schemes and hide their stolen goods, and which, of course, they do not make public, and which is not likely to be known by honest and true people. Except those employed as police or otherwise in aid of justice, as these captains were, of course it would not be spoken of at all. There might be slave traders in London knowing it very well, but they would be perfectly silent probably, and hardly mention it by name even in speaking one to another. It is very probable, therefore, that the place was not very well known; that when these persons spoke of the Gallinas, they might say the Gallinas on the coast of Africa; and a person might be very conversant with the geography of Africa in an honest way, who had not been active in putting down the slave trade, and yet might not know where it was, except that it was on the coast of Africa."

It is impossible more correctly to state, in stronger language, or more clearly, the possibility of the place of destination of a vessel being a slave trading place, and that exclusively, without in the least diminishing the great probability of its being unknown to the party in England who ships goods for that place as a commission-agent, by order and for account of somebody else abroad. Thus, the great probability of my statement before the Committee of the House of Commons of the ignorance of the character of the trade carried on at Gallinas was completely vouched for, and the observation, that those who knew were not likely to tell, and not likely to as much as name the place, was forcible in my favour, since the house had entered and cleared the Augusta *for Gallinas*, and not for *Africa*, as ships with destinations for the West Coast are generally dispatched, and as the Augusta might most certainly have been, had the house even suspected an improper object which required concealment. It is singular that, in the explanations prepared for instructing counsel, the case is stated in nearly the same terms as to the ignorance of the character of the place, as those used by Judge Maule. Merchants easily understand this, because it is the case more or less with every one. In shipping goods by foreign order and for foreign account to distant ports in all parts of the world, with which there is hardly any communication, and with which the shipper himself has none, and need not have any for the purpose of such a transaction, it most frequently happens, that the nature of the trade carried on at that particular port is very imperfectly or rather not at all known. In the multitude and the rapidity of operations which must be disposed of almost without thinking, the inquiry (not being either interesting or profitable, and of course quite unnecessary) is not made, or indeed as much as thought of, especially when heretofore, I believe, it will be acknowledged that it has not been considered that the nature of the trade carried on at any place could involve the mere shipper, without a connexion or any interest in that place, in the slightest responsibility.

But what follows? The character of the place is thus settled: "That it is itself a slave trading place appears to be very evident from the case on the part of the prosecution. Probably those honest persons, those honestly dealing persons, who know best about it, are those who have been called upon by their public duty to ascertain it. Such persons have been called, and they give it this character and description, and they state that it is distinguished from other parts of the coast of Africa; for on other parts of that coast, it is said, slaves are sold as one article of export, but that other things, such as palm-oil—I believe that is the principal thing—and ivory, and wood, and other things, are sold in immense quantities on the coast of Africa; but that that is not the case at the Gallinas. They might be carrying out goods to other parts of Africa, intending to bring home palm-oil, or slaves, as might be most profitable; they might intend to bring home an honest commodity, and not have to do with this dishonest and perilous commodity; but it appears difficult to conceive what a person, carrying a cargo of goods to the Gallinas, could intend to do with it, unless he intended to have those goods employed in the slave trade. The prisoner might say they were to be employed by others in the slave trade; that would be plain and simple: it is wrong, but it is a plain and simple account of that which was intended to be done. It is a place, as it appears, without any trade; and if there be an obvious plain interest in a person carrying goods to that place, it appears to me that it may be taken that they were for the purpose of the slave trade. If that be the plain and obvious inference, it appears to me that might be the inference very properly drawn by Colonel Nichol, that this was a slave adventure, unless the contrary were proved." Here the character of the place seems the only point upon which the observations of the learned Judge bear; and that character having been laid down as very probably indeed unknown to any one but the dealer in slaves, and the police employed against them, they do not seem to touch the prisoner. But at the same time an answer is suggested which the prisoner might give about what was intended, thus seeming to imply, that he ought to be furnished with evidence in answer, capable of accounting for what was intended, without which the full weight of an inference by one of the witnesses must remain, so far attaching to him the knowledge that he must necessarily be supposed to entertain of what was intended by others. I had said before the Committee, in the evidence read in Court, that the house knew nothing of what was to be done with the goods. Therefore, this not being admitted, it seems to follow that the law, as laid down by Judge Maule, requires some plain and simple account of what was intended to be done with the goods from the commission-agent in England who ships them by order and for account of a merchant residing abroad. It had before been laid down, that to ship the goods for slave trade purposes is an offence under the Act, if the shipper was cognizant of the intent: it is now said, that the port is an exclusively slave trading port, and it is not suggested that this was probably unknown, as it had before been said, to any but the dealer in slaves and the police employed against them, nor any account taken of the statement of the accused before the House of Commons, which had been read in Court, disclaiming the very possibility, as a mere shipping-agent, of any knowledge of what was to be done with the goods: the only answer suggested is one which may give a plain and simple account of what the merchant abroad intended to do with the goods at such a port. It seems to follow, therefore, that the mere shipping-agent in England is bound by the Act to be provided with such an account; and if he does not give it, the inference, to be drawn as to the object of the shipment from the character of the port, will not only attach to the adventure, but will cut deeper, since if you are bound to have and to produce a knowledge, and you do not produce it, it seems that the account is to be held not to be producible.

The notion that the Act of Parliament must be understood, not only as punishing a proved guilty knowledge, but as demanding from the accused party proof of an innocent knowledge of the plans and objects of a foreign merchant residing abroad, in respect of a transaction, in which the former has had no other share than that of a simple shipping agency in England, by order and for account of the latter, pervades the whole of the proceedings, and shows itself more clearly in the remarks that follow. "It is possible," continues the Judge, "that this might be an adventure, not slave trading; if so, nothing can be more simple than to prove it: Martinez & Co. might prove that it is an honest adventure. If it was a dishonest adventure, it could not be expected that Martinez & Co. should be called to give evidence at all; but if it were an innocent adventure, it would be very easy for them to be called. It is true that persons are to be convicted, not by evidence they did not produce, but by evidence produced against them—not on suspicion, but on conviction; but where such evidence is offered of the trade being slave trading, as is offered here, namely, that the vessel was loaded with goods" (in itself, as the learned Judge had formerly stated, not conclusive of guilt)— "that a cargo of goods was dispatched" (to which the same former observation applies) "to a place, where slave trading is the only known object for which vessels *ever* go" (known to slave traders and the police employed against them, as was also aptly remarked by his Lordship; although one of these, Captain Denman, seems to have known of 800 tons, according to his evidence (see p. 329); and upwards of 1,000 tons, according to his official dispatch to the Governor of Sierra Leone, dated 12th December, 1840[2], as having been landed at Gallinas, without being able to say that the object was slave trading)—"a slave-mart and nothing but a slave-mart—you have a case, though it is an answerable case; but if the answer, which if it exist could be easily given, is not given, it may very fairly be inferred that the vessel was proceeding on a slaving voyage, a voyage either for the purpose of bringing home slaves, or of landing those goods for the purchase of slaves."

[2] Vide "Report. West Coast of Africa. Part II, Appendix," &c. p. 460.

The learned Judge is still upon the point of the nature of the adventure, as indicated by the nature of the trade said to prevail at Gallinas; and as in the former observations, since the name of Gallinas has been laid down as probably conveying no information to any but slave dealers and the slave police, the prisoner seems to remain untouched. But then it is laid down that an answer, which of course somewhere must exist, could be easily given by the accused. How so? but that the law, this special Act of Parliament, must be so understood as to require the simple shipping-agent in England to prepare himself with a full knowledge of the plans and the objects of the foreign merchant abroad, who orders certain goods to be purchased and shipped for his account. The learned Judge has not lost sight that in the universal practice of law, a conviction is only justifiable by evidence produced—that is, produced against, not by that which the accused party does not produce: but he feels it his duty, under the Act of Parliament he was expounding, to warn the Jury that the case is not so to be treated; for the operation of that Act, when to be applied to a commission-agent in this country, shipping goods to a place about which such evidence is offered as that it is a slave-mart, and a slave-mart only, even although the knowledge of that fact has been previously stated to be most probably confined to dealers in slaves, and the police employed against them, upon whose testimony alone it stood before the Court—in such a case, when dealing with the 5th Geo. IV, the *onus probandi* lies with the accused. In the course of mercantile transactions, the commission-agent, who buys and ships goods by order and for account of a foreign merchant residing abroad, and to a port with which the former has no intercourse of trade whatever, would not be supposed nor could be expected to possess any further knowledge than that necessary to complete, in England, his own part of the transaction; but not so for the purposes of the Act in question. The reasoning seems to be this: here is a law which makes a certain knowledge guilty, if the object of the party abroad, originating the transaction be in deed and in fact a guilty one. In order to give force and strength to the operation of this law, it must be so laid down as to render necessary some knowledge of either an innocent or of a guilty nature, in the party residing in England, of the plans and objects of the party abroad by whose order and for whose account he has shipped goods to the port indicated to him. This or that knowledge must exist in the agent: he must be called upon to produce even the very foreign merchant himself, over whom the Court can give the accused no control, over whom he himself is not shown to possess any, and whose testimony after all could not be trusted; since that of the accused, as recorded before the Committee, is not. If in this, or in some other way, he does not prove knowledge of an innocent object, the object must be taken to be a guilty one; and as the law must be understood to require a knowledge, and he shows no innocent knowledge, the inference remains of a guilty knowledge: from which it seems evident that shipping agency business cannot be safely undertaken, as has been heretofore done, at least for merchants residing in countries in which slave dealing still exists, not only in Africa, but Cuba, Brazils, the United States, and other places. But merchants in England are required to master the whole object and plan of their correspondents abroad; and that the sincerity of his endeavours will be measured only by the result, is what common prudence will teach a man to expect from the machinery which is set on foot in order to apply to this Act of Parliament that notable remark, that *who wills the end wills the means*.

And thus, after having laid down that the Act requires a proof of innocence in the party accused, a knowledge of something innocent intended—which, if not given, must leave the inference of guilty knowledge, inasmuch as *no knowledge*, ignorance of the object, cannot be taken as an answer—the accused, if he cannot produce his correspondent, or if he did not possess himself at the time of making the shipment, of a plain and simple account of his plans, is left to the mercy of such inferences as may be drawn; and upon this view of the requirements of the Act of Parliament he is to be considered as withholding something which cannot be supposed to be favourable to him. This inference will not be counterbalanced—it cannot be when once admitted; it must either be destroyed by the plain and simple account of what the merchant abroad intended, or its edge will be blunted by nothing else. The accused's character may be "of the very highest," perfectly unassailable; the position he occupies in the mercantile profession may be very high, the profession itself in this country being reckoned on a level for honour and principle with the highest; and men of unblameable character, of considerable standing and independence, conscientious and upright, moving in society where good taste and right feeling prevail, are not likely to put their property, their character, their consciences, in jeopardy, especially by partaking in transactions to which their habits and feelings, and those of persons around them, stand opposed, and all that for very paltry advantage. It is pointed out by the learned Judge, that although a very grave charge, and of a very highly penal nature, still the slave trade—the dealing in slaves—"is a trade, which till a recent period was lawful for persons in this country, and many persons of very good character certainly did engage in that trade, and a great number of persons justified it. I suppose," he continues, "those same persons would now say it is not to be engaged in, because it is a prohibited thing—it is a regulation of trade enforced by very severe penalties made by this country—but that the dealing in slaves is in itself a lawful, right, good, and proper thing, which ought not to be prohibited. Those persons would now consider slave trading as a thing prohibited only by positive regulations. There is no one who does not at once perceive that practical distinction between them. There is no person who, in point of feeling and opinion, does not perceive the difference there is between a thing which is prohibited by positive law, and that kind of thing, against which, if there were no law at all against it, the plain natural sense and conscience of mankind would revolt. This trading in slaves, in the opinion of a great many persons, is itself an abomination, a thing which ought to be considered with the greatest horror, whether prohibited or not; but those who think it was right when it was not prohibited, probably do not think it so very bad if it be committed now, since it has been prohibited by law, only that it is to be avoided on account of the penalty to which it subjects the individuals engaged in it. This has some bearing on the question of how far considerations of character would have weight with respect to such an offence." The opinion entertained by the individual in question against the slave trade may be as strong as the strongest for any thing that appears, who has stated without its having been contradicted, that neither himself nor his family have ever been suspected of having the smallest interest in slave dealing, or in slave property, about which he has stated how his fathers have proceeded: an individual, who may, perhaps, have a very strong opinion as to the moral and religious duty of obedience to positive enactments by competent authority, and who said something to that effect in the evidence before the Committee of the House of Commons, which had been read in Court.

This as to the character of the party. As to the inducement, when it is alleged that the smallness of the agency commission charged shows that the transaction was considered to be one in the ordinary course of shipping business, that consideration is pressed down by the weight of the radical defect in not having given a plain and simple account of what was intended by the foreign merchant. "It is alleged," says the Judge, "that the profit on this transaction would be extremely small. I do not think that the petty gain of this one transaction is the matter, for it appears that Pedro Martinez & Co. do a great deal of business, and it is possible that whenever persons have a large and valuable business to conduct, *there is some small portion that the correspondent and agent would willingly get rid of if he could*; but he is not allowed to pick and choose, but he must take the whole." In short, a London merchant, of the character which has been described, is to be supposed as not at all unlikely to commit a felony, if the alternative be to lose a valuable connexion.

And thus, whilst the most unimpeachable character is not a proof to any extent against the suspicion of a felonious knowledge and intent, and whilst the token of innocence afforded by the charge of the ordinary rates allowed in legitimate business is not considered of weight—as a compensation in some other way is possible, and the disposition to barter conscience and duty for money is such a thing as people who conduct a large business are not quite unlikely to lend themselves to if they are not allowed to pick—so, likewise, the supposed extent of the connexion of the merchant is no bar to their being supposed anxious to retain one more under felonious conditions. Neither the superiority of his knowledge and education, nor his skilfulness, are likely to make him either apprehensive or disinclined to the commission of a crime, whilst these qualities render him obnoxious to the remark, "that it may very generally be taken, that people know what they are about, unless they can show there was some particular concealment, some hinderance to their knowledge;" "unless they," so accused, "can show," that they did not know (not if those who accuse them have shown that they *did* know), then all the qualities of character, station, extent of business, education, are against the accused; and unless the accused can show, that he had a knowledge of something innocent having been intended by the foreign merchant, any peculiar circumstances of the case, which may appear to be of a favourable nature to the accused, must be considered only in that light which may diminish the improbability of his having had a guilty knowledge. Thus, as the employment of the British flag for the purpose of dealing in slaves stares every body in the face, and was a very strong feature in the present case, not only against any knowledge on the part of the charterer of the vessel and shipper of the goods in England, but even against there having been any guilty intent in the merchant abroad, who had the choice of other flags equally secure and less easy of detection and punishment, the favourable inference hence arising must be neutralised. "If Jennings" (the master of the vessel) "was an adventurer, if he were, as suggested, a very clever and intelligent person, and very conversant with every thing to be done on this occasion, a competent master of the vessel, supposing the slave trade to be intended, a thing which requires qualities one is sorry to see exercised so ill— a great deal of courage, sagacity, and presence of mind, and an unscrupulous readiness to employ them for the commission of this felony, not to be found in everybody—a man of such a description would be the paramount object of a slave trader, whose aim would be, whoever the owner may be, to elude all search, so to manage the thing as that the cruizers of any country shall not stop him. Probably, if the adventure succeeds, it must succeed by such means, so that one sees a perfectly good reason why, consistently with this being a slave trading voyage, it may have been English owned." Not a word appears in the proceedings against the character of this man, neither does it seem intended by the learned Judge to impugn it, simply to say that *if* the man did possess the qualities of cleverness and courage attributed to him, these qualities being very serviceable for wicked purposes, it is to be inferred that they were intended to be applied to a slave trade adventure, since no plain and simple account of a lawful intent on the part of the foreign merchant has been given by the charterer in England, with whom the law is to be supposed to make a knowledge imperative. The prosecutor knew, although it was not before the Court, that this man had been tried for the very identical offence in this matter of the Augusta at Sierra Leone, and had been acquitted; for *the chief witness in this prosecution*, in which, be it observed, Jennings is coupled with me (see the indictment, page 211), *was the prosecutor in the proceedings against him before the criminal court of that colony*; and he himself stated before the Committee of the House of Commons (see Lieutenant Hill's evidence, page 84), that Jennings had been acquitted. And here, by the way, let it be noticed, that *Jennings is at this moment under a prosecution in London for the very crime for which he was tried at Sierra Leone and there acquitted*, the chief and really the only witness, upon whose sworn depositions before the Grand Jury here the bill against Jennings has been found, being the very same person who instituted the prosecution at Sierra Leone, which terminated in the acquittal of Jennings. And thus, while the individual so acting is at this moment on his way to take possession of his appointment as governor of the Gold Coast, the unfortunate man, who he knows cannot be tried a second time, is in prison.

Further, as the vessel had been admitted (how reluctantly may be easily seen) by one witness not to have been furnished with equipment of any sort for slaving purposes, and had been rescued from the attempt to raise a doubt upon this point, by the evidence of another witness, this is shown also as in no way serving the shipping-agent in England without giving the plain and simple account of what was intended by the foreign merchant residing abroad. "I should think it would be quite a matter of course, even if the vessel was intended to be sent to promote the slave trade, that she should not go out with shackles or leagers, or any thing of that kind on board; for if they are on board, the vessel would be at the mercy of any Custom-house officer."

The vessel had, however, been at Cadiz, where, according to the representation made on behalf of the prosecution she was really meant to go first, in order to provide herself with the slave instructions, which the Court would not receive, though strongly pressed, as evidence against the agent who had managed the vessel in England so far as chartering and loading her; and yet, although it had been said by Serjeant Bompas "that wherever a vessel leaves a place such as Spain, or some place where she may leave with impunity, with all her equipments complete," she does so; and although this vessel, which has been charged by the prosecution to have gone into Cadiz for the very purpose of helping the illegal object imputed: she is found not to have been there equipped—and that not from any great attention to the safety of the adventure, for the letters contended to be so clearly slave instructions for the voyage seem to have been there put on board—still the observation is not the less applied, that she was not equipped for the slave trade, because she could not have been so in an English port, without any reference to the fact that the prosecution had contended she could and would have so been at a Spanish port. There she had, however, touched; and that too, according to the prosecution, for the very express purpose of helping the illegal object in a manner more condemnatory than any other. The thing demanded from the prisoner is, however, a plain and simple account of the intent of the foreign merchant in this transaction, and without his being able to give that, every other circumstance which may be favourable to him, either vanishes away, or converts itself into a weapon against him.

Again, the counsel for the defence had put the following case to the Jury:—"You may be manufacturers of guns or gunpowder, or commission-agents living in this country, who, for the purpose of shipment, purchase those goods; in either case a party comes and says—I want 1,000 muskets and six tons of gunpowder to be shipped to a certain place on the coast of Africa. I ask you, are you first to consult the map to ascertain the place, and, having ascertained where it is, are you to go to Captain Hill or Captain Denman and inquire whether they have been upon the coast of Africa, and can tell you the character of the trade carried on there? Are you next, the person being a Spaniard or a Portuguese, to inquire whether they ever deal in slaves; and if you find they do, are you to say, I will execute no order you give me?"

Upon this the learned Judge remarks:—"That Zulueta & Co. stand in a very different situation from that of a person who is simply the manufacturer or dealer in goods, and who has those goods ordered, and who, inquiring Where shall I send them? is answered, Send them on board the 'Augusta,' now lying at Liverpool. It would be a strong thing from that circumstance to infer that a person sending those goods on board had any thing to do with slave trading; but that appears not to be the nature of this transaction. In regard to there being a slave trading, all that is done, is done by Zulueta & Co. It is not merely that they had goods sent on board the ship, but they chose the number of the goods to be sent on board the ship, goods which they had bought, for which they had negotiated; and they made out such charter-party, and that charter-party provides that the ship shall proceed to Gallinas on the coast of Africa."

In the case of the manufacturer of the goods, described as receiving an order and executing it, and shipping the goods on board a vessel for the Gallinas, it would be *strong* to infer that he had any thing to do with the slave trade. Why so, but because every one of these acts is compatible with ignorance of the objects that are or may be intended? Now, the learned Judge had previously established that the acts of buying and shipping, chartering, and dispatching, are not necessarily in themselves conclusive of guilt, which of course they are not; how, then, is the inapplicability of the comparison put by the counsel for the defence to be maintained, but by laying down the principle, that for the purpose of a defence under this charge, the commission-agent must, at all events, be required to be possessed of, and therefore to be able to give, a plain and simple account of what the merchant abroad intended; and this once laid down, nothing that comes short of it must be suffered to tell in his favour.

The preceding remarks are scattered over the whole of the summing up, and accompany a recapitulation of the particulars of the case. They are here brought together in succession, for the purpose of showing the manner in which the circumstances of the case, in a proceeding of this kind, are treated. It is very true that an introductory remark precedes, laying down "that it is necessary undoubtedly, on the part of the prosecution, that there should be a case made of knowledge, on the part of the prisoner, of the purpose for which this adventure was meant." The whole process which follows is of a nature which would appear contrary to this principle, unless with the qualification that the proof is to consist in the prisoner not giving himself a plain and simple account of something innocent meant by the foreign merchant residing abroad; and as if the law left no alternative to the shipping-agent, who buys and ships the goods in England by his order, but to do this; or, *ipso facto*, by not doing so, to stand self-convicted of the guilty knowledge.

Under this view of the requirement of the law, which I have now followed throughout this charge, the concluding remarks of the Judge seem to be dictated. "Now, inasmuch as there are two other partners, and it is probable there might be some other persons in the concern, there arises this consideration. It is true, supposing that there were a case made, but that the prisoner was innocent of it, that he could not call Martinez & Co. on that supposition, as he might on the supposition of there being no slave trading; for Martinez & Co. would not be innocent persons, and they would not be willing to come into this country and say, 'We carried on the slave trading, but it was disguised from our correspondent, Zulueta & Co.' If you think there is a case requiring an answer, the question then is, would there have been any difficulty in the prisoner calling his two partners, and others conversant with the business of the firm, and proving that Zulueta & Co. knew nothing at all about this, that they had not the least suspicion, that Martinez & Co. never communicated the fact to them, and that the illegal purpose was utterly unknown to them, for some reasons which the prisoner cannot give, but which his partners could? It would be extremely desirable they should do it, if the defence existed in point of fact." And lastly, the learned Judge concludes his address to the Jury, by directing their attention to the evidence of the character of the prisoner, remarking, that it is "a character I should say very strong indeed, and almost conclusive, supposing the case were one that did not admit of an answer in point of fact."

Here the same principle of demanding a justification of innocence is carried out, which pervades the whole of the summing up, and of every part of the management of the case by the Court. It is not said, in any one part of the charge, that the prosecution have made out either a case of slave dealing, or any knowledge of such a thing being intended, or known to be intended by the prisoner, against which a contrary case should be opened and proved; but only that evidence which the prisoner should give of innocence is pointed out; and, what is most remarkable, the following circumstance was not thought worthy of notice.

Mr. Fitz-Roy Kelly (the counsel for the defence) had in the outset, when Mr. Serjeant Bompas was opening the evidence for the prosecution, brought into Court every book, letter, and paper of the firm of Zulueta & Co., with the clerks in whose keeping these documents constantly are: they consisted of the journals, ledgers, letters, bill-books, memorandum-books, original letters of the house of Martinez & Co., of the Havannah, and Martinez of Cadiz, since 1839, one year before these transactions originated, up to 1841, one year after their termination; and, as will be found in page 303, Mr. Kelly made the following tender:—"I ought to add, as the notice to produce has been referred to, and is now upon the table, that the notice calls upon the prisoner, Mr. Zulueta, to produce all the books, documents, and accounts of his house, between certain dates, at all relating to the transaction in question; and all letters written, and copies of letters written by this house, or any body for them in relation to this matter. My Lord, every document there mentioned is here in Court, and in two minutes ready to be put upon the table.... The greater part are in Spanish, and the prisoner at the bar can distinguish them; but the clerks who kept these books, the corresponding clerk, and the clerk in whose handwriting they are, are ready to speak to any thing my learned friend may call for from the beginning to the end." This is not taken any notice of by the learned Judge, when pointing out that the prisoner should have called his own father and his own brother, the only partners in the house, to prove that Zulueta & Co. had no knowledge of any slave trading being intended, although the prisoner himself had so stated the fact to be before the Committee of the House of Commons, in the evidence which had been read in Court; and if the statement was objectionable, as being from the party now deeply interested himself, when in a very different situation, it is not perceived how that objection would not have held with tenfold strength at that moment against their evidence. Thus it remains on record, that nothing short of a plain and simple account of what the merchant abroad intends, made out by the defendant, will answer any purpose of the slightest advantage to himself. It is enough in the case of a vessel employed by an agent in England to carry goods, bought and shipped by himself, by order and for account of a foreign merchant residing abroad, if the prosecutor show a general slaving at the port of destination.

And thus have I disposed of the last point which I proposed to illustrate out of the summing up of Justice Maule, in order to show the position of merchants who have intercourse of business with countries wherein slavery, and the slave trade, is still permitted to exist.

I began by showing the facility afforded by the law to any individual whomsoever, who may choose to undertake a prosecution, not only without the consent, but against the recorded judgment of the Legislature, and the known opinion of those officers of the Crown who are especially charged with the prosecution of public offenders. I have shown, that this may be done by any man—whether from motives of private resentment, or of private interest, or of wanton malice—whether under a fanatical hallucination, or from a desire of vain-glory, or from a combination of all or of some of the very worst passions of the heart with the less inexcusable errors of the head, it matters not: the search for the particular motive operating in any one given instance is indeed unprofitable, and whilst it cannot do much towards reclaiming the perpetrator of the mischief, would but little improve the moral tone of mind of his victim, yet the fact itself remains unaltered, *viz.* that a prosecution of this kind, in the name of the Queen, which the forms of justice require to be used, and on the plea of a public spirit, may be taken up by any man in defiance of a recommendation to the contrary by the House of Commons, upon a case canvassed and decided upon by a Committee of that House, and against the opinion of the law officers of the Crown. It has also appeared, that to the general and very powerful objections which are suggested by the common sense and reason of mankind against this practical reversion to the state of savage life in which a man can take such means of attack upon his fellow-man as he thinks will effect his purpose best, with this sole difference, that the self-appointed public prosecutor may inflict even greater mischief with the weapon of the law than the savage with the knife, and more securely, this evil is added, *viz.* that this private avenger of public wrongs may adopt the form of a secret information before a Grand Jury, thus avoiding the necessity of appearing as the accuser, unless he chooses so to do, at his own most convenient time, and always preserving the secrets of his own statements, by means of which the first blow at all events will have been successfully, irremediably, and fatally inflicted, and thus placing himself above any responsibility on that account. Then it has been seen, that at this stage of the proceedings, and under all the ignorance as to the prosecutor and as to the depositions upon which he is charged, inseparable from the nature of the proceedings, a man, reputed honourable, as unsuspecting himself as unsuspected by his fellow-citizens, may be dragged from his office and from the bosom of his family, with imminent risk to his business, and with still more fearful effect upon his dearest connexions; and under the shock of his own feelings, which so awful a situation must naturally produce, is conducted as a common felon under charge of the police to the station-house, and thence to the Old Bailey, whence he can only be suffered to depart (of course in exactly the same state of ignorance under which he entered the Court), when the person who arrested him shall have consented, and on such terms as he shall consent to; and then only will he be allowed to return to his distracted family and prepare his defence—against what? against a technical definition of some facts in which he has played some part, but which being so defined as to square with the application which may be meant to be made of a certain Act of Parliament, is sure to bear no kind of resemblance to the real manner in which the said facts occurred, and of course none at all to the impression which they left on the mind of the accused, or to the form in which alone they can present themselves to his mind; and, therefore, such a definition can convey no information of the nature of the depositions secretly made against him, and cannot consequently assist him in preparing evidence against them. He must launch into the regions of imagination for every possible construction which may be given by any man to those facts which have been really done by him, and prepare evidence upon every one of such possible constructions, at an expense and amidst perplexity which may be supposed, and after all most likely to no purpose, for probably the construction to which the proof will be directed by the prosecution may be one against which no counterproof has been prepared; and indeed it will be so, for with this very object the proof will be directed to the construction least likely to occur to the accused, and that upon which a counterproof will be most difficult— for all which the nature of the Act of Parliament has been seen to afford peculiar advantages.

In this state of things the trial comes on. The facilities thus far given to an unknown accuser have been seen, and to so frightful an extent, that even if the trial proceeds no further, an amount of incalculable and irreparable evil and misery may have been perpetrated. These facilities, it has been further seen, are not at all balanced by the strictness of the requirements of the law from the prosecution, they are all applied against the accused. The definition of the crime by the Act of Parliament is itself loose and capable of an unlimited application, and it is understood and laid down in the very largest, thereby including acts which are notoriously and expressly admitted to be in themselves perfectly innocent: the only qualification is the *knowledge*. This is brought to a lower point in the scale, *viz. suspicion*. With a show of ingenuousness, as if to put down *a quibble*, which in Court sounds like a zeal for the truth, the question is made to be, not whether *you knew*, but whether *you suspected*; and next, whether *you had reason to suspect*; the tendency really being towards the real point, to which you are only being gently let down, *viz.* whether witnesses can be found who will say that they themselves *knew* very well a great many things, which ought therefore to have been known by yourself, and that therefore you must at least *have suspected*.

Then the prosecution is not limited to the proof of one particular charge: here it is suffered to remain quite at large—they need not define the act they mean to charge, whether it is this, or that, or any thing else, upon the accused. The knowledge of the intent, in which every lawyer in the land whom you may consult previous to entering into any operation, will tell you, *before you are indicted*, that the guilt consists, after being brought down to a lower point, as observed before, is made out to be, 1st, any knowledge, not the knowledge in the particular case; 2nd, the knowledge of *others*, not *your* knowledge; and the proof of it is no further put upon the prosecution than so far as to make out a case of *probable knowledge*, founded upon evidence of some general acts done by certain persons on other occasions, not the one in question, in distant countries—acts to which you are not shown to have been a party, or even probably acquainted with—persons in respect of whom all your proceedings in England are admitted to be in themselves, and as done towards them, perfectly innocent; such acts being done upon such other occasions by such persons in countries far away, little known, with which no regular means of communication exist—countries almost unknown to every one in England, and not at all proved to be known to yourself: and all this evidence given by individuals not in circumstances analogous to those in which the accused stands, but by individuals, and by no others, who in the exercise of a peculiar duty have sometimes visited the countries in question; and therefore leaving the whole of the case open to this remark, that whilst it is not at all shown, either from your own acts, or from the facts themselves, that you in England must necessarily *have known*, there is an evident impropriety in pushing the witnesses to the extent of proving, that nothing but what they said to have happened on other occasions in other places, could have been the ultimate issue of an unaccomplished speculation, intercepted by one of the witnesses, to his evident advantage.

It has lately been shown that such a case of probable knowledge, so made out, and so substantiated, will go to the Jury; and in going to the Jury nothing will avail you, as far as the law goes, but your being able to give "a plain and simple account of what was intended by a foreign merchant residing abroad," whom you must even bring over to give evidence of what he intended to do with goods shipped by yourself in England, in consequence of a simple order as a mere commission-agent, or to show an impossibility of your being aware of that intent whatever it may be. Without complying with one or other of these two requirements, your case shall go to the Jury, accompanied by every unfavourable inference; and what should have been for your advantage is turned against you. The readiness and openness of the party accused in giving every explanation upon the very first intimation of a suspicion existing on the subject—the credit attached by every one capable of correctly estimating those explanations, whatever circumstances of a favourable nature may lie on the very surface of the case itself—the respectability of the accused, his rank in society, and high character, as vouched by men of the first standing, and who have every opportunity of knowing him and his acts—his wealth, his education, his knowledge—qualities peculiarly adapted to this kind of felony, which is intimated to be the felony of the honest, the wealthy, the educated, the well-informed—all these things seem in the exposition of the law to be literally against him. Nevertheless, these circumstances, combined with the impression produced by the inquisitorial nature of the original proceedings, together with the irresistible force of that axiom, that "a man must be proved to be guilty, and not called upon to prove himself innocent," may—and thanks be to God, did, in the instance before us—blunt the edge of the murderous weapon brandished over the head of the accused.

There may be something so revolting in the whole conduct of such proceedings to the consciences of men, as to stand in the way of a conviction by an English Jury; but it has been seen in what way every other indignity may, at all events, be safely inflicted; and as affecting men and families of certain education and feeling—who, be it never forgotten, are the very parties said to be most obnoxious to the charge—a verdict of guilty need not arrive, to produce evils as great or greater than any penalties which it is possible for any human law to impose. And when it is considered—first, that the legitimate popular sense of words is distorted in order to call *slave trading* that, which is neither directly nor indirectly *dealing in slaves*; secondly, that under the guise of a question of fact, a very subtle metaphysical argument about the nature and the degree of knowledge in the mind of an individual, is the thing really submitted to minds the least likely to apprehend the very nice distinction upon which the decision must hang—and, lastly, when every means are industriously resorted to in order to make it appear that the crime largely prevails in the class to which the accused is likely to belong, and to represent that the only difficulty is to get over the technicalities of legal evidence, but that moral evidence abounds—when all these things are taken together, it is easy to discover how much even the failure of such a prosecution as this, facilitates the next attempt: perhaps it may be practically found that it does so, more than its success could have done.

The resolution of the London Committee of the Anti-Slavery Society of the 8th of December, which has been already quoted, broadly states the prevalence of the crime among British merchants; and another, of a still more recent date, besides repeating the same assertion in another form, clearly intimates that the obstacle to its being visited as it deserves, does not consist in the want of proof of the existence of the guilt, but in "the difficulty encountered in the course of the prosecution in an English Court of Law:" that is, in the technicalities of the rules of evidence, even after the stretch of these rules, which this particular Act of Parliament would, by the experience of the late proceedings, seem to demand.

These resolutions, just published, passed by the Committee on the 29th December, are as follows:—

"Zulueta's Trial.—At a meeting of the Committee of the British and Foreign Anti-Slavery Society, held at 27, New Broad Street, on Friday, December 29, 1843, George William Alexander, Esq., in the chair, the following resolutions were adopted:—

"I. That this Committee, regarding the recent trial of Pedro de Zulueta, Jun., on a charge of slave trading, in the Central Criminal Court, on the 27th of October last, and following days, as an event of the highest interest and importance, feel it their duty to express their sentiments on the state of things which has been developed by it.

"II. That, abstaining from all comment on the verdict of the Jury, this Committee regard the following points as brought out with great force by this trial, *viz.*—

"1. That articles of British manufacture are principally used on the coast of Africa in barter for slaves.

"2. That British merchants who are engaged in furnishing such supplies to slave traders are practical supporters of the African slave trade.

"3. That, although a British merchant may furnish supplies to the most notorious slave traders in the world, the evidence by which a charge of aiding and abetting the slave trade can be substantiated against him is of such a nature that it is extremely difficult, if not almost impossible, to prosecute such an offender to conviction.

"4. That the practice of aiding and abetting the slave trade by supplying goods to slave traders prevails to a considerable extent among British merchants, and that, by a portion of the mercantile community, it is not regarded with the sentiments due to its flagitious character.

"III. That this Committee regard in particular the last fact now stated with the deepest and most poignant regret; and that they earnestly invoke, not so much the fear of punishment as the sense of honour, of justice, and of benevolence, in the British community, for the correction of so great an evil.

"IV. That the difficulties encountered in the course of this prosecution in an English court of justice, and the extended ramifications of the slave trading interest which have been developed by it, have, in the judgment of this Committee, confirmed the principle held by the British and Foreign Anti-Slavery Society, that the only effectual mode by which the slave trade can be abolished is the abolition of slavery itself.

"JOHN SCOBLE, Secretary."

In these resolutions, the Committee describe the particular matter which they had under their consideration, *viz.* the supply of British goods. Not so in the previous resolution of the 9th of December (see page xxvi). In it a hope is expressed, that by the proceedings against Pedro de Zulueta, "a salutary check will be given to the notorious implication of British capital and commerce in that nefarious traffic." How this implication takes place is not pointed out. Upon the merits of the matters contained in these resolutions, it is not, of course, my intention to enter; I take them as they are put forth, for the only purpose which perhaps gives them any value or importance, *viz.* as expressions of the sentiments and opinions of people who show every disposition to sanction, and have the pecuniary means required in order to encourage or to assist others in the use of that power of private prosecution which every one possesses, even if they themselves are not inclined to exercise it in their own persons.

Now, although it is not distinctly stated in the resolution just quoted how this *notorious* implication of British capital is supposed to take place—not to say any thing at present about a most unjustifiable use of the word *notorious*, which, in these matters, is constantly made—the mode in which the implication takes place must be supposed to be large enough to be notorious—large enough, when even a check to it is made the object of hope and the subject of a resolution, which, as it conveys a serious charge against fellow-citizens, nothing but a very overwhelming sense of the necessity of a *check* could have induced the Committee to overcome the painfulness of publishing. The term could not properly apply to any direct concern in the slave trade; *that* would be something more than *implication*. It cannot be confined to the supply of goods, since this is a subject treated in a separate set of resolutions. It must be taken to apply to other operations also, such as occur in the progress of a mercantile intercourse with other countries in which slavery, or the slave trade, are permitted to exist, and must apply to all or any transactions with those countries, at least, unless a clear and distinct separation can be made that will render it quite certain and quite capable of proof that neither the slave trade nor slavery can possibly be forwarded directly or indirectly by the transaction. This is the only certain way of avoiding *implication*. This sense of the charge against British merchants at large, is perhaps the only one which can render either intelligible or practicable the observation which was so emphatically delivered by the learned Serjeant Bompas in his opening speech at the trial, that "if merchants in this country would not accept bills drawn by slave traders, if they would not send goods from this country to be employed for the purpose—in fact, the trade could not be carried on at all."

And whether this rather extraordinary assertion be or be not correct, I deal with it as with the resolutions of the Anti-Slavery Committee—it is quite enough, upon such a question, and with such momentous interests at stake, that such opinions prevail in certain quarters, and that the power exists of giving them that fatal effect which these proceedings reveal, in order to force upon us, as merchants, the consideration of whether any mercantile transactions whatsoever can possibly be carried on with countries wherein the slave trade or slavery exist, with any real safety to our persons and to our property, whilst things remain as they have been shown to be in the practical development of the law.

It is very true, that previous to the late elucidation of its working, there were such high legal authorities on the subject, as will be found in the pages immediately following this address; and even now, if a case is placed before the very highest counsel of the land, you will be told that *knowledge, wilful knowledge*, of the *guilty* intent can condemn the acts upon which you are seeking advice—that that, of itself, will condemn the most indirect—and nothing short of that can condemn the most direct act of abetting the slave trade. But, in order to make good a charge, the evidence of a *probable knowledge* is made up of those very acts which, without presupposing the knowledge, you had been told are innocent, perfectly legal, and such as you could perform. When once that case of probable knowledge is thus made out, you are called upon to meet it with a case of your own, in which you cannot allege, with any success, the innocent nature of your acts; for although those have been already declared to be innocent in themselves, they are also taken as evidence that you must be possessed of *a knowledge* of what they were intended to be made subservient to by a foreigner at some thousands of miles distant, in a country which to you may be *terra incognita*.

The question resolves itself therefore into one of prudence, about which you will be told by the learned Counsel, and properly told, that you alone can be, and you alone must be, the judge, *viz.* whether, under the state of the law which has been developed, it is safe to enter into any dealings, not which you know or suspect (this is *a fraud of the law*), but which *may be* rendered subservient, however indirectly by others, to a slave trading purpose. The letter of the law seems to speak of *knowingly and wilfully* aiding and abetting the slave trade, and so it is expounded by the highest legal authority of the land, when consulted upon any one case in perspective; but the practice renders this a most *egregious fraud* on the part of the law itself, which presents itself under false colours; for, whilst in theory it does not permit of any other advice being given for its observance than that just mentioned, in practice it has been seen how the proof of your knowledge is established, not by evidence produced against you, but by that which you do not produce when a case of probable *knowledge*, founded upon knowledge of others in totally different circumstances, has been made out.

These things speak for themselves and show what is the practical situation of merchants trading with countries in which dealing in slaves and slave negotiations are both legal and of common occurrence. I need not say, that the United States, Cuba, Brazils, and a large portion of Europe, without talking of Africa, fall exactly under this description. It has been admitted, for indeed it cannot be denied, that it is impracticable to draw a line of separation, in order to distinguish the illicit from the licit traffic, in countries where they both subsist, for they are interwoven and mix themselves with, and merge the one into, the other. This is perfectly clear, and indeed the only intelligible account of the matter. Under such a view of the nature of the thing—after what has been brought to light in the late proceedings as to the mode in which a man may be attacked, with ruin staring him in the face at the first onset, whatever the subsequent result may be, seized on—laid hold of at any, perhaps the most critical, moment—after what has been seen of the method in which his prosecution will be suffered to be carried on, and the manner in which the evidence will be made to bear, in order to prove the *knowledge* which constitutes the guilt—after seeing that no precaution can guard a man against the attack, and no endeavour to ascertain the real sense of the treacherous law, which speaks one thing and means a very different one—after seeing that as a merchant of wealth, character, and education, he carries in those very circumstances as many presumptions of guilt—after it has been shown that the only thing which can save him, according as the law is laid down and administered, is that which in the nature of mercantile transactions is, and must be in almost every case impossible—after all this, which the late proceedings have so strongly brought to light—there remains but one safe course, *viz.* to abstain from all mercantile intercourse with countries in which slavery or the slave trade exists.

The absurdity which appears on the face of such a statement as this just made, involving as it does the cutting off communication with half the world at least, and leaving the communication with the other half very much on the footing of an inconsistency, renders the accuracy of the rule, as a conclusion from the preceding reasoning, very suspicious. I appeal, however, to every candid and honest mind whether it be or it be not the conclusion which, but for its *absurdity*, (if so it is to be called) would be imperative, and such as could not be avoided without manifest want of honesty. If such is the real fact—if the conclusion is just and legitimate, and yet it leads to something absurd and wrong; then the principles upon which it proceeds must themselves be the *wrong-doers.* The state of the law, which leaves no other alternative than that of an impracticable absurdity on the one side, and on the other an exposure, imminent and threatening, to an indictment, followed up by the most terrible consequences, even if a conviction does not take place—must be wrong. It deserves a stronger epithet, lest it should be thought that by wrong is only meant *unwise*—it is positively of the very nature of a national crime—it is a deep moral stain upon the people who suffer this state of things to continue in all its hideous deformity, whilst the victims to such a state of the law could only be looked upon as barbarously sacrificed: the people tolerating its continuance, when once made aware of what was being done, could be considered only as a race of heartless, cruel tyrants. In the pursuit of a praiseworthy object it is very possible, and indeed it is not uncommon, for a nation no less than for an individual to betray itself into a very false position, which is made so much the more mischievous, because, in the case of the nation no less than the individual, people are found ready to take advantage of that position. But so soon as the evil reveals itself in this practical shape, the nation, quite as much as the individual, is called upon to remove the very possibility of a repetition of the act of oppression arising from that false position.

And what is the false position in which this country appears before the whole world in the matter before us? It is this. Here is a people with whom trade and manufactures form very important elements of wealth, independent of the justly admitted tendency of both to promote civilization—a most important, but not the present consideration—these people thrive largely by their mercantile intercourse with Cuba, with the Brazils, with Spain and with Portugal, with the United States, with Africa, so much so, that they cannot dispense with that trade. Those of their people who follow the commercial career in all its branches, their merchants, manufacturers, and ship-owners, and conduct the intercourse with those countries, materially contribute to the welfare and to the prosperity of every class of the community in which they live. They contribute not a little to the support of the State, and when an emergency arises, when the credit of the country and the honour of the Crown are at stake, they are among the first upon whom the call is made, and is not made in vain: and yet the state of the law among this people who derive the important benefits, which have not certainly been exaggerated, from a commercial intercourse with the countries just mentioned, is such as to place those of their fellow-countrymen, who conduct that intercourse, and are therefore nearest in contact with those countries, liable to be dragged from the scene of their labours, so vital to the prosperity of this people, as common felons, upon an indictment secretly procured and obtained; and their very acts, notoriously necessary for carrying on the very operations of commerce, which the country cannot dispense with, are in the first instance to form the presumption of the guilt, and afterwards the proof of it, unless they can prove them to be *not guilty*. It is true that this people have anathematized a branch of trade which subsists in those countries, and have expunged that trade from their code of licit pursuits at an immense sacrifice to themselves, and are determined to extinguish it among the nations of the earth, as far as it can be done by lawful means; but inasmuch as they cannot dispense with all other intercourse with other countries, although fully aware that from that intercourse the proscribed traffic must necessarily derive assistance (since it cannot be separated from any one licit pursuit in the countries wherein it prevails), they are bound so to construct the law as to protect the men who conduct that intercourse, against any attacks which may be founded more or less on the use to which others, and not themselves, may turn the acknowledged necessary and legitimate acts, without which the intercourse cannot exist. And if such be the meaning of the law, as I have no doubt whatever there is not one man in Great Britain at all acquainted with these matters, who has not been, to this moment, in the understanding that such and no other was the state of the case—if it be not meant that the intention is that a law shall be made with apparently one meaning, and to be used for a quite different purpose—when the perversion which it seems to authorise shall have been discovered, sharpened by the application of the right of private prosecution, and in the form of a secretly procured indictment, which destroys before it convicts—there is only one of these honest courses left—*either let the law—a clearer law—be substituted for that which exists, or let it be clearly explained; and, at all events, let the right of prosecution be placed exclusively in hands, and limited to a course of proceeding, which will afford some guarantee for its right use.* Let us cast away from us the worst features of the Inquisition.

It cannot be meant to leave matters so—that the nation shall be deriving all the benefits of commercial intercourse with the countries already mentioned, trusting to our desire for profit as merchants to get the better of our prudence as reasonable men—that we shall be content to run the risk of private prosecution, and secretly procured indictments, of arrest, imprisonment, ruin, disgrace, transportation, the sacrifice of all that is dear to a man on earth; and, therefore, that the nation will go on prospering by our labour, whilst we ourselves may be told that we need *only be a little more* careful. And all this, as if it was meant to be insinuated that if a victim is now and then made, it is expedient that it should be so; that it is not extremely harsh, since merchants are to be thought of only as men accustomed to risks, and therefore who get obdurate against adversity—as if it were assumed, that as to the victim so made, it is sure to be some one who has deserved his fate by a more than ordinary degree of temerity, by going a *little* too far, or by an act of rebellion against the attempt to fix the brand on his forehead, which really, when once we have suffered ourselves to be so far stigmatised, there can be little doubt will be designated as a degree of fastidiousness to which an exclusively money-making and money-loving race can have no just pretensions. You may trust to their rapacity (it would seem to be argued by this defamatory process, which before it is openly avowed must work its way by implying as much in action, as, if it were not too revolting, would be stated in as many words)—you may trust to their rapacity for any necessary amount of risk being encountered, and therefore no fear of trade being given up, because we make it a *little*—only just take care that it shall not appear too dangerous.

This is not, I am sure, the position which is meant to be taken by the country towards a profession heretofore deemed honourable, and which has become interwoven with the highest ranks of our society. It is not, it cannot be meant, that such be the state of things at home, as between the merchant and the country.

Neither is another position (in every moral point of view equally indefensible) to be taken by British merchants towards their correspondents abroad, even supposing it could last. It is well known and admitted, that a mercantile intercourse imposes a tacit contract between the two parties who carry on a correspondence, a breach of which can be visited by the law; that in the progress of the intercourse all acts mutually required within the mercantile usage, and not otherwise illegal or improper, shall be performed. If a man carries on a correspondence with another and a course of business, he is not at liberty, either as a matter of principle or of law, to break it off when and how he pleases. Are we called upon as merchants in England, either by the requirements of the law, or by public opinion, to encourage our foreign correspondents to send their sugars and their coffees, their tobacco and their cotton, their copper ore, their minerals, and other produce, to us in England, and when we are quite sure of our profits, when they begin to dispose of the proceeds of their property, and we fancy (which must be very soon, after what the late proceedings have exhibited) that we may render ourselves liable to a prosecution—are we then to turn round upon our correspondents, and say, "I cannot accept your bill until you show me that its proceeds are not going to buy slaves with?" "I cannot honour the credit you have opened in behalf of A, B, or C, because I see in the 'Anti-Slavery Reporter,' that 'he is a *notorious* slave dealer.'" Are we, when our correspondent sends an order to buy a ship which is on public sale, and which may be employed in any trade, and goods which you, reader, may happen to manufacture yourself—are we then to turn upon our correspondent and say, "Show to us satisfactorily that these things are not intended by you or any one connected with you, indeed that they cannot be used, in promoting the slave trade?"

And again, are we to trust to the circumstance of his being in our power, and to the odium which the simple imputation of slave dealing will attach to him, to bear us out in our justification, should he bring an action against us? Are we, upon receiving an order from our correspondent, to lay it before counsel for their opinion, which we have seen will advance us very little? Shall we disclose the name of our correspondent with the insinuation that he *may be* a slave dealer, or that we suspect him to be one, or that some one else suspects him, thus helping, as far as we are able, to put his property in peril, and to render every communication with him dangerous? Shall we advertise our counting-houses in England, not, as they have been hitherto considered to be, the symbol of security and good faith, but as nests of treachery, deceit, and suspicion? and shall our intercourse with foreign merchants assume the character of covert *espionage*? A state of things such as this, inflicting gross injustice, cruel injury, inexpressible degradation, upon one class of men, and that class of which England has had hitherto good reason to be proud—such a state of things at home, and so much scandal and disgrace abroad, is not, cannot be, contemplated without feelings of the deepest horror.

I denounce this state of things as involving a national crime—as attended with national disgrace; I denounce it as a stain which should be wiped off without delay from the character of a nation eminently jealous of its public as much as of its private morality, as an offence to the religious feeling which is not wanting among us; I appeal to the conscience of every man in Great Britain against this state of things. May I not take upon myself to say, that I make this appeal in behalf of a class which yields to no other of the community in high principle or right feeling—a class which is not at all below the standard of morality, religious convictions, tastes, education, which may be set by the most distinguished in this country? I do appeal to the Legislature and to the Government of the land, which do not make laws or maintain them as a snare or a trap against a particular class of their subjects. I appeal to the Honourable Members of the Committee of the House of Commons on the West Coast of Africa, before whom I appeared in 1842; I appeal to them as senators, as gentlemen, as men of honour and principle—I do appeal to all, whether the position of merchants in mercantile intercourse with countries in which the slave trade and slavery exist, should remain as it has been shown to be now by the late proceeding; whether the laws should not be made such, that, whilst we should be answerable for our own acts, and for our participation and consent in the wrong acts of others, we may not be undone before we are even heard in our defence; that we may not be required to prove ourselves innocent before we are proved to be guilty; and, above all, that the right of prosecution may be confined to such hands, and its use to such a procedure as will afford the British merchant a guarantee against private, malicious, secretly conducted attacks, and will make his personal security something more than a mockery. I make this appeal with the same confidence in the result, which my conscience felt when I stood before the British Jury, into whose hands it pleased Providence, by so unexpected a proceeding, to place, in point of fact, my very existence—the existence of all that is dear to me on earth—of much that the world has had opportunities to try and has stamped as honourable in character—of much, not the less valuable because the world can never know of it—the Jury upon whose verdict hung the honour of this country—a country for whose honour and estimation among the nations of the earth I must feel strongly—and from which a gross and cruel injustice would be doubly felt, bound to it as I am by those ties, which it has been attempted barbarously to tear asunder, but which it is only in the power of God to dissolve.

P. DE ZULUETA.

London, 17th January, 1844.

OPINIONS OF THE LEGAL AUTHORITIES
Referred to in

"1 & 2. There is not any thing in the Act of Parliament in question which renders illegal a commercial dealing on the coast of Africa, in usual lawful merchandise, though such dealing may be with a person known to gain his livelihood by dealing in slaves, and therefore of course, an owner or supercargo making a sale in the manner described to any such person, does not subject himself or the ship to any of the penalties of the Act.

"3. Independently of the above Act, an English owner, or master, or supercargo, or other person who engages in such commercial dealing as above described, is not guilty of any offence against the law, nor subject to any punishment.

(signed) "*Fred. Pollock.*"

"Temple, 8 June, 1842.

(Vide Report, West Coast of Africa, Part I, p. 344.)

"1. Unless the merchant knew, when he sold the goods, that they were used for carrying on the slave trade, I am clearly of opinion that he is not guilty of felony. The question of knowledge will be for the Jury, if the case is tried by a Jury, or by a Judge or Judges without a Jury, and will depend upon the evidence that is given either of direct knowledge, or that the circumstances were such that he must have known the destination and occupation of the vessel and her crew.

"2. It will appear from the statutes 11th and 12th, and 46th of Geo. III, c. 54, &c., that the merchant might be tried at Sierra Leone, and if so, I am disposed to think that the constituted authorities at Cape Coast would be warranted in apprehending him and sending him for trial to Sierra Leone, as the offence committed is felony.

"3. I hardly know what precautionary measures can be adopted by the Governor in cases where it is unknown whether the vessels are intended for the slave trade or not. The same articles that are used for bartering for slaves are no doubt also used in bartering for palm-oil, elephant's teeth, and other African products, and to prohibit all dealing in such articles of barter would be greatly prejudicial to the innocent trade carried on with Africa. The Governor can hardly do more than warn merchants not to deal in such articles with suspected vessels upon peril of the consequences.

(signed) "*W. Wightman.*"

"Inner Temple, July 8th, 1840.

(*Vide Report, West Coast of Africa, Part II, Appendix, &c.*, p. 25.)

"If a person fitted out a vessel to traffic with slave factories and settlements, and sold goods to those factories, out and out, though they were such as might be used for the slave trade, as well as the innocent commerce of the coast; and though, in point of fact, they were used in slave trading, he was of opinion that this did not amount to slave trading: whether it was a commendable use of capital or not, was a different question. If the goods sent out were of such a description that it could not be doubtful that they were to be used in the slave trade alone, such as a cargo of fetters or other implements that could only be employed in such a trade, he had stated that he deemed this much more doubtful, yet he was not prepared to say that it was an act of slave trading which would render the exporter of such articles liable to be tried for felony. But if goods were sent, whether of one kind or the other, whether of an ambiguous description, or plainly fitted for the slave trade alone, and the price of the goods was to depend (as the petitioners stated to be the fact) upon the slave trade, in which such goods were to be employed, he had stated that his opinion was that this was an act of slave trading, being in truth a partnership with slave traders, and the persons exporting such goods would be guilty of a felony within the meaning of the Abolition law."

(*Extract from* LORD BROUGHAM'S *Speech before the House of Lords, Oct. 5, 1841. Vide Hansard's Parliamentary Debates, Vol. LIX, fo. 1116.*)

DOCUMENTS,
&c. &c.

R. R. GIBBONS, ESQ., TO MESSRS. ZULUETA & CO.
HOUSE OF COMMONS.
Select Committee on West Coast of Africa.

Gentlemen, April 15th, 1842.

By Lord Stanley's desire I send you a copy of Dr. Madden's Report, on the Gold Coast, and its dependencies.

I am to add, that this is sent to you as being personally interested therein, but that you will be good enough to consider it as entirely confidential.

I have, &c.
R. R. GIBBONS.

The Report of Dr. Madden forms part of the Appendix to the "Report from the Select Committee on the West Coast of Africa[3]," and although the first official communication which was received by the house of Messrs. Zulueta & Co., it is not inserted, in consequence of its want of connexion with the chief subject of this publication. It is entitled, "Report of Her Majesty's Commissioner of Inquiry on the State of the British Settlements on the Gold Coast, at Sierra Leone, and the Gambia, with some Observations on the Foreign Slave Trading Factories along the Western Coast of Africa, in the Year 1841;" and sets forth its object as follows:—

"Pursuant to the instructions of Her Majesty's Secretary of State for the Colonies, the following matters were duly examined into, and the result of the best consideration that could be given to these subjects will be found in the following order:—

"1st. The state and condition of our forts and settlements on the Western Coast of Africa, their trade, population, resources, and government.

"2d. The facilities afforded in these settlements to the foreign slave traders resorting to them, by affording supplies in goods or stores that are essential to the trade.

"3d. The prospects and practicability of emigration from Sierra Leone to our West India Colonies.

"4th. The climate, salubrity, and nature of the locality of our settlements on the Western Coast of Africa: and in addition to these subjects, I have to add the consideration of two very important ones, not specified in my instructions, but which, in their execution, became part and parcel of them, and which I conceived I would not have done my duty had I left unnoticed, or taken no steps to remove the evils connected with them; these subjects are:—

"1. The existence of slavery in our settlements on the Gold Coast.

"2. The co-operation of British commerce with slave-trade interests, at the factories of notorious slave dealers on the Western Coast of Africa."

[3] Vide Part II, p. 9, et seq.

In treating of the last subject here mentioned, the following remarks occur:—

"It is very true the Consolidated Slave Law, the 5th of Geo. IV, comprehends every case of aiding and abetting the slave trade, that I have proposed to have still more formally and specifically prohibited; and there can be no question that any infraction of this law, whether by insuring slave property, selling goods for slave trading objects, lending money, or giving any species of assistance for the promotion of these objects in any court in England, where the case would be tried on its proper merits, and not decided on by a jury implicated or involved in the interests of slavery, that the offender would be convicted of the felony and punished. But few of those employed in judicial situations on the Western Coast of Africa have been persons belonging to the legal professions, and those who did belong to it, and were the advisers of our governors, have not been persons of very profound experience in the law, and the consequence has been that, with few exceptions, our authorities on the Western Coast of Africa hold the opinion that was entertained at Cape Coast as to the legality of aiding and abetting the slave dealers, of supplying them with the goods and stores essential to the purchase of the slaves. The Consolidated Slave Trade Act, of 1824, distinctly states in the very second clause, that it is unlawful 'in any manner to engage, or to contract to engage, directly or indirectly therein (the slave trade), as a partner, agent, or otherwise, or to ship, tranship, lade, receive, or put on board, &c.... knowing that such ship, vessel, or boat is actually employed, &c.'....

"In the 7th clause, with the customary verbiage, it is declared, that 'if any person shall knowingly and wilfully ship, or put on board of any vessel any money, goods, or effects, to be employed in accomplishing any of the objects hereinbefore declared unlawful, then and in every other such case the person so offending, and their procurers, counsellors, aiders, and abettors, shall forfeit and pay for every such offence double the value of all the money, goods, or effects so shipped, transhipped, laden, received, or put on board, or contracted so to be as aforesaid.'

"And by the 10th clause, the persons thus aiding and abetting the slave trade, are further declared to be felons, and shall be transported for a term not exceeding fourteen years, or confined and kept to hard labour for a term not exceeding five years, nor less than three years, at the discretion of the Court.

"The right and privilege heretofore exercised of suing in Vice-Admiralty Courts for the forfeitures or penalties incurred by the contravention of this law, are set forth in the 12th clause, notwithstanding any criminal proceedings that may have been instituted against the aiders and abettors of this trade. That the merchant in the case of the Dos Amigos had left himself subject to both sorts of proceedings there can be no doubt. In a case somewhat analogous to this, of recent occurrence, a British vessel, commanded by a British subject, the Augusta, dispatched by a London house, was captured by Lieutenant Hill, of Her Majesty's ship Saracen, having merchandise on board adapted for the slave trading factories, and having a direct destination to one of these. The vessel was condemned at Sierra Leone, but no proceedings have been taken in the Vice-admiralty Court in England by Lieutenant Hill, to recover the penalties incurred by this breach of the law. The notoriety of this vessel at all the factories on the coast of Africa had its weight in the tribunal where she was ultimately condemned for aiding and abetting the slave trade. In no respect was the evidence against this vessel stronger than that against the Cape Coast merchant, yet that vessel was condemned by the authorities at Sierra Leone, and the merchant is defended by those at Cape Coast. The Augusta, a notorious slaver, had only been captured and sent to England a few months before under the name of the Gollupchik, and under Russian colours, and she was found again on the coast, under the British flag, the property of London merchants. The Spanish slave trader, who was captain of the Gollupchik, when captured by the Saracen, and sent to England was subsequently taken near Whydah by Commodore Tucker of the Wolverine, while I was passenger on board that vessel, in another slaver called the Liberal; and from this man I learned particulars entirely corroborative of the documentary evidence found on board the Augusta. The recent relinquishment of the slave trade on the part of Don Theodore Canot at his slave factory at New Sesters, one of the principal slave dealers on the Kroo Coast, led to the giving up of his books and papers to Lieutenant Segrim, of Her Majesty's ship Termagant, with whom he entered into arrangements for renouncing his unlawful trade; and, on examining these books on board of Her Majesty's ship Wolverine, I found that a London house had long been in the habit of supplying stores and merchandise to his slave factory from their vessels on the coast. On the 4th of December, 1839, there is an entry of the arrival at his factory, for the purposes of trade, of the English brig Enterprise.

"1st January, 1840. There is an entry of the arrival of an English brig 'Corcyra,' belonging to another house in London, for the purposes of trade, and of having purchased of him 50 guns, 100 cutlasses, 100 large kettles, and 100 bars of irons.

"13th May, 1840. There is an entry of the re-appearance of the captain of the 'Enterprise,' at his factory, and having purchased from him 83 cruces of rice, or about 2,000lbs. weight, for which he paid 63 dollars, and 84 dollars for 21 guns.

"1st July, 1840. There is an entry of the arrival of the English schooner 'Gil Blas,' of London, and of having purchased two pieces of cloth, eight bars of tobacco, and one gallon of rum.

"On the 5th of December, 1840, Don Theodore Canot placed himself under the protection of the British flag, renounced his traffic, and gave up 104 slaves to Lieutenant Segrim.

"Lieutenant Hill, of Her Majesty's ship 'Saracen,' on the 14th January, 1839, visited the British vessel 'Medora,' and was informed by the master that he had just disposed at the Gallinas of 10,000 dollars' worth of goods to the factories there.

"Lieutenant Segrim, of the 'Termagant,' recently boarded the British merchant vessel 'The Guinea Man,' and the master admitted having just sold 500*l.* worth of goods to the slave trade factories at the Gallinas.

"A British trader, a man of colour, who has an establishment at Accra, has one likewise at Little Popoe, where he is known to dabble in this trade.

"This man was an agent of a mercantile house in London; and information reached me of his having embarked for Popoe some time ago, in the neighbourhood of St. Paul's, a number of slaves on board a British vessel then under discharge. On visiting this part of the coast in Her Majesty's ship 'Wolverine,' on my way to Princes' Island, we found at Great Popoe a British subject of colour holding a factory, from which Captain Tucker had information he had lately shipped a cargo of slaves. While at anchor off the shore, Captain Tucker addressed a letter to him on the subject, informing him of the report he had heard, and giving him to understand that, on any repetition of his illegal proceedings, he would destroy his factory and carry himself to Sierra Leone. He returned a submissive, and I must add a very proper answer, not denying the transaction alluded to, but promising faithfully in future to abstain from exporting slaves.

"I have noticed these circumstances, though not apparently bearing on the subject of this part of my Report, namely, the resources, trade, and government of our settlements on the Gold Coast, and the influence of the latter on the adjoining districts, in order to show the necessity there is for a new enactment to prevent the facilities that are now afforded by our commerce from supplying the slave trade factories with these commodities which are indispensable to the slave traders. It is evident that those factories are supplied with goods by British traders, and especially by London merchants, to a very great extent." ...

London, 31st July, 1841.

(signed) R. R. MADDEN.

———

COPY OF A LETTER
FROM
MESSRS. ZULUETA & CO. TO LORD VISCOUNT SANDON.

My Lord, London, 25 April, 1842.

A letter has been addressed to us under date of the 15th inst., by Mr. R. R. Gibbons, sending to us, at your Lordship's desire, a copy of Dr. Madden's Report on the Gold Coast of Africa, and its dependencies, and stating that this is done in consideration of "our being personally interested therein, but that we are to consider it as entirely confidential."

In common with all other merchants in this city, we may of course be said to possess more or less of a professional interest in all matters which relate to commerce.

As having occasionally executed shipping orders for ports in the coast of Africa, on foreign account, of lawful merchandise, lawfully, and therefore publicly cleared at Her Majesty's Customs, in lawful vessels, and as far as we, as mere shipping agents, could be supposed or expected to know, to the best of our knowledge, for no unlawful purpose, without any other interest or emolument in the operation antecedent or subsequent to the shipment than that of the simple and regular commission usually charged in, or legitimately connected with the invoice, and possessing no control, direct or indirect, over either vessels or goods, from the moment they left the shores of Great Britain, we may perhaps be supposed to feel a more direct interest in whatsoever throws light on the subject of trade with ports with which, in the course of our mercantile career, we may have had general business transactions, although they have not been either extensive or frequent.

Still more as shippers, in the form and capacity just described, and in no other, of a cargo consisting not only of legal, but even unsuspected merchandise on board the English schooner Augusta, Captain Jennings, the Report of Dr. Madden, as a document in which the capture of that vessel is alluded to, may also be supposed to form an interesting piece of information, whatever its merits may be in other respects.

Such is the nature and the extent of the interest which we acknowledge to possess in the Report of Dr. Madden, neither more nor less; and we submit that, in describing it as personal, a supposition is advanced which, considering the nature of that Report, we have reason to deem unfavourable to our characters, which the facts will not justify, and which we may say, even appearances will not warrant.

The Report brings together a number of transactions, not one of which have we even the remotest knowledge until the perusal of it, with the sole exception of the case of the Augusta. Now, as when looking at them together as a whole, and in conjunction with the other facts, most probably equally unknown to us, which in the course of the investigation now carried on before the Committee may be brought forward, there is no telling to what extent the association of our name with the matters of the Report may be carried, we have thought it right to explain to your Lordship what kind of interest we have no objection to be supposed to possess in the perusal of Dr. Madden's Report, or in the inquiry now before the Committee. Beyond casual shipments in the manner described, and the acceptance of credits opened at our establishments by parties abroad, in behalf of parties resident in that coast, we have not even one single correspondent, or have we even consigned or sold, or in fact transacted any business whatsoever, or had any intercourse with individuals resident in those parts. We possess no interest in the trade with them, and even the agency for buying and shipping, which now and then we have had, is so insignificant, that we look with the most perfect indifference, as may easily be believed by any one who knows any thing of our business, as to any future legislation which may be the result of the present Parliamentary inquiry, or, indeed, as to any construction which may be put upon that now in existence. It is not, therefore, with the view of in any degree influencing the deliberations of the Committee, or of offering any remark on the facts or on the opinions contained in Dr. Madden's Report, that we address your Lordship. Let the result of the labours of the Committee be what they may, and let the merits or the influence of Dr. Madden's Report be what it may, whatever legislation may emanate from these proceedings, as a matter of business, it is of no moment to us, and therefore it is not our intention to throw the weight of a feather in the balance. Our sole object is to place our position in its true light; and the simple fact of our possessing no interest whatever, either personal or otherwise, in any branch of trade with the coast of Africa, much less with that lamentable branch of it which, much before the law was carried to even its present extent, our firm has shunned in all its branches and ramifications during an existence in business of more than seventy years, independent of the consideration of its illegality, without partaking in many of the views entertained by others concerning it, but from the principle of not wishing to derive profit or advantage from the sufferings of humanity, whether avoidable or unavoidable.

We have, &c.

(signed) *Zulueta & Co.*

———

HOUSE OF COMMONS.
Select Committee on West Coast of Africa.
R. R. GIBBONS, Esq. to MESSRS. ZULUETA & CO.

Gentlemen, July 13th, 1842.

I am desired by Lord Sandon, the chairman of this committee, to forward to you copies of evidence taken before them, in which your house is mentioned; and I am to acquaint you that if you are desirous of making any statement thereon, either personally or by letter, the committee will be ready to receive the same.

I have, &c.

(signed) *R. R. Gibbons.*

———

MINUTES OF EVIDENCE
TAKEN BEFORE THE SELECT COMMITTEE ON WEST COAST OF AFRICA.

Veneris, 10° die Junii, 1842.

MEMBERS PRESENT.

Sir T. D. Acland.
Mr. Aldam.
Lord Viscount Courtenay.
Lord Viscount Ebrington.
Mr. Evans.
Captain Fitzroy.

Mr. Forster.
Mr. Hamilton.
Mr. Metcalf.
Mr. Milnes.
Mr. W. Patten.
Mr. Stuart Wortley.

LORD VISCOUNT SANDON in the chair.

Henry William Macaulay, Esq. called in; and further examined.

5003. *Chairman.*] Will you state what has been your connexion and acquaintance with the coast of Africa?—I went out to Sierra Leone first in the early part of the year 1830 as a merchant, and at the latter end of the year 1831 I was appointed one of the judges in the court of Mixed Commission; I then left business and devoted myself entirely to the business of the court; and I ceased to act as a judge on the 31st of December, 1839.

5004. Since what time have you been at home?—I remained on the coast a short time to recover my health. I was too unwell to move for some months, and then went to the Island of Ascension, from which I came home in the latter end of the year 1840.

5005. Will you state what the court of mixed commission consists of?—The Portuguese court consists of a British commissary judge and a Portuguese commissary judge, who have to decide upon every Portuguese case; in case of any difference of opinion between the two principal judges, the British commissioner of arbitration and the Portuguese commissioner of arbitration draw lots as to which of the two the case is to be referred to for final decision. In the same way, in the Spanish court, the British commissary judge meets the Spanish commissary judge, and in case of difference of opinion, the case is left to either the British or Spanish commissioner of arbitration, as the lot may determine.

5006. Are there any judges for other nations?—The courts at Sierra Leone are the Portuguese court, the Spanish court, the Brazilian court, and the Dutch court; but no court during my time has been perfect in the number of its judges except the Brazilian court.

5007. You mean by perfect, that the British judge has had to sit alone?—The treaties require that after a certain time, in the absence of any foreign judge, the British commissioner of arbitration shall act as the foreign commissary judge.

5008. Who is the British commissioner of arbitration; is he a distinct person from the British commissary judge?—Yes; the British court is always perfect.

5009. What does it consist of?—It consists of the British commissary judge and the British commissioner of arbitration; and the treaties point out how any vacancy, either by death or absence, is to be supplied; the governor in the first instance, attends for the absent judge, whoever he may be, and after him, the chief justice, and then the colonial secretary. It is left to those three officers; but I presume that if those three should all be ill, or their places be vacant by death, the office would then descend to the person next in seniority in the colonial government there; but we never went lower than the colonial secretary. The Brazilian court has been the only one perfect, and the British commissioner of arbitration has always sat in my time for the Portuguese and Spanish commissary judges. No case at all has occurred in the Dutch court.

5010. In case a vessel taken under the colours of any other nation were brought into Sierra Leone, how would that case be decided?—There are other treaties than those I have mentioned. A French case is sent to the French authorities under the French treaty, and in the treaties with all other nations that have treaties on the model of the French treaty, the vessels are handed over to their own judicial authorities.

5011. Within Sierra Leone?—The treaty points out where they are to be taken; if a French vessel is taken, it is sent to Goree.

5012. Then no vessels are brought in for adjudication to Sierra Leone but Dutch and Portuguese, and Spanish and Brazilian vessels?—Not for adjudication by the mixed commission; but there is the vice-admiralty court, which under the late act relating to Portugal, for the suppression of the slave trade, takes cognizance of vessels under that flag which are captured; and may take cognizance of any vessels under any flag that are captured in British waters, wherever they are taken, whether at Sierra Leone, or the Gambia, or any British settlement on the coast, and that has been rather frequent of late.

5013. The mixed commission court has jurisdiction over all cases which are brought within the limits of the treaty with Portugal, and the Vice-Admiralty Court in the Portuguese cases, over which we have assumed jurisdiction by Act of Parliament, that is to say, all cases of vessels captured south of the Line?—Yes; it is optional still for the captor to prosecute a Portuguese vessel, captured under the Act of Parliament, before the admiralty court, if he chooses, instead of bringing her before the mixed commission court, but the process is so much more summary with us, and the expense so much less, that that option is seldom taken.

5014. Will you proceed to explain what is the process which is pursued when a slaver is brought into Sierra Leone for adjudication?—Whenever a vessel appears in the harbour under any of the flags of which we can take cognizance, the marshal of the court goes on board, and he receives from the prizemaster who is on board an account of the capture, which he fills into a printed form, and he sends one of those printed forms to each of the judges, and one to the governor, immediately; in fact, generally before the vessel comes to anchor, and then the court is made aware of the vessel being in the harbour, and is prepared to make arrangements for the landing of the slaves, if there are any, generally the morning after its arrival, if it comes in the evening, or if it comes in early in the morning, the same day. The proctor for the captor brings the papers of the vessel before the court, and they are always accompanied by a declaration of the captor. All the forms of the court are very much the same as those of the Admiralty Court in England. If there are slaves, the proctor petitions for the admission of the vessel into court, and generally accompanies that by a petition to land the slaves; and since I have been there, in every case of inquiry the slaves were landed and handed over to the superintendent of the African department pending the investigation, and held in their character of slaves during the time that the vessel was passing through the court. The proctor then produces his witnesses, and they are examined upon printed interrogatories, which have been used ever since the court was formed. These questions are framed with a view to make out a case, and they always do prove slave dealing wherever it has existed, if the witness answers truly; and in an ordinary case, where slaves are on board, no defence is ever attempted, it is out of the question. Then as soon as the evidence is given, generally by the captain and one of the officers of the captured vessel, the proctor prays for publication; and when the monition which issues in the first instance, calling upon any persons to bring forward a claim if they have any against the capture, or to show cause why the vessel should not be condemned, is returned, trial is prayed for, and it takes place on an early day after arrival of the vessel; in an undefended case, and where the capture has been made properly by the man-of-war, the vessel is condemned, the slaves are emancipated at the same time; a commission of appraisement and sale issues, which directs the particular officer of the court who has the duty of conducting the auctions to expose both the vessel and the goods, and any thing that may be on board, to public auction, after due notice given. Those things are then sold, and the proceeds are divided equally between the British Government and the foreign government, and the proceeds are then paid into the commissariat, which settles with the Government at home, and they pay the money, or set it off against any claim they may have against the foreign government; but the foreign government has a claim to one-half the proceeds of the vessels and cargoes.

5015. Is there any large proportion of cases in which condemnation does not follow, and under what circumstances principally has condemnation not been the consequence?—There have been vessels restored for being seized, for instance, Portuguese vessels from the southward of the Line, contrary to treaty. In two cases there were vessels restored with upwards of 8,000*l.* damages against the captors in each case, making 16,000*l.*; and there was again one case of the Pepita, which I remember, when it was proved that the slaves had been embarked under circumstances that would not justify condemnation under the treaty; she was restored with damages. There have been several cases under the equipment article since the new slave treaty came into force, where vessels have been restored because the equipment was not deemed sufficient to warrant condemnation. There have been also vessels taken on the suspicion that black persons on board were slaves, who have been proved to be domestics, and not bought for the purpose of the traffic. There have been a variety of condemnations; but in any case where the treaty would not warrant condemnation, the vessel has been restored; and where the treaty required it, restored with damages.

5016. Have there been a considerable number of restorations; can you state, from statistics, the number?—I have statistics for two years; from the 1st of January to the 31st of December 1838, one vessel only was liberated.

5017. What number were condemned?—Forty-one; during the year 1839 there were two liberated, and 45 condemned; and in addition to those, there was a very large number of American vessels which were seized, with American papers on board, and which I refused to receive into court at all; there were some in 1838, and there was a large number in 1839.

5018. Can you state the number?—I think the number was 13; but the reports of the whole of those cases are in the Parliamentary Papers.

5019. Were they *bonâ fide* American?—I believe not American, in any one case, but sailing under the American flag, and with American papers, supplied to them by American authority.

5020. Where?—Almost entirely, I think, without one exception, at Havannah.

5021. Supplied by the American consul?—Yes; but I considered that as they sailed with those American papers, however wrongfully they might have been given by the American authority, we had no right to interfere with them.

5022. Mr. *Forster.*] Have not some vessels belonging to the States been condemned?—Yes; since my time.

5023. You were not a party to the condemnation?—I was not.

5024. Mr. *W. Patten.*] But in those cases which you mention, you had not the slightest doubt in the world that they would have been condemned if they had not American papers on board?—Certainly they would, with the exception of one case, which seemed to be a sort of experimental seizure: it was known that almost every vessel on the coast under the American flag, at that time was a Spanish vessel in disguise; and this vessel seems to have been seized in the hope that the captain and officers might be able to prove, by some evidence found on board, that she was really Spanish; but though we had access to the papers, we found nothing that would have condemned her if she had been prosecuted in the court; there was a deficiency of papers on board; the captain, perhaps had either destroyed them or concealed them, and we could not get at the proof that would have enabled us to condemn her as being a Spanish vessel; but none of the cases I speak of were prosecuted; I would not allow them to be libelled in court.

5025. So that those cases do not appear upon the records of the court?— No; but I took the opportunity of examining the papers, and sending home all the particulars to the Foreign-office, and the papers are copied in the Parliamentary Returns.

5026. Mr. *Forster.*] Will those seizures be matter of complaint on the part of the owners?—I do not know that any of those seizures have been matter of complaint; some of the seizures made subsequently have been.

5027. Seizures of vessels belonging to the United States?—Yes; but none of those that came before me have been made matter of complaint.

5028. Are you aware that there are several cases of condemnation that have been the subject of remonstrance with the British Government by the United States?—I believe the whole of them are.

5029. *Chairman.*] You have not heard that they complain of vessels being brought in for condemnation to Sierra Leone which you did not allow to be libelled in court?—No, except as regards the general right which was exercised. There has been no complaint with respect to a particular vessel, so far as I know; but complaints have been made of the right which was exercised by cruizers on the coast to board any American vessel and search it.

5030. Mr. *Aldam.*] Has the practice of the court been changed since your time?—Yes, it was changed the day that I left; there was an American vessel waiting at Sierra Leone for adjudication the day I left, and the officer suspecting, that if presented to me, I should refuse her in the same way as I had done the others, detained her till I left, and she was condemned by my successor under orders from Lord Palmerston.

5031. Then the orders from Lord Palmerston changed the practice of the court?—Yes.

5032. Do you know the nature of those orders?—The orders appear in the printed correspondence.

5033. Mr. *W. Patten.*] Can you state briefly the nature of the orders?—His Lordship stated that the Queen's advocate was of opinion that the court was justified in making use of information obtained by the search of vessels under the American flag. The court had decided, that having no right to search vessels sailing as American, and recognised as American by American authorities, they could not make use of any information which they obtained by unauthorised and illegal acts, and Lord Palmerston considered that they had a right.

5034. *Chairman.*] You held that the papers protected the vessel?—I did.

5035. Mr. *Forster.*] Then it is those condemnations which are appealed against at present by the American government?—I have not seen any appeal of the American government except against the general right exercised by the British cruizers.

5036. The complaint is, of seizing vessels as connected with the slave trade, which, from their papers, ought not to have been subject to that suspicion?—I am not aware of any appeal in any case of that kind.

5037. Mr. *Aldam.*] Have any vessels with strictly American papers been condemned?—You can hardly call them strictly American papers where the papers have been applied for, and given through fraud. The American authorities at the Havannah who gave them, knew very well that the vessel had no more claim to be styled an American vessel than a Dutch vessel.

5038. *Chairman.*] But as far as the documents themselves showed, those vessels were American?—Yes, they had an American register, just in the same form as any vessel sailing from New York, or Baltimore; indeed it was a copy of the same document.

5039. What indication was there in other papers taken, to lead you to know that the property was not *bonâ fide* American?—It appeared, from the very strict overhauling these vessels received from the cruizers, that in many of those cases there were papers on board showing that the man who appeared as the American captain was only a passenger, and that the 30 Spanish passengers who took out passengers' licences at Havannah were the real crew; and there were also instructions, found on board, to the pretended captain, what he was to answer to the cruizers when they boarded him. The whole thing was a complete fraud without any doubt whatever. There were many of those cases where it was quite plain that the vessels were only Spaniards in disguise; that they only kept the American flag until their cargo was ready. In some cases the vessels that were boarded one day by the cruizers under the American flag, were boarded two or three days afterwards with the Portuguese or Spanish flag hoisted, and full of slaves.

5040. And condemned?—Yes.

5041. What was the object of hoisting the Spanish or Portuguese flag?—If the vessels had been captured by a British cruizer with the American flag hoisted, he would have carried them into America; and if he did carry them into America, every man on board would have been hung as a pirate.

5042. Had he authority to do so?—It *was* done; the American authorities did not complain of it.

5043. Mr. *W. Patten.*] Were they hung in that case?—No, there were no slaves on board.

5044. Mr. *Aldam.*] Every ship of war has a right to capture a pirate?—Yes.

5045. The law of the United States recognizes slavery as piracy?—Yes, but it is not piracy by the law of nations, and indeed our own courts have decided most positively on that point, that the slave trade is not piracy by the law of nations; that it can only be punished by the municipal law of the particular country to which the vessel belongs.

5046. Mr. *Forster.*] The class of condemnations to which you have alluded are different from the cases which have taken place since you left, under the direction of Lord Palmerston?—No condemnations took place before the 1st of January, 1840; there were vessels condemned by me that were captured under the American flag, and with American papers, but they were taken in British waters, where British ships had a right to visit and search the vessel, and the captor might make use of any information he obtained in the search: when apparent American vessels were boarded on the high seas, we deemed that the captor had not that authority.

5047. *Chairman.*] What do you consider British waters on the coast of Africa; what would you for instance, on the Gold Coast, consider British waters?—The waters of a nation are those within gun-shot of the shore; generally reckoned three miles; it is the same all over the world.

5048. With regard to the Gold Coast, you are aware that our settlements consist of several forts; do you consider the whole line of coast, from end to end, along which our forts are planted, to be British water?—No, for there are foreign forts there mixed with ours; but in every case we have the sovereignty over three miles of the sea from our own possession, wherever it may be, and the only ports to which a vessel could go, have forts attached to them; a vessel lying at Accra, or lying at Cape Coast, would be within three miles of the fort.

5049. If she was sailing along the coast, should you consider her to be in British waters?—Where an indefinite authority is exercised along a line of coast, without any real right, I do not consider those British waters.

5050. You would consider as British waters only those which were a certain distance from the fort?—Yes; the difficulty occurred in the case of the Jack Wilding, one of the richest prizes that was made during the year 1839; she was seized lying in British Accra roadstead, and she was under the American flag; she was brought up to Sierra Leone, and defended, on the ground that, though the vessel was in British waters, she was within three miles of the Dutch fort, but we considered that that could not make any difference, that we could not allow slave trading within three miles of any acknowledged British fort, and we condemned the vessel.

5051. Have you seen practical evil arise from the mixed commission being fixed at Sierra Leone?—No, certainly not.

5052. Not as to the health of the slaves in the length of the voyage from the place of seizure to the place of condemnation?—I believe that there is a great misapprehension on this subject, which would be corrected by a mere reference to the statistics of the trade; there seems to be an impression that a very great majority of the cases of capture are made to the eastward of Cape Palmas, and in the bights, but a large number have been taken for many years past, and might always have been taken, to the westward of Cape Palmas, and in the neighbourhood of Sierra Leone.

5053. Is there any statement of the length of voyage of each vessel from the time of its seizure to the time of its condemnation?—I do not think there is any table drawn out; but in the printed reports the times and places of capture are stated, which comes to the same thing; because, where the vessels are captured in the immediate neighbourhood of Sierra Leone, the voyage is very short, and in going through the reports the number of days can be calculated. In the detailed reports which are given of each case, the date of the capture is always mentioned, and the date of arrival at Sierra Leone. In some cases the vessels are delayed after capture, and you could not get an exact account; but in most cases the difference between the date of capture and the date of arrival would be the length of voyage.

5054. Mr. *Forster.*] Has not the great bulk of the seizures been made in the bights and to the eastward of Cape Palmas?—Not a very large majority during the last year, and before that a large portion were made to the westward of Cape Palmas; and if that part of the coast had had the number of cruizers that it ought to have had, there would have been a much larger number of captures made there.

5055. *Chairman.*] You think that the slave trade has gone on with greater intensity to the westward of Cape Palmas?—With great intensity in the Gallinas, which was unnoticed for some years; and, indeed, that part of the coast was utterly neglected. The admiral and commanding officers seemed to fancy that the slave trade could only be carried on in the bights, but a great deal of slave trade was carried on to the westward.

5056. Where?—In Gallinas, principally, New Sesters, Sherboro'; those are the principal ports in that part; there are others smaller.

5057. For all those ports, of course, Sierra Leone you consider to be the most advantageous position?—Certainly.

5058. Mr. *Forster.*] But in speaking of the amount of slave trade carried on at those places which you have just named, do you speak of those in comparison with the bights, and also with the Spanish and Portuguese settlements to the south of the Line?—I speak of the amount of captures that have been made there. The south was left very nearly in the same state in which the north was. The cruizing of the squadron was almost entirely confined to the bights.

5059. To the south of the Line they could not cruize, could they?—Yes, they could cruize near the Portuguese settlements, for the court practically got over the article in the treaty under which captures were forbidden to the southward of the Line, by establishing, which they did in 1838, the principle, that the national character of any vessel was to be taken from the residence of the owner, the place where he carried on his mercantile business, and also from the course of trade in which the vessel was engaged; and as there could be no foreign Portuguese slave trade, for Portugal has no colonies to supply with slaves, we were sure to make the vessel either Brazilian or Spanish. She was captured under Portuguese colours, and with Portuguese papers, but the treaty had given us a right to search her any where, either north or south; it had not given us the right to detain her south of the Line, if she was *bonâ fide* Portuguese; but if captured as a Portuguese vessel under the Portuguese flag, and with Portuguese papers, she was sent up to Sierra Leone, and was almost certain to be condemned either as a Brazilian or a Spaniard.

5060. That decision was come to in 1838?—Yes.

5061. Before that time the impression had prevailed that the slave trade from the Portuguese settlements was protected?—There was no seizure to the south of the Line to render a decision necessary; vessels were seized immediately close to the Line, in several cases, and it was never thought of; that was before the Portuguese flag was so much used, and the cause of the Portuguese flag being so much used by slavers, was the Spanish treaty having given the right to seize, on the ground of equipment; that did not take place till 1836. I was at home in that year, and on my return in December 1837, I found that almost every vessel on the coast was sailing under Portuguese colours, and then we met this new circumstance by an alteration in the interpretation of the treaty.

5062. Mr. *Aldam*.] If the owner had been a *bonâ fide* Portuguese, would the vessel have been still condemned?—If the owner had been a Portuguese, resident in Havannah, we should have treated the vessel as a Spanish vessel; and if at Rio Janeiro, we should have treated it as a Brazilian vessel.

5063. But in the case of a Portuguese merchant resident in a Portuguese possession, and carrying on his business there?—We should have looked at the course of trade in which the vessel was engaged, and the Portuguese having no colonies would not require slaves.

5064. Mr. *Forster*.] Do you consider the Spanish and Portuguese settlements to the south of the Line the places at which the slave trade will be last overcome?—The part of the coast at which the slave trade is carried on depends entirely on the cruizers; you may knock up the slave trade on any part of the coast you please, if the cruizing is properly conducted. The largest slave trade on the coast was the slave trade at the Gallinas; by the system of blockade that Captain Denman adopted there, he completely destroyed it.

5065. That blockade must be continued to make it permanent in its results?—Yes; and he never went away for water or provisions, without leaving a vessel to supply his place. He could always regulate the time that he should remain, knowing of course, to a day, how long his water and provisions would last him.

5066. But to render that remedy effectual and permanent, vessels of war must continue at the Gallinas?—Yes; but if you blockade the rivers, where the slave trade has been carried on for a number of years, and completely shut up the slave trade for a year or two, you destroy the system of slave trade in that part.

5067. *Chairman*.] You think the machinery cannot be re-established in that part?—It may be re-established, but in the meantime there is no mart for the slaves; they are brought down and lodged in the barracoons, and the feeding of the slaves completely ruins the slave owner.

5068. Mr. *Forster*.] What is there to prevent the system being resumed there unless you continue the blockade of the place?—There is nothing.

5069. Then it is upon the blockade of the settlements that the success of the cruizers depends, and not upon the destruction of the barracoons?—Exactly; by blockade, I do not mean shutting out legitimate trade, but preventing any vessel fitted for the slave trade going in, and preventing any vessel with slaves coming out.

5070. *Chairman*.] Do you believe that if you blockade a port, materially interfering with the slave trade for a considerable period, you obstruct it even for some time afterwards?—I think you do; and I think the people are so accustomed to the goods which they procure from slave dealers that they will get them if they can by other means.

5071. Then you think, that if you can blockade for a certain time, and put an end to the power of procuring what the natives desire by the slave trade, that their taste will have to be gratified by lawful traffic, and that that will make it less necessary for them afterwards to have recourse to the slave trade?—Certainly.

5072. Mr. *Forster*.] By such destruction as took place in the case of Gallinas, do you not interfere with the course of the legitimate trade, as well as with the course of the slave trade?—I am not speaking of the destruction of a settlement.

5073. Had not the operations of Captain Denman the effect of destroying the stores, and in fact the whole settlement?—He destroyed the barracoons; but no one ever kept in barracoons any thing but slaves.

5074. Was not also a considerable property in merchandize destroyed?—Yes, so it appears by the Parliamentary papers. At that time there was no trade whatever carried on at Gallinas except in slaves; there was no legitimate trade at all, I believe.

5075. Do you mean that there was no legitimate trade carried on at the Gallinas previous to the destruction of that place by Captain Denman?—I believe, none whatever; there was certainly none with its nearest large port, which was Sierra Leone; the only trade carried on between the two places was of a very questionable character.

5076. Were not Hamburg vessels and other foreign vessels constantly in the habit of visiting Gallinas for the purpose of legitimate trade previous to the destruction of the settlement?—I am not aware that they did.

5077. I thought you told the Committee in a late answer, that there was no legitimate trade carried on there?—From Sierra Leone; but whether Hamburg vessels went direct to Gallinas, I do not know; from Sierra Leone, I do not believe that any legitimate trade was carried on with the Gallinas.

5078. What opportunities had you at Sierra Leone of knowing the course of trade to Gallinas?—I was in Sierra Leone, where there were a large number of small coasting vessels employed, and those who brought back produce did not go to Gallinas for it.

5079. But had you any opportunity of knowing the nature and extent of the legitimate trade there by foreign vessels, independently of Sierra Leone?—No; but I have always understood, (it is only from hearsay I mention this,) from the men-of-war on the coast, that every vessel they have found lying in the harbour there, has been engaged in the slave trade in some way or other, as American vessels bringing over goods from the Havannah for the supply of factories, or bringing out equipments to be carried away by slavers when they were full.

5080. You have stated that previously to the destruction of Gallinas by Captain Denman, no trade had been carried on between the Gallinas and Sierra Leone, except such as was of a very questionable nature?—I have.

5081. Was that questionable trade to a considerable extent?—No, not with Sierra Leone; but trading vessels that came along the coast have called at Sierra Leone, and gone down the coast afterwards, and probably put into Gallinas amongst other ports; but directly with Sierra Leone the trade was very little indeed.

5082. Up to what period did this questionable trade between Sierra Leone and Gallinas continue?—It continued as long as I was connected with the colony, that is, to the 31st of December, 1839; but we always looked with suspicion upon any merchant there that was connected with that place.

5083. Is it within your knowledge that up to that time the slave dealers, by themselves, or their agents, were in the habit of frequenting Sierra Leone, and making purchases there for the supply of Gallinas?—They generally made their purchases, I believe, through some merchant resident at Sierra Leone; one in particular; they generally had one merchant at a time, I believe, who was employed by them.

5084. *Chairman.*] Making purchases of prize goods?—Yes, and sometimes of vessels; a vessel that might be put up to auction there he would bid for, and have it sent down to Gallinas; and I have no doubt goods also.

5085. Was he a white merchant, or a black, who was so employed?—He was a white merchant, an English merchant.

5086. Who was he?—The name is mentioned in the Parliamentary Papers, as being connected with the purchase of a slave vessel, Mr. Kidd; and it is mentioned in connection with that of Mr. Zulueta, of London.

5087. Can you refer to the passage?—It appears at the 38th page of the class (B.) of the papers on the subject of the slave trade, presented to Parliament 1839-40. Zulueta, the gentleman in London to whom the vessel was sent, and who sold her again to her former Spanish owner, is a name well known on the coast in connexion with the slave trade; any man ought to have been careful of being connected with such a person as that. I have seen the same vessels over and over again in the slave trade; you can detect them when you get accustomed to the form and build of the vessels.

5088. Mr. *Forster*.] Were not those vessels sold to the best bidder?—Yes.

5089. Do not you think that the fault was with those who sold them originally, and not those who bought them?—No; you are not bound to suppose that a man will make a bad use of that which he purchases.

5090. Mr. *W. Patten*.] Are those vessels generally bought by the same person?—Mr. Kidd purchased vessels only during the latter part of the time I was there, for he was not in the colony when I first went there; he was looked upon as the person employed by the Gallinas slave dealers to transact their business at Sierra Leone.

5091. *Chairman*.] To purchase vessels and goods?—Yes.

5092. Mr. *W. Patten*.] Is Mr. Kidd the person you alluded to just now, who generally purchased the vessels at auction?—No, they were generally purchased by various people; he purchased a few of them.

5093. Mr. *Forster*.] Would Mr. Zulueta, if he had entered the auction-room, have been at liberty to bid for the purchase of that vessel?—Certainly; by the treaty it is required that the goods seized shall be exposed to public auction for the benefit of the two governments.

5094. How do you make it out to be criminal in Mr. Kidd to do that which it was innocent for the auctioneer on the part of the British Government to do?—The auctioneer is required to do it by his duty, he is appointed for that purpose under the Act of Parliament; he sells to any body who will purchase; of course, the responsibility of the employment of the purchase rests with the purchaser.

5095. Then it is the fault of the Government, not of the auctioneer?—It is not the fault of the auctioneer; nor do I consider it any fault of the British Government; it is no fault to purchase goods, but to use them unlawfully is wrong; it is the use which he makes of the vessel after purchasing it that is wrong.

5096. How could it be criminal in Mr. Kidd to sell the vessel to Mr. Zulueta when you see no fault in the British Government doing the same thing?—The British Government is obliged to do it under the treaty; there is no compulsion on Mr. Kidd to sell his vessel to a slave dealer, he may sell it to any body.

5097. According to that doctrine, the British Government is obliged to act criminally?—No, certainly not; I do not think it follows. The treaty requires that goods and vessels shall be exposed at auction; the responsibility of the employment of those goods or vessels which are sold, I think, rests with the purchaser; he may employ them lawfully, and I have purchased a vessel at auction myself, in former days, when I was engaged in business; but if I had taken that vessel and sold her to a slave dealer, I should think that I did wrong.

5098. But you admit that the public auctioneer would have sold the same vessel to the same party whom Mr. Kidd sold her to?—Certainly.

5099. *Chairman.*] You meant to say that the auctioneer had no choice to whom he should sell her, and Mr. Kidd had?—The auctioneer had no choice; the Act is imperative, and requires him to sell to the highest bidder, for the benefit of the two governments.

5100. Mr. *Aldam.*] Did Mr. Kidd sell his vessel to a slave dealer or to a Spanish house, who subsequently sold it to a slave dealer?—It appears in some of the records that in some cases he sold vessels direct to the slave dealers.

5101 Are those vessels worth more to a slave dealer than if used for any other purpose?—Certainly.

5102. How then is it possible to prevent the ships being applied to that purpose for which they are worth more than for any other?—Spanish ships are prevented from being used for the trade by being cut up when they are condemned.

5103. Mr. *Evans.*] But you have no power of doing so with the Portuguese ships?—No.

5104. Mr. *Aldam.*] Those vessels, from their small size, are not worth much for other trades?—There are some trades that they are adapted for, the fruit trade for instance, and they are employed in the smuggling of opium and such trades as those; they are not capable of carrying large burdens.

5105. In all cases it will answer the purpose of the merchant to give a larger price for those ships to be employed in the slave trade than for any other purpose?—Yes, probably.

5106. Viscount *Ebrington.*] Have you ever considered what the result would be of the British Government buying those ships in?—It would be impossible to buy them all in.

5107. All that are not liable to be broken up?—No. During last year, for instance, the number condemned was so large, that the Government, if they had bought them, could not have found a use for them.

5108. Mr. *Forster.*] Have you any doubt that those vessels have been sometimes knocked down by the auctioneer to agents of the slave traders on the coast?—It may have been so, and I have no doubt it has; I do not recollect a case at present, but I would have insisted upon it, as head of the court, that it should have been knocked down to any one who made the highest bid.

5109. It is your opinion also, that the prize goods have been frequently sold in the like manner?—Some portion of them, but certainly not the bulk of them.

5110. Was there any thing to prevent the whole of them being sold to the slave dealers, or the agent of the slave dealers?—Nothing whatever.

5111. Had you opportunities of observing, up to the time you left Sierra Leone, whether the agents of the slave dealers on the neighbouring coast frequently appeared in the market of Sierra Leone as purchasers of goods or vessels?—Not often; if the goods came into their hands it was through a third person generally. I have heard of Spaniards going down, and bidding for the vessels, but it was not an ordinary occurrence.

5112. Then you are of opinion that usually slave dealers at Gallinas did not visit Sierra Leone for the purpose of making purchases of goods or vessels?—Not in their own persons, they may have done it through a third party; but, perhaps, it would shorten the questions to state that the greater portion of the goods sold at the auctions captured from vessels in the slave trade were purchased by liberated Africans, by the hawkers there, and they made the best use of them. That a certain portion of the goods so purchased at auctions may get into the hands of slave dealers afterwards, is very possible; but I am convinced, from the description of goods which are sold, which may be used in lawful trade, and from the different appearance of the whole colony since goods were sold so extensively, that the greater portion of them are consumed in the colony, and are made use of in the lawful trade, by liberated Africans in the neighbourhood. I consider that the colony has been very much benefited indeed by those sales; that the condition of the liberated Africans has been very much improved by them, as has been very evident from the great wealth that has been stirring among them; and the liberated Africans have now not only completely bought out the Maroons and settlers, who were the original settlers of the place, but are gradually driving out the white merchants; and I think it a very great advantage, for they are able to live much more cheaply than the white men can do; they carry on their business at one hundredth part of the expense, and turn their money over very much more quickly.

5113. Are any precautions taken by the authorities at Sierra Leone to prevent slave dealers obtaining goods at Sierra Leone, either by public auction or in any other manner?—Certainly not.

5114. Mr. *W. Patten.*] You have stated that there was an illicit trade going on between Sierra Leone and Gallinas; are there any other circumstances than those you have mentioned, that you can adduce in proof of that?—None; in the trade that has been just referred to, of Spaniards and Portuguese at Gallinas sending up to purchase goods at auctions, they have done so, and they have been sent down to them through a third party, but it is seldom they appear themselves.

5115. You do not, of your own knowledge, know what is the connection between Mr. Kidd and any individuals at Gallinas?—No.

5116. Nor of any other merchant at Sierra Leone?—No.

5117. Do you believe that they act as commission merchants to purchase goods?—Yes; I suppose on commission.

5118. Is there any trade carried on by any merchant on his own account with the Gallinas?—I should think that very likely too; but it is impossible to know, for after vessels have gone outside the Cape they may carry their goods any where: you do not know what becomes of them.

5119. Mr. *Forster.*] Do you think it would be desirable to impose any restriction upon legitimate trade to Gallinas?—I think not; I think no restriction upon trade should be imposed, even on the intercourse between the two places.

5120. Mr. *W. Patten.*] How would you distinguish the legitimate from the illegitimate trade?—You cannot distinguish it; and there I think the danger lies of attempting to interfere with intercourse.

5121. Mr. *Forster.*] And therefore, in attempting to check or impede the one, you would do more harm than good in repressing and discouraging the other?—I think it very probable; I think it would be quite impossible to draw the line.

5122. But supposing it to be possible, do you think it would be, in fact, desirable to take any measures which would have the effect of checking the progress of legitimate trade?—Certainly not.

5123. Were there any Hamburgh vessels condemned at Sierra Leone?—Not in my time.

5124. Mr. *Hamilton.*] Do you think that the establishing such a blockade on the coast as you have alluded to just now, would have the effect of interfering with legitimate trade?—No, not such a blockade as I alluded to; I think the natives are well aware of the design for which the cruizers are on the coast, they would consider their presence rather as a protection, than otherwise, to the legitimate trade.

5125. Mr. *Forster.*] Were not large quantities of tobacco and rum sold at Sierra Leone from the prize vessels conveyed there leeward for sale to the Sierra Leone merchants?—Yes; I believe there were several cargoes of Brazilian tobacco and of spirits sent down the coast: I believe, principally to Badagry and that neighbourhood.

5126. That tobacco was, of course, especially imported on the coast for the purpose of the slave trade?—It was taken out of slave vessels; therefore, of course, it was.

5127. When it arrived at Badagry, it would consequently be very acceptable to slave dealers there?—Yes; but they had to pay for it.

5128. Mr. *W. Patten.*] Did you find when you were at Sierra Leone that the price paid for goods at auctions exceeded or was below the price of goods imported in other ways?—The necessary effect of such large quantities of goods being thrown on the market, and compelled to be sold at any rate to the highest bidder, was of course to lower the price; and I consider that the very cheap rate at which the liberated Africans were able to procure those goods, which, in former times, they could only obtain at a high price, was what formed the advantage which they derived from those sales.

5129. How do you account for it, that the merchants at Sierra Leone do not themselves purchase those goods?—They have not the money; in fact, they have no money at all. There are only one or two men that have any money in the place; they are almost all men who receive their goods from houses in England; they are generally very much in debt to the persons who send goods to them; and the only parties who have money in the colony, with the exception of two gentlemen, are liberated Africans, and many of the latter have very large sums.

5130. Mr. *Forster.*] Has the trade at Sierra Leone not, in your opinion, been a successful trade for some years?—It has been a successful trade for the liberated Africans.

5131. The question applied to British traders?—I cannot say; I have not been engaged in trade myself during that time; but I should think that the English traders must have suffered by the goods which were thrown on the market from slave vessels, whilst they had goods which were purchased at a much dearer rate to dispose of, and had not the money to purchase the low-priced goods there. But one case I can mention, where a white merchant at Sierra Leone had the funds to go into the market and compete with the liberated Africans; he has made a great deal of money by it, and the more in consequence of his means being so superior to those of the Africans; but that was because he had money: the losses of the others were because they had none.

5132. You have spoken of the advantages to the black population from the sale of those goods, which have led them to become hawkers and pedlars in the neighbouring country; it is the fact that the natives of Africa are very much disposed to that species of employment in preference to agricultural labour?—It certainly is so at Sierra Leone.

5133. Then the advantages derived from the encouragement thus given to them to embark in that species of employment in preference to the fixed pursuits of agriculture may be questionable on that ground?—I think not; I think if the liberated African can get money and can educate his family well, and procure all that he wants by trade, it is just as well as if he procured it by agriculture.

5134. Have you found them practically carrying on any regular system of agriculture voluntarily?—Not for export: there have been some articles cultivated, but to no very great extent: ginger, and pepper, and cassada, but cultivation has not been carried to any great extent for export at Sierra Leone.

5135. How do you account for cultivation and improvement having made so little progress in Sierra Leone after all the efforts of the party in this country, and all the money which has been expended upon it?—I doubt the proposition contained in the question; I think that they have made progress.

5136. Planting and cultivation is carried on there to a great extent?—No, it is not; but the people have other means of procuring what they require.

5137. Have any means been taken, or if taken, have they been successful, for promoting any regular system of agriculture or planting in the neighbourhood of Sierra Leone?—No, I think not, and I am very sorry for it; I think more might have been done in the way of premiums upon produce, and giving prizes for successful cultivation.

5138. In fact, has any thing been done in that way?—Nothing whatever, I believe, of late years. There was an agricultural society that existed many years before I went to the colony, which offered premiums, but the members of it died, and the scheme fell to the ground.

5139. The attempts of that society, in fact, were not successful?—No; it was before my time; I cannot speak positively to the efforts that were made; it is a great many years ago now.

5140. Can you distinguish the amount of captures to the south and north of the Line?—Yes; in 1838, 15 out of 30 vessels, either were captured, or took on board their slaves to the westward of Cape Palmas, or one-third of the vessels which were detained with full cargoes of slaves on board, or four out of seven, if we only look to the vessels detained in the West Indies. The whole, or very nearly, of the slave trade carried on in the north, or rather west of Cape Palmas, is for the supply of the island of Cuba, and generally on account of the Havannah merchants. In the following year, "of the 61 vessels which passed through the courts during the year 1839, three were captured in the West Indies, the remainder on this coast, eight to the southward of the Line, but none below the latitude of 4 deg. 58 min. south, and of 50 vessels captured north of the Line, 30 were met with to the eastward and 20 to the westward of Cape Palmas."

5141. Mr. *W. Patten.*] Does not the return distinguish from what part of the coast those vessels came?—Yes; it goes into all the particulars of the places from which they came, and the places to which they went, and to which they took their cargoes; 18 of the whole number had slaves on board, 11 having shipped their slaves in parts to the eastward of Cape Palmas, and seven to the westward of the same point, and the river where they shipped them is mentioned.

5142. Mr. *Forster.*] Supposing that the time should arrive when the greatest number of prize vessels should be brought from the southward, would you in that case consider Sierra Leone to be the place best adapted for the mixed commission?—If that arose from the slave trade being permanently at an end in the north, I should say, that the commission should certainly follow the course of the slave trade.

5143. Mr. *W. Patten.*] From the position you held, had you any information, officially or otherwise, of knowing the state of the slave trade to the south of the Line?—No, except what I got from papers found on board detained vessels, and from conversation with naval officers.

5144. From information so obtained, were you led to believe that the slave trade on the coast of Africa, taking both the east and west coast, had increased or decreased during the period you were there?—It had decreased in the bights, so as to be almost entirely destroyed at one time.

5145. The question refers to the coast on the south of the Line?—When it was suppressed to a great extent in the bights, it was driven both north and south of the bights; the old slave trade rivers in the bights were the principal places frequented by slave vessels, but the whole efforts of the cruizers were directed to that point, and the trade was almost entirely suppressed in those rivers, the Bonny and many others.

5146. You had no information which could enable you to judge whether the slave trade on the whole had increased or decreased during your residence at Sierra Leone?—I should say, that it decreased during the last two years I was there, from the immense number of captures that were made.

5147. It has been stated by a witness on the Committee, Captain Bosanquet, that in his belief, the slave trade south of the line, has increased materially during the last 10 years?—I think Captain Bosanquet refers to the eastern coast.

5148. Captain Bosanquet stated that he was, at two periods, on the coast, and that at the last period he found the slave trade going on with much more violence than at the first?—The effect of the suppression of the slave trade in the bights was to drive the slave trade both north and south, and it increased in the north and south, but I should say that the whole extent of the slave trade had decidedly decreased during the last two years.

5149. Do you think that it is a very material decrease?—I do.

5150. Do you know any particular places on the coast to which slavers have resorted, more especially since it has been so much checked on the west coast north of the Line?—It increased to the south; there have been many more Brazilian captures made in the rivers immediately south of the Line, of late years, than there were before; but the great diminution in the bights has not been made up by the increased slave trade either north or south.

5151. Mr. *Stuart Wortley.*] Will you explain what period you refer to when you use the expression, "of late years"?—In the years 1835 and 1836, it began to diminish, and in 1837 there was hardly any slave trade at all in the bights.

5152. Then, I understand you to say that there has been an increase of captures south of the Line since the years 1835 and 1836?—Yes, there has been.

5153. Could the capture of vessels under Portuguese colours have taken place till 1836?—It could have taken place if the same rule had been applied then as was applied in 1838.

5154. But in fact were there any captures made?—No, the rule was not applied till 1838.

5155. Then when you speak of the increase of captures since 1835, you mean that the practice of making captures south of the Line has been introduced since that period?—Yes; and I would observe with respect to that, that the Act of Parliament for the suppression of the Portuguese slave trade really did very little good. I am alluding to the Act which was passed in order to catch vessels south of the Line, because we already dealt with them in the way I have mentioned, and the only trade the Act could possibly affect, was the trade carried on between the Portuguese islands off the coast and the main-land.

5156. Sir *T. D. Acland.*] Do you mean Prince's Island?—Prince's Island and St. Thomas.

5157. Mr. *W. Patten.*] Seeing that the sale of those goods at auctions conduces in some degree to the continuance of the slave trade on that coast, can you point out any other means by which those goods can be disposed of without contributing to the encouragement of that trade?—I do not see how it is possible to form regulations which shall follow the goods through all the hands into which they pass.

5158. Sir *T. D. Acland.*] Could they be sold elsewhere?—Yes, there is trade on the coast; but I think it would be very injurious to interfere with trade.

5159. Mr. *Patten.*] Do you think that if the captors of the slave vessel were allowed to take the vessels and cargoes, they having been condemned, and sell them in any other country, they might not make greater gains than they do by selling them on the spot?—It is possible that they might make greater gains, but it would be impossible for the court to allow goods that have been once submitted to their jurisdiction regularly to pass into other hands for disposal. When the goods are condemned, they are placed under the authority of the marshal, to be dealt with according to the decision of the court; it cannot allow that decree to be carried into effect by any other than its own officers.

5160. According to the present law, it cannot; but do not you think that arrangements might be made by which the parties making the capture might derive greater benefit from the capture, by being enabled after the condemnation to dispose of the goods in another country?—I think the captors would not benefit by such a regulation; it would take them away from their cruizing stations, where they have an opportunity of making other captures.

5161. Have you not heard complaints made by the captors of the very little benefit they obtain from it?—Yes; but I think without good grounds.

5162. Can you state what is the highest amount that you have heard of paid to a cruizer for the capture of a slaver?—I do not know any thing of the reward given in England; it does not come before us in any way whatever; that is an affair between the captor and the Government. But it is not the captor, strictly speaking, that is injured in this case; for the captor, as far as the court is concerned, has no interest whatever; the goods are not condemned as a prize to the captor, but as a prize to the British and foreign Governments, and the British Government may pay or withhold its moiety, if it pleases. It generally gives it to the captor, but it is in its power to pay any smaller sum. The captor has no claim, except upon the bounty of Government, with respect to the goods sold at auctions.

5163. But does it not come to this, that the remuneration paid to the captor depends upon the value of the cargo which he captures?—Where a captor has seized a cargo, it does; but cases vary very much; for instance, many vessels are seized quite empty, without any cargo; many vessels come over without any cargo, I should say the great proportion. Where a vessel is full of slaves, the interest of the captor is not affected, because the bulk of his remuneration depends upon the head-money he gets for the slaves.

5164. Can you account for this circumstance, that in a return made to Parliament, in the list of vessels that have been sold, it appears that the proceeds or effects of one vessel have amounted to 1,108*l.*, and the charges on the sale have amounted to 585*l.* out of the 1,108*l.*?—It seems very enormous, but I must know the circumstances of the case.

5165. This is the passage, "On the following cases of slave trade vessels sent in for adjudication to the commission courts of Sierra Leone by Captain Tucker of Her Majesty's ship Wolverine, the charges here detailed were made: The San Antonia Victirioso, a Brazilian vessel, the proceeds and effects of that sale were 1,108*l.*, and the charges on the sale were 585*l.*"?—I cannot account for it; it did not happen in my time; I should know the name of the vessel if it had.

5166. *Chairman.*] Can you, from your knowledge of the usual course of proceeding, explain the circumstances under which such a charge could have arisen?—No; I know what the expenses are likely to be, and I might account for a portion of it in that way.

5167. Mr. *W. Patten.*] Will you state the expenses in detail?—The expenses on Brazilian vessels were enormous, owing to the duty that was levied at Sierra Leone by the customs, on spirits and tobacco. The spirits and tobacco that are sent in Brazilian slave vessels are of a very inferior quality indeed, and the duty levied is very high; in many cases exceeding the value of the goods; so much so, that I took it upon myself a short time before I gave up my situation, to abandon the whole of several cargoes of spirits and tobacco to the custom-house, because the goods would not sell at the auction for the amount of the duty. I thought that the captors had great reason to complain; but subsequently to that, an Act was passed by the Governor in Council there, which was brought in by myself, to meet this exigency, and since that time I do not think that the captors have any reason to complain about the duty levied on those goods.

5168. *Chairman.*] What was the nature of the Act you allude to?—It put on an *ad valorem* duty instead of a fixed duty; the value of the articles alluded to was so small, that when you put a fixed duty upon them, a duty that was framed to meet tobacco and spirits from England, which were of a very different quality, they were hardly worth any thing beyond the duty; and I should suppose that was the principal cause of the heavy charges now referred to; but I know nothing of the case.

5169. Mr. *W. Patten.*] To take another case: the Palmira, a Spanish vessel was captured, the effects produced 1,824*l.*, and 582*l.* were the charges?—That is not in my time.

5170. *Chairman.*] Do you explain that by the same circumstance?—No; not knowing any thing of the circumstances of the case, I cannot explain it; the vessel may have been detained for several months at the desire of the captor; but I am quite sure that, with the exception of one or two items, and heavy items, of which the captors, I think, *had* a right to complain, and over which the court had no control, the expenses were not unreasonably heavy.

5171. What other items had they reason to complain of besides the one you have mentioned, of the heavy duty upon the article?—With regard to translating documents. I pressed this evil very strongly upon the Government at home, and they have remedied that since. It was found that very great benefit arose to the court from translating all documents almost that were found on board detained slavers, because, in consequence of those translations, we were able to condemn many vessels which would have escaped if it had not been for the translation of papers found on board former vessels, which gave a full history of the transactions in which those vessels subsequently taken were engaged. The translations were made at a heavy expense, and were included in the captor's expenses, and it could not be avoided; it fell very heavily, indeed, upon the captors; and I recommended that the translator should be adopted by the court, and paid in the same way as other officers of the court, and that his remuneration should be charged in the contingent expenses, which are borne equally by the British Government and the foreign Government, so as to relieve the captors altogether. The court felt a delicacy when they would have wished to have a translation of particular papers, in having it done, because the expense fell so very heavily upon the captors.

5172. Mr. *W. Patten.*] Doctor Madden recommends that "the captors should be allowed to furnish their own interpretation of the documents that require to be translated, subject to the approval and revision of the British Commissioners?"—That is impossible, you can never allow a man to interpret in his own cause. If you left it to the captor to decide upon what papers he would have translated, he would have none translated, if the condemnation of his vessel was secure without it; but now there is no inducement to captors to withhold papers, because the whole expense of the translation is at present borne by the Government.

5173. *Chairman.*] In consequence of suggestions made to the Government here?—Yes; in consequence of suggestions made in 1839.

5174. Mr. *W. Patten.*] Doctor Madden also says, "in many cases more than half the prize-money that the captors had reason to expect is swallowed up in the charges made by the various officers at Sierra Leone employed in taking care, and ultimately disposing of the effects of the captured vessel." Do you know what are the charges that would come under the other charge?—Yes.

5175. Can you distinguish those from the charges you have mentioned?—In the case of an empty Spanish vessel, it is not at all likely that the captor will receive much from the sale of the vessel or effects, because the vessel is cut up into a number of different parts, and those are sold for fire-wood in a country where fire-wood is tolerably plentiful; and, therefore, the expenses that are incurred previously to cutting up, will absorb any thing that can be derived from the old vessel cut up and sold as fire-wood. As far as the goods are concerned, the only charge, besides the duty, is the commission of the commissioner of appraisement and sale, which the captor would have to pay whoever sold the vessel, without having the security which he possesses now of having a good man, or the richest merchant in the place as the person answerable for the money, because in appointing the commissioner of appraisement and sale, the Court takes bond to a very large amount, that he shall account properly for the proceeds of the goods sold; he charges the ordinary commission, 5 per cent., and 2½ per cent. for expenses; and I believe that there is no other charge except the pay of the Kroomen, employed as labourers, and the marshal.

5176. Mr. *Forster.*] Do you think Dr. Madden's complaint upon the subject correct?—"The intervention of the whole present establishment of marshals, collectors, surveyors, interpreters, harbour-masters, agents, storekeepers, canoe-hirers, and victuallers of captured ships' crews might be dispensed with." I do not know what he means by "marshals;" we have only one marshal for the court. There is only one collector of customs, and with him we have nothing to do; he is the officer of the Crown, who collects the same duties from these vessels as he would do from any other vessels; we have no control over him; he is independent of the court; the surveyor is not employed by the court, but subsequently to the condemnation of the vessel, he is employed by the captor to survey, in order to enable him to make a claim according to the tonnage, through his agent in England; that is a question with which we have nothing to do. The interpreter is paid by the court; he gets 5s. for each examination, or something of that kind; he is a poor man; they could not get it cheaper done, and there is no hardship in that. The harbour-master charges exactly the same for a prize-vessel as he does for an English vessel; there is a regular fee, under an Act of the Governor and Council; we do not collect it. I do not know who are meant by "agents," or "storekeepers," or "canoe-hirers;" I do not know whom he refers to there.

5177. Mr. *W. Patten.*] You do not know of any charges connected with those departments that you have read over?—I know nothing about "agents" and "storekeepers." There may be a charge where goods are kept, but I do not recollect a cargo ever having been kept, for it is landed and sold immediately; the auctioneer is obliged to sell it under the regulations within a certain time. There are canoes employed to land the cargo by the marshal and by "victuallers of captured ships' crews." I do not know whom he means.

5178. Is there any expense thrown upon captured vessels in case of slaves being brought on shore, for the maintenance of the slaves after they are put on shore?—I mentioned in the early part of my evidence that on their being landed they were handed over to the liberated African department, to be kept as slaves until adjudication. They are fed by the liberated African department at the ordinary rate at which the other liberated Africans in the yard are fed; and when the vessel is condemned, the liberated African department brings to the marshal his account for feeding them, at the same rate which is charged for other liberated Africans; I think it is 1½d. per head per day, or something of that kind; and there is a further charge, I think, of 4d. or 6d. per day in the hospital; those are expenses over which the court has no control.

5179. Is any of that charge made upon the share which goes to the captors?—Yes; it comes out of the proceeds of the vessel; they pay half, as it were; it goes in diminution of the moiety which goes to the British Government.

5180. Mr. *Evans.*] The captor has no claim upon that?—The captor has no claim upon it, except from the bounty of Government.

5181. *Chairman.*] But the Government does generally hand over its moiety to the captor?—Yes.

5182. Then by whatever amount that moiety is diminished, the captor's share is diminished?—Yes.

5183. Mr. *W. Patten.*] If any means could be discovered of doing away with those great expenses on the sale of captured vessels, do not you think that it would give great stimulus to cruizers on the coast?—I do not think they require a stimulus; but I do not think it is possible to diminish the charges materially in the shape of duties, which is the heavy item. In translating the papers, they have been already relieved, and also in a great measure from the duties; and I really do not think that there is any change that can materially diminish the expenses, so as to have the services properly performed.

5184. *Chairman.*] Those are services which must be performed by somebody, which can hardly be performed at less expense than they are now performed, and if the expenses are to be defrayed, they must be defrayed by the Government or by the captors?—Yes: certainly.

5185. And the Government gets the moiety of the proceeds, but out of its bounty habitually makes over that portion to the captor?—Yes.

5186. You do not think it unfair that the bounty should be diminished by those expenses, not being extravagant expenses, in your opinion?—The bounty granted by Act of Parliament is not diminished. Cases do happen sometimes, as the case of the Passos, where the expenses exceed the proceeds, and in those cases the Government pays the difference, leaving the bounty perfectly free to the captor. None of the expenses go in diminution of the bounty given by Act of Parliament.

5187. But this is a sort of premium given beyond the bounty?—I suppose it was given to enable them to pay the expenses, but they get something beyond the expenses, and the bounty comes to them entire, not suffering any diminution from the general expenses, and the proceeds go in payment of the expenses.

5188. Mr. *W. Patten.*] Do they get the bounty in all cases?—Yes, in all cases captured under the treaties.

5189. If the vessel has no slaves on board, do they receive the bounty?— Then they get the bounty on the tonnage of the captured vessel.

5190. Mr. *Stuart Wortley.*] You have been speaking of cases in which there are slavers captured on board the prizes; in cases where there are no slavers captured on board the prizes, is there any charge made on the proceeds of the vessel on account of the crew?—The crew of a slaver brought into Sierra Leone never consists of more than three, therefore the expense cannot be very great; the adjudication generally takes place on the eighth day after arrival, and there is a regular sum which is given day by day in money to each man; as far as I recollect it, the captain and mate get 3*s.* a day, and the other man 2*s.*

5191. Whatever the amount of that charge is, it is made against the proceeds of the vessel?—Yes.

5192. Sir *T. D. Acland.*] Do you recollect sending a despatch home in December 1838, giving your opinion upon the state of the slave trade?— There is a despatch here upon the subject.

5193. Does that despatch refer to the subject of this country retiring from the contest which it has so long carried on?—Yes, I think it does, but I can find the passage.

5194. Can you state what the opinion was?—The opinion expressed was, that unless more effectual means were taken for the suppression of the traffic, that perhaps more harm than good was done by the exertions that we had made previously; but since that time a very great alteration has taken place; I expressed my opinion with regard to an increase of the force on the coast, and the occupation of British territory that belonged to us, where we were supplanted by the slave traders, at Bulama especially, and also as to the punishment of the crews engaged in the slave trade.

5195. Have any of those measures which you recommended been carried into effect?—The Portuguese have been driven from Bulama, and a much more effectual method of cruizing has been followed; very superior vessels have been employed.

5196. Have you now any doubt of the propriety of continuing our policy?—Certainly not: with regard to cruizing under the present system, I would propose increasing the force still, and employing a certain number of steam-vessels; indeed, there are several measures that I might propose. The occupation of Bulama was referred to; I think that would be an important measure; it was urged very strongly in that despatch to which I have been referred, and the commander of the Brisk, Captain Kellett, then for the first time visited the place, and drove the Portuguese slave traders from it, and carried away the slaves who were kept in the barracoons there. Another proposition was, sending home foreign crews, and perhaps I may be allowed to read the passage containing it:—"The only other suggestion which we shall at present offer is, the adoption of means to secure the punishment of persons implicated in slave trade adventures. As things are now managed, the confiscation of a slave vessel affects only the owner or the underwriters; and the parties who navigate the condemned vessel are constantly seen to embark again, on a second illegal voyage, a few days after the termination of the first. The complete personal impunity which attends the agents by whom illegal slave trade is carried on, combined with the high wages by which their services are secured, renders the slave trade, notwithstanding all its inconveniences, the most desirable employment for the Spanish and Portuguese sailor. On this subject we beg leave to refer your Lordship to Class A., 1824-1825, pages 142 and 143; and to Class A., 1836, pages 217 and 218. The plan which we now propose for adoption, with regard to slave vessels captured on this coast, and condemned at Sierra Leone, is applicable, with some modifications, to similar seizures in other parts of the world; but its effect may be tried here in the first instance. Both the Portuguese and Spanish treaties require that the captain, and a part, at least, of the crew, of a captured slave ship should be left on board; and this clause, whilst it sanctions the present almost invariable practice of sending up only the master, and one or two of the seamen, of a detained vessel, as witnesses before the mixed courts, and landing the remainder of the crew, as soon as possible, at the nearest or most convenient port, equally permits the detention of the whole of the crew, if it should be thought necessary, and we now beg leave to recommend the latter course, with a view to ulterior proceedings against all the guilty parties. The hulk already fixed at Sierra Leone may be used as a temporary receptacle for such prisoners; and one small steamer, or vessel of war, might be constantly employed in conveying the prisoners from this place to England, to obtain the orders of Her Majesty's Government as to their delivery, at Lisbon (if Portuguese), or at Cadiz or some other port (if Spanish). Portugal and Spain are both bound by treaty, as well as by their own law, to punish their respective subjects, 'who may participate in an illicit traffic in slaves,' and 'to assimilate, as much as possible, their legislation in this respect to that of Great Britain;' and those powers will thus enjoy the opportunity of fulfilling their obligations. The punishment of the guilty persons might be strongly urged by the British ambassadors; but whether punished or not, we are persuaded that a more severe blow would be given by this proceeding to foreign slave trade than it has ever yet received. No less than 687 Spanish and Portuguese sailors were engaged in navigating the 30 vessels which came before us last year. All these men have long since returned to their former occupation; but had they been withdrawn, as we propose, from their old haunts and pursuits, carried to Europe far from their slave trading connexions, fined, imprisoned, and otherwise punished, and left to find their way back as best they could to Cuba and Brazil, the alarm which would have been thereby caused amongst the many thousands of seamen engaged in the same manner, would have done more to check and injure the illegal traffic than any means that have been adopted for the last twenty years."

5197. Mr. *Forster*.] In the paper you have just read, the necessity of increased measures for the punishment of the crews of slave vessels is alluded to; you are not aware, probably, that it is in evidence before this Committee, that those crews, being landed on the coast at the nearest point to that at which the capture took place, not above one in ten of them escape death from destitution and want, in which case you would probably think the punishment sufficient?—I was not aware of the fact; but still I would have *that one* sent home.

5198. *Chairman*.] You would rather have the regular punishment of the sailors?—A total withdrawal of the men from the place where their slave trading occupation leads them, even if they are not punished in Portugal and Spain, would have a good effect; they would be withdrawn so completely from the line of their ordinary business, that the expense of their finding their way to the Havannah or the Brazils would deter them from engaging in such voyages, except at extravagantly high wages.

5199. Mr. *Aldam*.] Why could not they work their way back?—But they still would be losing the enormous wages that they would obtain on board a slave ship.

5200. Mr. *W. Patten.*] Do you happen to know the wages given on board the slave ships?—They vary a little; but the wages of a common sailor I have known to be 5*l.* a month. I should say a common seaman on board one of those vessels would obtain, taking the value which the slaves fetch, 7*l.* or 8*l.* a month on a successful voyage.

5201. Of course, those sailors undertake those voyages, and obtain that enormous remuneration on account of the danger they run to life and limb, from coming into the hands of our cruizers?—Yes; English sailors would, until lately, have been hung if we caught them on board a slave vessel, and, therefore, we see no English sailors in that trade; but you would have men of all nations volunteer into it, if it were not for the danger they ran.

5202. There is nothing in the trade itself, except the danger that they run from our cruizers, which would lead to such enormous wages?—Nothing whatever; they may be exposed to very great inconveniences, and if you increase the inconveniences in the way I proposed, the wages would double, probably; the rate of wages depends upon the danger and inconvenience.

5203. Do you think that all the parties usually engaged in the slave trade are perfectly aware that they run the risk of being put on shore in case of capture, and of having to undergo great peril of their lives before they can return to their homes?—It is known in all the slaving ports; it has been the universal practice ever since the cruizers were on the station to land the crews; indeed it cannot be otherwise with the small vessels that we have on the coast. To venture to take fifty or sixty scoundrels like the crews of those vessels, on board such a ship, would be madness.

5204. Have you had your attention called to the very great hardship which some of those crews have sustained when put on shore?—It has not come before me in any way whatever; I have no knowledge of it at all; I attended this Committee some time ago, and I heard of one case, where it was mentioned that they were starved, but that is the only case I have heard of.

5205. Can you suggest any alteration by which they could be put on shore and subjected to very great personal inconvenience, without the dreadful loss of life that we have heard of?—I think they were as badly off when they were landed at Prince's, which is a Portuguese settlement, as they are at any other place.

5206. Would it increase the expenses very materially, or be a very material inconvenience, to fix upon certain points of the coast at which the crews could be landed before the vessels were sent to Sierra Leone for judgment?—I do not think it could be done; it would take the cruizer out of his ground, and would inconvenience him greatly; the object is to keep the vessel efficient for the cruize, and keep him on the ground; an empty vessel might run out, in order to be taken, while the full slaver got away.

5207. If the regulation were adopted, that a cruizer taking a slaver in certain districts, which should be detained, should be obliged to land the crew at particular places; would that be practicable?—I do not think it is possible.

5208. Mr. *Forster*.] Independently of the feeling of humanity towards the crews themselves, do you not think that the example of such treatment must have a very bad effect in the eyes of the natives of the coast of Africa, as showing them an example of inhumanity on the part of those who profess to be acting solely in that way from motives of humanity?—I have never known a cruizer act inhumanly; I heard of one case the other day, where they were starved, but it was stated in that case that it was owing to the refusal of the Portuguese factories to support them.

5209. Mr. *Stuart Wortley*.] In the paper you have read, it was stated that there were 687 sailors engaged in navigating 30 slave vessels; a short time since you stated that with respect to ships condemned at Sierra Leone, there were seldom more than three or four connected with the navigation of a vessel; will you reconcile those two statements?—They only leave those three or four on board; they land all but those who are required as witnesses at Sierra Leone.

5210. There are no individuals belonging to the slave crew retained on board?—None, but those who are required as witnesses.

5211. Then those individuals of whom you spoke, as being charges against the vessel, were individuals retained as witnesses?—Yes.

5212. *Chairman*.] Do you think that the price paid to the Spanish or Portuguese Governments, as the case might be, would suffice for the maintenance of the crews of those vessels?—Yes, it would be only rationing them for the voyage across.

5213. And paying for their passage?—Now we pay continually out of the foreign moiety for the passage; at least the commissariat does.

5214. That is for the captain and mate; but here you are supposing several hundred instead of 20 or 30?—The rationing of the commissariat commences the moment we cease to have any thing to do with the vessel; the day the vessel is condemned, there is given to the commissary a list of the men who will come upon him for rations, and as long as they remain in the colony they will come upon him daily; when a number of vessels have been captured, and at one time we had 37 vessels lying in the harbour at the same time, they would cause a great drain upon the provisions, which are sent out only to meet ordinary contingencies; in that case the commissary went to the expense of hiring vessels to send those men away, and charged those expenses, in the same way as he would have done the rations, against the share of the foreign government.

5215. If you brought the crew to Sierra Leone you would increase the expense of maintenance very considerably?—Yes.

5216. You still consider that the moiety given to the foreign government would cover such expenses?—Yes, if vessels continued to be taken as they have been in the last few years, they would do so certainly. The only case in which I should conceive that the expense would exceed the moiety, is where very few vessels are condemned, and where you would have to run across with a very few passengers.

5217. This could be done by the existing treaty, without the necessity for any fresh negotiation?—Yes.

5218. Captain *Fitzroy*.] What becomes of the remainder of that moiety which goes to the foreign government, the part which is not used in paying for the maintenance of those men?—I believe there are always accounts going on between the governments at home, and it is used in England in some way that I am not aware of; the Treasury disposes of it either by paying it over to the agent of the foreign government here, or in some other way.

5219. Is the foreign moiety paid to our Government?—The whole of it is paid to the commissary at Sierra Leone; he has accounts with the Treasury; there are regular accounts which are made up as between the British Government and the foreign government, showing the exact sum that is due by the English Government to the foreign Government for their moiety.

5220. Mr. *W. Patten*.] Looking to the general nature of the vessels that are sold at Sierra Leone, do you think that they would bring by auction as large a price if sold in the West Indies, as they would sold at Sierra Leone?—Yes, I think they would.

5221. Do you think they would bring a larger price?—There have been vessels sold at the West Indies, but there was not any material difference in price; it would depend a good deal upon the island to which they went; in some islands there might be no great demand.

5222. *Chairman*.] There is a good deal of small traffic, is there not, along the coasts of the West India islands?—Yes; I should think the chances are, that the prices vessels would fetch in the West Indies would be higher than at Sierra Leone.

5223. Mr. *W. Patten.*] Suppose the station was established at the West Indies, would there not be the security that they would be sold without being made use of again for the slave trade?—There might be. I have strongly recommended that vessels should be sent to the West Indies, when they have cargoes on board; that the slaves should be landed in the West Indies, and the vessels, of course, might be sold there when sent over.

5224. *Chairman.*] You would bring them to Sierra Leone for adjudication?—Yes; there could not be a mixed commission established under the present system in the West Indies; because the treaty requires that there shall be one mixed commission on the coast of Africa, and another in the West Indies, and we have one there already at Havannah.

5225. You would think it a very material advantage, looking to the slave trade, if those sales could take place at the West Indies instead of on the coast of Africa?—No; the advantage that I was alluding to, is an advantage for the supply of labour in the West Indies, but not with regard to the supply of vessels, because the vessel might soon run across the Atlantic, and get into the hands of the slavers, as at present.

5226. If a person wished to obtain those vessels bought in the West Indies, for the encouragement of the slave trade, he would buy them at a great disadvantage as compared with the price which he now pays at Sierra Leone?—Yes; but notwithstanding the higher price in the West Indies, it is not likely to be such a price that the owner would not be able to get much more from the slave dealers than anybody else.

5227. If the sales of the prize vessels and the prize goods were made in the West Indies rather than at Sierra Leone, would they be less serviceable in the encouraging the slave trade?—Those particular goods would.

5228. Would the absence of that mode of supply be in any way an obstruction to the slave trader?—Certainly not.

5229. Are they got at those prize sales at a cheaper rate than they are directly from the merchants?—The price goods obtained at public auctions is much lower than you would buy them for in one of the shops.

5230. Then by so far as the prize sales in Sierra Leone do furnish a cheaper article to the slaver than the regular sale would do, so far they are an assistance to his trade?—The cheapness of goods sold at Sierra Leone is useful to all trades as well as to that.

5231. But if those sales did not take place at Sierra Leone, they would not be supplied so cheaply as they are?—It is a very small portion of assistance they receive; but so far as it goes it is an assistance.

5232. A vessel sold at Sierra Leone, is more easily convertible to the purposes of the slave trade, than if it were sold in the West Indies?—More easily, but not much more so, because the vessel might be run across at once.

5233. Is there not more demand for vessels in the West Indies than at Sierra Leone?—Certainly, and therefore the price would be higher.

5234. Captain *Fitzroy.*] Is there not also an advantage in having men disposable, ready to man those ships when purchased?—Yes.

5235. Mr. *Forster.*] Are not the cases very few in which they would man the vessels at once again?—I have known cases of that kind.

5236. But are not the cases comparatively rare?—Yes.

5237. *Chairman.*] Who generally are purchasers of prize vessels?—The greater portion are purchased on speculation; the number sold now is not at all, in proportion to the number taken, what it was before the Spanish treaty, under which most of the vessels are condemned, require that the vessels should be cut up, but some are bought on speculation, and come into the fruit trade, and others go into the Mediterranean trade; others are bought by slavers.

5238. Mr. *Evans.*] Do you know any thing of the slave ship Almirante, for which vessel the sum of 600*l.* was offered by an officer of Government, to be used as a tender, which offer was not accepted, and the vessel was sold at 1,500*l.*, and immediately went down to the Bonny and took away 600 slaves from that port?—The Almirante was captured before my time at Sierra Leone, but I think it is very likely, because such things were taking place continually.

5239. Mr. *W. Patten.*] When you were at Sierra Leone, you have stated in your evidence already, that the liberated Africans were carrying on the trade with much greater advantage than the white merchants, in consequence of the price at which they obtained goods at public auctions?—Not entirely in consequence of that, but that has been one great means to assist them. For many years past, before those prize goods were sold at Sierra Leone, the liberated Africans had gradually been working themselves into notoriety; most of them are very much addicted to trading, and the persons whom they have supplanted are a lazy, indolent, worthless set, who cannot compete with them at all, and having completely driven out of the market the Maroons and settlers, they are now gradually driving out the white merchants.

5240. There is then this additional disadvantage in those auctions at Sierra Leone, that they are destroying the trade of the white merchants of the place, by the other merchants being able to purchase goods at a price which is not remunerating to the British merchant?—I consider it a great advantage.

5241. Is it not a great disadvantage in one respect, that it is discouraging the trade between England and the coast of Africa at that particular point?—No, I think quite the reverse; the supply of goods will be the same whoever are the receivers, and the extent of our export to Sierra Leone will not be diminished by altering the colour of the merchants there.

5242. But if it should be desirable to establish a general trade with that part of the coast in a legitimate way, does not the sale of goods at those public auctions, at materially reduced prices, offer a great impediment to English merchants conducting trade upon that part of the coast?—I think its first effect might be that; but its ultimate effect, I think, would be far different. I think the great point is to encourage the use of such articles, and to increase the desire for them; and the British goods will always, in competition, beat out the foreign goods from the market.

5243. Has it not pretty much the same effect there that a very large sale, under a bankruptcy in England, has upon the trade in this country?—I think not, to the same degree there; because what you require there, in order to create a demand for goods of good quality is, to allow the people to have the use of something superior to what they would have without those sales.

5244. *Chairman.*] But the goods sold at those prize sales are articles of an inferior kind, are they not?—The goods that are sold there are very much the same as those that are used by the natives in their own trade, and probably many of them are British manufacture.

5245. You think that it is an advantage to the trade ultimately, that those forced sales, at unnaturally low prices, should be made within the colony, producing a taste which will be gratified by a more regular trade?—Yes.

5246. Though they may interfere with the regular trade in the colony?—That is only for a time.

5247. Mr. *Aldam.*] Are the goods English goods?—The principal part of them are.

5248. *Chairman.*] Those forced sales have had a very injurious effect upon the regular trade of the place, have they not?—Yes, upon the shops; at the same time they have raised into wealth, and brought forward still more prominently than before, the liberated African hawkers.

5249. Have they created a class of native traders who have extended commerce inland further than British trade by itself, in its natural course, would have done?—Yes, certainly; the trade between Sierra Leone and the Sherboro', and the rivers in the neighbourhood of Sierra Leone, has been very much more brisk in the large canoes that are employed by the liberated African traders, since goods have come in so cheaply.

5250. Therefore you think, incidentally to the regular trade, advantage has been given by these forced sales, which have created tastes which would not have existed under other circumstances?—Yes.

5251. Mr. *Forster.*] The brisk trade which you have spoken of between Sherboro' and Sierra Leone would be with those goods; a trade chiefly with the slave dealers in that quarter?—All are slave dealers, if they can be, beyond British jurisdiction; but what the Sierra Leone traders receive in exchange for goods are rice, and other articles of produce, which are consumed in the colony; for though rice is the principal food of all who can afford to pay for it, there is no rice raised in the colony; and therefore a trade of some kind is required to be carried on, in order to procure the means of subsistence.

5252. *Chairman.*] The colony has not the means of supporting itself?—No.

5253. Mr. *Forster.*] Though those goods may be sold to slave dealers in those districts, you think that it is a legitimate and desirable trade for the English merchant?—Yes.

5254. Mr. *Evans.*] Have you not stated that the black merchants at Sierra Leone have more capital than the English?—There are hardly any English merchants; there are agents of English houses. The black merchants have twice as much capital as the resident English agents, but there is one merchant, Mr. William Cole, who is carrying on business on his own account, and he went into the market, he did not hold back and oppose the thing, as was done by the other English traders, but he entered into competition with the black traders, and made a good deal of money by it.

5255. In Sierra Leone merchants who had capital to employ would have considerable advantage over the agents or merchants who had not the money to lay down?—Yes.

5256. Mr. *Forster.*] Was not the want of money you have alluded to on the part of the English merchants, mainly owing to having their stores filled with English merchandize, which was rendered completely unsaleable by the quantity of prize goods thrown into the market in the way you have mentioned?—I think not, because Mr. Cole was in just the same circumstances; he had the largest store in the town; but he had more money than the others; he had money in his pocket instead of being in debt in England, and instead of sending home money as others were obliged to do to pay their accounts in England, he reserved his money to purchase cheap goods in the colony.

5257. Had he a large stock?—Yes, he had; but he took advantage of the circumstances that occurred, and made his profit by them.

5258. Would it answer the purpose of the trader at Sierra Leone to keep a large quantity of goods and money on his hands?—If Mr. Cole had known of those prize goods coming in such large quantities he would not have purchased goods from England, but he happened to have those goods in store as the other merchants had, and he happened to have money also, and he took advantage of the prize goods coming in, but there were very few merchants in that position.

Martis, 14° die Junii, 1842.

MEMBERS PRESENT.

Sir T. D. Acland.
Mr. Aldam.
Viscount Courtenay.
Mr. Denison.
Mr. W. Evans.

Captain Fitzroy.
Mr. Forster.
Mr. Hamilton.
Mr. Milnes.
Mr. W. Patten.

LORD VISCOUNT SANDON, IN THE CHAIR.

Henry William Macaulay, Esq. called in, and further examined.

5261. *Chairman.*] Do you wish to make some remarks upon Dr. Madden's Report, page 14?—I do. He states that liberated Africans at the prize sales at Sierra Leone "buy up the coppers, guns, and ship's stores of vessels for the British agents of the slave traders of the Sherboro' and Gallinas residing at Freetown, and thus they acquire a taste for this illegal traffic." Now he might have known, if he had made any inquiry at Sierra Leone, that coppers are never sold at public auction, or any kind of equipment for the slave trade. The subject is referred to by Colonel Doherty in his reply to Dr. Madden's Report. He gives a positive contradiction to that statement, and I can confirm the contradiction.

5262. To what are the sales confined?—To the vessels and the goods found on board, and to the tackle, apparel, and furniture; that is the term used in the condemnation; but coppers, irons, and any other articles that may be used again in the slave trade are always brought up to the commission-office or warehouses. It is the interest of the Mixed Commissions to gain every single copper they can; for, when broken up, the coppers are sold, and supply funds from which the repairs of the boat used in the service of the Mixed Commission are paid; that is, the boat used to carry about the officers of the court in the harbour.

5263. Do you mean that the accommodation which the officers derive is dependent upon that?—No; but they are constantly afloat. During the time that a vessel is there the marshal is required to visit her three times a day.

5264. But is the accommodation dependent upon its being derived from this source?—No; whenever that copper fund is insufficient, the repairs of the boat are paid out of the funds of which the foreign governments pay a portion; but the money derived from the sale of the coppers is appropriated to that purpose, and there is a regular account kept of the sale of those coppers that are broken up. There never was an instance of a copper being sold at public auction, or any equipment.

5265. Have you any reason to believe that this practice does lead to the encouragement of the slave trade?—I have none whatever.

5266. Have you reason to believe that any of the parties, either British or native, living at Freetown, are in any way sharers in the proceeds of slave transactions?—They may sell goods to the slave traders.

5267. Are they sharers in the proceeds of slave goods?—I believe not; I cannot say for certain, because we have a shifting population of Spaniards and Portuguese passing through the colony; but I should say no resident whatever shares in such proceeds. It is a thing which one cannot know, because of course such a transaction would be concealed if it existed.

5268. Are you not aware of any British agents of the slave traders; are you aware of the existence of agents of the Sherboro' and of Gallinas residing in Freetown?—Yes, of persons purchasing vessels on account of slave traders, and I have no doubt purchasing goods also.

5269. What is the interest in the transaction which such persons have?—A commission, I presume.

5270. Mr. *Forster.*] In your former evidence, you have mentioned a merchant, of the name of Kidd, as acting as agent for the purchase of prize vessels on behalf of the slave traders at the Gallinas; in your opinion, was Mr. Kidd singular in that respect?—I do not recollect any other person employed in that way during my time.

5271. Is it within your knowledge that merchants, who were members of the Council of Government at Sierra Leone, have been engaged in similar transactions?—Never, to my knowledge; but I would also mention, as Mr.

Kidd's name has been spoken of, that, since the last meeting of the Committee, I have met with his name accidentally, in connexion with another transaction of the same kind, in the printed Parliamentary Papers, and therefore I may refer to it. It is the case of a vessel sold to a slave trader, a vessel called the Ligeira, which was captured a second time, and brought into Sierra Leone a very short time after she left the port; it appeared that in the meantime Mr. Kidd had carried her from the colony and sold her to a slave trader, and she was captured almost immediately afterwards. The case is reported at page 101 of Class (A.) of the Slave Trade Papers, for 1839-40.

5272. *Chairman.*] Would it not be desirable, if possible, that all the vessels taken in the slave trade should be broken up?—Certainly, it would be the best thing that could possibly be done; and in those cases where it appeared to the court, during the latter part of the time that I administered the mixed courts there, that a vessel could have been condemned either as a Portuguese or a Spaniard, in all these cases we condemned her as a Spaniard, in order that she might be cut up after her condemnation; for the slave traders were seriously injured by being deprived of the means of getting off the coast and getting slaves again.

5273. Mr. *W. Patten.*] In the case of the breaking up of a vessel, do the captors get any prize money?—Yes, they get a bounty on the tonnage of that vessel; she is measured by the surveyors before being broken up, in order to ascertain her tonnage by the new mode of measurement, and upon that measurement the captors are paid the bounty in England.

5274. It is immaterial to the captors whether the vessel is broken up or sold again, so far as their private interests are concerned?—Except that the vessel sells whole for much more than she does when she is broken up for fire-wood.

5275. Is the vessel valued only as fire-wood when broken up?—They get only a moiety of the proceeds of the broken parts, in the other case they get a moiety of a vessel fit for sea, with all the rigging perfect.

5276. You do not coincide with Dr. Madden, who recommends that a vessel when captured should be put into the possession of the capturing officer to be disposed of?—It would be quite impossible; the foreigners would very justly complain of us if we left the vessel in charge of the officer when once brought before the court. It appears by a paper, which I have seen this morning only, that already they complain of irons and other things, to condemn the vessel, being put on board after the arrival of the vessel at Sierra Leone. Now, if during the time the vessel was passing through the court, and during the time when the marshal now has charge of her, in order to prevent any thing of that kind happening, you left the vessel to the officer, who is interested in putting three or four shackles on board, which is quite sufficient to condemn the vessel, I think they would have just cause to complain.

5277. What Dr. Madden recommends is, that when the vessel has been condemned it should be put at the disposal of the commanding officer on the post, for the exclusive use of the service of the navy?—A small number of the vessels condemned might perhaps be beneficially made use of, and the new Act authorises the purchase of vessels when the commanding officer may think it right to purchase them; but having had that option, he of course only purchased such vessels as were required; we had 60 odd vessels in 1839 before the court; what would the navy have done with all those vessels?

5278. Mr. *Forster.*] Had many of those vessels cargoes on board?—Yes.

5279. *Chairman.*] Should you think it would be advisable to sell the vessels under bond that they should not be employed in the slave trade for a certain period?—The law is now almost as stringent as any bond could be.

5280. In what way?—Dr. Madden seems to suppose that vessels may be fitted out in Sierra Leone, and may lie in British waters equipped for the slave trade; but any one at Sierra Leone would have told him that no vessel could possibly lie there equipped for the slave trade; the authorities are so particular, that even in many cases vessels were seized and brought before the court if they were supposed to have a few gallons too much water in them. There is an exceeding jealousy on the subject, as indeed appears by some of the papers which have been presented.

5281. Mr. *Forster.*] Before what court is a vessel, taken in British waters, equipped for the slave trade, brought; the Court of Admiralty or the Court of Mixed Commission?—If she is prosecuted under the Act of Parliament, she is prosecuted of course in the Vice-Admiralty Court.

5282. Is there not a rule on that subject, and are not all vessels taken in British waters on suspicion of being engaged in the slave trade prosecuted in the Admiralty Court?—No; it remains with the captor, if there is a treaty which will reach the vessel, to prosecute her under that treaty before the Mixed Commission Court, if she is a Spaniard or a Portuguese, or before the Admiralty Court, for a breach of the municipal law, because she violates both the treaty and the municipal law, and therefore he has the choice of the one court or the other.

5283. In your last evidence you spoke of a vessel captured of the name of Jack Wilding, at Accra, upon that ground; in which court was she prosecuted?—Before the Mixed Commission Court, but the captor had the option of prosecuting her before the Admiralty Court; the expenses are so much less in our court, and the proceedings so much more rapid, that he preferred bringing her before ours.

5284. Is not the evidence taken before the Mixed Commission Court transmitted to England?—Yes; and it is published by the Foreign Office.

5285. But the evidence in trials before the Vice-Admiralty Court is never made public?—It is not, and a very great disadvantage it is, for this reason: our ability to condemn many of the vessels that were condemned in 1839 depended very much upon evidence found on board vessels brought before the court; this evidence conclusively proved the employment in the slave trade of other vessels not then before us, which were afterwards captured. Now, all evidence of that kind, which might be made use of subsequently in the condemnation of other vessels, is completely shut up from the public or from general knowledge, by the proceedings before the Vice-Admiralty Court being never made public. In the Mixed Commission Court papers can be invoked by the proctor which have been filed in a particular case against another vessel that is subsequently prosecuted.

5286. *Chairman.*] Is there no advantage in the secrecy of such papers?—None whatever.

5287. The proceedings before the Mixed Commission Court are public in themselves, and are published afterwards?—The examinations are not public, but strictly private in the first instance, but they are read in open court at the trial of the vessel, and they are sent home to the Foreign Office; an abstract of the evidence of every witness is given.

5288. The evidence taken before the Vice-Admiralty Court is not published in any way?—No.

5289. Is it communicated to the Mixed Commission?—No.

5290. Mr. *Aldam.*] Are the proceedings of the Vice-Admiralty Court there carried on in the same form as the proceedings of the Admiralty Court here?—Yes, very much the same.

5291. With any greater degree of secrecy?—No, but here the public papers publish them; we have no newspapers there to publish accounts of the proceedings.

5292. *Chairman.*] Would there be an advantage if the proceedings of the Vice-Admiralty Court were always communicated to the Mixed Commission?—Yes; and I recommended at the time when vessels began to go so frequently to the Vice-Admiralty Court, in 1839, that we should be informed of the papers filed in that court.

5293. Would there be any difficulty or objection to that?—There is no establishment of clerks connected with the Vice-Admiralty Court to supply copies at all, and it is not the custom of the judge of the Vice-Admiralty Court to report his proceedings home.

5294. Mr. *Evans*.] Do you think that the Mixed Commission Court has sufficient power for the objects for which it is instituted?—I think that they have. They have been rather shy of exercising it sometimes, but I believe that they do possess much more power than they ever exercised.

5295. You have no improvement in the court to suggest?—No. There seemed to be a deficiency of authority in the marshal a short time ago; but that was supplied by a local Act, which gave him all the power which the marshal of the Vice-Admiralty Court possesses.

5296. *Chairman*.] It is stated by Dr. Madden, in page 14, that the new interests which he supposes to be created in the minds of the British residents, especially in the minds of the liberated negroes, "have a very unfavourable influence upon them when employed in public situations, or called upon to act as petty juries in our courts." He states, "if the case is one which involves the interest of a slave dealer, no matter what his nation, the disposition of a jury thus composed is invariably to give a verdict in favour of the slave trader, unless the chief justice should take extraordinary pains to make them do their duty honestly and impartially." Do you know instances in which this has operated?—No; I believe it never operated in any case.

5297. What are the cases in which slave dealers come before juries in Sierra Leone?—Slave dealers have come before them, and been convicted and executed; I never knew an instance of a man who ought to have been convicted escaping.

5298. He mentions here an instance of a vessel, the Gollupchik, being captured and being sold, and becoming the property of certain London merchants, and being again sent out with a cargo of goods for the slave trade factories of Gallinas, under British colours, and commanded by a British subject. "The vessel," he says, "was condemned by the Mixed Court of Justice at Sierra Leone, and the English captain was committed for trial at the ensuing assizes. The grand jury found a true bill against this man on the clearest evidence, but the petty jury, all of whom were persons of colour, returned an unanimous verdict of acquittal, which was received by the coloured persons in the court, and by some others of similar sentiments, with decided tokens of approbation." Are you acquainted with that case?—Not at all; without knowing the case it would be impossible to say whether the jury were right or wrong; I have known cases where they have discharged persons accused of slave dealing, and where they were right. In the case referred to by Mr. Hartung of the Echo, the jury thought that the prisoner was not liable to conviction; but I never knew in my time any man who ought to have been convicted of slave dealing escape.

5299. Generally speaking, did you find the coloured juries do their duty in all cases?—Certainly; they do their duty very well.

5300. Mr. *W. Patten.*] Is it from any particular class that juries are selected?—The grand juries are selected from the most respectable inhabitants of Freetown, and the petty juries from shopkeepers and the reputable class of traders.

5301. Viscount *Courtenay.*] Who selects them?—The sheriff.

5302. *Chairman.*]—Has the office of chief justice been frequently vacant?—It has been vacant several times since I was in the colony, and an acting chief justice has been appointed.

5303. Who has acted in the interval?—During one interval, Mr. Melville, who was Queen's advocate at the time, and Mr. Carr, who was also Queen's advocate, and who is now chief justice, officiated on another occasion.

5304. Were they gentlemen who had a legal education?—Both of those persons had; but there were two other instances in which the office was held by men who had no legal education; once by a merchant, and a second time by the collector of customs.

5305. Was that under the necessity of the case?—Yes.

5306. Mr. *Forster.*] How long did the collector of customs hold that office?—A very long time; he held it from the death of Chief Justice Rankin until the appointment of Mr. Carr as chief justice, which was probably a year and a half after.

5307. Mr. *W. Patten.*] Do you know what year it was in?—From August 1839 till, I think, the end of 1840, or the beginning of 1841.

5308. Mr. *Forster.*] It is a part of the duty of the chief justice to deliver the gaol at the Gambia, is it not?—Yes.

5309. Are you aware whether the acting chief justice visited the Gambia for that purpose during the 18 months in question?—Certainly; while I was there Mr. Hook visited it.

5310. Do you know how frequently, in each year, it is the duty of the chief justice to deliver the gaol of the Gambia?—There is no time appointed; but I consider it a great disadvantage both to the Gambia and Sierra Leone, having only one chief justice for the two places.

5311. You are not aware whether the Gambia has not been left for a period of 12 months without a gaol delivery?—No; I think it is possible that it might be the case between the early part of 1838 and 1839, or between the beginning of 1839 and the beginning of 1840. There is very great difficulty in getting any person in a colony like that to fill the situation of chief justice, I mean from among the residents in the colony.

5312. Are you aware of the cause of the office having been vacant for the period of 18 months?—No, not at all; I suppose that the Colonial Government could not find a proper person to send out. One barrister who was appointed was drowned before he reached Sierra Leone.

5313. You are not aware that the applications have generally been extremely numerous for that office whenever it has become vacant?—No.

5314. Mr. *Aldam*.] What is the system of criminal law in force in the colonies?—The law of England.

5315. Is it modified at all?—Very little; if it is modified, it is modified by local Acts passed by the Governor and Council.

5316. Mr. *Evans*.] Do you think it a good thing to appoint men of colour to such high offices as those of chief justice or Governor, in any colony where many English gentlemen reside?—Certainly, if they are fit for the situations; but at Sierra Leone there is no feeling whatever except amongst one or two individuals, on the subject of colour; indeed I believe that the most popular man at the present time, and almost during the whole time when I was there, was a man of colour, and who was afterwards Lieutenant-governor; that was Dr. Ferguson, a man, I believe, universally beloved there.

5317. Mr. *Forster*.] Do you think that the natives have the same confidence and respect for a person of that description, as for a white officer?—I think so; at Sierra Leone, certainly.

5318. Mr. *Aldam*.] Practically, do you find a great number of men of colour who are fit to fill high situations in the colony?—There are not so many men of colour as white men fit to fill the high situations; but some of the highest situations have been filled in my time by men of colour, and well filled.

5319. *Mr. W. Patten*.] Have you any other observation which you wish to make upon Dr. Madden's Report?—At page 28, on "The result of the efforts at present in use for the suppression of the slave trade," Dr. Madden mentions "The disappointment the captors experience at seeing all their arduous efforts for hindering the slave trade factories from receiving their supplies from the foreign vessels engaged in this trade completely nullified by the proceedings of our own merchants and commanders of merchant-vessels, who supply them with the identical goods and stores which they capture the foreign vessels for conveying to the coast." Now I wish particularly, with reference to that statement, to say, that foreign vessels are never captured for having *goods* of any description on board of them. There appears to have been some error entertained as to the grounds on which the vessel called the Dos Amigos, which has been mentioned before, was condemned. That vessel was condemned at Sierra Leone, and in the report which the Commissioners made to Government, they stated that the Dos Amigos had been allowed to lie in Cape Coast Roads fully equipped for the slave trade. It seems to have been supposed that our complaint was, that she was carrying *goods* for the supply of the slave trade; but no vessel, either British or foreign, has ever been condemned at Sierra Leone on account of the description of goods that she was carrying.

5320. What is the object which you have in calling the attention of the Committee to that statement; is it to deny that statement?—There is a good deal of evidence in the papers before the Committee on the case of the Dos Amigos. The impression seems to have been, that the complaint of the mixed commission court at Sierra Leone against the Governor of Cape Coast Castle, was, that he allowed a vessel to trade at Cape Coast, which was afterwards captured there as a slave trader. Now the ground of complaint was quite distinct, namely, that he allowed a vessel with *equipments* on board for the slave trade to be in a British harbour with impunity; it had nothing to do with the goods whatever.

5321. *Chairman.*] You do not believe that it would be lawful to seize and condemn a foreign vessel for conveying to a slave trader goods and stores that are not included in the equipment article?—I do not.

5322. Therefore the expression is incorrect that our commanders of British cruizers must "experience disappointment at seeing all their arduous efforts for hindering the slave trade factories from receiving their supplies from the foreign vessels engaged in this trade completely nullified by the proceedings of our own merchants and commanders of merchant vessels who supply them with the identical goods and stores, which they capture the foreign vessels for conveying to the coast"?—It is impossible that they can feel disappointment about what never happened.

5323. Mr. *W. Patten.*] Is it your opinion that the law can be altered upon this subject for the better?—I think not; any alteration would, I think, be for the worse. In the next paragraph Dr. Madden states, that he considers it would be desirable that the men-of-war vessels on the coast should only be employed two years. I do not think that any naval officer would agree with him in that respect; it is not till they have been two years on the coast that they become acquainted with the arts of the slave dealers, and thoroughly efficient in the suppression of the slave trade.

5324. In short, it requires considerable experience to ascertain the best means of capturing the slavers?—Certainly; but on all questions relating to service on the coast I would recommend that a naval officer should be examined.

5325. *Chairman.*] Dr. Madden suggests, "that instead of head-money, or the bounty of 5*l.* paid for the capture of each slave, the pay of men and officers should be doubled, and the promotion of the former advanced in proportion to the time of service required for it on any other station in a double ratio." Are you of opinion that any inconvenience arises from the present system of head-money?—I do not think any inconvenience has been found to arise; it was supposed at one time, and stated rather positively in the House of Lords, that such an effect had been produced, but a refutation of the statement was given the same year, for instead of full vessels being taken, there was not one out of 20 that was taken with slaves on board.

5326. You think that the remuneration to the officers is put upon the best and fairest footing now?—I would not say that, because I think the officers are not remunerated sufficiently for empty vessels at present; the sum received for the capture of an empty vessel is so very small, and the sum received for the capture of a full vessel so much larger, that there is no comparison whatever between the two cases; and there is more good done by the capture of an empty vessel, and the service is just as arduous.

5327. Have you ever thought of any other system that could be adopted?— I have suggested an alteration of the bounties on this scale. It appeared that about three times as many vessels were captured under the equipment treaties, as were formerly taken, when only vessels full of slaves were allowed to be captured; and I thought that the remuneration for an empty vessel should be so calculated, that it should amount to about one-third of what the officer would receive if he took a full vessel with the average number of slaves on board. There would be no difficulty in making the calculation, and it would be only fair to the officers to give them that advantage.

5328. No such alteration has been made?—No.

5329. Mr. *W. Patten.*] You would not diminish the head-money to officers when they captured a vessel full of slaves?—No; it has been diminished very greatly the last 12 years, from 10*l.* to 5*l.* a head.

5330. What would be the effect of putting all vessels on the same footing, whether having slaves on board or being empty?—There would be no difficulty.

5331. *Chairman.*] Would it not be fairer to make the remuneration independent of the casual circumstance of whether the vessel was full or empty?—Yes; it would be taking away the advantage which the officers now enjoy with full vessels, but I think it would be a fair thing.

5332. Mr. *Forster.*] Are officers entitled to the head-money on slaves taken on shore?—No; the difficulty in that case is, that when taken on shore they are British subjects, if they are taken in British territory, and the British law will not acknowledge that they could be slaves. The difficulty was found some time ago, when a naval officer went to Bulama and captured several hundred slaves who were detained there by the Portuguese; he proceeded in the Admiralty Court, but the judge said, These men are not slaves, they are taken on British territory. The British law will not allow that any person can be a slave on British soil; so that the captor was deprived of his head-money.

5333. A considerable number was taken at the Gallinas by Captain Denman?—Yes.

5334. Will Captain Denman be entitled to head-money upon those persons so captured?—He has never received any thing for them, but I hope he may; if there is any fund from which remuneration on the ordinary scale can be granted, it would be desirable that such cases should be dealt with in the same manner as they would be if brought under the terms of the Act.

5335. Mr. *Evans.*] If the remuneration was on the tonnage of the vessel, supposing it was on the same scale as it is now, would that be a just way of taking it?—Yes; a remuneration on the tonnage, whether full or empty, would be fair, but the scale should be very much raised; at present it is miserably low.

5336. I am supposing that it was raised to the average of the present remuneration for capturing full and empty vessels?—That would be an improvement.

5337. Mr. *W. Patten.*] Is there not more difficulty in capturing a vessel with slaves on board than in capturing an empty vessel?—There is much less difficulty in capturing a vessel with slaves on board.

5338. Are not more exertions used when a vessel has slaves on board?— They run away in both cases; but the vessel is impeded greatly whilst she has her cargo of slaves on board, and there is more chance of capture, and the chase is less likely to be long, than with an empty vessel.

5339. *Chairman.*] The security of condemnation is greater?—Yes.

5340. You stated that there was a difficulty in remunerating the officers when slaves were taken on shore, on the ground of their being considered as British subjects; does that apply to Gallinas?—No; the question did not apply there, but to Bulama, because we claimed the sovereignty of that island. There is no remuneration, under any Act of Parliament, for slaves released under those circumstances which occurred at the Gallinas.

5341. Might there not be some question altogether, whether the release of slaves on shore was within the proper functions of a cruiser?—There might, under some circumstances; but in the case referred to it was a voluntary act on the part of the chief of the country releasing those slaves; they were detained there by persons whom the chief considered as his enemies, by whom he was kept in control, and he was relieved from their control by the Wanderer. There was a positive application made by the chief of the country.

5342. Then it was not, properly speaking, a duty imposed upon the commander engaged upon that station?—No, it would be only a duty under peculiar circumstances.

5343. Therefore such a practice would naturally not be contemplated by any Act of Parliament?—No.

5344. Mr. *Forster.*] Do you consider the chiefs of the Gallinas opposed to the slave trade?—No.

5345. How did they happen to apply for relief against the slave dealers?—An illegal act had been committed by those chiefs on the subjects of Sierra Leone, and when redress was demanded the excuse offered by the chiefs was, that they were held in subjection by the resident Spaniards there, and that they could not afford the relief which was required by British subjects, or even prevent British subjects being carried into slavery, in consequence of the control which was exercised over them by the Spanish and Portuguese slave traders.

5346. Do you yourself believe that excuse to be true?—I believe that it was stated; I have no means of judging of its truth.

5347. *Chairman.*] It was a justification for the interference of Captain Denman?—Exactly. By the papers presented to Parliament it appeared that some women and children at Sierra Leone, as far as I recollect the case, were taken down to the Gallinas, and were known to be there, and Captain Denman was instructed by the Governor of Sierra Leone to go in and demand their liberation, and also to remonstrate with the chiefs for the offence which had been committed; and also to inquire how it was that British men-of-war boats going into the river were refused all supplies, were not allowed to water, and were even prevented having intercourse with American and other vessels lying in the river. The principal chief then complained of the treatment which he received from the Spaniards and Portuguese, and he requested to be released from their control, and Captain Denman complied with his request.

5348. Mr. *Aldam.*] Were there any British subjects found among the slaves captured at the Gallinas?—None that I am aware of, except those particular ones that Captain Denman demanded, and whom he recovered.

5349. *Chairman.*] Do you believe that there are any instances of kidnapping out of the territory of Sierra Leone?—Very few.

At page 34 of Dr. Madden's Report, there is this passage: "The charges made for the disposal of these effects," that is, goods sold by public auction, "the captors state, and I believe with truth, are extremely heavy; and in many cases more than half the prize money that the captors had reason to expect, is swallowed up in the charges made by the various officers at Sierra Leone, employed in taking care, and ultimately disposing of, the effects of the captured vessel. On the following cases of slave-trade vessels sent in for adjudication to the Commission Courts at Sierra Leone, by Captain Tucker, of Her Majesty's ship Wolverine, the charges here detailed were made." Then follows the schedule; five out of the nine vessels mentioned in that schedule were sold, while I was in the court, and with respect to those five I obtained the heads of the charges yesterday from the Foreign Office. The Vigilante is the first; the charges were 99*l*. 1*s*. 4*d*., and in that case the sum paid to the collector of customs for duty was 18*l*. In the Pampeiro, the charges were 63*l*., the duty was 12*l*. In the Passos, the charges were 22*l*. 8*s*., and the proceeds very small; but in that case the vessel was destroyed at Prince's Island, and there were also slaves on board, and the whole of those charges, for the vessel was only in port a few days, consisted of the feeding of the slaves, and the duty on the goods which were found on board, and the marshal's expenses. The reason of the small amount of proceeds was, that there was no vessel, and only a few goods that were brought up in the man-of-war; only a few pieces of cloth, and such things. In the case of the Firmeza, the charges were 1,014*l*. 7*s*. 5*d*., but of that sum the duty paid to the customs was 775*l*., and the translations were 18*l*.; so that about 800*l*. was paid by the marshal on those accounts out of 1,014*l*.

5350. Mr. *W. Patten*.] The translations do not then appear to be of that onerous nature to the captor, which Dr. Madden, in the previous part of his statement, says that they are?—They are very heavy in some cases: I have known them as high as 60*l*. and 70*l*. In the Emprendador the expenses are 351*l*. 19*s*. 1*d*.; of that sum 172*l*. was paid in duty, and 33*l*. in translations, making 205*l*. out of 351*l*. Then the other expenses are the five per cent. to the auctioneer, the marshal's charges for taking charge of the vessel, and boats and labourers landing cargo, and also a premium of about six or six and-one-eighth per cent. difference between the English money and the currency.

5351. Viscount *Courtenay*.] Are those fees fixed by a scale settled by the court?—The fees were fixed by a regular scale, that has been drawn up on the model of the schedule of fees paid in the Vice-Admiralty Courts, which was approved of by Dr. Lushington and two other gentlemen connected with the Admiralty Court in England, and which schedule was sent out to all the Vice-Admiralty Courts of our colonies, as the rule by which they were to be guided. In many cases our charges were less; but in no case, I believe, were they more than directed in that schedule.

5352. *Chairman.*] Since those heavy charges which are alluded to by Dr. Madden have been incurred, the duties, which are one principal source of expense, have been modified according to your recommendation?—They have.

5353. What would have been the result of the reduction in that case of the Firmeza, where the duties appear to have been 775*l.*?—The reduction would have been very great indeed. Without knowing on what articles the duty was imposed, I cannot say; but the duty was changed from a fixed to an *ad valorem* duty; and in the case of the tobacco and spirits of that vessel, the reduction would have been very great; probably it would have struck off 500*l.* at least of the 775*l.*

5354. That evil, therefore, is met to a considerable degree?—The evil is met as much as can be expected; indeed, I do not think that there is any thing whatever now that the captors have to complain of.

5355. It cannot be expected that the goods should be sold for the benefit of the captor, free of duty, in a colony where other articles imported pay duty?—No, certainly not.

5356. Viscount *Courtenay.*] Is it in the power of the proctors to make additional charges upon those parties?—The arrangement between the proctor and the captor is left to themselves; the court attempted once to interfere with the charges of the proctors, but they were instructed that it was a matter which they had no control over.

5357. Is that settled by a certain rule of etiquette?—It is settled by practice; there is a certain charge that is made for every vessel now, whether she is troublesome or not; but it is a matter over which the court can have no control whatever.

5358. Are the proctors Europeans?—There have seldom been more than three or four at one time practising.

5359. *Chairman.*] Are they men of education?—Yes; the Queen's advocate is generally one, and the one who gets the most practice; and there are others who are practising attornies in the other courts, who act as proctors in the Mixed Commission Court.

5360. Are they universally Europeans, educated in England?—I believe every one has been educated in England, and is an European; there is one of them that was born in the West Indies, I believe, but educated in England.

5361. Mr. *Forster.*] Have the officers of the Mixed Commission the patronage of any of the appointments on the spot?—Of all.

5362. *Chairman.*] Do they appoint the proctor?—The proctor petitions to be admitted; and latterly, for the last year or two that I was there, I made them undergo an examination, for I found that one or two were applying to be admitted as proctors of the court in order to escape serving on juries, and I therefore made them submit to an examination on the treaties, and on the decisions of the Mixed Courts, and it checked the practice.

5363. At what time were those charges made which are specified in Dr. Madden's Report?—The five cases out of the nine that I have referred to occurred in 1839, the others subsequently to my leaving the colony.

5364. When were those modifications made which would affect the statement which Dr. Madden has made?—They came into effect after the five cases occurred on which there are those high charges; they came into effect in December, 1839.

5365. Previously to Dr. Madden's visit to Sierra Leone?—Yes, some time previously.

5366. Have you any further observations to make upon Dr. Madden's Report?—In page 35 is a passage to which I was referred at the last examination: "The intervention of the whole present establishment of marshals, collectors, surveyors, interpreters, harbour-masters, agents, storekeepers, canoe-hirers, and victuallers of captured ships' crews, might be dispensed with without inconvenience to the public, and with some advantage to the individuals who are interested in the disposal of the effects." A great many of those persons do not exist in connexion with our court at all.

5367. Can you state what is the real establishment connected with the adjudication of slave vessels?—There is one marshal; he is paid by fees, on the principle of the schedule that was drawn up in England for the regulation of the Vice-Admiralty Courts in the colonies, and which are very low, I think almost too low; the collector we have nothing to do with; he is the Queen's officer: as regards the surveyors, we have two surveyors in cases of vessels which are prosecuted for equipment to examine the equipment of the vessel, and to report, and they get a fee for that examination; in cases of vessels taken full of slaves no surveyors are required; it is only in cases of vessels seized for equipment.

5368. That is an officer absolutely necessary for the ascertainment of the facts?—Yes, because we could not allow a man to give evidence in his own case upon such a point as that.

5369. What is the fee?—I think the fee is two guineas a day during his employment; and in order to obtain the services of a respectable man who will go through the disagreeable duty which is imposed upon him in examining a vessel equipped for the slave trade, overhauling her in every part, and whose testimony can be positively relied upon, I do not think that a smaller fee ought to be paid.

5370. Does the survey occupy more than one day?—If it occupies more than a day, he gets another two guineas, but I do not recollect any case of that kind.

5371. What is the interpreter?—There is one interpreter, who interprets between the witness and the registrar when the witness speaks in a foreign language, and I believe he gets 5s. on an examination; he is a poor man; it is very trifling.

5372. Is the harbour-master an officer of the court?—No. Agents we have none. There is no storekeeper; the marshal lands the goods, and under some peculiar circumstances, where they have to be held over for sale, they may be stored, but I think such a thing has hardly occurred in my time.

5373. Canoe-hirers, who are those?—There are canoes employed to land the cargo.

5374. That is a duty which must be discharged and paid for at the ordinary rate in the colony?—Yes.

5375. "Victuallers of captured ships' crews," who are those?—We have no such men; the marshal victuals the ship's crew at the regular rate laid down, 3s. for the officers and 2s. for the men; there are generally only three persons in each case thus provided for.

5376. Is that any thing beyond the absolute expense necessary for the object?—You cannot in a colony where food is so dear lodge and feed an European in a respectable line of life for less than 3s. a day.

5377. Mr. *W. Patten.*] Would you recommend the uniting of any of those offices together?—The only three officers we have are the marshal, the surveyor, and the commissioner of appraisement and sale, who is not mentioned here, and their offices cannot be united.

5378. *Chairman.*] Dr. Madden recommended that "the effects of the captured vessel, prior to adjudication should remain in them under the charge of the captors"?—They always do remain in the vessel; Dr. Madden mentions this as a change that ought to take place, but nobody ever thought of landing a vessel's goods before condemnation, because if the vessel is restored she goes out with all the goods in her. He then says, "On condemnation they should be delivered over by the captors to the collector of the customs, and this part of his service be included in the remuneration of his general duties." The court could have no control over the collector of the customs, and how he would perform the duty more cheaply than the marshal I do not know; those goods must be landed under the control of the court, and kept under the control of the court till they are sold.

5379. What are the charges on the sale which are alluded to?—The custom-house duties and the auction duty, and those already mentioned.

5380. The custom-house duties are the duties which you alluded to as having been subsequently reduced?—Yes.

5381. Which did press upon the goods in proportion to their quality?—Yes; Dr. Madden says in the last sentence, "I beg to be understood as not meaning to attribute, in the slightest degree, to these gentlemen the disadvantages of the system that is adopted for the disposal of the effects of the condemned vessel. This system has grown up to its present amount of abuse, I believe, without their sanction, and I should think, from what I have seen of these gentlemen, it exists without their approval." It does not; if there had been any abuse I should have been responsible for it, of course, during the time that I was there; but I believe no abuse whatever existed which the court could control. In the case of translations, we had no translator till we applied to the Government, and indeed the necessity did not arise till lately, because when you could only capture vessels full of slaves, you did not require any translations; I believe there is no abuse whatever, and it certainly is not without the sanction of the court, if it exists.

5382. Viscount *Courtenay*.] Is there any storehouse belonging to the Vice-Admiralty Court, where goods, supposing them to be of a suspicious character, if landed, are kept?—There is a storehouse connected with the mixed commissions, where the coppers and shackles, and the iron fittings for the open hatchways, are lodged.

5383. Under whose charge is that?—It is in the residence of the registrar; the registrar is required to be a resident officer, on account not only of the books and papers which he has constantly under his charge, but on account of the equipments of condemned vessels, which are also kept by him.

5384. It would be, therefore, very irregular that any of those equipments should be kept in any place but under the custody of the registrar?—Certainly.

5385. Supposing this to have been stated, that a number of leg-irons and other things, which had been landed from a slave vessel condemned in the Vice-Admiralty Court, had been deposited in a public shed on the wharf, and that they had been neglected by the officer of the Vice-Admiralty Court, whose duty it was to have put them in a place of safety; if that was so, should you say that that was irregular and unusual?—It cannot happen in our court; if such a thing were to happen, the marshal would be immediately dismissed; but the thing never happens, because there is a regular system of duty; but the Vice-Admiralty Court has no office, it has no storekeeper, and no means of carrying on its duty efficiently.

5386. What would have been the regular course in such a case as that mentioned in this paper?—I do not know what course the Vice-Admiralty Court would pursue, but with us, equipment articles are landed and carried up to the registrar. There were several rooms, when I left, completely filled with these things, and occasionally, when the Government requires coppers for the use of the Liberated African Department, we hand them over to them, and they are supplied to vessels carrying over recruits to the West Indies; but in no case do the coppers from the condemned vessels go to anybody that we do not know will make a good use of them.

5387. Is the same person that is marshal of the Mixed Commission Court marshal of the Vice-Admiralty Court?—No; it is a rule that is laid down very strictly, not to allow any sort of connexion between the two courts, as it would only produce irregularity and confusion.

5388. *Chairman.*] Have you any other observation to make upon Dr. Madden's Report?—In the last sentence of his Report he says, that parties should not be allowed to become purchasers of slave ships, or the equipments of condemned slavers, unless they "enter into a bond that such ships or equipments shall not be employed in slave trade objects, on pain of incurring the penalty of fine to the amount of double the value of the property thus employed." Now the Act of Parliament positively requires, that if any equipments are on board a vessel, a bond shall be given, and that no vessel shall be cleared out by the custom-house unless a bond is given.

5389. Is there any thing in the present state of the law which makes it illegal to sell a vessel bought at Sierra Leone immediately into the hands of a person who shall employ her in the slave trade?—Nothing whatever.

5390. Mr. *W. Patten.*] Is there not an Act of Parliament which does prevent any body knowingly dealing with a slave dealer?—Yes, there is; but the difficulty would be to prove the guilty knowledge of the fact, that the man to whom the vessel is sold intended to employ that vessel in the slave trade.

5391. Mr. *Forster.*] What Act of Parliament do you allude to when you say that there is an Act which forbids persons selling a vessel or goods to slave dealers?—The 5 Geo. 4, c. 113.

5392. Mr. *W. Patten.*] In that Act of Parliament, does the word "knowingly" apply to knowledge of the fact that the parties are slave dealers, or of the fact that the goods so sold are to be employed in the slave trade?—To the latter. The second clause of that Act declares that it shall not be lawful to ship, tranship, and so on, or to contract for the shipping or transhipping to be employed in accomplishing any of the objects or the contracts in relation to the objects, which objects and contracts have hereinbefore been declared unlawful; but by the 7th and 10th clauses penalties are imposed only upon a party upon its being shown that he "knowingly and wilfully" shipped and laded goods to be employed in the slave trade.

5393. It does not apply to his knowledge of the fact of the man being a dealer in slaves?—I am not aware that it does; a great deal may come under the general term of "aiding and abetting" the slave trade; but in all the penal clauses of that Act the words "knowingly and wilfully" are introduced.

5394. How do you account for the governor of a British colony commencing his proclamation with these words: "Whereas by the laws of Great Britain, and more particularly by the provisions of the Act of Parliament passed in the fifth year of the reign of his late Majesty George the Fourth, all British subjects are prohibited in the most express and positive terms, and under the most severe penalties, from aiding, abetting, or trading with, directly or indirectly, all or any vessels or vessel engaged, or about to be engaged, in the slave trade, or fitted with that view and purpose"?—The prohibitory clauses of the Act are very strong indeed; they would seem to comprehend every kind of dealing with slave traders; but it is the penal clauses which would prevent convictions.

5395. *Chairman.*] If you could convict the party selling the vessel to the slave dealer with a guilty knowledge of the purpose to which the vessel was to be appropriated, you have in the Act of Parliament all that can be required?—Yes.

5396. Mr. *W. Patten.*] Does the same observation apply to goods?—To every part of the Act. I believe in every instance where prohibitions are given in the Act the penal clauses referring to the prohibition contain the words "knowingly and wilfully."

5397. *Chairman.*] Therefore those acts are all of them unlawful, but the difficulty is in proving the guilt?—Yes. You may possibly prove the guilty knowledge by letters found on board the vessel.

5398. If you could ascertain that any merchant at Sierra Leone sold vessels or goods to a party, knowing that such vessel was to be employed in the slave trade, he might be convicted under the Act of Parliament?—Yes; he would be prosecuted and convicted under the 5th of Geo. 4.

5399. Mr. *W. Patten.*] Should you imply that this was guilty knowledge, that the vessel should be sold to a notorious slave dealer on any part of the coast, who was perfectly known to have no legitimate traffic of his own?—That is a legal question which would be decided in the common law courts, whether a guilty knowledge might be implied from particular circumstances, though it could not be proved directly.

5400. Mr. *Forster.*] You have given an opinion upon the construction of the words "knowingly and wilfully" used in the Act of Parliament; upon what authority have you given that opinion?—The Act cannot be misunderstood; I think no person can read it without seeing the meaning of it, whether lawyer or not.

5401. To sell goods or vessels to Pedro Blanco, for example, would that, in your opinion, bring a party within the meaning of the Act?—No, not unless you could prove that he sold them knowing that they were to be applied to an unlawful purpose.

5402. *Chairman.*] The difficulty, then, is not in understanding the purpose and object of the Act, but in proving the offence?—Yes; the difficulty is in proving the guilty knowledge, and that is the only difficulty.

5403. Sir *T. D. Acland.*] Was not the principal design of that Act to prevent persons from aiding in fitting up vessels for the direct and notorious purpose of engaging in the slave trade, and for no other purpose?—Yes, it was one object.

5404. Therefore, would not any person selling shackles, or any thing else that was notoriously employed in procuring slaves, or in exchange for slaves, be brought under the Act?—If you could prove that at the time he made them he contemplated that they would be employed in the slave trade, he would be brought within the purpose of the Act.

5405. If he sold shackles to vessels engaged in the slave trade?—I should think he would be brought within it then, because the guilty knowledge would be properly inferred in that case; but shackles may be made in England, and kept on board merchant vessels to be employed on the crew.

5406. Mr. *Forster.*] You do not think, then, that the intention of that Act was to prevent British subjects and British capital from being engaged in partnership, or having an interest in the slave trade itself, and nothing beyond that?—Yes, I think the intention of the Act was to prevent such engagements.

5407. Do you think that it goes beyond that?—I think that is all we require, that they should have no connexion with the traffic.

5408. How would you bring the party within that Act who sold goods, having no interest or partnership in the transaction to which they were subsequently applied?—In that case I think the Act would not reach him.

5409. What becomes, then, of the guilty knowledge of which you have spoken so much?—No guilty knowledge can be proved against the party in the case you suppose.

5410. *Chairman.*] But it may exist?—Yes, it may exist; but unless you can prove it, the penalties of the Act would not reach him.

5411. Do you conceive that the act of selling a vessel or goods that may be hereafter employed, or that shall be, to the knowledge of the person selling them, employed in the slave trade, falls within the meaning of the Act, unless that person is to have a share in the profits of the transaction?—Yes, I believe it does include that; I think that it forbids aiding and assisting in every way, even as servants, or employed in boats.

5412. Mr. *Forster.*] Then you think that a British subject selling goods to Pedro Blanco, or any other slave dealer, with the impression on his mind, or, in fact, the conviction on his mind, that those goods would be employed in the slave trade, would come within the meaning of that Act?—Yes certainly; but the difficulty would be in the proof of the guilty knowledge. Such an act as that is certainly intended to come within the Act; not that I would recommend that those words, "knowingly and wilfully," should be taken out entirely; I think it might be a dangerous thing to do so; but I am speaking of what, in my opinion, the meaning of the Act is, namely, that it is absolutely necessary in every case to prove the guilty knowledge, in order to bring the party accused within the penalties of the Act.

5413. In what way would you prove the mental impression upon the man's mind?—There is the difficulty.

5414. Do you think that any British Act of Parliament would impose penalties for the mental impression upon a man's mind?—I have stated that I am not prepared to say whether or not the words "knowingly and wilfully" might be advantageously omitted from the Act, but a guilty knowledge may be inferred from particular circumstances.

5415. Then you consider that that Act of Parliament is an Act against constructive slave trading?—No.

5416. *Chairman.*] You consider it to be an Act against aiding and abetting the slave trade in as many ways as the Act of Parliament can reach it?—Yes; there is no Act that I ever read that is so general and comprehensive in its terms; but unfortunately it is limited, as it must be limited, in its application.

5417. Mr. *Forster.*] Can you quote the authority of any British lawyer for the opinions you have expressed with respect to the construction of that Act?—Yes, I have heard opinions expressed on the subject from the Bench at Sierra Leone repeatedly, and by educated lawyers.

5418. In the case of a British merchant selling goods to a person who was known to have no other means of gaining his livelihood, except by the slave trade, the party selling the goods would in your opinion be liable to the penalties of that Act?—It is the same thing in that case; you must prove guilty knowledge, direct or implied.

5419. In selling goods to a man who has no other means of gaining his livelihood than by applying those goods for the purposes of the slave trade, there can be no doubt of the guilty knowledge?—I should think not; but if I were a juror I should have to satisfy my own conscience that there was a guilty knowledge. I am no lawyer; this is only the opinion of a private person.

5420. Can you conceive a stronger proof of guilty knowledge than such a transaction as that would furnish?—I think I should decide that there was a guilty knowledge, taking the case supposed, that the seller knew there was no other way in which the purchaser would employ the goods sold to him than in the slave trade; if I were a juror I think I should find him guilty in that case under the Act of Parliament; I should consider the guilty knowledge to be proved.

5421. *Chairman.*] You appear to be in favour of the proposal for taking bond from the person selling the vessel, that such vessel shall not be employed within a certain period in the slave trade?—That they should take bond that the vessel should not be immediately sold to a slave dealer; but the difficulty would be in following the vessel through successive transfers.

5422. Can you suggest any means of so framing that bond as to escape the difficulty which pervades the enforcing the provisions of the existing Act of Parliament, on account of the necessity of establishing guilty knowledge?—I think I could to a certain extent. The case once came before me at Sierra Leone; I was consulted by one of the officers of the Mixed Commission Court on the subject of the sale of a vessel of his; he knew perfectly well that if he had sold that vessel to a slave dealer, we should immediately dismiss him from his situation, and he came to consult me respecting the person who had offered to buy the vessel. He had inquired about him, and there was some sort of suspicion, and I told him that I could not allow him, as an officer of the court, to sell this vessel to that person, unless he took bond to a sufficient amount that the vessel should not be sold again to a slave dealer, so that if the vessel, whilst in the possession of the person to whom he sold her, should be captured, the bond should be considered as violated, and he should be liable to the penalty. But I do not think you can carry the restriction beyond the first purchaser: but if the vessel, whilst in the hands of the first purchaser, should be seized for slave dealing, the penalty of the bond might be enforced.

5423. But would you not find it difficult to make that effective, from the facility that exists for the transfer of the vessel to other parties?—Yes; I do not think the restriction could be carried beyond the first purchaser.

5424. Would reaching the first purchaser be any great additional difficulty in the way of employing the prize vessels in the slave trade?—It would in Sierra Leone be a difficulty to some small extent; because, where only one or two persons are engaged in purchasing vessels to be afterwards sold to slave dealers, it is not likely that there would be any intermediate person between the seller and the Spanish or Portuguese purchaser at Gallinas, or any slave station in the neighbourhood.

5425. Would it not be very easy to establish a system of third persons acting as a medium between the slave dealer and the purchaser, who should protect the purchaser at the prize sale from the penalties of such a bond?—It might be done; but the difficulty would in that case be, to get two men to endure the odium of such employment; the difficulty would be doubled.

5426. Could not a vessel be sold to a subordinate party at Sherboro' or Gallinas, not the slave dealer, but the agent of the slave dealer, who might be compelled immediately to hand over the vessel to the slave dealer?—It might be done.

5427. Mr. *Forster.*] Would you propose, by bond or otherwise, to make it illegal that the purchaser of a prize vessel at Sierra Leone should sell that vessel, on her arrival in London, to the Spanish merchants Messrs. Zulueta & Co.?—No; I would not certainly render it illegal.

5428. Then that being your opinion, in what way can you imagine any restriction to be devised for the purpose of regulating the sales of the vessels after they may be purchased at Sierra Leone?—I have mentioned that the restriction could only last, in my opinion, whilst the vessel remained in the hands of the second purchaser; that is, the person who purchases her from the highest bidder at the auction; I do not think you could follow her beyond that.

5429. Then you would prevent the actual purchaser at Sierra Leone from selling the vessel to Messrs. Zulueta & Co. in London?—No, I would not.

5430. Then where is the value of the restriction you would impose?—The value is this, and it is not of great value, that if that vessel, whilst sailing under the name of Zulueta & Co. is captured and condemned as being engaged in the slave trade, you will come upon the person who sold that vessel to Zulueta & Co. for the amount of the bond.

5431. You think it would be just to make the first purchaser of the vessel responsible for the subsequent employment of that vessel, after he had sold her to Messrs. Zulueta & Co.?—Yes, as long as it remained in the hands of Zulueta & Co.; and I would mention further, that an advantage which I did not perceive before would result from it, that the man who sells the vessel in the case supposed to Zulueta, would not be very happy under such a sale, unless he got a security from Zulueta for the amount of the bond, and in such a case, whenever doubtful characters came forward as purchasers, the amount of the bond would be an addition to the price paid for the vessel.

5432. When a prize vessel is brought into the public market in London, why should this vessel be subject to regulations different from any other vessel in the London market?—Because the vessel being purchased at Sierra Leone, at one of our sales, would be likely to be a vessel fitted for the slave trade, and for nothing else.

5433. But is it not well known that there are many vessels in the London market equally well adapted for that purpose as many of those vessels?—I think not.

5434. Sir *T. D. Acland.*] Do you not think that if a bond were given under penalty of forfeiture, if in the course of a certain time, say one, two, or three years, that vessel were detected as being engaged in the slave trade, the party giving the bond would take very good care to keep her out of that mischief?—Yes, I think he would.

5435. Would he not take very good care that the vessel should not get into hands through which that risk could be brought upon himself?—He would be interested in doing so.

5436. *Chairman.*] Other parties would secure themselves upon each successive transfer by successive bonds to the amount of their own liability?—The amount of the bond might be more than the value of the vessel considerably.

5437. Mr. *Forster.*] Then the result of that would be that there must be a series of bonds running through all the subsequent sales of the vessel?—Yes.

5438. Mr. *W. Patten.*] You have stated that in your opinion the breaking up of all the vessels would be far preferable?—Yes, the breaking up of all the vessels would be one of the best things that could possibly be done.

5439. *Chairman.*] What proportion of the vessels that have been taken within your knowledge have been so broken up?—It is only since the Spanish treaty came into operation in 1836 that they have been broken up at all; since that time more than two-thirds of the vessels condemned have been broken up.

5440. Sir *T. D. Acland.*] Would it be possible to fix the bond upon the vessel itself?—No; I do not think it would.

5441. *Chairman.*] You have seen a good deal of the effects of British trade upon the coast of Africa, especially as connected with Sierra Leone?—I cannot say that I have seen very much, but I have seen something.

5442. You have seen that British manufactures are, to some extent at least, employed as instruments of barter for slaves?—Yes.

5443. Indirectly through Brazil and Cuba, and from England, goods are sold to persons who would use them in barter for slaves?—Yes.

5444. Therefore, to a certain extent, British trade gives facilities for the slave trade?—Yes.

5445. Do you conceive that it would be possible, with advantage to the cause of putting down the slave trade, to have any further restrictions upon British trade on the coast of Africa: do you believe that it would be advisable to prohibit absolutely dealing in lawful articles with slavers or with slave factories?—I consider it to be undesirable to impose any restrictions.

5446. Will you state your reasons?—I think that no restrictions whatever could be drawn up applying to any description of goods that might not materially interfere with the legitimate trade.

5447. And you believe that it would be a serious injury to the people of Africa, and to the cause of civilization in Africa, if lawful trade were interfered with and impeded?—I do; I would not have any restrictions whatever upon the commercial intercourse of our vessels, to which only of course our law would apply, with any port on the coast, whatever her character was with regard to slave trading.

5448. You conceive that although some additional facility to the slave trade may arise from the lawful traffic, on the balance much more good accrues?—I think so. I think there are positive advantages in gaining an entrance for our vessels to those ports where the slave trade is carried on: that information of the character of the people and of their mode of trade is obtained, and facilities offered to the squadron cruizing on the coast and visiting those rivers; and also that at any time, if, from the checks given to the slave trade by more stringent cruizing in that part, the natives should be desirous of turning their attention to lawful commerce, there are the means of doing it at once ready to their hands. It might happen anywhere that legitimate trade, from strict cruizing, would become a desirable one for the natives; but they would not have the means of carrying it on if British vessels were forbidden to enter those ports.

5449. Is it desirable that the natives should see a lawful trade offered to them by the parties and nations who are now connected with the unlawful traffic themselves?—I think it is.

5450. If you prohibited the access of English vessels and English trade to the suspected ports, should you be able under any existing treaties, or should you be likely to be able under any future treaties, to prohibit the access to those ports of foreign vessels engaged in the supply off lawful articles?—I do not think it could be done.

5451. Unless you could so prohibit the access of foreign vessels, you could not in any way prevent the supply of those articles which are requisite to be used in barter for slaves?—No.

5452. Then, on the whole, you would gain nothing in the way of interruption to the slave trade, and you would lose many advantages for the obstruction of the slave trade which you now possess by the free access of English vessels even to the suspected ports?—That is my opinion.

5453. Sir *T. D. Acland.*] May not the carrying on of legitimate commerce, even with slave-dealing natives, be used as a means of inducing them by negotiation to give up dealing in slaves?—It may be so, certainly.

5454. *Mr. Forster.*] How did this merchant at Sierra Leone come to be regarded with suspicion and mistrust who traded to the Gallinas, if, in your opinion, such trade is beneficial for the civilization of Africa, and the suppression of the slave trade?—I have not stated that exactly; I would not impose any restrictions by law on the entrance of any vessel, whether for lawful or unlawful purposes; but such freedom does not release the merchant who sells his goods, knowing that they will be employed for the slave trade, from the responsibility of doing so.

5455. You would prevent merchants and vessels frequenting such places as the Gallinas, if it was to be inferred that they could not go there and dispose of their goods without being subject to the charge of being aiders and abettors in the slave trade?—I think that it is very desirable that some regulations should be drawn up for the guidance of the men-of-war on the coast, with regard to vessels engaged in traffic; there appears to be a sort of impression now, that it is their duty to interfere with all vessels trading with slave-trading ports, and it is quite a misunderstanding on their part.

5456. Mr. *Aldam.*] If there is an establishment formed, where both the lawful and the unlawful traffic is carried on in goods, do you think it is desirable to prevent English vessels from trading to that establishment?—I think it is undesirable.

5457. *Chairman.*] It is suggested in Dr. Madden's Report, that there should be some further acts of treaty, with a view of developing the resources of the colony?—I quite agree with Dr. Madden in that. In the year 1836 I was before a Committee of the House of Commons, when my evidence went particularly to that point. I thought that the policy of the British Government in rejecting territory, when they had legally and properly acquired it, and confining themselves entirely to the peninsula of Sierra Leone, was very injurious.

5458. The peninsula of Sierra Leone does not afford adequate employment and resources?—I think the employment and resources are sufficient for the population at present, but the land is not so fertile as the land that we then possessed, and which the Government at home required the Government there to give up, and restore to the natives; also the destruction of our sovereignty and property in that country will not allow us to take cognizance of slave-dealing transactions occurring in that territory.

5459. Mr. *Forster.*] Do you think it desirable to extend the limits of the colony at Sierra Leone?—I do.

5460. Do you think that there would be any difficulty in effecting that extension?—None whatever.

5461. Do you think that it would impose upon the British Government any great expense or responsibility to carry that out?—I do not think it would.

5462. *Chairman.*] Would it be desirable for the trade of the colony, if possible, to extend the limits of it, so as to give to a larger portion of the produce of the soil the advantage of British growth in the English markets?—I do not think advantage would be derived in that way; because no produce that is now brought down to Sierra Leone, and passes through Sierra Leone to England, is considered as foreign produce, either teak wood, palm-oil, rice, or any thing else.

5463. Does teak, for instance, take its character from the port of Sierra Leone?—Yes.

5464. Is it landed there?—Teak that is embarked in the river Sierra Leone is put on board the vessel in British waters.

5465. Where?—At Banee Island Roads.

5466. What distance from Freetown is that?—About fifteen miles.

5467. Is it floated down so far, and then put on board at that place?—Yes.

5468. Have you considered the question of emigration from the coast of Africa to the West Indies?—I have.

5469. Will you state generally what opinion you have formed on it?—I have formed a very favourable opinion of it. On the 15th of February 1841, at the desire of Lord John Russell, I expressed my views fully upon this subject, in a communication which I then made to the Colonial Office; I stated the classes from whom emigration might be expected, and though this was before any scheme of emigration was carried into effect, nothing has occurred since which has at all altered my opinion; and indeed just what I then expected has happened. It was supposed that there was a considerable desire on the part of the inhabitants to emigrate; such a desire I stated did not exist; that a few liberated Africans had been anxious to go to the country from which they had been taken as slaves, to join their friends, and that many Maroons had been anxious to go back to the West Indies, from which they had been taken, and where they had friends; but that beyond that, there was no general desire for emigration; that if such desire was requisite, it would be necessary to create it. That there was no difficulty at any time thrown in the way of persons anxious to leave the colony by the Governor and Council there; that on the contrary, just before I left, an application had been made by a party of liberated Africans to the Governor asking him to send them back to Badagry, on the coast, and the Governor and Council replied, that they might go if they pleased; but that the Government would not be at any expense in sending them. A few did go and returned, and since that time emigration has been going on to a considerable extent to Badagry, and at present there are a large number of liberated Africans there, who are finding their way across to the Niger; and in a letter I received a few days ago from a gentleman at Sierra Leone, he mentions that liberated Africans are still going to Badagry, and that it is likely to become an important place. There were a few Maroons, before emigration was encouraged by any agents from the West Indies, who purchased a vessel at Sierra Leone and went over to Jamaica, and their arrival was mentioned by Sir Charles Metcalfe, in one of the despatches which was received before my letter was written. I recommended that two persons should be selected from each of the principal tribes of liberated Africans, and sent over to the West Indies to report upon the prospects that were held out to emigrants by the colonies there, and that their wives and families should be supported during their absence, and also themselves paid a certain monthly allowance until their return; and I have no doubt that if that plan had been followed, a very large emigration from Sierra Leone would have taken place, and I regret much that it was not done.

5470. Are there at Sierra Leone chiefs who exercise a considerable influence over the liberated Africans?—Every tribe of liberated Africans has some chief man who represents its interests on all occasions, and who, in case of any difference with the Governor or other persons, stands forward to represent it.

5471. Do they generally fall into location according to the tribes from which they come?—No, they are mixed in the villages; the Governor pays no attention to that; he locates successive importations of negroes according to the wants of the place, and the land which is to be given away, without reference to nation.

5472. But subsequently those belonging to the same tribe co-operate?—They keep very much to their own nation.

5473. So that there are in the colony of Sierra Leone persons who exercise an influence over different portions of the population, according to the tribe that they come from?—Yes; I recommended that two persons should be chosen from each of the principal tribes, and sent over. And it appears from evidence that I heard given here the other day, that it was the non-return of such persons from Trinidad which prevented any further importation into that colony. I may perhaps be allowed to read a part of the letter which I wrote to the Colonial Office: "Evils of a serious nature may be anticipated if the collection and embarkation of African emigrants be left in the hands of private speculators, or even of the salaried agents of the different West India colonies, some of whom, at least, would be more anxious to signalize their zeal and success by the number of passengers whom they might ship, than cautious and scrupulous as to the means by which they are procured. Persons like the Maroons and liberated Africans mentioned above, who purchase or hire their own vessel, and pay their own passage, may of course go where they please, without question or obstruction, and they are little likely to go wrong. But with regard to negroes from the western coast of Africa, for whom a free passage will be found to the West Indies, in order that they may help to supply the deficiency of labourers so seriously felt there at present, I beg respectfully to recommend that the shipment of all such emigrants be positively restricted to the British settlements on the coast; that it there take place only with the sanction of Government, under the direct control and superintendence of the British emigration agent, and in exact conformity with the regulations issued for the guidance of that officer, and that it be confined to negroes who have been resident not less than 12 months in a British colony. Beyond the limits of British jurisdiction there is no part of this coast, except Liberia and the Kroo country, where the West India agents could obtain emigrant labourers from any other class than either the domestic slaves or the slaves prepared for sale to the slave traders; and when it is considered that, from causes which I need not now stop to explain, the price of a slave at the Gallinas, the largest slave mart in Africa, and close to Sierra Leone, has latterly been only 10 dollars a head, the necessity of confining the shipment of emigrants to British territory will be sufficiently evident. I cannot understand the reasons set forth by the Commissioners of Emigration as the ground on which they recommend that the emigrants should have been resident upwards of a twelvemonth in the colonies previous to their embarkation." The precaution is nevertheless highly important; it will prevent the possibility of slaves from the territories which surround our small colonies being brought into our settlements, by their masters, merely for the purpose of being offered as emigrants to the West India agents. A chief, or the representative of a chief, from the Bullom shore, or from the Timany country, may very well supply the West Indian agent at Sierra Leone with 40 or 50 emigrants, on receiving a bonus of 10 dollars for each. This would probably be looked upon as a bounty, well bestowed for the advantage of procuring so many labourers and as a small addition to the expenses attending their collection and transport; but the supposed bounty would actually be the price and purchase-money of so many slaves; the slaves would be presented to the Government superintendent as free emigrants, and the payment of their purchase-money would be an affair known only to the parties concerned in it. With regard to liberated Africans (as long as they continue to be located at Sierra Leone) and Kroomen, there would appear to be less necessity for requiring that they should have been resident for a year previous to embarkation; but I would still apply the same strict rule to all, making however a year's service on board a British man-of-war (in the case of the Kroomen) equal to a year's residence in a British colony. Such strictness in this case can hardly be regarded as needless scrupulosity. In dealing with this delicate question, I presume it will be desired not only to satisfy ourselves that we have taken every precaution for the prevention of abuse, and for the protection of the negro emigrants, but to preserve our proceedings from the possibility of exception, or even suspicion on the part of other powers; and cautiously to avoid every practice, however innocent in itself, which may be dexterously accepted as a sanction of abuses which we have been forward to censure and oppose. I may here refer to the long correspondence which took place between the Foreign Department and the Netherlands Government on the subject of the African recruits enlisted at Elmina for service in the Dutch East India possessions; and to the recent capture, by a British man-of-war, of a French vessel employed, under the sanction of her Government, in collecting negroes on the coast to form black troops in the French colonies on the coast of Africa and in the West Indies. In the first case it was evident that the bounty which was paid by the Dutch Government for each recruit, to the person who produced him, was actually the purchase-money of a slave, and our senior naval officer in the Bights very properly gave notice to the Governor of Elmina, that any vessel with such recruits on board, if fallen in with by our cruizers, would be captured and sent to Sierra Leone for condemnation; and if brought there I should certainly have condemned her; and in the second case, the collection of recruits for the French Government, owing to its being entrusted to private speculators and contractors, immediately degenerated into open and undeniable slave dealing. "In the papers which I have received, little reference is made to any other emigrants than agricultural labourers, which is of course the class chiefly, if not exclusively wanted; I allude to this circumstance, because there are some classes at Sierra Leone which would supply no agricultural labourers, but only mechanics, schoolmasters, traders, boatmen, &c. The population of Sierra Leone, which in round numbers I take to be about 60,000, consists of about 1,200 Nova Scotia settlers, 1,200 Maroons, 50,000 liberated Africans, 7,600 Kroomen and strangers: 60,000. The Nova Scotians, or settlers, as we generally term them, would yield no field labourers, nor do I think that you would obtain any from the Maroons, though a large number of the latter would be very glad to be re-conveyed to their friends and relations at Jamaica, free of expense; a fair supply of mechanics, &c., might however be obtained from both classes. Of the liberated Africans, none of the more prosperous would, in my opinion, be inclined to emigrate, and at any rate they would not add to the number of the field labourers in the colonies. The people to whom I refer are hawkers, traders, and mechanics, and are generally drawn together and settled in Freetown and its neighbourhood, where they live in comfort and even luxury. It is to the remaining portion of this valuable body that we must principally look for emigrants, if we are to obtain them at all at Sierra Leone; and, if prudence and caution be used, I see no reason to doubt that a large number of them (quite as many as it will be proper for the colonies where they are now located to lose) may eventually be induced to remove to the West Indies. I would beg to propose that the four or five principal tribes of liberated Africans should be called upon, by means of influential persons of those tribes resident in Freetown, to select each two men in whom they have confidence; and those eight or ten delegates should be furnished with a passage to the West Indies and back, free of expense, in order that they may examine and ascertain for themselves the prospect which emigration offers. They should be used well on the voyage, should receive 2*l.* a month during their short absence, and their wives and families should be supported (a very trifling expense) during the same period. Let this plan be adopted and properly carried out, and I have no doubt whatever that it will be completely successful. The Kroomen, amongst whom I include the Fishmen, are so peculiar a race that they must always be considered by themselves. Their national peculiarities are very remarkable, and distinguish them almost as much from every other African tribe as they do from the Europeans. But it will be only necessary to notice those which affect them as emigrants. In the midst of a slaving district, they are never enslaved, and they navigate and work on board the Spanish and Portuguese slavers with perfect confidence and safety. Every man-of-war on the station ships has a certain number of these people according to her rating, and there are never less than 400 of them embarked on board the different vessels of the squadron at any one time. All the timber vessels, and indeed almost all other vessels on the coast engage Kroomen to do the heavy work, which Europeans cannot attempt with safety in that climate. They are to be met with wherever work is to be had or wages are to be obtained; they labour with astonishing energy, cheerfulness, and perseverance; and they are distinguished by frugality and parsimony. At Sierra Leone we have a shifting Kroo population of several hundreds, who are employed by the merchant vessels, and at the factories up the rivers, and by the merchants and other residents in Freetown; and the superior value of their labour as compared with that of liberated Africans is proved by the fact, that whilst the wages of a Krooman are from 9*d.* to 1*s.* per day, those of a liberated African are only 4*d.* a day, and yet the former is preferred. As agricultural labourers the Kroomen have never yet been tried either at Sierra Leone or anywhere else that I am aware of, but there is no doubt that, with their industry and intelligence, they would easily and rapidly acquire the necessary practical skill. From this description it may be supposed that the Kroo country is likely to supply our most valuable emigrants for the West Indies; but two objections may be made by the Colonial Governments to receiving Kroomen at all: one is, that they will not permanently settle anywhere but in their own country; and the other is, that they never carry their countrywomen away from home with them. Sierra Leone is the great mart for Kroo labour, and has been much frequented by that people during the last 30 years, and yet a Kroo woman has never been seen amongst us. The Krooman who leaves his own country in search of employment, will always return home at the end of three or four years, with the goods, the produce of his labour, which he has collected during his absence; part of the property thus acquired he presents to the king or head man of the town or district to which he belongs, and with the remainder he builds a house, procures a wife, clears a farm, and supports himself for about a year or 18 months. His holiday being over, he leaves his house, farm, and property to be attended to by his wife and his relations, and absents himself from home for another term of three or four years, at the expiration of which time he again returns with the fruits of his exertion to make a new present to his chief, to obtain another wife, and to add to the dimensions of his farm. This process is repeated several times, until the wanderer has acquired what is by him considered competent wealth, when he settles in his own country for the remainder of his life. The Kroomen are too valuable a class of labourers to be lightly thrown out of the scheme of emigration. If means of transport are provided, their numbers in the West Indies may eventually be kept up to several thousands. In that case the requirement respecting women must be dispensed with in their favour, and they must be assured that at least one opportunity will be afforded to them during every year of returning to their own country; nor would the people object to pay a limited sum (say eight to ten dollars) for their passage, finding themselves in provisions, as they do with us. Should it be deemed advisable to secure the services of these people, I would beg to propose that the same plan should be pursued with respect to them as I have recommended in the case of the liberated Africans, and that two head Kroomen and two head Fishmen should be selected to accompany the other African delegates from Sierra Leone, enjoying all the advantages of free passage and monthly pay conceded to their fellow-passengers. The Kroomen, however, unlike their companions, would leave behind them in the colony no wives and families to be supported during their absence. In Liberia there are several thousands of black American emigrants, some of whom are very poorly off, and might be disposed to remove to the West Indies; but it would be matter for consideration, whether it would be advisable, for the sake of the small supply which could be thus obtained, to depart from the rule of confining the shipment of negro emigrants to the British settlements on the coast, more especially as the distance between Sierra Leone and Liberia is so short, that many of the disappointed colonists from the latter have lately established themselves at Freetown. But the number of emigrants which can be obtained from all these sources, indeed the number of free labourers on the western coast of Africa compared with the great demand for labour in Trinidad or Demerara is so insignificant, that I would earnestly recommend a plan for the location and settlement in the West Indies of all slaves hereafter embarked by decrees of the various courts of mixed commission and mixed courts of justice, established under treaties between Great Britain and foreign powers for the suppression of the slave trade. This, however, is a subject not embraced in the papers which have been submitted for my perusal." Then follow the rules for the emigration agent.

[Adjourned till To-morrow, at One o'clock.

Mercurii, 15° die Junii, 1842.

MEMBERS PRESENT.

Sir T. D. Acland.
Viscount Courtenay.
Mr. Denison.
Mr. Evans.
Captain Fitzroy.

Mr. Forster.
Sir R. H. Inglis.
Mr. W. Patten.

LORD VISCOUNT SANDON, in the chair.

Henry William Macaulay, Esq., called in; and further examined.

5474. *Chairman*.] Do you wish to correct any portion of your previous evidence?—I do. In reply to question 5176, in reference to Dr. Madden's statement about the surveyors, I said, "The surveyor is not employed by the court, but subsequently to the condemnation of the vessel he is employed by the captor to survey, in order to enable him to make a claim, according to the tonnage, through his agent in England." There are two classes of surveyors; the one referred to in this reply: the other, which I ought to have mentioned also, are the surveyors employed by the court to see to the equipment of the vessel, and this survey takes place before condemnation. I referred to the latter surveyors yesterday in my evidence; but I mentioned only the surveyor employed by the captor to measure the vessel for the tonnage in my former examination, and it would appear as though I had on the first occasion understated the officers of the court. We have two surveyors employed by the court in equipment cases, not in the case of vessels laden with slaves. There is another correction I wish to make: in the answer to question 5087, I stated that "It appears that it is a regular thing, sending vessels to him, that is to Mr. Zulueta: if they come to England to him, he sends them to Cadiz, and they get out again to the Havannah, and come again into the trade." My answer was intended to describe only the course of that particular transaction, and not to apply to any other case.

5475. I observe in answer to 5087, to which you refer, you state that Zulueta "is a name well known on the coast in connexion with the slave trade, and any man ought to have been careful of being connected with such a person as that." Will you state distinctly what charge it is you intended to make against Mr. Zulueta in those expressions?—Zulueta was known at Sierra Leone as the correspondent of the largest slave dealer on the coast, Pedro Blanco; all the bills which Pedro Blanco drew upon England were drawn upon Zulueta, and passed current in the colony of Sierra Leone with Pedro Blanco's name on them, and Zulueta's as the drawee. Zulueta was also subsequently found to be engaged in connexion with a slave vessel called the Gollupchik.

5476. Will you state who Pedro Blanco is?—He is a merchant who has now retired to the Havannah, but who was engaged for a long series of years in the Gallinas, as the principal person carrying on the slave trade there; his name occurs, for years together, in the case of very nearly every slave vessel captured off the Gallinas.

5477. Have you reason to know whether he was solely engaged in the slave trade?—His sole occupation was the slave trade.

5478. You think, therefore, that Zulueta's known connexion with Pedro Blanco should have deterred any person who was unwilling to have aided or abetted the slave trade from having any transaction with him?—Certainly.

5479. Mr. *Forster.*] Are you aware that the house of Zulueta & Company is one of the first Spanish houses in this country, and perhaps in Spain?—I am aware that it is a very large house.

5480. You are consequently aware that it has commercial correspondence and transactions with most of the principal houses at Havannah and in the south of Spain?—I think it is very likely; I am not aware of it; but I know it to be a large mercantile house.

5481. That being the case, do you not think that bills might be drawn by Pedro Blanco on Messrs. Zulueta & Company without any direct correspondence between that house and Pedro Blanco himself, but accepted by order and on account of houses residing in Spain or in the Havannah?—It is quite impossible that Mr. Zulueta should have been ignorant of the only trade in which Pedro Blanco was engaged.

5482. But might not those bills be drawn without Messrs. Zulueta & Company having any direct account with Mr. Pedro Blanco?—Yes, it is possible.

5483. Then supposing a slave vessel were purchased at Sierra Leone and sent to this market for public sale, do you see any thing extraordinary in the party to whom the sale of that vessel is intrusted in London selling her to one of the first Spanish houses in this country?—If it was an Englishman who sold the vessel to the party to whom Mr. Zulueta sold her, I should think it very extraordinary indeed, because it was perfectly well known that Pedro Martinez, to whom she was sold, was a slave dealer.

5484. Then you think a London merchant who is intrusted with the sale of a vessel on the part of his correspondent in Africa, and whose duty it is to take that vessel to the best market, would be justified in refusing an offer for the vessel from Messrs. Zulueta & Company?—I think it would be his duty to do so, because the chances would be ten to one that she very soon afterwards would be employed in the slave trade.

5485. Then what justification, in your opinion, would that agent in London be able to make to his correspondent for refusing to sell the vessel to the highest bidder?—If the correspondent was an honest man, I think he would be perfectly well satisfied with the representation of his agent that the acceptance of such an offer would necessarily involve the introduction of the vessel immediately afterwards into the slave trade.

5486. But supposing the agent to act in that manner, would that prevent Messrs. Zulueta & Company buying the same vessel in a circuitous manner in this market?—No, it might not.

5487. *Chairman.*] Have you any thing further to say with regard to the connexion of Zulueta with the slave trade?—I would refer to his connexion with the Gollupchik, which was lately captured. In that case, it appeared that the vessel went out direct to the Gallinas from London.

5488. But you would not object to a British vessel trading lawfully with a slave trade factory?—No.

5489. What is there then in this transaction which gives it a guilty character?—Mr. Zulueta's former connexion with the Gallinas slave traders shows, that his course of trade with the Gallinas was one liable to exception.

5490. But what is there to prove that he dealt with the slave traders in other than lawful goods?—They would be *lawful* goods, certainly.

5491. Do you consider it to be unlawful or improper to deal in lawful goods with a man who is engaged in the slave trade?—I do not consider it unlawful, but I do consider it improper; I say not unlawful, because you cannot prove guilty knowledge, but highly improper to sell goods to persons who, the seller must be aware, will employ them in the slave trade afterwards.

5492. Do you hold it to be against the purport of the Act to deal in lawful goods with persons engaged in the slave trade?—It is not against the purport of the Act for a merchant to deal with any one, unless he is aware that that person is engaged in the slave trade, and that the goods that he sells will be employed for slave trade purposes.

5493. Then that which is against the purport of the Act in your opinion, is to deal in goods, which goods will be used for unlawful purposes?—Yes.

5494. The mere trading in lawful goods, in itself you would not consider unlawful, or against the purport of the Act?—No.

5495. What evidence have we that Zulueta knew that in dealing with Pedro Blanco the goods he sold would be used for the barter of slaves?—Any body engaged in the Spanish trade would be aware that Pedro Blanco was the largest slave trader in the world.

5496. How would Messrs. Zulueta be paid for those lawful goods by Pedro Blanco?—I am not aware that he ever sold any goods to Pedro Blanco; the

Gollupchik did not arrive off the Gallinas till after Pedro Blanco had left; he left I think in the latter part of 1838.

5497. It was a slave trade factory at the Gallinas with which Zulueta was dealing?—It was with the Gallinas.

5498. In the case of dealing with a person who had no other business than that of the slave trade, how would the payment be made?—In gold; in doubloons generally.

5499. There would be no payment in produce?—No; and that is the way in which all trade of that description is paid; there have been vessels going down from Sierra Leone and trading with the Gallinas and other slave ports, and the returns which they bring for their goods are doubloons.

5500. And you would infer from the circumstance of bringing doubloons, and not the produce of the country, that there was at least strong suspicion that it was an unlawful traffic?—A strong suspicion; I would not say more than that.

5501. Mr. *Forster.*] Suppose Messrs. Zulueta & Co. to receive an order from their correspondent at Havannah to supply a cargo of British merchandise to Pedro Blanco at the Gallinas, and these goods are shipped and are regularly cleared at the custom-house in England, do you consider that an illegal shipment?—The illegality depends upon the guilty knowledge. I consider it an improper transaction, because he must know the character of the person to whom he sends the goods.

5502. Do you think that Messrs. Zulueta & Co. would have been justified as merchants in refusing to obey the instructions of their foreign correspondent in a case of that kind?—I think that a man who viewed the slave trade in a proper light would have considered it improper to be so engaged.

5503. How could Messrs. Zulueta consider that illegal which was publicly allowed to be done by the custom-house authorities in this country?—The criminality depends upon the guilty knowledge, as to which the custom-house cannot decide.

5504. Then it is upon those grounds that you designate Messrs. Zulueta & Co. as connected with the slave trade?—Upon the grounds that I have stated altogether.

5505. *Chairman.*] Do you consider a merchant trading with King Peppel, a notorious slave trader in the Bonny, and receiving the produce of the country in exchange, to be acting against the purport of the Act of Parliament?—No, certainly not; because there there is a legitimate trade carried on alongside of the slave trade.

5506. Then you do not look merely at the person dealt with, but at the object for which the traffic is carried on?—Just so: I would designate as improper any trade carried on by a person who knew that the goods he sold would be employed in the slave trade.

5507. Mr. *Forster.*] If you consider it lawful for a British merchant to sell goods to so notorious a slave dealer as King Peppel, on what ground do you consider it illegal for Messrs. Zulueta & Company to ship a cargo of goods to Pedro Blanco or to Gallinas?—In the one case the trader receives his return in produce, and in the other case he sells goods which he knows will be employed in the slave trade, and for which he receives a return in money.

5508. How do you know that he is paid in money?—I do not know that Zulueta ever shipped goods to Pedro Blanco.

5509. Would you consider it legal if he did?—I think I have answered that question before, that the illegality depends upon the guilty knowledge of the party concerned, and that is a question for a jury to decide, if he is put upon his trial.

5510. Then that depends upon your construction of the Act of the 5th of George the Fourth?—Yes; no one can read the Act without understanding its purport.

5511. And you think the same principle applies in the case of slave vessels?—Yes.

5512. Mr. *Wortley.*] You stated just now that you were not aware that Messrs. Zulueta ever shipped any goods to Pedro Blanco; did you not previously state that that was one of your reasons for believing Messrs. Zulueta to be connected with the slave trade?—No; the ground I stated was the bills which Pedro Blanco drew upon them, which bills were current all along the coast, and I have seen some of them at Sierra Leone; they were drawn by Pedro Blanco on Zulueta; the transactions which gave rise to those bills I do not know.

5513. Mr. *Forster.*] Do you consider the shipment of goods referred to in the case of the Gollupchik an illegal shipment?—It was after my time; but I presume that it was illegal, because the vessel appears to have been condemned.

5514. *Chairman.*] The legality or illegality will depend upon circumstances, which are not before you?—Yes; all that I know of it is from this report.

There is a gentleman here to-day who seized the vessel, Captain Hill; he will explain all the circumstances.

5515. Mr. *Forster*.] Do you consider that any vessel laden in this country, and legally cleared at the custom-house for a slave factory on the coast of Africa, is seizable as being engaged in an illegal transaction?—She is seizable, but if the captor seizes her wrongfully, the person seized would have a claim for damages. She is certainly seizable by any man-of-war, but her condemnation would depend upon the fact whether or not the captor made out a case.

5516. *Chairman*.] The mere fact of conveying goods to a slave factory would not be ground of condemnation, would it?—Certainly not.

5517. Mr. *Forster*.] Upon what ground can a vessel conveying a cargo of legal merchandise to the Gallinas be condemned?—On the ground of guilty knowledge, if it can be proved.

5518. Mr. *W. Patten*.] And that guilty knowledge would have to be left to the jury?—Yes.

5519. *Chairman*.] You have been asked upon the case of the Almirante, in question 5238; can you in any way state what the transaction was, and are you able to give any explanation of it?—All I remember respecting that transaction is, that a merchant at Sierra Leone, of the name of Benjamin Campbell, on my arrival in Sierra Leone, in 1830, spoke to me about a sum of 500*l.*, not 600*l.*, that was due by him to Mr. Kenneth Macaulay, who was at that time dead—he died in 1829—for a vessel that Mr. Campbell had purchased from him. I did not know of that vessel having gone into the slave trade till it was mentioned just now.

5520. The sale was made by Mr. Kenneth Macauley to Mr. Campbell?—Yes.

5521. Mr. *Forster*.] Was not Mr. Campbell an agent of the house of Macaulay & Babington?—No, not at that time; he had been one of the clerks in the house, but many years previously; he had long ceased to have any connexion with the house, I suppose about five years. He was in business for himself at the time, and in rather a large way of business.

5522. Mr. *W. Patten*.] At Sierra Leone?—Yes.

5523. *Chairman*.] You have spoken in your despatch, which you read at the last meeting of the Committee, of an extended scheme for promoting emigration from the coast of Africa to the West Indies; will you explain that more fully?—I would propose that the negroes should be sent to the West Indies after emancipation, in the same way as they have been of late years sent to the different colonies there from Havannah. Dr. Madden, who has made this Report, was the person appointed by Government, and specially sent out for the purpose of superintending the emigration of the emancipated negroes from Havannah to the different West India islands, and he would be able to give to the Committee all the details of the regulations which were adopted and sanctioned by the Government. I am not aware of the rules that were laid down for his guidance; but it appears in the slave trade papers of former years, during the time that the Duke of Wellington was Foreign Secretary, that he required a certain proportion to be observed between males and females, and also that negroes should be examined by a medical man, and no unhealthy ones sent; there were other regulations also by which he was bound; all the negroes that he could get he sent to Trinidad in the first instance, and I believe he sent some afterwards to Honduras and other places.

5524. Should you propose that they should remain a certain time in the colony before they were removed to the West Indies?—No, certainly not; I would have the removal take place immediately after emancipation. There is an emigration agent established at Sierra Leone, so that the whole machinery is ready at hand at once.

5525. How would you propose that the expense of transport across the Atlantic should be defrayed?—There would be no difficulty whatever about the expense, because the colonies to which they are sent would gladly pay any expenses of removal. The difficulty that the Government would experience would be, in distributing the negroes among the different colonies; but any West India colony would gladly pay the expense of removal of any number to their own shores.

5526. What is usually the expense incurred on account of each liberated African under the existing system at Sierra Leone?—The commissariat issues notice of tenders; when recruits are sent across from Sierra Leone to the West Indies, which they are continually to supply the West India regiments, it is open to any persons who have vessels unemployed to tender for their removal; and if the Government undertook to remove the negroes, I suppose it would be done in the same way.

5527. What is the expense now incurred for the maintenance of a liberated African at Sierra Leone?—He is maintained for six months; the allowance has been varied from 1d. to 2d. a day; but I believe now it is 1½d.

5528. Are you aware of the expense of transporting them across the Atlantic?—I am not aware what has been charged; but whatever the expense was, the colony receiving the negroes would be very happy to pay it.

5529. You conceive that it would be a material advantage to the liberated Africans to be placed in a West India colony, rather than maintained for six months by Government, and afterwards thrown upon their own resources in Sierra Leone?—It would be an advantage in every way; an advantage first to the British Government in saving the expense of their maintenance; it would next be an advantage to the negroes, who are removed to a West India colony; and it would be a very great advantage to the colony of Sierra Leone, because, though it may be well able to support its present population, yet I think that further importations at any rate, unless the colony is extended, should be stopped. The advancement of the people who are now located there, is also considerably retarded, by having fresh importations of savages thrown amongst them from time to time, as they are, when slave ships are condemned.

5530. Is it possible to have a society of the extent of Sierra Leone otherwise than materially disturbed in all its moral and social relations by 4,000 or 5,000 uncultivated negroes from various quarters being thrown upon them at certain periods?—I think it is greatly injured by it.

5531. Is there any amount of capital in Sierra Leone ready to take up and give adequate employment to that influx of population?—No, not immediate employment; the people would themselves find employment to a certain extent, and I will not say how many more could be introduced safely so as to find employment; but all who are there can find employment, and can provide themselves with all the necessaries and conveniences of life if they choose.

5532. Are there the means, except in trade, of providing for more than the mere necessaries of life?—Agriculture is open to them to follow, if they have sufficient inducement.

5533. Is there sufficient opportunity afforded, from the state of agriculture in the colony, for raising more than is necessary for the sustenance and common maintenance of the labourer?—No, not at present; agriculture is not followed at all there for export; there are a few articles that are not worth mentioning that are raised, but there is no such system of agriculture for export followed that they could embark in agriculture at once.

5534. Then you conceive that both the social and moral condition of the negroes there would be improved, as they are now constituted, if they were placed in the West Indies instead of in Sierra Leone?—I think so; both for those who are left at Sierra Leone, and for those who are removed, it would be better.

5535. Do you think that it would be desirable to give the negro the option whether he would go to the West Indies or not?—Certainly not; it is never done now, and the Act of Parliament does not even contemplate such an option being given; the negro is taken to Sierra Leone, and located there, without his opinion or wishes being consulted, and in the same way he might be transported to the West Indies.

5536. Mr. *W. Patten.*] Is it obligatory in some of the treaties to take them to Sierra Leone?—The new Spanish treaty requires that they shall be established in a territory of the country to which the cruizer that has made the capture belongs.

5537. *Chairman.*] But must not the adjudication be on the coast of Africa?—Not necessarily; Spanish vessels may be condemned at Havannah; and in some cases when Portuguese vessels have been captured in the West Indies, the slaves have been sent to Jamaica, and various other islands in the West Indies; and when the vessel is sent over to Sierra Leone, she comes over to us without the slaves; the slaves having been landed in the first instance, so as to save them a second voyage across the Atlantic; but with regard to vessels seized in the West Indies, which are liable to condemnation under the Spanish treaty, the Havannah court would condemn them, and the slaves would then be sent as Dr. Madden has sent them, to one of our West India colonies.

5538. Do you conceive that foreign powers would entertain, or be justified in entertaining, any objection to such a distribution?—No, they would not entertain it, and I do not think that they would be justified in entertaining it; on the contrary, it was the case in former days that the vessels that were condemned by the court at Havannah had their slaves located in the island of Cuba; but the planters cried out against it very loudly; and it was at their suggestion and their request that we sent away the negroes to our own West India colonies.

5539. By the treaties it is arranged that the captured negroes should be planted within the colonies of the capturing party?—It is stipulated in the seventh Article of the Portuguese treaty and the old Spanish treaty: "As to the slaves, they shall receive from the mixed commission a certificate of emancipation, and shall be delivered over to the government on whose territory the commission which shall have so judged them shall be established to be employed as servants or free labourers." The Act never contemplates any option whatever being exercised by the persons seized, because it allows of their being drafted into the army or navy, without any reference to their own will.

5540. Would the possible objection of foreign nations be stronger if we engaged in a system of colonial emigration from the coast of Africa, from other points than Sierra Leone?—I mentioned yesterday that we could not go beyond the limits of British jurisdiction in procuring emigrants, without appearing to give a sanction to those practices for which we have been complaining against other nations of late years, both the French and Dutch.

5541. In placing the emancipated slaves in islands where they would be engaged in cultivating sugar, you would be in fact compelling the slave trader to put down the slave trade itself in a great degree?—Yes; I think that a great advantage, causing our efforts for the suppression of the slave trade to operate in encouraging the cultivation of sugar in our own colonies.

5542. In as far as it went, it would cheapen the very produce, the dearness of which now constitutes the great inducement for carrying on the slave trade?—Yes; the best way of putting down the slave trade is our cultivating that produce in such a manner that it can compete with slave-grown produce; and every thing that we do in adding to the difficulty of carrying slaves across the Atlantic, adds to the price of labour and the price of sugar in the slave-growing colonies.

5543. Every thing that we do with a view to encourage the lawful produce, and to induce the negroes of Africa to get what they require in a lawful way, diminishes the temptation to carry on the slave trade, and co-operates with the cruizers in putting it down?—Certainly. There is a passage with respect to enlisting negroes who are condemned by the courts, without any reference to their own will; it occurs in the 22d clause of the Act of 5 Geo. 4, c. 112: "It shall be lawful for His Majesty, his heirs, and successors, and such officers, civil or military, as shall, by any general or special order of the King in Council, be from time to time appointed to receive, protect, and provide for such persons as shall be so condemned, either to enter and enlist the same, or any of them, into His Majesty's land or sea service, as soldiers, seamen, or marines, or to bind the same or any of them, whether of full age or not, as apprentices, for any term not exceeding seven years, to such person or persons, in such place or places, and upon such terms and conditions, and subject to such regulations as to His Majesty shall seem meet, and as shall by any general or special Order of His Majesty in Council be in that behalf directed and appointed; and any indenture of apprenticeship duly made and executed by any person or persons to be for that purpose appointed by any such Order in Council, for any term not exceeding seven years, shall be of the same force and effect as if the party thereby bound as an apprentice had himself or herself when of full age, upon good consideration, duly executed the same." It leaves no option whatever with the party bound.

5544. You think vessels could always be taken up to meet the arrival of emancipated negroes?—The chartering of vessels would, I think, offer no difficulty at Sierra Leone. There are, I believe, now, but there certainly would be, in case such a plan was adopted, agents from the different colonies which are anxious to obtain negroes, who would be always ready to secure vessels for their transport across the Atlantic.

5545. Would not this be of advantage in opening a communication from the West India islands with the coast of Africa, and encouraging the intercourse between the two countries, and the free interchange of products, to the advancement of the civilization of Sierra Leone, and through it, of Africa?—In almost all cases where vessels have gone across to the West Indies with recruits from Sierra Leone, the vessels have gone on from the West Indies to England, taking a cargo from the West Indies to England.

5546. Then it would only have the effect of increasing the advantageous resort of vessels to Sierra Leone generally?—That would be one effect.

5547. Would it not have an effect on Sierra Leone, by giving an advantageous freight to vessels frequenting it?—Yes, it would have that effect.

5548. If it were considered desirable, would there be any difficulty in giving to the negroes, after emancipation at Sierra Leone, the option of remaining in the country or of going over to the West Indies?—I think it would be undesirable to introduce a new practice where no option is now given, and where the persons are not qualified immediately after emancipation, to form any opinion whatever.

5549. Mr. *Forster.*] Do you think that it would be good policy to give retired allowances to all public officers who have served a certain number of years on the coast of Africa?—I think it would.

5550. The officers of the Mixed Commission Court, I believe, are the only officers who enjoy that advantage?—I think the colonial chaplain does, but by favour, not by right; there are no officers who serve under colonial governments who are entitled to pensions; it is a rule of the service, which is stated positively in their printed regulations.

5551. But considering the danger to health in that climate, you are of opinion that it would be for the benefit of the service, and also consistent with justice, that some allowance, in the shape of pension or otherwise, should be made to officers serving there?—I think so. There is one other point that I would beg to refer to, and that is rather personal. It was stated by a witness in evidence on the 24th of May, that there was a party in the colony of Sierra Leone who had great influence in the Colonial Office; that this party was an individual; that the suspicion of the witness, Colonel Findlay, did not apply to more than one individual, and that that individual was myself; and that he found, during the time that he was governor of the colony, that the contents of despatches sent from the Colonial-office to Sierra Leone were known in the colony by that party before they came to his hands, and that he was consequently, and owing to that, impeded in carrying on his government. Now I would only mention, with regard to this statement, that I never received one single line all the time I was in the colony, which was 11 years, from any person connected with the Colonial-office, either directly or indirectly, on any subject whatever; and that I never wrote one line to any person in the Colonial-office during that period, except one letter of introduction, which I gave to an officer of the 31st regiment, who wanted to travel in Africa; I gave to this gentleman a sort of certificate that he was a man of mild and conciliatory manners; that was the only letter that I wrote to the Colonial-office, and I never received one line upon any subject from any party in the Colonial-office, not even in reply to the letter of introduction just referred to.

5552. Mr. *Forster.*] You had no correspondence with the Colonial-office during your residence in Africa, directly or indirectly?—None whatever, or with any person connected with the Colonial-office.

5553. Mr. *W. Patten.*] Colonel Finlay, in his evidence, referred to a party existing in the colony; are you aware of two distinct parties existing in the colony?—I am aware of one party that existed in the colony during the time that he was there, and that is a long time ago, a party that opposed his government, because they thought he was a bad Governor. I was one of that party certainly, while I was a merchant. As soon as I became a government officer I abstained from any public demonstration of feeling or opinion, but as a merchant, and before I entered upon my public duties in the Mixed Commission Court, I certainly took the means that every man is allowed to take to show that I did not approve of his proceedings.

5554. But was that party a political party, or was the party connected solely with the circumstances of the colony itself?—It was merely with relation to the colony; they did not care at all about Whigs and Tories out there; they had their colonial politics to attend to.

5555. Mr. *G. Wood.*] Did the discontent originate in political or commercial views?—It originated in consequence of measures which were considered oppressive upon individuals; it was upon local matters altogether.

5556. Mr. *Forster.*] Do you consider that it originated in commercial questions?—Certainly not.

5557. Were you a government officer at the time that the transaction took place which led to Colonel Finlay's recal?—I think I was; I think the imprisonment of Mr. M'Cormack occurred in 1832; I entered upon my office in 1832; I think it was after I became a government officer. After I became a judge I took no public part in opposition to any government, however bad it might have been.

5558. You took no part in that transaction which led to Colonel Finlay's recal?—I took no public part; I may have given advice to my friends.

5559. Did not a trial arise out of those transactions, in which you were a witness?—No; no trial at all occurred, and therefore I could not have been a witness in any.

5560. *Chairman.*] Have you read the remarks of Colonel Doherty on the Report of Dr. Madden?—I have.

5560*. Do you concur in the views which he has taken of the points alluded to?—In almost every particular.

5561. Is there any material point upon which you differ from him?—I think only two: one, with respect to the Kroomen, whose residence in the colony Colonel Doherty thought was injurious, and interfered with the resident liberated Africans; I do not agree with him in that respect; I think that they should not be interdicted at all from coming to Sierra Leone, nor should their numbers be limited.

5562. You believe them to be advantageous to the colony?—Yes.

5563. And, by their example, to the liberated Africans themselves?—Yes, I think even to them, as setting an example of industry, which they would do well to imitate.

5564. Do you concur in opinion with Colonel Doherty as to the character of the Kroomen; he speaks of the Kroomen as men never to be trusted, never converted to Christianity, and likely, wherever they may be, to exhibit a bad example in that particular; do you concur in that?—I agree in opinion with Colonel Doherty, that they would not be converted to Christianity. I do not think them dishonest when they are well treated. I never heard of an instance of any liberated African being converted to the Pagan opinions of the Kroomen; I believe such a thing was never heard of.

5565. You believe that they are more difficult of conversion than other Africans?—It is quite impossible, if I may say so of any body; there never was an instance known of a Krooman being converted.

5566. To what do you attribute that peculiarity?—To their constant return, as I mentioned yesterday, to their own country. They never think of settling any where but in their own country. There is no instance of a Krooman settling any where but in the Kroo country.

5567. Do they not settle at Fernando Po?—No; no more than they settle in Sierra Leone.

5568. Mr. *G. Wood.*] Do they all retire to their own country in their old age?—Yes. I have known a great many of them; indeed, I was very partial to them, and had a good many in my employ. Governor Doherty rather discouraged their employment, which I thought unwise, but that was one slight point on which I disagreed with him.

5569. *Chairman.*] Have you never heard of their being converted at Cape Palmas by American missionaries?—No.

5570. Mr. *G. Wood.*] Are you aware of any persevering and continuous efforts having ever been employed?—No, I cannot say that I am; but they are thrown into our colony very much under the same circumstances that the liberated Africans are, who become Christians, almost universally.

5571. *Chairman.*] The liberated Africans are more settled?—Yes.

5572. And are therefore more exposed to the influence of those around them?—Yes; but the Krooman also resides at Sierra Leone, and is never away more than once in three or four years, but the periodical return to his own country, and to his old habits, is I think a great cause why it is so difficult to christianise him.

5573. Mr. *Wortley.*] Is there any mode of accounting for those remarkable peculiarities in the Kroomen?—No; I think they are kept distinct by the habit of the country, never allowing the women to leave the country, and thus inducing the men constantly to return.

5574. Is there any distinction of race to be observed between them and other tribes?—Yes, a most striking difference.

5575. Is there any reason to suppose their origin to have been different from the origin of the rest of the inhabitants of Africa?—One would suppose so from their being totally different in colour and habits.

5576. Mr. *G. Wood.*] Has their language been analysed with a view to see whether that affords any indication of their being from a different stock?— No. An opinion seems to have been expressed by Governor Doherty against allowing Mahomedans to exercise their religion. I differ from him there also; but I think, with those two exceptions, as far as I recollect it, I agree with the remainder of the Report.

5577. Viscount *Courtenay.*] Bearing in mind the remarks which are made in that Report upon the subject of schools, do you concur with him generally in those remarks, or do you wish to add any thing?—I quite concur with him, particularly with regard to the pay of the teachers; I think the pay certainly is on too low a scale at present to secure the services of good teachers.

5578. What is your opinion as to the practice which seems to exist of separating the children of liberated Africans from the Creole children?—I think any separation of that kind is undesirable.

5579. Is it apparently justified by any difference of natural talent between them as a class?—No; but there is a very great difference between the colony-born children and those who have been introduced into the colony at a later age; those who have been born and bred in the colony are very superior.

5580. Is the result of this separation that liberated African children make much less progress in education generally than the other children?—Yes; I should think that is the effect.

5581. Are they taught English?—Yes, they all speak English.

5582. Mr. *G. Wood.*] Does it give birth to any permanent feelings of enmity between the two classes of children?—No.

5583. Mr. *W. Patten.*] I observe in one of the recent slave treaties, which sets out the duties incumbent upon the master to whom negroes are apprenticed, the first duty is, that the apprentice shall be maintained in proportion to the employment done, and shall be supplied with such clothes as are usual according to the custom of the colony; during your residence in Sierra Leone was that attended to by the authorities there?—I think that the whole system of apprenticeship there was bad; it was required by the indentures, but the indentures were very imperfectly fulfilled.

5584. There are six different classes to be attended to upon this point; first, with regard to food; secondly, with regard to instruction in the Christian religion; and according to that second article they must be baptized before the expiration of the second year of apprenticeship; was that at all looked to?—No, I do not think it was. In many cases you could not carry it out, because the person who was apprenticed came there not as a child, but grown up, and the clergyman would then take upon himself to decide whether he was a fit subject for baptism or not.

5585. But the authorities in the colony did not see in any way that that was done?—No.

5586. The next is, "that the apprentice should be vaccinated as soon as possible after being delivered into the charge of the master, and that in sickness he shall have proper medical advice and be treated with due care and attention, and that in case of death, he shall be decently buried at the master's expense?"—There is no obligation of that kind with regard to negroes in Sierra Leone; this is a treaty that does not refer to Sierra Leone.

5587. This is in the treaty that was signed in 1839?—It did not come into operation at the time I was in Sierra Leone; there is a treaty somewhat similar; the last treaty with Spain, which requires that attention shall be paid to emancipated negroes.

5588. You stated that you thought the apprenticeship system was very bad?—Yes, I think the whole system of apprenticeship at Sierra Leone is bad, and ought to be done away with.

5589. Mr. *G. Wood.*] What system would you substitute for it?—I would not object to apprenticing children to artizans and to master tradesmen, but I certainly would not apprentice them to other persons.

5590. *Chairman.*] Your system of disposing of the liberated Africans in the West Indies would, of course, get rid of the difficulty attending upon the future?—Yes.

5591. Mr. *G. Wood.*] But supposing that system not to take place, what system should you think preferable to the system of apprenticeship now prevalent in Sierra Leone?—There can be no system introduced that would not entail considerable expense upon the Government.

5592. *Chairman.*] Would you throw the adults upon their own resources at an earlier period than at present?—No; I think the time (six months) for which the Government now support the adults is as short as it could possibly be, and I do not think they could shorten that by one day.

5593. Mr. *G. Wood.*] You stated that no other system could be substituted but what would be attended with considerable expense; do you think it would be worth while to incur that expense?—I do not think the present system should be continued, whatever the expense might be of substituting another system for it.

5594. What system would you recommend as a substitute for it?—The system that must be substituted for it, in case of the apprenticeship being done away with, would be keeping all the children, as they now do many of them, landed from slave vessels, in the schools till they are old enough to be thrown upon their own resources.

5595. *Chairman.*] Making them, in fact, boarding-schools?—There is a boarding-school in many of the villages; in the villages the liberated African children are lodged and fed by the manager, but that is only the children who are not apprenticed.

5596. You would have all the children put into boarding-schools?—I see no other way at present of disposing of them, if they are not apprenticed.

5597. Mr. *G. Wood.*] Had the change of system that you alluded to reference to an altered system with regard to the adults?—No; I would not alter the system with regard to the adults, except, perhaps, by extending the period two months, during which they should be maintained by Government.

5598. That would be an extension from six months to eight months?—Yes; at any rate, while the Government continues to use their services, as they do at present, when they are employed for three months after their arrival labouring upon Government works, and are prevented from employing themselves upon farms.

5599. Mr. *Forster.*] In answer to question 5208, in your former evidence, with respect to the system of landing the crews of captured slavers, you said, "I have never known a cruizer act inhumanely. I heard of one case the other day where people starved, but it was stated in that case that it was owing to the refusal of the Portuguese factories to support them." Had you any opportunity at Sierra Leone of observing the system pursued in this respect by our cruizers?—I have mentioned that the only portion of the slave crews that we saw at Sierra Leone were those who were sent up as witnesses.

5600. What case is this which you allude to as having heard of?—It was a case I heard of in this room, mentioned by some gentleman connected with the Bonny trade.

5601. Are you aware whether there are any Spanish or Portuguese factories in Bonny?—I am aware that there were some slave factories there formerly.

Lunæ, 27° die Junii, 1842.

MEMBERS PRESENT.

Sir T. D. Acland.
Mr. Aldam.
Captain Fitzroy.

Mr. Forster.
Mr. W. Hamilton.
Mr. Milnes.

VISCOUNT SANDON, IN THE CHAIR.

Captain Henry Worsley Hill, R. N., called in; and examined.

7109. *Chairman.*] What has been your connexion with the coast of Africa?—I commanded the "Saracen" on the coast of Africa from October 1837 till January 1841.

7110. What part of the coast have you cruized along?—The first eight months I was in the Bight of Benin; after that I went to the Cape of Good Hope and Madagascar, returning to Sierra Leone in December 1838; and continuing on the coast between Cape Palmas and Portendique till June 1841.

7111. Has the character of the system of cruizing altered during that period?—On the Sierra Leone side, certainly. Latterly, we established a very close blockade.

7112. Have you been engaged in descents on the coast?—Yes, at Gallinas, and at Sea-bar.

7113. At Gallinas you were engaged with Captain Denman?—Yes.

7114. At Sea-bar, were you by yourself?—The "Ferret" was there likewise.

7115. What were the circumstances of your operations at Sea-bar?—I had had a boat blockading Sea-bar, where there was a noted slave factory, and my boat's crew had required water, and on landing to procure water, the king, Harry Tucker, refused water without I paid for it at a most exorbitant rate, about a dollar a gallon he demanded; and I was authorized by the Governor of Sierra Leone to endeavour to effect a treaty, that had been sent out from the Home Government with the chiefs of that part of the coast. I landed for the purpose of endeavouring to effect this treaty, and also to inquire into the cause of the king's refusing my boat's crew water. The slave factory belonging to Mr. François is close to the usual place of landing, being close to the water; it is at the southernmost entrance of the Sherboro' River. On landing I found that every person had left the factory; after a short time, I succeeded in getting a messenger to go to the king, who was represented to be in the bush, and requested that he would come to see me, assuring him that I had come upon a friendly mission. He refused; I then wrote to him for the same purpose; after waiting some time, several people appeared at the borders of the wood, armed, and one man advanced and came to me, and told me that Mr. François, the slave merchant, and the king had armed the slaves for the purpose of coming down to attack us, but that they preferred giving themselves up to us, and going to Sierra Leone to be made free, and asking if I would receive them on board; I of course told them yes, as many as would come, and I think about fifty came down armed with muskets and cane knives. They procured for themselves a canoe; I had not room in my own boats for them. They represented that they had been very ill-used by the slave-factor, Mr. François, flogged and beaten, and kept in irons, and confined closely in the barracoons; and when they were in the boat they expressed their delight, by clapping their hands and singing in their country manner. I had determined upon destroying the barracoons, but I thought it better if I could induce the slaves to do it themselves, it would be setting a better example. Upon its being mentioned to the slave who could speak English (there was only one who could speak English), he mentioned it to the others, and two or three immediately volunteered from the troop, to go up and burn the barracoons and the factory. They went and set fire to it in about twenty places, and the place was destroyed. I was told afterwards that this was followed by another slave factory being burnt on the opposite side of the river the following day, by the slaves themselves.

7116. Who was this Mr. François?—He is a slave factor, who has resided a long time at Sea-bar; I believe he was once in the French navy as a foremast man, but I am not certain.

7117. Was he living under the protection of the native chief there?—He was living in the chief's territory; therefore, I suppose he was there with his sanction and knowledge; I had been there before, and I had seen the chief in Mr. François' house.

7118. Mr. *Forster.*] Do not you think it was setting rather a dangerous example to tell the natives to destroy property under such circumstances?—No, I thought I was setting a good example, or I should not have done it.

7119. You think they could fully appreciate the motives and views with which you acted?—Undoubtedly.

7120. Do the natives condemn the slave trade themselves?—They carry the slave trade on; if they did not carry it on, there would be no slave trade.

7121. Then on what ground of moral right could they account for your destroying this property for the reason that it was with the view of doing away with the slave trade, a trade which they do not consider morally wrong?—They can easily, I think, appreciate the view with which the slaves were armed to come down and attack Her Majesty's boats, who went there with friendly intentions.

7122. *Chairman.*] Those whom you got to destroy the barracoons were slaves themselves?—They were slaves, who had been armed to come and attack us, and they came and placed themselves under British protection, and begged to be taken to Sierra Leone.

7123. You think they would understand why you sent them to destroy the means of imprisonment;—I think so, certainly.

7124. Mr. *Forster.*] You carried them to Sierra Leone?—I carried them to Sierra Leone, and entrusted them to the protection of the governor.

7125. *Chairman.*] Do you know any thing of the circumstances under which those slaves had come there?—They were Mr. François' slaves, and I imagine they must have been purchased in the way in which all the slave factors purchase their slaves; they are brought down from the interior.

7126. Mr. *Forster.*] Have you given any similar advice to the native chiefs, or the natives, on any other part of the coast, to destroy the property of slave dealers?—I have advised the whole of the chiefs that I have had any communication with to discontinue the slave trade, the sale or barter of negroes to Europeans.

7127. *Chairman.*] Was there property in those barracoons that were destroyed?—There was very little property; I think the goods must have been removed from the slave factory some time previously.

7128. Sir *T. D. Acland.*] The use of those barracoons was distinctly for the purpose of keeping up the traffic in slaves?—The slaves had been confined there, according to what I learned from those I received on board, on the previous night, to the number of between 300 and 400. There were a vast number of shackles and chains, with which they had been chained, and the slaves had been removed out of the barracoons on the approach of my boats.

7129. Therefore the property destroyed was only such as was used for the most criminal purpose?—There was no property destroyed but what was used for the slave trade. In fact, there was very little property besides the buildings; every thing had been removed.

7130. Mr. *Forster.*] You think the natives could draw the distinction between property of that description and other property which you yourself might feel inclined to respect?—I think the natives could draw the distinction between property intended for the slave trade, belonging to a foreign slave dealer who had settled in the country for the express purpose of carrying on the slave trade, which the natives know is contrary to the laws of his own country, and contrary to the laws of all Europe.

7131. But when they see those persons settle in their own country, with the sanction and under the protection of their chiefs, do you think that, under those circumstances, to teach them such a want of respect for property can have a beneficial tendency in the country generally, where it must have been witnessed by other natives, and known to other natives besides those which you have mentioned as being engaged in this transaction?—I think it must have a beneficial effect on the natives of the country where it takes place.

7132. *Chairman.*] In doing this did you act under specific instructions, or upon your own responsibility?—Upon my own responsibility; I have received the approbation of the Admiralty.

7133. Did you receive any general instructions to attack slave factories wherever they were not under an European flag?—Not while I was on the coast.

7134. Mr. *Forster.*] Did you visit the Rio Nunez?—Yes.

7135. Do you know two chiefs there of the names of Sallafou and Sarra?— Sallafou is the chief of the Narrow country, and Sarra is the chief of the Kikandy country.

7136. Did you advise those chiefs to get possession of the goods of any slave vessel that might come within their reach, and any property that might be in them?—I think it is very likely that I advised those chiefs, while I was in their country, to discontinue the European slave trade and to prohibit slave vessels from coming to their country.

7137. But you did not advise them to seize slave vessels or slave cargoes?—I advised them to prohibit slave vessels coming to their country, and not to allow the slave trade.

7138. But you did not advise them to use every means in their power to get possession of any property belonging to a slave dealer that might come within their reach?—They could not get possession of any property, or slave vessel, if they followed my advice of not allowing them to come to their country to trade for slaves. There was no slave vessel, nor did I see any factories, in the Nunez, or any signs of the slave trade being carried on there.

7139. But they could not prevent slave vessels coming into their country without being in contact with them, and therefore having the means of seizing them?—Their seizing slave vessels and goods would be an act of their own. I remember no advice being given them by me, that they were to lie wait, or endeavour to seize vessels that they supposed to be engaged in the slave trade, or to seize goods on board those vessels, or to use any fraudulent means of getting those goods into their possession.

7140. Then if they have made your advice a pretext for seizing property in vessels belonging to Frenchmen in their rivers, they have done so falsely?—They never received any advice or recommendation from me to seize goods or vessels belonging to the French or any other nation. When I was in the Nunez there were three English merchants and four French merchants with me. The origin of my going there was owing to a war existing between King Sarra and the Nallow chief, which had stopped the trade of the river. There had also been some outrages committed upon an English vessel; the captain of one English vessel had been forcibly made to pay between 60 and 70 dollars, and another English vessel had been fired on by the natives. I entered into treaties with the chiefs that French and English property should be respected. The merchants were present at both interviews with those chiefs, a Foolah chief, with about 100 or 120 Foolahs, who had been sent down from the Foolah country, was also with me, and assisted in making king Sarra refund 64 dollars which he had taken from this English captain, which money I delivered to the Governor of Sierra Leone; and on leaving the river both the English and French merchants expressed themselves very much satisfied with what I had done. There was no advice given by me to either of the chiefs but in the presence of those merchants.

7141. *Chairman.*] Did you find, in the course of your cruize, assistance given to the slave trade by English merchants?—I detained an English vessel bound to the Gallinas, freighted through the agency of Messrs. Zulueta, of London, on behalf of Pedro Martinez, of the Havannah, consigned to some notorious slaving establishment at the Gallinas.

7142. What was the result?—I sent the vessel to Sierra Leone; she was tried in the Vice-Admiralty Court, and condemned; the master was also tried at the sessions at Sierra Leone. The grand jury found a true bill against him, and I have every reason to believe the petty jury would have found him guilty, had the Queen's advocate, who conducted the prosecution, represented the master as also the owner. But upon the trial he was tried merely as the master, and the jury acquitted him on the supposition that the master of a vessel might be ignorant of the trade in which she was engaged; but he being master and owner, and having been to the Gallinas on two previous voyages, and delivered cargoes, consigned in one instance to the notorious Pedro Blanco, and in another instance to another slave merchant; had this appeared, I have every reason to believe he would have been convicted. It is my opinion the house of Zulueta have aided and abetted the slave trade for a number of years, by acting as agents for slave dealers. There is a case on record, very nearly similar to this, of the brig Arrogante, which was sent out to the Havannah, and represented to the English Government by the English consul at the Havannah.

7143. You mean by the same house?—By the same house.

7144. What is the nature of the interest which the house of Zulueta have in these transactions?—They appear as agents only.

7145. What is the nature of their agency?—I will state the whole case of the vessel. I have copies of the principal papers with me in London, if the Committee should wish to see them. The "Augusta" was originally the "Goluptichick." The "Goluptichick" was detained by me off Gallinas under Russian colours, with a crew composed solely of Spaniards. Her course of trade for two years had been wholly confined to Spanish ports and the coast of Africa. I had information of her taking a cargo of slaves from the coast a few months previously to my capturing her; I sent her to Sierra Leone, and attempted to try her in the Spanish and British Mixed Commission Court, under the treaty with Spain. She was refused to be admitted into the court, being under Russian colours and papers. I then determined upon sending her to England, being convinced that this vessel could not be trading lawfully from Russia, Russia having no colonies to which it was possible she could be carrying slaves. The vessel was perfectly equipped for the slave trade.

7146. What year was this in?—This was in 1839. The master of the vessel, rather than be sent to England, told me he would prove that the vessel was Spanish property, and gave me a certificate to that effect. I tried a second time to get her into the Mixed Commission Court, and failed, and then sent her to England. She was detained in England by the English Government for some time, and I believe given up to the Russian authorities; but I have received no official information on the subject. The vessel was sold at Portsmouth to a Mr. Jennings, but by the papers found on board her this purchase appears to have been effected by Zulueta & Co. The vessel proceeded to Liverpool, and shipped a cargo through the agency of Zulueta, on account of P. Martinez, of Havannah, which cargo was to be delivered at the Gallinas, to three notorious slave dealers. I found her at the Gallinas, and immediately seized her, when she was tried, as I have related, at Sierra Leone. An appeal has been entered before the Privy Council, and is now pending. In the trial at Sierra Leone the master and owner, Mr. Jennings, did not defend the vessel, which is an extraordinary thing, because the master and owner of the vessel, when she was tried before the Vice-Admiralty Court at Sierra Leone, ought to have defended her.

7147. Mr. *Hamilton*.] Was she equipped for the slave trade the second time?—No, she was not.

7148. Captain *Fitzroy*.] Who defended her?—She was not defended at all.

7149. Sir *T. D. Acland*.] This is the second time that she has been tried at Sierra Leone?—This is the third time. The case of the Arrogante is very nearly similar; it is to be seen in the Papers laid before Parliament in 1839 or 1840.

[Adjourned to Wednesday next, at Half-past Twelve o'clock.

————

Mercurii, 29° die Junii, 1842.

MEMBERS PRESENT.

Sir T. D. Acland.
Mr. Aldam.
Viscount Courtenay.
Captain Fitzroy.

Mr. Forster.
Mr. W. Hamilton.
Sir R. H. Inglis.
Mr. Milnes.

Captain *Henry Worsley Hill*, R.N., called in; and further examined.

7150. *Chairman.*] When you were last examined, you were stating the cases in which you conceived that British merchants had given assistance to the slave trade?—Yes; I stated the case of the Augusta having been detained by me.

7151. Are there other cases which have come to your knowledge?—Not of vessels being engaged in the slave trade.

7152. Are there any other instances in which you have ascertained that English merchants had aided or abetted the slave trade?—A representation in a private way was made to me by the governor of Liberia, that an English vessel had supplied Mr. Canót at New Cestos, with goods and arms. He mentioned among other things, two or three pieces of brass ordnance, with which Mr. Canót was supposed to be fortifying his slaving establishments.

7153. Was that case investigated?—No, I could not gain sufficient proof. I went on board the vessel, and the master of the vessel did not deny having landed goods at Theodore Canót's establishment, but I could find nothing amongst her papers or her custom-house cockets that went to convince me that guns and things had been taken out from England consigned to Mr. Canót. It did not come to any thing, it was merely a representation made by the governor of Liberia, as a set-off to the complaints that were daily made of the American flag covering the slave trade upon the coast; but I could find nothing whatever that justified me in supposing that that vessel came out with her cargo consigned to Mr. Canót.

7154. Do you know of any other case?—No, I know of no other case.

7155. Have you received assistance in the prosecution of your duty upon the coast from English vessels engaged in trade, in the way of information or otherwise?—In one or two instances I have.

7156. Of what nature?—Merely giving information of vessels which they had seen on the coast, which they suspected of being engaged in the slave trade.

7157. Have you ever received obstruction from them?—No, I have not.

7158. Mr. *Forster.*] You have spoken very strongly of Messrs. Zulueta & Co. as connected with the slave trade; are you aware that those gentlemen act very extensively as agents for foreign houses in Cuba, in Spain, and in Brazil, as Spanish merchants?—I have no means of ascertaining that.

7159. The cargo of the Augusta, which you seized, was shipped at Liverpool, where Messrs. Zulueta & Co. have a house?—It was.

7160. Did you find any prohibited goods in that cargo which had been shipped at Liverpool?—None.

7161. That cargo having been shipped at Liverpool, composed of lawful goods, and legally cleared by the custom-house officers there, in what way do you consider Messrs. Zulueta & Co. criminally implicated in such a transaction?—The custom-house officers at Liverpool may be totally ignorant of the trade carried on at the Gallinas, and also totally ignorant of the trade carried on by Pedro Martinez & Co. at the Havannah.

7162. Suppose Messrs. Zulueta & Co. to have received orders from their foreign correspondents to ship those goods; in what way do you consider them bound to know the history and pursuits of the person to whom they were directed to consign them at the Gallinas?—I should certainly think they are bound to be cautious that they did nothing contrary to the laws of the country in which they were residing.

7163. But unless they knew that those goods were to be applied for the purchase of slaves on the coast of Africa, in what way do you consider them bound to exercise any caution, and above all, to refuse to comply with the orders of their correspondents?—I certainly think they are bound to use every caution that they do not act contrary to law.

7164. Who were the parties to whom they were consigned at the Gallinas?— The goods were consigned to be delivered to Don José Alvarez, and Don Angel Ximenes, and Don José Perez Rola, all noted slave dealers.

7165. *Chairman.*] Have Messrs. Zulueta direct intercourse with the coast of Africa themselves, as merchants, or are they only agents?—I have never met a vessel belonging to Messrs. Zulueta & Co. on the coast of Africa.

7166. They are shipping agents in England, obeying orders given them by their correspondents abroad?—I have never known Zulueta & Co. to be employed in any mercantile transactions on the coast of Africa, except with regard to Spanish slave merchants. I have never seen their names in any vessels that I have boarded, engaged in innocent traffic.

7167. Do you conceive that a shipping agent is bound to make himself acquainted with the pursuits of the parties to whom he ships lawful goods?— I think, as far as regards the slave trade on the coast of Africa, it is the duty of a merchant residing in England, to be cautious that he does not do any thing that will at all be acting contrary to the Act of Parliament for the Abolition of the Slave Trade.

7168. Supposing he had consigned goods to the Bight of Benin, for instance, where many of the greatest dealers in produce have been till lately dealers in slaves; can you conceive that he would have been engaging in unlawful traffic in complying with such orders from his correspondent?—If the goods were to be consigned to a port where innocent traffic was carried on, and to merchants who carried on that traffic as well as the slave trade, of course it would admit of great doubt to what purpose those goods would be applied; but, in this case, the goods being consigned to those three people at the Gallinas, a port where no trade but the slave trade has been carried on for a considerable number of years, I think it materially alters the position of the parties in the shipping of the goods.

7169. Then the innocence or otherwise of the transaction depends, in your opinion, upon the knowledge on the part of the shipping agent in England of the exclusively slave-dealing character, of the trade carried on from any point of the coast of Africa to which the goods may be consigned?—I think not exactly.

7170. Supposing the Gallinas had carried on a trade to the extent of 100 pieces of ivory annually, would that have been an innocent transaction which you now consider to have been a culpable one?—I think it might admit of a doubt whether there was a possibility of the goods shipped being employed in innocent traffic; but I think, being shipped to a place like the Gallinas, there can be no doubt whatever to what purpose the goods would be applied.

7171. Is not the nature of the traffic carried on from different points of the coast of Africa, shifting and varying from time to time; at one time exclusively in slave dealing, at other times partly in slave dealing and partly in produce; and at other times wholly in produce; according as the efforts of the English merchants have prevailed more or less. Would it not, therefore, according to this view, require constant reports to the shipper in England of the state for the year of the different points of trade on the coast of Africa, to enable him to know whether he could with safety carry on trade with any one place?—I think the slave trade has been at the point to which the vessel in question was consigned to deliver her cargo, so fully established, that it can admit of no doubt whatever as to the trade in which that vessel was employed. But it may happen, at many places on the coast, that a doubt might exist. For instance, if a merchant were established on the coast, carrying on the joint traffic of exchange of the produce of the country as well as the slave trade, it certainly would admit of a doubt. But I think it is the business of the merchant residing in England to make himself acquainted with the character of the persons on the coast of Africa to whom he makes consignments, especially seeing the attempts that are making and have been made for the suppression of the slave trade.

7172. You observe that the case in question is not the case of a merchant carrying on a direct trade with a slave dealer, but a merchant obeying the orders of his correspondent, to make consignments merely as his shipping agent?—I think myself it depends in a great measure upon the place to which the cargo is to be delivered. I think at New Cestos, for example, there might be a doubt to what trade the cargo would be applied; but there are many cases which will not admit of a doubt. Now if a merchant has been in the habit of acting as agent to a foreign house for a length of time, I think he must somehow acquire a knowledge of the trade which this foreign merchant is embarked in. I think it becomes the duty of the merchant to endeavour to make some inquiry, because the Act of Parliament is very decisive; it says, "Or in any other manner to engage or contract to engage directly or indirectly therein as a partner, agent or otherwise, or to ship, tranship, lade, receive or put on board, or to contract for the shipping, transhipping, lading, receiving or putting on board of any ship, vessel or boat, money, goods or effects to be employed in accomplishing any of the objects or the contracts in relation to the objects, which objects and contracts have hereinbefore been declared unlawful." The law is very decisive.

7173. Mr. *Forster.*] What are the objects and contracts which have been previously declared unlawful?—"For any persons to deal or trade in, purchase, sell, barter, or transfer, or to contract for the dealing or trading in, purchase, sale, barter, or transfer of slaves or persons intended to be dealt with as slaves."

7174. Do you consider the lawful shipping of goods at Liverpool a dealing in slaves?—A lawful shipment of goods cannot be unlawful.

7175. But if the shipment had not been lawful, would not the custom-house officers at Liverpool have seized the goods?—It is possible that the custom-house officers at Liverpool may be ignorant of what caused the shipment of the goods to be unlawful.

7176. But the custom-house officers cannot be ignorant whether the goods which they pass at Liverpool are lawfully shipped?—The parties and the port to which the goods are to be delivered of course stamp the character of the trade in which they are sent out.

7177. *Chairman.*] Would it be convenient if the custom-house officers were informed from time to time to what ports vessels might clear with safety, and to what they might not?—I think in the case of such a port as the Gallinas, it would have been convenient, and perhaps have been attended with some benefit, had the custom-house officers in our different ports in England been made acquainted with the trade that was there carried on, to prevent goods being shipped direct for that port; but that again would be evaded by shipping goods, as is frequently done, for the coast of Africa, without specifying any port.

7178. Do you conceive that the destruction of the barracoons is very effectual in putting down the slave trade?—I think that in many cases it would be attended with great benefit to the suppression of the slave trade, almost in every instance; but great care should be exercised in doing it.

7179. In what respects?—That the establishments should be decidedly ascertained to be slaving establishments, so as not to destroy any establishments that might be erected where innocent traffic was carried on, but only the slaving establishments that were *bonâ fide* for the express purpose of slaving.

7180. Have you found any feeling of irritation created among the natives upon the coast by that mode of proceeding?—No; I was frequently at the Gallinas after the barracoons at the Gallinas were destroyed, and I thought a good feeling was springing up amongst the chiefs for the establishment of commerce and the cultivation of their soil. They certainly expressed a wish that the barracoons and the slaving establishments in the neighbouring states should be destroyed as well as their own.

7181. Do you conceive that the slave trade is popular with the natives of all classes, or that its profits are principally confined to the chiefs?—I think it is popular with the natives of all classes.

7182. Mr. *Forster.*] If it is popular with all classes, how do you account for their expressing a wish that the barracoons should be destroyed?—That followed after their own barracoons had been destroyed; they wished their neighbours' barracoons to be destroyed likewise; they expressed their delight very openly when I went to the Gallinas after the establishments at Sea-bar had been destroyed.

7183. Supposing them to feel any irritation upon the subject, do you think it likely that it would be to the officer of a ship of war that they would communicate those feelings?—Perhaps not, directly; but I think the officers on being on shore would very easily observe if their feelings were unfavourable.

7184. *Chairman.*] Had you any communication with the slave dealers themselves upon the subject of this method of putting down the slave trade?—Yes; I saw, I think, the most intelligent of the slave dealers that were established at the Gallinas, I think it was Don Angel Ximenes, who told me that it was impossible for him to carry on the slave trade, if this plan was followed up; that he was ruined by it; and that he intended immediately going to America, and that he had recommended the other slave dealers to do the same. Two or three of them, I know, left Africa immediately, and one other man left the Gallinas territory and settled in the neighbouring states, with the intention of trying to carry on the slave trade again.

7185. Has the introduction of the Equipment Article led, as a matter of necessity, to carrying on the slave trade by the collection of slaves in barracoons, ready for the descent of any slaver, who can no longer now hover in sight, and remain waiting for the collection of slaves during its stay there?—Yes; slave vessels now come across from the Havannah in every way ready equipped for embarking their slaves at an hour's notice; they appear off the coast, and in one or two instances, I have heard that in two hours their cargoes have been put on board them.

7186. Barracoons have now become an essential part of the existing system of the slave trade?—They have always had barracoons.

7187. Mr. *Milnes*.] Do you think the slave trade is popular among the lower classes?—Yes, I think it is in those parts of Africa where they have known no other trade; that has been the trade by which they have derived all the principal articles that have almost become necessary to them.

7188. *Chairman*.] Have you seen instances where, upon the extinction of the slave trade, legitimate trade has taken its place?—I heard various reports of its having done so at the Bonny and at Benin; at the Bonny particularly. Again, Mr. Spence, in the River St. George's, established himself and introduced innocent trade, and I believe totally expelled the slave dealers; it had a very beneficial effect in those three places.

7189. Was that a case where lawful traffic had the effect, without the assistance of cruizers, of expelling the slave trade, or was it in co-operation with them?—I think in co-operation with the cruizers. Mr. Spence took a great deal of pains, and if he had known of a slave vessel coming into St. George's, he would have immediately informed the cruizers, and in fact he had so much influence with the chiefs immediately around him, that he prevented them from carrying on the slave trade. The slave trade cannot be carried on without the sanction of the chief, and in fact in almost every case it is done by the chief of the district himself; he is the principal slave dealer, receiving a certain emolument from the slave dealers coming to his place to trade.

7190. When you speak of the co-operation of the cruizers with Mr. Spence's efforts, you mean that the cruizers protected Mr. Spence in his operations, but not that they were preventing the slave trade at the time by a blockade?—Exactly.

7191. Have you heard since the destruction of the slave factory at the Gallinas, or at Sea-bar, whether lawful trade has taken the place of the slave trade?—When I was last at the Gallinas, one of the chiefs showed me a sample of cotton that he was cultivating, and he promised that he would collect as much as he could for the purpose of carrying on innocent trade: he had then, I think, at the time I am speaking of, six or eight large packages in his house, and he said, that in the course of time, he could produce any quantity. He seemed to be honest in his intentions.

7192. Viscount *Courtenay*.] Was it wild or cultivated cotton?—He told me that he had cultivated it; and it appeared to me to be particularly good; it was much finer than any I have seen elsewhere.

7193. Mr. *Aldam*.] Did you see any cotton cultivated?—No, I did not see any cultivated; this was up the country, 10 or 12 miles up the Gallinas River.

7194. Would it be practicable to collect a considerable quantity of wild cotton?—No; I think the wild cotton is so much scattered, that without cultivation they could not collect any quantity.

7195. *Chairman*.] Had you any conversation with the chief upon the advantage with which the people might be employed in raising produce rather than their being sold as slaves?—Frequently I endeavoured to instil into their minds the advantages they would derive from giving up the slave trade, and employing their own slaves in tilling the ground, and collecting cam wood, and any thing the country might produce. I think in many parts of the Gallinas the country is capable of being cultivated to a great extent. I am now speaking of King Siacca's Town, which is 10 or 12 miles up the river.

7196. Do you think it would be of advantage, either for the suppression of the slave trade, or for the encouragement of the lawful trade to have factories or forts planted at particular points?—I think, decidedly; I think if factories were established along the coast, it would materially lead to the suppression of the slave trade, and also to the cultivation and improvement of Africa generally; I think particularly on the coast from Sierra Leone to Cape Mount, which has been the chief slavery district on that part of Africa.

7197. Have you had reason to know whether there would be facilities or otherwise for the purchase of sites for settlements of that description from the native chiefs?—I think there might be a little opposition made in the first instance, which might easily be overcome. I remember one of the chiefs of the Gallinas telling me that he would have no objection to see the English settle there; but others again did not seem so desirous of it. Again, at Cape Mount the chief was very anxious that the English should establish themselves, and carry on trade there; and when I was last at Cape Mount the English flag was flying. The American governor of Liberia came up, and was very desirous that the American flag should be likewise hoisted, which the chief refused; he showed a decided preference to the English.

7198. Is there a coasting traffic established along the coast to any degree from point to point, and is any part of it carried on by the liberated Africans of Sierra Leone?—I think not; I think the coasting trade of Sierra Leone to the southward does not extend beyond one or two towns in the Sherboro' River, where they go for cam wood, which is particularly good there. To the northward the canoes trade to the River Scarcies, and occasionally, I think, as far as the Pongos. But those boats that go to the Pongos always incur the suspicion that they are all more or less carrying goods for the slave dealers in the Pongos; but as far as regards the immediate coasting trade of Sierra Leone, it is very much confined.

7199. You would be glad to see the services of a steamer secured for Sierra Leone?—I think it is absolutely necessary.

7200. Sir *T. D. Acland*.] And also for the Gambia?—And for the Gambia likewise. I think it is absolutely necessary for the Gambia, to communicate between St. Mary's and M'Carthy's Island. For instance, it occurred while I was at the Gambia that information arrived from M'Carthy's Island of the natives having attacked the island, and before troops could be sent up, or I could get up in a sailing vessel, many days elapsed, where a steam-boat would have done it in a day and a half. Steam-boats would also be particularly useful for the suppression of the slave trade.

7201. Is there any other point besides Sierra Leone and the Gambia where you think they are particularly wanted?—I would say, generally along the coast, for the suppression of the slave trade, I should say that it would require half-a-dozen steamers to protect the coast between the Gambia and the southernmost slaving ports on the western coast of Africa.

7202. Where?—Down to Benguela. I think about half-a-dozen steam-boats would be sufficient.

7203. Sir *R. H. Inglis*.] What is the average passage by steam and the average passage by sailing vessels between the Bight of Benin and Sierra Leone?—It depends a great deal upon the season of the year. I think from the Bight of Benin to Sierra Leone the average passage in sailing vessels is about a month.

7204. Have you experience sufficient to enable you to state to the Committee the average passage by steam-vessels?—No, I have not.

7205. What is the extreme length of passage between the Bight of Benin and Sierra Leone in a sailing vessel; the question having reference particularly to a sailing vessel taking slaves on board for adjudication before the court at Sierra Leone?—I have heard of vessels being a very long time, three months; I think I remember slave vessels that have taken between two or three months to get up from the Bight of Benin to Sierra Leone; but I think that is a very rare occurrence; usually the passage is made in about a month.

7206. In all seasons?—In all seasons; I think a month is the average passage.

7207. Sir *T. D. Acland*.] What is the shortest?—I think I have heard of its being done in a fortnight.

7208. Sir *R. H. Inglis*.] What is the average passage across the Atlantic, from the Bight of Benin to the Havannah?—From five to six weeks; but I think it is done in less time; I think I remember a slaver telling me, that he did it in something less than a month, but I think from five to six weeks is the average passage; the great difficulty is getting immediately off the coast.

7209. *Chairman*.] Are the winds mostly on shore?—It depends a great deal on the season of the year.

7210. Would there be any difficulty in a vessel lying off Cape Palmas, if it were thought desirable, for the purpose of regulating any emigration that might proceed from those parts?—I think there would be no difficulty in a cruizer remaining off Cape Palmas; in lying at anchor there would be danger, but not in keeping under weigh.

7211. Sir *T. D. Acland*.] Do you think that it would be possible for a naval officer to undertake the service of clearing vessels for the West Indies, having ascertained that the natives embarked on board came with their free will, without any fraud or compulsion?—I think the local authorities could do that better than a naval officer.

7212. The question refers to those parts where there are no local authorities; and it proceeds on the supposition that no vessel could be received with emigrants in the West Indies without a clearance from the British officer commanding a certain range of coast: could a British officer in the first place lie off and on, and in the next place, could he discharge the duty of ascertaining whether the emigrants on board any vessel submitted to his examination, were or were not engaged on that voyage without fraud or compulsion?—I think he would have no other means of ascertaining, but what he was told by the natives themselves.

7213. What course would he pursue; would he muster the emigrants on deck, and be able to ascertain from them the circumstances under which they were embarked?—Of course he would have to muster the negroes, and he would question each whether they embarked with their free will for the purpose of emigration; but to do that, he would require an interpreter, and perhaps amongst the number, there might be a great many who spoke different languages; therefore there would be as many interpreters required, as there were different languages; and after all, those people might declare that they had not been asked, and probably place the naval officer in a very awkward predicament. He would be subject entirely to the African, who might tell half-a-dozen different stories in the course of so many months. It would be a very difficult measure to carry out.

7214. *Chairman.*] If they were only to embark Kroomen or inhabitants of the coast, do you think he would have any difficulty in ascertaining whether they were free agents or otherwise?—With Kroomen or Fishmen, I think none whatever; because in the Kroo country and in the Fish country the slave trade is not carried on, or if it is carried on, it is so slight that we hardly know any thing about it.

7215. Mr. *Aldam.*] Is there more than one language spoken by the Kroomen and the Fishmen?—There is some difference of language, but still they understand one another.

7216. One interpreter would be sufficient with the Kroomen and the Fishmen?—I think so.

7217. *Chairman.*] Would the officer on the station be able to distinguish Kroomen and Fishmen from the natives of the interior?—Decidedly, any person could.

7218. So that if he were instructed to sanction the emigration only of Kroomen and Fishmen, he would be in no danger of confounding them with any other tribes?—No, they are so distinct a class; they are perfectly different from any other natives. They differ materially in appearance, and manners, and language, and every thing.

7219. Then if the emigration were confined to those classes, you do not apprehend that there would be any difficulty in preventing that emigration from assuming the character of slave trade?—I think there would be no difficulty in the Kroo country and in the Fish country. The difficulty would be on the part of the coast where the slave trade is known to have been carried on, and where, from the slave trade having been carried on, the different tribes are so very much intermixed.

7220. Sir *T. D. Acland.*] Could it in that case be done by the commander of a fort on shore, who if he had time, would be able to ascertain the facts?—I think it would be an undertaking of great trouble.

7221. Mr. *Forster.*] Have you made any other seizures on the coast of Africa than the Augusta?—Several.

7222. Did you seize a vessel called the Sénégambie at St. Mary's?—Yes, I seized a vessel called the Sénégambie in the river Gambia.

7223. On what ground was that seizure made?—On account of being equipped for the slave trade.

7224. Were you aware at the time you seized her that she had been chartered by the governor of Senegal for the voyage in which she was engaged?—I do not know whether I knew that at the time of making the seizure, or whether it was immediately afterwards, but the impression upon my mind is, that the owner told me in the custom-house that he was going to Bissao for a cargo of negroes.

7225. Did he not show you his papers and engagements, or rather did you examine them yourself?—The papers of the vessel when I seized her were in the custom-house. The vessel had been in the port of St. Mary's two or three days.

7226. Did you not examine the papers?—I went to the custom-house for the purpose of examining the papers, and there I met Mr. Marbeau, the owner of the vessel, who told me the vessel was going to Bissao for a cargo of negroes.

7227. Did he not inform you that the negroes were for the service of the French government?—Afterwards I received copies of an agreement entered into between Mr. Marbeau and the governor of Senegal, transmitted to me by the governor of St. Mary's.

7228. When did you receive them?—While I was at St. Mary's.

7229. Before or after you had seized the vessel?—I think two or three days after I had seized the vessel; but those papers are printed in the correspondence, and they give much better information upon the subject. I have nothing to guide me but my recollection.

7230. Were there any mechanics or persons on board of her from the shore, at the time you seized her?—Yes; there were some mechanics on board of her belonging to St. Mary's, who were employed in caulking and fitting the vessel for her intended voyage. There were also on board of her three small children, who I thought were under most suspicious circumstances, belonging to St. Mary's.

7231. Did you think the carpenters and caulkers, who were engaged on board the vessel from shore, were there under suspicious circumstances?—No, they were employed on board the vessel, fitting the vessel for her intended voyage to Bissao for a cargo of slaves. The Sénégambie was partly equipped for the slave trade; she was lying in a British port, equipping for a cargo of slaves, where she had been for two or three days; the equipments were quite sufficient to condemn her, and she was condemned at Sierra Leone. She was absolutely lying in a British port equipping; she was to get provisions, and she had carpenters and men at work upon her belonging to the colony.

7232. Sir *T. D. Acland.*] Was she preparing false decks?—The slave-deck was partly laid, not wholly laid; she was being generally equipped for the voyage she was going on.

7233. *Chairman.*] Were the carpenters laying the slave-deck?—I cannot say exactly what the carpenters were doing; I did not see them laying the slave-deck; but she was fitting out for her intended voyage to Bissao. There was a slave-deck partly laid, and part of it to be laid, and I believe they would have finished it.

7234. Were the planks ready for completing the slave-deck lying there?—I think they were.

7235. Sir *R. H. Inglis.*] But you are certain that part of her slave-deck was laid?—Yes.

7236. Sir *T. D. Acland.*] Did you seize her upon the ground of her partial equipment?—Her equipment was the ground upon which I seized her.

7237. *Chairman.*] And it was the ground of her subsequent condemnation?—It was; the equipment was perfectly proved.

7238. Mr. *Forster.*] Do you wish the Committee to understand that that vessel was chartered by the governor of Senegal for a voyage to Bissao, and that she was not fitted out for that voyage at Senegal?—That I cannot say; I found her partly equipped, and lying in a British port, equipping for her intended voyage. She was so far equipped for the slave trade that there were ample grounds for my seizing her; and she was there caulking, fitting, and preparing for sea. She was to receive provisions for her intended voyage from the colony of St. Mary's; at least, so I was informed by the supercargo.

7239. How do you account for the vessel coming from the neighbouring French settlement of Senegal to fit out for the purpose of receiving those negroes at the Gambia?—It is a most extraordinary thing, in my mind, that a vessel should sail from a French port, only distant 50 or 60 miles, and come to an English port, and there remain for two or three days, with people at work upon her, caulking and repairing her, and fitting her for sea.

7240. Mr. *Aldam.*] Had she had bad weather?—No, nothing at all of the sort; by the vessel's papers she was not out of Goree more than one day before she arrived at the Gambia; I think less than one day.

7241. Mr. *Forster.*] Do you wish the Committee to understand that the vessel did not arrive at the Gambia with all her fittings for the voyage?—I have before stated that the vessel was lying in the Gambia, caulking and equipping for her intended voyage. It is impossible for me to state whether she brought her slave-deck with her to the Gambia, or whether she procured her slave-deck at the Gambia; but if she came to the Gambia with all those equipments on board, I would ask what can be thought of our custom-house officers at the Gambia?

7242. Do you think the custom-house officers at the Gambia would very readily conceive themselves entitled to seize a French vessel, chartered by the governor of Senegal?—The vessel being chartered by the governor of Senegal could have nothing to do with the laws that prevail in a British port. The French governor of Senegal cannot be regarded in an English port; our own laws are what are to govern our officers. The custom-house officers' duty was to seize a vessel that was acting contrary to the laws of a British port.

7243. Therefore you think it was no excuse for the custom-house officers that she was employed in the service of the French government?—None whatever, because the custom-house officers, in all probability, would be perfectly ignorant of that circumstance, as I was myself. I seized her, and I was not aware she was employed by the French government till I had seized her one or two days.

7244. Sir *R. H. Inglis.*] The last question, and your last answer, have assumed that the vessel was employed in the service of the French government; is that what you wish the Committee to understand in respect of a vessel chartered by the governor of Senegal: might it not have been a speculation, on the part of the governor, as an individual, not involving any responsibility on the part of the government of France?—Undoubtedly it is very possible that it might have been a speculation on the part of the governor of Senegal without the knowledge of the French government; but in the case of a vessel equipped for the slave trade in a British port, whether she is employed by the governor of Senegal, or the governor of Bissao, or the governor of any nation, cannot in any way affect our laws.

7245. Mr. *Aldam.*] Was this vessel, which was fitted up for the purpose of procuring negroes for the French service, fitted up as an ordinary slave ship?—As an ordinary slave ship.

7246. There were the same means of restraint?—Precisely; iron bars across the hatchway, and the usual equipment of a slave vessel.

7247. So that it appeared that men were intended to be kept under restraint upon the voyage?—Certainly.

7248. Mr. *Forster.*] Were there any slave-irons on board?—I do not at this period remember very minutely her equipment, but there was quite sufficient ground to authorise my seizing the vessel.

7249. What were those carpenters doing on board?—They were at work upon the vessel.

7250. Can you describe the work they were doing?—I cannot do that: they were performing their work as carpenters.

7251. *Chairman.*] Do you recollect whether they were caulking outside, or performing work inside the vessel?—I saw them at work, but I do not remember whether they were caulking the outside or the inside; but I see in my report that she had caulkers on board belonging to St. Mary's, who were caulking and equipping her.

7252. Mr. *Forster.*] When you found that those carpenters belonged to St. Mary's, did you send them on shore?—No, most assuredly not.

7253. Did you seize them with the vessel?—I sent them up with the vessel to Sierra Leone, and put them into the court with the vessel; and with respect to the three children that were on board, I considered, from their age, that they could be in no way connected with the equipping of the vessel, or otherwise concerned in the vessel beyond a general suspicion arising in my mind of what was intended to be done with those children, and I therefore sent them on shore to the governor of the Gambia, that he might make such inquiry respecting those children as he might judge proper.

7254. Did you consider that those carpenters, working for hire on board a vessel in the harbour, were justly chargeable with a participation in the slave trade?—They were found on board the vessel, and I considered it was necessary that I should send them with the vessel before the Vice-Admiralty Court.

7255. Did you consider them as assisting in the equipment of the vessel?— They were assisting in the equipment of the vessel, and it was with that view I sent them up; and, moreover, their evidence, if the court had required it, would have been necessary to show that the vessel was absolutely equipping in a British port; but perhaps the vessel would have been condemned without it.

7256. What was the result of the trial?—The vessel was condemned.

7257. Mr. *Forster.*] If the vessel was so fully equipped for the purposes of the slave trade, as you stated, how could the evidence of those carpenters be necessary at Sierra Leone?—I have stated that the vessel was partly equipped, and was completing her equipment in the port of St. Mary's; those carpenters being on board, I considered that it was necessary that I should send them to Sierra Leone for the court to decide in what way they were punishable.

7258. Were not representations made to you from the shore that those people were carpenters belonging to the settlement, hired by the master of the vessel, and in no way answerable for his proceedings, or for the destination of the vessel?—No official representation was made to me; perhaps some merchant, or some person connected with some mercantile houses on shore might have told me so, but I certainly paid no attention to it, nor did I consider myself bound to pay attention to any thing of the sort.

Had an official representation been made to me from the governor, of course it would require my greatest attention; but if an officer in the execution of his duty is to be guided by every person that he may meet in the settlement telling him this, that, or the other, there would be no possibility of his ever performing his duty.

7259. But at all events you knew that they were native workmen, belonging to the British settlement at the Gambia?—Yes; I knew that from their own story. I sent them up with the vessel, and put them into court with the vessel, and moreover acquainted the lieutenant-governor of the Gambia officially that I intended doing so.

7260. Were they put in prison upon their arrival at Sierra Leone?—I was not at Sierra Leone when the vessel arrived. To the best of my knowledge they were confined about a month.

7261. *Chairman.*] Were they condemned?—I do not know.

7262. Mr. *Aldam.*] Were they confined preparatory to trial, or after sentence?—I forget, for I was not at Sierra Leone at the time; but I believe it was the Vice-Admiralty Court that confined them.

7263. Mr. *Forster.*] Do you know whether the carpenters were tried or not?—I do not know; I was not at Sierra Leone during the trial of the vessel, but I believe I arrived at Sierra Leone the very day that the vessel was condemned in the Vice-Admiralty Court.

7264. Did you make no inquiry as to the fate of those carpenters?—No, I did not, because I left Sierra Leone, I think, the day after the vessel was condemned, for Portendique, and I had no time to make inquiry on either of the two days that I was at Sierra Leone. I knew that the vessel was before the Vice-Admiralty Court who would decide upon the merits of the case.

7265. Was there a French gentleman also on board the vessel when you seized her?—There was a French person on board, whom I believed to be the supercargo, and, I rather think, was the brother of Mr. Marbeau.

7266. Did you find that he was the supercargo of the vessel?—He told me that he was the supercargo; and I believe that he was the brother of Mr. Marbeau, the owner.

7267. Was he not a passenger from Senegal to the Gambia?—It is impossible for me to say what he was.

7268. Had he been on shore at the Gambia previously to your seizing the vessel?—It is impossible for me to say.

7269. Did you carry a French gentleman from the Gambia to Sierra Leone, without making inquiry into his character and pursuits, and his connexion with that vessel?—All persons who were found on board the vessel, as I have before stated, with the exception of three black children, I sent to Sierra Leone, because I could not tell, of course, what he was doing in the vessel; he might be a French gentleman, or he might be there for the purpose of purchasing slaves; or he might be, for what I could tell, the very person who had got on board the three children, who, I have before stated, I thought were placed in a very suspicious position. My duty was to send everybody found in the vessel I had captured, on the suspicion of slave dealing, before the court appointed to adjudicate upon such cases.

7270. How did you consider him to be connected with those three children?—What I stated was, that he might be; I have not said that he was; I stated that I knew nothing about him, but finding him in the slave vessel, I sent him with the slave vessel before the court.

7271. You sent the three children on shore?—Yes; everybody else I sent before the court; and if any person in the world had been on board the vessel I should have sent him in the same way; if an English merchant had been on board, that merchant would have gone with the vessel likewise before the court; the court is to decide upon the legality or illegality of the conduct of persons found under such circumstances.

7272. *Chairman.*] You conceive that that vessel, by her equipment was clearly seizable, as engaged in the slave trade?—Yes, or else I should not have seized her; I took upon myself a great responsibility in seizing her.

7273. And under those circumstances you felt yourself called upon to send every person found on board the vessel for adjudication before the proper court?—Yes; if I had not done so, I should have conceived that I laid myself open to the charge of not doing my duty.

7274. Sir *T. D. Acland.*] When you find a vessel reasonably suspected of being engaged in the slave trade, you think those who are found on board are liable to the same suspicion?—In the case of a vessel seized amenable to the British law.

7275. Sir *R. H. Inglis.*] Did you not find on board the vessel a contract between Marbeau and Pellett on the one hand, and the French governor on the other, to deliver a certain number of "passengers" at Goree?—This contract for "Blacks" was forwarded to me by the lieutenant-governor of the Gambia, one or two days after I had made the seizure, which contract I sent to the Vice-Admiralty court, with the vessel; every paper connected with the vessel, as well as the contract, was laid before the court.

7276. Mr. *Forster*.] Were you aware that she was engaged by the French government before you sent her from the Gambia?—I had seen this contract, which was entered into by the French governor of Senegal, but not the French government.

7277. Was the French gentleman, M. Pellett, put in prison also upon his arrival at Sierra Leone?—I have stated that I know not what was done by the court at Sierra Leone. Not being in Sierra Leone at the time the vessel was at Sierra Leone, I cannot say; but, to the best of my belief, the whole of them were put in prison.

7278. Sir *T. D. Acland*.] Have you known instances of persons in authority under other governments being engaged in slave dealing?—The charge has been frequently repeated very strongly of the governor of Bissao being engaged very frequently in slave dealing, and I verily believe it myself, because I have frequently detected vessels with papers given by the governor of Bissao, which vessels were equipped in every way for being engaged in the slave trade; and I have also some recollection of some papers being found from the governor of Bissao, detailing how some slaves that he had sent from Bissao were to be disposed of.

7279. That slave dealing being contrary to the law of his own country?—That slave dealing being contrary to the treaty between England and Portugal.

7280. Therefore the mere fact of finding the name of a governor upon the papers would not be a complete warrant for the lawfulness of the traffic in which the vessel was engaged?—I should pay great respect to the name of the French governor, but I should be very cautious how I regarded the name of the governor of Bissao, because I have seen so many instances of papers in which his name has been used to cover slaving transactions.

7281. Mr. *Forster*.] Was the captain of the Sénégambie a black or a white man?—I think a black man was represented to me as the captain.

7282. Mr. *Aldam*.] You spoke of the desirableness of having forts upon the African coast, upon the territory of the native chiefs. What establishment would it be necessary to have in any such fort?—I should think if the forts were small and well built, a very few men would be sufficient; I should fancy the best form of fort to be erected would be a Martello tower, that they might have one gun upon a pivot, so that for the defence of the fort it would require very few men.

7283. How many whites?—I should say half white and half black; I should say a dozen men altogether.

7284.—Would not one or two white officers be sufficient, the rest of the men being black?—That would do if you could insure white officers living, but the danger is of one dying, and in that case to whom would the charge of the fort devolve. It would be necessary to have a sufficient number of white people, that you might always insure one person to be in command.

7285. Are there no sub-officers blacks, whom you might entrust with a command of that kind, subject to the visits of the captains of men-of-war upon the station?—I think not at present; I think Africa would require to be much further advanced in civilization before it would be prudent to trust a fort entirely to black men.

7286. And it would generally happen that those forts would be built upon an unhealthy part of the coast?—It is almost impossible to select any part of the coast of Africa as being healthy. One spot may be more healthy this season than another; but there is very little difference upon the coast. The coast of Africa, from the Kroo country up to Senegal, is generally composed of a low swampy mangrove line of coast. Those mangroves extend frequently from 25 to 30 miles into the interior. There are spots like Sierra Leone, Cape Verde, and Cape Mount, where you can find high land; but generally speaking it is all a swampy mangrove coast.

7287. The spots you would select for those forts for commercial purposes would generally happen to be unhealthy?—It would naturally so occur, because they would require to be near the mouths of the principal rivers, for drawing the exports down from the interior; but I should think that the communication would be drawn down better from the interior by opening some communication, or making an agreement or treaty with some of the inland powerful chiefs, such as the Foolahs, who are by far the most enlightened race that I have seen, and much more advanced towards civilization than the people in any other part of Africa that I have been in.

7288. Sir *T. D. Acland.*] Does Teembo belong to them?—Yes.

7289. Mr. *Aldam.*] Would you contemplate in that case having a fort some distance up the river?—No; in the River Nunez, to which I allude with respect to the Foolahs, I do not think it would be necessary, because the petty chiefs immediately at the mouth of the Nunez, who are now likely to give trouble, would be kept in order by them; I think a treaty entered into with the Foolah chief, would in a great measure ensure our trade with the Foolah country. Through the means of the Foolah chief we should be enabled to carry on trade independent of the petty chiefs, through whose territory the trade now has to pass.

7290. What kind of treaty would you make with those chiefs?—The object of it would be to bind the Foolah chief down to afford protection and security to our commerce, and to people settling in his country, for the purpose of carrying on trade.

7291. And you think it would be easy to obtain such a treaty?—I think so; I judge from the opinion given me by a Foolah chief, whom I met in the Nunez, and who expressed himself desirous that the white people should not leave the River Nunez, and said that he would be very happy to escort me up to Teembo, that the Foolah Almaamy would be very happy to see me.

7292. Over what extent of country would the influence of this chief extend?—The Foolah country is now very extensive. The kingdom of Kikandy is in some measure tributary to the Foolah country.

7293. Mr. *Forster.*] Were you at Sierra Leone when the affair of the Hamburgh vessel, the Echo, took place?—I was at Sierra Leone while the Echo was there.

7294. Did you apply to the captain of the Echo for some of his crew?—I met some of the crew of the Echo, who came to me and expressed a wish to enter the Saracen for Her Majesty's service, and on meeting the captain of the Echo, I mentioned to him that those people had done so; but I had no idea of entering the crew, as they were all foreigners.

7295. Sir *T. D. Acland.*] How far is the Nunez navigable?—For vessels drawing 10 feet water to Debucca, a distance of 50 or 60 miles; and for large canoes I should think much higher.

———

HOUSE OF COMMONS.
Select Committee on West Coast of Africa.
R. R. GIBBONS, Esq. to MESSRS. ZULUETA & Co.

Gentlemen, July 15th, 1842.

I send you herewith a copy of evidence given by Captain Hill, of a later date than that I sent on a previous occasion.

I am, &c.

(signed) R. R. *Gibbons.*

———

MEMBERS PRESENT.

Sir T. D. Acland.
Mr. Aldam.
Viscount Courtenay.

Captain Fitzroy.
Mr. W. Hamilton.

VISCOUNT SANDON, in the chair.

Captain *Henry Worsley Hill*, called in; and further Examined.

7958*. *Chairman.*] Have you something which you wish to add to your evidence on the case of the Augusta?—Yes; I wish to state, with respect to my detaining the Augusta, the grounds on which the seizure was made, as far as my memory will admit of my going, and I feel myself at liberty to disclose to the Committee. On going on board the Augusta, amongst the letters and papers that were seized by me, I found a letter, dated "London, 20th August 1840." This letter is a reply to a letter written by Captain Jennings from Portsmouth, stating, "We cannot exceed 500*l.* for the vessel in question, such as described in your letter; if you cannot, therefore, succeed at those limits, we must give up the purchase." This letter is signed Zulueta & Co. By this letter, it certainly appears to me that the vessel was purchased by Zulueta &, Co., or intended to be purchased by that firm. The next letter is dated "London, 26th of September 1840," addressed to Captain Thomas Jennings, Portsmouth; the signature of this letter was cut out on my finding it. It acknowledged the receipt of Captain Jenning's letter of the following day, observing "that the sum remitted would not be sufficient to cover the expenses, to clear the ship, and requesting that Captain Jennings would write the next day, stating the sum that was necessary, that it might be forwarded to him by the post of Monday night, to enable the ship to sail for Liverpool on Tuesday or Wednesday at furthest." The signature cut out. But there is a note to the letter: "According to our Liverpool mode, note, you will go on shore to the Salt House Dock." The next paper I would allude to, is the charter-party of the vessel, dated London, 19th October 1840, wherein it is mutually agreed, between Mr. Thomas Jennings, master and owner of the good ship or vessel called the Augusta, and Messrs. Pedro Martinez & Co. of Havannah, that the ship shall load from the factories of the said Messrs. Pedro Martinez & Co. a cargo of legal goods, and shall proceed therewith to Gallinas, on the coast of Africa, and there deliver the same; after which she may be sent on any legal voyage between the West Indies, England, Africa, or the United States, according to the directions of the charterer's agents. The freight to be paid on unloading and right delivery of the cargo, at the rate of 100*l.* sterling per calendar month. The necessary cash for the ship's disbursements to be furnished to the captain free of commission; the captain being indebted to the charterers in certain sums, as per acknowledgment elsewhere. The freight earned by the vessel to be held as general lien for such sums." This is signed Thomas Jennings, for Messrs. Pedro Martinez & Co. of Havannah, Zulueta & Co.

7959*. Jennings is the owner of the vessels?—Yes.

7960*. And Zulueta appears as the agent to Messrs. Pedro Martinez & Co., chartering Jenning's vessel for certain purposes?—Yes; by the extract from the first letter it appears that Zulueta bought the vessel; by the second letter he pays the expenses of the vessel; but the charter-party is made out by Thomas Jennings, as the owner of the vessel.

7961*. Sir *T. D. Acland.*] Then Zulueta acts as agent for Messrs. Pedro Martinez & Co.?—Yes; the next paper, I will read the extract from is marked "Additional Memorandum of Charter-party;" which commences, "I Thomas Jennings, captain and owner of the ship Augusta, declare I have received from Messrs. Pedro Martinez & Co. of this city, 1,100*l.* sterling, for the disbursements of the said ship, the fitting out and provisions, which I engage myself to repay, with the earnings of the same, namely, all the earnings of the ship, will be accounted for and applied to the said Messrs. Pedro Martinez & Co., they furnishing the cash for all expenses, crew's wages (including 15*l.* per month for my salary as captain). At any time when the said gentlemen may think proper to close the charter-party, I will deliver to them, or their representative, a bill of sale for the said ship, and all her appurtenances, to cover the balance due to them in the said account." It states, that Mr. Thomas Jennings is no way responsible for the settlement of the above-mentioned debt, but with the said ship and her earnings, and that Messrs. Pedro Martinez & Co. will take on themselves the insurance and risk on the vessel. This paper is dated London, 21st October, 1840, and signed "Thomas Jennings." The next paper is the bill of lading, which states the cargo to be shipped by Thomas Jennings, of Liverpool, in the Augusta, lying in the port of Liverpool and bound to Gallinas: 20 hogsheads of tobacco, 60 cases of arms, one case of looking-glasses, 10 casks copper ware, 134 bales of merchandize, 1,600 iron pots, 2,370 kegs of gunpowder, to be delivered at Gallinas to Don Alvarez, Don Angel Ximenez, and Don Jose Perez Rolla. This is dated Liverpool, 10th November 1840. The vessel had no register, but a sailing licence from the Commissioners of Her Majesty's Customs, wherein Thomas Jennings, of No. 2, James-street, Limehouse, is represented to be the owner, and that the vessel is to be employed in foreign trade. There is also an account current between Messrs. Zulueta with Thomas Jennings, master of the Augusta, amounting to 339*l*. 16*s*. 9*d*., the chief part of which is for the disbursements of the vessel. I further state to the Committee, that ten letters were found on board this vessel, dated Cadiz, and addressed to three notorious slave merchants at Gallinas: in one of these letters, addressed to Señor Ignacio Perez Rolla, at Gallinas, dated Cadiz, 30th November 1840, is a paragraph to the following effect: "In a letter, dated London the 21st instant, which I have just received from Messrs. Zulueta & Co., merchants, in London, I had the pleasure of receiving a bill drawn by you on them for 250*l*., which I this day place to their credit, waiting your advice of the same." This letter is signed "M." but no name. The other letters were all on slave business; not a word of any innocent trade, but the whole directing how slaves were to be shipped on board various vessels.

7962*. Who were they signed by?—All signed in the same way.

7963*. Signed "M."?—Yes, and to the best of my recollection, every vessel to which they referred was captured by Captain Denman and myself.

7964*. Where were these letters dated from?—From Cadiz; the Vanguardia was captured by Captain Denman; the Uracca by myself, the Diana also; the other vessel referred to in the letters is the Gabriel, which vessel fired upon the boats of Her Majesty's vessel Termagant, killing three or four of her crew, and has been since captured by the Acorn, Captain Adams. Therefore these letters at once show that the three persons to whom they were addressed, residing at Gallinas, and who were the parties to whom the Augusta was consigned, were most extensively engaged in slave dealing. No other letters were found on board the Augusta but those that related to slave dealing.

7965*. The Augusta had touched at Cadiz on her way out from England?—Yes, and landed part of her cargo at Cadiz, although it was consigned to be delivered at Gallinas.

7966*. What are the inferences that you draw from these papers?—That Zulueta, by the letter of the 20th of August, 1840, advanced the money for the purchase of the vessel; that by the letter of the 26th of September, that Zulueta advanced the money to defray her expenses and fitting out, necessary before she proceeded to sea; that Mr. Jennings was put in as the owner, when in fact he was not the owner; that Zulueta was perfectly aware of this, and that he chartered the vessel to carry a cargo on behalf of Messrs. Pedro Martinez & Co. of Havannah, a notorious slave dealer, which cargo was to be delivered to three notorious slave dealers at the Gallinas; that afterwards these notorious slave dealers at Gallinas were to have the direction of the vessel for the future proceedings; and, moreover, that at any time Messrs. Martinez, or their agents, thought proper to close the charter party, the vessel was to be given up to their agents, by which means, a ship bearing English colours was certainly employed by notorious slave dealers; she was to be directed in her voyage by slave dealers; and she was, at any time these notorious slave dealers thought proper to name, to be given up to them entirely. This transaction, with the purchase of the vessel, and a person put in as the nominal owner who was not the owner, cannot but stamp a character that the vessel was engaged, with the knowledge of Zulueta, in some trade that they were desirous should not be discovered.

7967*. Mr. *Forster.*] Inform the Committee in what way you connect Messrs. Zulueta & Co. illegally with any improper transaction there, or what part of the transaction which you have detailed it was not competent for foreign merchants to perform as agents in this country; mention which part they were not bound to perform, provided they received instructions from their agents at Havannah to do it, having money in their hands to make a purchase of the vessel and ship the goods?—Messrs. Zulueta must be aware that it is contrary to law to act as agents, or otherwise, for the shipment of goods that are to be employed in the slave trade; they were bound to do no thing illegal; they are merchants residing in England, and they must conform themselves to the laws of England, and they cannot, by the laws of England, plead ignorance of those laws.

7968*. *Chairman.*] You conceive it would be unlawful for an agent in this country to ship goods to be employed in the slave trade?—Yes.

7969*. Mr. *Forster.*] How is a merchant acting in this country in pursuance of orders from his correspondent abroad to know what that correspondent means to do with the goods which he purchases on his account and ships at Liverpool?—In this case I think it is plain that Messrs. Zulueta entered into a scheme for chartering and purchasing a vessel, and putting in an owner, and establishing a British character to a vessel that he could not be ignorant was to be engaged in the slave trade, or in some trade which, for reasons that Messrs. Martinez may have, that they wished to keep in the back ground, and that secrecy alone ought to have called from Messrs. Zulueta a degree of vigilance, and more particularly a vessel being bound to a place on the coast of Africa, where, if they had taken the slightest trouble in the world, they must have known there were no constituted authorities or custom-house officers, or any persons of an European nation who could ascertain if she was engaged in legal trade.

7970*. Then, in fact, you think it is imperative on the English merchant, before he executes the orders of his foreign correspondent, in any matter relating to the trade between Brazils, Cuba, and the coast of Africa, to send out and inquire the character of the party with whom the transaction is connected on the coast of Africa?—I have stated nothing of the sort; but I have endeavoured to be particular in making it appear that this vessel was chartered to a place where there were no constituted authorities. A vessel to be chartered to the Brazils or Cuba, or any country where authorities existed in the colony of a recognized nation, would materially alter the position of Messrs. Zulueta; but Messrs. Zulueta, as I before stated, residing in England, it became the duty of that house to be guarded that they did not break the laws.

7971*. Do you speak of this as a matter of prudence and taste on the part of Zulueta & Co., or as an act of criminality?—As far as I am able to give my own opinion, I believe that Messrs. Zulueta were perfectly criminal; at least they had a perfect knowledge of what they were doing. I think I am borne out in that by the secrecy they have endeavoured to purchase, and putting in a false owner. Messrs. Zulueta have been for a number of years agents to the notorious Pedro Blanco; they have also before this purchased and sent out to the Havannah a notorious slave vessel called the Arrogante, which circumstance was represented by Mr. Tolme, Her Majesty's consul at the Havannah, to the English Government, and is also in the printed correspondence laid before parliament, either for the year 1839 or 1840. In fact, there can be no want of evidence to show that Messrs. Zulueta had for a length of time been agents to slave dealers; and I think it is impossible that any merchant can be an agent and ship cargoes of goods without ascertaining some knowledge of the party for whom they are shipped.

7972*. in the first place, you assume that it was illegal for Messrs. Zulueta & Co. to ship these goods to Alvarez at the Gallinas; are you quite sure that that is not a gratuitous assumption of law on your part?—I am speaking from my own belief; I cannot say what the law is, but I am speaking from my own belief, and the inferences I can draw from the vessel's papers. I think the papers are quite conclusive to the mind of any man that Zulueta was cognizant of what he was doing; but as far as it is an illegal transaction it is not for me to judge, but the judge of the Vice-Admiralty Court of Sierra Leone did think it illegal, and condemned the vessel; and, moreover, the man who is put forward as captain and owner did not defend the vessel on her trial.

7973*. Are you quite sure he had the means to do so?—He cannot plead as an excuse that he had not the means, for the owner of a vessel in a British port, with a cargo worth between 4,000*l.* and 5,000*l.*, I think, could always manage to raise 30*l.* or 40*l.* for the defence of his vessel.

7974*. Was that cargo in his possession, or was it under seizure at the time you speak of?—The vessel and all was seized by me, but still there was the captain and the owner present, and nothing was touched until the condemnation took place.

7975*. How could he offer security and raise money on a seized ship and cargo?—To say how he is to do so is not for me; I am not a mercantile man, but I only observe, that it is most extraordinary that the owner of a ship, with a cargo on board, cannot, in a British port, raise 50*l.* for the defence of that vessel.

7976*. But how can you affect any wonder on that subject, when you yourself admit that you do not know how he was to do it?—I have already stated that I am no mercantile man, and to say how these things are done, I cannot.

———

MINUTES OF EVIDENCE
TAKEN BEFORE
THE SELECT COMMITTEE ON WEST COAST OF AFRICA.
Mercurii, 22° die Junii, 1842.

MEMBERS PRESENT.

Mr. Aldam.
Sir T. D. Acland.
Captain Fitzroy.
Sir Robert H. Inglis.

Mr. Milnes.
Mr. W. Patten.
Mr. Stuart Wortley.

Captain the Honourable *Joseph Denman*, R. N. called in; and Examined.

6540. *Chairman.*] Will you state what your service on the coast of Africa has been?—My first acquaintance with the coast of Africa was in the year 1834, when I took over a slave vessel from Rio Janeiro. In the year 1835 I commanded the Curlew, upon that coast, for a considerable period; and for the last two years I have been in charge of the coast between Cape Verde and Cape Palmas. I was the senior officer upon that district.

6541. What has been the course of the slave trade since your acquaintance with the coast of Africa; has it decreased in extent, or changed its direction?—Since my first acquaintance with the coast, the slave trade has changed in many most important particulars, both with regard to the locality and with regard to the method in which it has been carried on.

6542. Will you state first, as to the locality, in what respect it has changed?—In the year 1835, when the Equipment Treaty came into force, the effect was, in a great measure, to drive the slave trade into the south latitude, where it was carried on with perfect impunity, under the flag of Portugal, by the then existing treaty. They then found that upon the north coast they could carry on the slave trade, by using the flag of Portugal, exactly as before.

6543. By the north coast, you mean north of the equator?—Yes: but from the end of the year 1839 they have been equally shut out from the Portuguese and from the Spanish flag. Up to that period no check whatever had been effected. Since that period I conceive that the slave trade has diminished to one-half what it was before.

6544. Not only north of the equator, but along the whole coast?—Along the whole coast of Africa. The whole amount of the export of slaves from Africa is, in my opinion, now, not one-half what it was previously to the Act of 2 Victoria, empowering us to capture Portuguese ships fitted for the slave trade. The effect of all former changes had been to throw the slave trade under the flag of Portugal, where it received a perfect protection in the southern latitude, and in the northern latitude was on the same footing on which it had been always since the trade was first established.

6545. Does the trade seem now to look to any flag to cover itself under?—They seem to have been deprived of every flag they could possibly look to; they no longer receive protection from any flag.

6546. Not from the American?—Not from the American flag, decidedly, except indirectly.

6547. Do you conceive that the present system, if carried on with the same amount of force, will reduce the slave trade to a still greater extent?—My opinion is, that the system of blockade is that which alone can be successful under any circumstances, but that to render it effective we want a considerable increase of force; with an increase of force I believe that in three years the slave trade may be demolished and exterminated.

6548. Sir *T. D. Acland.*] In the south as well as in the north?—Yes; there is no longer any difference since the 2nd of Victoria.

6549. *Chairman.*] Do you contemplate a blockade of the whole coast?—I contemplate the blockade of those parts where the slave trade is carried on.

6550. Do you believe that a material check to the trade, or an extirpation of the trade for two or three years, in any one place, makes it difficult to resume it afterwards, if the interference of the cruizers is suspended?—It turns the trade into another course. When once the trade is interrupted at any place, people are not in the habit of sending traders up the country for slaves, and traders from the interior cease to bring slaves down to them there, and there is great difficulty felt in resuming it; and in almost every instance legitimate commerce comes in, and the wants of the natives are supplied by those means; but I would not in such cases suspend the interference of the cruizers altogether, until the slave trade should be entirely eradicated.

6551. You believe that when the slave trade is checked for a period, legitimate commerce grows up in its place, and the desire to resume it is diminished?—I think the desire to resume it is diminished, in the first place, principally on account of the difficulty of resuming it. I believe that all over Africa the natives prefer the slave trade to any other trade.

6552. But you conceive that the lawful trade co-operates with the efforts of the cruizers?—In speaking of lawful trade I think it is necessary to state, that in my opinion the only legitimate trade of Africa, in the strict sense of the term, is that wherein goods are paid for in produce; all other trade, more or less, is connected with the slave trade.

6553. You mean that the money by which goods are paid for can only have been acquired by the slave trade?—Universally by the slave trade; dollars are brought upon the coast by no other means.

6554. Mr. *Forster*.] Those dollars and doubloons being diffused over the coast, in what way would you propose to stop the circulation of them?—I do not propose to stop the circulation of them.

6555. *Chairman*.] When you say "lawful trade," you mean trade which you would consider as free from any connexion with the slave trade?—Trade which is altogether unconnected with the slave trade.

6556. Where it is a mere exchange of goods for produce, you see no connexion with the slave trade?—No connexion whatever.

6557. But where you see an exchange of goods for money, there you conceive there is at least a suspicion of the slave trade?—I do not think that an individual receiving dollars or money upon the coast should of necessity be suspected or accused of engaging in or conniving at the slave trade in any way; I merely say that such transactions do indirectly partake and mingle with slave-trading transactions.

6558. Because the money is brought upon the coast originally only by the slave trade?—Yes.

6559. But the parties receiving the money may be totally exempt from any connexion themselves with the slave trade?—They may be certainly unconnected with the slave trade altogether.

6560. Wherever the slave trade is carried on, there probably money will be found?—Invariably.

6561. And therefore those who deal in lawful goods, in places where the slave trade is also carried on, will probably receive money in the course of their transactions?—In many places altogether money.

6562. What is the change in the system of blockade at present, as compared with the former system?—Under the former system we had no power over the ship until the slaves were actually on board. The consequence was, that if a man-of-war lay in a port full of slavers, as I have seen Whydah, with ten or a dozen slavers at one time, so long as the man-of-war was in sight they would not ship their slaves; directly the man-of-war was out of sight they shipped their slaves; and every vessel in the harbour would weigh their anchor and set sail. The cruizer would probably chase the wrong ship, and after having chased 100 miles would be laughed at by the master of her, and told that he only did it as a *pasatiempo*.

6563. Then the change of system is essentially dependent upon the power of seizing under the equipment treaty?—Yes, entirely; the system of blockade is only effective in consequence of that change in the powers of the cruizers.

6564. Sir *T. D. Acland.*] The equipment treaty allows you to enter rivers, and to board ships even while lying in the river?—The equipment treaties do not give any new rights as regards places.

6565. Under that treaty you may examine slavers lying in the river, and seize them there?—The sole difference is this, we might have searched them formerly as we may search them now, but we could not seize them before unless slaves were on board.

6566. *Chairman.*] Are you acquainted with the condition of the leeward coast?—I have not been on the leeward coast since the year 1835.

6567. You cannot speak to the condition of that coast as to the slave trade?—I can state that then it was carried on to an enormous extent; that I knew 20 sail of vessels to be there, and that under those former treaties every one of those 20 escaped with full cargoes of slaves.

6568. You have been cruizing the last two years to the north of Cape Palmas?—I have.

6569. What are the points that have been principally the resort of the slave trade during that period?—The Gallinas, to an enormous extent; New Cestos, which lies to the southward of Mesurado, between Mesurado and

Cape Palmas; Sea-bar at the Sherboro' river; the rivers Pongas, Bissao, and Cacheo.

6570. Which should you say have been the places from which the slave trade has been carried on with the greatest vigour?—The Gallinas, immeasurably more than any other place; but at Bissao, since the destruction of the Gallinas, owing to the great difficulty of cruizing there, it has increased, and no doubt will increase more, unless proper measures are taken.

6571. What is the great difficulty of cruizing off Bissao?—There is an inland navigation, a chain reaching from Bissao to the sea upon the north. There are innumerable islands to the south, amongst which there are seven or eight different passages by which the slavers could escape; and there is the Portuguese settlement of Bissao, under which a slaver may lie with perfect impunity under the Portuguese flag. From all those circumstances, there is the greatest difficulty in the cruizers operating effectually there.

6572. You have not the right of capturing under the walls of either a Spanish or a Portuguese fort?—No, we cannot supersede their municipal laws; all we can do is to remonstrate with the authorities.

6573. But you may seize as soon as the vessel is out of their waters?—Yes; but they take care never to go out when you are in the neighbourhood; they can get the most perfect information by canoes.

6574. Would steamers be especially adapted for cruizing on that coast?—I consider two steamers indispensable for eradicating the slave trade between the isle of Bulama and Bissao, assisted by two cruizers at least; but a yet more important object is the occupation of the Bulama island, from which the slavers have received the greatest possible assistance, and the occupation of which would directly intercept the principal supply of slaves. It is an island not only of immense importance as regards commerce, but also of extraordinary fertility.

6575. Is it salubrious?—I cannot say that any part of the coast of Africa is salubrious, but I have no reason to believe that it is less so than other parts; this inland is one of the last importance; I do not think it is possible to appreciate it without seeing Captain Belcher's chart.

6576. What is the importance of that island to commerce?—It is at the mouth of all the rivers; the river Nunez, which is a river of vast importance, in my opinion, and the Rio Grande, and the Rio Pongos. It intercepts the trade with Bissao completely.

6577. Do those great rivers open out a fertile country?—I think not, generally; I think the banks are generally very swampy near the sea; but there is a very large inland trade brought down the river, both in slaves and produce: the slaves are carried almost entirely to Bissao.

6578. Sir *R. H. Inglis.*] You have referred to the occupation of the island of Bulama, as furnishing by its geographical position a most important station for the prevention of the slave trade, was not it selected by Captain Beaver for that purpose, and was not its almost proverbial unhealthiness the cause of its abandonment?—I believe there was a great deal of prejudice upon the subject; I believe, moreover, that the settlement was most injudiciously selected for health, and I think, besides, that if you compare it with certain periods at Sierra Leone, and every other part of the coast, there will be found periods quite as unhealthy at other places as at Bulama. I think Captain Beaver's account of the island fully explains the causes of the sickness. It was very much from the misconduct of the people. I know that when orders came out to declare the sovereignty of Great Britain over that island, 1,600 persons at Sierra Leone volunteered to me to go there to settle it at a time when the emigrant ships could not get a man, so high was the impression of the people as to its advantages.

6579. Mr. *W. Patten.*] Are none of the other islands so well situated?—None to be compared to this, and this is the only one over which we have any claim.

6580. In point of health how are the other islands as compared with Bulama?—I have no means of judging, being inhabited by barbarous piratical people, with whom we have no sort of intercourse at present; the policy of the Portuguese is to keep all the persons surrounding their settlement in the most barbarous state.

6581. Mr. *Aldam.*] What is the nature of the land on the opposite coast?— All swampy, I believe.

6582. Then is not the island necessarily unhealthy?—No, I think not; I think that if the sea coast on the western side of the island was occupied, it would not be so; it is certainly not more swampy than the Gambia itself, and many other settlements.

6583. Mr. *Forster.*] You attribute the failure of Captain Beaver to the inadequacy of the means that he employed rather than to the fault of the island?—I think it was a great deal owing to that; I think there is no proof that the island is unhealthy to the extent supposed, and I believe the island might be immediately peopled by blacks.

6584. Have you in the course of your cruizing on the coast of Africa seen any part that appeared to you to be so eligible for a settlement as the island of Bulama?—I have already stated in as strong terms as I am able, the importance of the island, in my opinion, in every respect; there may be places that I should suppose to be more healthy; for instance, Sierra Leone itself, is apparently the most healthy part of the whole coast, but there seems to be great doubt whether it is so.

6585. Mr. *Aldam*.] If the opposite coast is swampy, would not fever almost always prevail there when the wind sets from the land?—I am not at all able to say what causes fever, for we find it under all circumstances; you find sometimes swampy places less unhealthy than high places.

6586. Mr. *Forster*.] Did you land on the island of Bulama?—Yes.

6587. Have you seen any considerable portion of the island?—No, I have not, excepting the coast.

6588. Is it your opinion that there is open ground there?—I found the ground under cultivation, and therefore only told the people that it was a British island; I thought it would have been injudicious to remove them and let jungles spring up before the Government took possession of it.

6589. You saw no extraordinary obstacle to the cultivation and improvement of the island?—Decidedly not; I think it is the most favourable spot for cultivation I have seen upon the coast of Africa.

6590. Have you been up to the river Nunez or the river Pongas?—I have been up the Nunez and the Pongas.

6591. To what distance?—I went up the Nunez as high as Kacundy, about 40 or 50 miles in a direct line; it is where the British factories are; it is the place to which all the trade of the Foota-Jallon nation is brought.

6592. Did you land upon the banks of the river?—Yes; I was five days in the river altogether.

6593. Did you see any thing of the state of the cultivation?—I had no means of judging; I do not believe the exports of the produce raised in the neighbourhood of the river itself at all important; the important commerce is that which is brought down from Foota-Jallon; and the opportunities I had of judging gave me the highest impression of the state of that country. I think they are far superior to any other African people I have ever had the means of acquiring a knowledge of; they are a Foolah nation, in the Foota-Jallon country; Teembo is the capital.

6594 Mr. *Forster*.] You found those British factories depending entirely upon the protection of the natives, without any British establishment to assist them?—I went up for the purpose of affording them protection; there is no

Government establishment of any sort, nor do I think it desirable there should be.

6595. Sir *T. D. Acland.*] What is the ground of that opinion?—That the river is exceedingly unhealthy; and my opinion is that the Government influence would be quite as well supported by occasional visits by steam ships, and Bulama would afford support to the trade, if colonized.

6596. *Chairman.*] What kind of settlement do you contemplate upon the island of Bulama?—A colony of black people, with any traders there that choose to go there, supported by a small fort, with a detachment of the African corps.

6597. Sir *T. D. Acland.*] Under the English Government?—Under the English Government.

6597*. And visited by steamers?—And visited by steamers and cruizers.

6598. Mr. *W. Patten.*] What time does it require to go from Sierra Leone to Bulama?—It depends a great deal upon the time of year; I should say, generally, the passage might be made in less than three days.

6599. Do you recollect the distance?—I am not quite sure; 200 miles, I should think.

6600. Sir *T. D. Acland.*] Would you have this colony dependent upon the Government of Sierra Leone?—Yes, I think decidedly.

6601. Mr. *Forster.*] Tn preference to its being attached to the Gambia?—It depends upon the facility of communication between the two; whichever the communication is most easy with, I should say it should be connected with. I am not prepared to say at this moment with which the communication is most easy.

6602. Sir *T. D. Acland.*] But at all events you think it should be dependent upon one or the other, not separate?—I think so.

6603. Mr. *Forster.*] You were understood to say that the country up the River Nunez, and the River Pongas, is swampy in the interior?—The mouths of the rivers are swampy, but up the Nunez there is good rising ground; the Pongas is a succession of creeks joining each other.

6604. Did you become acquainted with the fact up the Nunez of the growth of coffee on the mountains?—I became aware of the fact of coffee growing in whole forests, which have been hitherto neglected in consequence of the duties amounting to a prohibition.

6605. Is it your opinion that the slave trade is carried on in the Nunez to any material extent?—The Portuguese settlement of Bissao has small boats and canoes collecting slaves, together with produce, as far down as the north bank of the Sierra Leone river; there are many of those boats and canoes employed in the Nunez, but to the best of my belief no vessel has carried slaves from thence for several years, except in one instance, where, under the plea of recruits, the French took away a cargo.

6606. *Chairman.*] The canoes go about picking up a few at a time, and collecting them into a store, as it were, at Bissao and Cacheo?—At Bissao and Cacheo; I have no doubt that there are also barracoons upon the Bissagos islands, but I had no opportunity to examine as to the fact.

6607. Mr. *Forster.*] You do not consider the British factories in Rio as at all responsible for those proceedings?—Decidedly not; I have no reason to suppose that they are.

6608. How do you account for so few cruizers having generally visited that part of the coast hitherto?—Because the station which I had charge of has generally been very short of cruizers; the only means of communication was by boats, and owing to the long exposure, and the fatigue it occasioned, it invariably cost the lives of about a fourth of the people employed, whereas a steamer might do in one day what boats take four or five days to do.

6609. *Chairman.*] How would you provide fuel for the steamers in those parts?—I am not aware how far wood might be substituted for coal; I think in that part wood certainly might be used, because they would be able to take in supplies so frequently.

6610. They would have no long distances to go?—Not in that district.

6611. So that they need never be far removed from the depôts?—Precisely; there might be depôts at Bulama, and at the Gambia, and at Sierra Leone; the great difficulty is the engineers; you are obliged to have white engineers at present, but there is no sort of reason why black people of Sierra Leone should not be brought up for the purpose. There are numbers sufficiently educated for the purpose, and with proper instruction, in the course of a few years, they would supersede the necessity for white engineers.

6612. Mr. *Forster.*]—Have you not found the natives rather remarkable for the quickness and facility with which they learn mechanical operations of that kind?—I have found them quite equal to white people in that respect, possessing great intelligence, and quickness, and shrewdness, making allowance for their want of education and barbarous habits in general.

6613. Mr. *Wortley.*] Did you ever consider how far it would be possible to establish an effective blockade upon the coast which has been the scene of the slave trade by means of a combination of steamers and sailing cruizers?—I believe that by such means, by taking certain districts of the coast pointed out by particular circumstances, and effectively and continuously blockading those parts, and then moving from point to point, leaving a smaller force to prevent the slave trade from reviving, that system would be perfectly effective in the course of three years, supposing the forces to be increased.

6614. Sir *T. D. Acland.*] From what point to what point?—I speak merely of the West Coast, I have no knowledge of the East; but I have no hesitation in saying that it might be effected from Cape Verde down to the northern part of our Cape of Good Hope dominions.

6615. Mr. *Wortley.*] In order to accomplish that object are you able to state what you imagine would be the necessary force of steamers and cruizers?—I should say that steamers are only necessary in particular parts; I should say that six steamers would be quite enough.

6616. *Chairman.*] And how many sailing-vessels?—There are now upon the coast sixteen sailing-vessels; I would increase them by at least one-half; I would withdraw all the cruizers now employed in checking the slave trade on the other side of the Atlantic; I consider them, as regards the suppression of the slave trade, as entirely useless.

6617. Do you know what number are employed on the other side of the Atlantic?—On the other side of the Atlantic they have various other duties to perform; I can scarcely say that any of them are exclusively employed in this service.

6618. Mr. *Wortley.*] But the whole number there is rendered large by having this service to perform?—Yes.

6619. Can you say what number it would be possible to dispense with, in case the slave trade service were discontinued on the other side of the Atlantic?—I cannot answer this question, as they have various other duties to perform, and are not exclusively employed against slave trade.

6620. When you said that you would increase the number of cruizers by one-half, did you mean that you would increase it by one-half, including the number of steamers that you propose to have?—No, excluding those; I would make the present 16 vessels 24, and have six steamers in addition.

6621. And you think that if there were a force of that kind employed upon the West Coast of Africa, it would have the effect of entirely suppressing the slave trade?—If a proper system of blockade were adopted, I have no doubt of it.

6622. *Chairman.*] Do you consider that it is useless, towards putting down the slave trade, to capture slave vessels off the coast of Brazil or the West

Indies?—My opinion is, that any captures there are such utter chance that they do no good whatever, as on that side not one vessel out of ten can ever be captured, and wherever it is reduced to a chance at all, the profits are sufficient to keep up the slave trade. My opinion is, that the only way in which the slave trade can be stopped is in the interior of Africa. Every slave vessel that sails with her cargo of slaves has already done all she can to keep the slave trade going in Africa. The native dealer has his profit upon them; he does not care where she goes to, or what becomes of the slaves afterwards.

6623. Mr. *Forster.*] Is not a slave vessel captured on the western side of the Atlantic, equally a loss to the slave dealer as a slave vessel captured on the eastern side of the Atlantic?—My opinion is, that the amount of loss to the slave dealer is of little consequence, seeing that it is the result of chances which, in that quarter, must be always immensely in favour of the slave dealer, and that, compared with the chance of escape, the chance of capture is nothing; the profits are so large that the risk will be readily incurred.

6624. *Chairman.*] You think that the chance of escape is much greater with cruizers on the western side of the Atlantic than on the eastern?—My opinion is, that if the slaves are once on board, the mischief is already done.

6625. Mr. *Aldam.*] Do you think that the only effect of capturing a slave ship off the coast of America, is to increase the price of slaves, and that any increase which that can cause, the planters can still afford to pay?—The capture of a slave ship after her slaves are on board inflicts a heavy loss on the owners; but while embarkation can be effected to any extent, slave trade can never be stopped. The mere fact of keeping cruizers on the American side of the Atlantic is in itself an absolute proof of the want of success of our efforts, and the strongest argument in favour of the system I recommend. While slaves can be introduced, planters can afford to pay almost any price.

6626. Mr. *Wortley.*] Do you think it would be possible to suppress the slave trade by any system pursued in the interior of Africa, without an effectual suppression of the trade upon the coast?—The only way in which I contemplate the suppression of the slave trade in the interior of Africa, is by the suppression of the embarkation of slaves.

6627. As long as the temptation upon the coast exists, do you think it impossible to put an end to the slave trade in the interior?—Precisely; as long as embarkation takes place, that temptation continues, and the slave trade of the interior remains untouched.

6628. *Chairman.*] Has not the cruizing off the coast of Africa the additional advantage of protecting British trade incidentally, and showing to the natives before their eyes that the English flag is actively exerted to put down that traffic, which advantages would not be secured by cruizing on the western side of the Atlantic?—Certainly, it is one of our first duties to protect British trade, and in that respect I have no doubt it is useful, as well as in the suppression of the slave trade.

6629. Is it not of considerable advantage in a traffic like that upon the coast of Africa, that the British power should be pretty frequently displayed?—It is highly necessary.

6630. *Chairman.*] Supposing even the chance of capture to be equal in the two cases, has not cruizing off the coast of Africa the further advantage of checking or entirely preventing the horrors of the middle passage?—If you capture a full vessel upon the coast of Africa, she has nearly the same voyage to Sierra Leone from many parts: it depends upon circumstances.

6631. Sir *R. H. Inglis.*] You have stated that the slave trade is a favourite trade throughout Africa; would, therefore, the prevention of the slave trade, whether on the east or on the west of the Atlantic, remove the temptation in the one case more than in the other?—My opinion is, that the temptation is removed alone by throwing difficulties in the way of embarkation; because, as long as the native can sell his slaves, he does not care where they go to; he goes and buys more slaves.

6632. *Chairman.*] Would you think it advantageous if the cruizers were allowed to fit up one of their prizes as a cruizing tender?—It would be undoubtedly of great advantage, but it would be contrary to the treaties.

6633. To all the treaties?—I think to all the treaties; and it would be open to great abuses.

6634. What abuses?—I think you would have young midshipmen and people cruizing away in those vessels, and getting into scrapes, by improperly searching foreign vessels.

6635. You regard the duty as one of rather a delicate nature, which is not to be entrusted to subordinate officers?—The most difficult and the most delicate that a British officer can be entrusted with; the immense mischief produced by an indiscreet search, by giving offence to foreign nations, has been very much experienced.

6636. Do not the treaties require that officers of a certain rank shall alone be empowered to carry out the search?—That is the case in most of the treaties.

6637. Mr. *Wortley.*] Has not there been an improvement of late years in the class of vessels employed in cruizing?—Very great; I believe that for some years they have been replacing the old brigs with a superior class of vessels; fast sailing vessels, which are quite equal to the slavers in sailing qualities.

6638. Are you aware whether that change has been followed by a perceptible increase of efficiency in the service?—That change was about contemporaneous with the change by the Act of the 2d of Victoria; you cannot distinguish between the effects of the two.

6639. According to your observation, should you say that the present class of vessels is an efficient class for the service for which they are employed?— Decidedly; there are still a few of the old class, but they have been always replaced at the expiration of their term of service by efficient vessels.

6640. How are they in point of sailing as compared with the generality of slavers?—They are generally superior; I commanded one for two years, and I never chased a vessel that I did not overhaul; some got away from darkness coming on, but I had the advantage in point of sailing in every instance.

6641. What vessel was that?—The Wanderer, a 16-gun brig.

6642. *Chairman.*] What are the respective functions that you would assign to the sailing-vessel and to the steamer, the two acting in combination?—The steamer, I think, should be probing the rivers and ranging about the coast; the sailing-vessel should be as much as possible a fixture at the place where the slaves are put on board, which should never be left unguarded for an hour. The steamer should be employed in going from place to place to see whether from new places they are making arrangements to embark slaves, and also for carrying provisions and water, and in chasing; but steamers could not entirely blockade, because they are so much more frequently obliged to leave their stations for supplies.

6643. Mr. *Wortley.*] What was the system you generally pursued in the course of your service; did you pass your time principally in stationary blockade, or were you upon a moving cruize?—When I took charge of the station, the orders I issued to the other cruizers (as well as what I practised myself) were, to maintain the principle of blockade; and if they chased a vessel off a certain port where slaves were shipped, never to lose sight of that port; but if they could not catch the vessel without losing sight of it, to go back again, for she was sure to come back again, and there was no harm done. If, on the other hand, the chase is continued to any distance, other vessels might get in and ship slaves; and even the very one pursued might dodge the cruizer at night, and run in and effect her escape with a cargo.

6644. Mr. *Aldam.*] Then where would you place the six steamers you propose to have?—I would have two between Cape Mesaduro and the river Gambia, principally stationed at the Bissagos; but those operations I speak of would very soon alter the character of the trade, and it would be removed from point to point. I think there should be two more steamers, perhaps, between

Cape Formosa and Cape Palmas, and two more to the southward of those points.

6645. Mr. *Forster.*] Do you think they could be navigated with wood fuel entirely?—I am not prepared to answer that question, but I think not; I think coal would be required upon most parts of the coast.

6646. Mr. *Aldam.*] What would be the size of the steamers necessary, the tonnage, and the power of the engine?—The steamers on the coast of Africa ought to be small steamers, not drawing more than five or six feet water.

6647. *Chairman.*] Might not the slave vessels be useful as tenders sometimes after condemnation?—Under the treaties we are not empowered to buy them. In the Act of 2d Victoria, there is a clause by which the Government can take any captured vessel that they please for the purpose of a tender,—one was established by me under that clause by orders from the Admiralty,—but not to cruize; simply to convey the prize crews to their proper ships.

6648. Mr. *Forster.*] Do not you consider the British settlements on the coast of Africa an important assistance in the suppression of the slave trade?—I consider that the settlements on shore have done some service in that way, but not half so much as they might have done.

6649. *Chairman.*] Will you state the grounds of that opinion?—With regard to Sierra Leone, I have no hesitation in saying, that the slave trade has derived great advantage from it, and that the British influence does not extend there much beyond the limits of the colony as regards this object. The entrance of the Sherboro' river has on one side of it Sierra Leone, and there is a slave trade carried on there, and that has been owing to the view which the Government took of General Turner's proceeding in 1826, the consequence of which has been to prevent future governors from attempting similar plans.

6650. What were those plans?—To obtain the sovereignty of the coast down as far as the Boom Kittam river, which lies on the south side of the Sherboro', and from thence, I believe, to Cape Mount.

6651. Mr. *Forster.*] Had he already entered into treaties for that purpose?—He had already got possession as far as the Boom Kittam, and the Government ordered that that should be relinquished again.

6652. *Chairman.*] In what way has Sierra Leone lent assistance to the slave trade?—The slave vessels have been repeatedly purchased there by people, notoriously agents of Pedro Blanco, and others at Gallinas, and they have gone back into his hands.

6653. Mr. *Forster.*] Do you think the settlement of Sierra Leone was so much responsible for that as the system under which the vessels were sold?—I think the individuals who purchased slave vessels for slave dealers were very much to blame, and it is only to be regretted that no punishment could be inflicted upon them.

6654. Sir *R. H. Inglis.*] By the law at present the slave vessels must be broken up?—Not in all cases. Under the British law, the Act of the 5th George the 4th, vessels are not broken up, so that if a vessel is condemned in British waters by the British law, she is sold, and probably goes into a slave dealer's hands the next day, which is the case also with vessels condemned under the Brazilian treaty.

6655. Mr. *Forster.*] Are you aware that those vessels are sold by auction to the highest bidder?—I am perfectly aware of that; that is according to the treaties under which they are condemned: it is no fault of the authorities of Sierra Leone nor of the Mixed Commission Court; the authorities are compelled to allow her to leave the port afterwards.

6656. If an agent of Pedro Blanco, or even Pedro Blanco himself, went into the auction room and bid the highest price he would get the vessel?—I suppose so.

6657. *Chairman.*] It is in that respect that you consider that Sierra Leone has afforded facilities to the slave trade?—It is in that respect; but, at the same time, I cannot conceive Pedro Blanco having the audacity to go into the sale room for such a purpose, or the authorities letting the vessel under such circumstances sail out of port.

6658. How could the authorities stop the vessel going out under the charge of Pedro Blanco himself, as well as under the charge of his agent?—I think the facts would be almost sufficient to prove that she was engaged in the slave trade; but there would be a difficulty, unless she had equipments about her.

6659. Mr. *Forster.*] You would not propose to punish the auctioneer who sold the vessel to the agent of Pedro Blanco?—No, he could not be responsible; he would be acting as a Government agent.

6660. Mr. *Aldam.*] If a vessel was purchased on behalf of a slave dealer at Sierra Leone, where would she clear for?—Probably for the Cape Verd Islands. I know two cases where the vessels cleared for the Cape Verd Islands; one of them I captured. I will state an instance of the way in which vessels not broken up pass into the slave trade again. The Republicano, a prize of the Fantome, was condemned at Sierra Leone; she was purchased by an individual known to be engaged in the slave trade; I went on board her and saw what her object was, that she was going to carry slaves, and I detained her.

6661*. The purchaser was a man known to be engaged in the slave trade?—Yes, and I detained her. When I went away myself I left orders with my agent, on no account to let her go without a decree of the court; but he thought that we could not prove sufficient to justify her detention, and he let her go. The purchaser then proceeded to the Cape de Verd Islands, and fitted her out for the slave trade, and she was taken off the Gallinas by Captain Hill, of the Saracen, perfectly equipped as a slave ship.

6662*. Who was the slave dealer?—He was an American; I forget his name.

6663*. Do you mean to say that he was a resident at Sierra Leone, carrying on the slave trade?—No; but I merely mention that as an instance of the way in which captured vessels, when not broken up, are afterwards employed again in the slave trade. I do not say that he was amenable to British law.

6664*. *Chairman.*] Was it the actual slave dealer who made the purchase in Sierra Leone?—He was a man known very well to be closely connected with a slave vessel lately condemned.

6665*. What was the nature of his real or supposed connexion with the slave trade?—I cannot exactly call to mind the proof of the fact; but that it was so a reference to the printed correspondence will show.

6666*. Mr. *Aldam.*] Whose name appeared as owner; was the owner of the ship that you captured a Spaniard or a Portuguese?—It was a Spanish master; she appeared as the property of the American who had made the purchase.

6667*. *Chairman.*] Have there been instances in which a slave dealer in his own person has come to Sierra Leone and made purchases of this kind?—In the case I have just mentioned he had been already brought to Sierra Leone in some vessel, but he was not known as Pedro Blanco was; but I believe there would be no means of preventing them from taking the vessel away, unless equipment was on board.

6668*. Has the colony of Sierra Leone in any other way contributed to the maintenance of the slave trade, besides the facilities which it has afforded of purchasing ships which have been condemned?—I have no doubt that some degree of communication has been kept up between the slave dealers in the neighbourhood of the Gallinas and the Sherboro', and parties in Sierra Leone.

6669*. Have you reason to know that any liberated Africans have engaged in slave dealing?—I have no actual knowledge of any such circumstance; I have no doubt that many, I have proof that some, liberated Africans have been sold again into slavery.

6670*. To any extent?—I am not able to say to what extent; I should think to a considerable extent, from cases which have fallen within my knowledge.

6671*. Sir *R. H. Inglis.*] Do you believe that they have been kidnapped?—I am unable to say whether they were kidnapped or not; I should think it most likely.

6672*. *Chairman.*] What are the cases with which you are acquainted?—There were three cases at the Gallinas. There was one case in the Pongas, where I went up and liberated a girl who had been carried off.

6673*. Had those persons been carried off from within the district of Sierra Leone, or in the course of their traffic along the coast?—The one in the Pongas had been carried off from the colony of Sierra Leone, and one of them had been taken away as a servant, and left as a pawn; in fact a slave. The other two had been taken when out of the colony.

6674*. Was the case which you alluded to as having occurred within the colony itself, a case of kidnapping or abduction conducted by inhabitants of Sierra Leone?—I have Sir John Jeremie's letter here upon the subject. By the Timmanees, I see, is the statement in the letter.

6675*. Then this is a case in which some strangers entered the country and carried off some of the inhabitants of Sierra Leone?—So it appears from the letter.

6661. Sir *R. H. Inglis.*] Then you wish the Committee to understand nothing more than that Sierra Leone has been the scene of incursions made with a view to carry persons as slaves from that part of Africa, as might have been the case from the Bonny?—I stated my belief that a considerable number had been kidnapped also by the people of Sierra Leone, and sold to natives who have carried them away, often in canoes.

6662. But you do not attribute that to any overt acts, or any neglect of the Government?—By no means; I think it is almost unavoidable under the circumstances.

6663. *Chairman.*] You have no reason to know that a system of kidnapping prevails in the colony, though individual instances may have occurred?—I have no reason to know it; but I have reason to believe that it did exist to a considerable extent, more particularly formerly, when a great number were landed from slave ships; but now that is reduced to a small number.

6664. In those instances of kidnapping you imagine that they were the acts rather of strangers to the colony than a system pursued by the inhabitants of the colony?—In many cases I think they were the acts of inhabitants of the colony, who had kidnapped people, or seduced them from the colony, and then sold them to the slave dealers.

6665. Upon what ground do you imagine that kidnapping does exist to a considerable extent in the colony?—I have heard the thing repeatedly stated with great confidence, and I think those instances go to prove it; when I went into the Gallinas I found 90 slaves, and of those 90 two were British subjects.

6666. Mr. *Forster.*] Could such a system have been carried on without the consequences of it becoming obvious to every person resident at Sierra Leone, and acquainted with the number of captured negroes in the neighbourhood?—I believe that it might at times, when there was a great influx of those black people; my opinion is, from what I have heard, but I am not able to enter into the facts very closely, that the apprenticeship system at Sierra Leone is extremely defective, and that the whole system of supervision over the liberated Africans, as well as of the apprentices, is also exceedingly bad, and open to great abuses.

6667. *Chairman.*] Would it not be the duty of the police magistrates of the district to see that there was no diminution of numbers by kidnapping?—I am not aware that there are any district police magistrates, except the superintendents of the villages.

6668. Do not those superintendents exercise the functions of magistrates?—I do not know; but they are very often taken off by sickness, and villages are frequently left without proper people to take charge of them; and I believe, in my own mind, that the system of kidnapping has gone on to some considerable extent.

6669. Mr. *Forster.*] But your opinion upon that subject is founded merely upon report?—Yes; and upon information I have received in conversation.

6670. Mr. *Aldam.*] Do you think that there is any remedy for that evil?—I think the only remedy would be to exercise more supervision over the liberated Africans, by having a larger Government establishment to some extent, and a better class of people employed.

6671. *Chairman.*] Have any other settlements given facilities to the slave trade besides Sierra Leone?—Not directly, to my knowledge; the trade of the Gambia is principally with Bissao, and at Bissao there is a great slave trade, and legitimate trade, or rather produce trade going on hand-in-hand together; the merchants of Bissao purchase quantities of slaves and quantities of produce; and again, goods supplied by the merchants at the Gambia are paid for in produce and in money; those goods, undoubtedly, are more or less used by the slave dealers in the slave trade.

6672. Sir *R. H. Inglis.*] The case to which you referred as within your own knowledge, of a person detained in the Gallinas as a slave, taken from Sierra Leone, was the case forming a subject of the Parliamentary Papers of the year 1841?—No; another case; that was a case where she had gone voluntarily into the country, and been detained.

6673. Mr. *Aldam*.] How many white people would be necessary to manage the establishment on the island of Bulama?—I do not see the absolute necessity of one white person, unless it be the officer commanding the detachment; but at the utmost, three or four, independently of those who chose voluntarily to settle in order to trade.

6674. Mr. *Forster*.] You appear to entertain a doubt whether the British settlements already on the coast have rendered as much service as they might have done for the suppression of the slave trade?—I spoke more particularly of Sierra Leone; at the same time, the connexion of the Gambia trade with the slave trade is a fact that there is no doubt about.

6675. Sir *T. D. Acland*.] Do you also include the settlements on the Gold Coast?—I have no knowledge of the Gold Coast settlements.

6676. Then your remark does not apply to them?—No.

6677. Mr. *Forster*.] When you speak in terms of disapproval of the transactions which you say have taken place between Sierra Leone and the Gallinas, do you wish the Committee to understand that you would recommend that the intercourse between Sierra Leone and the Gallinas should be put a stop to?—There is now no intercourse whatever between Sierra Leone and the Gallinas, and there has not been any for the last few years; I speak of former years.

6678. Would you think it desirable that there should be a commercial intercourse between Sierra Leone and the Gallinas?—Undoubtedly I think a commercial intercourse is the only means of eradicating the slave trade; it is the best auxiliary of the cruizers.

6679. And your opinion would be the same with respect to the intercourse between the Gambia and Bissao, that it is desirable that commercial intercourse should be continued and extended if possible between those two places?—Yes, and that it should be separated as much as possible from the slave trade.

6680. *Chairman*.] How do you distinguish the lawful from the unlawful trade carried on in a place where both are going on together?—It is almost impossible to distinguish them; for instance, at Bissao the principal slave dealer is also the principal produce dealer, Caetano or Kyetan Nossolino, with whom all the merchants at the Gambia have dealings; in my opinion, that is not a very beneficial trade, because it is not a direct trade with the natives at all; it is a trade between the slave dealer and the British merchants; he buys produce, with which he procures slaves; his principal trade is the slave trade, and he derives great advantages from his commerce with the Gambia in his slave trade.

6681. Would he not have the same facilities of getting the goods necessary for the slave trade from other sources?—He would not have the same facility; it would be much more difficult for him to get it from any other quarter, I apprehend.

6682. Mr. *Forster.*] Do you mean that it would be difficult, supposing the supply from the British settlements at the Gambia were cut off?—I think it would be more difficult.

6683. *Chairman.*] Could you stop an American or a Hamburgh vessel going in with the same produce?—Certainly not, nor would I stop an English vessel, but I should wish to consider the means by which we might separate the legitimate trade from the slave trade; my opinion is, that the separation would be best effected by the occupation of Bulama, which would put our merchants in a better position to trade themselves direct with the natives.

6684. You consider then that the trade with Bissao is now thrown too much into the hands of one man, who becomes a monopolist of the trade, and who derives advantages from it in carrying on the slave trade, which would not be derived if we had an entrepôt of our own, to which the natives could resort for goods?—I do; instead of the trade passing all through his hands, I would endeavour, by the occupation of such places as Bulama, to create a rival trade between the English merchants and the natives, instead of goods going, as they now do, through the hands of Caetano and other slave dealers.

6685. You would not, by a legislative enactment, endeavour to prevent a communication by British merchants with slave dealers, but you would rather open other means of trade which were less likely to be objectionable in their results, and thus rival the slave dealers?—Where produce trade existed to any extent at all, I would trust to such measures for the separation of the two; but there are some places where there is no produce trade whatever, where, from one year's end to another, not a single piece of ivory, or a single gallon of palm oil is exported. The Gallinas is a case in point; it is very true that British vessels can supply goods to the Gallinas, but there is, I think, a scandal in our ships supplying goods there, which does infinite harm to our claim on other nations to abolish and make an end of the slave trade.

6686. Mr. *Forster.*] How would you introduce British trade in produce at the Gallinas unless you encouraged British traders to go there?—The fact is, that wherever the slave trade exists people never turn to legitimate traffic at all, unless the slave trade is insufficient to supply their wants, or until the slave trade is stopped, or at least checked, by forcible means. When the slave trade no longer supplies what they want they are compelled to labour and raise produce, and they are then ready enough to engage in lawful trade; but the goods now brought are as much slave trade almost as the slaves that are exported.

6687. Are you not aware that in some places on the coast the slave trade has been in a great measure, if not entirely, suppressed by the force of commerce alone?—I do not know of any instance; in every case the first step has been the suppression or the check of the slave trade, and then, and not till then, do the natives labour to raise produce.

6688. Have you been to Popo lately?—I have been to Popo; the cruizers at Popo first checked the slave trade, and then the slave dealers preferred Whydah, which is in the neighbourhood, and they have since taken to legitimate trade at Popo.

6689. Are you aware that there was a considerable slave trade formerly from the Rio Nunez?—I am not particularly acquainted with the slave trade that has been carried on from thence; I know that in the year 1835 there was no great amount of slave trade from thence.

6690. You are not then aware that since the establishment of British factories there, the slave trade has entirely disappeared excepting in the way you have referred to, by the visits of Portuguese canoes picking up slaves in the neighbourhood?—I consider that simply produced by the fact of Bissao being a more convenient place; slavers lie there in perfect security under the walls of the Portuguese fort; they prefer bringing their slaves from the Nunez, which they do in great numbers, in canoes to Bissao, to shipping them direct from the Nunez, from whence the passage and the escape is much more difficult than from Bissao.

6691. Is it your opinion then that the slavers would have the same facility in procuring slaves at the place or near the place where a British factory was established, as in any other part of the coast where no such establishment existed?—I consider that the British factory would never, unassisted, put down the slave trade in any way; I can answer for the statement that I received from Mr. Benjamin Campbell, a merchant in the Nunez, and formerly in the Pongas, a man of great intelligence and great experience: his statement to me was, that directly a slave vessel came in, his factory was abandoned; that nobody would come near him when she was there; that the natives invariably preferred slave commerce to legitimate commerce.

6692. Are you not aware that the whole of the Gold Coast is at present dependent upon our settlements for the suppression of the slave trade, and that if those settlements were removed, the slave trade would be immediately resumed there?—I have no doubt whatever that the settlements on the Gold Coast have put down the slave trade, but that has been not by the unassisted force of commerce; it is because they have an establishment and force, and are able to govern the natives; it is not like a single merchant upon the banks of a river forming a factory. I have a letter from Mr. Campbell here, in which he states that when the natives hear of a slave vessel in the Pongas or Bissao, they accuse the British merchants of driving away their trade. That I believe to be an error on their part, especially as Mr. Campbell, in the same letter, states that Caetano has two white agents in the river purchasing slaves for him. I believe the reason that they go to the Bissao is because they are more secure; but the slave trade with the Nunez is by no means given up; dozens of canoes go every month with slaves.

6693. None are shipped there?—They are shipped in the canoes, and they are taken to Bissao, because Bissao is a more convenient place for sending them off.

6694. Would they not be shipped from Rio Nunez but for the presence of the British factories?—I think they may throw some doubt over the minds of people as to the probability of giving information, and so on; but I believe the reason that the slave dealers prefer Bissao is what I have stated; viz. the difficulty of escaping from the Nunez.

6695. If British factories, without a British fleet or any British force, can have a beneficial tendency in suppressing the trade, does it not follow that settlements with a British force, and British authority to support them, would be still more efficient in suppressing that trade?—That is undeniable; and I allow that the influence would be beneficial in conjunction with the naval force, but I deny the power of unassisted British factories in putting down the slave trade; I do not believe that there is a single instance of it on the whole coast.

6696. Then if British factories and British commerce cannot have that influence, you apprehend that a large British force will continue to be necessary upon that coast?—That is not what I have stated; what I have stated is, that they have never, unassisted, put down the slave trade; wherever it is put down commerce instantly springs up: and there is the strongest reason to suppose, that when the slave trade is put down generally, commerce will be established throughout Africa; and when legitimate trade exists as a habit of the people, in the course of time I look to that legitimate trade putting an end to the slave trade for ever.

6697. Mr. *Wortley.*] Your observation and experience have led you to the decided conclusion that all attempts to suppress the slave trade by inducing the natives to betake themselves to legitimate traffic would be abortive, unless the direct suppression of the slave trade was effectual?—Unless the slave trade was checked by other means; when it is checked, commerce begins, and extends by degrees.

6698. *Chairman.*] How would you carry out the principle of separation; would you proceed to prohibit certain places which you considered to have no other traffic than the slave trade till the slave trade should have been to a certain amount checked, if not extirpated from that place?—My opinion is, that there is a change required in the law. At present, English merchant ships may supply slave factories, known to every soul at Sierra Leone to be slave factories, and yet if they cannot prove that the person who sold those goods for the purpose of buying slaves, did actually and positively know in his own mind the fact of those goods being certainly to be used in the slave trade, there can be no conviction.

6699. In a case such as that of Canôt, who is a great produce dealer, as well as a dealer in slaves, would you prohibit intercourse with him?—I would not prohibit intercourse with any body: but in every case where it was clearly proved that goods were sold to a person who it was well known could only use those goods in the slave trade, and the slave trade alone, that man's character being perfectly notorious, I think that British vessels supplying him with goods, ignorant of his character, and from the want of the exercise of reasonable care and precaution, so aiding and abetting the slave trade, should be subject to the penalties of the Act.

6700. Speaking of this as a legal question to be provided for by Act of Parliament, how would you decide the proportion of produce trade which should entitle a foreign slave dealer, under such an Act of Parliament, to carry on intercourse with British traders; unless you could define that, would it not be easy for every slave dealer wishing to have that intercourse, to carry on a trade in produce, however small, sufficient to bring him within the permission given to deal with persons carrying on trade lawfully as well as unlawfully?—I do not think that it would be desirable to apply the provision very strictly; I think it would be very injudicious to be searching and inquiring in every case, whether the proceedings were of this character or not; but where there is a glaring and an unquestionable case, such as any English merchant sending goods to a slave ship, or to a factory where there is no other trade, I think he should be punished, and I think that it is highly important to the position which England holds upon this question with regard to foreign nations; my proposition is, that if from want of reasonable care he did not know that which was a notorious fact to every body else, he should be subject to the penalties.

6701. Sir *T. D. Acland.*] The trade of which you are speaking is that which is carried on with factories, notoriously used for the purpose of the slave trade; would you apply the law to such places?—I can mention a case which I think is a very strong one, the case of the Gallinas, where, to my certain knowledge, cargoes to a great extent were brought under the American flag, and other flags, solely for the purpose of purchasing slaves, the freight for all those cargoes being paid for in the Havannah, and without one single atom of produce being exported in return. Now in my opinion it was open under the Act for a British merchant ship to have carried all those goods to the Gallinas instead of an American with perfect impunity, and such a course of trade would bring the utmost scandal upon the English name, and the utmost doubt upon the sincerity of our wishes to put an end to the slave trade. You could not probably have proved to the satisfaction of juries at Sierra Leone, that they were knowingly aiding and abetting the slave trade.

6702. Mr. *Forster.*] Then to render such a law effectual you must induce all nations to enter into a common league to carry it out?—I think not; my view is, that England must leave to other countries the control of their own merchant vessels; but especially considering the situation she holds with regard to the slave trade, I think she is bound to prevent such a direct system of aiding and abetting slave trade on the part of English vessels.

6703. Do you think, if England were to do so, that it would have any real tendency to prevent the slave trader obtaining a supply of goods?—Certainly not; as in this instance he got all those goods without the assistance of the British flag; but had the British flag been used, I think it would have been an abominable disgrace.

———

Veneris, 24° die Junii, 1842.

MEMBERS PRESENT.

Sir T. D. Acland.
Mr. Aldam.
Viscount Courtenay.
Mr. E. Denison.
Captain Fitzroy.

Mr. Forster.
Mr. W. Hamilton.
Sir R. H. Inglis.
Mr. Milnes.

VISCOUNT SANDON, in the chair.

Captain the Honourable *Joseph Denman*, R. N. called in; and further
Examined.

6742. *Chairman.*] You mentioned that there had been a considerable change
in the means employed for putting down the slave trade, within the last two
or three years: and you mentioned, in the first instance, a different system of
cruizing pursued in consequence of the Equipment Treaty. Has there not
been another means lately introduced, by means of destroying the slave
factories upon the coast?—The slave factories of the Gallinas were not
destroyed as a part of the powers with which I was invested. It was in
consequence of peculiar circumstances, which I took advantage of for the
purpose.

6743. What was it that entitled you to make that attack?—For a long series
of months, the people upon the shore had been guilty of the most inhuman
conduct towards my boats, conduct which a state of war would not justify,
and which would be a fair subject of war if committed in any civilized
country.

6744. You grounded your attack upon information received of the detention
in slavery, by the son of the chief of the Gallinas, of two of Her Majesty's
subjects of the colony of Sierra Leone?—I did; but I had long previously
intended to destroy the barracoons and the slave factories, if I found the case
to be what I supposed it was, upon the grounds that I have before mentioned.

6745. What were those grounds?—The inhuman treatment of my boats. I
can show the Committee letters from the officers reporting the treatment
they had received. The circumstances detailed in those letters were reported
to me by the commander of the ship as having occurred some time
previously to the destruction of the factories. This is the report of the officer
in the boat; he wrote me this letter subsequently to the affair, at my desire,
the circumstances having been stated before. He was entrusted with one of
the Rolla's boats. He says, "I stood out for the purpose of reconnoitring, it
blowing a strong breeze, with a head sea. I had not proceeded above three
miles from the Alexander," an American brig, "when the boat was
unfortunately stove, and it was with great difficulty she was kept afloat by
constant baling with three buckets, until we arrived alongside the Alexander,
the captain of which vessel kindly allowed us to hoist her on board for the
purpose of repairing. Subsequently the captain of the Alexander going on
shore to wait on his consignees, they very strongly expressed their
disapprobation at his having rendered any assistance to a British cruizer's
boat, and at the same time regretted that he had not left us to sink or swim.
Had the captain complied with their wishes, which had been communicated
to him previous to this accident, the only resource left us would have been

to attempt beaching the boat, which, owing to the boisterous state of the weather, would have been almost impossible, and probably attended with loss of life to all or most of the crew, the bar at the time being perfectly impassable, and not the slightest probability of keeping the boat afloat for any length of time by means of baling." That is signed by Mr. George Marriott, mate. In consequence of this prohibition, refuge was repeatedly refused to my boats by friendly vessels disposed to succour them, and had any boat subsequently been in the same condition, she would have been left to drown with all her hands. My whole knowledge of this was from the circumstances reported to me by different officers.

6746. Were there other cases of the same nature?—Other cases of the same nature, produced by threats of the persons on shore, which prevented American and French vessels in the roads, otherwise disposed to do so, having done so before, from affording refuge to our boats under almost similar circumstances. But no case was so strong as that of the boat sinking.

6747. Mr. *Forster.*] Were those things done by the authority of the native chiefs, or by the authority of the Spanish slave dealers?—Before I went into the river I had no means of knowing; but I considered that the chiefs of the country were responsible for the treatment of cruizers in their waters according to the law of nations.

6748. It appears by the correspondence that the detention of a woman named Try Norman and her child were the grounds you chiefly relied upon to justify that proceeding?—I might have gone upon either ground. I preferred choosing the ground of the detention of that woman and her child; first, because it was an outrage of a far graver nature even than those I have described, which had occurred in the anchorage; and secondly, because it would enable me at once to go to the barracoons to get out all the slaves, to endeavour to find out whether Try Norman and her child were among them.

6749. By which of the chiefs was this woman detained?—By a man of the name of Manna, the eldest son of King Siacca.

6750. Did he assign any reason for detaining this woman and her child; did he justify himself in anyway?—It was impossible that he could justify himself in any way. I considered that the woman Try Norman was as much a British subject as any person in this room. I can see no distinction between his making a slave of her and his making a slave of any white person.

6751. Did he attempt any justification?—He attempted a justification which was utterly unsatisfactory. His justification was, that the person to whom she had been an apprentice had owed him money and that was the ground of his excuse, as appears in the printed correspondence.

6752. Do you know the name of the woman who, he said, owed him money?—I know nothing of it but by his own statement; the woman's name was Rosanna Gray.

6753. You have read the correspondence?—I have.

6754. Is there not a letter from this Prince Manna, complaining that one of his wives, whom he had sent to Sierra Leone for instruction, had been made a prostitute by this Mrs. Gray?—So it appears in his letter.

6755. Did not his detention of this woman and her child arise out of that transaction?—Such was his statement.

6756. Did you inquire, when you arrived at Sierra Leone, whether there was any ground for that statement?—I did make some inquiry about it, and Mrs. Gray stated that the girl had run after the men herself. I put the correspondence into the governor's hands, and requested him to afford such redress to Prince Manna as the case might require.

6757. But you ascertained that she had been under the care of Mrs. Gray?—There was no doubt of that fact, I believe.

6758. Then, at all events, you destroyed those factories and barracoons on your own responsibility, and not by virtue of any treaty with Spain?—I destroyed those barracoons upon my own responsibility, because I found that the Spanish slave dealers had been the persons who had been the cause of the inhuman treatment of my boats at sea, in the first place; in the second place, I found in those barracoons two British subjects. The destruction of the barracoons and factories was done through the medium of the consent of the native chiefs.

6759. *Chairman.*] Did you not act in some degree under instructions from the governor of Sierra Leone?—The governor of Sierra Leone had no power to give me any instructions; he merely mentioned the circumstances, and requested me to take the necessary measures for redeeming this woman; I considered that a stronger ground to go upon than that which I before intended to go upon, and I therefore adopted that which appeared most advantageous.

6760. Mr. *Forster.*] Did the native chiefs grant that authority to destroy the property of the Spaniards voluntarily?—Decidedly; they agreed to destroy it themselves, upon the grounds stated in the correspondence.

6761. It would appear by the correspondence that they showed great unwillingness to meet you and confer with you on the subject of your mission, when you arrived there?—For the obvious reason, that Prince Manna felt, that having held a British subject in captivity, he was in a very awkward position; I think that is explained in my letter to Governor Doherty.

6762. In the letter of the 20th of November you call upon King Siacca to "destroy their factories, and their contents, or consent to Captain Denman's doing so, and that he will deliver up the slaves who have been carried into the bush from the factories." You mean that he consented after you had made a requisition to this effect?—Undoubtedly; a requisition to that effect was made, because he stated that the white slave factors had got him into the scrape without his knowledge, and without his authority; and also because I found them in possession of British subjects for the purpose of exportation.

6763. The first article of your treaty with him stipulates that he shall totally destroy "the factories belonging to these white men, without delay," and in a sort of postscript to the treaty, you promise him the forfeiture of the goods belonging to the Spaniards that were deposited in the Spanish stores?—I made no promise of the sort. The postscript states, that King Siacca having declared that the white slave dealers have acted in defiance of his laws, he considers their goods are forfeited to him; for that reason my demand for their destruction was withdrawn, and I consented that he should take possession of them.

6764. In point of fact, they received as the reward of their consent, the whole of the property belonging to the Spaniards that was found in the stores at the Gallinas?—No, it was not so, for the treaty was already entered into before this permission was made; and, moreover, at the time this treaty was made they had already taken possession of the goods out of all the factories but one.

6765. But, at all events, they got the goods as the result of their proceedings?—They undoubtedly got the goods. I do not mean that the chiefs got the goods, but the people in general got the goods.

6766. Do you think that the Spaniards were settled there with the approbation or consent of the chiefs?—I believe that the Spaniards did settle there, in the first instance, with the consent of the chiefs; but I believe that they afterwards became very powerful, and were exceedingly hated by the chiefs. I had various complaints from the natives of the haughty and disgusting treatment which they received from the Spaniards.

6767. If they were so averse to the settlement of those Spanish slave dealers, how did it appear to be necessary to insert an article in the treaty, binding King Siacca that no white man should ever for the future settle in his country for the purpose of slave dealing?—I thought it desirable to prevent the possibility of the slave trade being re-established by the white people, as it had been before established.

6768. Captain *Fitzroy*.] Does it follow, that because the chiefs were averse to those Spaniards living with them, that they should also be averse to every other white man who might come there?—I thought there was a very considerable chance of the slave trade being re-established by white men afterwards.

6769. And therefore you took such steps as you thought best to prevent any similar settlement?—To prevent any similar settlement, and to give us a right to compel them to send them out of the country again if ever they should resume such practices. It was a precautionary measure.

6770. Mr. *Forster*.] Does it not seem somewhat inconsistent with the seventh article of the treaty, which stipulates that "no white man from Sierra Leone shall settle down in King Siacca's country without his full permission and consent"?—It seems to me quite in accordance with the other principle. I say, "No white man shall sit down as a slave trader." King Siacca, upon the other hand, in order to insure himself against his country being taken possession of by the English, proposes this, which I accede to. It was a proposal of the chiefs on the part of the King Siacca.

6771. Does it not imply that the king was averse to allow British traders to settle there from Sierra Leone?—I think it bears upon its face that he was averse, for the reason I have before stated.

6772. *Chairman*.] Did you feel yourself entitled, by King Siacca's country having been made the means of carrying on a slave trade, through which some of Her Majesty's subjects had been made slaves, to make stipulations which should prevent the recurrence of such an outrage for the future?— Not only entitled, but bound to do so.

6773. And you conceived that one of the most effectual means for that purpose would be to prevent other white men, foreigners, from taking advantage of King Siacca's country as a position from which to carry on a trade which endangered the safety of Her Majesty's subjects and their free passage into that neighbourhood?—I will state the principle upon which I acted, and the relation in which I considered that we stood towards King Siacca. In the first place, the outrages and inhospitality committed in his waters I considered him responsible for; secondly, I considered him responsible for holding Sierra Leone people in his country as slaves for the purpose of traffic. Upon his declaring that he knew nothing of those acts, I considered it perfectly just that the punishment should be visited upon the persons who had committed those crimes, and who had been the cause of those crimes.

6774. And you felt yourself entitled, if the king professed an inability to prevent others from taking advantage of his territory for purposes injurious to the security of British subjects, to take means yourself for securing such objects?—I entered into a treaty for the purpose of preventing future proceedings of the description that had already occurred, and enabling me to meet such cases if they should recur.

6775. Mr. *Forster.*] Is it not your opinion that it has been owing to the preference given to Spanish slave dealers that British merchants have not sooner established themselves at the Gallinas, and carried on commercial pursuits there?—In my Report to the Governor of Sierra Leone upon the state and prospects of trade in the Gallinas, in page 15 of the Printed Papers, I say, "When the English slave trade was abolished, considerable traffic sprung up and was rapidly increasing when the Spaniards commenced the slave trade in about 1817. From that time legitimate commerce gradually withered, and was at length totally annihilated by the establishment of a permanent slave factory in-shore, about 15 years ago, by Pedro Blanco, at that time mate of a slave vessel. Since then the slave trade has been the only pursuit, and during the long period that has since elapsed, not enough produce has been exported to form the cargo of the smallest coasting vessel."

6776. Had there been any legitimate trade carried on at the Gallinas previous to your operations there?—A passage in the letter I have just read states my opinion upon that subject, derived from information from the chiefs themselves.

6777. *Chairman.*] You mean by legitimate commerce, the exchange of manufactures for produce?—Exactly; and I stated that there was no legitimate commerce, because there was no produce whatever. Might I be allowed to refer to a question and answer that I understand has been put referring to the Gallinas. I have been informed that this question was put to Mr. Peters: "You do not think Captain Denman's observations upon the subject practically of any value." Now I beg to observe that Mr. Peters can never have seen my observations upon the subject. The answer of Mr. Peters is, that I thought I had put an effectual stop to the slave trade in the Gallinas, and that many others thought so.

6778. Mr. *Forster.*] In a letter to the Governor of Sierra Leone, dated the 12th of December, you say that the people at the Gallinas "have already, in a wild state, but of the finest quality, cotton, indigo, pepper, and palm nut, the sugar cane and tobacco, which they are enabled to cure. Salt is procured in considerable quantities, and there is no doubt that coffee would flourish as well as at Sierra Leone and Monrovia." Do you wish the Committee to understand that if a trader from Sierra Leone were to go there with goods, he could obtain in exchange for them any of those articles you have enumerated?—With regard to the tobacco there is a misprint; instead of "enabled to cure" it should be "unable to cure." I have stated in the same letter that no cultivation whatever did exist, and that I used every effort to persuade the chiefs to cultivate the soil. My information was derived from the chiefs as to the existence of these articles.

6779. *Chairman.*] Do cotton, indigo, pepper, palm nut, the sugar cane, and tobacco, grow there in a wild state, and are they of good quality?—It is a fact that I derived from the unanimous declaration of the chiefs of the country.

6780. Mr. *Aldam.*] Are there any means of carrying on any considerable commerce at the present moment?—Certainly not. It must begin upon a small scale, as elsewhere; it does not spring at once into a considerable commerce.

6781. Mr. *Forster.*] Are you of opinion that there is nothing questionable in the proceedings of our navy in destroying the property of foreigners in a foreign country, and encouraging the native chiefs in those proceedings, with reference to the moral effect of it upon the minds of the chiefs and the natives?—It depends entirely upon circumstances. If aggressions have been committed against persons belonging to Sierra Leone (and I can conceive no aggressions or injuries so great as that of making British subjects slaves), I consider that those people are in every respect entitled to the same protection as white people. Indeed I consider that the liberated Africans of Sierra Leone have peculiar claims to the regard and protection and favour of England. I see no distinction whatever between them and British subjects. Supposing three British subjects had been held in this way, I conceive it would have been highly improper to have allowed such a proceeding to pass unnoticed.

6782. *Chairman.*] You rest your proceeding at the Gallinas, not upon the general ground of using means for putting down the slave trade, but upon the specific offences committed by the chiefs of the Gallinas against British subjects settled at Sierra Leone, and their inhospitality to your crews upon the coast?—Precisely so.

6783. Therefore you do not consider that you are making a precedent for indiscriminate descents upon the coast, wherever a slave barracoon is established, for the purpose of destroying it as a means of putting down the slave trade?—In the proceeding adopted by me at the Gallinas, the grounds were exactly those stated in the preceding question. At the same time I conceive that the destruction of barracoons and slave places not in settlements belonging to European powers, would be justifiable all over the coast. Nothing of the sort had been done before, and therefore I did it under very heavy responsibility. I could not have struck out a new line without some special grounds to go upon.

6784. Should you consider yourself entitled, without any of those peculiar grounds for the interposition which the proceedings at the Gallinas gave you, to make a descent upon any point of the coast under the jurisdiction of a native chief, where slaves were collected for the purpose of exportation, and destroying those barracoons, and insisting upon the slave trade being given up?—I should think myself perfectly justified in doing so whoever the slave factor might be. Whether it would be borne out by my instructions from the Admiralty would depend upon what those instructions were.

6785. You would conceive yourself, if you were an officer on that station now, entitled to pursue that as a general method of putting down the slave trade?—I should certainly have pursued it had I remained.

6785*. Do you conceive yourself entitled to do this under instructions, under treaties, or entirely upon your own responsibility, without any direct authority?—I consider that it might have been done upon my own responsibility entirely, upon the footing that the law of nations can afford no sort of recognition of the dealing in slaves by Spaniards in a foreign country. And secondly, that those persons were criminals by their own laws, and could not look to protection from their own government. So long as the slave trade was clearly and distinctly separated from legitimate trade, I consider that such proceedings would have been perfectly justifiable.

6786. Supposing a native chief had collected slaves in barracoons upon his own territory for exportation, should you then have felt yourself justified in destroying such places?—I should have considered myself justified in following the same system there, upon the ground that the native chiefs are not recognized amongst the nations of the world; they are in a barbarous state, and the law of nations, in my opinion, cannot apply to them further than for their own good and their own protection, and I should have considered the destruction of those buildings and the taking off the slaves as an act most directly and most importantly tending to their own good and benefit.

6787. Captain *Fitzroy*.] It has appeared in evidence before this Committee that the Pluto sailed from Fernando Po, under orders from the Admiralty, to destroy any barracoons or other slaving establishments that she might meet with in various parts of the coast, not being the property of Europeans; were similar instructions issued to the officers on that coast while you were there?—I saw instructions to that effect a few weeks before I left that coast.

6788. From the Admiralty?—From the Admiralty.

6789. *Chairman.*] Have you been at the Gallinas since?—Yes, I have been three or four times at the Gallinas.

6790. Has the effect of what you did been to put down the slave trade, or to what extent has it done so?—It has nearly broken up the system then followed, except as regards the south-east branch of the river, upon which a place called Soolimane stands; there was, when I was at the river, a small factory there, which I did not destroy, as I had no case against it, and this is the factory which Captain Blount has recently destroyed. In the part where I went, it does not appear that any slave trade has sprung up again.

6791. You conceive then that if this process is followed, it will be effectual for its object?—My opinion is, that in such a part of the coast as the Gallinas, blockade alone is quite sufficient to stop the slave trade. These measures, of course, render the operation of the blockade more quick. But I had kept a blockade up at that place for nearly a year, during which only two vessels had escaped. Nearly 20 vessels had been captured, and they were reduced to despair. Every American vessel generally used to inform my officers that the slave dealers declared they could not carry on the trade under the pressure of a blockade so maintained. The blockade during a great part of the time, both at Cestos, where similar results were produced, and at the Gallinas, was carried on for the greater part of the time at the Gallinas by my ship alone, and at Cestos by the Termagant alone, under my orders.

6792. During that blockade, did you prevent the access of any vessel bringing goods into the country?—I interfered with only vessels equipped for the slave trade; goods to purchase the slaves I could not interfere with. Had they been brought in British vessels, I should certainly have seized those vessels; but I should have been very doubtful whether conviction would have followed under the penal clauses, where the necessity of proving the knowledge of the party is so difficult.

6793. But you would have taken the risk?—I should have felt it my duty to take that risk.

6794. Mr. *Aldam*.] Did any British vessels attempt to go in during that period with goods?—No, not while I was there.

6795. *Chairman*.] Did any vessels of any nation come in with lawful goods during that period?—There is a list of them in the correspondence.

6796. Mr. *Forster*.] Then if a British vessel, laden with lawful merchandise, had attempted to enter the Gallinas, you would have seized her?—Not so, exactly; but if British vessels had come under the same circumstances as American vessels did, with cargoes consigned from Pedro Blanco to Thomas Buron, both notorious slave dealers, to be paid for at the Havannah, or in dollars there, I certainly should have seized them.

6797. How could you have known how the goods were to be paid for?—I should have considered it a clear case of aiding and abetting the slave trade, as clear as it is possible for any thing to be.

6798. How could you have learned that the goods would be paid for at the Havannah in dollars?—I think it is immaterial whether they were paid for in dollars at the Havannah or at the Gallinas; but the fact that they were not paid for in produce, and that it was distinctly putting goods into the hands of the Spaniard Buron to buy slaves with, would, in my opinion, make it a clear case of aiding and abetting the slave trade.

6799. *Chairman.*] And you would argue, from those circumstances, that guilty knowledge could not be absent?—Guilty knowledge could not be absent, in my opinion, in such a case. It may repeatedly happen that, in default of proving their guilty knowledge, people may escape; whereas every one but the criminal himself perfectly well knows the character of the trade which is going on, and which alone could be going on at such a place. Sierra Leone juries are exceedingly careful to have the fact of the knowledge imprinted upon the mind of the culprit proved to them; and unless it is proved they will not convict.

6800. Mr. *Forster.*] At all events, you would have assumed the guilty knowledge, and seized the vessel under the supposed circumstances?—I should; and had I not done so, I think my conduct would have been open to a court-martial.

6801. You have stated that you think the slave trade can be effectually prevented, and was effectually prevented, by a blockade at the Gallinas?—It can certainly be effectually prevented, and was effectually prevented to such an extent that during 9 or 10 months but two vessels escaped, and about 20 were captured.

6802. Then it was not necessary, for the purpose of putting down the slave trade there, to destroy the Spanish property?—My reflection in such a case always would be, the miseries that the slaves on shore were enduring in consequence of this; and I should always be eager to take every opportunity of relieving them from it. It would be undoubtedly the most effectual measure possible.

6803. The using means to put down the slave trade, or to throw difficulties in the way of the slave trade, carries a moral justification with it, which no one can question; but do you think the means you took in that case were altogether justifiable, upon the ground of example to the natives, and the native chiefs; do not you think they might misunderstand those proceedings, and that it might lead to conduct on their part prejudicial to the interests of British commerce?—I think not in any way whatever; I think the operation would be the opposite.

6804. *Chairman.*] Are you aware that any British commerce has followed since those operations against the Gallinas?—No, it has not; I knew very shortly afterwards that they were endeavouring to re-establish the slave trade about there, and I kept the blockade up, intending to knock them down immediately the fine season commenced, and that has been done by Captain Blount.

6805. Mr. *Forster.*] From your experience in Africa you are aware of the great importance of setting all ranks of the natives a high example of honour, and equity, and honesty, in all dealings and transactions; and the question is, whether the effect of those proceedings in that point of view may not render them open to objection. Is it not your opinion, considering that they are not themselves opposed to the slave trade, that they might be at some loss to understand, on any principle of justice, why you should be at liberty to destroy the property of a Spaniard who favoured the trade which they also favoured, and they not be at equal liberty to destroy the property of a British merchant who was opposed to them on the subject of the slave trade?—They are perfectly well aware that the one trade is a legal trade and that the other is a prohibited trade; and they are, moreover, perfectly sensible of the injustice of the custom of selling their fellow-creatures.

6806. *Chairman.*] You find them open to feelings of that nature?—Perfectly; the *argumentum ad hominem* always tells very well with them.

6807. Mr. *Forster.*] In your opinion, do they consider the slave trade a crime?—They do not consider it a crime, because it is not against their laws; but they perfectly well know that it is opposed to every principle of justice, that it is founded upon the grossest injustice and cruelty, and that it is productive of the utmost misery.

6808. How could they reconcile it to their notions of justice that you should destroy the property of Spaniards for doing that which is legal according to their own civil institutions?—Because they are perfectly aware that the Spaniards are carrying on a contraband and prohibited trade, and therefore they are not surprised to find that their vessels are captured; nor are they much surprised when they find that their slaves on shore are emancipated. The one is just as easily to be reconciled to their minds as the other.

6809. *Chairman.*] Have you found, among any of the native chiefs with whom you have had to deal, a feeling against this as an act of injustice?—No, I cannot say that I have, in any instance. On the contrary, I have a letter from the chiefs of Sea Bar, distinguishing their position altogether from that of the Gallinas people, and, upon that ground, begging that I would not come and burn them down.

6810. Do you think they are aware that the slave trade, if carried on by any European nation, is a trade in itself illegal?—They are perfectly aware of it.

6811. Mr. *Aldam*.] How do the chiefs at Sea Bar distinguish between their case and the case of the Gallinas?—It is rather a difficult letter to understand. It was sent off with two ducks, which I believe were poisoned for my benefit. It is a long letter. It alludes to General Turner's endeavours to get possession of their country, and then points out that it is not under the English laws, and that they have received intelligence from the Gallinas that I have burnt and destroyed the Spanish factories, and that it is my intention to come to Sea Bar and do the same; and it ends with something like a threat, that if we did do it, we might be insulted by their people, which they should be sorry for.

6812. Will you have the goodness to deliver in the letter?—

[*The same was delivered in, and read as follows:*]

"Sea Bar." On Her Majesty's Service.

To Deman Esq., Commander of Her Majesty's brig Wander.

Hon. Sir, 2 December 1840.

Be it known to you and all other officers commanding Her Majesty's vessels cruizing on this part of Africa, particularly off Sea Bar, that we the undermentioned gentlemen of this country, do with the greatest honour to you and all Her Majesty's subjects, do relate and acquaint you of our poor late and respected father, Mr. James Tucker, chief of this country, which I have no doubt the Government knows the same, as he told them when they consulted together with Messrs. Rendall, Macauley, Campbell, and several other gentlemen of the colony of Sierra Leone, when with intention to put him under the controul of the English laws, but which he did not consent to, stating that it was his living throughout all his ancient family, and he had no other means for his livelyhood, yes certainly the inhabitants of the colony of Sierra Leone trade in this river, but their trade is no profit nor benefit to us in this country, although they receive a great assistance from this country, but however we have received intelligence from the Gallinas that you the subject of Her Majesty's have burnt and destroyed all the Spanish factories in that country, and that it is your intention coming down here at Sea Bar, and will act the same here as have done with Gallinas, so therefore we the under gentlemen of this country do beg and warn you with the greatest friendship towards Her Majesty's subjects to acquaint you that this part of the country is very different with the Gallinas, as the land is our and all the standing property and building is belonging to us, and in case they should be destroyed and burnt down on account of foreigners, it cannot be an injury to them, but to us in the country; we very knows that it is a law between the different nations of Europe for diminishing that traffic, but however it dont concern with us as they comes to us, if you meet them outside to sea, but coming in the rivers and destroying places, so therefore hearing such news from Her Majesty's subjects about this country and taking as friends, and if you coming on any purpose you dont let us know in the country and burn any place belonging to us; as we do honour the English colour for fear of coming in such a manner, perhaps some of our subjects might do what may be an insult to the English flag, and we dont wish such a thing to be between us, so therefore we beg you all to allow us the liberty of relating to you the aforementioned laws of this country, and hoping it will not be an offence to you.

We remain, &c.

Tessana Town,
2 December 1840.

}

Henry Tucker.
Johnny Tucker.
Jack Tucker.

6813. *Chairman.*] Did you have intercourse with those chiefs after that letter?—No, I did not. The rainy season was coming on, and I was compelled to go to another part of my station.

6814. Captain *Fitzroy.*] Did Governor Doherty make a requisition to you, that you should take those measures with respect to the Gallinas which you have described?—The only requisition from Governor Doherty to me was, to recover the woman and her child, who had been made slaves of by Prince Manna.

6815. Did Governor Doherty express himself satisfied, or otherwise, with the result of your expedition to the Gallinas?—In the first letter in the correspondence before the Committee, a despatch to Lord John Russell, Governor Doherty expresses, in the strongest way, his satisfaction.

6816. Sir *R. H. Inglis.*] Having received the approbation of the local government near the scene of your exploit, have you also received any expression of approbation on the part of Her Majesty's Government, either on the part of the Colonial-office, or of the Admiralty, or of both?—The Colonial Secretary and the Foreign Secretary both expressed, in the strongest terms, their approbation of my proceedings. My despatches to the Admiralty did not arrive till the middle of July. They had, however, previously approved of my conduct, although they had declared that they could not entertain the question with reference to promotion, as the despatches had not come to them. The despatches sent through the senior officer arrived at the Admiralty in July, and I was promoted in August.

6817. Were you promoted by the Admiralty with reference to those services?—No, I cannot say that; I think they may also have considered that as affording some claim, from the tone of letters which I have seen, not addressed to myself, by the Foreign and the Colonial Secretaries.

6818. But the approbation of the Colonial Secretary and of the Foreign Secretary was absolute?—It was absolute.

6819. And the approbation of the Admiralty may be inferred from the fact of your promotion?—That approbation was expressed, in the first instance, by them before they received the despatches, from what had appeared before Parliament.

6820. Mr. *Aldam.*] Has the Admiralty issued orders for other officers in similar cases to follow the same course?—I think the Admiralty has done so.

6821. Mr. *Forster.*] You wish the Committee distinctly to understand that you think such means as you resorted to would not have the effect of offering a bad example to the native chiefs, which they might imitate, and under some pretext or other to seize upon British property?—I think not; I think no example in the natives engaged in the slave trade can possibly make them worse than they are while such traffic is there pursued, nor is there a possibility of improvement until it is stopped.

6822. You think that, when the slave trade is once put down, British settlements planted at the parts where it has been carried on will keep it down?—I think eventually legitimate trade will keep it down; I do not limit it to British settlements only, although British settlements would undoubtedly have a good effect for that object.

6823. Then if a British settlement had been founded at the Gallinas on the completion of your operations there, you think the slave trade would have been permanently suppressed?—Undoubtedly I think so, if founded on good principles.

6824. In your last examination you spoke in terms of strong condemnation of the traders upon the coast having any commercial dealings with persons suspected of being engaged in the slave trade; now, without requiring from a naval commander an intimate or practical knowledge of the principles of commerce, it may nevertheless be reasonable to ask you, after the strong opinions you have expressed, how British trade in Africa could possibly be successfully carried on in competition with foreigners under any restrictions such as you have pointed at?—The restriction that I recommend is, that there should be such a change in the law as to enable us to seize and to condemn any vessel that trades with a notorious slave factory, there being no other trade but the slave trade there prosecuted; also, against the supply of slave ships with goods for the purposes of their traffic, and also against the sale of vessels calculated for the slave trade to slave dealers. In my opinion, those three practices should be stopped.

6825. Do you know Senor Caetano, at the Bissao?—I know who he is, well.

6826. You have stated in your former evidence, that Senor Caetano dealt both in produce and in slaves; how would you act in his case?—I have stated that it would be impossible to distinguish in such cases.

6827. You are aware that slavery and slave dealing are extensively carried on in Cuba?—Undoubtedly; the slave trade to a much diminished extent of late.

6828. And you are aware that it is equally the case in Brazil?—I am aware that it is also the case in the Brazils.

6829. And also in the southern states of the North American Union?—I have no reason to believe that any slave trade whatever exists there, except the slave trade from one part of the coast to another; I believe that no new slaves are introduced.

6830. Are you aware that they buy and sell slaves throughout the southern states of the Union?—Yes; I am speaking of the external slave trade; slavery implies the right of selling slaves within their territory; I mean that they have no external slave trade, to the best of my belief.

6831. Do you draw any distinction between slaves sold and shipped from Virginia to New Orleans, as compared with slaves shipped from the coast of Africa?—Unquestionably; they were at Virginia in the same condition as they are again at New Orleans; it is merely a change of locality in the same country or state, quite distinct from the African slave trade.

6832. Are the slaves shipped from the coast of Africa in the same condition in the West Indies as they were in previously to their being shipped from the coast of Africa?—No, decidedly they are not; they are in a very different condition in Africa from what they are in the West Indies; they are not equally slaves; their condition is entirely different. The whole bearing and meaning of the trade is as different as possible, in my opinion.

6833. Do you draw any distinction, in a moral point of view, between selling and shipping men from the state of Virginia to the Mississippi, as compared with selling and shipping men from Africa to the West Indies?—I consider the case is altogether different; as distinct as possible.

6834. Do you consider that there is any difference in a moral point of view?—Yes, I think there is a difference in a moral point of view. In my opinion, the distinction between commerce with slave states in America and commerce with slave factories in Africa is this: the commerce with the slave factories in Africa, in the cases I have before contemplated, goes there entirely for the purpose of purchasing and making men slaves: the commerce with the slave states of America has no such tendency whatever; the slaves are already property. In my opinion, there is the broadest distinction between the cases.

6835. Then you disapprove of selling goods to persons connected with the slave trade on the coast of Africa, not on account of the moral difference of the act, but on account of the difference of the tendency and consequences of that act?—I consider that, in every case, the dealings of British merchants with slave dealers, although their produce trade may be mixed with the slave trade, is, in a very high degree, objectionable and improper; but, at the same time, I do not think that we can separate them; I do not think it would be politic, or for the benefit of Africa, or for the cause that England has in hand, to endeavour to carry the distinction between them too far.

6836. But if it be wrong or immoral to have dealings with persons engaged in the slave trade, is it not equally wrong for a British merchant to ship and sell goods to a slave merchant in Cuba and Brazil, as it is to sell goods to a slave dealer on the coast of Africa, so far as the moral question is concerned?—I think so, decidedly, supposing those goods are intended to go into the slave trade, and it is known that they will go into the slave trade.

6837. Are you not aware, from your observation on the coast, that most of the goods, if not all, the cotton goods in particular, brought to the coast of Africa by Spanish and Portuguese slave dealers, are manufactured in this country?—I am perfectly aware of it; I consider this highly objectionable, in the same way as the mixed trade upon the coast is; but I do not think it would be wise to interfere with it.

6838. The Committee cannot but highly appreciate and deeply sympathise with your benevolent feelings on this subject; but do you consider yourself sufficiently familiar with the searching effects of commerce, to pronounce a sound opinion on the collateral tendency of trade to supersede the slave trade on the coast of Africa, even when carried on with persons connected with the slave trade?—I consider myself perfectly qualified to give opinions, so far as I have given them. The opinions I have given, I feel myself perfectly qualified to give, and to support.

6839. *Chairman.*] You do not see any indirect advantage in dealing with persons solely engaged in the slave trade, by means of lawful goods, sufficient to counterbalance the direct evil of the facilities given by that means to the slave trade?—The case of the Gallinas, I think, is a perfect answer to the question; no good whatever is derived from the exchange of the commodities of the civilized world for slaves. There is no export of produce in that district of the coast. I conceive that this commerce has no good effect whatever.

6840. You think it promotes no industry?—On the contrary, it annihilates it.

6841. Mr. *Forster.*] You have stated that there has been no British commerce carried on there to any extent?—In the Return which I have already referred to, in the 14th page of this correspondence, is given an account of the trade which formerly did exist, and which, under the withering influence of the slave trade, has been utterly destroyed. There is no doubt that there was considerable export trade at one time from the Gallinas; they exported rice, and they exported produce. Now they are obliged to import rice to feed themselves; cattle, which were formerly abundant, are now hardly to be procured, and then only at an enormous expense. They used to get cattle from Sierra Leone. Indeed, the only case I know of any communication with Sierra Leone, while I was last on the coast, was, in one or two instances of very small boats, not above six or seven tons, which had in one instance cattle and sheep on board. In the second instance I did not search her.

6842. You have stated that the Gallinas has been principally supplied with goods for the slave trade by foreign ships, and not by British traders?—That has been my statement.

6843. You have stated also that you would have felt it your duty to prevent English trading vessels entering there?—Under certain circumstances, which I have detailed.

6844. Are you not of opinion that if British commerce had been encouraged there, and more particularly if a British settlement had been formed there, British commerce would have been of material assistance in discountenancing and putting down the slave trade at the Gallinas?— Legitimate commerce at the Gallinas has been eradicated and annihilated by the sole influence of the slave trade. It existed there, and the slave trade annihilated it. Had a British settlement been formed there, the results might have been different.

6845. *Chairman.*] Do you think the results would have been different if the same goods had been brought by English ships carrying on the same trade as the foreign ships?—I do not see, had they been brought in the same way as the goods were brought in the foreign ships, how any difference would have been made. It would have been the same unmixed evil as it has been when carried on under the American flag.

6846. Mr. *Forster.*] Then it is only by the formation of British settlements that you think the advantages of British commerce could be fully realized there?—I think the advantages of legitimate commerce will commence when they make their minds up that the slave trade will no longer supply them with what they have been hitherto accustomed to receive, and that that might be further assisted by the formation of a settlement, I have no doubt whatever.

6847. Sir *R. H. Inglis.*] Have you any means of knowing how the slaves in the barracoons at the Gallinas were procured for the slave market; whether they were born in slavery, or were made slaves for the mere purpose of sale?— The fact that the general system of society in Africa is slavery, I believe is universally admitted. Those people were brought down from the interior to meet the demand upon the coast.

6848. Do you mean the Committee to understand that in your opinion they were born slaves, and brought up to the slave market, or that, having been free, they were made slaves for the slave market?—In my opinion they were all born in a state of domestic slavery, answering to a sort of villeinage in the early periods of our own history. But my belief is, that no African chief dare sell his domestic slaves in this way, except occasionally under the pretence of crimes committed, or of debts owing; they are generally, I fancy, either kidnapped or taken in wars, or in the ways I before mentioned.

6849. The kidnapping and the wars being for the purpose of supplying the slave market?—Undoubtedly, in my opinion.

6850. *Chairman.*] Do you derive your information of the internal condition of the Africans from investigations of your own, or from what you have read?— Partly from inquiries I made while in shore at the Gallinas and up the Nunez.

6851. You do not believe that, generally speaking, the chiefs, the owners of slaves in Africa, have the right of selling their own slaves?—By no means; I believe they dare not do it; that the population would at once rise against it.

6852. Mr. *Aldam.*] Do you consider that the slaves are generally prisoners taken in wars that have incidentally arisen, or that there are wars carried on for the purpose of making slaves?—I believe both to a great extent; I believe that wars are frequently begun for the purpose of taking prisoners and making slaves, and frequently by agreement between two chiefs, who dare not sell their own people. They go to war in order to take each other's people.

6853. Mr. *Forster.*] Did you hear of instances of that kind while you were in the country?—I have heard statements of that kind from persons conversant with the country up the rivers, and also from the natives.

6854. Captain *Fitzroy.*] Referring to the letter which you have produced from the chiefs of Sea-bar, was that letter written by a native?—It was written undoubtedly by a negro, whether a native of Sierra Leone, trading to Sea-bar, or whether one of the chiefs there, I cannot say; but I have seen natives write infinitely better than that.

6855. It is signed by Henry Tucker; who was that Henry Tucker?—He was one of the chiefs of the country in the neighbourhood of Sea-bar; they are a family who have dominion there.

6856. Was that chief, Tucker, educated at Sierra Leone?—I cannot say; I believe he was, but I am not sure about it.

6857. (To Captain *Hill.*) Are you aware by whom that letter was written?—I was at Sea-bar frequently, and have frequently seen Harry Tucker, and have also seen a person whom he introduced to me as his secretary, who, on conversation, I ascertained to be Harry Tucker's son, and this son was writing letters for him; and I asked his son where he learned to write, and he told me that he was educated at Sierra Leone; and Harry Tucker also told me, that he sent two or three of his sons to Sierra Leone to learn to read and write.

6858. Then, it is your belief that that letter was written by a son of a native chief, who was educated at Sierra Leone?—Yes.

6859. Mr. *Aldam,* to Captain *Denman.*] Where is Sea-bar?—It lies between Sierra Leone and Gallinas. It is the passage between the south-eastern end of the Sherboro' Island and the main land.

6860. Captain *Fitzroy.*] Is "Sea-bar," the place named in the letter, the same as the River "Shebar," in the map?—It is the same.

6861. Mr. *Hamilton.*] Had you any opportunity of making any observation as to the climate of the Gallinas; how far it would be fit for Europeans to live there?—As far as my observations went, they were rather favourable, for I went in at not a very good time of the year, and, out of upwards of 100 men, I think that only two or three deaths occurred. I believe only two men died after having been on shore a week.

6862. Going up in the boats?—Yes.

6863. Is the ground swampy, or is there any high ground in the neighbourhood?—The ground is rather low, but some of the islands are as healthy as any of that part of Africa; indeed, the contrast between that river and some of the rivers we afterwards went up, at a more favourable season, was remarkable.

6864. Mr. *Milnes.*] Did you not fall in with a vessel called the Echo, bringing a cargo of goods to the Coast of Africa?—I did, a Hamburgh vessel; I think it was on the 11th of December.

6865. Had you any reason to suspect her of having any connexion with the slave trade?—The officer who was sent on board her found that her cargo was consigned from the Havannah, I think from Charles Tyng to Mr. Canôt, a slave dealer at New Cestos, and she had also on board a Spanish supercargo, affording strong ground for suspecting her, indeed proof, that she was engaged in aiding and abetting the slave trade.

6866. Do you regard any commerce in which ships might be engaged with a slave factory as necessarily abetting the slave trade?—Not all commerce; but I consider that if she were sailing with goods consigned from one slave dealer to another she would be aiding and abetting the slave trade.

6867. *Chairman.*] You mean that there could be no doubt of the guilty intent of the parties?—There could be no doubt of the guilty intent of the parties to aid and abet the slave trade.

6868. Mr. *Forster.*] Are you of an opinion that a Hamburgh vessel could not lawfully enter into a charter-party to the Havannah, to convey goods to a slave factory on the coast of Africa?—I think that where a Hamburgh vessel is carrying a cargo under the same circumstances I have described, it forms the strongest reason to suspect that she may be doing still worse.

6869. Mr. *Milnes.*] You searched that Hamburgh vessel?—Upon the 11th of December; it was late in the evening when I boarded her. The officer returned to me, reporting after a very imperfect search, indeed after no search, that he found on board nothing to condemn her, and that he had given a certificate to that effect.

6870. Do you think that that certificate was prematurely given?—No, that the search that I had to institute was under the treaty, and therefore I considered her entitled to a certificate, although I certainly intended, if I fell in with her again, to search her more perfectly, as I was not satisfied upon the subject; all I could say then was, that nothing was found.

6871. What time did the first search take?—It was not a search, it was a visit; it did not amount to a search; it was a visit to the ship, and some little examination, perhaps lifting the hatches; it was in one sense a search, but a most imperfect search; it did not occupy above half an hour.

6872. Did you afterwards see Mr. Canôt, upon the subject of that vessel?—I afterwards saw Mr. Canôt, not upon the subject of that vessel; he mentioned to me that he expected a vessel with a cargo.

6873. Under what circumstances did you search the Echo a second time?—Upon our arrival at New Cestos, considering her exposed to the worst suspicions, after I found that she was consigned to Mr. Canôt, I caused a most perfect search to be instituted; the hold was cleared, and she was thoroughly searched for slave equipments. It should be observed, that the right of search is never carried to anything like this extent, except in cases justifying the strongest suspicion.

6874. How long did that search take?—I think from the 15th to the 18th of December.

6875. Were you then satisfied by the result of that search that there were no grounds for seizing the Echo?—I certainly found nothing, in my opinion, to convict her; at that time there was nothing detected on board her to warrant detention; had there been, I should have detained her of course.

6876. Did you or your master entrust to the captain of the Echo certain captured Spaniards, to take to the Havannah?—When I was about to sail from New Cestos, I allowed a prize crew of Spaniards, who had been captured in a prize, to go on board this vessel, to endeavour to get a passage back to their own country.

6877. Did you use any persuasion to Captain Soms to call at Sierra Leone, as he states in the papers you have seen?—I never was on board her in the first place, and I never saw Captain Soms; in the second place, the master, on returning on board the Wanderer, told me, that he had advised the captain of the Echo to go to Sierra Leone with the view of getting passengers; subsequently, when I heard that the vessel was captured, I recollect distinctly saying to the master, "Oh, they will think you have betrayed them into the hands of the Sierra Leone government." The advice was given without my authority, and without my knowledge until afterwards; but I saw no harm in the advice.

6878. Could the Echo have incurred any culpability with regard to the slave trade between the time when you examined her and her seizure at Sierra Leone?—Very possibly.

6879. How?—She might have entered into an arrangement to carry away a cargo of slaves from another part of the coast; she might have equipped herself for slave dealing; it does not at all follow because she was apparently free from liability to capture when I was on board her, that she should not have done something subsequently that rendered her so.

6880. You do not consider your having declared her to be innocent to be a sufficient ground for saying that she was not guilty at Sierra Leone at a subsequent period?—It was certainly no sort of guarantee against the consequences of any future proceedings that she might choose to take.

6881. Sir *R. H. Inglis.*] It was not either a retrospective or a prospective guarantee; it was a guarantee only that on the 11th of December, when you visited her, she at that time had no *primâ facie* evidence of being engaged in the slave trade; is that your impression upon the subject?—It was no particular guarantee, but it was a certificate which the treaties, under the authority of which I searched her, declared that I was to furnish her with; it was a certificate to the effect that the treaty required.

6882. *Chairman.*] Was that certificate a security to her against any further search by any other man-of-war on the station?—It would probably operate against any further search, because they would not take the trouble to do it unless they had some new reason to suspect her; they would have no wish to cause unnecessary vexation.

6883. Is the certificate intended, in your view, to operate as a security against further trouble?—I think there are two motives for the certificate; one is, that there may be no concealment as to the ship which may have committed any wrong in the exercise of the right of search upon her; and secondly, to act as a sort of certificate with regard to others that may fall in with her; but if others have reason still to doubt her, in spite of that certificate, they are perfectly at liberty to search her again.

6884. Did you hear what became of the Echo afterwards?—I did not hear of her detention at Sierra Leone until the end of March, I think the 28th of March; I visited Sierra Leone a few days after I had boarded her, but before her arrival.

6885. Did you not hear that she was condemned?—I heard that she was condemned.

6886. Upon what ground?—My knowledge upon the subject is merely hearsay; all that I know is, that an officer of the Wanderer was at Sierra Leone, and I mention it in order to show that Sir John Jeremie was not moved by interested motives in seizing her, he was anxious that this officer should seize her as a prize to the Wanderer.

6887. Has the Governor any interest in seizures?—He has a proportion of the proceeds.

6888. Mr. *Forster.*] And he would be entitled to a proportion of the proceeds of the Echo when condemned at Sierra Leone?—Yes.

6889. Mr. *Milnes.*] Did you ever fall in with any other Hamburgh vessel engaged in abetting the slave trade?—I fell in once with the Argus, at the Gallinas, when she was landing casks. I considered that a suspicious circumstance, although one not warranting seizure. I never met with any other.

6890. Have you ever heard that eight or any other number of Hamburgh vessels had proceeded from Hamburgh for the purpose of abetting the slave trade, or being engaged in it?—I think decidedly not.

6891. Mr. *Forster*.] If the Echo had been an English vessel, would you have seized her under the circumstances in which you found the Echo?—Undoubtedly, under the circumstances of the trade which she was carrying on.

6892. Mr. *Milnes*.] Do you mean after the first or after the second search?—The search told nothing. It was the fact of her carrying goods from one slave dealer to another, with a Spanish supercargo on board, that would have proved to me that she was aiding and abetting the slave trade.

6893. Would you have seized her upon the knowledge of that fact alone?—Undoubtedly, if she had been an English vessel.

6894. *Chairman*.] But being a foreign vessel, you did not think that ground sufficient to act upon?—Being a foreign vessel, I could not apply the English laws to her case. I could only apply the treaty to her case, and I held that according to the treaty only equipment would warrant a seizure, or slaves.

6895. Mr. *Milnes*.] Would you have had a right to seize that ship under those circumstances simply from the fact of her having a foreign supercargo?—Not upon that fact, but upon the fact of her carrying goods from one slave dealer to another slave dealer to buy slaves with.

6896. How do you know that it was to buy slaves with?—From the fact of their being both engaged in the slave trade.

6897. Was Mr. Canôt at that time avowedly engaged in the slave trade?—Mr. Canôt had, a very few days before the arrival of the Echo, given up all his slaves and abandoned the slave trade. It was a mere accidental circumstance their finding that Mr. Canôt was not then carrying on the slave trade.

6898. *Chairman*.] They were consigned to him under the expectation that he was a slave dealer?—At the time the consignment took place he was a slave dealer, and no one at that time could have contemplated so sudden a change on his part.

6899. Mr. *Milnes*.] But at the time the Echo was there, Mr. Canôt was not engaged in the slave trade, and was under British protection?—Mr. Canôt had, a few days before, given up his slaves and abandoned the slave trade.

6900. But the parties who chartered the Echo could not have been aware of that fact?—They could not possibly have been aware of that fact.

6901. Sir *T. D. Acland*.] Mr. Canôt was known to be concerned in the slave trade at the time the consignment was made?—Perfectly.

6902. Mr. *Forster.*] You do not think that Mr. Canôt in abandoning the slave trade, was at all influenced by the prospective arrival of this vessel, with a view to possessing himself of the cargo?—I do not see how he could have been influenced by that; because, under the circumstances, I could not have seized her, whether he had been carrying on the slave trade or not. On the other hand, although he had turned from the slave trade, yet, had I found any equipment upon her, I should have seized her. It made no difference whatever.

6903. Did he immediately avail himself of the services of the British squadron to remove the goods from New Cestos, the place to which they were consigned, to Monrovia?—It would be necessary to explain what had taken place at New Cestos with reference to Mr. Canôt, to understand what took place with respect to those goods. Mr. Canôt, on the 8th of December, voluntarily delivered his slaves to Lieutenant Seagram, commanding H. M. S. Termagant, stationed by me to blockade the place. Lieutenant Seagram then sailed, to land those slaves at Sierra Leone, carrying with him reports upon the subject for my information. I met at New Cestos his boats, and not having received any information from him, but only from the officer in charge of the boats, verbally, I left an order for him to the following effect: that if he was persuaded of Mr. Canôt's integrity of purpose, and provided the slave trade was at an end, he was to afford him convenience and protection, and to assist him in establishing a factory for Redman & Co. at Cape Mount. After my departure, the goods consigned to Mr. Canôt were, I believe, landed at his factory, the supercargo being on board, and ready to object if there was any thing improper about it; and they were subsequently, according to the orders I had left, protected by Lieutenant Seagram, when embarked from the beach, the natives showing every disposition to resist the departure of Mr. Canôt.

6904. Mr. *Milnes.*] Did you hear any thing at Sierra Leone about a buoy, in which the papers of the Echo were said to have been concealed?—I saw a buoy at the registrar's office, at the Vice-Admiralty Court, which was hollowed out with a scuttle, and I was told that the papers had been concealed in this buoy. I should state, that on searching the Echo, there was no search for papers, because papers under the treaty with Hamburgh would not have been sufficient to condemn her. Equipments were what I searched for.

6905. Would any papers that you could have found have been sufficient to condemn her under the treaty with Hamburgh?—Had I found papers distinctly proving that she was intended to take slaves, I should have taken upon myself the responsibility of sending her to Hamburgh for trial, according to the treaty; because, although not according to the letter of the treaty, I believe the spirit of the Hamburgh treaty is entirely true and just, and I believe it would have been enforced.

6906. Would any papers found upon her in British waters cause her to be condemned, which would not cause her to be condemned if found in other waters?—Papers found upon her in British waters, proving her to be engaged in the slave trade, might certainly condemn her under our laws, as coming under our jurisdiction.

6907. Mr. *Forster*.] Did the registrar inform you that the hollow place in the buoy was intended to conceal papers, or that papers were found concealed in it?—He told me that papers had been concealed in it. He did not say that they had been found there, but that it had been used for that purpose.

6908. Did he say that papers of that nature had been found in it at Sierra Leone?—No, I think not.

6909. Mr. *Milnes*.] Have you known many instances of the crews of men-of-war boats remaining on board during a search of that kind, and conducting themselves improperly, taking articles out of the cargo for their own use?—Extremely rarely. In this instance I am aware that some of my ship's company misbehaved themselves; but they, well knowing the punishment that awaited them, managed to desert.

6910. Did you order the return of the goods which they had taken?—There were no goods taken; I believe there was a bottle or two of champagne drunk.

6911. Did you order the men for punishment?—The men escaped; the master did not bring them back with him. They both died shortly afterwards, or rather one died and the other one was very badly wounded in the Termagant's boats, and never returned to the Wanderer.

6912. Is it not very difficult to prevent the men from committing those abuses?—I think not when the officers are strictly vigilant; but upon this occasion Mr. Elliott had been induced to go on shore by some representations of Mr. Canôt, who wished to prove to him that his intentions were honest and upright as regarded his abandonment of the slave trade; and that accounted for it.

6913. Were the men left by themselves?—No, they were not; there were the officers of the Termagant employed also, in whose charge they were left.

6914. Mr. *Forster*.] What means do you suppose the master of the Echo would have at the Havannah of knowing the character and pursuits of Mr. Canôt, to whom he was consigned upon the charter-party?—If he had made the smallest inquiry, he could not have been in doubt for a moment.

6915. Where should he have made inquiry?—In the Havannah; Mr. Canôt was as well known in the Havannah as Pedro Blanco himself.

6916. Is it the duty of a merchant captain in search of trade at a foreign port to make inquiries as to the character and pursuits of his consignee in another country?—Applying it to an English captain, I should say that he was just as much bound to ascertain that he was not engaged in the slave trade as an apothecary, when he sells arsenic, is bound, as far as in him lies, to ascertain that it is not intended to poison any body.

6917. Mr. *Milnes.*] Is it common for a ship to be condemned, and for the captain at the same time to be declared not guilty of aiding and abetting in the slave trade?—It occurs frequently, upon the very principle of the difficulty of proof of the individual being wilfully and knowingly engaged in the slave trade.

6918. Is it supposed that a vessel can be engaged in the slave trade without the cognizance of the captain?—Engaged in the slave trade indirectly, as the Hamburgh ship, the Echo, was, I think is possible; it is very unlikely.

6919. You would say generally, that where the ship was condemned and the captain escaped, it was through some want of legal proof?—Through the want of bringing home the proof of his having actual knowledge of the tendency of the trade in which he was engaged.

6920. *Chairman.*] Upon whom would the loss fall of the condemnation of the ship?—Upon the owners of the ship.

6921. The owners being in Hamburgh?—The owners being in Hamburgh.

6922. What control would they have over their ship in the Havannah, except through the medium of the captain?—They might have an agent there, who might be ordered to allow her to be taken up for freight to any part of the world, and who might send the goods on board; and the master might not know what part of Africa he was going to till the moment before he loosed sails.

6923. But a guilty knowledge on the part of some party is necessary to the condemnation of the vessel, is it not?—Yes, it is.

6924. In such cases as those, would the articles have nothing on the face of them in the character of equipment, to serve the purposes of the slave trade?—Not necessarily.

6925. Where can the guilty knowledge reside which shall condemn the vessel and the goods consigned, if the captain is supposed not to have possessed it?—The guilty knowledge, in my opinion, might be presumed. It is the duty of owners to take care that their ships are not turned into pirates or into smugglers, and if they are turned into smugglers or pirates, they must take the consequences; and so if they break other laws I conceive.

6926. Mr. *Milnes*.] Do you know other instances of ships being condemned, and the captains acquitted?—Yes; the Augusta, captured by Captain Hill, was a case of that description.

6927. Mr. *Forster*.] Is it not equally an offence on the part of the captain?—Undoubtedly so, if a guilty knowledge can be proved against him.

6928. You cannot prove a guilty knowledge in the case of the ship?—I think you may be able to show that the persons owning the ship or acting as agent for the owners may have had a guilty knowledge, where the master had no guilty knowledge.

6929. Mr. *Milnes*.] But you cannot legally sell the property of the captain when the captain himself is declared to be not guilty?—If the vessel was declared guilty by a proper court, undoubtedly that is a consequence of the condemnation.

6930. Would the individual property of the captain himself be included in the condemnation?—I believe the doctrine always has been, that the whole property on board the ship is vitiated by her being engaged in the slave trade. But these questions are all questions as to the construction of the Act of Parliament of the 5th of George the 4th, which I do not feel competent to interpret in this manner, although I see my way clearly enough to act upon it.

6931. Mr. *Forster*.] Do you consider that the mere conveyance as a common carrier of goods from the Havannah to the coast of Africa, is an act of slave dealing?—Not the common carrying of goods: but if she is carrying goods from Pedro Blanco to Mr. Canôt, I do not call that a common act of carrying. It is the act of carrying goods for a specific purpose between two persons engaged in a criminal trade.

6932. Mr. *Milnes*.] Could not Pedro Blanco and Mr. Canôt have mercantile communications which should be of an indisputably legal character?—They might, but they indisputably have no such commerce except in the smallest degree possible. There was some little palm-oil trade carried on by Mr. Canôt. I believe Mr. Canôt's evidence was not taken upon the question, but Mr. Canot made no secret of the purposes to which that cargo would have been applied by him.

6933. Mr. *Forster*.] Supposing arsenic to be conveyed from London to Manchester, and there made an illegal use of, would you consider the carrier responsible in that case?—No, but I think that supposed case applies to the carriage of goods from England to the Havannah, and not from the

Havannah to a slave factory in Africa. If you suppose the case of the person at the place to which the arsenic was sent, and the person who sends it, both being employed in poisoning people, I should think in that case the carrier would be culpable, supposing him to be aware of the fact.

6934. Do you consider it illegal for an English vessel to convey a cargo of merchandise from the Havannah to a person engaged in the slave trade on the coast of Africa?—Supposing they are sent by a person engaged in the slave trade.

6935. Do you consider it illegal for an English vessel to convey a cargo of goods to a notorious slave dealer at the Havannah?—No, I do not.

6936. On what ground do you draw the distinction between the two cases?— I think the one is more directly aiding and abetting the slave trade than the other; the other is in a much more remote degree. I have before stated that I thought it was morally wrong.

6937. Mr. *Milnes.*] Do you recollect whether the fitting up of the vessel was such that it could have taken back a cargo of slaves, supposing Mr. Canôt had still been concerned in the slave trade?—She would only have had to get a few casks and a few planks, and she might have taken back 700 or 800 slaves with the greatest ease Any vessel can be fitted up as a slaver.

6938. Then your impression is that that vessel arrived there expecting to find Mr. Canôt engaged in the slave trade, and was disappointed at finding that he had abandoned it?—Undoubtedly, they still supposed him to be engaged in the slave trade; but how far the disappointment went I cannot say. The goods were landed to him still, although there was a supercargo on board, which is a strong reason to suppose that Mr. Canôt was not robbing his employers, as was suggested.

6939. Mr. *Forster.*] Was it not the fact, that it was not till after they had been landed that the goods were removed to Cape Mount?—But they had been promised to be removed before. The promise was given that his goods should be removed to Cape Mount, under the protection of the British flag, because it was well understood that the natives would resist the removal of Mr. Canôt; they wanted to have a slave dealer.

6940. What back cargo could the Echo have taken from Mr. Canôt, except slaves?—She could have taken nothing approaching to a cargo; there were a few casks of palm oil, but wholly insufficient for the cargo of such a vessel.

6941. *Chairman.*] Could she not have taken money?—She could have taken money or bills, but nothing in the shape of cargo.

6942. Is not the greater part of the slave trade on the coast of Africa carried on upon the principle of one vessel bringing a cargo and taking back money, and another vessel being employed to take away slaves?—It is. In most of those cases, the principal slave dealer is resident at the Havannah; and in all cases almost the freight of the former is paid for in the Havannah. There is no money or goods taken out in the vessel intended to carry back slaves.

6943. There is nothing, in the course of the slave trade on the coast of Africa, which leads you to imagine that a vessel which carries goods to the coast must necessarily intend to carry slaves back?—No; there is only one instance which I know, when I was upon the coast during the last two years, of such an attempt. With respect to Mr. Canôt, there is one fact with regard to his conduct which is highly in his favour. Some time after the slaves were delivered up, the natives got some goods from him, and tried to endeavour to induce him to resume the slave trade. They went and bought 50 slaves with those goods. He gave information on the subject, and through him the slaves were delivered up to Lieutenant Seagram. Throughout his whole conduct I have the strongest reason to suppose that he is most perfectly honest in his intention of abandoning the slave trade. He has always given me the fullest information with regard also to the resumption of the slave trade at New Cestos.

6944. *Chairman.*] You had a good deal of intercourse with Mr. Canôt?—A good deal. I used to receive communications from him, giving me information with respect to the slave trade.

6945. What appears to have been the moving cause to induce him to abandon the slave trade?—I have reason to believe that he had for some time contemplated it; but the immediate cause was, that under the blockade he found that he could not follow out the commerce; that he could not get the slaves away.

6946. Mr. *Forster.*] Was the captain cognizant of Mr. Canôt having abandoned the slave trade previously to the landing of the cargo?—He states it himself in his complaint. He states that it was so; that he saw the English flag flying.

6947. Do not you consider that strong proof, that the captain of the Echo was no party to the slave trading transactions going on between the shipper and the consignee?—I can only suppose that the property was Mr. Canôt's, and that he as an honest man felt himself bound to give it to him. Had it been Pedro Blanco's own property, sent by him for Mr. Canôt to buy slaves with, I think the property would not have been allowed to be landed.

6948. If the captain had been in the secret as to the transactions between the house at the Havannah and Mr. Canôt, the captain, to protect the house in the Havannah, finding that Mr. Canôt had abandoned the slave trade, would not have delivered the goods?—He was paid for his freight. I suppose he did not care what became of the goods. Had he not landed the goods, he would have had to carry them back; he would have been unable to take freight back.

6949. Mr. *Milnes.*] Was none of the freight landed?—I believe all that was consigned to Mr. Canôt was landed after I sailed.

6950. How would Mr. Canôt have paid for it?—I have no idea how it was paid for. There are three theories to choose amongst; one is, that he robbed his employer's goods without any set-off; another is, that his employers owed him something equivalent at least to the value of the goods; and the third is, that they were his own property. I refused to enter into the subject with him at all; I had nothing to do with his slave transactions; had it been amenable to seizure I should have seized it.

6951. Captain *Fitzroy.*] Does the slave trade increase or decrease, at the time of the senior officer on the station being changed?—It has generally been observed in the printed correspondence of the commissioners, and also from the observations of the officers on the coast, that the senior officers not having a practical knowledge of the coast, upon their first arrival there the cruizing is much less efficient for a certain time. It requires a long time for an officer to understand the duties of the coast.

6952. You have understood that frequently changing the officers is injurious to the suppression of the slave trade?—Such is my opinion; I think that three years is the proper time for an officer to be employed there. I think the service would suffer if they were removed more frequently.

6953. How long, speaking generally, does it take for an officer to acquire a tolerably competent knowledge of the duties on that coast?—Several months, certainly.

6954. Are the cruizers now obliged to leave their stations frequently, to get provisions?—They are obliged to leave their stations generally once in three or four months for that purpose, and during that period, of course, the slavers frequently escape. The period is longer or shorter, according to the distance of the depôts.

6955. Do not the slave traders generally obtain accurate information of the periods at which the cruizers will probably be absent?—They frequently do so by reasoning, and by observing the time at which the cruizers have received their supplies.

6956. Does the present state of the Bounty Acts afford due encouragement to exertions for the prevention of the slave trade, or might an alteration be made which would do more justice to those who are affected by those Acts?—In my opinion the present system of bounties is upon an extremely bad footing. It affords a great premium upon the capture of full vessels over empty vessels; whereas I believe the slave trade is to be stopped by the prevention of embarkation.

6957. How could the Act be altered, in your opinion, so as to make less difference between full vessels and empty vessels?—My opinion is, that there should be no difference whatever between them; that they should be paid upon the tonnage a bounty, calculated upon the average between the profit of a full vessel and an empty vessel of the same tonnage; that there should be no more head-money whatever; that the proceeds should not go to the captors; that the proceeds should go to the Government; that the reward of the captors should be only upon the tonnage.

6958. Abolishing head-money altogether?—Abolishing head-money altogether.

6959. *Chairman.*] Do you conceive that Sierra Leone is well situated as a place for adjudication, under the present circumstances of the slave trade?—I think that it is the best place, under the present circumstances of the slave trade.

6960. Captain *Fitzroy.*] Can you suggest any improvement in the rigging of the ships employed on the coast, or in the boats with which they are furnished?—The cruizers employed upon the coast have the same masts and sails precisely in them as they would have in the North Sea, their duties lying altogether in the Tropics. In my opinion, with the same masts, a large increase of canvass, by making the sails squarer, would be of the utmost advantage.

6961. Are the boats now used the best adapted for that particular service?— I think every vessel, capable of carrying them, ought to carry two long six-oared galleys at her quarters, and that those that carry boats amidship should have as large boats as they can stow, and that they should be built so lightly as to be able to keep pace with the galleys. A much larger proportion have been captured by boats than by cruizing.

———

Lunæ, 27° die Junii, 1842.

MEMBERS PRESENT.

Sir T. D. Acland.
Mr. Aldam.
Captain Fitzroy.

Mr. Forster.
Mr. W. Hamilton.
Mr. Milnes.

VISCOUNT SANDON in the chair.

Captain the Honourable *Joseph Denman*, R. N., called in; and further examined.

6962. *Chairman.*] Can you give the Committee any information with regard to the Kroo Coast; first as to the extent of the Kroo Coast?—The Kroo Coast, I conceive, begins at the river Cestros, the place known as St. George's, where Mr. Spence had established a factory several years ago, which has been recently abandoned. The Kroomen occupy only five towns upon the coast at different places between the river Cestros and the Grand Cestros; to the northward of that the Bassa people lie intermixed with the Fishmen, and, occupying all the coast to the southward of the Grand Cestros, are the Fishmen, a different people from the Kroomen; they are often confounded with them, but there is a broad distinction between them. Intermixed with the five Kroo towns are many Fish places. The Kroomen occupy the interior of the country more than the Fishmen; the Fishmen are entirely upon the coast. Below Grand Cestros they are all Fish towns. The Fish people are much more numerous than the Kroomen. At a place called by the Fishmen Saucy Town, the natives from the interior fought their way down to the beach.

6963. What were they?—We have no means of knowing; they are quite different from any other races that we know of; at this the Fishmen are exceedingly angry, as they consider that they have a title to all the trade upon the coast. They have prohibited all trade with this place, and have committed many outrages against British vessels and others who have traded there in spite of their prohibition. The Fishmen are perfect pests to the trade upon the coast; they require keeping in order very much.

6964. Are they principally Kroomen or Fishmen who enter on board Her Majesty's ships?—More Fishmen than Kroomen; we cannot employ them together.

6965. Is it the same with reference to mercantile vessels?—I am not aware, but I think the Fishmen are generally preferred, as they are more at home with boats and more accustomed to live on the water than the Kroomen.

6966. Do you call those principally Kroomen or Fishmen that live at Sierra Leone?—Both classes exist there, but I am not aware in what proportions; the Kroomen are preferred for domestic purposes; they are much more capable of attachment to white people.

6967. Have you any idea what the population is, whether of Fishmen or of Kroomen?—The population of the coast of Fishmen is much greater than that of Kroomen, but I always understood that the Kroomen ran a long way into the interior, and were an agricultural race; indeed if it was not so, I do not see how they could possibly exist against the hostility of the Fishmen, as their numbers on the sea-coast are very inferior; they are almost always at war.

6968. Are both Fishmen and Kroomen exempt from becoming slaves?— They are exempt from becoming slaves; at the only slave factories upon the coast, between Sierra Leone and Cape Palmas, Gallinas, and New Cestos, the work was entirely carried on by Fishmen, but they have a great objection to being slaves themselves; they are in the habit of sacrificing their enemies taken in war to the Fetish tree.

6969. Are you speaking of Fishmen or of Kroomen now?—Both; I have had opportunities of knowing that that is the fact.

6970. Do those parties bring slaves from distant parts in the interior, or is it upon neighbouring tribes that they make inroads in order to procure slaves?—I do not think the Fishmen or Kroomen are in the habit of collecting slaves at all; but they are very willing to lend themselves out to slave factories, to assist them in carrying on the traffic in every way.

6971. And to allow their territory to be made a place of embarkation for slaves?—I believe not; indeed there is no embarkation of slaves in their territory; nor nearer than Young Cestos.

6972. Sir *T. D. Acland*.] Their willingness to hire themselves out to slavers is merely as a means of active employment?—Exactly so.

6973. Not from any preference to that employment?—They prefer it, I believe, because they are better paid for that than any thing else.

6974. *Chairman*.] Have you had any opportunity of knowing the domestic condition of the Kroomen or the Fishmen; whether they are under the obligations of slavery to any parties?—No, there is no slavery in the Kroo or Fish country, although the system of every headman having his boys under him approaches something to it. The headman receives all the wages of all the boys under him; whether that is from family connexion, or from political institution, I do not know, but the headman receives all the pay of all the boys. A headman on board a man-of-war, for instance, will have 20 men under him, and he receives the whole of their wages.

6975. Do you always take on board a headman, for every number of Kroomen or Fishmen that you engage?—It is absolutely necessary to have a headman to keep them in order; he generally chooses all the people, we leave it to him to choose them. If Fishmen and Kroomen happen to be mixed up in the same party there are always quarrels and disturbances, indeed there is no getting on with them, so strong is the antipathy.

6976. Sir *T. D. Acland.*] Do you think, from what you know of those people, that they would be disposed to engage themselves as labourers in the West Indies, if proper means were taken to acquaint them with the nature of the service?—If proper means were taken, I have not the least doubt they might get thousands of them; the thing necessary is to produce confidence in their minds, and that would best be done by some man-of-war upon the coast taking over some of the headmen, upon a promise that they should be returned by the same ship.

6977. *Chairman.*] You believe that they have confidence in a man-of-war?—I believe they have the greatest confidence in a man-of-war, and also in the English people; but they might fancy that abuses might take place, and that they might be made slaves of, unless they had the evidence of some of their own people.

6978. Sir *T. D. Acland.*] Do you think it would be possible for a man-of-war to discharge the duty of securing against any possible abuse in their embarkation?—I do not think it would be at all necessary to have a man-of-war for that purpose. I think you might safely leave them to take care of themselves. The only purpose for which a man-of-war need interfere, would be to give them a feeling of confidence in the first instance. They might object to go over in any thing but a man-of-war. I think the first impression is all that a man-of-war would be required for.

6979. Do you think these people might not take others with them against their will?—I think not; I do not think they hold slaves in any way; the mark of the race is so very distinct, that other races could not be mixed with them as emigrants without detection.

6980. *Chairman.*] You think that the connexion between the chiefs and those companies of boys is rather a voluntary connexion, for the purpose of protection, than one of compulsion?—It is a voluntary connexion, because it exists equally strongly at Sierra Leone as any where else.

6981. Sir *T. D. Acland.*] Have you any doubt that the commanders of one of Her Majesty's ships could effectually prevent any embarkation of the natives against their will?—I do not think there would be the smallest necessity for a man-of-war to superintend the coast, except at first.

6982. Supposing no landing were allowed in the West Indies without a certificate of one of Her Majesty's officers, would it be easy for the officer, before he gave such a certificate, to take effectual security against being imposed upon by the delivery of a person without his full consent?—It would be very easy to ascertain the fact; but the Kroo and Fish race are so distinct from all others, that I do not think there is the smallest apprehension of its taking the form of slavery.

6983. You mean so far as regards any embarkation from that part of the coast?—Yes, in British ships.

6984. Would it be equally safe on other parts of the coast?—It would be impossible in other parts, without perpetuating the slave trade, in my opinion.

6985. *Chairman.*] What would be the difference between the two cases?—There are no other races upon the coast who leave their country voluntarily to labour. The only way in which it could possibly be expected that the natives would be obtained from any other part of the coast would be upon compulsion and upon sale, upon positive sale and nominal manumission afterwards, before embarkation; but that would hold out the same inducements to internal slave trade in Africa as the slave trade to Brazils or Cuba.

6986. Sir *T. D. Acland.*] You think it would be impossible to guard against fraud in that case?—It would be impossible to establish such a plan without perpetuating the slave trade.

6987. *Chairman.*] On the Fish Coast, and on the Kroo Coast, you would not apprehend that the advantage given by any little presents to the chiefs on the departure of any of their people for the West Indies, might induce them to bring negroes from other parts of the country for the purpose of emigration?—I think negroes from other parts of the country would be immediately distinguished from the Kroomen.

6988. The security, then, you think would consist in the external marks of the Kroo and Fish people?—Yes. Moreover, the Kroomen and the Fishmen, on landing in the West Indies, would be always able to tell their own story; to speak English enough to make their case known.

6989. You do not mean that the Kroomen living inland speak English?—I suppose not; but all that I have ever seen have managed to make themselves understood; indeed I think it is possible they might have some idea of the English language inland, it is so universal amongst all that I have seen. It would be very easy to follow the plan supposed, to have a man-of-war stationed in that quarter, and known to be at a certain place; it would be very easy to require every emigrant ship to visit her, and receive a certificate from the captain before she sailed for the West Indies.

6990. Would you feel any difficulty in ascertaining certainly, against possibility of fraud, that those people were *bonâ fide* volunteers?—There would not be the smallest difficulty.

6991. *Chairman.*] You would call up the men and be able to ask them, either directly in English, or through interpreters, the circumstances under which they embarked?—Yes.

6992. And ascertain their knowledge of the object of the embarkation?—Yes; nothing would be more easy or more certain.

6993. Sir *T. D. Acland.*] Supposing any man embarked were to say that he did not wish to go, what would you do with him?—He must give his presents back that he has received and go back himself.

6994. If he had been sent on board by compulsion, would he not run some risk on his landing?—I think it altogether repugnant to the customs of the country to force people on board; I do not think it is a thing at all to be apprehended.

6995. Mr. *Aldam.*] You think there would be no more difficulty in emigration from the Kroo Coast to the West Indies than in emigration from England to Canada?—There would be scarcely more difficulty; I should feel quite confident, that with the commonest care upon the part of the Governments in the West India islands, such a thing could not be abused.

6996. You think the one is as liable to abuse as the other?—Yes: I think the emigration from the coast of Africa would require a little more looking after.

6997. But the captain of a man-of-war might perform every duty that the emigration agent now performs in an English port?—Yes; I think a man-of-war stationed in the neighbourhood might do so.

6998. Sir *T. D. Acland.*] Do you think the Kroomen would be willing to leave their families?—I think they would be perfectly willing to remove without their families; you could not get them to take their families.

6999. For what length of time?—For three or four years; they have the greatest objection to remove their women; indeed it is impossible for any race to be more obstinately attached to their own habits and prejudices than the Kroo and the Fish races.

7000. Therefore their engagement would be of a temporary nature?—There is scarcely such a thing known as a Krooman to be absent from his country more than seven years.

7001. Mr. *Aldam.*] Would their absence in the West Indies, and the habits they would be likely to acquire there, tend to improve the manners of the people at home, upon their return?—I think it would have that effect to some small extent.

7002. And to introduce civilization?—To a very small extent; I do not think that much could be expected without other means.

7003. Sir *T. D. Acland.*] Have they any means of education?—None whatever.

7004. *Chairman.*] They have no contact with any white men, except some that come for the purpose of trading upon the coast?—And at the settlements of Sierra Leone and Liberia.

7005. Sir *T. D. Acland.*] Do they take opportunities of acquiring instruction on board ships?—No, I think not, except what they must learn to do their duties.

7006. Do they show any disposition to learn to read and write?—Not at all.

7007. Do you think that having learned the cultivation of sugar in the West Indies, they would be likely to introduce the same cultivation in their own country?—I think that at present they are not sufficiently enlightened to make it very probable.

7008. *Chairman.*] Would the effect of considerable emigration from the Kroo Coast be to raise the rate of wages of the Kroomen employed in the navy, and on board merchant ships?—I should think very probably it might have that effect, but the wages now paid on board ships of war are much higher than are paid anywhere else.

7056. *Chairman.*] Have you considered the subject of the removal of the Mixed Commission Court from Sierra Leone?—I have. I have heard that the places named as preferable are Fernando Po, Accra, and Ascension. The first is a foreign possession, and not to be purchased, therefore utterly out of the question. The second has dangerous anchorage; no harbour or place for breaking up ships, no territory for location, no market for goods, and no community of which liberated Africans could become a part. The third is a desert, the 150 persons now living there being victualled, as at sea, on salt provisions. Since 1839, at the latter end of which we were for the first time enabled really to attack the slave trade, the number of Africans liberated by the Mixed Commission Court has been extremely small; and this diminution may be regarded as a test of success, the grand object being to guard the coast and prevent the embarkation of slaves. In 1840 the number emancipated at Sierra Leone amounted to but 732, and in the first half of 1841 to but 291, and of these not one-sixth died between capture and emancipation. Sierra Leone is far preferable to any other place for the location of liberated Africans, there being already a large and prosperous community, comprising natives of every African race, who receive among them their newly-emancipated countrymen, and regard them with the utmost sympathy, assisting them in every way, and instructing them in the language and customs of the colony. It frequently happens that near relations are again united, and the transports of joy on such occasions well vindicate the African from the charge so often repeated. The marked inferiority of the liberated

Africans who have been sent to the Gambia is owing to their small numbers, in a community having no sympathies with them, and from whom they are as much separated as from the white inhabitants; and I would ask whether intercourse with the Fantees of the Gold Coast would civilize or improve them to a greater extent?

7057. What is your opinion as to the advantage of transporting the slaves as soon as they are emancipated, from Sierra Leone to the West Indies?—The treaties embodied in the Act of the 5th of Geo. 4, provide that slaves shall be located in the territory of the nation of the capturing cruizer. This provision is fulfilled, when slaves captured by a British cruizer are emancipated at Sierra Leone. When slaves so captured are emancipated at Havannah, they should be removed to whichever of the British West India islands it is honestly believed they will be best placed for their own welfare and happiness. I utterly deny the right to consult the interests of any other parties whatever in their location. It has been argued that it would be beneficial to Sierra Leone to send negroes after emancipation in the West Indies, and that the Act in question authorises the Government to compel slaves emancipated under its provisions to serve in the Army or Navy, or to send them where it pleases. But to carry this provision out to its full extent would be but to perpetuate their slavery, contrary to the whole spirit of the Act; nor could the forcible removal of these poor creatures from an asylum containing thousands of their countrymen, and possibly many of their near kindred, be rendered justifiable by any consideration whatever. I have seen a cargo of slaves, after the completion of one voyage across the Atlantic, condemned to another for their own supposed benefit; and I can bear witness to the horror of the victims, when they found themselves once more on the "middle passage."

7058. What circumstance do you allude to?—The vessel which I stated before, that I took from Rio Janeiro to Sierra Leone, a slave ship, with a cargo of slaves which had arrived there, and had been there seized. Further I would say, let the subject be considered with regard to foreign governments. The Dutch government not long ago purchased slaves at Elmina, who, after nominal enfranchisement, were forcibly transported to the island of Java. It is undoubted, that a vessel employed in carrying them would be subject to capture by a British cruizer, and condemnation at Sierra Leone. Had such a case occurred, and the negroes after emancipation been immediately transported to Trinidad, or to Demerara without their own consent, how could such a transaction be vindicated in the eyes of Europe? Voluntary emigration from Sierra Leone may very properly be encouraged by all fair means. The number of emigrants cannot, however, amount to any considerable extent, compared with the wants of the West Indies.

7059. Mr. *Forster*.] Are you well acquainted with the land in the neighbourhood of Accra?—No; I have not been to Accra. I only know that the British settlement is confined to the walls of the fort.

7060. Are you aware of any difficulty that would arise in acquiring territory in the neighbourhood of Accra?—I believe there would be no difficulty; but it is the fact that we have no territory now.

7061. But if it were deemed advisable to establish the Mixed Commission Court there, are you aware of any difficulty in acquiring territory for the purpose of locating the liberated Africans?—No; I believe that territory might be obtained if it were desirable in other respects. But I believe it is not desirable in other respects.

7062. Captain *Fitzroy*.] Have any liberated Africans been employed at Ascension; and if so, how have they conducted themselves?—I have a letter from a gentleman who was adjutant in the Island of Ascension, under whom those Africans were employed, Lieutenant Wade. I beg leave to state that in this letter, as regards the first party to which he alludes, from my own knowledge I can say that he has very much understated the difficulty that existed with them. They were very troublesome in every way. He expressed to me verbally, in the strongest terms, the contrast between the people who had not received the benefit of residence at Sierra Leone, and those who had.

[The letter was delivered in, and read as follows:]

Sir, London, 23 June, 1842.

I have the honour to address to you the following facts relative to the liberated Africans employed by Government on the Island of Ascension, and which you may be pleased to lay before the African Committee for their information.

The liberated Africans attached to the establishment are 33 in number, and are relieved every three years if they wish it; they are paid in three classes. The first class receive 6*d.* and the lowest 4*d.*, according to their merits; they receive a full ration of provisions, but no spirits, except the head man, who is paid and victualled as the marines.

I was three years on the island, the last two as adjutant, and as such these people were more immediately under my control; and therefore I am enabled to speak confidently as to their general conduct.

I found them easily managed, especially the last party which arrived in December 1840, who being residents at Sierra Leone for many years, were most useful and intelligent men; most of them had learned to read and write, and several had been brought up to trades and were industrious; whereas the former party, who were sent direct from the slave-yard (as it is commonly termed), were difficult to instruct, owing to their ignorance of the English language.

Each man is permitted to bring his wife.

I have, &c.

To Captain the Honourable
Joseph Denman, R.N.

(signed) *Jno. Wade*, Lieut. R.N.

7063. Mr. *Forster.*] As you appear to consider Sierra Leone as a desirable place for landing and locating the liberated Africans, how do you account for so little progress having hitherto been made in agricultural improvement and in carrying civilization into the interior from that part, up to the present time?— I consider that the liberated Africans of Sierra Leone have made a wonderful advance, comparing them with their condition when landed from the slave ships.

7064. Is it not the fact that no progress has been made in cultivation or in planting in the neighbourhood of Sierra Leone?—No advance has been made because there has been no inducement held out to them; but the people have made wonderful strides, in my opinion, in civilization, and the condition of the liberated Africans is quite extraordinary, comparing them with the state in which they were landed, considering the very short time that has elapsed since the first Africans were liberated there from the slave ships.

7065. Is it not upwards of twenty years that the system has been going on there, and would not that afford ample time for greater improvement than is perceived there at this moment?—Considering the great numbers that during the twenty years have been landed from the slave ships, and their condition, I think the advance is more than could have been expected, considering that no inducement has been held out to agricultural pursuits.

7066. Are you acquainted with the banks of the Gambia and the land in the neighbourhood of our settlement there?—I have been in the Gambia a good deal; I cannot say that I have any perfect knowledge of the banks of the river.

7067. Would you think that the Gambia affords a more desirable location than Sierra Leone for cultivation?—I think, perhaps, for that particular object it may, but I am not at all sure of that.

7068. *Chairman.*] Sierra Leone furnishes very little exportable produce of its own?—I am not aware that it exports any thing of its own, but the country we are about to purchase affords means of raising produce, if it is encouraged; I mean the Quia country.

7069. You think it desirable that the limits of the colony of Sierra Leone should be extended?—I think undoubtedly, both up the river and coastwise; I consider that the plans of General Turner were in the utmost degree wise and enlightened, and it is very much to be regretted that they were not followed up.

7070. Sir *T. D. Acland.*] When you say coastwise, do you mean north or south?—I think south to Cape Mount, where a settlement is already established, I would purchase the sovereignty, and establish one or two settlements between Cape Mount and Sierra Leone.

7071. Including the Sherboro'?—Including the Sherboro'; Boom Kittam General Turner already had. With regard to the Gambia I should wish to observe, that to bring forth the resources of that colony a steamer on the river is indispensably necessary, and in my opinion she would pay her own expenses, if she were allowed to carry light goods up and down for the merchants, as a sort of packet.

7072. *Chairman.*] Would there be any difficulty in manning a steamer almost entirely with blacks, so as to expose very little, if any, white life to the risks attending the navigation of the river?—For the services of colonial steamers, I believe they might be entirely manned with black people, and in the course of a few years, even with black engineers.

7073. Mr. *Forster.*] Are you aware that the French have two or three steam boats generally on the Senegal?—I am aware that the French have steamers, that they are exercising the utmost rivalry against British commerce upon the coast, and that they derive the greatest possible advantages over British commerce by the use of those steamers.

7074. *Chairman.*] Is there any thing at present to prevent the establishment of mercantile steamers, either at Sierra Leone or at the Gambia, as a private venture?—As a private venture, certainly not; but it would not be worth the while of any individuals to make the speculation.

7075. Sir *T. D. Acland.*] Are the French steamers government steamers?— They are government steamers attached to the colony of Senegal.

7076. *Chairman.*] What sized steamers would be required for the purpose that you contemplate?—I should say very small steamers for the Gambia itself; as small as the London boats that run above bridge; but their services would be required entirely for that river, and perhaps for the Casamanza.

7077. Mr. *Forster.*] Would not a steamer on the Gambia be very important for the Government communication with Macarthy's Island, and generally up the river?—It is the only way that settlements up the river can be supported or protected in my opinion; it would have the effect of quadrupling the force there now, and it is the only means by which we can, in my opinion, bring out the resources of the upper parts of the river, which are so great.

7078. *Chairman.*] Is the force of the current generally so strong as to render it extremely difficult to navigate up the stream with sailing vessels?—It frequently takes a week or 10 days to get a good-sized vessel up to Macarthy's Island, where now our highest settlement is; but we should have one still higher.

7079. You conceive that there are immense resources up the river?—I do; I believe that a supply of gum might be obtained at the Gambia equal to that which we have been deprived of by the French at Portendique, if proper measures were taken. At Portendique, for the last two years, there has been no trade at all.

7080. Mr. *Forster.*] In your former evidence, in answer to question 6674, in reference to the importance of British settlements for the suppression of the slave trade, you say "I spoke more particularly of Sierra Leone, at the same time the connection of the Gambia trade with the slave trade is a fact that there is no doubt about;" are the Committee to understand that you mean that Sierra Leone and the Gambia are on the same footing in that respect?— I think they have assisted the slave trade in very different ways; one way in which they have both assisted, is by the sale of vessels to the slave dealers; but the trade in the Gambia goes hand in hand with the slave trade of Bissao, as I before stated; at Sierra Leone it has been more directly by the sale of vessels, and some few goods passing down through their hands to the Gallinas and elsewhere.

7081. Will you have the goodness to explain to the Committee your meaning in saying that "the connection of the Gambia trade with the slave trade is a fact that there is no doubt about"?—I should have said the external trade of the Gambia; the trade up the river is another thing. As regards the external trade of the Gambia, the greater part of the trade is through the hands of notorious slave dealers, who sell produce, and give money to the Gambia merchants, and who in return receive goods from the Gambia; and those goods are the means again of purchasing slaves and produce; that is a connection which I consider is a very direct one.

7082. *Chairman.*] You do not mean, that merchants trading at the Gambia are themselves personally interested in any slave trade adventures, or have any share in the profit or loss of such transactions?—No; I have no reason to suppose that such is the case directly.

7083. Sir *T. D. Acland.*] Do you mean to say that the goods so furnished to the slave dealer are essential to the maintenance of the slave traffic?—I believe they might get goods elsewhere, if those were not supplied by the Gambia merchants.

7084. But still goods from some part are essential to the maintenance of the slave traffic?—Indispensable; all their slaves are bought with British goods.

7085. *Chairman.*] Could they not obtain their slaves solely with money?—I think not.

7086. Sir *T. D. Acland.*] What is the state of civilization of the people upon the Gambia?—The banks of the Gambia have been disturbed for several years by a man of the name of Kemingtang, and a great deal too much forbearance has been used towards him. I do not think the people in general upon the banks are in an advanced state of civilization, by any means.

7087. Its progress has been interrupted by this man's disturbance?—This man has occasioned mischief, but I do not think it was making progress to any extent.

7088. Mr. *Forster.*] You appear to distinguish between legitimate and illegitimate trade by the mode of payment; that is to say, according to whether the payment is in money or in produce?—I have already said that, strictly speaking, in the strict sense of the term, "legitimate trade," that is, trade which has no communication with the slave trade in any way whatever, is that in which goods are exchanged for produce.

7089. Would you recommend or expect that a trader on the coast of Africa should refuse dollars in payment of his goods to any body?—In cases where he knew that no use could be made of those goods but to purchase slaves, I think he would be bound to do so; and I think if he did not he should be subjected to the penalties of the Act.

7090. Supposing the British traders of Bissao were to refuse money from the Spaniards, would you recommend that they should refuse money also from the natives in exchange for their goods?—I have stated that I do not recommend that they should refuse money from any body, except in cases where the trade must necessarily be going on to supply the slave trade exclusively. In cases where slave trade and produce trade exist together, I do not think it would be possible, and I do not think it would be desirable to endeavour to prevent the trade from going on; I have stated that fully in the former part of my evidence.

7091. *Chairman.*] You would, if possible, devise some means by which English trade, although in lawful goods, with settlements purely confined to slave trading, such as the Gallinas, should be prevented?—Precisely; that is my view.

7092. As long as the prize vessels are sold at Sierra Leone, will there not be great practical difficulty in preventing those vessels getting ultimately into the hands of the slave dealers, whether you can prevent it at the first hand or not?—I think the longer the interval that elapsed before they got into the hands of the slave dealers, the better. I think that British subjects selling vessels adapted only for the slave trade into the hands of notorious slave dealers, should be rendered subject to penalties; but I admit the difficulty of preventing the eventual return of such vessels into the hands of slave dealers.

7093. You think it very desirable, if possible, that the system of breaking up vessels should be further extended?—I think it should be applied universally to slave ships.

7094. Is there any English law which you would wish to see amended in that respect?—Under the Act 5 Geo. 4, under which a vessel in British waters would be condemned for carrying on the slave trade, there is no provision for breaking up the vessel; and consequently vessels condemned under that Act are sold to the highest bidder. I certainly think it is desirable that a clause should be inserted in the act for the purpose.

7095. Mr. *Forster.*] You have stated in your former evidence that the public auctioneer is obliged to knock down the vessel to the highest bidder. Would you recommend that the public auctioneer should be subject to penalties for selling a vessel to the agent of a slave dealer?—I have before stated that he is not subject to penalties; he is a Government agent employed according to law.

7096. Captain *Fitzroy.*] You have stated that the cruizers should be withdrawn from the western coast of the Atlantic, their efforts against the slave trade there being comparatively ineffectual. Can you give any further reason for that opinion than the one you have expressed?—The cruizers upon the coast of Cuba or Brazil, cruize under much greater disadvantages than they formerly did upon the coast of Africa, before the Equipment articles came into force; and moreover, the immense number of merchant vessels always in sight about those parts of the coast is, I think, another reason against attempting to suppress the slave trade upon that side of the Atlantic. And there is besides another subject of greatly increased importance, the inconvenience that would arise from the exercise of the right of search in that quarter.

7097. *Chairman.*] You mean to say, that in consequence of coming into contact with a much greater number of vessels of different descriptions, the right of search, if exercised there, would be more obnoxious, and lead to greater difficulties with the countries upon whose vessels we should exercise it?—It could never be fully exercised with regard to the vessels that were there, and the exercise of it would involve 50 searches for one upon the coast of Africa.

7098. In the one case you only have to search the African trade, in the other case you have to search the whole trade of those countries on the American coast?—Yes.

7099. Captain *Fitzroy*.] You have stated the disproportion between the emolument derived by the captains of cruizers from the capture of slavers after the embarkation of the slaves, compared with that derived from the capture of empty vessels, to be very great, and altogether unjust; can you give the Committee any further information upon this subject?—I have here an account of two vessels, captured under the Equipment articles by me, one measuring 57 tons and the other 43 tons; the aggregate of the proceeds of both these vessels for distribution to the captors was 576*l.* 6*s.* 5*d.* Another vessel of 48 tons was captured by me, with slaves on board; the proceeds for distribution upon this single vessel amounted to 1,654*l.* 19*s.* 5*d.*, nearly three times as much as the two empty ships, measuring together 100 tons.

7100. *Chairman*.] Can you state how many slaves could have been carried by the two empty ships, in case they had been allowed to have been filled?—There might have been 700 slaves in those two ships.

7101. Sir *T. D. Acland*.] How many were there in the other?—Forty-eight tons and 350 slaves. With regard to the capture of these vessels, the empty vessels were captured upon the principle of blockade, a service of the most harassing, tiresome, and arduous description. The full vessel was, as it must be in most cases, captured by chance.

7102. How would you propose to arrange it?—I would take the whole of the sums payable upon captured vessels during any given year, and upon that I would calculate what it amounted to per ton, and I would give that bounty for the future upon every vessel, as a substitute for the head-money, for the payments now made.

7103. Captain *Fitzroy*.] You have stated in your former evidence, that, six weeks after you were at New Cestos destroying the slave factory, a slaver was there again; can you offer any explanation of that circumstance?—The slave factory at New Cestos was abandoned in December 1840. The factories were left standing, to form a palm-oil factory, at the request of some British traders. I however understood that the prince was endeavouring to get a slave-dealer to re-establish himself in this factory, and I therefore, in the middle of April, burned down the buildings. On the 8th of June a new factor arrived from the Havannah and landed his goods, but no slaves were taken away till October. Three or four days after the slaves were carried off the blockade was re-established, and there could be no more.

7104. It has been stated, in answer to question 5968, that you thought you had put an effectual stop to the slave trade at the Gallinas by the destruction of the factories; was that your own opinion?—I beg to refer the Committee to the third paragraph from the bottom of a letter in the correspondence relative to the Gallinas, at page 9, in which I state that "I believe they will endeavour still to prosecute the slave trade."

7105. Mr. *Forster.*] Is it your opinion that the British traders on the coast of Africa, and those connected with them, are more deeply interested in the suppression of the slave trade than any other class of British subjects?—In general they are; but there are some instances in which particular merchants derive great advantages from the connexion. There can be no question that it is for the interests of commerce that the slave trade should be put down; but there may be particular instances where British merchants derive great profits from their connexion with it.

7106. But generally, you are of opinion that the British merchants are decidedly interested in the trade being put down?—I have no doubt of it at all.

7107. *Chairman.*] You believe that wherever the trade in slaves is put down, a more profitable trade might be carried on in its place in the form of manufactures in exchange for produce?—Undoubtedly more profitable, both to the natives and to the persons trading with them.

7108. When you speak of individuals being interested, you mean that there are individuals incidentally benefited by the commerce which the slave trade gives rise to in that country?—Precisely; that is what I mean. For instance, supposing the slave traders at the Gallinas had been supplied by a British commercial house, that probably would have been more profitable to them than any prospect of produce trade after the slave trade of the Gallinas was destroyed.

———

Lunæ, 25° die Julii, 1842.

MEMBERS PRESENT.

Sir T. D. Acland.
Mr. Aldam.
Viscount Courtenay.
Viscount Ebrington.
Captain Fitzroy.

Mr. Forster.
Sir R. H. Inglis.
Mr. Wilson Patten.
Mr. G. W. Wood.

VISCOUNT SANDON in the chair.

Captain the Honourable *Joseph Denman*, R. N. called in; and further examined.

10646. *Chairman.*] What evidence had you of those parties being British subjects whom you brought back to Sierra Leone?—I found them in the barracoons mixed with other slaves for exportation; I took them to Sierra Leone; they were examined, both speaking English, by the Governor of Sierra Leone in my presence; the opinion of the Governor of Sierra Leone was, that it was most undoubtedly the fact that they were British subjects; one was a liberated African and the other a Creole, born in Sierra Leone.

10647. Mr. *Forster.*] Do you consider them, under those circumstances, as fairly and properly entitled to the appellation of British subjects?—As completely as any person in this room.

10648. Was the circumstance of your finding them at the Gallinas the ground upon which you took your proceedings there and burnt the place?—It was the principal ground of those proceedings; the grounds have been already stated in my former evidence; I think that was the most important ground.

———

EVIDENCE OF PEDRO DE ZULUETA, JUN., ESQ.
TAKEN BEFORE
THE SELECT COMMITTEE ON WEST COAST OF AFRICA.

Veneris, 22° die Junii, 1842.

MEMBERS PRESENT.

Sir T. D. Acland.
Mr. Aldam.
Viscount Courtenay.
Captain Fitzroy.
Mr. Foster.
Mr. W. Hamilton.

Sir R. H. Inglis.
Mr. Milnes.
Mr. Wilson Patten.
Lord Stanley.
Mr. G. W. Wood.

VISCOUNT SANDON, in the chair.

Pedro de Zulueta, Jun. Esq. called in; and examined.

10370. *Chairman.*] You have seen some statements that have been made to this Committee upon the subject of a transaction in which your house was engaged; have you any observations to offer upon it?—I received from the Clerk of the Committee a letter accompanying a copy of certain evidences, which are Mr. Macaulay's evidence of the 10th of June, the 14th of June, and the 15th of June; and Captain Hill's evidence of the 29th of June, the 4th of July, and the 6th of July. I would beg, first of all, to refer to the letter which I had the honour to address to the Chairman. My reason for wishing to be examined before this Committee was, that the statements contained in the evidence which I have mentioned are all of them more or less incorrect, some of them totally so. I will begin by stating what has been the nature of our, I will not say trade, for we have not had a trade ourselves, but of our connexion with the shipment of goods to the coast of Africa. We have been established as merchants for upwards of 70 years in Spain, for nearly 20 years in this country, and we have had connexions to a large extent in Spain, and in the Havannah, and in South America, and several other places; among them we have had connexions or commercial intercourse with the house of Pedro Martinez & Co. of the Havannah, and with Blanco & Cavallo of Havannah. With them we have carried on a regular business in consignments of sugars and of cochineal, which they have made to us; and in specie received by the packets from Mexico and other places. We have several times acted for them here in this country, buying raw cotton for instance at Liverpool, and re-selling it very largely; that has been principally with Pedro Martinez & Co.

10371. They are general merchants?—They are general merchants, and their transactions with us have been of that nature. As general merchants we have bought stock here for them rather largely; and in the course of those transactions we have received orders from Don Pedro Martinez & Co. of the Havannah, and from Don Pedro Martinez of Cadiz, to ship goods for the coast of Africa; never from Pedro Blanco, and never from Blanco & Cavallo.

10372. Have you received orders from Pedro Martinez for shipments for the coast of Africa?—Yes; in the course of business we have received orders to ship goods upon the funds in our hands belonging to them; and we have shipped the goods described in the letter, and sent the bills of lading to Pedro Martinez; but beyond that we have never had any returns from the coast of Africa, nor any control of any kind from the moment the cargoes left the ports of this country.

10373. You have had no interest in the result of the venture?—No, nor any notice, nor any acquaintance, nor any correspondence with any one upon the coast; we have never had any kind of knowledge, either subsequently or previously, of the shipments, except the mere fact of buying the goods and shipping them.

10374. Your whole interest was a commission upon the transaction— Entirely. The extent of those transactions has been so limited in the course of nearly 20 years that we have been in this country, that the amount of the invoices that we have sent out has been something like 20,000*l.* or 22,000*l.* in the course of all that time. That is one part of the operations we have performed. The other operations are the acceptance of bills drawn by people on the coast; among them Pedro Blanco when he was there, upon ourselves, on account of Blanco & Cavallo, of Havannah, upon funds which Blanco & Cavallo had in our hands: for instance, the people at the Havannah, or in Spain, open a credit with us, and we accept the bills of the parties on that credit with us, just the same as we should do with any other correspondent in any other part.

10375. You would have funds in your hands, arising from some commercial transactions between you and the Havannah merchant or the Cadiz merchant; and Pedro Blanco, upon the coast of Africa, would draw upon the credit of those funds, being authorised by the Cadiz or the Havannah merchant?—Yes; and if Pedro Blanco had drawn 5*s.* beyond that, we should have protested, and in some instances we have protested. With regard to the vessel alluded to in this Report, the Augusta, our part in that concern has been simply that which appears from one of the letters: that is to say, Pedro Martinez, of Cadiz, had made choice of Jennings to buy the vessel, and lent him money to buy the vessel; because Pedro Martinez wanted him to have a vessel in the trade, for the purpose of taking his goods to their destination. I have now described the three kinds of operations in which we have been concerned, and our knowledge of all of them terminated with the execution of the orders of our correspondents. We had nothing more to do than to follow the orders of the purchaser in shipping the goods. With regard to the purchase of the vessel by Jennings; Jennings is a man who has been employed some time by Martinez; he has served Martinez as a chartered captain, and Martinez having been satisfied with his services, agreed to lend him that money on the security of the vessel, provided it did not exceed a certain amount; which was all the interference we had with it, just to see that a certain amount was not exceeded, 500*l.* or whatever it was.

10376. Then you were to furnish Captain Jennings with money for the purchase within a limited amount, say 500*l.*, credit being given to him upon you by Pedro Martinez, of Cadiz?—That is just the point.

10377. Captain *Fitzroy.*] The Augusta being purchased by money advanced by your house for Martinez & Company of Cadiz; and she then became the property of Pedro Martinez?—No, she became the property of Jennings; the money was lent to Jennings, and he bound himself by giving security on the vessel to answer for the amount. It is a mercantile operation which is not unusual.

10378. Mr. *Forster.*] You advanced the money to Captain Jennings for the purchase of the vessel, Jennings transferring the vessel to you as a security for the amount so advanced?—That is just the description of operation, which is a very general one in business.

10379. *Chairman.*] What is the object of such an operation?—I know very little or almost next to nothing of the operations in those parts of the world; but the object of such an operation I apprehend to be this: a vessel chartered with a stranger must be governed by the different clauses of the charter-party; the charterer must be limited to time and to places; and by Martinez having the vessel owned by a man with whom he could have a better understanding than with others, he might always send more advantageously articles from the Havannah to the Gallinas, and from here to the Gallinas. When I say articles, I mean legal articles.

10379*. What advantage would there be in Mr. Jennings taking the articles rather as the owner than as captain under Martinez; was not he commander of the vessel as well as owner of the vessel?—Yes.

10380. He is made the owner, instead of being captain?—He is the owner as well as the captain of the vessel; he stands indebted to Martinez, and gives a bottomry bond for the vessel.

10380*. Does Mr. Jennings upon this transaction make all the freight to his own profit?—Certainly, whatever he does is to his own profit.

10381. He is not, then, an agent for Martinez?—No, he is a person to whom Martinez lends the money to buy the vessel; whatever profit he derives is his own. Martinez has this advantage, which to a mercantile man is very perceptible, that he has got a charter with a man who stands in that relation towards him which gives him a sort of control over the vessel. If I as a stranger charter a vessel for Martinez, and he has spent one, two, or five days more in landing goods than the charter-party allows, I should make a claim for it; I should say, "You must keep to the charter." Now, when Jennings is indebted to him for the favour of a loan for the vessel, he is not upon a similar footing.

10382. So that he gets the vessel more under his own control?—Yes; in saying this I am putting an hypothetical case, but I do not know the mind of Martinez himself.

10383. Mr. *Forster.*] You acted in this transaction merely as agent in the usual manner, as you would have acted for any house in any part of the world?—Exactly; if Martinez had told me, "You have got 500*l.* in your hands, pay that to Captain Jennings," I should have known nothing more of the transaction; I should have paid the money. But Martinez did not wish to go beyond a certain amount; and he says, "You exercise control, do not allow the man to pay more than 500*l.* for the vessel."

10384. But beyond the purchase of the vessel and the shipment of the goods, the other arrangements and the subsequent transactions were entirely between Jennings and Martinez & Co.?—Most assuredly; except with the order of Martinez, I do not know how we could have done any thing with him in any way.

10385. Captain *Fitzroy.*] Though the process of hypothecating a vessel may be usual between British merchants, is it usual to cover a transaction of Spanish slave trade with the British flag, by means of such an arrangement as that described to have taken place in the case of the Augusta?—In order to answer that question, it seems to me that it is fair that I should ask where is the transaction of covering, and where is the slave trade transaction? I know positively of my own knowledge, that there is no such thing at all connected with the Augusta. If I had an opportunity, I could make my affidavit of that.

10386. Sir *T. D. Acland.*] Do you mean that you know that the Augusta was not engaged in any slaving transactions during the voyage upon which she left Liverpool?—Most assuredly not; in fact my testimony is hardly required of that, because every thing proves that. When she was detained, it was never said that she was upon a slaving operation at all. Before she left this port, after she was bought, she was completely rendered useless for that purpose.

10387. *Chairman.*] The charge is, that she was engaged in carrying goods to a person engaged in the slave trade; not that she was engaged in the slave trade herself?—I most certainly say that I do not know whether the person is so engaged or not.

10388. Captain *Fitzroy.*] Is it usual to cover a transaction of Spanish trade with the English flag?—I am not aware that a Spanish merchant is prohibited chartering an English vessel.

10389. But is it lawful to employ the British flag to cover a vessel that is not owned by a British subject?—I say that that vessel is owned by a British subject.

10390. Sir *T. D. Acland.*] By whom?—By Captain Jennings.

10391. Was not the money with which she was purchased, the money of Pedro Martinez?—It seems to me that English captains and English subjects are not prohibited from borrowing money from Spaniards; she was bought with money lent by Pedro Martinez to Captain Jennings for the purpose.

10392. Do you mean that the money was a loan to Captain Jennings, at the time he paid it for the vessel?—It was a loan to Captain Jennings.

10393. Do you mean that the ship was then Captain Jennings's property?—It was.

10394. Was it in his power to sell that ship at any port he pleased?—There was a mortgage upon the vessel.

10395. Mr. W. *Patten.*] You have stated that yours is an agency trade?—It is so; and in the multitude of business, any one can understand that 20,000*l.* in 15 or 20 years, can only be a mere trifle in the business of any merchant, without laying claim to a large business; and in following that business, we have executed shipping orders.

10396. To what part of the coast of Africa has that business been chiefly conducted?—I believe, almost exclusively to the Gallinas.

10397. Have the goods that Mr. Martinez has ordered to be sent to the Gallinas, been all sent to the same individual?—No, to different individuals; sometimes to Pedro Blanco, who was for a certain time an agent of Pedro Martinez on the coast, and sometimes we have sent a bill of lading drawn in this way to order; we have sent it to Pedro Martinez as a voucher against his account.

10398. Do you know the nature of the trade of Pedro Martinez at the Gallinas?—I know from general report that Don Pedro Martinez himself is supposed to deal in slaves, and I believe it is so.

10399. Is he known at the Havannah as a dealer in slaves?—I do not know, but I believe so; I do not know why it should not be known at the Havannah, if it is known in other parts.

10400. *Chairman.*] Is a ship which is hypothecated, liable to be foreclosed at any moment, at the discretion of the mortgagee?—It depends altogether upon the terms of the mortgage; if the mortgagee says, "You must give me the money when I ask for it," of course he must sell the vessel if he has not got any thing else; he would always have to deduct whatever freight had been earned. When the security may be called upon to be effective, depends upon the nature of the transaction between the parties.

10401. Mr. *Forster*.] Your house had nothing to do with any letters that might be put on board the Augusta after she sailed from this country?—Nothing whatever.

10402. The Augusta was seized on the coast of Africa, on the charge of slave trading?—I believe that was the case.

10403. Did you not appeal against that condemnation?—Yes, there is an appeal by the owner.

10404. Before the Privy Council?—Yes.

10405. That appeal is not yet decided?—I believe not.

10406. Sir *T. D. Acland*.] You stated that your transactions with Africa for Martinez have amounted to about 20,000*l.* in 15 or 20 years. What has been the amount of your whole transactions with Blanco & Martinez of the Havannah during that period?—Perhaps 100,000*l.* or a larger sum. For instance, we have received more than 40 or 50 cargoes of sugar from the Havannah, consigned to us, and cigars; and we have received bills of lading of specie shipped at Mexico to be sold here, and bar gold, and things of that sort.

10407. Mr. *Wood*.] Have you reason to suppose that the whole of that large commerce is subservient to the carrying on of the slave trade by the house of Blanco & Martinez at the Havannah?—I do not know; I know that they have large transactions in general business. I know that a short time ago I got 40,000*l.* or 50,000*l.* of Spanish bonds in the market for Martinez. I know that he is a large speculator in Spanish bonds and in securities of state.

10408. Is that speculating in Spanish bonds on account of the house at Cadiz, or the house at Havannah?—Speaking technically, I should say it was on account of the Cadiz house.

10409. The question related to the commerce of the Havannah house?—Pedro Martinez is a Havannah merchant. But with regard to Havannah merchants, we have received large consignments of sugar, cochineal, and sometimes Mexican goods, brought to Havannah and shipped to us here.

10410. In what course of business have the proceeds of those consignments been disposed of; have they gone in sending supplies to the coast of Africa?—Out of that large amount of money 22,000*l.* is the amount of all the goods that we have sent to the coast of Africa in 20 years.

10411. Of all descriptions?—Of all sorts and kinds; I have gone through the invoice-book and found them out.

10412. Have the proceeds generally been disposed of by drafts from the parties themselves to your house?—By the parties at Havannah, when the exchange turns to their advantage.

10413. Have you reason to suppose that a large portion of the trade that they carry on at the Havannah is the slave trade?—I had no reason to know any thing of the kind; I have known more of their transactions with the slave trade since these things have been mooted than I ever knew before; I have had more knowledge of these things lately than I ever had in my life before; and when I say "I," I beg to state that I ought to state "we," for all my partners are in the same situation.

10414. Have you been employed by the house at the Havannah to ship manufactured goods from this country to Havannah, suitable for the African trade?—We have sometimes shipped goods to the Havannah of the same kind as those that were in the "Augusta;" cotton goods and other things of that sort.

10415. Has that been recently?—In the course of our operations.

10416. How many years ago?—In the course of these 15 or 20 years that we have been engaged in business with them; all that I could see in a moment by my books.

10417. Have you sent any goods of that description to the Havannah recently?—Not very recently; I think not for some years.

10418. Have you sent any goods of that description since you first began to send goods out direct to the coast of Africa?—They have been mixed; I cannot draw a distinction between the two destinations; some have gone to the Havannah, some to the Gallinas.

10419. Have those supplies of English manufactured goods, which heretofore went to the Havannah, to be used there for promoting the slave trade, been more recently sent direct from this country to the coast of Africa?—No, I do not think that is the case; I should think the contrary is more likely to be the case, but I think we have shipped in some months, or in some years, partly to the Havannah, and partly to the Gallinas.

10420. If the coast of Africa be their ultimate destination, will not they go out at a cheaper cost to the owner if they go direct from this country, than if they go circuitously first to Havannah, and then to the coast of Africa?—I think that is very doubtful indeed, because the freights to Havannah are so miserably low that I believe they can be taken for almost nothing; in

Liverpool, English vessels loading for Havannah, load for any thing you will choose to give them.

10421. Has the trade of Pedro Martinez increased or diminished the last few years in that particular kind of goods?—I think it is neither more nor less: I think it is just about the same. I believe for the last three or four years it has been less altogether to both places, but it has diminished equally; I cannot say when it is increased in the one part or diminished in the other.

10422. How long have you conducted the trade upon the coast of Africa?— As I said before, I do not think we have conducted any trade on the coast of Africa, either legal or illegal.

10423. How long have you acted as agents for Martinez, on the coast of Africa?—As long as we have had any connexions with Martinez; it is part and parcel of other operations; that is to say, in the multitude of other operations that have intervened we have shipped goods as I have said.

10424. Did that part of your operations for him spring up after your first connexion with Martinez had commenced?—No, it is part of a mass of business all mixed up together.

10425. Mr. *Forster.*] In the extensive transactions of your house, these shipments, whether to Havannah or the coast of Africa, form a very trifling proportion?—I can only leave the Committee to judge for themselves as to that, after what I have stated.

10426. Mr. *Wood.*] What is the firm of the house at Havannah?—Pedro Martinez & Co.; the Cadiz house is Pedro Martinez only, without the company. Blanco & Carvalho was the firm some time ago: it is now Blanco & Co.

10427. Are the answers which you have given in relation to one of these houses equally applicable to both of them?—There is some difference between them: but in regard to the general business of both of them, what applies to the one applies to the other. I have the same general business with both, and the smallest part of the business has been the shipment of goods, whether to Havannah or to the coast of Africa. The shipments apply to Martinez only.

10428. Have you shipped English manufactured goods direct to the coast of Africa, on behalf of both those houses?—Such goods as were in the Augusta I have shipped for one party only. With regard to the house of Blanco & Carvalho, and the house of Pedro Martinez & Co., with both of them I have carried on a general large business. But to Blanco & Carvalho I never shipped a single piece of goods of any kind, except some sugar mills to the Havannah;

and with regard to the house of Pedro Martinez, we have shipped such goods as those by the Augusta.

10429. From your general knowledge of the trade of the house of Pedro Martinez & Co., is it your opinion that the goods which you so shipped to the coast of Africa were destined to be employed in the slave trade?—I do not know; they may be, for any thing that I know.

10430. Has it come within your knowledge that the house of Martinez & Co. are exporters from Africa of the native produce of Africa?—No, because I never tried to get any knowledge of their transactions there of any sort.

10431. Have you ever received consignments from them, or on their behalf, of palm-oil, gold dust, or ivory, from the coast of Africa?—Never; we never have received any thing from the coast of Africa whatever. With regard to all these transactions, it will perhaps appear strange to the Committee that I should not know more of the coast of Africa, having shipped things there; but if we had shipped to the amount of 100,000*l.* to the coast of Africa, or carried on any considerable trade there, we should certainly have known more about the coast of Africa; but in transactions of a very large amount, an invoice occasionally of about 2,000*l.* or 3,000*l.* of goods was a thing that we sent as a matter of course, and did not trouble our heads about, especially as the remuneration we got was a mere trifle, not of itself worth pursuing, if it had not been for the general business we had.

10432. *Chairman.*] Is there any other part of the evidence which has been given that you wish to observe upon?—It is asked here, in Question 5086, "Who was he?" the answer is, "The name is mentioned in the Parliamentary Papers as being connected with the purchase of a slave vessel, Mr. Kidd; and it is mentioned in connexion with that of Mr. Zulueta of London." Now, as to Mr. Kidd, the very first thing I ever knew or ever heard of his name was to see it here. I never heard of his name at all. I never had a letter from him or through him, or knew any thing of the man whatever. That is with regard to myself. With regard to my partners, I can say the same; I have been making inquiries about it. My father knew there was such a man upon the coast, but I did not know even that, though I have managed all this business. Our house never had a letter from the man, or knew any thing about him.

10433. You have no connexion with Mr. Kidd in any way?—No, nor any knowledge of him. Then in the next answer it is said "Zulueta the gentleman in London to whom the vessel was sent, and who sold her again to her former Spanish owner, is a name well known on the coast in connexion with the slave trade." Now what is known on the coast I really cannot pretend to say; but I believe that not many persons can say that which I can say, that neither myself, nor my father, nor my grandfather, nor any body in our firm, has ever had any kind of interest of any sort, or derived any emolument or connexion from the slave trade. My father had at one time an interest in a bankrupt's estate at the Havannah, upon which he was a creditor. There were some slaves on the estate, and they formed part of the property assignable to the creditors, and my father got the slaves assigned to him; because the other gentlemen and the creditors were not of the same opinion, he got them assigned to him, and made them free; and that is all the connexion we have ever had with any slaves in the world. I do not know how far that may be considered irrelevant to the point, but I state it because we are here mentioned three or four times as connected with slave dealers, as a name well known in connexion with the slave trade. That sort of statement is rather a difficult thing to deal with.

10434. If it is meant to insinuate by these observations that you ever had any other connexion with the slave trade, than being the shipping agent of goods which were sent to a man who was a dealer in slaves, you entirely deny it?— I assure the Committee, that although I have a general notion as to what interest Blanco and Martinez have in slaves, yet, if I was put upon my oath to make any particular statement, I really could not, because I do not know it. Of course I believe it; but my personal knowledge amounts only to that which the knowledge of what we read in a newspaper amounts to.

10435. There was nothing upon the face of the transactions which you had with those parties which spoke of a connexion with traffic in slaves?— Nothing whatever. It is well known, that, fifty years ago, it was in the ordinary course of business in Cadiz to insure operations in slave trading. My house at that time were underwriters, and it was notorious that a policy of that kind would never enter the doors of our house; and nobody would come to offer such a thing to us upon any terms. It is notorious, both here and in Spain, that we set our faces distinctly against having any interest of any kind in the slave trade.

10436. It is further stated, "It appears that it is a regular thing sending vessels to him, that is to Mr. Zulueta; if they come to England to him he sends them to Cadiz, and they get out again to the Havannah and come again into the trade." Have you any observation to make upon that?—It is all untrue, the whole of it; I never received a vessel from those gentlemen; there has been nothing of the kind.

10437. Have you any thing further to state upon the subject?—There are several things I have marked; for instance, such as this, "You are not bound to suppose that a man will make a bad use of that which he purchases." If I wished to put my statement upon that footing, I should have done with it in a moment, for I knew nothing of the use they were put to. I bought goods, but as to what use was made of them I knew nothing whatever. But that is not the position which I wish to assume. It is said here that we sent goods or vessels to Pedro Blanco. To that I say, that we never sent either goods or vessels to Pedro Blanco. In answer to Question 5474 it is said by Mr. Macaulay, "I stated 'that it appears that it is a regular thing sending vessels to him, that is to Mr. Zulueta; if they come to England to him he sends them to Cadiz, and they get out again to the Havannah and come again into the trade.' My answer was intended to describe only the course of that particular transaction and not to apply to any other case." I never received a single vessel from the coast of Africa at any time, nor any body for us.

10438. Mr. *Forster.*] Then that statement is entirely untrue?—Totally, from beginning to end; we never did so, and nobody for us; and nobody to our knowledge, or with our connivance; I deny it in the most distinct manner. In answer to Question 5487, Mr. Macaulay is asked, "Have you any thing further to say with regard to the connexion of Zulueta with the slave trade?" The answer is, "I would refer to his connexion with the Gollupchik, which was lately captured. In that case it appeared that the vessel went out direct to the Gallinas from London." That is the same vessel as the Augusta, which I have already explained; it formerly bore the name of Gollupchik.

10439. *Chairman.*] Have you been concerned in the purchase of vessels frequently for Pedro Martinez or Pedro Blanco?—We have sometimes bought such vessels here as we could resell at the Havannah, such as the Arrogante, which we have bought.

10440. Upon orders?—Partly on orders, and sometimes on our own account on speculation.

10441. Mr. *Wood.*] For what particular trade were they calculated when they reached the Havannah?—I think for the same trade which they were calculated for when they were sold here.

10442. For the conveyance of merchandise?—As well as any thing else. They were sold here publicly.

10443. Mr. *Forster.*] If it was legal for them to be sold here, you considered that it was legal for you to buy them?—I never had any doubt of the legality of buying here, or of selling them again afterwards.

10444. Mr. *Wood.*] But the questions appertaining to the carrying on of the slave trade do not confine themselves within strictly legal grounds, but they have other more important considerations attaching to them?—As to that point, there may be a difference of opinion; I would be very sorry indeed, for the sake of catching the approval of other persons, to make a disclaimer of any particular set of opinions whatever; but I believe the only point with which the Committee have to do, is the legal point. As to the moral point, it seems to me, that I am to judge of that; upon that point, I think I have stated quite enough, having stated distinctly that I never had any connexion, nor derived any profit from the slave trade whatever.

10445. Sir *T. D. Acland.*] You have stated in your letter, that your principle is, that of "not wishing to derive profit or advantage from the sufferings of humanity, whether avoidable or unavoidable," and you have acted upon that principle?—That is the principle upon which we have acted.

10446. And you do not find that acting upon that principle has interfered with the fair success of your commerce?—I do not think it would; if it would, we should not care much about that, because we are in a position which is well known to many persons here, as well as to persons abroad. In 5495, Mr. Macaulay is asked, "What evidence have we that Zulueta knew that in dealing with Pedro Blanco, the goods he sold would be used for the barter of slaves." I have said, that I had nothing to do with him; I never sold any goods to Pedro Blanco. The answer here is, "Any body engaged in the Spanish trade would be aware that Pedro Blanco was the largest slave trader in the world." It may be so, that he is the largest in the world; but I can only say that the largest is very little, if that is the case, for I have spoken of 22,000*l.* as being the amount of the bills we have paid for him, which I have here (*producing the same*), to the order of several houses established in Sierra Leone, for goods, I suppose bought for him, amounting to about 22,100*l.* I only mention this with reference to the notoriety of his being such a large slave dealer, that it was impossible to shut your eyes to it. Then with respect to what is said in answer 5502, I only wish to remark upon this, that what I have answered already I believe applies to this. It is said, "I think that a man who viewed the slave trade in a proper light, would have considered it improper to be so engaged." I have observed already upon that, that the propriety or impropriety of our conduct is a different thing from the question whether we have been legally or illegally engaged, although the question with which I am now concerned is a general disclaimer of any participation in the slave trade.

10447. You agree with Mr. Macaulay's opinion, "That a man who viewed the slave trade in a proper light, would have considered it improper to be so engaged"?—I do not know whether my opinions would agree with Mr. Macaulay's upon this subject, but I think that a man who in any way tried to elude the laws of his country, would be acting against his conscience in the highest degree; that is my impression of it, and that is what I mean to say; and with regard to the slave trade, I mean to carry out that which I have stated in my letter, that I look upon it as an evil, and I would wish to add nothing to that evil in any way, but to diminish what I could of it. As to the moral criminality of all the parties, I suppose that depends upon other considerations. Then in the Evidence of Captain Hill, in answer to question 7161, it is stated here, "the Custom-house officers in Liverpool may be totally ignorant of the trade carried on at the Gallinas, and also totally ignorant of the trade carried on by Pedro Martinez & Co. at the Havannah." All our shipments have been made through the Custom-house, giving the destinations of the vessels and every thing, and what we did was illegal; we should consider ourselves not justly treated altogether, in being allowed to do that which we say we are going to do, and then after it is done being told it is illegal, although before it is done we have the very sanction of the parties to do it, because we have no concern in it beyond the shipment, and the shipment is publicly made. In answer to Question 7165, it is said, "I have never met a vessel belonging to Messrs. Zulueta & Co. on the coast of Africa." Of course, we never had one, and therefore he never could meet with one. Then in answer to Question 7958*, Mr. Hill states that he found a letter, dated London, 20th of August 1840, stating, "We cannot exceed 500*l.* for the vessel in question, such as described in your letter; if you cannot therefore succeed at those limits, we must give up the purchase." But he says, "there is a note to the letter, which says, 'According to our Liverpool mode, note, you will go on shore to the Salthouse Dock.'" Now I have been looking at our letter-book, and I am quite willing to suppose that the person who has stated this might not wish, of course, to state any thing that was incorrect; but this is altogether unintelligible to me. The Salthouse Dock is well known to every person acquainted with Liverpool; it is one of the docks in which vessels go and unload, and that is all. Our house might say that our custom was to send our vessels there; we generally do; but I do not understand this at all.

10448. *Chairman.* You do not understand what bearing it has upon the question?—I think the words must be badly copied; there is no such thing in our letter-book as it appears here; it is quite unintelligible to me.

10449. Sir *T. D. Acland.*] Is the other part of the letter correct, which is stated as bearing date the 26th of September 1840?—Yes.

10450. Have you referred to your own copy of the letter?—Yes, and it is not in our copy; but I can conceive our saying to the captain of the vessel, go into the Salthouse Dock, because we generally send our vessels there.

10451. Had you ever employed Jennings before?—Jennings had had charge of vessels before, chartered by Martinez, and hence the connexion between Martinez and Jennings. There are some captains in all trades, that make a great deal of difficulty about every thing, and others that do not; of course, merchants like to deal with those that do not, more than those that do.

10452. *Chairman.*] It would appear from Question 5087, that your name is supposed to have been mentioned in a Parliamentary Paper, as connected with a slave trade transaction. Will you refer to page 38, in Class B. Paper of 1839 and 1840, which is the place referred to in the answer, and see if there is any trace of your name in that transaction?—I do not find my own name there; I only find an allusion at the bottom to the name of Pedro Martinez, but in a manner in no way connected with me, and stating a circumstance which I never knew. In Question 7965*, it is stated, "The Augusta had touched at Cadiz on her way out from England?" The answer is, "Yes, and landed part of her cargo at Cadiz, although it was consigned to be delivered at Gallinas." Now Captain Hill, who has given this answer, must have known why she touched at Cadiz, and why she discharged part of her cargo, for it must be in the log-book of the vessel. It was because she was nearly wrecked in her passage; she put into Cadiz in distress, and there she landed a part of her cargo, which was tobacco which was rotten, and sold for the benefit of the underwriters. Now that has not been stated here, but I think Captain Hill must have known it, because it is in the log-book of the vessel which he took.

10453. *Chairman.*] And the log-book he must have read?—I should think so; because if he has not done that he has done nothing. All I mean to say is that it is, an *ex parte* statement.

10454. Sir *T. D. Acland.*] It was not intended when she left England, that she should put into Cadiz?—Most certainly not; all the facts of the case show that she went there because she was obliged. I have not seen the log-book, but it must be there; because in the log-book the captain is bound to enter those things, and whoever captured the vessel must have seen the log-book of course. In answer to Question 7967*, it is said, "Messrs. Zulueta must be aware that it is contrary to law to act as agents or otherwise for the shipment of goods that are to be employed in the slave trade; they were bound to do nothing illegal; they are merchants residing in England, and they must conform themselves to the laws of England, and they cannot by the laws of England plead ignorance of those laws." Now I and my partners are British subjects, and therefore we are bound by the law, and we must obey the law; and I say that to endeavour to elude the law is criminal in my estimation of things. In the answer to Question 7970*, it is stated, "I have endeavoured to be particular in making it appear that this vessel was chartered to a place where there were no constituted authorities." I think that in the Gallinas there are constituted authorities. It is the first time that I ever heard that it is illegal for any merchant to ship goods for any places without ascertaining beforehand whether there are constituted authorities there. I believe that if they like to send goods to any place, they may do it; and as to the fact of there being constituted authorities in the place or not, I do not see what that has to do with the question; besides, there have been such things as treaties made with persons at the Gallinas, so that there must be some constituted authorities there. But I do not know why I should be called upon to know whether there are constituted authorities at the port or not. Then it is stated, in answer to Question 7971*, "As far as I am able to give my own opinion,

I believe that Messrs. Zulueta were perfectly criminal, at least they had a knowledge of what they were doing. I think I am borne out in that by the secrecy they have endeavoured to pursue in putting in a false owner." I have answered all that before. I state again, that all the secrecy and mystery of the thing lies in supposing other things different from what appear. Then it is said, "In fact there can be no want of evidence to show that Messrs. Zulueta had for a length of time been agents to slave dealers." Mr. Blanco and Mr. Martinez may have been engaged, as I have stated, in slave operations; and I have stated that we conducted their general business here.

10455. Mr. *Forster.*] Is not Pedro Blanco a partner in a commercial house at the Havannah who are general merchants?—Yes, I have stated that before.

10456. Captain *Fitzroy.*] Have you ever discounted any bill drawn by Pedro Blanco on Pedro Martinez &. Co. for goods delivered for them on the African coast at the Gallinas?—I have accepted bills drawn by Pedro Blanco and others from the Gallinas upon our house, and paid them to the order of several houses in Sierra Leone and houses in London. I have paid them in money that I had in my hands resulting from the general transactions of business, which I have explained. But discounting would be this, if I had paid those acceptances before they were due, and received some consideration for them; that I never did, but I might have done it in the case of these bills.

10457. Were those bills negociated through your hands in payment of goods delivered at the Gallinas?—No; they were drawn generally with the advice attached to them, saying, I have drawn a thousand pounds upon you for account of Blanco and Carvalho, or Blanco &, Co., at the Havannah.

10458. Mr. *Wood.*] By whose orders were you desired to honour it; was it by the order of Pedro Blanco at the Gallinas?—No; by the house at the Havannah or by the house at Cadiz; sometimes the one and sometimes the other. Blanco had a house some time ago in Malaga, as a general merchant, occupied in shipping the fruits of the country and oil to the United States, &c. &c. In answer to Question 7961*, the following is stated:—"In one of these letters, dated Cadiz, 30th of November 1840, is a paragraph to the following effect: 'In a letter, dated London, the 21st instant, which I have just received from Messrs. Zulueta & Co., merchants in London, I had the pleasure of receiving a bill drawn by you on them for 250*l.*, which I this day place to their credit, waiting your advice of the same.'" There is here certainly a mistranslation of some kind, because it says that this man receives a bill upon us, and credits it to us, which is of course contradictory in the very terms of it, because if the bill was remitted to this man upon us, he would have debited it to us, and not credited it. But altogether there is some confusion about it; I suppose arising from the mistranslation of the documents, because the fact is this, the bill is one of the bills I have already mentioned, drawn from the Gallinas upon ourselves, to the order of a third party. It is a bill drawn at the Gallinas upon ourselves, on account of the credit, and therefore it could never have been received by the person in Cadiz. It must have been presented to us here, and in fact so it was; the bill is here. I wish to show that that letter is perfectly inaccurate.

10459. Sir *T. D. Acland.*] Can you give the Committee any information upon this: "The other letters," nine of them, "were all on slave business: not a word of any innocent trade, but the whole directing how slaves were to be shipped on board various vessels." How do you account for this vessel carrying letters upon slave business?—I account for it in this way: first of all, it is impossible for us to answer here what letters will be put on board a vessel at Cadiz; but there is very seldom any communication between Cadiz and the Gallinas; whatever letters there were must have gone by such random occasions as arose. As to the fact that whoever wrote those letters is engaged in the slave trade, the letters will speak for themselves.

10460. *Chairman.*] Those letters were not prepared in the expectation of the arrival of this vessel, because this vessel was not destined to that port, and was only driven there by stress of weather?—Most certainly. I will add one circumstance in proof of that. The vessel was supposed to have been lost, from the circumstance of a boat having been found upon the coast with the name of T. Jennings upon it, and it was supposed that it was a boat belonging to the vessel; it was, in fact, a boat from the vessel, but the vessel had not been lost; therefore the vessel was quite unexpected in Cadiz by every soul. It went there from stress of weather, and nothing more. Then it is said, in answer to Question 7972*, "I think the papers are quite conclusive to the mind of any man that Zulueta was cognizant of what he was doing; but as far as it is an illegal transaction, it is not for me to judge; but the Judge of the Vice-Admiralty Court of Sierra Leone did think it illegal, and condemned the vessel; and moreover, the man who is put forward as captain and owner did not defend the vessel on her trial." Now, as to the statement of his being a false owner, I have already stated that he was not. But then, again, with regard to the other part of the business, the man did not defend it, because he was prevented from defending it.

10461. How was he prevented from defending it?—He had not money to defend himself. It appears from the protest that the vessel was condemned without allowing Thomas Jennings to say any thing in her defence. I will deliver in the protest, which shows that that was the fact. (*The same was delivered in.*) As to his not having money, it is said that he might have raised money upon the cargo; but there is no one can entertain any doubt as to the palpable contradiction of such a statement, because to raise money upon a cargo, which was seized, over which he had no control, is to me quite unintelligible.

10462. Mr. *Wood.*] You have spoken of some bills drawn upon your house by Pedro Blanco, and you were understood to say that they were drawn some of them, in favour of Sierra Leone houses. Can you inform the Committee the names of the houses at Sierra Leone in whose favour they were drawn?— I have no objection to do so, but I feel loath to mention names. I could have mentioned many names; we are not the only correspondents in London of Blanco and Martinez. With regard to those houses at Sierra Leone, I should be sorry to introduce names, because I know the pain I have had from mine being introduced here, but still there is no secret in the thing.

10463. You have given the committee the names of parties drawing the bills, and on whose account they were drawn, and you speak of their being drawn in favour of Sierra Leone houses; have you any objection to furnish the names of the houses in whose favour they were drawn?—I say that I have no objection, except that I should not like to introduce names unnecessarily; but the bills are in my hands, and any gentleman can look at them who chooses; they are at the disposal of any body who likes to look at them.

[*The Witness produced the bills.*]

Sabbati, 23° die Julii, 1842.

MEMBERS PRESENT.

Sir T. D. Acland.
Mr. Aldam.
Viscount Courtenay.
Viscount Ebrington.
Captain Fitzroy.

Mr. Forster.
Mr. Milnes.
Mr. Wilson Patten.
Mr. G. W. Wood.

VISCOUNT SANDON, in the chair.

Pedro de Zulueta, jun. Esq. called in; and further examined.

10464. *Chairman.*] The Committee understand that you have some further observations to make upon the evidence which has been given with reference to your house?—With reference to the destination of the Augusta, from

Liverpool to Gallinas, and the fact of its having put into Cadiz unforeseen, and unpremeditated altogether, in consequence of stress of weather, I omitted to mention a circumstance which will put the thing beyond doubt, and it is this: an insurance was made at Lloyd's, from Liverpool to the Gallinas, and it is well known that, of course, we should have forfeited the insurance by going to any other port except from the peril of the sea, and the British consul at Cadiz is well aware of the circumstance, because he is Lloyd's agent there; and therefore he had to interfere in the whole proceeding; without his sanction nothing could have been done. We have called upon the underwriters upon that account, and it has been paid, and which would not have been paid without its being proved. I stated yesterday that the transactions of my house with Pedro Martinez & Co. of the Havannah, with Blanco & Carvalho of the Havannah, and with Pedro Martinez of Cadiz, had amounted in the 20 years to 100,000*l*. I was afraid of overrating the amount; but on reference to the books of the house, I find that our transactions with them in 20 years have amounted to 400,000*l*. out of which the 22,000*l*. that was mentioned is the whole amount of goods that have been shipped by their order for the coast of Africa.

10465. Can you state how much of the 22,000*l*. has accrued within any given period; is it distributed equally over the whole 20 years, or has it grown up in the last four or five years?—In the last few years it has decreased, but otherwise it is spread over the whole number of years. In such a length of time it forms to our minds a mere speck. In the last six months our transactions with the house of Pedro Martinez of Cadiz amount to already 30,000*l*., and with Pedro Martinez of the Havannah to nearly the same amount. With the house of Pedro Blanco & Co. of the Havannah, the amount has been 15,000*l*. for what has passed in the last six months, and with the houses generally at Cuba, throughout the island, it amounts to 100,000*l*. altogether, arising entirely from cargoes of sugar, and from tobacco, and remittances of bills from there in carrying on banking operations, upon which they draw again, which are negotiated in the Havannah and sent to houses in London to cash, and remittances of drafts on the Spanish treasury at the Havannah, and bills of lading of specie and bullion, and such things, from Mexico. I state these things only to show the nature of our trade, and I have been particular, because as these are large amounts I wish to show what they arise from. Another fact escaped my attention yesterday, and it is this, that Don Pedro Martinez is owner of several large vessels of 300 tons and 400 tons, which are in the trade of sugar, tobacco, and such things, with us, in England and with Cadiz.

10466. Have you bought other vessels for him than those which have been employed in the slave trade?—Yes, decidedly so; there was the Star, Captain Jennings. That vessel was sent from here to the Gallinas, precisely the same as the Augusta has been sent. She delivered her cargo; she went from thence to Cape Coast, I believe, and from there to Madeira; she received a cargo of wheat; she came back to Spain, and she was sold at Liverpool to a third party, not Martinez, or any body connected with him; in fact, she was sold for very little. The object of that vessel was just the same as the Augusta, to maintain a legal trade with Gallinas; that is, within my own knowledge.

10467. Mr. *Aldam*.] What is the description of legal trade that was carried on?—Sending out goods to be sold at those places, and to go to other ports, not to carry any cargo from there to the Havannah.

10468. There has been a good deal of evidence, in which it has been stated that no legal trade is carried on with Gallinas?—I could not say what trade there is at the Gallinas of a legal nature, but I know that those vessels would have taken nothing if there was nothing legal to take, from that place to the Havannah, or to any other place; I am aware that my answers upon this point must be deficient, because I am really very ignorant of the trade of the West Coast of Africa.

10469. Do you suppose that the vessels would be used to carry on a legal trade?—Most certainly I do; because persons find it worth while to send goods there constantly. The Committee will observe, that what the application of the goods is afterwards I cannot say, but I speak of the fact of the vessels having gone there with the intention of returning to the Havannah to bring a cargo of some description here, to pay a freight, and then to go again with the same kind of goods to Africa.

10470. *Chairman*.] You have stated before, that you have cleared out for the Gallinas from Liverpool?—Yes.

10471. In carrying on operations of that kind, should you have ever thought it necessary to exercise any disguise as to what part of Africa you were clearing out for?—Not at all.

10472. You did not imagine, that in being the instrument of sending lawful goods to any part of Africa you were doing any thing which required concealment?—Nothing at all of the kind; and the proof of that is, that in the bills of entry in Liverpool any body could see our names as consignees of the vessel, and see entries made in our names of every thing.

10473. Is not there a document officially published daily in London and at Liverpool, stating the daily entries at the Custom-house of all goods shipped, with the description of the goods, and the name of the port and of the shipper?—Yes, there is.

10474. Is not this printed from time to time in the public papers?—It is in general circulation; there is hardly any merchant in Liverpool or in London who is not possessed of one. The Liverpool entries are reprinted in London, Liverpool being such an important place of business. The bill printed in London contains also Liverpool, Hull, and Bristol.

10475. So that every such transaction is perfectly notorious to every one?— Notorious to every one who chooses to read the public papers. There is another thing which escaped me till I came into the room this morning. As I have been in the business from my childhood, I know every thing that is going on in it. The Arrogante, after we sold her at the Havannah, was sent to Vera Cruz with a cargo of Spanish paper, spirits, raisins, &c. &c., such as is sent for the South American trade, for the purpose of breaking the blockade of Vera Cruz, which she did break and went in. It was asked in question 7147, whether the Augusta was equipped for the slave trade the second time; the answer was, "She was not." I wish to state, that before any goods were put on board of her, it was our express wish and order that every thing in her that was fit for that trade should be taken down, and the vessel put in the same condition as any other merchant vessel; and we should not have loaded any thing in her if that had not been done. It is stated in the evidence that the Augusta was consigned to three notorious slave dealers; now we had never in our lives heard of the name of any one of the parties to whom she was consigned.

10476. You mean that the first time you heard their names was when the order to ship those goods was given to you?—Yes, and the circumstance of three consignees is a regular thing with distant consignments, such as South America and Africa. There is such an uncertainty attending the residence of parties in those places, that we invariably put a second and a third consignee in addition, in case the first should not be in the way.

10477. Mr. *Forster*.] Some bills were referred to in your former evidence drawn by Mr. Pedro Blanco upon your house; have you any objection to put those bills before the Committee?—Not any. And I ought to state now, as I have been looking at the bills more closely, that they are not all drawn to the orders of Sierra Leone houses, but to the orders of other Spaniards, and those people endorsed them to the Sierra Leone houses. This does not alter the case materially, but for the sake of accuracy I mention it.

10478. You will put them in for the inspection of the Committee?— Certainly.—(*The same were delivered in.*)

10479. You only hesitated in giving the names yesterday from motives of delicacy, not from any motive of concealment?—Yes, I do not wish to withhold any thing, but I am indisposed to introduce any name. I have no wish to conceal any thing whatever. I have been consulting with my partners upon this subject, and I have a request to make to the Committee. Our position is one which is certainly an unpleasant one. I think that what I have stated will have proved to the satisfaction of the Committee that we have not in any way intended to elude the law. Now our situation is this, with reference to any future transactions we have no valid reason to give our correspondents for not executing an order. The Committee will have to make their report, and several gentlemen have given their opinions as to how the law is to be altered. I, for my part, am not competent to give any advice upon the subject, but I would only wish that whatever law is made, it should be clear and distinct as to what a man might to do, and what he is not to do. The trade that we have carried on with the Gallinas, at least the shipments we have made, are perfectly unimportant to us in itself, as is evident from the amount; but at the same time, with regard to the correspondents that we have accounts with, we are placed in this dilemma, that we must refuse fulfilling their orders without giving them any valid reason, unless we should be able to say, Sir, we cannot fulfil your order because the law of this country prohibits that we should ship any goods that are liable to be applied to that purpose, to persons who may at any time have had any dealings, or are suspected of having had any dealings of that description. To us it is indifferent which way the legislation turns upon this subject, so long as we know what it is. But supposing it legal for a man to ship goods to a port, are you then to be liable to have the vessels captured, and what to us is worst of all, to be brought into a kind of notoriety as being engaged in slave dealing, which is exceedingly unpleasant to our feelings. That is a consideration which I hope the Committee will look to.

10480. You wish that the law should be made clear for your guidance, to enable you to understand what course you are to pursue with your correspondents?—Yes, in what I have to do with them. I do not mean to say that if a man ships goods knowingly to slave dealers, for the purpose of being exchanged for slaves, I do not mean to say that the law does not reach him now. My own impression is, that it might do so; at all events the morality of the thing would be very questionable; but we want something more than that; that is not enough. Here is my case, which, if true, proves that we have not done any such thing, and yet we are liable to all this unpleasantness.

10481. You want something also to plead with your correspondents, as a reason for not complying with any order they may send?—Exactly.

10482. You feel that at the present moment the law is in an unsatisfactory state, that doubts have been raised upon the subject, which as merchants you are desirous of seeing quieted by some declaration, one way or another?—I do; for instance, I may on going home find an order; and I assure the Committee that after all that has occurred, after all this unpleasantness upon the subject, I should be in an awkward position. I might have to throw up my correspondents without any valid reason, because of course goods may be shipped to them by other parties, which I should refuse to do; and they may do it legally, because they may send those goods to the Havannah or to any other such place, and then my correspondents could not say that I had any valid reason to refuse.

10483. If there were any obstruction interposed in the way of export from this country directly to the coast of Africa, you would rather desire that it should be at the English Custom-house, before the goods went out, than that it should be left in uncertainty, to be decided upon the coast of Africa?— Exactly; that is my impression. At the same time I am not stating that that would be wise or expedient, or proper, or any thing of the kind; but I say this simply because I do not wish it to be brought into question that we elude the law; not that we break it, because that would be a question before a court of justice; but before men of honour, I do not wish to be open to the imputation of eluding the law.

———

REPORT
FROM THE SELECT COMMITTEE
ON THE
WEST COAST OF AFRICA.

———

Martis, 22° die Martii, 1842.

Ordered, THAT a Select Committee be appointed to inquire into the State of the British Possessions on the West Coast of Africa, more especially with reference to their present Relations with the neighbouring Native Tribes.

———

Mercurii, 6° die Aprilis, 1842.

A Committee was nominated of,—

Lord Stanley.
Viscount Sandon.
Lord John Russell.
Sir Robert Harry Inglis.
Mr. E. Denison.
Mr. Forster.
Sir Thomas Acland.
Mr. Milnes.

Mr. Charles Buller.
Mr. Hutt.
Captain Fitzroy.
Earl of March.
Viscount Ebrington.
Viscount Courtenay.
Mr. George William Wood.

Ordered, THAT the Committee have power to send for Persons, Papers, and Records.

Ordered, THAT Five be the Quorum of the Committee.

———

Mercurii, 11° die Maii, 1842.

Ordered, THAT Mr. Stuart Wortley, Mr. Evans, Mr. Wilson Patten, Mr. Aldam, Mr. William Hamilton, and Mr. Metcalfe, be added to the Committee.

———

REPORT.

THE SELECT COMMITTEE appointed to Inquire into the State of the BRITISH POSSESSIONS on the WEST COAST OF AFRICA, more especially with reference to their present Relations with the neighbouring Native Tribes, and who were empowered to Report their Observations, together with the MINUTES OF EVIDENCE taken before them, to The House;——HAVE considered the Matters to them referred, and have agreed to the following REPORT:

YOUR COMMITTEE, previous to reporting the result of their Inquiries into the subject which has been submitted to them by Your Honourable House, think it desirable to state the circumstances which led to their appointment. In the course of the Year 1839 information was communicated to the Marquis of Normanby, then Secretary of State for the Colonies, that a Spanish Slaver, the Dos Amigos, had, a short time previous to seizure, been allowed to trade freely at Cape Coast, a British Settlement on the Gold Coast, and had been supplied there by a British Merchant, a Magistrate, with some of the Goods, not Equipments, requisite for carrying on her unlawful Traffic. This information led to further inquiry, in the course of which it appeared that such practices were not unusual, and that Captain Maclean, the Governor, appointed by the Committee of Merchants in London, on whom the charge of the Settlements of the Gold Coast had been devolved by Parliament, in the Year 1828, did not consider himself entitled to interfere with the Traffic of any Vessel of a friendly Nation, whatever her purpose, coming to purchase Goods, in themselves lawful, within the waters of a British Settlement. In consequence of this information, Lord John Russell, then Secretary of State for the Colonies, concurring with his predecessor, gave strong Instructions for the discontinuance of this practice, and for the punishment of it as illegal, expressed his opinion that it was desirable the Government of these Settlements should be resumed by the Crown, and instructed Dr. Madden, a gentleman who had formerly been employed as a Stipendiary Magistrate in the West Indies, and subsequently in the Mixed Commission at Havana, to proceed as Commissioner to the Gold Coast, and the other British Settlements on the West Coast of Africa, for the purpose of investigating these and other matters connected with the administration and condition of these Settlements. He was at the same time instructed to inquire into, and report upon, the Prospects of Emigration from Sierra Leone to the British West India Colonies.

The Reports which were the result of this gentleman's inquiries, involving materially the interests of Humanity and of Commerce, and impeaching gravely the character of individuals engaged in the British Trade with Africa, in a manner which seemed to call for further investigation before any conclusion could be fairly come to upon the questions at issue, have been laid before Your Committee, have in fact formed the basis of their proceedings, and are published with this Report; but in publishing them, Your Committee beg to state, that while they do full justice to the value of much of the information contained in them, and to the zeal and diligence of Dr. Madden, they do not concur in all his conclusions, or intend to warrant the accuracy of his statements. His inquiries were conducted over a vast surface of Coast in a short period, and under circumstances of considerable interruption from health disordered by the climate, and in many instances he apparently found himself compelled to take his information from third parties, the accuracy of whose statements and the correctness of whose opinions he had not the opportunity of testing.

In many of his recommendations they concur; on some, and those of no slight importance, they have come to an opposite opinion; but thinking it would be more convenient that they should give their own conclusions upon the whole subject submitted to them in a consecutive form, rather than in the shape of a commentary upon his Reports, they beg to submit the following statement and recommendations to The House, as the conclusions at which they have themselves arrived.

GOLD COAST.

In the first place, then, we recommend that the Government of the British Forts upon the Gold Coast be resumed by the Crown, and that all dependance on the Government of Sierra Leone should cease.

We fully admit the merits of that Administration, whether we look to the Officer employed, Captain Maclean, or to the Committee under whom he has acted, which, with the miserable pittance of between 3,500*l.* and 4,000*l.* a year, has exercised, from the four ill-provided Forts of Dixcove, Cape Coast, Annamaboe, and British Accra, manned by a few ill-paid black soldiers, a very wholesome influence over a Coast not much less than 150 miles in extent, and to a considerable distance inland; preventing within that range external Slave Trade, maintaining Peace and Security, and exercising a useful though irregular Jurisdiction, among the neighbouring Tribes, and much mitigating and in some cases extinguishing some of the most atrocious practices which had prevailed among them unchecked before. We would give full weight to the doubts which Captain Maclean entertained as to his authority, until specifically so instructed, to prevent vessels, suspected of being intended for the Slave Trade, but not having Slaves on board, from trafficking in lawful goods within his jurisdiction; and we do not infer from that circumstance, that the Government of these Forts had any partiality for an abominable Traffic, which, on the contrary, they have done much to check; but we think it desirable, for the sake of enlarging the sphere of usefulness of these Settlements, and of giving greater confidence in the character and impartiality of their Government, that it should be rendered completely independent of all connexion with Commerce, by a direct emanation of authority from the Crown, and that it should be placed, with increased resources, in direct and immediate communication with the general Government of the Empire.

We recommend, further, the reoccupation of several of the Forts, such as Apollonia, Winnebah, and Whydah, abandoned in 1828, when the Government was handed over to the Committee of Merchants, and the reconstruction of others, on however small a scale, on other similar points. In some cases the climate will be found to be not worse, in others better, than on other parts of the coast of Africa; but this evil may be very much mitigated, if not entirely removed, by the employment of such Europeans only as are already inured to a tropical climate, and of British Subjects of African descent, who, we believe, may now be found, either within our African Settlements or our West India Colonies, fitted for almost every branch and grade of service[4]; and we look upon such Establishments as of high importance, not for the extension of Territory, but of that control over the Slave Trade, and wholesome moral influence over the neighbouring Chiefs, which we have described as having been exercised by the existing

Forts, and which is much needed at those places to which we have particularly alluded, as well as others.

The Judicial Authority at present existing in the Forts is not altogether in a satisfactory condition; it resides in the Governor and Council, who act as Magistrates, and whose instructions limit them to the administration of British Law, and that, as far as the Natives are concerned, strictly and exclusively within the Forts themselves; but practically, and necessarily, and usefully, these directions having been disregarded, a kind of irregular jurisdiction has grown up, extending itself far beyond the limits of the Forts by the voluntary submission of the Natives themselves, whether Chiefs or Traders, to British Equity; and its decisions, owing to the moral influence, partly of our acknowledged power, and partly of the respect which has been inspired by the fairness with which it has been exercised by Captain Maclean and the Magistrates at the other Forts, have generally, we might almost say, uniformly, been carried into effect without the interposition of force. The value of this interposition of an enlightened, though irregular, authority, (which has extended, in some cases and with advantage to humanity, even to an interference in capital cases,) is borne witness to, not only by parties connected with the Government of the Settlements, who might be suspected of a bias in its favour, but also by the Wesleyan Missionaries, and even by Dr. Madden, who, objecting to its undefined extent, and to the manner in which, in some respects, it has been carried out, yet still bears high testimony to its practical value, to its acknowledged equity, and to its superiority over the barbarous customs which it tends to supersede. Even the duration of imprisonment, of which he complains, has been usually adjudged to offences which would have incurred a severer penalty in most civilised countries, and would certainly, if left to the arbitrary decision of native chiefs, or to the "wild justice" of private revenge, have been punished by death, and that frequently of the most cruel kind. Still, however, it is desirable that this jurisdiction should be better defined and understood, and that a Judicial Officer should be placed at the disposal of the Governor, to assist, or supersede, partially or entirely, his judicial functions, and those now exercised by the Council and the several Commandants in their magisterial capacity; but we would recommend, that while he follows in his decisions the general principles, he be not restricted to the technicalities of British Law, and that altogether he should be allowed a large discretion.

[4] The gentleman lately Acting Governor of Sierra Leone, and the Queen's Advocate there, are both gentlemen of colour: and it appears that an Akoo, lately a liberated African, is now on his way to England, to be ordained a clergyman of the Church of England, having been instructed in Greek under the care of the Church Missionary Society established in the same colony.

It is to be remembered that our compulsory authority is strictly limited, both by our title and by the instructions of the Colonial Office to the British Forts, within which no one but the Governor, his Suite, and the Garrison reside; and that the Magistrates are strictly prohibited from exercising jurisdiction even over the Natives and Districts immediately under the influence and protection of the Forts. All jurisdiction over the Natives beyond that point must, therefore, be considered as optional, and should be made the subject of distinct agreement, as to its nature and limits, with the Native Chiefs, and it should be accommodated to the condition of the several Tribes, and to the completeness of the control over them, which by vicinage or otherwise we are enabled to exercise. Their relation to the English Crown should be, not the allegiance of subjects, to which we have no right to pretend, and which it would entail an inconvenient responsibility to possess, but the deference of weaker powers to a stronger and more enlightened neighbour, whose protection and counsel they seek, and to whom they are bound by certain definite obligations.

These obligations should be varied and extended from time to time, and should always at least include (as many of the Treaties now in existence on that Coast already do) the abolition of the external Slave Trade, the prohibition of human sacrifices, and other barbarous customs, such as kidnapping, under the name of "panyarring," and should keep in view the gradual introduction of further improvements, as the people become more fitted to admit them.

In this arrangement we should find the solution of our difficulty in regard to Domestic Slavery, and a modification of it under the name of "pawns," which has prevailed within these settlements, not actually within the Forts, but within their influence, and even in the hands of British subjects. To them indeed they have been already prohibited; but although the system of pawns, which is properly an engagement of service voluntarily entered into for debt, and terminable at any time by the payment of the debt, is one which "does not seem abstractedly unjust or unreasonable[5]," yet as liable to much abuse, and much resembling slavery, it should be the object of our policy to get rid of it, even among the Natives; and in the places more immediately within the influence of British authority, we believe there will be no difficulty in limiting it at once, both in extent and duration, and probably, ere long, in abolishing it, by arrangements such as we have above suggested. Some caution, however, must be exercised in this matter on account of the close intermixture of Dutch and Danish with the British settlements, though perhaps it might be possible to induce them to co-operate in such arrangements as might be thought desirable for the improvement of the neighbouring Tribes; and great facility and advantage would certainly arise from such co-operation, if it could be secured.

[5] Despatch of Sir G. Grey, 4. Dec. 1837.

With regard to the judicial arrangements, a plan has been suggested by which a Supreme Judicial Officer might be placed at Ascension, at Fernando Po, where no authority of any kind exists, and one is much needed, or at some other Island off the Coast, visiting, with the aid of a steamer, the various Settlements on the Gold Coast periodically, as well as the Trading Stations in the Bights of Benin and Biafra, and exercising in the latter a very wholesome influence in the adjustment of disputes with the Natives, which, for want of such interposition, occasionally lead to consequences injurious to the British character and to the interests of Commerce. But Your Committee are aware that difficulties might arise in carrying out this suggestion, more especially on account of the necessity for prompt decision in most cases in which the Natives are concerned; and therefore are not prepared at present to do more than call attention to the suggestion.

We would here acknowledge the great services rendered to religion and civilisation on this Coast by the Wesleyan body; they have even established a friendly communication with the barbarous court of Ashantee, which promises results important in every way; and, indeed, little in the way of religious instruction would have been done without them. But we should recommend that further provision should be made for these objects, by the appointment of a Colonial Chaplain, and by encouragement to schools of a higher class than any which are found there at present; to which, among others, the neighbouring Chiefs should be invited to send their sons to receive an education which might fit them to be of benefit to their own people directly, if they returned to their families, or indirectly, if they remained, by entering into connection with British interests. Some officer also should be appointed, whose duty should be to take care of the effects of intestate persons, to verify the character of vessels entering the ports, and to attend generally to the fiscal regulations of the Settlements.

We beg also to call attention to the suggestion, that we should endeavour to secure the co-operation of our Dutch and Danish neighbours, in licensing the canoes which ply along that coast, as they seem to afford considerable facilities to such Slave Trade as still exists along the Leeward Coast.

The Military also should be somewhat increased in number; and their condition, as recommended by Dr. Madden, should be improved.

A scheme for an establishment such as we have been proposing, will be found in the evidence of Mr. Hutton, one of the Council of the Committee of African Merchants, who now govern these settlements. To the details we do not pretend to give our sanction; but we beg to call attention to it, as showing that all the objects which we have been recommending may be attained at an expense far short of that which was incurred for these settlements when they protected instead of, as now, controlling the Slave Trade, or even when they were last under the direct management of the Crown. Indeed in itself it is of but trifling amount when compared with the objects to be attained, and we are confident that the increased expense will be well repaid, both directly by the diminished necessity for naval force upon the Leeward Station, and indirectly by the increase of commerce, which will be the certain consequence of extended influence over very important nations, including the kingdoms of Dahomey and Ashantee, of an improving population, and of the continued and still more complete suppression of the Slave Trade on that Coast, once infamous as the principal scene of its operations.

GAMBIA.

For the purposes of trade and useful communication of every kind with the interior of Africa, the Settlement in the Gambia seems to possess advantages far beyond those of any other British Settlement on the Coast of Africa. It has that which in all countries, but more especially in Africa, where no means of land carriage exist, save the backs of slaves, is of the highest value, the command of a noble river, navigable for vessels of considerable tonnage for several hundred miles into the interior; and it would appear as if a little fiscal encouragement to its products and those of its vicinity,—together with the employment of Steamers, which we would earnestly recommend, both for the suppression of the Slave Trade at the mouths of the neighbouring Rivers and for keeping up communication, both commercial and official, with the Settlement of Macarthy's Island, (which is itself nearly 200 miles up the river) and with the countries still higher up,—would draw out untold resources for a useful and honourable commerce, and even restore to us some portion of the gum trade which we have lately lost.

As in the case of the Gold Coast, we recommend the entire separation of this Government from that of Sierra Leone. The dependence, which has hitherto existed, has been the cause of great inconvenience, and seems to possess no advantage. The Laws of the Settlement have been enacted by those who are little acquainted with its concerns. Their Gaol has depended for clearance on the uncertain arrival of a Chief Justice from a distance of 500 miles, and by a voyage of above 20 days; and in the case of the death of one Chief Justice, two years elapsed before a criminal, confined under a charge of murder could be brought to trial, and then, owing to the delay, the witnesses had returned to Europe, and no evidence could be found. Even if a regular Steam Communication were established, though the amount of the evil would undoubtedly be thus diminished, yet still the uncertainty of life in such a climate should not be forgotten; and we would recommend the appointment of a distinct Judicial Officer in each Settlement, who should have authority to act in case of vacancy in either.

The Governor should have the assistance of a Council; but under the circumstances of the Settlement, we recommend that he should have full power to act on his own responsibility, and even contrary to their advice; every Member of the Council, including the Governor, in such cases, as in India, recording the reasons of his opinion for the information of the Government at home.

We would earnestly recommend to consideration the propriety of reestablishing the former British Settlement on the Island of Bulama. Its climate is certainly unhealthy; but we are not aware that it is more so than that of Sierra Leone or of some other places on the Coast. It might be principally, if not entirely occupied, by British subjects of Negro race; and its position, both for checking the Slave Trade of Bissao and its neighbourhood, and for drawing out the legitimate resources of several noble rivers, would be invaluable.

We would also suggest the erection of small Blockhouses, whether up the Gambia itself, or along the Coast, as at Cestos and the Gallinas, on points where British commerce is superseding the Slave Trade, as they would protect the lawful trade, and prevent the re-appearance of the Slave Trade where it has been extinguished, or is dying away.

SIERRA LEONE.

In regard to the machinery by which this Colony is governed, Your Committee have no specific recommendation to offer.

In the course of their investigations, questions have arisen connected with its past management and administration, more especially on the subject of the party spirit of a peculiar nature, which is alleged to have acted injuriously in regard to it both on the Colonial Office at home and on the internal transactions of the Colony itself; questions mixed up with topics of a personal nature, and which, in spite of the facilities for a full investigation which were offered by the Colonial Office, Your Committee would have found it impossible, within their limited time, even if it had been their proper province, to follow out. On these points, therefore, not having the means either of forming themselves a satisfactory opinion, or furnishing The House with the means of forming one, they have thought it due, not less to the questions themselves than to the individuals concerned, not to report the Evidence; and they are the more induced to pursue this course, in that they are thus not prejudging any inquiry into this subject, if in a future Session it should be the pleasure of The House to engage in it.

In regard to the future, much will depend on the decision which shall be come to as to several points which have been under our consideration; such as the continuance at Sierra Leone of the Courts for Adjudication of Prizes taken in the Slave Trade, the disposal of the rescued Slaves, and the question of Emigration from Africa generally.

Now it is hardly necessary to remind the House of The Resolution come to by a Committee which sat upon this subject in 1830, which distinctly condemned the location of the Mixed Commission Court at Sierra Leone as highly inconvenient for the purpose, on the ground of its situation, not only at so great a distance as 800 or 1,000 miles from the places where the Slaves to be adjudicated were then principally captured, but also so far to windward, that captured ships were sometimes eight or nine weeks, and on an average upwards of five weeks, on their passage from the place of capture to Sierra Leone, occasioning a loss of the captured Slaves amounting to from one-sixth to half of the whole number, whilst the survivors were generally landed in a miserable state of weakness and disease. Such undoubtedly was the case then, and had been the case then for many years, and has been still the case, though in a somewhat less degree, since the Report of that Committee. We regret that means should not have been taken earlier to remedy this crying evil. As the Slave Trade however now exists, that evil is no doubt much diminished. By the provision introduced into our more recent Slave Trade Treaties, the Cruizers of the contracting parties are authorised to seize Vessels merely on the evidence of their equipment, without making it necessary to wait till Slaves are actually on board, and thus a much smaller number of Slaves is brought for adjudication and exposed to this kind of middle passage. Moreover the exertions and improved quality and system of our Cruizers, the depressed condition of the sugar-planters of Cuba and Brazil, the extension of legitimate traffic, and other causes, have succeeded in diminishing altogether the amount of Slave Trade; and the scene of its greatest activity, North of the Line, lies now within a moderate distance of Sierra Leone, or to the windward of it. The reasons, therefore, for removing the Courts of Adjudication from that Colony are not what they were. If, however, one place of adjudication only is still to be assigned, and only one place of release, to the wretched victims of the Slave Dealer, we believe that Ascension, or one of the Portuguese Islands, would on the whole be best adapted for that purpose, as being more convenient than Sierra Leone to the Bights of Benin and Biafra, and to the Portuguese Settlements South of the Line, now the principal seats of the existing Slave Trade, and (owing to the set of winds and currents in that direction) as being easy of access even from the farthest extremities of the Windward Coast, where any Slave Trade is carried on. We are aware, however, that these are arrangements which can only be made in conjunction with Foreign Powers, and that they involve many considerations which have not been fully before us. They are, however, of high importance to the interests of humanity, and we cannot do less than invite the best attention of Her Majesty's Government to the subject.

The next point we have alluded to, that of the place and manner of locating the Africans who are liberated from the captured Slave Ships, is so closely connected with the question of Emigration from Africa generally, that this seems to be the proper opportunity for discussing that important subject. Before, however, they go further, Your Committee desire to say a few words as to the point of view from which they have felt it their special duty to look at it. On another Committee has been devolved the charge of examining it in its bearings on the prosperity of the West Indies: we consider it our peculiar duty to look at it as affecting the interests of Africa only, whether of its Natives generally, or specially of those who come into our hands and under our protection in the course of our attempts to put down the Slave Trade. Now, the investigation alluded to as devolved upon another Committee of Your honourable House, is no doubt one of the highest importance, even to the interests of the African himself; inasmuch as we have it on the highest authority, that the diminished supply of Sugar from our West India Colonies, consequent on Emancipation, gave an extraordinary stimulus to the Slave Trade for the supply of Cuba and Brazil; and the best aid for its discouragement, and the best chance for its total extinction, would undoubtedly be the diminution of inducement to carry it on, which would arise from the production of Sugar by Free Labour in the British Colonies on lower terms. But, as more immediately within our province, we have thought it our duty to confine our inquiries upon this subject to three points: 1st. Whether, indeed, there are any considerable materials for a free Emigration from Africa to the West Indies; 2dly. Whether it would be desirable for the African to make the change; and, 3rdly. Whether it could be carried on, and how, without reasonable apprehension, or even a possibility of creating or encouraging a new Slave Trade.

Now, as to the first point, we may briefly say, that on the Gold Coast few materials for a perfectly free Emigration, or for Emigration of any kind, appear to exist. The devastations of the Slave Trade, and of the wars connected with it, though it has now ceased there entirely for nine or ten years, are yet too recent to allow of the existence of any very crowded Population, or any adventurous habits; and all, save the Chiefs and a few dwellers on the coasts, who have engaged in the various pursuits of commerce under the protection of the British, the Dutch, and Danish settlements, are Slaves, though their Slavery, like that of Africa generally, is not, as to labour, of a very grievous kind. As we proceed up the Coast, we fall in, between Cape Palmas and Cape Mount, with a very singular race of men, consisting of many small tribes, known commonly by the collective name of Kroomen, scattered along a considerable range of shore; much given, though not exclusively, to maritime pursuits; forming part of the crew of every English man-of-war and merchantman on the coast; known by a distinctive external mark, and neither taken as Slaves themselves, nor making

Slaves of others. Their numbers are uncertain, but are undoubtedly considerable, and seem to be increasing, and their confidence in the English character is ascertained. But it seems doubtful whether permission for large numbers to leave their shores could be obtained without some present to their Chiefs; and their attachment to their own country, and their present habits of migrating only for a period, and without their families, make it also doubtful whether they would ever become permanent settlers elsewhere, or indeed remain away from home for a longer period than two or three years. Upon this point we would refer, in addition to other Evidence, to that which was given before us by two or three of these men themselves.

Passing by Sierra Leone for the moment, we come to the British Settlement of the Gambia, and here we find about 1,500 Liberated Africans, whom the British Government has removed thither from Sierra Leone, from whom of course not much emigration could be expected, though some, for they have little employment there. But we find there a periodical Migration from a considerable distance up the River in two tribes of Serawoolies and Tilliebunkas, who come in numbers to do all the severe labour of the Settlement, and having saved their earnings return to their homes, apparently free to come and go without restraint or obligation of any kind. Their case may be considered as somewhat resembling that of the Kroomen, and as offering materials for a temporary Emigration in the first instance, though possibly hereafter, on further experience, for one of a more permanent character. We now return to Sierra Leone, and here we find the Liberated Africans and their descendants, in number from 40,000 to 50,000, a body of Kroomen, in numbers which are variously stated from 1,000 to 5,000, who, like the Serawoolies in the Gambia, do all the hard labour of the Colony, and between 1,000 and 2,000 of a mixed population, who, like the Kroomen, have come into the Colony of their own accord. We have also to deal here with those who may hereafter be the subjects of adjudication on their release from Slave Ships, or who may hereafter come into the Colony, if it should be permitted, for the purpose of Emigration. These are the materials for Emigration to the West Indies which have presented themselves, and progressively, if it were permitted, encouraged, and successful, they would probably prove to be considerable.

The next question is, whether it would be a desirable change for these people to be in the West Indies rather than in Africa. Now for this object we desired that statements might be prepared for us, founded principally on Official Documents, acquainting us with the state of things, the condition of society, the temporal, the moral and religious advantages which would be enjoyed in three of our principal Colonies, to which we beg to refer in our Appendix, but from which we insert here a few Extracts, as sufficient for the present occasion.

JAMAICA.

"Of the actual condition of the labouring population of Jamaica, and consequently the condition which would be accessible to the African immigrants, Sir C. Metcalfe gives the following description, in his dispatch to Lord Stanley of the 1st November, 1841:

"With respect to the labouring population, formerly slaves, but now perfectly free, and more independent than the same class in other free countries, I venture to say, that in no country in the world can the labouring population be more abundantly provided with the necessaries and comforts of life, more at their ease, or more secure from oppression than in Jamaica; and I may add, that ministers of the Gospel for their religious instruction, and schools for the education of their children, are established in all parts of the island, with a tendency to constant increase, although the present reduction of the Mico schools is a temporary drawback."

"Of the means afforded for the religious and moral instruction of the population of Jamaica, Sir C. Metcalfe, in this dispatch, makes the following statement:

"I turn from the cheerless prospects of proprietors to a more pleasing feature in the present order of things. The thriving condition of the peasantry is very striking and gratifying. I do not suppose that any peasantry in the world have so many comforts, or so much independence and enjoyment. Their behaviour is peaceable, and in some respects admirable. They are fond of attending Divine service, and are to be seen on the Lord's day thronging to their respective churches and chapels, dressed in good clothes, and many of them riding on horseback. They send their children to school and pay for their schooling. They subscribe for the erection of churches and chapels; and in the Baptist communities they not only provide the whole expense of the religious establishment, but by the amount of their contributions afford to their ministers a very respectable support. Marriage is general among the people. Their morals are, I understand, much improved, and their sobriety is remarkable.

"For these very gratifying circumstances we are indebted to the Ministers of Religion in the Island of all denominations. Church of England, Church of Scotland, Moravians, Wesleyans, Baptists, Bishop, Clergy, and Missionaries, all exert themselves, and vie with each other in amicable rivalry to do good to their fellow-creatures. The number of Churches, Chapels, and Schools built and being built in every part of the Island, affords a most pleasing and encouraging sight. In this respect the prospects of the Island are very cheering, and the liberal support afforded to useful Institutions, and the encouragement given to Religious Teachers, without any bigoted exclusions, are creditable to the Island Legislature, and every part of the Community."

The Reports of the Magistrates[6], which will be found in the Parliamentary Paper 1842, concur in representing the great efforts which are made in promoting Religious Instruction.

[6] Statement given in by W. Burge, Esq., Agent for Jamaica.

"The annual charge defrayed by the Colony of Jamaica, for the support of the Ministers and Schools of the Church of England, was, in 1836, 53,260*l.* 14*s.* 5*d.* currency, or 31,956*l.* 8*s.* 8*d.* sterling money, as will appear by a Paper laid before Parliament in 1837, and which will be found referred to in Evidence before the Committee of The House on the West India Colonies. Since the Year 1836 an increase has been made; and in the Years 1839 and 1840, an addition of 14,000*l.* sterling per annum was made to the charge. The total annual charge, therefore, defrayed by the Colony for that part of the Ecclesiastical and School Establishment, connected with the Church of England, exceeds 45,000*l.* sterling money. But this Establishment is still further extended by occasional Grants by the Assembly of Jamaica, by Parliamentary Grants, and by certain Religious Societies in England, and by individuals there and in Jamaica. In addition to this Establishment, very extensive means of Religious Instruction are afforded by the Presbyterian, Moravian, Wesleyan, and Baptist Missions, established in Jamaica, and those schools and places of worship are thickly spread over the Colony, and large contributions for supporting and extending these Schools are derived from Parliamentary Grants, from Grants by the Assembly of Jamaica, by charitable institutions, and by private individuals here and at Jamaica."

BRITISH GUIANA.

"If I were not convinced that the unhappy Africans are benefited by the transfer to this colony, I should not so urgently press the continuance of the countenance of Her Majesty's Government to that effect. I have, in my residence on this coast, seen that the Africans from Sierra Leone are far from being in the civilised state I should have anticipated; that their condition must, therefore, here be improved; how much more so then must the pure savage be raised by being brought amongst his own colour, who are in a high progressive state of civilisation[7]."

[7] Extract from the Dispatch of Governor Light to Secretary of State, dated 21 Sept. 1841, Parl. Paper, 1842, p. 85.

"Religious instruction administered at 57 places of public worship. Each parish has at least two parochial schools under the superintendence of the minister. Each missionary has a school attached to his domicile, and nearly all the principal plantations in the colony, if at a distance from the schools, maintain a school for the instruction of their labourers' children, free of expense.

"An annual grant has been made by the colony in aid of the education of children of the labouring population in the rural districts, amounting to 13,333 dollars."

"The average rate of wages for agricultural labourers is about 5-12ths of a dollar per task; a day's task is understood to be seven hours, but is generally performed in four or five hours by an industrious man; any extra time or labour is paid for additional."

"House-room, garden ground, medicine, and medical attendance, have hitherto been granted free; all other requisites are provided by the labourers themselves[8]."

[8] Parl. Paper, 1842, p. 120. Extract from Report of Committee on Emigration.

TRINIDAD.

"By Mr. Latrobe's Report in 1839, it appears there were 35 Day and Evening Schools, and 14 Sunday, of all denominations; whereas, by the Return of the Society for the Propagation of the Gospel, the Established Church alone has now 28 Schools, and it is calculated that the present number in all is not less than from 50 to 60. As regards Churches and Chapels, there are no less than 18 connected with the Established Church, 11 Roman-catholic, 4 Wesleyan, and 1 Presbyterian, together 34, for a population of from 50,000 to 60,000 souls; this would give a School for every 1,000 souls, and a Church for every 2,000.

"In the Colonial Estimate for this year, there is a provision of 1,660*l.* for the Established Church, and for the Roman-catholic 3,236*l.*, as fixed expenditure, besides 5,865*l.* towards building Churches, and 1,937*l.* towards Education."

"The soil of Trinidad is a rich marl that requires no manuring whatever, and of such soil there are fully one million of acres in brushwood and forest. Were there only a sufficiency of labour every British market might be amply supplied with Sugar from this one Island; hence, Foreign Sugars would be excluded, and the Slave Trade, as it refers to Great Britain at least, would be practically discouraged.

"In Trinidad too, Christian Ministers can live and labour with far less risk of health and loss of time. Government is also extremely willing to give half the amount required for the erection of Chapels, School-houses, Teachers' Salaries, &c. in any part of the Island where we may have even a small Society of Emigrants.

"It is therefore my deliberate conviction that the people would gain an accession to their religious privileges by quitting any part of Western Africa for the Island of Trinidad.

"But again I think that the worldly circumstances of the Emigrants would be considerably advanced. The labourers may very easily earn half a dollar per day on their arrival here, and in a couple of weeks, that is, as soon as they fully understand the nature of the work, the able-bodied may make a dollar. A house and garden are given to every labourer. On these particulars Mr. David and the labourers who have returned with him will be able to satisfy you[9]."

[9] Extract from Letter addressed by Rev. J. Blackwell, Wesleyan Minister in Trinidad, to Wesleyan Ministers at Sierra Leone.

Now after looking at such a picture, drawn from the most unsuspected sources, we cannot doubt that, whether for the homeless Negro just rescued from the hold of a Slave Ship, or for the ignorant and uncivilised African who comes down to our Settlements to pick up a small pittance by the hardest labour, and to return with it to his barbarous home, it would be of the highest advantage, it would be the greatest blessing, to make such an exchange. But how is it with the Liberated African of Sierra Leone, who has been enjoying perhaps for years the fostering care of the British Government? Now to that Government, beyond his rescue from the Slave Ship, and emancipation from future Slavery, and a temporary sustenance, and his being placed within the reach of Missionary efforts, to which it has not contributed, the Liberated African cannot fairly be said to owe much. To the invaluable exertions of the Church Missionary Society more especially, and also to a considerable extent, as in all our African Settlements, to the Wesleyan body, the highest praise is due. The former expend nearly 7,000*l.*, the latter nearly 2,000*l.* annually upon the Religious Instruction of the Colony. By their efforts nearly one-fifth of the whole population, a most unusually high proportion in any country, are at school, and the effects are visible in considerable intellectual, moral, and religious improvement,—very considerable under the peculiar circumstances of such a Colony. But a few ill-supported Schools and one Chaplain is all that has been contributed by the Government to the religious and moral improvement of those of whom she has undertaken the protection, and their social improvement has been unattempted. No Model Farm has been established, no instruction in Agriculture has been afforded. The rate of wages, when any are earned, which is chiefly by a few in the neighbourhood of the towns, is 4*d.* to 7*d.* a day, and with this and a little cultivation a sufficient subsistence, though nothing more, is gained. The extent of good soil is limited; the inhabitants wander out of the Colony for the subsistence which they cannot find within it. There is little industry, there are small facilities for trade, as the Colony itself produces little to export save a little arrow-root and ginger, and the River which it commands is only navigable for 30 or 40 miles to any useful purpose, and supplies no article but timber and camwood. With such a climate, therefore, and thus circumstanced, the Colony can never invite the residence of planters or of merchants of considerable capital, or become a favourite with officers, either civil or military, of a higher order. What elements of prosperity, therefore, can it have? The Government has not done much, but under any circumstances the Colony must be an artificial creation. The Government ought to have established a Model Farm, or in some way communicated agricultural knowledge; and we would recommend that it should be attempted even now. But, after all, what is that to the magnificent Model Farms which would surround the African in the West Indies?

We need hardly add more to prove that it would be well for the African, in every point of view, to find himself a Free Labourer in the free British West India Colonies, enjoying there, as he would, higher advantages of every kind, than have fallen to the lot of the Negro race in any other portion of the globe.

We pass the question, though not absolutely to be lost sight of, that, in Sierra Leone, the newly liberated African is a burden to the British Government as well as to himself; and that, in the West Indies, not only would his own condition be improved, but he would become a source of wealth and prosperity to the Empire. But we must not omit the advantage to Africa, of the probable return to her soil of many of her own sons, enriched with civil and religious knowledge, and bringing back with them wealth, and the means of wealth and civilisation; "that reflux of the West upon the East, in moderate numbers, and managed with caution," in the words of Sir John Jeremie, "to which we must look for the civilisation of the East."

But Your Committee had next to consider, whether, in achieving this object, any danger existed of creating a real, or plausible suspicion of a real, Slave Trade under another name.—Under proper regulations, they think there is not. A free passage may be offered to the African already settled within the colony, and to the Free Settler or other Native, who shall have remained long enough in the Colony to give the authorities sufficient time to ascertain the circumstances under which he came, and to assure themselves that they were entirely free from all suspicion of fraud or force. To such as thus leave their homes, a free passage back at the end of a certain period, say three or four years, might be promised, with full permission to them to return at any time at their own expense. To the homeless African, newly liberated, the option should be given of settling at once in the West Indies, if he please, with permission to return hereafter at his own cost, or of removing from Sierra Leone, or of remaining in it on the first adjudication, if he undertake for his own maintenance, or can find friends or relations who will undertake it for him.

With regard to the Kroomen, however desirable they may be as labourers, and however advantageous the object may be to themselves, we are not prepared in the first instance to recommend other facilities for emigration than those which we have suggested to be offered to other Natives who might desire to make use of a British Settlement as a point of departure[10]. If they should desire, as it appears that it is not improbable they may, to make a Migration across the Atlantic, with their habits they will find no difficulty in making their way, for the purpose, to Sierra Leone, where some hundreds or even thousands of their brethren habitually reside, some of whom have already emigrated to Guiana, and seem to be as active in the field, as we have long found them to be on the sea, and to be well pleased with the experiment.

[10] On this point, however, we beg to refer to the important evidence of Capt. Denman, who thinks that on account of the peculiar character of the Kroomen, emigration, with common precaution, might be conducted from their coast without risk of abuse. *See* Q. 6995, *et preced.*

If it should hereafter be thought desirable to form any Settlement on the Kroo Coast, however small, it might facilitate arrangements similar to those which we have recommended for the other Settlements. Or they might possibly hereafter be embarked from the Coast itself under the superintendence of a man-of-war. (*See* Capt. Denman.)

The same door might be opened, under the same precautions, from the Gambia; but with regard to the Gold Coast, the supply of labour there not appearing to be more than necessary for the wants of the country, we would not recommend any peculiar facilities to be afforded.

The expense of the Emigration would of course be defrayed by the Colony to which each successive band of Emigrants was directed.

All this of course cannot be secured from abuse without the strictest superintendence of some Government authority; which we believe, dealing as it would do only with British Settlements, would be substantially effective. But we would earnestly recommend, that it should rather be undertaken altogether by the Government itself. In that way only can perfect security be given and felt against the abuses which might arise from the competition of the Agents of rival Colonies; in that way only can perfect confidence be given, whether to the African himself, or to the public opinion of England and the civilised world, that nothing shall be done which shall even bring suspicion upon a reputation, of which we are justly jealous, of which we can still be proud, and which it is of the highest importance that we should sustain. But under these sanctions, whether we look to the effect of the prosperity of our Free Colonies in discouraging the Slave Trade, or to the advantage of placing the African in that position where he will be most likely to raise himself in the moral and social scale, and to react beneficially upon the destinies of his Mother Country[11], Your Committee cannot but strongly urge upon Parliament not only not to prohibit the Emigration of Free Blacks from our African Settlements to our West India Colonies, but to encourage and promote it by the authority of Government, under the sanctions and regulations above suggested, or such other as further consideration may supply.

[11] To prove that this expectation is not altogether even now unsupported by facts, we beg to quote a passage from a letter in the Appendix, from Messrs. Anderson & Co.: "Demerara, 30 April, 1842. The Superior is off to day for Sierra Leone; 68 people have gone in her, including children, and with the exception of three or four, who are old soldiers, the whole of them are people who came seven or eight years ago from the Bahamas, (liberated Africans?) and they return to their native country with a good deal of money; three of them have not less than 5,000 dollars each."

As we have said before, the way in which this question is disposed of will affect materially other questions connected with the internal administration of the Colony.

If Emigration should go on to any great extent from the settled Population of Sierra Leone, which we believe it might without in any way injuring the condition of the Colony, but rather the reverse, (for the rate of Wages would probably rise, and it appears that it is not the successful and thriving who are inclined to go), it will probably be possible to dispense with some of the Establishment which is now requisite for watching over the interests of the Liberated Africans. If, on adjudication, they are mostly located in the West Indies, the much-discussed question of the best means of disposing of them, of the necessity of maintaining them, as now, for six months, or the expediency of leaving them at once to their own resources and the charity of their countrymen; the question of the best means of disposing of the Children, and the ever-new devices of successive Governors for escaping from the inevitable evils of apprenticing them to persons on whose character no dependence can be placed, will be got rid of; and the British Government will be relieved from the necessity of attempting to overcome the obstacles which nature seems herself to have interposed at Sierra Leone, in the way of ensuring a prosperous condition to the objects of its humane care.

We now come to the question which has of late excited so much interest and feeling, that of the facilities which British Commerce is charged with having furnished to the Slave Trade, and to the extent and nature of the connexion which exists between them; a question which must be considered dispassionately and soberly, rather with a view to what is best for the object upon the whole, and to what is practicable, than to what might at first appear to be desirable, and what might be perhaps a partial good, producing possibly, in other ways, a greater evil. *Now, in the first place, it is fair to state that we have no evidence, or reason to believe, that any British Merchant concerned in the trade with the West Coast of Africa, either owns or equips any vessel engaged in the Slave Trade, or has any share in the risks or profits of any Slave Trade venture. The charge is this, and it must be admitted, that whether by selling condemned Slave Vessels back to Slave Dealers, which is the rarer case, or, which is the more common, by selling to Slave Dealers lawful goods, which are afterwards employed in barter for Slaves (whether circuitously by sale to Merchants in Cuba and Brazil, or directly on the Coast of Africa), the British Merchant and Manufacturer does, in common with the Merchants of other nations, furnish very considerable facilities for the Slave Trade.*

It must further be admitted, that owing to the equipment article in our recent Treaties, which has prevented the actual Slaver from hovering on the Coast in safety, a large portion of the goods necessary for the Slave Trade is driven into Vessels innocent in their apparent character, but subserving the purposes of the Slaver; and that, in consequence, a somewhat larger portion of this kind of traffic may possibly now pass directly from the English or other Merchant to the Coast of Africa, than heretofore, when those supplies went round by Cuba and Brazil in the Slavers themselves, without risk of capture.

Now an opinion has prevailed, and that in very influential quarters, and it runs through Dr. Madden's Report, that at least such direct dealing is illegal, and punishable under the Statute of the 5 Geo. IV, c. 5; and if not so already, the same parties would urge on Parliament to make it so by new enactment; and some even would extend it to all connexion, however indirect, in which a guilty knowledge of the destination of the goods or of the Vessel could be presumed. Now this view of the Act is not unnatural, owing to the general and comprehensive nature of its language, and to the desire which must naturally exist to understand it in as comprehensive a sense as possible for the obstruction of so odious and detestable a traffic as the Slave Trade. But looking closely at the language of the Act itself, and to the interpretation put upon it by the Law Officers of the Crown, as alluded to by the Under Secretary of the Colonies, in his letter to Dr. Madden, April 1842, and to the opinion of the Attorney General in the case inserted in the Evidence, *we cannot affirm it to be illegal now*, and we shall presently state to The House why, however reluctantly we may come to the conclusion, *we are not prepared to recommend that it should be made so.*

Now in the first place, it is difficult to consider or to make that illegal, which is and has been done at Sierra Leone for years, by a Court of Judicature, (in doing so, acting under Treaties and under the sanction of an Act of Parliament, namely,) selling publicly, and to the highest bidder, Prize Vessels and Prize Goods condemned for Slave Dealing, indiscriminately, and without precaution or restriction, to persons of all descriptions, including

Slave Dealers themselves, and which, in regard to vessels at least, had been practised in that Colony by persons of high character and station unreproved. But if it should be made illegal hereafter to sell a Vessel to a party concerned in the traffic in Slaves, the next question, and one that a Legislative body must consider, is, in what manner shall such a prohibition be enforced? A bond that the Vessel shall not be disposed of to a Slave Dealer has been proposed; but how shall the Vessel be prevented from passing very shortly from hand to hand till it reaches an unlawful owner? and is it not unwise for the Law to attempt that which it has so little means of effectually enforcing? There seems no remedy for this, which at Sierra Leone, in the heart of the Slave Trade, and where the Vessel is often sold for half its value, is an evil substantially as well as in feeling, but that of extending the provisions of those Treaties which direct that a Slave Vessel shall be broken up, not sold, and altering our own Municipal Law to the same effect.

But in regard to goods and merchandise, should the Committee advise The House to make such dealing illegal? Now all the witnesses, even those who advocate this view most strongly, admit that legitimate trade, by which is meant the exchange of merchandise for produce, is most beneficial to Africa, and co-operates materially with the cruizer in his operations, whether directly by the assistance and information with which the British trader supplies him, or indirectly by diminishing the necessity of a trade in Slaves, as the means of procuring European or other goods; they admit that nothing therefore would be more injurious to the interests of Africa, than to interfere materially with the operations of lawful commerce. It appears, moreover, that in every place on the Coast North of the Line, (to which limits our inquiries have mainly been confined,) with the exception of perhaps two or three points, a lawful trade of more or less extent is or has been carried on contemporaneously with, and often, nay generally, by the same persons as, the Slave Trade: they have told us that the same goods, such as cottons, rum, tobacco, guns and gunpowder, are employed in both trades; and that, although those employed in the Slave Trade are often of an inferior description, yet that quality alone will not furnish the means of distinguishing between one and the other, and that, practically, there are no means of making such a distinction; they have told us that any restriction on traffic which they would recommend, must therefore be confined to places or persons *solely* or *principally* concerned in the Slave Trade, and that the law should not attempt to interfere with any other. The question still remains, how this is to be carried out?

With regard to those places, where the Slave Trade has been extinguished, no difficulty will arise; but with regard to those places, not few in number nor of slight importance, where, as in Bissao now, and as it has been and may be again, in the Brass and Bonny Rivers, the most important marts for lawful trade upon the Coast of Africa, a trade in produce and slaves is carried on together and by the same persons; or where, as in Whydah and Popo, a trade in produce has been gradually growing up and gaining upon the Slave Trade in proportion as the enterprise of the British merchant pushes on the one and the vigilance of the British cruizer checks and cripples the other, how should the Legislature deal with them? Shall they be lawful or unlawful ports or persons? What is to legalise the traffic in such cases? What proportion, or what positive amount, of lawful traffic? But, indeed, how is the lawful traffic to spring up at all under such circumstances of exclusion?

Some witnesses have argued, that this question of degree need not be defined but may be left to be solved by the practical sense of a jury. By what jury? In England or at Sierra Leone? Under what uncertainties and obstructions would the most scrupulous trader deal with the Coast of Africa, if, for the misinterpretation of such instructions, as the nature of such a case will admit, by a supercargo, his vessel and goods are liable to be brought some hundreds or thousands of miles out of their course, to have the question decided by a jury, whether some person or some factory dealt with was *principally* or not engaged in the Slave Trade, it being unlawful if *principally*, lawful if *partially*, in some unknown and varying proportion, so engaged.

The question for the Legislature to consider is, whether it is worth while to do all this, to infuse so much risk and uncertainty into a trade which it wishes to encourage, which it looks to as one of the main instruments for the civilisation of Africa, for the sake of interfering with so small a proportion of the facilities which commerce, permitted at all with Africa, under her present circumstances, must of necessity afford more or less to the Trade in Slaves. For unless all other countries can be persuaded to take the same view, it must indeed be a small proportion, and little indeed will have been done towards the object; an obstruction will merely have been raised for such length of time as may be required for conveying the same goods from England or from foreign countries through other channels. It would be merely a transfer, and a transfer to parties less friendly to the object, and less under control. We have had ample evidence, that foreign vessels already carry on this trade to a considerable extent; nor is there any right by existing treaty with foreign nations, nor can it be expected, that we should obtain it, to interrupt foreign vessels engaged in such a traffic. But indeed, how would it be carried out? The right of search, in any shape, is one, as we know by experience, that requires the greatest delicacy in carrying out with the ships of friendly nations. But what kind of search must that be, which would seek to ascertain, on board of an apparently innocent vessel, innocent in her build and in her equipment, and freighted with innocent goods, whether the destination of such goods was not made unlawful by some document hidden in the most obscure recesses of the vessel? How prolonged, how minute, consequently how irritating at all times, how vexatious, if unsuccessful; how likely to be unsuccessful, if not guided by more obvious indications; how likely consequently to lead to disputes and collisions among nations, most injurious, if not fatal to that harmonious co-operation for the common object which is so absolutely essential to success. It must not be lost sight of how large a share of these evils must be inflicted on those who are engaged in our own lawful commerce, if such a search be applied to them.

Now if we were bound by a rigid principle to do this, these arguments must be rejected, as not affecting a case of conscience; but in this case we are not trying the value of a rigid principle. The principle would be intelligible which dictated the absolute interdiction of all commerce with every place from which a single Slave was exported; or, further still, with every place from which a Slave Trade was carried on, such as Cuba and Brazil; or if it dictated a prohibition to send goods where there was a probability that they might be exchanged for Slaves. But this arbitrary and uncertain limitation, so little capable of being referred to strict principle, and yet so injurious to lawful commerce, can only rest on the ground of its expediency, of its tendency to attain or promote the object; must submit to be tried by that test, and so tried will be found wanting. It is no doubt galling to a zealous and gallant officer, engaged in the service of his country and humanity in watching anxiously a well-known slaver's haunt, to see foreign vessels, still more vessels bearing his own country's flag, passing inwards and supplying those goods, though innocent in themselves, which are the medium of an atrocious traffic; it is not surprising that under such circumstances that feeling should have arisen which appears in Dr. Madden's Report, and in the Evidence of several, especially the naval, Witnesses. It is a feeling natural and honourable in itself; and we hope that the English merchant, animated as he is by the same feelings of horror for the Slave Trade, will endeavour to extend the influence of those feelings through the whole circle of his transactions. But we cannot recommend that a provision so difficult to be carried out, so vexatious and yet so ineffectual for its object, should be made the subject of Legislation.

Happily in this great work we need not despair. The measures lately adopted have done much. The evidence of all the Naval Officers as well as Commanders of Merchant Ships, concurs in stating, that North of the Line, over a coast of many thousand miles, the Slave Trade, with the exception of a few points in the neighbourhood of Sierra Leone and the Gambia, is virtually extinct. And the continuance of these measures, well guarded and considered in all their details, as well as extended, together with such as we have recommended in different parts of our Report, give fair ground for hoping for ultimate success. Under this head we would venture to recommend that none but the swiftest vessels should be employed; that some of the best Prizes should be converted to the purposes of the service; that

Steamers should be engaged in watching the intricacies of Islands, and the mouths of Rivers; that the system of paying by Head-money, so unjust to gallant men[12], or, perhaps, by Bounty at all, should be reconsidered, and possibly replaced by higher pay and the prospect of promotion. Encouragement and ample protection, at the same time, should be given to lawful trade in every shape[13]; and the Settlements which we hold, or which we may form, upon the coast, should be kept open indifferently to all nations as to ourselves, that they may see, and be compelled to acknowledge, that in all we are attempting for Africa, we are only endeavouring to provide a feast of which all may equally partake; and seeking, as the reward of our exertions, no advantage to ourselves save that which may fairly fall to our lot from a proportionate share of a more abundant table, spread out for the common benefit of all.

[12] As an instance of the injustice of this system, we beg to refer to a case cited by Captain Denman (Q. 7099), in which it appears that the capture of two vessels, of the aggregate capacity of 80 tons, which would have held 700 slaves, was remunerated with no more than 576*l.*, because they were empty; while that of a single vessel, of little more than half that tonnage, brought in 1,654*l.*, because she was full. Thus the least laborious and dangerous, as well as the least effective service, receives the highest reward.

[13] Perhaps one or two vessels might have this specific duty assigned to them, apart from the general operations of the Cruizers connected with the Slave Trade.

IN THE CENTRAL CRIMINAL COURT.
REGINA *v.* ZULUETA.

Counsel for the Prosecution.

MR. SERJEANT BOMPAS.
MR. SERJEANT TALFOURD.
MR. PAYNE.

Counsel for the Defence.

MR. FITZ-ROY KELLY.
MR. CLARKSON.
MR. BODKIN.

PROCEEDINGS
INSTITUTED AGAINST
PEDRO DE ZULUETA, JUN., ESQ.

From the moment I left the Committee of the House of Commons, on the 23d of July, 1842, I never again heard of this matter until Wednesday the 23d of August, 1843.

On that day, between two and three o'clock in the afternoon, I was sitting at my desk in the private room of Zulueta & Co.'s office, 22, Moorgate Street, in the City of London, when a clerk came into the room to announce that a gentleman of the name of *Scoble* wished to see me. "Do you know him? He says that he is not known to you." Upon this I went out into the clerks' office and found the individual, thus calling himself, standing outside the counter. I asked him his business, and he replied that *he did not call upon his own business.* He asked me, in a pointed and distinct manner, if my name was Pedro de Zulueta, which of course I instantly acknowledged. "*I do not call on my own business, but to introduce a person who wishes to speak with you. Shall he see you here, or at your house?*" "I should like to know first who he is; what is his name?" "*You do not know him, his name is Brown.*" "I do not recollect any person of that name," I replied. "*He is below, if you like to see him.*" The first impression on my mind was that the whole was some ridiculous mystery about some great trifle, and I thought I could not dispose of it better or more quickly than by seeing the man, so suiting the action to the word, I said, "I will go and see who he is," and opened the door which leads from the office into the landing-place at the top of the stairs. No sooner was I outside the door than the individual, calling himself *Scoble*, addressed me in a tone different from the insinuating manner in which he had done before—not rude, but solemn—"The fact is, Sir, that a true bill has been found by the Grand Jury against you for felony, and there is an officer below to take you into custody. I did not like to state this before the clerks."

The first impression I received at hearing these words I cannot give any account of, but it certainly struck me as the whole thing being a trick. "What do you say, Sir?" I asked; and the assertion was repeated, adding that the charge was slave trading. Then I was still more confirmed that there was some trick in the case. I asked the policeman, who was within the house and apparently in the act of ascending the stairs, to be called up, which Mr. Scoble did, and both were shown by me into the private through the public office. My father was sitting in the next room, and when I tried to make him understand the case, seeing the policeman and Mr. Scoble, he received the same impression of the whole being a trick, which raised his indignation at the audacity, and made him address Mr. Scoble very angrily. Mr. Scoble was evidently anxious to leave the room; and the policeman, to whom he gave strict directions about what was to be done with me, having assured me that the thing was in earnest, that I must go with him, I opened the private door for Mr. Scoble, who left the office repeating his injunctions to the officer, that I must be taken directly to the station-house, where Sir George Stephen would immediately go.

We had never before heard Sir George Stephen's name, and my father thought he might be a magistrate. He tried to ascertain from the policeman by whose authority he was acting, but we could not obtain from him any thing that we could understand. He waited until Mr. John Lawford, of the firm of Messrs. Lawford, of Drapers Hall, our solicitors, arrived, and then we proceeded to the Garlick Hill Police Station-house. There Sir George Stephen appeared: he did not know me, and asked which was Pedro de Zulueta. When my name was mentioned, I answered to it, and then he preferred the charge as will be found in the succeeding page.

Mr. Lawford spoke aside with Sir George Stephen, for the immediate and pressing question was the bail. Sir George expressed a firm determination *to resist bail to any amount.* Then the dreadful thought was, what was to become of my family, since it never has happened, that I have been absent without their being acquainted with all the circumstances; and I do not think I have slept one night out of my house while in town. The late hour made it quite unlikely that with opposition to the bail, and as counsel must be heard, that I could escape passing the night in Newgate. Mr. John Lawford, with the greatest kindness and feeling, expressed to me that such was his fear. My reply was, that they might do what they pleased with me, only that my wife should be seen to, for I was quite sure of the result of her hearing suddenly of such an occurrence, together with my not going home. Sir George coldly remarked, that "it must already be known at home, for he had sent there to take me, in case I had not been taken at the office." The agony, which such a statement caused, was perceptible, and one of the officers in the room remarked, that I needed not apprehend any thing, as all the officers could do, would be to watch the house.

I was conveyed very late to the Court at the Old Bailey, where I sat until nearly nine o'clock in suspense as to what would be the result of the application for bail, and next whether the persons approved of could be found at so late an hour. It was not until late, that the former was granted; and after considerable difficulty, and the impossibility of finding one of the two bail offered, the other was accepted as sufficient by the Court, together with my own recognizance. I then went home at about half-past nine o'clock at[209*] night to my afflicted family in a condition, which, as I believe it unprecedented when all the circumstances of my case are considered, so I hope and trust may never fall again to the lot of any man who lives in that happy and undescribable feeling of habitual security, which in this country we so dearly value as the precious privilege and the certain possession of every man who has not contemplated and is not aware of a breach of the law. Thus will it have been reserved to me, in the British dominions, to experience this peculiar method of receiving a wound in the heart, which, although time and the sympathy which has been so kindly expressed may allay, I alone can know how unlikely it is that any lapse of time can altogether cure.

As I would not state a fact with any greater appearance of certainty than what I really possess, I ought to add, since I *now* have seen the name of Mr. *John Scoble* mentioned as that of the Secretary of the Anti-Slavery Society, that as I never saw before or have seen since, that I am aware of, *the Scoble*, who acted in this to me ever memorable occasion, I cannot tell whether they are both one and the same person.

———

Extract from the Book kept at the Station-house on Garlick Hill, containing the Entries of Charges made on Wednesday, August 23, 1843.

Hour 3. 50.—PEDRO DE ZULUETA (32), 22, Moorgate Street, brought in by P. C.[14] 489, —— Tye, charged by Sir George Stephen, 17, King's Arms Yard, Coleman Street, with Felony (*Slave Trading*); also with Conspiracy, a true Bill having been found against him at the C. C. Court on both of the above charges.

(signature of person charging) "GEORGE STEPHEN."

[14] P. C. means Police Constable.

———

(*From the Anti-Slavery Reporter.*)
CENTRAL CRIMINAL COURT.
WEDNESDAY, AUGUST 23, 1843.
(Before the Recorder.)
EXTRAORDINARY AFFAIR.

The Grand Jury having, in the course of the day, returned true bills against Pedro de Zulueta the younger, of the parish of St. Mary-le-Bow, merchant, Thomas Jennings, and Thomas Bernardos, late of the same place, mariners, for felony,

Mr. *Clarkson* applied to his Lordship under, as he said, circumstances[210*] of a rather peculiar character. Two bills had been found against Mr. de Zulueta for felony and misdemeanor. He was a highly respectable merchant of the City of London, and he was charged with conspiring, with other persons, to fit out a ship for the purpose of trading in slaves. The proceedings before the Grand Jury were of course entirely *ex parte*, and no application had been made to any magistrate. The first intimation which Mr. de Zulueta had of the fact was his being taken into custody, and he knew nothing of the nature of the charge beyond what was entered in the police-sheet.

The *Recorder* asked, was the defendant present?

Mr. *Clarkson* said he was in custody, and was on his way to the Court.

The *Recorder* asked, what was the application which Mr. Clarkson wished to make?

Mr. *Clarkson* said he wanted the defendant to be allowed to give bail.

Sir *G. Stephen*, who, it appeared, was the solicitor for the prosecution, stated that the charge against Mr. Zulueta was founded upon the Act of the 5th of Geo. IV, which declared the offence imputed to the prisoner to be felony. In answer to the Court, he added that the charge was framed under that section of the Act which rendered the party convicted liable to the penalty of transportation for fourteen years.

The *Recorder* said that if the learned counsel intended to enforce his application for bail, he apprehended that it would be incumbent upon him to show more reason for such a course than the mere statement that the party had been taken by surprise.

Mr. *Clarkson* trusted that the circumstances he had stated would be considered sufficient by the Court. The fact of the defendant being so suddenly arrested and placed in confinement would cause the greatest distress to his family. He was prepared to put in bail to any amount.

The *Recorder* inquired if there was any objection to bail being taken?

Sir *G. Stephen* was understood to say, that in consequence of the circumstances of Mr. Zulueta, there was some doubt whether he ought to be admitted to bail.

Mr. *Clarkson* assured the Court that Mr. de Zulueta had not the slightest indisposition to take his trial; but, on the contrary, he had the greatest anxiety to have the matter investigated. His only wish, in applying to be admitted to bail, was to prevent the misery and inconvenience to which his family would be subjected by his being prevented from returning to them. He especially wished to save the anxiety of the female branches.

The *Recorder* suggested that the case should be dealt with in the ordinary manner, and that affidavits should be prepared in support of the application.

At this stage of the proceedings the prisoner entered the Court, in custody of an officer.

Mr. *Clarkson*, after some communication with Sir G. Stephen, addressed the Court, and said that he believed no objection would be offered to bail in the sum of 5,000*l.*

The *Recorder* said he thought that would be quite sufficient.

Mr. *Clarkson* said the defendant would enter into his own recognizance in 3,000*l.*, and give two sureties in 1,000*l.* each.

It was then arranged that this amount of bail should be put in upon the indictment for felony; and with regard to that for misdemeanor, the defendant should give his own recognizance in 100*l.*, and two sureties in 50*l.* each.

The indictment was then read. It charged the prisoner and the two other persons with having feloniously equipped and employed a certain vessel, called the Augusta, for the purpose of trading in slaves. In other counts the parties were charged with equipping the vessel for the purchase of slaves, and for the purpose of purchasing persons to be dealt with as slaves.

Mr. de Zulueta pleaded not guilty to both indictments.

He then, in default of two sureties, entered into his own recognizance in 6,000*l.*, and one surety in 2,000*l.*, to appear when called on.

———

INDICTMENT FOR FELONY.

THE QUEEN,
v. }
ZULUETA & OTHERS.

CENTRAL CRIMINAL COURT

To wit.—The jurors for Our Lady the Queen, upon their oath present that PEDRO DE ZULUETA the younger, late of the parish of Saint Mary-le-Bow, in the City of London, merchant and commission agent; THOMAS JENNINGS, late of the same place, mariner; and THOMAS BERNARDOS, late of the same place, mariner, heretofore and after the 1st day of January, in the year of the reign of our Lord 1825, to wit, on the 1st day of November, in the 4th year of the reign of Our Sovereign Lady Queen Victoria, with force and arms, to wit, at London aforesaid, and within the jurisdiction of the said Court, did illegally and feloniously *man, navigate, equip, dispatch, use, and employ a certain ship or vessel,* to wit, a ship or vessel called the "Augusta," in order to accomplish a certain object, which in and by a certain Act of Parliament, made and passed in the 5th year of the reign of his late Majesty King George the Fourth, intituled "An Act to amend and consolidate the laws relating to the Abolition of the Slave Trade," was and is declared unlawful, that is to say, *to deal and trade in slaves,* contrary to the form of the statute in such case made and provided, and against the peace of Our Lady the Queen, her crown and dignity;

2. And the jurors aforesaid, upon their oath aforesaid, do further present that the said Pedro de Zulueta the younger, Thomas Jennings, and Thomas Bernardos, after the 1st day of January, in the year of our Lord 1825, to wit, on the 1st day of November, in the 4th year of the reign of Our Sovereign Lady Queen Victoria, with force and arms, to wit, at London aforesaid, and within the jurisdiction of the said Court, did illegally and feloniously, and against the form of the statute in such case made and provided, *fit out, man, navigate, equip, dispatch, use, and employ a certain ship or vessel,* called the "Augusta," in order to accomplish a certain object, which in and by a certain Act of Parliament made and passed in the 5th year of the reign of his late Majesty King George the Fourth, intituled "An Act to amend and consolidate the Laws relating to the Abolition of the Slave Trade," was and is declared unlawful, that is to say, *to purchase slaves,* contrary to the form of the statute in such case made and provided, and against the peace of Our Lady the Queen, her crown and dignity;

3. And the jurors aforesaid, upon their oath aforesaid, do further present that the said Pedro de Zulueta the younger, Thomas Jennings, and Thomas Bernardos, after the 1st day of January, in the year of our Lord 1825, to wit,

on the 1st day of November, in the 4th year of the reign of Our Sovereign Lady Queen Victoria, with force and arms, to wit, at London aforesaid, and within the jurisdiction of the said Court, did illegally and feloniously, and against the form of the statute in such case made and provided, *fit out, man, navigate, equip, dispatch, use, and employ a certain ship or vessel*, called the "Augusta," in order to accomplish a certain object, which in and by a certain Act of Parliament made and passed in the 5th year of the reign of his late Majesty King George the Fourth, intituled "An Act to amend and consolidate the Laws relating to the Abolition of the Slave Trade," was and is declared unlawful, that is to say, *to deal and trade in persons intended to be dealt with as slaves*, contrary to the form of the statute in such case made and provided, and against the peace of Our Lady the Queen, her crown and dignity;

4. And the jurors aforesaid, upon their oath aforesaid, do further present that the said Pedro de Zulueta the younger, Thomas Jennings, and Thomas Bernardos, after the 1st day of January, in the year of our Lord 1825, to wit, on the 1st day of November, in the 4th year of the reign of Our Sovereign Lady Queen Victoria, with force and arms, to wit, at London aforesaid, and within the jurisdiction of the said Court, did illegally and feloniously, and against the form of the statute in such case made and provided, *fit out, man, navigate, equip, dispatch, use, and employ a certain ship or vessel*, called the "Augusta," in order to accomplish a certain object, which in and by a certain Act of Parliament made and passed in the 5th year of the reign of his late Majesty King George the Fourth, intituled "An Act to amend and consolidate the Laws relating to the Abolition of the Slave Trade," was and is declared unlawful, that is to say, *to purchase persons intended to be dealt with as slaves*, contrary to the form of the statute in such case made and provided, and against the peace of Our Lady the Queen, her crown and dignity;

5. And the jurors aforesaid, upon their oath aforesaid, do further present that the said Pedro de Zulueta the younger, Thomas Jennings, and Thomas Bernardos, heretofore and after the 1st day of January, in the year of our Lord 1825, to wit, on the 10th day of November, in the 4th year of the reign of our Sovereign Lady Queen Victoria, with force and arms, to wit, at London aforesaid, and within the jurisdiction of the said Court, did illegally and feloniously, and against the form of the statute in such case made and provided, *ship on board a certain ship or vessel*, called the "Augusta," *divers goods and effects*, to wit, 29 hogsheads of tobacco, 6 cases of arms, 1 case of looking-glasses, 10 casks of copper ware, 134 bales of merchandise, 1,600 iron pots, and 2,370 kegs of gunpowder, to be employed in accomplishing a certain object which was in and by a certain Act of Parliament, made and passed in the 5th year of the reign of his late Majesty King George the 4th, intituled, "An Act to amend and consolidate the laws relating to the Abolition of the Slave Trade," declared unlawful, that is to say, *to trade and deal in slaves*,

contrary to the form of the statute in such case made and provided, and against the peace of Our Lady the Queen, her crown and dignity;

6. And the jurors aforesaid, upon their oath aforesaid, do further present that the said Pedro de Zulueta, Thomas Jennings, and Thomas Bernardos, heretofore and after the 1st day of January in the year of our Lord 1825, to wit, on the 10th day of November, in the 4th year of the reign of Our Sovereign Lady Queen Victoria, with force and arms, to wit, at London aforesaid, and within the jurisdiction of the said Court, did illegally and feloniously, and against the form of the statute in such case made and provided, *ship on board of a certain ship or vessel*, to wit, a ship or vessel called the "Augusta," *divers goods and effects*, to wit, 29 hogsheads of tobacco, 60 cases of arms, 1 case of looking-glasses, 10 casks of copper ware, 134 bales of merchandise, 1,600 iron pots, and 2,370 kegs of gunpowder, to be employed in accomplishing a certain object, which was and is in and by the said last mentioned Act of Parliament declared unlawful, that is to say, *to purchase slaves*, contrary to the form of the statute in such case made and provided, and against the peace of Our Lady the Queen, her crown and dignity;

7. And the jurors aforesaid, upon their oath aforesaid, do further present, that the said Pedro de Zulueta the younger, Thomas Jennings, and Thomas Bernardos, heretofore and after the 1st day of January, in the year of our Lord 1825, to wit, on the 10th day of November, in the 4th year of the reign of Our Sovereign Lady Queen Victoria, with force and arms, to wit, at London aforesaid, and within the jurisdiction of the said Court, did illegally and feloniously, and against the form of the statute in such case made and provided, *ship on board a certain ship or vessel*, to wit, a ship or vessel called the "Augusta," *divers goods and effects*, to wit, 29 hogsheads of tobacco, 60 cases of arms, 1 case of looking-glasses, 10 casks of copper ware, 134 bales of merchandise, 1,600 iron pots, and 2,370 kegs of gunpowder, to be employed in accomplishing a certain object, which was and is in and by the said last mentioned Act of Parliament declared unlawful, that is to say, *to deal and trade in persons intended to be dealt with as slaves*, contrary to the form of the statute in such case made and provided, and against the peace of Our Lady the Queen, her crown and dignity;

8. And the jurors aforesaid, upon their oath aforesaid, do further present that the said Pedro de Zulueta the younger, Thomas Jennings, and Thomas Bernardos, heretofore and after the 1st day of January, in the year of our Lord 1825, to wit, on the 10th day of November, in the 4th year of the reign of our Sovereign Lady Queen Victoria, with force and arms, to wit, at London aforesaid, and within the jurisdiction of the said Court, did illegally and feloniously, and against the form of the statute in such case made and provided, *ship on board of a certain ship or vessel*, to wit, a ship or vessel called the "Augusta," *divers goods and effects*, to wit, 29 hogsheads of tobacco, 60 cases of

arms, 1 case of looking-glasses, 10 casks of copper ware, 134 bales of merchandise, 1,600 iron pots, and 2,370 kegs of gunpowder, to be employed in accomplishing a certain object, which was and is in and by the said last mentioned Act of Parliament declared unlawful, that is to say, *to purchase persons intended to be dealt with as slaves*, contrary to the form of the statute in such case made and provided, and against the peace of Our Lady the Queen, her crown and dignity.

INDICTMENT FOR CONSPIRACY.

THE QUEEN
v. }
ZULUETA & OTHERS.

CENTRAL CRIMINAL COURT

To wit.—The jurors for our Lady the Queen, upon their oath, present that PEDRO DE ZULUETA the younger, late of the parish of St. Mary-le-Bow, in the City of London, merchant and commission agent; THOMAS JENNINGS, late of the same place, mariner; and THOMAS BERNARDOS late of the same place, mariner, heretofore and after the 1st day of January, in the year of our Lord 1825, to wit, on the 1st day of November, in the 4th year of the reign of Our Sovereign Lady Queen Victoria, with force and arms, to wit, at London aforesaid, and within the jurisdiction of the said Court, *did covinously conspire, combine, confederate, and agree together illegally and feloniously*, and against the form of the statute in such case made and provided, *to fit out, man, navigate, equip, dispatch, use, and employ a certain ship or vessel*, to wit, a ship or vessel called the "Augusta," in order to accomplish a certain object, which in and by a certain Act of Parliament, made and passed in the 5th year of the reign of his late Majesty King George the Fourth, intituled "An Act to amend and consolidate the Laws relating to the Abolition of the Slave Trade," was and is declared unlawful, that is to say, *to deal and trade in slaves*, contrary to the form of the statute in such case made and provided, and against the peace of Our Lady the Queen, her crown and dignity;

2. And the jurors aforesaid, upon their oath aforesaid, do further present that the said Pedro de Zulueta the younger, Thomas Jennings, and Thomas Bernardos, after the 1st day of January, in the year of our Lord 1825, to wit, on the 1st day of November, in the 4th year of the reign of Our Sovereign Lady Queen Victoria, with force and arms, to wit, at London aforesaid, and within the jurisdiction of the said Court, *did conspire, combine, confederate, and agree together illegally and feloniously*, and against the form of the statute in such case made and provided, *to fit out, man, navigate, equip, dispatch, use, and employ a certain ship or vessel*, called the "Augusta," in order to accomplish a certain

object, which in and by a certain Act of Parliament, made and passed in the 5th year of the reign of his late Majesty King George the Fourth, intituled "An Act to amend and consolidate the Laws relating to the Abolition of the Slave Trade," was and is declared unlawful, that is to say, *to purchase slaves*, contrary to the form of the statute in such case made and provided, and against the peace of Our Lady the Queen, her crown and dignity;

3. And the jurors aforesaid, upon their oath aforesaid, do further present that the said Pedro de Zulueta the younger, Thomas Jennings, and Thomas Bernardos, after the 1st day of January, in the year of our Lord 1825, to wit, on the 1st day of November in the 4th year of the reign of Our Sovereign Lady Queen Victoria, with force and arms, to wit, at London aforesaid, and within the jurisdiction of the said Court, *did conspire, combine, confederate, and agree together illegally and feloniously*, and against the form of the statute in such case made and provided, to *fit out, man, navigate, equip, dispatch, use, and employ a certain ship or vessel*, called the "Augusta," in order to accomplish a certain object which in and by a certain Act of Parliament, made and passed in the 5th year of the reign of his late Majesty King George the Fourth, intituled "An Act to amend and consolidate the Laws relating to the Abolition of the Slave Trade," was and is declared unlawful, that is to say, *to deal and trade in persons intended to be dealt with as slaves*, contrary to the form of the statute in such case made and provided, and against the peace of our Lady the Queen, her crown and dignity;

4. And the jurors aforesaid, upon their oath aforesaid, do further present that the said Pedro de Zulueta the younger, Thomas Jennings, and Thomas Bernardos, after the 1st day of January, in the year of our Lord 1825, to wit, on the 1st day of November, in the 4th year of the reign of Our Sovereign Lady Queen Victoria, with force and arms, to wit, at London aforesaid, and within the jurisdiction of the said Court, *did conspire, combine, confederate, and agree together illegally and feloniously*, and against the form of the statute in such case made and provided, *to fit out, man, navigate, equip, dispatch, use, and employ a certain ship or vessel* called the "Augusta," in order to accomplish a certain object, which in and by a certain Act of Parliament, made and passed in the 5th year of the reign of his late Majesty King George the Fourth, intituled "An Act to amend and consolidate the Laws relating to the Abolition of the Slave Trade," was and is declared unlawful, that is to say, *to purchase persons intended to be dealt with as slaves*, contrary to the form of the statute in such case made and provided, and against the peace of Our Lady the Queen, her crown and dignity;

5. And the jurors aforesaid, upon their oath aforesaid, do further present that the said Pedro de Zulueta the younger, Thomas Jennings, and Thomas Bernardos, heretofore and after the 1st day of January, in the year of our Lord 1825, to wit, on the 10th day of November, in the 4th year of the reign

of Our Lady the now Queen, with force and arms, to wit, at London aforesaid, and within the jurisdiction of the said Court, *did conspire, combine, confederate, and agree together knowingly, wilfully, and feloniously to ship on board of a certain ship or vessel*, to wit, a ship or vessel called the "Augusta," *divers goods and effects*, to wit, 29 hogsheads of tobacco, 60 cases of arms, one case of looking-glasses, 10 casks of copper ware, 134 bales of merchandise, 1,600 iron pots, and 2,370 kegs of gunpowder, to be employed in accomplishing a certain object, which was and is and by a certain Act of Parliament, made and passed in the 5th year of the reign of his late Majesty King George the Fourth, intituled "An Act to amend and consolidate the Laws relating to the Abolition of the Slave Trade," declared unlawful, that is to say, *to trade and deal in slaves*, contrary to the form of the statute in such case made and provided, and against the peace of Our Sovereign Lady the Queen, her crown and dignity;

6. And the jurors aforesaid, upon their oath aforesaid, do further present that the said Pedro de Zulueta the younger, Thomas Jennings, and Thomas Bernardos, heretofore and after the 1st day of January, in the year of our Lord 1825, to wit, on the 10th day of November, in the 4th year of the reign of Our Lady the now Queen, with force and arms, to wit, at London aforesaid, and within the jurisdiction of the said Court, *did conspire, combine, confederate, and agree together knowingly, wilfully, and feloniously to ship on board of a certain ship or vessel*, to wit, a ship or vessel called the "Augusta," *divers goods and effects*, to wit, 29 hogsheads of tobacco, 60 cases of arms, 1 case of looking-glasses, 10 casks of copper ware, 134 bales of merchandise, 1,600 iron pots, and 2,370 kegs of gunpowder, to be employed in accomplishing a certain object, which was and is in and by the last mentioned Act of Parliament declared unlawful, that is to say, *to purchase slaves*, contrary to the form of the statute in such case made and provided, and against the peace of Our Sovereign Lady the Queen, her crown and dignity;

7. And the jurors aforesaid, upon their oath aforesaid, do further present that the said Pedro de Zulueta the younger, Thomas Jennings, and Thomas Bernardos, heretofore and after the 1st day of January, in the year of our Lord 1825, to wit, on the 10th day of November, in the 4th year of the reign of Our Sovereign Lady the now Queen, with force and arms, to wit, at London aforesaid, and within the jurisdiction of the said Court, *did conspire, combine, confederate, and agree together knowingly, wilfully, and feloniously to ship on board of a certain ship or vessel*, to wit, a ship or vessel called the "Augusta," *divers goods and effects*, to wit, 29 hogsheads of tobacco, 60 cases of arms, 1 case of looking-glasses, 10 casks of copper ware, 134 bales of merchandise, 1,600 iron pots, and 2,370 kegs of gunpowder, to be employed in accomplishing a certain object, which was and is in and by the said last mentioned Act of Parliament declared unlawful, that is to say, *to deal and trade in persons intended*

to be dealt with as slaves, contrary to the form of the statute in such case made and provided, and against the peace of Our Sovereign Lady the Queen, her crown and dignity;

8. And the jurors aforesaid, upon their oath aforesaid, do further present that the said Pedro de Zulueta the younger, Thomas Jennings, and Thomas Bernardos, heretofore and after the 1st day of January, in the year of our Lord 1825, to wit, on the 10th day of November, in the 4th year of the reign of our Lady the now Queen, with force and arms, to wit, at London aforesaid, and within the jurisdiction of the said Court, *did conspire, combine, confederate, and agree together knowingly, wilfully, and feloniously to ship on board of a certain ship or vessel*, to wit, a ship or vessel called the "Augusta," *divers goods and effects*, to wit, 29 hogsheads of tobacco, 60 cases of arms, 1 case of looking-glasses, 10 casks of copper ware, 134 bales of merchandise, 1,600 iron pots, and 2,370 kegs of gunpowder, to be employed in accomplishing a certain object, which was and is in and by the said last mentioned Act of Parliament declared unlawful, that is to say, *to purchase persons intended to be dealt with as slaves*, contrary to the form of the statute in such case made and provided, and against the peace of our Sovereign Lady the Queen, her crown and dignity;

9. And the jurors aforesaid, upon their oath aforesaid, do further present that the said Pedro de Zulueta the younger, Thomas Jennings, and Thomas Bernardos, after the 1st day of January, in the year of our Lord 1825, to wit, on the 1st day of November, in the 4th year of the reign of our Sovereign Lady Queen Victoria, with force and arms, to wit, at London aforesaid, and within the jurisdiction of the said Court, *did conspire, combine, confederate, and agree together feloniously to engage in the trading and dealing in slaves*, contrary to the form of the statute in such case made and provided, and against the peace of our Lady the Queen, her crown and dignity;

10. And the jurors aforesaid, upon their oath aforesaid, do further present that Pedro de Zulueta the younger, Thomas Jennings, and Thomas Bernardos, after the 1st day of January, in the year of our Lord 1825, to wit, on the 1st day of November, in the 4th year of the reign of our Sovereign Lady Queen Victoria, with force and arms, to wit, at London aforesaid, and within the jurisdiction of the said Court, *did conspire, combine, confederate, and agree together feloniously to engage in the trading and dealing in persons intended to be dealt with as slaves*, contrary to the form of the statute in such case made and provided, and against the peace of our Lady the Queen, her crown and dignity;

11. And the jurors aforesaid, upon their oath aforesaid, do further present that the said Pedro de Zulueta, the younger, Thomas Jennings, and Thomas Bernardos, after the 1st day of January, in the year of our Lord 1825, to wit, on the 1st day of November, in the 4th year of the reign of our Sovereign

Lady Queen Victoria, with force and arms, to wit, at London aforesaid, and within the jurisdiction of the said Court, *did conspire, combine, confederate, and agree together feloniously to engage in the purchase of slaves*, contrary to the form of the statute in such case made and provided, and against the peace of our Lady the Queen, her crown and dignity;

12. And the jurors aforesaid, upon their oath aforesaid, do further present that the said Pedro de Zulueta the younger, Thomas Jennings, and Thomas Bernardos, after the 1st day of January, in the year of our Lord 1825, to wit, on the 1st day of November, in the 4th year of the reign of our Sovereign Lady Queen Victoria, with force and arms, to wit, at London aforesaid, and within the jurisdiction of the said Court, *did conspire, combine, confederate, and agree together feloniously to engage in the purchase of persons intended to be dealt with as slaves*, contrary to the form of the statute in such case made and provided, and against the peace of our Lady the Queen, her crown and dignity.

———

Names of Witnesses endorsed on both the Indictments before the Grand Jury.

Sir GEORGE STEPHEN.	*[Solicitor.]*
JOHN BROWN.	*[Clerk of the Admiralty.]*
Lieutenant HENRY WORSLEY HILL, R.N.	
The Honourable Captain JOSEPH DENMAN, R.N.	
Colonel EDWARD NICOLLS.	
EMANUEL EMANUELS.	*[Of Portsmouth.]*
WILLIAM THOMAS.	*[A Clerk at Messrs. Glyn & Co., Lombard Street.]*
ABRAHAM DE PINNA.	*[Notary Public.]*

———

(From the Anti-Slavery Reporter.)
CENTRAL CRIMINAL COURT.
THURSDAY, AUGUST 24, 1843.
THE CHARGE OF TRADING IN SLAVES.

Mr. *Clarkson* applied to their Lordships to take the bail for Mr. de Zulueta, arranged by the Recorder on the previous evening. He explained that only one of the sureties having been present, and the hour too late to obtain the other, Mr. de Zulueta had been enlarged upon giving his own recognizance in 6,000*l.*, and one security in 2,000*l.* He was now in Court with Mr. Glyn, the well-known banker, and Mr. Wilcox, who were ready to enter into the sureties of 1,000*l.* each, Mr. de Zulueta himself being ready to give his personal recognizance in 3,000*l.*

Mr. *Payne*, who was retained for the prosecution, had no objection.

Mr. *Clarkson* then applied to have the trial, both for the felony and the misdemeanor, postponed to the next session.

Mr. *Payne* consented.

Mr. de Zulueta then entered into the requisite securities.

AFFIDAVIT
OF DEFENDANT AND MR. EDWARD LAWFORD
IN SUPPORT OF
APPLICATION FOR WRIT OF CERTIORARI.

REGINA
v.   } Sworn, 8th Sept. 1843.
ZULUETA.

IN THE QUEEN'S BENCH.

PEDRO DE ZULUETA the younger, of the city of London, merchant, and EDWARD LAWFORD, of Drapers Hall, in the same city, gentleman, attorney for the said Pedro de Zulueta the younger, severally make oath and say, And first this deponent, Pedro de Zulueta, for himself, saith, that he, this deponent, is a merchant of London, and has been so for the last eight years, and as such engaged in large mercantile transactions with houses in different parts of the world, but particularly at Cadiz, and the Havannah. And this deponent saith, that he is engaged in such business in partnership with his this deponent's father and brother, and that this deponent's said father and grandfather were engaged in such business for seventy years and upwards, and that their said house of business is and always has been of good repute as honourable merchants, and that this deponent has always occupied the rank and station of a gentleman, and has always associated with gentlemen and merchants of the first respectability. And this deponent further saith, that on Wednesday, the 22nd day of August last, while this deponent was sitting in his counting-house in Moorgate street, in the city of London, he was, about three o'clock in the afternoon, to his great surprise taken into custody by a policeman, in consequence, as he was then informed, of a true bill having been then found against him for felony at the sessions then being held of the Central Criminal Court. And this deponent saith, that upon being taken to the said Court, and the said indictment being exhibited to him, he found it to be an indictment against this deponent, and against one Thomas Jennings, mariner, and one Thomas Bernardos, mariner, for illegally and feloniously manning, navigating, equipping, dispatching, using, and employing a certain ship or vessel called the Augusta, in order to accomplish a certain object, which in and by a certain Act of Parliament, made and passed in the 5th year of the reign of His late Majesty King George the Fourth, intituled "An Act to amend and consolidate the Laws relating to the Abolition of the Slave Trade," was and is declared unlawful, and for other illegal offences against the said Act of Parliament. And this deponent saith, that he is not guilty of the offences charged against him by the said indictment, or of any or either of them, and that he never did, directly or indirectly, man, navigate, equip, dispatch, use, or employ the said ship, or any other ship, to accomplish any of the objects declared by the said Act to be unlawful, and that he is not, nor ever was, directly or indirectly, in any way or manner interested in the said ship or her earnings, or the profits of any voyage made or to be made by her. And this deponent saith, that when he was so taken into custody he was altogether ignorant that any proceedings whatever had been, or were about to be, taken against him in reference to the said ship, or to the offences charged by the said indictment. And this deponent saith, that there had been no previous examination or inquiry before any magistrate in reference to the said charges, and that he was then, as he is now, altogether ignorant of the evidence upon which such true bill was found, and has no means whatever of ascertaining, except as appears by the said indictment, what facts he is charged with. And this deponent saith, that upon his being so taken into custody and removed to the Central Criminal Court then sitting, upon a representation of the facts made by his counsel to the Recorder of London, then presiding as judge of the Central Criminal Court, it was ordered that he, this deponent, should be admitted to bail himself in the sum of 3000*l.*, with two sureties in the sum of 1000*l.* each, to take his trial upon the said indictment, and that he forthwith pleaded Not Guilty to the said indictment; and that inasmuch as by reason of the lateness of the hour in the evening at which such order was made, he was unable to procure two sufficient persons as bail, the Recorder permitted him to enter into his own recognizance in 6,000*l.*, with one surety in 2,000*l.*, conditional for his completing the bail on the following morning pursuant to the said order, which this deponent accordingly did. And this deponent saith, that the said indictment now stands for trial at the next session of the Central Criminal Court. And both these deponents say, that they believe that this is the first instance of an indictment for felony preferred in this country under the said statute, and that they believe that questions upon the true meaning and construction of the said statute, and other and difficult questions of law will arise upon the trial thereof. And these deponents say, that in the judgment and belief of these deponents this is a case which ought to be tried by a special jury of merchants. And this deponent, Pedro de Zulueta the younger, saith, that he is desirous of having the assistance of the most eminent counsel upon the trial of this indictment, and that he has retained for that purpose one of the most eminent of Her Majesty's counsel learned in the law, but that he is informed and believes that such counsel will not attend at the Central Criminal Court. And this deponent saith, that if he shall be permitted to remove this indictment by *certiorari* into this honourable Court he will have the assistance of such counsel, and he will apply for a special jury, and will take all necessary steps for having the same tried by a special jury, and for being defended therein by such eminent counsel as aforesaid, with the least possible delay. And this deponent, Pedro de Zulueta the younger, further saith, that the facts and circumstances relative to the using and employing the said ship or vessel called the Augusta, upon the occasion to which the said indictment has reference, formed one of the subjects of an inquiry in the year 1842, by a Select Committee of the Honourable House of Commons appointed to inquire into the state of the British possessions on the West Coast of Africa, and that three of the witnesses whose names appeared on the back of this indictment, (that is to say) Captain the Honourable Joseph Denman, Captain Henry Worsley Hill, and Colonel Edward Nicolls, were examined before such Committee. And this deponent saith, that it appears by the printed minutes of the evidence taken before the said Committee, and this deponent believes the fact to be, that the said Henry Worsley Hill captured the ship Augusta off the Gallinas, on the coast of Africa, and that the said Thomas Jennings, then the owner and master of the said ship, was tried in Her Majesty's Court of Sierra Leone upon a charge similar to that now charged against him and against this deponent, and that the said Thomas Jennings was by such Court on such trial acquitted. And this deponent saith, that he is one of the mercantile correspondents in London of the mercantile house of Pedro Martinez & Co., of Cadiz and the Havannah, and that the nature of his commercial dealings with the said houses of Pedro Martinez & Co. is confined to the usual mercantile business of purchasing and selling, in this country, for the said Pedro Martinez & Co., lawful goods and merchandise, and usual mercantile banking transactions, and that he has no sort of connexion with him or with any other house, either here or abroad, as to any dealings in, or in relation to, slaves or the slave trade.

<table>
<tr><td>Sworn by both the deponents, Pedro de
Zulueta the younger, and Edward Lawford,
at my Chambers, Rolls Garden, Chancery
Lane, this 8th day of September, 1843,
Before me,
T. ERSKINE.</td><td>} </td><td>PEDRO DE ZULUETA, Junior.
EDWARD LAWFORD.</td></tr>
</table>

NOTE.—*The learned Judge, to whom the application was made for a Writ of Certiorari, did not see fit to grant it.*

———

CENTRAL CRIMINAL COURT.
MOTION TO POSTPONE THE TRIAL OF THE INDICTMENT.
THE QUEEN *versus* ZULUETA AND OTHERS.

Proceedings at the Central Criminal Court at the Old Bailey, before the Honourable Mr. Justice ERSKINE and the Honourable Mr. Justice CRESSWELL.

(Thursday, 21st of September, 1843.)

Mr. *Clarkson.* My Lords, I consider it my duty to take the earliest opportunity of bringing under your Lordships' consideration the case of the Queen *v.* Zulueta.

Mr. *Payne.* My Lords, Mr. Serjeant Bompas leads me for the prosecution in this case: he is not here now, but will be here in a moment.

Mr. Justice *Erskine.* This is an application only.

Mr. *Clarkson.* Yes, my Lord; I will give my learned friend every advantage I can. We have given him a copy of our affidavit, in answer to which an affidavit has been sworn, I understand the effect of which is this, that Captain Hill—

Mr. Justice *Erskine.* What is the ground of your application?

Mr. *Clarkson.* The absence of material witnesses. I do not mean to trouble your Lordships at any length. My application to your Lordships is to postpone the trial of these indictments, upon the ground of the absence of material witnesses from Spain, without whose evidence the defendant cannot safely go to trial, and that application is founded upon an affidavit, a copy of which has been supplied to the gentleman on the other side some days ago. It was supplied immediately upon the sitting of the Court. One of the witnesses who had been sent for, and who was not expected to arrive, having arrived within the last two days, and this indictment having been preferred without any application being made to a magistrate, or without any notice to the gentleman himself. My learned friends have made an affidavit in reply; and in order to save your Lordships hearing two speeches from me, it will be better for your Lordships to hear what my learned friends have to say in opposition to this application and then to hear me in reply.

Mr. Serjeant *Bompas*. My learned friend seems to assume that the trial will be put off as a matter of course.

Mr. Justice *Erskine*. He has stated the ground of his application, namely, the absence of material and necessary witnesses, and he leaves you to state his affidavit, and comment upon it as you please.

Mr. Serjeant *Bompas*. My learned friend has not quite correctly stated his affidavit when he says his application is founded upon the absence of material witnesses.

Mr. Justice *Erskine*. The affidavit had better be read.

Mr. Justice *Cresswell*. Have you got a copy of it?

Mr. *Payne*. Yes, my Lord.

[A copy of the affidavit was handed to his Lordship.]

The affidavit was then read by the Clerk of the Arraigns as follows:—

In the Central Criminal Court.

The Queen *v.* Pedro de Zulueta the younger, and others.	}	ON INDICTMENT FOR FELONY.

The same
v.   } ON INDICTMENT FOR MISDEMEANOR.
The same

Pedro de Zulueta the younger, of No. 22, Moorgate Street, in the City of London, merchant, and John Lawford, of Drapers Hall, in the said city, gentleman, attorney to the said Pedro de Zulueta, severally make oath and say,—And first, this deponent, Pedro de Zulueta the younger, for himself saith, that the above mentioned indictments are preferred against this deponent, and against one Thomas Jennings, mariner, and one Thomas Bernardos, mariner, the first mentioned of such indictments being for illegally and feloniously manning, navigating, equipping, dispatching, using, and employing a certain ship or vessel called the "Augusta," in order to accomplish a certain object, which in and by a certain Act of Parliament, made and passed in the 5th year of the reign of his late Majesty King George the Fourth, intituled "An Act to amend and consolidate the Laws relating to the Abolition of the Slave Trade," was and is declared unlawful; and the last mentioned of such indictments for conspiring to do, &c. And this deponent saith, that he was taken into custody on the 23rd day of August last in consequence of the said indictments having been found against him. And this deponent saith, that upon his being so taken into custody and brought to the Central Criminal Court then sitting, the Recorder of London then presiding as judge of the said Court, ordered that he this deponent should be admitted to bail himself in 3,000l., with two sureties in the sum of 1,000l. each, to take his trial upon the said indictments; and that he thereupon pleaded "Not Guilty" to the said indictments, and entered into the said recognizances. And this deponent further saith, that when he was so taken into custody he was altogether ignorant that any proceedings whatever had been or were about to be taken against him in reference to the said ship, or to the offence charged by the said indictments (there having been no previous examination or inquiry before any magistrate in reference to the said charges), and that he was then, as he is now, altogether ignorant of the evidence upon which such indictments were found, excepting that this deponent has been informed that the charges contained in these indictments arise out of transactions in respect of which this deponent was examined in the year 1842 before a Committee of the Honourable the House of Commons. And this deponent further saith, that Joseph Toplis, who was the managing clerk of this deponent's house of business at Liverpool at the time of the transactions in question, was and is a most material witness for this deponent, and most essential to enable this deponent to prepare his defence to these indictments. And this deponent saith, that at the time when these indictments were preferred the said Joseph Toplis was at Gibraltar. And this deponent saith, that on Saturday the 26th day of August last, being the third day after the said indictments were preferred, and being the first possible opportunity which this deponent had of communicating with the said Joseph Toplis, this deponent's house of business wrote and sent a letter to him the said Joseph Toplis, requiring him to repair to England immediately, as well for the purpose of giving his evidence on the trial of these indictments as in order that the said Joseph Toplis might enable this deponent to procure such other necessary evidence for the defence of this deponent, as the knowledge of the said Joseph Toplis in relation to the transaction out of which these indictments arise might enable him to obtain. And this deponent, John

Lawford, for himself saith, that in consequence of the absence of the said Joseph Toplis, and in consequence of this deponent's belief that the said Joseph Toplis could not arrive in time to enable this deponent to prepare for the trial of these indictments, this deponent, under the advice of counsel, wrote and sent a letter to Sir George Stephen, the attorney for the prosecution, in the words and figures following:—

THE QUEEN v. ZULUETA.

Dear Sir, Drapers Hall, 11th September, 1843.

You will probably not be surprised to hear that it will require considerable time to collect and prepare the materials for Mr. Zulueta's defence, and you will therefore be pleased to consider this as a notice of our intention to apply to the Court for a postponement of the trial. We think it right thus early to inform you of our intention, that neither you nor your witnesses may be put to unnecessary expense or inconvenience, and we anticipate no objection on your part to a proceeding so manifestly reasonable.

We are, dear Sir,
Your very obedient servants,

Sir George Stephen.

(signed) *Ed. Jno. & H. S. Lawford.*

And this deponent saith, that in reply to such letter, this deponent received a letter from the said Sir George Stephen, in the words and figures following:—

THE QUEEN, v. ZULUETA.

Collins, 12th September, 1843.

Prince's Risborough.

My dear Sirs,

Personally I should have no objection to deferring the trial, and so far as your own convenience is involved in the delay, it would give me much pleasure to consult it. But this is a case in which I feel restrained from exercising the least discretion, and must therefore leave the matter to the decision of the Court. My briefs are delivered, and, with one exception, my witnesses are subpœnaed; but that exception is the most expensive, and therefore to save you that expense, I will not subpœna him until Monday, if you will write me word that you will consent to the trial being at all events deferred till Thursday. I put it thus, because I apprehend that the Court will only accede to your application on terms of your paying the costs of the day. Have the goodness to address your answer to me here. Yours very truly,

Messrs. Lawford, Drapers Hall. *George Stephen.*

And this deponent, Pedro de Zulueta the younger, further saith that the said Joseph Toplis, in consequence of the aforesaid requisition on the part of this deponent, came away from Gibraltar forthwith, and arrived in London on Sunday evening last, the 17th day of September instant. And this deponent further saith, that it will be absolutely necessary for the said Joseph Toplis to repair to Liverpool for the purpose of procuring the attendance of divers persons who are necessary witnesses on behalf of this deponent, who are not known to this deponent, and whose names this deponent had not the means of procuring until he had communicated with the said Joseph Toplis. And this deponent saith, that by reason of the shortness of the time since the arrival of the said Joseph Toplis, and the necessity of his repairing to Liverpool and elsewhere, to seek for and procure the necessary evidence in support of the defence of this deponent, it will be impossible for this deponent to be prepared with such evidence in time for the present session. And this deponent, John Lawford, for himself saith, that he has been retained as the attorney of the said defendant, and that he has diligently applied himself to the preparation of the defendant's case, and that he is advised by counsel, and verily believes that it will be absolutely necessary for this deponent to procure the attendance of the witnesses above referred to, and of others who he is informed and believes are resident at Manchester, Liverpool, and Glasgow, and also of some of the crew of the said ship Augusta. And this deponent saith, that he has been informed and believes that the defendant, Thomas Jennings, has been already tried for this offence at Sierra Leone, and acquitted thereof. And this deponent saith, that he has reason to believe that it may be necessary to procure the attendance of witnesses from that settlement as well as from Spain, and other distant places. And this deponent saith, that by reason of the shortness of the time which has elapsed since the said indictments were preferred, and by reason of the entire ignorance of this deponent of the evidence against the defendant, Pedro de Zulueta the younger, it has been utterly impossible for this deponent to complete the preparations for the defence in time for the present sessions. And this deponent further saith, that from the time of the said bills being found to the present time this deponent hath been in constant communication with the said other deponent with a view to his defence, and that no time whatever has been lost in preparing for such defence; but this deponent saith, that by the reason of the circumstances hereinbefore stated this deponent hath been wholly unable to prepare the brief for the defence.

(signed)

Pedro de Zulueta.
John Lawford.

Sworn in Court, 19th September, 1843.

Mr. Serjeant *Bompas*. Your Lordships will probably wish to hear the affidavit in answer, before I make any observations upon that which has just been read.

Mr. Justice *Cresswell*. Have you a copy of it?

Mr. *Payne*. Yes, my Lord.

[*A copy of the affidavit was handed to his Lordship.*]

The affidavit was then read by the Clerk of the Arraigns as follows:—

In the Central Criminal Court.

The Queen,
v.   }   FOR FELONY.
Pedro de Zulueta, and others.

The same,
v.   }   FOR MISDEMEANOR.
The same.

Henry Worsley Hill, of Great Rider Street, in the parish of St. James, Esquire, a Commander in Her Majesty's Navy, and Sir George Stephen, of King's Arms Yard, in the city of London, the solicitor for the prosecution, severally make oath and say,—And first, the said Henry Worsley Hill for himself saith, that he is under orders to proceed to the Gold Coast on the western coast of Africa, to assume the government thereof with the least possible delay, and that arrangements are now in progress for this deponent to depart by the end of this present month. And this deponent also saith, that the public service will sustain considerable inconvenience by any delay on the part of this deponent in proceeding to Africa as aforesaid at the time now appointed, and that he this deponent has no expectation or hope of obtaining further leave of absence. And this deponent, Sir George Stephen, for himself saith, that the said Henry Worsley Hill is a most material witness on behalf of this prosecution, and that without his evidence this deponent cannot safely proceed to trial; and this deponent, Sir George Stephen, further saith, that he has perused a copy of the affidavit of Pedro de Zulueta the younger, and John Lawford, made in these matters, and that in consequence of the misdirection of the same, as this deponent believes, he, this deponent, did not receive a reply to his letter of the 12th of September, 1843, set out in the said affidavit, and therefore proceeded in his preparations for trial. And this deponent saith, that he is ready to proceed to trial at the present session of this Court. And this deponent further saith, that he has caused another witness in this matter to come over from Paris, where such witness is permanently domiciled, and that such last mentioned witness incurred much inconvenience and expense in so coming, and that as he habitually resides out of the jurisdiction this deponent has no means of compelling him to appear again, should the trial of these indictments be deferred. And this deponent saith, that the evidence of such last-mentioned witness is most material. And this deponent further saith, that he has subpœnaed three other witnesses to come to London from a great distance, one of whom is a sailor, and another of whom is an officer of rank in Her Majesty's navy, and that the evidence of all the said last mentioned witnesses is most material, and that the said indictments cannot be safely tried in their absence, but that from the nautical profession of two of them, this deponent believes it to be very doubtful if he will again be able to compel their attendance. And this deponent further saith, that he has also subpœnaed another witness who habitually resides at Seville in Spain, and who is about to return to Seville, as this deponent is informed and believes as soon as the trial is over, and this deponent is informed and believes that the evidence of such last mentioned witness is material. And deponent saith, that he has no hope of again collecting together so many important witnesses whose professional avocations necessarily render their simultaneous presence in this country very uncertain. And this deponent further saith, that the said defendant, Pedro de Zulueta the younger, cannot have been taken by surprise by these indictments, because the said Pedro de Zulueta the younger, volunteered, as this deponent is informed and believes, to be examined as a witness before the Select Committee on the West Coast of Africa, and was so examined on the 22nd and 23rd days of July, 1843, when the nature of the case upon which this prosecution is founded was stated to the Committee, and the said Pedro de Zulueta admitted that he had received copies of the evidence given by Captain Hill on the 29th of June, the 4th of July, and the 6th of July previously. And this deponent saith, that the said Pedro de Zulueta the younger, did upon such examination admit that the house to which he belongs had been charged with criminality, and with having for a length of time been agents to slave dealers, and the said Pedro de Zulueta the younger avowed his reason for wishing to be examined before the Committee to be, that the statements contained in the said evidence were incorrect. And this deponent lastly saith, that in another part of such examination, the said Pedro de Zulueta the younger, in answer to the question, "Is there any other part of the evidence which has been given that you wish to observe upon?" after denying all knowledge of a person of the name of Kidd, adds, "With regard to my partners, I can say the same. I have been making inquiries about it; my father knew there was such a man, but I did not know even that, though I have managed all this business."

(signed)

H. W. Hill.
George Stephen.

Mr. Serjeant *Bompas.* My learned friend, Mr. Clarkson, has called upon me to make some observations upon this affidavit. I should not in addressing your Lordships at all wish to object to the postponement of this trial, if it could be considered even by the defendant or his counsel more advantageous to him that it should be postponed, could I consent to it without feeling that the trial could not fairly take place at any other period. I cannot help thinking, while your Lordship is looking at this affidavit, that it is one such as has been rarely produced before a Court, in order to found an application for the postponement of a trial. This indictment was preferred above a month from this time; that is, four weeks from this time. It is true, as has been stated, that no inquiry took place before a magistrate, but when long before that period at which the inquiry could have been instituted, if such had taken place, this matter had been inquired into before a Committee of the House of Commons, when Mr. Zulueta appeared before that Committee, and stated that he had had the management of all the business, and appeared in order to explain the transaction—

Mr. *Clarkson.* No.

Mr. Serjeant *Bompas.* I will refer to the words of the affidavit.

Mr. *Clarkson.* I beg pardon.

Mr. Serjeant *Bompas.* When it appears that that inquiry had taken place before a Committee of the House of Commons, this proceeding cannot have been instituted without ample notice of all that is to be now inquired into, as far as any party, under the circumstances, charged with felony, can be supposed to know the nature of the evidence to be brought against him. And what is the foundation of this application? Not that some material witness is absent—some material witness whom they have subpœnaed, and whom they know to be material, and whose attendance they cannot obtain; that is not the foundation of the application. The ground of the application is, that a person of the name of Toplis, who was managing clerk to Mr. Zulueta, was absent at Gibraltar, at the time the indictment was found. It is not even that he has not arrived: he arrived on Sunday and is now able to give any evidence that the defendant may require. It is said, that he is able to make communications in respect to the evidence of persons, whose names were not known to the defendant till he arrived, and upon whose absence the application was founded, and that it is now requisite to send for some witnesses from Liverpool, and I hardly know where. The affidavit is very singularly sworn; and when my learned friend says, "from Spain," and so on, there is no such statement to be found in it. That which is stated is, that it *may* be necessary to send for various witnesses, that it *may* be necessary to procure the attendance of witnesses from the settlement of Sierra Leone, as well as from Spain. My learned friend, in citing it, said, that they were to obtain witnesses "from Spain." The affidavit is, that it *may* be necessary to have witnesses from Spain—that it *may* be necessary to have witnesses from Africa, so that there is no statement whatever that there is any witness in Spain who would be wanted or can be expected, or that there is any witness in Africa who will be wanted or who is expected; there is no such statement at all. The statement is, "That it will be absolutely necessary for the said Joseph Toplis to repair to Liverpool for the purpose of procuring the attendance of divers persons, who are necessary witnesses on behalf of this deponent, who are not known to this deponent, and whose names this deponent had not the means of procuring until he had communicated with the said Joseph Toplis." Certainly that is a statement of a very extraordinary kind: no doubt it was put into the affidavit, believing it to be true, but the statement made by Mr. Zulueta before the Committee of the House of Commons was, that he had had the management of the whole of the business; and to suppose that there is a witness in Spain, that there is a witness in Gibraltar, Mr. Toplis, and that they can make no inquiry as to the names of the individuals till he comes over, is the most extraordinary statement ever laid before a Court. As far as this affidavit goes, it does not appear that they have taken the slightest steps in order to ascertain by any inquiry as to any witnesses or any transactions; but Mr. Toplis is to go to Liverpool to hunt out for witnesses. Who they are does not appear: not any persons who are certain to be witnesses, but that he is to go to Liverpool to hunt out for witnesses who may be—

Mr. Justice *Cresswell*. And whose names the deponent could not procure till Mr. Toplis came.

Mr. Serjeant *Bompas*. "And whose names this deponent had not the means of procuring until he had communicated with the said Joseph Toplis." He could hot tell certainly who Joseph Toplis would require till he had communicated with him; but that he could not have ascertained whether any witnesses were necessary for his defence would not appear satisfactorily to your Lordships. It is a case that will require examination by the Court, in order to do that which would be the object of the Court, to have the case most fairly and properly inquired into. Your Lordships see of necessity that the witnesses for the prosecution are witnesses in a situation not easy to be obtained upon any future occasion. There is one who is under orders to proceed abroad in order to take the government of the Gold Coast: there are others who are officers in the navy.

Mr. Justice *Erskine*. What was the date of the inquiry before the House of Commons?

Mr. Serjeant *Bompas*. 1842, my Lord.

Mr. Justice *Erskine*. Your affidavit states 1843.

Mr. Serjeant *Bompas*. It is a mistake, my Lord. It should be 1842.

Mr. Justice *Erskine*. Subsequently to that inquiry was any notice given to the defendant that it would be made the subject of a prosecution?

Mr. Serjeant *Bompas*. No notice, my Lord, till the bill was found.

Mr. Justice *Erskine*. What was the date of the transaction to which the indictment refers?

Mr. Serjeant *Bompas*. There was then an appeal pending before the Privy Council.

Mr. Justice *Erskine*. What was the date of the transaction to which the indictment refers? I want the date of the occurrence.

Mr. Serjeant *Bompas*. 1840; the end of 1840 and the beginning of 1841. The capture of the vessel, to which reference was made, was in February, 1841. She left England on the 9th of November, 1840. She was captured: there was a proceeding in the court abroad; she was condemned, and there was an appeal before the Privy Council.

Mr. Justice *Cresswell*. The ship sailed from Liverpool?

Mr. Serjeant *Bompas*. Yes, my Lord.

Mr. Justice *Erskine*. With a cargo of some sort. One question will be, whether it was a cargo adapted to the trade upon the African coast, or for dealing in slaves.

Mr. Serjeant *Bompas*. No doubt.

Mr. Justice *Erskine*. Was Mr. Toplis the managing clerk at Liverpool?

Mr. Serjeant *Bompas*. Yes, my Lord. It is stated that he was the managing clerk at Liverpool; but to suppose that the shipment of any firm at Liverpool to say that they can obtain no evidence of that shipment except by a managing clerk, is such a statement as can hardly be credited of any merchant. That is the statement; but they do not state any circumstances to explain it. That it is necessary to have his managing clerk to state the names of the parties concerned in the shipment, it is one of the most extraordinary statements ever made. Upon this statement your Lordships will have to consider the foundation of the application, and your Lordships will take into view all the circumstances of it. This case is to be proved, as it must necessarily be, by various officers in the navy besides Captain Hill, who is about to go out as governor of the Gold Coast; by officers in the navy, and sailors, and foreigners, now here ready to give their testimony.

Now, my Lord, there is one circumstance singularly deficient in this case, and without which there has never been a case in which the trial of any cause has been put off. The affidavit does not give the slightest suggestion when they are likely to be ready to take their trial; so that it is utterly impossible that the trial can be available, if they are to come when the witnesses for the prosecution may be scattered over the whole world: the prosecution may be gone through, but it would be a mere formal statement. I am willing to give due weight to every argument on behalf of a person charged with an offence, in order that the charge may be fairly and properly tried in respect to him; but at the same time there are duties on behalf of the prosecution. The crime cannot be inquired into unless there are the means to procure the evidence. If these witnesses are here, and this party has not taken the means which he might have done to have the trial now take place, and if he does not give us the slightest information when it is to be tried; if a person charged with an offence is to choose the time for trying it, every trial of this kind would be an utter abortion, because unless the witnesses for the prosecution are here it is impossible there can be a fair trial.

Now there is not a statement, there is no pretence, why the witnesses for the defendant could not have been here at the present time. To say that there were no means of knowing the general nature of the charge, and knowing the whole substance of the defence, and having the whole matter fairly considered and put into form before the Court, is what you cannot believe. Your Lordships cannot believe, that though Mr. Toplis may have been an important witness, that the general subject of the charge inquired into was not generally known, and that all the witnesses for the defence, such witnesses as were thought necessary, must not have been generally known to the defendant. There may have been a witness whose name was known only to Mr. Toplis; there may have been one or more, but it is impossible that the case might not have been got up with the exception of Mr. Toplis's evidence, and might have been ready for trial on this day. But if they have utterly neglected to take any step till last Sunday, the time as I understand it, they have no right to come now and ask your Lordships to put off the trial. There is no statement of any sort or kind of any individual witness necessary, except those suggested to be at Liverpool. Mr. Toplis could not know the witnesses abroad more than any other gentleman. Suppose there are witnesses abroad—have there been any, the slightest step taken to bring them here? What steps have been taken? He says there are witnesses from Africa: when are they to be here? when will they come? when is the trial to take place? There is not a single intimation of the time when they will be ready to take their trial. It is to be put off till the witnesses for the prosecution are scattered, and it is impossible to have the trial. Undoubtedly it is difficult to have a number of witnesses of this description ready before the Court, and to get their testimony together. But what do they say? They say that it may be necessary to get some of the sailors of the Augusta. Was Mr. Toplis necessary for that? Why have they not taken any step to get the evidence of those witnesses? They do not appear to have taken any one step to be prepared for this trial, although then knowing that it was a matter of difficulty to collect a number of witnesses like these. If it is to be held that they can at their discretion from time to time put off the case, it is a mere abortion to attempt to prosecute any person, however guilty, in the situation of Mr. Zulueta. However important it is for the defendant—and I would not wish to withhold that from the consideration of your Lordships—it is equally important for the public good, and as well worthy of your consideration. It would be with the utmost difficulty, if there is any probability of doing it at all, that the witnesses could be got together again. If they had taken every step, and gone down to inquire at Liverpool, and proceeded as far as they could and had the means in their power, and yet could not be ready, that would be some ground for the application; but they do not appear to have taken any step—they appear to have relied upon putting off the trial, considering that that would be as good a protection as any witnesses could possibly give them.

I certainly do feel that there is a ground of opposition to this application which has never failed when there is no suggestion at all in the affidavit of what time they expect to be ready for trial. I believe there has never been a case in which a party has not given the Court some reason to believe that, if the trial is put off, they will be ready to try at a given time: on the contrary, here it is put as if it was quite loose—there *may* be some witnesses from Spain and Africa, though they have had a month during which they might have made inquiries.

I have thought it right to submit these observations to your Lordships, both for the sake of the prosecution and the defendant. If the prosecution is well founded, it is of the utmost importance that it should proceed; on the other hand, it is no doubt of importance that the other side should have an opportunity of bringing the case before the Court in all the views of which the case is capable: but the case is one in which your Lordships must see the great inconvenience to the prosecutors, and the difficulty of getting the witnesses together, and I trust your Lordships will feel that it is one which ought not to be adjourned; but if it be adjourned, it must be to some fixed time at which it must be understood that the case will come on.

Mr. *Payne*. My Lords, I will add but two or three words to what Mr. Serjeant Bompas has already addressed to your Lordships. I must say that I never in the course of my experience met with a paragraph in an affidavit to postpone a trial similar to the first paragraph in this affidavit; it is merely this, "That it will be absolutely necessary for Joseph Toplis to repair to Liverpool for the purpose of procuring the attendance of divers persons who are necessary witnesses on behalf of this deponent, who are not known to this deponent, and whose names this deponent had not the means of procuring until he had communicated with the said Joseph Toplis." Now it is generally required, in affidavits of this description, that if you do know the names of the witnesses, and where they are to come from, that you should state them to the Court, that the opposite side may be in possession *bonâ fide* of the nature of the defence. If Mr. Zulueta had sworn that he did not now know the names of the witnesses, there would be some reason for not putting in the names; but he does not say that—he says he did not know them till Mr. Toplis came. Mr. Toplis came last Sunday night: he could furnish the names; and if he had put the names of the witnesses and the places they were to come from in the affidavit, instead of "divers witnesses," it might be in the usual form upon which the Court may sometimes postpone a trial. I say that that expression is not sufficient. I say that the Court are entitled to have information of the names of the persons necessary as witnesses, in order to bring the case within the ordinary rule.

Then, my Lords, the only other part of the affidavit which has not been noticed by my learned friend, and which may be touched upon on the opposite side, is the affidavit of the attorney that he has not been able to prepare the briefs. Mr. Zulueta having stated that he was the person who managed all this business, he must have possessed information sufficient to enable the attorney in four weeks to prepare the briefs; and if he has not furnished that information, it is owing to neglect on the part of Mr. Zulueta. Their affidavit is loose and defective—ours is precise. We say we do not think we can get Captain Hill again: he states, that he is under orders to sail. Under these circumstances, we must bow to what the Court think right to decide; but we consider that a case has not been made out to justify the Court in granting this application.

Mr. *Clarkson*. My Lords, in answer—

Mr. Justice *Erskine*. You cannot ask for any further postponement beyond the next sessions.

Mr. *Clarkson.* I did not think that your Lordships would assume jurisdiction to postpone it beyond that.

Mr. Justice *Erskine.* We cannot listen to that part of the application with respect to the witnesses from Spain or Sierra Leone; they are not stated with sufficient accuracy.

Mr. *Clarkson.* I quite feel that, my Lord; I only wish to say this, that if my learned friend comes here to ask for the costs of the day, or for what my learned friend calls terms—

Mr. Justice *Erskine.* That is not necessary.

Mr. *Clarkson.* There is some mistake about it; such a thing was never heard of here: but there is this observation to be made in answer to the greater part of what my learned friends have said—for twelve months and more have these parties who are prosecuting been taking steps, and yet to this hour nobody knows who they are, no name has been furnished: for twelve months have they been about that which they now call upon a respectable merchant of London to meet in a month; and two or three years have elapsed since the vessel was condemned.

Mr. Justice *Erskine.* It is the duty of the Court to take care that the ends of justice shall not be defeated by too easily yielding to applications of this nature; but it is equally the duty of the Court to take care that a man charged with a felony shall not be brought to his trial until, he is able to present such an answer as the circumstances of the case will admit of.

It appears that the offence with which the defendant is charged is alleged to have been committed in 1840. The grounds for charging Mr. Zulueta with participation in that offence may have originated in the examinations before the Committee of the House of Commons in 1842. If it did then originate, the parties who conduct this prosecution must have known what the foundation of that accusation was, and if they intended to charge Mr. Zulueta with that offence, and particularly if they meant to support it upon the testimony of witnesses who might be absent at a future time, they ought to have taken steps by which to have secured the attendance of the defendant, and have taken him before a magistrate, and examined the witnesses there. But it appears, though this examination took place in 1842, no steps are taken in the prosecution till August 1843, and that is just upon the eve of the departure of one of the witnesses, from which circumstance the Crown, it is said, cannot avail itself of his presence, because he is going upon a public mission to some other part of the world. This is a prosecution of a singular character, and the Crown will take care that the ends of justice are not defeated by their sending away an officer whose testimony is necessary for the establishment of such a charge. I do not believe there is any risk of the ends of justice being defeated by his absence.

Then is it fair to call upon the defendant now to present himself to the Court? It appears that a person of the name of Toplis had the management of this business at Liverpool, where the circumstances are said to have originated which form the foundation of this charge; he is abroad, and from the year 1842 no notice is given.

Mr. Serjeant *Bompas*. The Privy Council did not decide.

Mr. Justice *Cresswell*. We have nothing to do with the Privy Council.

Mr. *Clarkson*. There is no decision by any body. It is no prosecution by the Crown.

Mr. Justice *Erskine*. I was not saying any thing imputing improper motives to the prosecutors, but stating facts, that no notice had been given to the defendant. If, in the year 1842, any notice had been given to Mr. Zulueta that this prosecution was to be instituted, then if he had sent Mr. Toplis abroad, he would have no right to avail himself of that circumstance; but in the absence of any notice of that sort, he had a right to assume that the evidence before the House of Commons was satisfactory, and that there was no ground to institute a prosecution, and he might then fairly send his clerk abroad. Then it appears, that, having been sent abroad, immediately the prosecution was instituted a letter was sent to him, in consequence of which he returned to this country: he only arrived on Sunday last; and it is impossible, from the state of the facts, that Mr. Zulueta could be in a state to prepare the requisite instructions for counsel, and get those witnesses necessary to enable him to proceed with his defence. We therefore think that this trial should be postponed till the next sessions. We do not yield to the necessity suggested of sending to Spain or Sierra Leone; there is no sufficient ground for that laid in the affidavit.

Mr. *Clarkson*. The form will be, that your Lordships will be pleased to respite the recognizances of Mr. Zulueta and his bail to the next sessions.

Mr. Justice *Erskine*. Yes.

(The recognizances were enlarged, and the parties left the Court.)

TRIAL
OF
PEDRO DE ZULUETA, JUN., ESQ.,

AT THE CENTRAL CRIMINAL COURT, OLD BAILEY,
ON FRIDAY, 27th OCTOBER, 1843,

BEFORE

The HONOURABLE Mr. JUSTICE MAULE,
The HONOURABLE Mr. JUSTICE WIGHTMAN,

AND

Mr. COMMISSIONER BULLOCK.

———

Copy from Mr. Gurney's Short-hand Notes of the Proceedings on the Trial of this Indictment.

———

THE QUEEN,
v.   } INDICTMENT FOR FELONY.
PEDRO DE ZULUETA.

Mr. *Kelly.* My Lord, with respect to Mr. Zulueta, it is very important that I should be able to communicate with him from time to time as the trial proceeds. May I ask of your Lordship some indulgence to permit him to sit near his counsel?

Mr. Justice *Maule.* What is the charge?

Mr. *Kelly.* The charge under prosecution is felony; the felony being, the fitting out a ship with certain objects declared by statute to be illegal, namely, those of slave trading.

Mr. Justice *Maule.* I should wish that Mr. Zulueta, and every one else, should have the liberty of sitting by his counsel, but that is impossible. I understand an application was made in the case of a person of the name of Trotter.

Mr. *Kelly.* It has been done; there are many precedents. I do not ask it on the ground of any difference of rank or condition, but because the justice of the case requires it, particularly as he is a foreigner, a Spaniard, and many of the documents which will have to be referred to in the course of the proceeding are in the Spanish language, that I should be enabled to communicate with him. It is not at Mr. Zulueta's own instance I make the application, but for my own assistance in the conduct of the defence.

Mr. Justice *Wightman*. A similar application was made in the case of Captain Douglas.

Mr. *Kelly*. That was not an application by counsel for the convenience of counsel, in aid of the justice of the case, but on the ground of his being an officer in the British army. That, if granted, might establish a distinction which ought not to be established; but in the case of Horne Tooke, where it became necessary for the merits of the case that there should be a constant communication between the counsel and the prisoner, it was permitted.

Mr. Justice *Wightman*. What was the charge against him?

Mr. *Kelly*. High treason. A case, I may venture to say directly in point, except that that was a weaker case than this, for this is a case of a foreigner, a Spaniard; and, as I have observed, most of the documents to which it will be necessary from time to time to refer, are in the Spanish language, and it is impossible I can do justice to his case if I cannot communicate with the prisoner so as to understand their effect.

Mr. Justice *Maule*. Have you the 9th vol. of Carrington & Payne? The difficulty stated is, that though the prisoner cannot come to his friend, his friend may go to him.

[*The 9th vol. of Carrington & Payne's Reports was handed to his Lordship.*

[*The Witnesses on both sides were directed to leave the Court.*

Mr. Justice *Maule*. Have you got the case of the King *v.* Tooke?

Mr. *Kelly*. No, I have not the book here, my Lord; but I remember the case.

(The Report was produced.)

Mr. Justice *Maule*. In the Report in the State Trials of the case of Mr. Horne Tooke, to which you have referred, it appears that he claimed as a matter of right, the being permitted to sit near his counsel. The Lord Chief Justice says, "That is an indulgence which I have hardly ever known given to any person in your situation." The Lord Chief Justice at that time was Lord Chief Justice Eyre. Mr. Horne Tooke says, "I am perfectly aware that it is unusual, but I beg your Lordship to observe that every thing in the course of these proceedings is likewise unusual. I beg your Lordship to consider that the proceedings upon the last trial will fill, as I am well informed by the short-hand writer, 1,600 close printed octavo pages. That trial lasted nine days; eight days trial, and one day between. The nature of the indictment is such, that it has been impossible for me to guess what would come before your Lordship: it has been equally impossible for me to instruct my counsel; they cannot know the passages of my life, and from what I have seen on the last trial the whole passages of my life, and those which are not passages of my life, but are only imputed to me, will be brought before you: how is it possible for my counsel to know those particular facts which are only known to myself? If ever there was a case where indulgence was fit to be granted, it is this; yet your Lordship will forgive me for saying that I claim it as my right by law, and do not ask it as an indulgence." After more argument to that effect, the Chief Justice says, "Mr. Tooke, you have been furnished with that which the law considers as the necessary means to enable you to make your defence; you have had counsel assigned to you; they have had, or might have had, access to you at all seasonable hours; that is what the law allows you. You have taught the Court not to use the word indulgence, and you have pointed out to them their duty, that they are to give no indulgence. I am apprehensive that it would be considered as an extraordinary indulgence if the Court were now to do that which you ask, because that is not done to other prisoners; it was not done to another prisoner who went immediately before you, who had the same stake that you have, nor is it done to all other prisoners who do come to this bar, and therefore the Court are not permitted without doing injustice to others to grant that which you ask upon the ground upon which you ask it." Then he goes on—"But you have mentioned another circumstance extremely material, and which will, in my mind, warrant the Court to do that which you think they ought not to do, to indulge the prisoner. You have stated the condition of your health, and that in the place in which you stand your health will suffer: the Court has no desire to put you under any difficulties; they wish that you should be enabled to make your defence in the best way imaginable; and if the situation in which you stand is really likely to be prejudicial to your health, and therefore likely to disable you from making your defence in the manner you might otherwise make it, I shall put it to my Lords to consider, whether you may not be indulged with that which you have now asked.

"Mr. Tooke—The Court will forgive me only for saying, that if, on the footing of indulgence, the Court shall not think fit to grant what I ask, I hope I shall not, after that decision, be barred from my argument upon it as a point of law." Then the Chief Justice says—"You must state your whole case upon any matter that arises at once: the proposing it first in one shape, and then going on to state it in another, is carrying us on without end; if you mean to argue this as a point of law to be sure we are ready to hear you." Mr. Tooke: "I beg your Lordship not to misunderstand me; I did so mention it at first, and did ask it not as an indulgence, if your Lordship will be pleased to recollect: I did mention, that if there were objections I should then argue it in point of law, thinking that I am well entitled to it by the principles, by the letter, and by the practice of the law: I did not mean to change my ground; I beg your Lordship will be pleased to recollect I excluded the idea of indulgence: I did not mean to take first one ground and then another, but I thought it possible I might save the time of the Court, therefore I left it to your Lordship to collect the sense of the Court even upon the score of health, which your Lordship mentions, to save time, and not to waste the time. I understood very well that after a decision I should not be permitted to argue it, and therefore I mentioned that, but not to change my ground; and therefore if your Lordship should find upon the score of what you call indulgence, I suppose in a different view of the word that I am accustomed to take, I rather understand that your Lordship means you are willing to grant it me upon the score of my health, in that case I do not desire to waste the time of the Court; provided it is granted to me, I am very happy and shall be glad to avoid the argument, if your Lordship will be only pleased to give me some intimation of your opinion." The Chief Justice, after consulting with the other judges, says:—"Mr. Horne Tooke, I have consulted my Lords the Judges who are present, they feel themselves extremely disposed to indulge you on the score of your health; they think that it is a distinction which may authorise them to do that in your case which is not done in other cases in common; they cannot lay down a rule for you which they would not lay down for any other man living, but if your case is distinguishable from the case of others that does permit them to give you that indulgence which you now ask"—Then Mr. Tooke says:—"I am very much obliged to your Lordships, and am very well content to accept it as indulgence or any other thing. Undoubtedly it is very acceptable to me, and very necessary for my health; I am glad to save the time of the Court." On that ground, after having attempted it on the ground I have stated, he was removed to the inner bar.

Now that case seems, I think, to establish that it is, in the judgment of the several judges who were here upon that occasion, a thing which ought not to be done unless under very special circumstances, and we ought to be on our guard against doing that which might have the appearance of treating one kind of felony, and one rank or class of persons, in a different way from another; or of intimating that, because a person is somewhat of a superior rank, he is to be treated in a different manner; and we are anxious not to do it in the way of favour or on any such ground as that, and we feel that we cannot grant this on the ground on which you put it. This seems to my learned brother and myself to be the same in fact as Mr. Tooke's, though not quite so strong—a desire in the party to communicate with his counsel, which will exist in every case. It was not thought sufficient in that case: he was indulged only on the ground that his health was such that it would suffer from his remaining in the ordinary place: and here no such cause is alleged.

Mr. *Kelly*. It is my duty to acquiesce in the decision of your Lordships. I beg to say I did not put this on any distinction of rank.

Mr. Justice *Maule*. No; that we understand perfectly, and the Court is disposed not so to put it. I said, that lest there should be a feeling, though it was not put so, that there might be a distinction drawn between this and any other case on that ground. What other difference is there between Mr. Zulueta, charged with felony in slave trading, and any other person coming to that dock, charged with any felony of any other character, requiring wealth and capital to carry it on?

Mr. *Kelly*. I did not desire, in the least, to press it on that ground; on the contrary, I disclaimed it: I mentioned that which was the principal ground— that the documents are all in a foreign language; and that which I submitted to your Lordship was entirely my own suggestion, and not Mr. Zulueta's: I acquiesced at once, as I ought, in your Lordship's decision.

Mr. Justice *Maule*. The Court is so constructed that you can approach Mr. Zulueta, though he cannot approach you.

(The Defendant took his place within the Bar, and was arraigned on the Indictment for Felony.)

Clerk of Arraigns. How say you, are you Guilty, or Not Guilty?

Defendant. I am Not Guilty.

Clerk of Arraigns. If you object to any of the gentlemen who are called, you may make the objection before they are sworn; and it is my duty to inform you that you have a right to be tried, being a foreigner, either by a jury of half foreigners and half English, or by a jury entirely English.

Defendant. I have no wish; I am as safe in the hands of Englishmen as of any body.

The following Jurymen were called and sworn:—

1. John Foote.
2. William Jackson.
3. Robert Nagle.
4. Charles William Knight.
5. Michael Jones.
6. Richard Jessop.
7. William Hawksworth.
8. James Gillard.
9. Edward Findlay.
10. James Parker.
11. John Godfrey.
12. James Gordon.

(The Jury were charged with the Prisoner in the usual form.)

Mr. Serjeant *Bompas*. Before I make the address which it will be necessary to make to the jury, will your Lordship allow me to apply on behalf of a witness, a gentleman who took the notes in short-hand of what took place before the Committee of the House of Commons? I, of course, do it with the consent of the counsel on the other side; it is, that he may be now examined, which will remove all question as to the propriety of the proceeding; that he may be now sworn and state that this blue book contains a correct account of what took place: that will, of course, be subject to such objections as may be made by my learned friend.

Mr. *Kelly*. My Lord, I understand that Mr. Gurney's presence is required, for the purpose of justice in Wales, under an order from the Home Office. I perfectly agree, that it shall be taken upon his evidence that this blue book contains a true account of what took place before the Committee, subject to any objections as to the admissibility of the evidence, the matter standing as if Mr. Gurney had given his evidence in its proper order.

Mr. Joseph *Gurney*, sworn. Examined by Mr. Serjeant *Bompas*.

Q. Did you attend as short-hand writer before the Committee of the House of Commons, at which these proceedings were taken in short-hand?—*A.* I did.

Q. Is this book printed from your short-hand notes?—*A.* Mr. Zulueta's evidence. I took the evidence of Mr. Zulueta; not the whole.

Q. Did you take the evidence of others?—*A.* Yes; of some others.

Mr. Serjeant *Bompas*. On behalf of the prosecution we admit that the other parts are taken from the short-hand notes: we shall want the evidence of Mr. Zulueta.

May it please your Lordship,

Gentlemen of the Jury,—It is my duty to call your attention to a case of very considerable moment. I am quite sure you will feel that all cases, in which the liberty and welfare of any person standing as a prisoner at the bar before you are concerned, are matters of considerable importance; but I cannot but think that this is one which will deserve your very particular attention. The case is, to you and to most persons, one of a novel description as a matter of trial. It is very rarely indeed, that offences under the Act to which your attention will be directed can be brought before a jury as the subject of their investigation. It necessarily will include a variety of facts, some of them being in some degree complicated; and it requires, therefore, that careful discrimination which I am quite sure you will be quite ready to give. To the prisoner, of course, it is of paramount importance, standing here before you upon his trial on such a charge as that which has been presented against Mr. Zulueta, and calls for the utmost possible attention. I do not consider that I should keep from you one thing which has been mentioned already in your hearing, that the prisoner at the bar is a person of wealth, and rank, and station. He is a merchant of the city of London. I am quite sure that that cannot make any difference in your consideration of the case, unless by increasing that interest which necessarily is excited by the respectability in life of the person who is standing before you on his trial, exciting you to greater vigilance to see that perfect justice is done as between him and the law. I am quite sure that you will see, that if he be innocent, you will, as you would in respect of every individual who stands before you upon his trial, take care that he shall not be convicted; but if, on the other hand, the evidence, when it is laid before you, shall satisfy your minds that he is guilty, it can in no manner or degree lessen the guilt of a person against whom such facts shall be produced, that he is in a station which should teach him better to obey the law of his country. So far as any such topic can be urged, on the one side or the other, to excite your utmost anxiety and most careful vigilance to ascertain the truth, I, on behalf of the prosecution, should feel that it is of great importance it should be exercised, because the truth, and that alone, ought to be, and I trust in all cases is, the object desired by the public prosecutor.

Gentlemen, the kind of charge is one that will require your very particular attention. The prisoner stands charged, "that he did illegally and feloniously man, navigate, equip, dispatch, use, and employ," that is, that he did employ—that is the particular term to which I would direct your attention—"which in and by a certain Act of Parliament made and passed in the 5th year of the reign of his late Majesty King George the Fourth, intituled 'An Act to amend and consolidate the Laws relating to the Abolition of the Slave Trade,' was and is declared unlawful, that is, to deal and trade in slaves." The other counts vary the charge in some degree, but in nothing that I believe will be material for your consideration, except that in the four latter counts he is charged with shipping goods on board the same vessel for the purpose of accomplishing the same object.

Gentlemen, it is now happily a matter of history of some considerable period back, that there was a contest in this kingdom by those who were anxious to put an end to what they rightly considered one of the greatest crimes staining human nature. On the 25th of March, in the year 1807, was accomplished that victory, I may say for humanity, by which, as far as the laws of this country could accomplish it, this kingdom was separated from that course of crime, which probably is almost the greatest blot that rests upon human nature; I mean, that that Act was passed which is called "the Act for the Abolition of the Slave Trade."

Gentlemen, you are aware that before that time persons of wealth—for persons of wealth alone could engage in such an occupation, and unfortunately that which was called the slave trade was a source of great wealth—before that time no doubt persons of wealth engaged in that trade. That Act, as far as regarded any public Act, of course extinguished them; but from time to time, from that time to this present moment, though not of course engaged in public or in the immediate visible commerce which was the subject of condemnation by that Act, it has been more or less continued, and the course of the law has been from time to time by more and more stringent penalties as far as possible to put an end to it as respects this country; and it is impossible that you should not be aware that one great object of this kingdom in all its negotiations with all foreign countries is, as far as possible, to create one great combination among all the civilized part of mankind, uniting in extinguishing that which is a crime on the part of all engaged in it; and therefore it has become above all other things the duty of this Government, as far as relates to any individuals living within this kingdom, to the utmost possible degree to put an end to any connection with it of any sort or kind, and to prevent any persons who continue in this kingdom, and are subject to its law, from being in any way whatever connected with that which is considered a crime of the greatest magnitude; and it is with that view that the Act of Parliament which you have heard mentioned in the indictment, the Act of the 5th of George the Fourth, chap. 113, was passed, in order as far as possible to extinguish all connection of any individuals in this kingdom with the slave trade, and by a severe penalty to put an end to any such transactions. Indeed, when we consider the penalty, it is such as shows that the Legislature intended to render the punishment most severe: it is a penalty which subjects every person connected with that trade to transportation for fourteen years. But every single individual who, through any connection with that trade, is torn from his friends in Africa, and sent in the miserable way in which they must necessarily, if they survive the horrors of the voyage, be removed from that country to an interminable life of slavery—every individual suffers double and treble the penalty which is inflicted upon the criminal engaged in the trade; and therefore I feel satisfied that we shall not consider that penalty too severe, provided only the offence is fully proved: and the severity of the punishment ought to excite, I admit, to the utmost degree, your watchfulness to see that it is fairly and satisfactorily brought home to any man, because I take it any person on behalf of the prosecution who calls the attention of a jury to the enormity of any crime, does it under the most anxious caution that, in proportion as the crime is great, so the jury ought to extend their utmost care and attention to see that it is fairly and satisfactorily made out.

Gentlemen, you are aware that in cases of this kind the transactions must necessarily extend over some considerable time. The distance of the place to which the transactions ultimately relate, the difficulty of obtaining from Africa the various documents necessary to be produced to ascertain the guilt or innocence of the party, necessarily occasions the lapse of some considerable time; and in the present case it will be necessary for me to refer to transactions that extend over several years. In this particular case a trial took place in respect of the vessel in Africa, and afterwards in England, which necessarily occupied some considerable time; and no doubt the necessity of obtaining the requisite documents occasioned the delay for a still further lengthened period.

Gentlemen, the charge made against the prisoner is, that he employed a vessel in order to accomplish, that is for the purpose of accomplishing, the dealing in slaves, and that he sent goods for the purpose of accomplishing that object, namely, the trading in slaves; and the nature of the charge, which I will mention generally before I enter into the particulars of the evidence, is this, that the prisoner at the bar employed a vessel—and you will of course hear the manner and mode in which that was done, and observations will occur to you on the detail of the facts—that he sent goods in that vessel to supply persons who are merchants in slaves, individuals holding slaves in Africa, to enable them to keep the slaves while they were there, and to provide the means for bartering those slaves, so as to enable them to transmit them to Cuba, or the Havannah, as the case may be. Of course it need not be said for one moment that openly and publicly in this kingdom no man could do that, which to the eyes of all would appear to be dealing in slaves; it would be the object of attention of every man: and it is necessary I should detail the evidence I have, in order to show first, that this vessel named the Augusta, and the goods which were shipped on board that vessel were in fact for the purpose of supplying a factory situated at the Gallinas, a port on the Coast of Africa, and that the prisoner at the bar knowingly and willingly was the person who had employed the vessel, knowing that it was employed for that purpose. Of course the persons who were employed, the persons more deeply interested, were persons residing abroad; but we charge (and before you convict the prisoner you must be satisfied of that fact) that he knew the object, and lent himself to that object, and shipped the goods with that view.

Gentlemen, to give you an account of the progress of this vessel, I must direct your attention so far back as the year 1839. In the year 1839 a vessel, the Augusta as she has been since called, was then trading under the name of the Gollupchick, under Russian colours, fully equipped for slave trading. At that time she was captured by a gentleman, who will be called as a witness before you, Captain Hill, and taken into Sierra Leone as a vessel trading in slaves, of which there was no doubt. I have stated to you that she was sailing under Russian colours. At that time the captain on board was named Bernardos, one of the three persons named in this indictment, though not present. He was the captain, and the crew were entirely Spaniards. The Russians, you probably know, have not settlements requiring the dealing in slaves. She was taken to Sierra Leone to be condemned, it being believed that the Russian colours were employed merely as a pretence. The court before which she was to be tried was a mixed commission of Spanish and British. That court considering that they had no right to try the case of a vessel trading under Russian colours, she was not then condemned; the case was not there inquired into. It is sufficient to say that she was brought over from Sierra Leone to England with her crew, and with a number of the British crew who had taken her in there. Bernardos being the captain of her, he and his own Spanish crew came to England in that vessel. She was then perfectly equipped as a slave trader. Upon her coming to England the Russian consul claimed her as a Russian vessel. She was then sold at Portsmouth. She was sold to a person of the name of Emanuel, who purchased her for 600*l.*, paying 30*l.* as the auction duty; the expense therefore would be 630*l.* Upon her being sold, part of the balance of the purchase-money was paid to Bernardos, which had been expended on account of the vessel.

When this vessel was brought to this port, a letter was written by Mr. Zulueta: the contents of that letter I have no means of knowing; we can do no more than give evidence of the writing of that letter. I shall show a letter was written; it will be for the prisoner at the bar or not to produce that letter. She was sold, as I have mentioned, to Mr. Emanuel; and upon that we have a letter written by the prisoner at the bar, Mr. Zulueta, to Thomas Jennings, in respect of the purchase of that vessel, and I will call your attention to that letter. The letter is dated London, the 20th of August, 1840. It is a letter that was found in the vessel when she was subsequently captured by Captain Hill. The letter is in these terms, dated "London, 20th August, 1840," directed to "Thomas Jennings"—Thomas Jennings is one of the three persons indicted: he was the person who was captain of the vessel, and was captured in the vessel subsequently—"Sir, in reply to your letter of yesterday, we have to say that we cannot exceed 500*l.* for the vessel in question, such as described in your letter, namely, that excepting the sails the other differences are trifling from the inventory. If you cannot therefore succeed at those limits, we must give up the purchase, and you will please act accordingly. Zulueta and Company.—Captain Jennings, Portsmouth." The purport of this letter is, that Zulueta and Company would purchase the vessel if they could get her for 500*l.*, but that they would give no more than 500*l.* for the vessel. Gentlemen, in fact I shall be able to prove to you that this being dated the 20th of August, 1840, very shortly after that, I believe on the 29th of August, Messrs. Zulueta paid for that vessel 650*l.*; and the way in which they paid that for it was this—they gave a check to Bernardos, the captain of her when she was captured under the name of the Golupchick, whom I shall prove to have received the money at the bank in London, and to have gone down to Portsmouth, and together with Jennings to have gone to Emanuel, and paid this money to Emanuel for the purchase of the vessel. There will, I believe, be no doubt whatever that that money came from the prisoner at the bar, Mr. Zulueta; for I shall be able to show that that very same money received by Bernardos, the very same notes amounting to 650*l.* were paid to Emanuel at Portsmouth. There will be therefore no doubt that the money was paid by the prisoner at the bar.

Gentlemen, the vessel remained for some time at Portsmouth; she remained there, I believe, till the beginning of October. There will be no doubt what was her object. Immediately after her purchase—almost immediately after— I shall be able to show you, by its having been found in the vessel, that there was a letter written by Bernardos—

Mr. *Kelly.* Surely you are not going to read letters found in the vessel, without connecting the defendant with the vessel or with the letters.

Mr. Serjeant *Bompas.* If you object to the letter, I will state the ground on which I conceive it is evidence.

Mr. *Kelly.* I object to no letter written by Mr. Zulueta or any of his clerks; but letters found months after, when all his connection with the vessel had ceased, surely you cannot read.

Mr. Serjeant *Bompas.* I shall show that this letter was on board the vessel at Portsmouth on the 25th of September, 1840—a letter written by the man who received the money for the purchase of her to the captain, who was to conduct her to Africa: of course there are two facts here which it will be necessary I should prove; first, that her destination was the Gallinas; and secondly, that her object was to assist in the dealing in slaves: and it shall be my object to show, or I shall fail and you will give your verdict for the prisoner, that this was with the knowledge of Mr. Zulueta.

Mr. *Kelly.* Show that by proper evidence, but do not read letters which are not evidence.

Mr. Serjeant *Bompas.* I have a right to read this letter; you may object, if you please.

Mr. *Kelly.* I do object, because it is impossible with effect to object to it hereafter. Here is a gentleman on his trial for felony: I do not object to the reading of any letters from his house of business, though they may not have been written by himself; I do not object to any letter being read which was written by Mr. Zulueta himself, or any letter which my learned friend, Mr. Serjeant Bompas, can undertake to say Mr. Zulueta had seen or known; but letters written by third persons, over whom he had no manner of control—letters written by a person included in this indictment, but not on his trial, and which I have no means of explaining—cannot be evidence. Mr. Zulueta has no means of explaining this letter, the writer of which was unknown to him: and I submit that it would be more fair, and more according to the ordinary course of business in this country, if my learned friend were to arrive at the facts, which he says he can prove, by that which is properly evidence, and to leave the reading this letter to a separate discussion on any argument which may then be raised as to its reception in evidence.

Mr. Serjeant *Bompas*. I do not object to my learned friend interposing in objection to the reference to this letter, because I am willing to admit that it is desirable to exclude every effect which might be produced by the reading of a document which may be objectionable; and while it is my duty to open that which I feel to be evidence against the prisoner, I will not open any thing as to which I feel a substantial doubt. The letter I am now proposing to put in is a letter written by Mr. Bernardos, the man who received the money after that first letter I have mentioned, and after all which occurred with respect to the purchase, and it has reference to certain objects in respect of his destination, and giving him—not instructions in the sense of ordering him—but directions and instructions as to the course of that voyage. My object is to show, that at the time the vessel was at Portsmouth, the destination was fixed, and he received direction in that respect from a person whom I have so connected with Mr. Zulueta as to show that that man Jennings was the purchaser with the money of Zulueta of this very vessel, Jennings being the captain, and ultimately one of the owners; and I shall show directions from Mr. Zulueta. I cannot conceive how that can be objected to.

Mr. *Kelly*. I undertake to say not a shadow of doubt shall remain on your Lordships' minds that this is not evidence when the facts are before the Court. To be opening the contents of the letter, under such circumstances, I submit is not justified.

Mr. Justice *Maule*. Brother Bompas, I do not think this is so clearly evidence that it should be opened to the Court. It is very difficult to decide whether a document is evidence or not till the facts are brought before us.

Mr. Serjeant *Bompas*. Gentlemen, I am quite willing to be wholly under the control of the learned judges in the conduct of this case. I would not myself, as I think I ought not, to open that which is really substantially doubtful, and if I had felt this so, I would not have mentioned it at all.

Mr. *Kelly*. I am quite sure that my learned friend would not have done so if he had felt that it was open to objection. I am quite sure that my learned friend from the first desired that nothing should be stated, which in his opinion could not be brought home to the defendant himself.

Mr. Serjeant *Bompas.* After the observation of Mr. Kelly, I will say no more with respect to this. I have to prove two things; first, what was the object of this vessel. I have to prove what it was intended to do. It may or may not in many instances be shown that there was the hand of Mr. Zulueta in what was done; but if I show to your satisfaction that he was aware of the circumstances, and was one of the parties, it is not necessary that I should show that his was the hand by which every individual act was done: therefore, I beg to keep these two things quite distinct. I shall show what was the object and destination of the vessel; and undoubtedly I shall show you, or I fail in this case, that he was conscious of the object and intention of the employment of the vessel.

Gentlemen, upon the vessel, at the time she was at Portsmouth and when she was sold, there were on board her part of the equipments which had previously existed of the Gollupchick. In order in one way to equip a vessel directly for slave trading—to put her in a situation in which she could take slaves in—it is necessary that there should be the means of very considerable supplies of water. There are commonly leagers. It is not necessary there should be leagers, unless when the occasion requires the carrying an extraordinary supply of water; where that is required, it is necessary there should be the means of carrying such a quantity of water in the vessel; and there were on board this vessel leagers—that is, large vessels containing many hundred gallons of water, ten or twelve or fourteen feet in diameter. At Portsmouth several of the leagers then on board were taken to pieces, and the staves and heads left on board the vessel. You are aware that it would be quite impossible for such a vessel, with leagers, or any fittings up of that kind, to leave this kingdom in order to go to a place on the coast of Africa, where it is known the slave trade is carried on; it would be quite obvious what their object was; and these vessels were accordingly taken to pieces, and the materials left in the vessel.

It was observed, also, that the vessel afforded the means of having slave decks placed. Where a vessel leaves a place, such as Spain, or some place where she may leave with impunity with all her equipments complete, they have slave decks in the vessel—that is, decks with about two-and-thirty inches from one deck to another, in which the slaves lie. These they were not able to set up under these circumstances; but there are decks placed that as many as possible may be carried. These decks could not be existing in this country: they could not be allowed to go from this country. There are, however, places, and some screw-bolts where they can be placed, and by which they could be fastened: they might be speedily put in on the coast of Africa, so as to fit the vessel for carrying slaves there: of course it could not be done here, but the screw-bolts might be put in, and the slave decks fixed in an incredibly short space of time; and thus she might be immediately prepared for receiving the slaves when she was in Africa.

I shall also, I believe, show that a person was applied to at Portsmouth to enter to go to the coast of Africa. When she was there, letters were received by Jennings; and I shall prove certain circumstances by a witness, who I shall call before you, who was present when the vessel was taken, a letter found on board her, which was written from London: and I may state that at once, as my learned friend has admitted that whatever was written by the house would be evidence against the prisoner at the bar; and I should state that he himself said before the Committee of the House of Commons on his examination, that he himself had the management of the whole of this business. I will read the exact words—"I have managed all this business;" therefore there can be no doubt that what came from the house he is responsible for. The letter to which I will call your attention was received on the 26th of September, 1840.

Mr. *Kelly*. My learned friend will pardon me for a moment. I have said I shall not think it right, in a case of this sort, to interrupt my learned friend in any attempt he may make to read documents which proceeded from the house, but I must not therefore be taken to agree to their admissibility.

Mr. Justice *Maule*. You will not consider the admissibility of the evidence as established until it is offered in evidence.

Mr. Serjeant *Bompas*. Of course every thing I read, you will consider subject to proof. If I have been misled in any fact, you will remove it from your minds. Not that I would state any fact, if I did not believe it to be founded in truth. This is dated—"London, 26th September, 1840. Captain Thomas Jennings, Portsmouth. Dear Sir,—We have received your letter of yesterday, whereby we observe that the sum we have remitted you will not be sufficient to cover all the expenses to clear the ship. We much regret you have omitted mentioning the sum you require, which prevents our remitting you the same by this very post, thus causing a new delay in leaving that port, so contrary to our wishes. You will therefore write to us to-morrow, that we may receive your reply on Monday morning, informing us of the amount necessary to finish paying all your accounts and expenses, to remit you the same by Monday's night post, in order that you may be able to sail for Liverpool on Tuesday or Wednesday at the furthest. You must not omit stating the amount required; and waiting your reply, we remain, very truly, dear sir, your obedient servants." Then the signature which was to that letter is cut out. Then it says, "According to our Liverpool house notice"—the prisoner, Mr. Zulueta, is connected with a house at Cadiz, as well as a house in London—"According to our Liverpool house notice you will go there to the Salthouse Dock," superscribed "Captain Thomas Jennings, Broad Street, Portsmouth." That letter was regularly received in the course of business, as to which business Mr. Zulueta says, "I managed it." I believe I shall show you the handwriting of a part of it; but the signature was cut out. I believe I shall show it was cut out previous to its being found.

This being the letter, Mr. Zulueta having furnished the money for the purpose for which it was demanded, and having desired that Captain Jennings will send up an account of all the money expended, and that he should go to the Salthouse Dock at Liverpool; accordingly he went to the Salthouse Dock at Liverpool. It is impossible Mr. Zulueta's name should be mentioned as the owner of a vessel used for such a purpose. It is quite clear, that if he knew it, his name would not be used as the owner of the vessel, and therefore this vessel was purchased in the name of Thomas Jennings. How far he was really the owner you will be able probably to form an opinion from the remainder of the evidence with which I shall furnish you. When it was purchased, no papers of any kind were handed over. She was a condemned vessel. She was bought without any register, and taken as a Russian vessel, and there being no evidence of ownership, she was purchased as such.

Gentlemen, she went to Liverpool; and when she went to Liverpool, I shall have to call your attention particularly to what took place at Liverpool. At Liverpool a charter-party was entered into, to which I will call your attention:—"Memorandum of the charter-party. London, 19th October, 1840. It is this day mutually agreed between Mr. Thomas Jennings, master and owner of the good ship or vessel called the Augusta, of the burthen of   tons, or thereabouts, now lying at the port of Liverpool, and Messrs. Pedro Martinez and Co., of Havannah, merchants." Pedro Martinez and Co. were merchants, having a house at Cadiz. It will appear from Mr. Zulueta's own statement that they had a house also at the Havannah, that they were known slave dealers. According to Mr. Zulueta's own evidence, he believed at the time they were slave dealers.

Mr. *Kelly*. If you say that, I beg you to read the evidence. He never did say that.

Mr. Serjeant *Bompas*. "Do you know the nature of the trade of Pedro Martinez at the Gallinas?—I know from general report that Don Pedro Martinez himself is supposed to deal in slaves, and I believe it is so." That is at page 682, question 10398.

Mr. *Clarkson*. That is an examination in 1842.

Mr. *Kelly*. These are statements made in 1842. Have the kindness to read the answer to 10413, in the next page.

Mr. Serjeant *Bompas*. Every word he said in evidence will be read; but an interference in that form and that manner is not proper, and I shall not submit to it.

Mr. *Kelly*. I merely meant to correct what I supposed to be an inadvertent mistake.

Mr. Serjeant *Bompas*. My learned friend is quite right to interfere, if he thinks I am under a mistake. My object is to call your attention to what he said at the time; every word will be read to you, and you will form your own opinion upon it. "Is he known at the Havannah as a dealer in slaves?—I do not know, but I believe so; I do not know why it should not be known at the Havannah, if it is known in other parts." My learned friend will make his own observation upon that, I shall read that as evidence before you; you will consider whether it is sufficient proof that he knew that Martinez & Co. dealt in slaves.

Gentlemen, I was reading to you the charter-party of the ship: it proceeds in these words—"That the said ship being tight, staunch, and strong, and every way fitted for the voyage, shall, with all convenient speed, load from the factors of Messrs. Pedro Martinez & Co., a cargo of legal goods, which the said merchants bind themselves to ship, not exceeding what she can reasonably stow and carry over and above her tackle, apparel, provisions, and furniture; and being so loaded, shall therewith proceed to Gallinas, on the coast of Africa, or so near thereunto as she may safely get, and deliver the same; after which she may be sent on any legal voyages between the West Indies, England, Africa, or the United States, according to the directions of the charterers' agents (restraint of princes and rulers, the act of God, the Queen's enemies, fire, and all and every other dangers and accidents of the seas, rivers, and navigation of whatever nature and kind soever, during the said voyage, always excepted). The freight to be paid on unloading and right delivery of the cargo, at the rate of 100*l*. sterling per calendar month that the ship may be so employed, commencing with this present month, all port charges and pilotages being paid by the charterers, and   days on demurrage over and above the said laying days at   pounds per day. Penalty for non-performance of this agreement 500*l*. The necessary cash for ship's disbursements to be furnished to the captain free of commission. The charterers to be at liberty of closing this engagement at the end of any voyage performed under it on settling the freight due to the vessel. The captain being indebted to the charterers in certain sums as per acknowledgment elsewhere, the freights earned by the vessel to be held as general lien for such sum, and in any settlement for such freight, the said advances to be deducted from the vessel's earnings.—THOMAS JENNINGS."

Then, here is the addition to the charter-party:—"I, Thomas Jennings, captain and owner of the ship 'Augusta,' of this port, hereby I declare, I have received from Messrs. Pedro Martinez & Co., of Havannah, through Messrs. Zulueta &, Co., of this city, 1,100*l.* sterling for the disbursements of the said ship, her fitting out and provisions, which I engage myself to repay with the earnings of the same, according to the charter-party entered this day with the said gentlemen, and under the following conditions:—1st. All the earnings of the ship will be accounted for and applied to the said Pedro Martinez & Co., they furnishing the necessary cash for all expenses, repairs, provisions, and crew's wages, including 15*l.* per month for my salary as captain. 2nd. At any time, when the said gentlemen may think proper to close the charter-party, I will make out the account, and deliver to them, or to their representatives, a proper bill of sale for the said ship and all her appurtenances, to cover the balance due to them in the said account. 3rd. That I am in no other way responsible for the settlement of the above-mentioned debt, but with the said ship and her earnings; and that the said Messrs. Pedro Martinez & Co. will take on themselves the insurance and risk on the vessel.—THOMAS JENNINGS."

Now, Gentlemen, it will be most material for you to consider the effect of this charter-party, and what is called the loan. It is nominally chartered by Thomas Jennings, as the captain of the vessel, to Pedro Martinez & Co. through Zulueta & Co.; and Zulueta & Co. are the persons employing that vessel: there can be no doubt of that. Now what is the effect of these two documents? Is it that Jennings is the real party who engages to pay? No such thing. "I am in no other way responsible for the settlement of the above-mentioned debt, but with the said ship and her earnings; and that the said Messrs. Pedro Martinez & Co. will take on themselves the insurance and risk on the vessel." So that he is not in the slightest degree indebted to them: he is not bound to pay, but it is only that he is indebted to them on the vessel. Can he say I will pay you the money and keep the vessel? No; whenever Messrs. Martinez & Co. choose, the vessel is to be made over to them. Can he make over the vessel and apply the money to his own use? No; he has only 15*l.* a month, and can be required to make over the vessel whenever they please. But that would be the ordinary transaction in peace time; the money would be advanced to him; the vessel would be the security for it at any one moment at which Martinez & Co., or their representatives—that is, Messrs. Zulueta & Co.—might call upon Jennings to deliver up the vessel to them. He is always accountable to them for the earnings of the vessel, and he is in no respect personally responsible. The question you will have to decide is this: Is this a method by which it shall appear that Thomas Jennings is the owner of the vessel, so that no other person shall have a right to say that he is the owner? He is to appear to be so; but the other parties have a right to say, "Give the vessel up to us;" he borrowing, but having nothing but the vessel; he being to receive his wages of 15*l.* a month as captain. It will be undoubtedly a very material consideration whether this is matter of concealment; a mode in which Jennings is to be made the apparent and not the real owner, or whether he is the real *bonâ fide*, owner. It is clear he would be in no respect responsible under this arrangement entered into at Liverpool. You will have, in connexion with the evidence, to examine the statement made by Mr. Zulueta. The letters, which will be read, undoubtedly treat Zulueta & Co. as purchasers on behalf of Martinez & Co.; and the charter-party is made by them as agents for Martinez & Co., by which the factors are to ship these goods for Africa as agents for Martinez & Co.

Gentlemen, the vessel went to Liverpool; she was there loaded in the ordinary course, according to the account given by Mr. Zulueta in his evidence. He is asked, "You did not imagine that in being the instrument of sending lawful goods to any part of Africa, you were doing any thing which required concealment?—Nothing at all of the kind; and the proof of that is, that in the bills of entry in Liverpool any body could see our names as consignees of the vessel, and see entries made in our names of every thing." No doubt, gentlemen, according to that charter-party, if it was a *bonâ fide* charter-party, shippers might ship goods on board the vessel in their name; every thing would be in their name; and the papers on board that vessel might be in the name of Zulueta, and not in the name of Captain Jennings: but if Captain Jennings was the owner of the vessel, and Messrs. Zulueta the factors of Martinez, he would have only to receive the goods shipped on board that vessel by Messrs. Zulueta. It is clear a cargo was put on board that vessel, and if she was going on a legal voyage, there is no reason why every thing should not be in the name of Messrs. Zulueta, and why the ship's papers should not be in their names as the owners of this vessel. But all the ship's papers were made out in the name of Thomas Jennings; the bill of lading is made out as shipped by Thomas Jennings; and none of the shipments are made by these factors, who, according to the charter-party, were to ship the whole. No doubt it will be for you to consider how far that is a wilful act of concealment or not.

Gentlemen, this vessel was going to the Gallinas. The Gallinas is a port in Africa, about 200 miles from Sierra Leone. It is necessary you should know the nature of that port. It will be impossible but that persons engaged in trade should know the nature of that port. It is a settlement, or rather a native State, that consisted of a harbour and a river, and it is called the Gallinas. The sole trade carried on there is the slave trade. It consisted of a few, I think there were five, of what are called barracoons. It is hardly necessary I should state that a barracoon is a place in which slaves are kept; that slave traders by attacking a village, or other means, take possession of the people, who are taken down to warehouses erected for their use—barracoons as they call them—places where they are kept until an opportunity arises, whereby they may be shipped off either to the Havannah or to Cuba: the two great places to which slaves are sent from this place are the Havannah and Cuba. The place consists of five barracoons, as they are called; five warehouses, where the slaves are kept. It is not a trading place in any other way. Slaves are purchased by the barter of cotton goods or other goods from England, or by doubloons, which are raised by drawing bills on persons in England. There is no other trade but the mere slave trade. In the barracoons and places, these unfortunate people are kept until an opportunity arises for selling them, to be disposed of either in Cuba or the Havannah. One was kept by a person of the name of Rolo, another by a person named Ximines, another by Alvarez, another by a person of the name of Buron, and another by a person of the name of François. This vessel and cargo therefore were dispatched to a place which was wholly a slave trade establishment. There is no other trade whatever. I believe there was not at that time, nor had been long before. Since the slave trade has been stopped there, it is somewhat a different thing; but at that time it was a place used entirely for the slave trade, and the goods which were sent there were used for barter, and the doubloons for which the bills were drawn were employed in the purchase of slaves. The three consignees of this vessel were the three persons I have first mentioned, three persons having barracoons in the Gallinas. It is possible that a name of a fourth may appear in the evidence. You will remember that the fourth is named Buron. The vessel therefore went out from England with a cargo consigned to these three persons, Rolo, Ximines, and Alvarez.

Gentlemen, when the vessel got some little distance from England, I believe a hundred miles from Cork, she encountered a considerable gale: upon that the captain determined to go to Cadiz; the wind was unfavourable for Cadiz: she was about a hundred miles from Cork, and there was a perfect facility of going to Cork or to Falmouth, where they might have arrived in the course of a day. It would take 18 or 19 days to go to Cadiz, I believe 19; but the captain determined to go to Cadiz, the crew resisted this, and they came to the determination that some of the crew should be discharged at Cadiz, Mr. Zulueta having a house at Cadiz, and Mr. Martinez too; and it was at Cadiz she received the dispatches which were found on board, as to the consignees, as to what was to be done with the shipment on board, and what was the object of the shippers. Part of the goods appear to have been landed there by the firm of Zulueta & Co., and Mr. Zulueta received an award for the injury which had occurred, the injury the cargo had sustained in that gale. I believe the principal part of the tobacco was landed. It will appear by the bill of lading the shipment of goods was by these three persons. The tobacco was landed by Mr. Zulueta of the house in Cadiz, and the house in London received compensation for the loss upon that, they having shipped the same in London.

Gentlemen, the vessel afterwards sailed from Cadiz. She arrived, I believe, about the 6th of December, and sailed in the early part of January. She was captured on the 7th of February, 1841, by Captain Hill, when she came near the coast of Africa. It happened that Captain Hill, whose duty it was to capture those vessels, either Spanish or English, which had dealings in slaves, met with her, and he was not a little surprised at seeing so soon a vessel he had captured as a slaver, under the name of the Gollupchik, come under English colours with a new name. He boarded her, and saw Jennings on board. She was not then, of course, to use the technical term, equipped as a slave trader; she having sailed from England with goods on board, it was impossible she should be. He asked to whom she was consigned: Jennings refused to tell.

Mr. *Kelly*. Are we to have the conversations with Jennings, the master, long after the felony is supposed to have been committed by Mr. Zulueta in England? Is the conversation with every person, in every quarter of the world, to be given in evidence?

Mr. Serjeant *Bompas*. I am not going into any conversation between the master and the captors, merely the simple fact. Captain Hill being about to seize the vessel, the dispatches of the vessel were at length brought out with great reluctance; the captain, however, delivered up the letters, and told Captain Hill those were the letters to the consignees. They are letters with certain directions.

Mr. *Kelly*. My Lord, I must object again to what I conceive is most irregular on the part of my learned friend, who is proposing to give in evidence that which took place between Captain Hill and Jennings. My learned friend has opened a very complicated case, and now my learned friend attempts to describe the contents of papers given by the house of Martinez & Co. to the captain, some months after the vessel had sailed from England. Mr. Zulueta, at the bar, is charged with a felony in having equipped and employed this vessel for the purposes of the slave trade. My learned friend is opening the case against him on the charge of felony, and he is supposed to be affected by instructions given by other persons months afterwards—persons in Cadiz, over whom he had no control—instructions which he never saw until they were alluded to in certain proceedings in which he had no concern whatever. My learned friend is stating a part of the contents, and stating them most incorrectly. I apprehend Mr. Zulueta is undoubtedly liable for the consequences of any act he has done, any act he has sanctioned, any thing done by his firm with his knowledge; but that he cannot have used as evidence against him papers delivered months after the supposed commission of the crime, and long after he could have interposed—months after the vessel left England. My learned friend knows he has no evidence affecting the defendant touching her afterwards; but he is opening the contents of papers given by a foreign merchant months afterwards.

Mr. Justice *Wightman*. I did not understand Brother Bompas to state that the prisoner was aware of the contents of those papers.

Mr. *Kelly*. My learned friend does not pretend now to state that, but he describes them as containing instructions given to the captain; they were not instructions given to the captain.

Mr. Justice *Wightman*. He does not state that they were.

Mr. Serjeant *Bompas*. It is important that the objection should be made, if at all, now. The evidence no doubt is most important, and I thought it was possible that my learned friend might object. It is fair to the understanding of the case that the objection should be stated, and I am obliged to my learned friend for taking the objection now, if it was to be taken. I wanted to call his attention to it, not wishing to allude to the contents of those documents unless they are admissible in evidence; but it will be quite impossible to call the attention of the jury to these facts, unless I know whether the evidence is admissible.

Mr. Justice *Maule*. How can we decide that until we know what they are?

Mr. Serjeant *Bompas*. My object is to offer them as evidence in the case, and therefore to open them as evidence.

Mr. *Kelly*. My learned friend is stating what I did not understand him to state before, and therefore your Lordship will allow me to place this point of the case on its proper basis. When he is opening this part of the case, in order that if there is no doubt on the admissibility of the evidence it may be at once taken, I do at once make the objection; and I think your Lordship will pardon my saying a few words more on that which my learned friend considered rather an interruption, or a protestation, than an objection. My learned friend charges Mr. Pedro de Zulueta with having committed a felony, that felony having been committed in England in the months of July, August, and September; that is, that Mr. Zulueta equipped and dispatched a vessel, and shipped goods on board that vessel, for the purposes of the slave trade. That vessel left England, I think, in the month of October—

Mr. Serjeant *Bompas*. The 9th of November.

Mr. *Kelly*. We shall have no dispute on those facts. That vessel, purchased under circumstances which will probably appear more clearly in evidence. It is stated by my friend that Zulueta and Company purchased the ship; no doubt the house of Zulueta and Company interfered as agents for the house of Martinez and Company. That vessel was dispatched from England, and left England in the month of November, 1840. Whatever the prisoner at the bar has done in respect of the dispatching of that vessel, was done and completed then. The crime, if he committed any, was completed before the month of November, 1840. That is the charge upon which he is now on trial. I quite agree that, if since November, 1840—if instantly he had held any conversation—if he had written any letter—if he had held any conversation that might be used against him as evidence of the purpose for which he used and dispatched that vessel, which he had dispatched in the month of November, 1840—

Mr. Justice *Maule*. With respect to that portion of the opening of my Brother Bompas, the question is pretty much the same as with respect to that mentioned before.

Mr. Serjeant *Bompas*. Will your Lordship just hear how I present it?

Mr. Justice *Maule*. It is open to the same mode of dealing with the matter depending on the question—whether it is so clear that it will be admissible, when it comes to be offered in evidence, as that it ought to be stated. If Brother Bompas proposes to argue that, he may go on now.

Mr. *Kelly*. I am in your Lordships' hands; it is immaterial to me when I am heard. I was only going to add, which will go much to the argument, that on a common civil case, something written, said, or done by another person in a distant country, some months after the time when he is said to have committed the offence charged, is no evidence against him. If it were, Mr. Zulueta might have (as I believe he was), he might, with the rest of his firm, have been engaged in shipping goods on a lawful merchandise according to the British laws, in consonance with natural equity and right, and the character of the transaction might be completely changed. I can very easily imagine a case in which a British merchant—nay, a British trader of any kind—may ship a quantity of muskets to the coast of Africa, or the coast of Spain: nothing can be more simple than the proposition—a trader may ship a quantity of muskets to Africa, to Spain, or to France; he receives the goods, and ships the goods; and now he has done all, and the ship sails; and he may have died after the shipment; another person possesses himself of those muskets, and he employs them in war against the Queen of Britain—Is that to be used in a criminal charge of felony against him? But that is just the case here. These gentlemen of this house of Zulueta and Company are concerned in shipping a quantity of goods—I might have taken the objection whether as principal or agent, but I will not raise that—here is the ship, and here are the goods; they ship them for the coast of Africa: the shippers remain in England; they have nothing more to do with the transaction; the vessel putting in to Cadiz, whether by previous design or stress of weather I will not say; another person, over whom the shippers have no more control than they have over the inhabitants of the kingdom of Spain, give certain orders, which I will suppose contemplate an illegal object—Are those to be used as evidence against the shippers here on a charge of felony? My Lord, I have done; I shall wait until I hear how my learned friend can justify the giving that in evidence against Mr. Zulueta.

Mr. Serjeant *Bompas.* My Lord, if I had any reasonable doubt that I could give this in evidence before your Lordships, I conceive I ought not to interfere with the view your Lordship has thrown out with respect to the letter I before tendered; but I apprehend there can be no doubt. I may be mistaken in the view I have taken: I may be wrong.

Mr. Justice *Maule.* Unless you feel it quite material to the case to state the nature of the evidence you propose to offer, I should think that in a matter of this kind it might be advisable to abstain from the statement of it. The circumstances which a learned counsel proposes to offer in evidence ought to be such as leave no doubt in his mind that he shall be able to bring them home to the prisoner, or that which is not ultimately made evidence against the prisoner may make an impression which is not justified. If you have any doubt that you shall be able to make this evidence, Mr. Kelly is justified in his objection, and so long as there is a doubt whether it is admissible, the Court think it is not fit it should be stated. If in your opinion that is doubtful, you have a right to be heard; but if you consider this as likely to be a long case, it will be desirable to abridge it so far as you can, to bring it within such a compass that it may receive the attention of the jury, and that time should not be unnecessarily occupied in these discussions.

Mr. Serjeant *Bompas.* Gentlemen, I am always most ready to adopt the suggestion which the Court are kind enough to hold out. I feel that a counsel, standing for the prosecution, stands in a somewhat different situation from another person, and their Lordships, sitting to do justice, and fairly taking care that if there be a doubt, that doubt shall be taken for the benefit of those charged with a crime. I feel that as to the admissibility in evidence, if there is a doubt, it ought not to be stated to the jury. It is not for me, as counsel for the prosecution, to say that their admissibility is perfectly certain. It would be very hard if the view taken by counsel in a criminal prosecution were not to be regulated by the judgment of the Court. It is enough that I should state, that, in my opinion, it will be necessary that these letters should be admitted in evidence, and that you should direct your attention particularly to them. It will place an additional obligation on the learned judges at a future stage, if I am not allowed to call your attention to them, to see that they are so brought before you as that you should understand them. There is no weight intended to be given to the evidence beyond that to which it is entitled, but it will be my duty to bring them fairly to your understandings, when I tender them, that you may see the bearing of them. The reason of my offering them in evidence will be given when I do offer them in evidence. This is not a decision that they are not admissible in evidence, but that it is better I should not open to you what may leave an impression which ought not to be made, unless I show that this is evidence. By the course taken, if this is not evidence, there will be no impression made. There is no doubt that very great importance to the prosecution will rest on the decision of this question; it will have a very great effect in the decision of the question, whether from this time or not there may be perfect and absolute impunity to any person who chooses to conduct a trade of this kind, provided only he is not so unwise as to advertise himself before-hand as a man who has connexion with the ultimate procedure of the vessel. Gentlemen, at present this matter is perfectly in debate. I shall offer this to you in evidence, and then it will be shown how it applies. This vessel, as I was stating when I mentioned certain things found on board, was captured by Captain Hill, was carried to Sierra Leone, and from thence brought home to England, and there was an end of the voyage.

Gentlemen, one material question that you will have to consider when the case is before you is—What was the object of the destination of the vessel? For what purpose was the vessel sent to the Gallinas? Was she sent for the purposes of fair trade, or was she sent to the Gallinas with goods to be used for the purposes of the slave trade? No doubt the vessel would not be perfectly equipped on going from Portsmouth; but the state of the vessel then you will have to consider, and I believe I shall be able to show that at that place the leagers were taken to pieces and put on board in such a manner as that they could be easily put together when she got out, and that there were existing in the vessel a very considerable number of shackles usually used for the purpose of confining slaves. You are aware that the slaves, the male slaves, are almost always put into this situation between the decks, and confined also by shackles. I shall be able to show that the leagers were taken to pieces and stowed on board the vessel, and that there were a very large number of shackles on board the vessel. Now, what was the object in going to the Gallinas? If any directions which were given in respect of that object are not brought out, you must find it out as well as you can in the circumstances of the vessel. She was going to the Gallinas. Mr. Zulueta was acting on behalf of a person whom he admits he believed to be dealing in slaves. The whole view of the case must be left in some degree to you, after all the evidence laid before you, supposing the evidence to which I have called your attention to be ultimately received.

Gentlemen, it will be my duty to call your attention to the evidence which Mr. Zulueta volunteered before the Committee of the House of Commons, and I can only say you will have to keep it in mind as applicable to the other evidence if it is admitted. If it is not admitted, you will take it as it is applicable to the case. I have mentioned one or two sentences, and my learned friend has interfered to represent that I was giving the effect of that evidence unfairly before you. I shall call your attention to the material parts, and leave you to apply it to the rest of the evidence. He was examined on the 22nd of July, 1842. It would appear, from the questions proposed to him, that some persons had made statements before the Committee of the House of Commons, which, being intended to reflect upon him, had been inclosed to him for his consideration, and that he felt himself obliged to appear to meet those statements. That is the way in which the evidence was given. He was not summoned before them—they could hardly summon him to give an account of that which was intended by previous evidence to reflect upon him; but, under those circumstances, he went before the Committee of the House of Commons. The Chairman says, "You have seen some statements that have been made to this Committee upon the subject of a transaction in which your house was engaged; have you any observations to offer upon it?—I received from the Clerk of the Committee a letter accompanying a copy of certain evidences, which are Mr. Macaulay's evidence of the 10th of June, the 14th of June, and the 15th of June; and Captain Hill's evidence of the 29th of June, the 4th of July, and the 6th of July. I would beg first of all to refer to the letter which I had the honour to address to the Chairman. My reason for wishing to be examined before this Committee was, that the statements contained in the evidence which I have mentioned are all of them more or less incorrect, some of them totally so. I will begin by stating what has been the nature of our, I will not say trade, for we have not had a trade ourselves, but of our connexion with the shipment of goods to the coast of Africa. We have been established as merchants for upwards of 70 years in Spain, for nearly 20 years in this country, and we have had connexions to a large extent in Spain, and in the Havannah, and in South America, and several other places; among them we have had connexions or commercial intercourse with the house of Pedro Martinez & Co. of the Havannah, and with Blanco & Cavallo, of Havannah. With them we have carried on a regular business in consignments of sugars and of cochineal, which they have made to us; and in specie received by the packets from Mexico and other places. We have several times acted for them here in this country, buying raw cotton for instance at Liverpool, and re-selling it very largely; that has been principally with Pedro Martinez & Co." "They are general merchants?— They are general merchants, and their transactions with us have been of that nature. As general merchants we have bought stock here for them rather largely; and in the course of those transactions we have received orders from Don Pedro Martinez & Co., of the Havannah, and from Don Pedro Martinez, of Cadiz, to ship goods for the coast of Africa; never from Pedro Blanco, and never from Blanco & Cavallo." "Have you received orders from Pedro Martinez for shipments for the coast of Africa?—Yes, in the course of business we have received orders to ship goods upon the funds in our hands belonging to them, and we have shipped the goods described in the letter, and sent the bills of lading to Pedro Martinez; but, beyond that we have never had any returns from the coast of Africa, nor any control of any kind from the moment the cargoes left the ports of this country." "You have had no interest in the result of the adventure?—No, nor any notice, nor any acquaintance, nor any correspondence with any one upon the coast; we have never had any kind of knowledge, either subsequently or previously, of the shipments, except the mere fact of buying the goods and shipping them."

It is quite correct that they had had communication, as will appear subsequently by evidence in respect of this vessel; they actually received the amount of the insurance on the damaged goods landed at Cadiz. "Your whole interest was a commission upon the transaction?—Entirely. The extent of those transactions has been so limited in the course of nearly 20 years that we have been in this country, that the amount of the invoices that we have sent out has been something like 20,000*l.* or 22,000*l.* in the course of all that time. That is one part of the operations we have performed. The other operations are the acceptance of bills drawn by people on the coast; among them Pedro Blanco when he was there, upon ourselves, on account of Blanco & Cavallo, of Havannah, upon funds which Blanco & Cavallo had in our hands; for instance, the people at the Havannah, or in Spain, open a credit with us, and we accept the bills of the parties on that credit with us just the same as we should do with any other correspondent in any other part." You will hear probably in evidence who this Pedro Blanco was. I shall prove that he was a person extensively engaged in the trade in slaves.

Then the evidence proceeds:—"You would have funds in your hands, arising from some commercial transactions between you and the Havannah merchant or the Cadiz merchant; and Pedro Blanco, upon the coast of Africa would draw upon the credit of those funds, being authorised by the Cadiz or the Havannah merchant?—Yes; and if Pedro Blanco had drawn five shillings beyond that, we should have protested, and in some instances we have protested. With regard to the vessel alluded to in this Report, the Augusta, our part in that concern has been simply that which appears from one of the letters: that is to say, Pedro Martinez, of Cadiz, had made choice of Jennings to buy the vessel, and lent him money to buy the vessel; because Pedro Martinez wanted him to have a vessel in the trade for the purpose of taking his goods to their destination."

Gentlemen, it is always satisfactory in a case of this kind to know, if a person be charged with any offence, as Mr. Zulueta was, that a copy of the evidence is sent to him; and when a person under such circumstances makes a statement, it is satisfactory to know that if that statement be true, it can be perfectly and easily proved by him, that there is no doubt about it. No doubt evidence must be given sufficient to charge the prisoner with the offence before he can be called upon for his defence; but if he makes a statement, it is satisfactory to know that, if there is a defence, it is absolutely in his power. Mr. Zulueta is one of a firm; there is no difficulty therefore in proving all their transactions. If he has letters limiting him to 500*l.*, there are means of proving that beyond all question.

He goes on: "I have now described the three kinds of operations in which we have been concerned, and our knowledge of all of them terminated with the execution of the orders of our correspondents. We had nothing more to do than to follow the orders of the purchaser in shipping the goods. With regard to the purchase of the vessel by Jennings; Jennings is a man who has been employed some time by Martinez; he has served Martinez as a chartered captain, and Martinez having been satisfied with his services, agreed to lend him that money on the security of the vessel, provided it did not exceed a certain amount; which was all the interference we had with it, just to see that a certain amount was not exceeded, 500*l.* or whatever it was." "Then you were to furnish Captain Jennings with money for the purchase within a limited amount, say 500*l.*, credit being given to him upon you by Pedro Martinez, of Cadiz?—That is just the point." There is no doubt, gentlemen, as it would appear, that the letter I have read to you had been published, and was known to Mr. Zulueta, in which he writes and tells Jennings that they will not proceed in the purchase further than 500*l.* Certainly it was not known at that time that we should have the means of showing them that there was in fact no such limit to the purchase adopted, and that that letter could not be used for the purpose, for Mr. Zulueta does actually give 650*l.* for the purchase of that vessel.

He is then asked—"The Augusta being purchased by money advanced by your house for Martinez and Company, of Cadiz; and she then became the property of Pedro Martinez?—No, she became the property of Jennings; the money was lent to Jennings, and he bound himself by giving security on the vessel to answer for the amount. It is a mercantile operation, which is not unusual." If it had been a mere loan and mortgage of the vessel, there can be no doubt of the fact; but it is for you to say whether that is the nature of the transaction. "You advanced the money to Captain Jennings for the purchase of the vessel, Jennings transferring the vessel to you as a security for the amount so advanced?—That is just the description of operation, which is a very general one in business." Then he goes on to describe the transaction: "What is the object of such an operation?—I know very little, or almost next to nothing, of the operations in those parts of the world; but the object of such an operation I apprehend to be this: a vessel chartered with a stranger must be governed by the different clauses of the charter-party; the charterer must be limited to time and to places; and by Martinez having the vessel owned by a man with whom he could have a better understanding than with others, he might always send more advantageously articles from the Havannah to the Gallinas, and from here to the Gallinas. When I say articles, I mean legal articles." "What advantage would there be in Mr. Jennings taking the articles rather as the owner than as captain under Martinez; was not he commander of the vessel as well as owner of the vessel?—Yes." "He is made the owner, instead of being captain?—He is the owner as well as the captain of the vessel; he stands indebted to Martinez, and gives a bottomry bond for the vessel." Gentlemen, the documents I have offered to you, which are the charter-party and the other papers relating to the vessel, do not amount to a bottomry bond; if there was one, there can be no difficulty in the prisoner proving it to you.

Then he is asked: "Does Mr. Jennings upon this transaction make all the freight to his own profit?—Certainly; whatever he does is to his own profit." That certainly was not the fact; for he was obliged to give up the vessel whenever called upon. "He is not, then, an agent for Martinez?—No, he is a person to whom Martinez lends the money to buy the vessel; whatever profit he derives is his own. Martinez has this advantage, which to a mercantile man is very perceptible, that he has got a charter with a man who stands in that relation towards him which gives him a sort of control over the vessel. If I, as a stranger, charter a vessel for Martinez, and he has spent one, two, or five days more in landing goods than the charter-party allows, I should make a claim for it; I should say, 'You must keep to the charter.' Now, when Jennings is indebted to him for the favour of a loan for the vessel, he is not upon a similar footing." "So that he gets the vessel more under his own control?—Yes; in saying this I am putting an hypothetical case, but I do not know the mind of Martinez himself."

Then he is asked: "You acted in this transaction merely as agent in the usual manner, as you would have acted for any house in any part of the world?—Exactly; if Martinez had told me, 'You have got 500l. in your hands, pay that to Captain Jennings,' I should have known nothing more of the transaction; I should have paid the money. But Martinez did not wish to go beyond a certain amount; and he says, 'You exercise control, do not allow the man to pay more than 500l. for the vessel.'" Gentlemen, the letter treats it as a purchase for Zulueta. There may or may not be those directions; if there were, it is in his power to prove them; and it should be recollected that there was not time to get fresh instructions after the declaration that he could not exceed 500l. before he paid 650l. for it: it is only in a few days. If a man says, when charged with theft, "I bought the goods of such a person," that is no evidence at all, unless, he proves that he bought them, which he may easily do if it is the fact. So here, if the prisoner says, though this letter, which purports to be the letter of instructions for the actual purchase, limits it to 500*l.*, I received directions from Martinez to purchase at 650*l.*, that is proved with perfect facility, for it must be by letter, and there are other persons in the firm who can prove it for him. "But beyond the purchase of the vessel and the shipment of the goods, the other arrangements and the subsequent transactions were entirely between Jennings and Martinez & Co.?—Most assuredly; except with the order of Martinez, I do not know how we could have done any thing with him in any way." That of course will be proved.

Then it goes on: "Though the process of hypothecating a vessel may be usual between British merchants, is it usual to cover a transaction of Spanish slave trade with the British flag, by means of such an arrangement as that described to have taken place in the case of the Augusta?—In order to answer that question, it seems to me that it is fair that I should ask where is the transaction of covering, and where is the slave trade transaction? I know positively of my own knowledge that there is no such thing at all connected with the Augusta. If I had an opportunity, I could make my affidavit of that." He is asked again: "Do you mean that you know that the Augusta was not engaged in any slaving transactions during the voyage upon which she left Liverpool?—Most assuredly not; in fact my testimony is hardly required of that, because every thing proves that. When she was detained, it was never said that she was upon a slaving operation at all. Before she left this port, after she was bought, she was completely rendered useless for that purpose." Now leagers and things of that kind must be taken to pieces, for she would not be allowed to have those on board; but the staves forming them were left on board in a state in which they might very soon have been made ready for use. When the question comes, whether she was engaged in a slave trading transaction, you are to examine the grounds of the prisoner's denial with reference to the other parts of the testimony, and how far that can be relied upon.

This question is then put: "The charge is, that she was engaged in carrying goods to a person engaged in the slave trade; not that she was engaged in the slave trade herself?—I most certainly say, that I do not know whether the person is so engaged or not." "Is it usual to cover a transaction of Spanish trade with the English flag?—I am not aware that a Spanish merchant is prohibited chartering an English vessel." No doubt a Spanish merchant is not; but if an Englishman knows that that vessel is being chartered for a slave trading transaction, and he is one of the persons chartering her for that purpose, I have no hesitation in stating that he is guilty under this Act of Parliament, for he is chartering a vessel to accomplish that illegal object; and if merchants in this country would not accept bills drawn by slave traders, if they would not send goods from this country to be employed for the purpose—in fact, the trade could not be carried on at all. Then he is asked:

"But is it lawful to employ the British flag to cover a vessel that is not owned by a British subject?—I say that that vessel is owned by a British subject." "By whom?—By Captain Jennings." It is for you to say whether that is a covert, or a *bonâ fide* ownership. "Was not the money with which she was purchased, the money of Pedro Martinez—It seems to me that English captains and English subjects are not prohibited from borrowing money from Spaniards; she was bought with money lent by Pedro Martinez to Captain Jennings for the purpose." Of course there can be no difficulty in showing that that was lent by persons connected with that firm, if it is true; if it is not true, of course it will not be shown.

Then he is asked: "Do you mean that the money was a loan to Captain Jennings, at the time he paid it for the vessel?—It was a loan to Captain Jennings." "Do you mean that the ship was then Captain Jennings's property?—It was." "Was it in his power to sell that ship at any port he pleased?—There was a mortgage upon the vessel." "You have stated that yours is an agency trade?—It is so, and in the multitude of business, any one can understand that 20,000*l.* in 15 or 20 years, can only be a mere trifle in the business of any merchant, without laying claim to a large business; and in following that business, we have executed shipping orders." "To what part of the coast of Africa has that business been chiefly conducted?—I believe almost exclusively to the Gallinas." I believe you will find the Gallinas is simply a slave trading place, and nothing else. "Have the goods that Mr. Martinez has ordered to be sent to the Gallinas, been all sent to the same individual?—No, to different individuals; sometimes to Pedro Blanco, who was for a certain time an agent of Pedro Martinez on the coast, and sometimes we have sent a bill of lading drawn in this way to order; we have sent it to Pedro Martinez as a voucher against his account." "Do you know the nature of the trade of Pedro Martinez at the Gallinas?—I know from general report that Don Pedro Martinez himself is supposed to deal in slaves, and I believe it is so." All his goods have been sent to the Gallinas. "Is he known at the Havannah as a dealer in slaves?—I do not know; but I believe so. I do not know why it should not be known at the Havannah, if it is known in other parts." "Is a ship which is hypothecated liable to be foreclosed at any moment at the discretion of the mortgagee?—It depends altogether upon the terms of the mortgage. If the mortgagee says, 'You must give me the money when I ask for it,' of course he must sell the vessel if he has not got any thing else." Read on in the same way this document, "but he is not bound to give the money in any shape or form." "He would always have to deduct whatever freight had been earned. When the security may be called upon to be effective, depends upon the nature of the transaction between the parties." "Your house had nothing to do with any letters that might be put on board the Augusta after she sailed from this country?—Nothing whatever." "The Augusta was seized on the coast of Africa on the charge of slave trading?—I believe that was the case." "Did you not appeal against that condemnation?—Yes, there is an appeal by the owner." "Before the Privy Council?—Yes." "That appeal is not yet decided?—I believe not." "You stated that your transactions with Africa for Martinez have amounted to about 20,000*l.* in 15 or 20 years. What has been the amount of your whole transactions with Blanco and Martinez of the Havannah during that period?—Perhaps 100,000*l.* or a larger sum. For instance, we have received more than 40 or 50 cargoes of sugar from the Havannah consigned to us, and cigars; and we have received bills of lading of specie, shipped at Mexico, to be sold here, and bar gold, and things of that sort." "Have you reason to suppose that the whole of that large commerce is subservient to the carrying on of the slave trade by the house of Blanco & Martinez at the Havannah?—I do not know; I know that they have large transactions in general business. I know that a short time ago I got 40,000*l.* or 50,000*l.* of Spanish bonds in the market for Martinez. I know that he is a large speculator in Spanish bonds and in securities of state." "Is that speculating in Spanish bonds on account of the house at Cadiz, or the house at Havannah?—Speaking technically, I should say it was on account of the Cadiz house." "The question related to the commerce of the Havannah house?—Pedro Martinez is a Havannah merchant. But with regard to Havannah merchants, we have received large consignments of sugar, cochineal, and sometimes Mexican goods, brought to Havannah, and shipped to us here." "In what course of business have the proceeds of those consignments been disposed of; have they gone in sending supplies to the coast of Africa?—Out of that large amount of money 22,000*l.* is the amount of all the goods that we have sent to the coast of Africa in 20 years." "Of all descriptions?—Of all sorts and kinds; I have gone through the invoice-book and found them out." "Have the proceeds generally been disposed of by drafts from the parties themselves to your house?—By the parties at Havannah, when the exchange turns to their advantage." "Have you reason to suppose that a large portion of the trade that they carry on at the Havannah is the slave trade?—I had no reason to know any thing of the kind; I have known more of their transactions with the slave trade since these things have been mooted than I ever knew before; I have had more knowledge of these things lately than I ever had in my life before; and when I say 'I,' I beg to state that I ought to state 'we,' for all my partners are in the same situation." "Have you been employed by the house at the Havannah to ship manufactured goods from this country to Havannah, suitable for the African trade?—We have sometimes shipped goods to the Havannah of the same kind as those that were in the Augusta; cotton goods and other things of that sort." "Has that been recently?—In the course of our operations." "How many years ago?—In the course of these 15 or 20 years that we have been engaged in business with them; all that I could see in a moment by my books." "Have you sent any goods of that description to the Havannah recently?—Not very recently; I think not for some years." "Have you sent any goods of that description since you first began to send goods out direct to the coast of Africa?—They have been mixed; I cannot draw a distinction between the two destinations; some have gone to the Havannah, some to the Gallinas." "Have those supplies of English manufactured goods, which heretofore went to the Havannah, to be used there for promoting the slave trade, been more recently sent direct from this country to the coast of Africa?—No, I do not think that is the case; I should think the contrary is more likely to be the case; but I think we have shipped in some months, or in some years, partly to the Havannah, and partly to the Gallinas."

Then comes a statement as to the mode of carrying on the trade, which will be read to you, but I do not think it necessary to read it now. "Have you shipped English manufactured goods direct to the coast of Africa, on behalf of both those houses?—Such goods as were in the Augusta, I have shipped for one party only. With regard to the house of Blanco & Carvalho, and the house of Pedro Martinez & Co., with both of them I have carried on a general large business. But to Blanco & Carvalho I never shipped a single piece of goods of any kind, except some sugar mills to the Havannah; and with regard to the house of Pedro Martinez, we have shipped such goods as those by the Augusta." "From your general knowledge of the trade of the house of Pedro Martinez & Co., is it your opinion that the goods which you so shipped to the coast of Africa were destined to be employed in the slave trade?—I do not know, they may be for any thing that I know."

Now, gentlemen, I would humbly submit, that if they have that reason to know, that they do believe that the goods are so employed, and if they send the goods, it is not for them to shut their eyes and say, "I do not know." It is like the case where a person receives stolen goods and no questions are asked, and he gives money in exchange for them. Such a person is as much guilty of receiving stolen goods, as if the person who brought them told him the fact. As to hundreds of persons whom you try for receiving stolen goods, they do not know, they cannot know positively that they are taken out of such a house; but they are delivered to them in such a way, or are concealed in such a way, that there is no doubt they were dishonestly come by, and that is as good evidence as if they had known where they were stolen. So it is not enough for a person to say, "I do not know; they may not for aught I know." If he believes, and you are satisfied that he must have been aware of the fact, then the case is clear; it is no defence to say, "I shut my eyes, and do not know; they may be for aught I know."

Then it is asked: "Has it come within your knowledge that the house of Martinez & Co. are exporters from Africa of the native produce of Africa?— No, because I never tried to get any knowledge of their transactions there of any sort." "Have you ever received consignments from them, or on their behalf of palm oil, gold dust, or ivory, from the coast of Africa?—Never; we never have received any thing from the coast of Africa whatever. With regard to all these transactions, it will perhaps appear strange to the Committee, that I should not know more of the coast of Africa, having shipped things there; but if we had shipped to the amount of 100,000*l.* to the coast of Africa, or carried on any considerable trade there, we should certainly have known more about the coast of Africa; but in transactions of a very large amount, an invoice occasionally of about 2,000*l.* or 3,000*l.* of goods was a thing that we sent as a matter of course, and did not trouble our heads about, especially as the remuneration we got was a mere trifle, not of itself worth pursuing, if it had not been for the general business we had."

Then the question is put: "Is there any other part of the evidence which has been given that you wish to observe upon?" and he answers, "It is asked here in question 5086, 'Who was he?' the answer is, 'The name is mentioned in the Parliamentary Papers as being connected with the purchase of a slave vessel, Mr. Kidd; and it is mentioned in connexion with that of Mr. Zulueta, of London.' Now, as to Mr. Kidd, the very first thing I ever knew or ever heard of his name was to see it here. I never heard of his name at all. I never had a letter from him or through him, or knew any thing of the man whatever. That is with regard to myself. With regard to my partners, I can say the same; I have been making inquiries about it. My father knew there was such a man upon the coast, but I did not know even that, though I have managed all this business. Our house never had a letter from the man, or knew any thing about him." Then it is asked, "You have no connexion with Mr. Kidd in any way?—No, nor any knowledge of him. Then in the next answer it is said, 'Zulueta, the gentleman in London, to whom the vessel was sent, and who sold her again to her former Spanish owner, is a name well known on the coast in connexion with the slave trade?' Now what is known on the coast I really cannot pretend to say, but I believe that not many persons can say that which I can say, that neither myself, nor my father, nor my grandfather, nor any body in our firm, has ever had any kind of interest of any sort, or derived any emolument or connexion from the slave trade. My father had at one time an interest in a bankrupt's estate at the Havannah, upon which he was a creditor. There were some slaves on the estate, and they formed part of the property assignable to the creditors, and my father got the slaves assigned to him; because the other gentlemen and the creditors were not of the same opinion, he got them assigned to him, and made them free; and that is all the connexion we have ever had with any slaves in the world. I do not know how far that may be considered irrelevant to the point, but I state it because we are here mentioned three or four times as connected with slave dealers, as a name well known in connexion with the slave trade. That sort of statement is rather a difficult thing to deal with." "If it is meant to insinuate by these observations that you ever had any other connexion with the slave trade, than being the shipping agent of goods which were sent to a man who was a dealer in slaves, you entirely deny it?—I assure the Committee, that although I have a general notion as to what interest Blanco and Martinez have in slaves, yet, if I was put upon my oath to make any particular statement, I really could not, because I do not know it. Of course I believe it; but my personal knowledge amounts only to that which the knowledge of what we read in a newspaper amounts to."

Now, gentlemen, we know too the trade of these parties in the Gallinas. If the prisoner believed that these goods were sent out for the purpose of carrying on the slave trade, and he did send them out, and you are satisfied that the name of Jennings was used as a mere cover, and the whole affair shows his knowledge, then I apprehend he is guilty within this indictment; and it is no defence to say, "If I were put upon my oath, I could not swear that the parties were slave dealers, because I do not know it." If these goods were sent out in order to accomplish the trading or dealing in slaves, if that was the object of it, the statute says it is criminal, and the party is liable to punishment, for that is all that is ever done in England: the parties who engage in the actual transactions must necessarily reside in Africa. What was meant to be prevented, was the sending any thing out from this coast that could be so used. It is not sufficient to say, "I believe these might be used for the purpose of slave trading:" that would not affect him.

Then he is asked, "There was nothing upon the face of the transactions which you had with those parties, which spoke of a connexion with traffic in slaves?—Nothing whatever." Why, would any human being believe that there would be any thing said of the kind? That would of course be kept secret. The vessel would not reach her destination, if it was avowed that she was going out for the purpose of slave trading. "It is well known, that, fifty years ago, it was in the ordinary course of business in Cadiz to insure operations in slave trading. My house at that time were underwriters, and it was notorious that a policy of that kind would never enter the doors of our house; and nobody would come to offer such a thing to us upon any terms. It is notorious, both here and in Spain, that we set our faces distinctly against having any interest of any kind in the slave trade."

Then it is put as a question: "It is further stated, 'It appears that it is a regular thing sending vessels to him, that is to Mr. Zulueta; if they come to England to him, he sends them to Cadiz, and they get out again to the Havannah and come again into the trade.' Have you any observation to make upon that?— It is all untrue, the whole of it; I never received a vessel from those gentlemen; there has been nothing of the kind."

The question is: "Have you any thing further to state upon the subject?—There are several things I have marked; for instance, such as this, 'You are not bound to suppose that a man will make a bad use of that which he purchases.' If I wished to put my statement upon that footing, I should have done with it in a moment, for I knew nothing of the use they were put to. I bought goods, but as to what use was made of them I knew nothing whatever. But that is not the position which I wish to assume. It is said here, that we sent goods or vessels to Pedro Blanco. To that I say, that we never sent either goods or vessels to Pedro Blanco." Now that is certainly very extraordinary, for a very little while before, when the question was put to him, "Have the goods that Mr. Martinez has ordered to be sent to the Gallinas been all sent to the same individual?" he answered "No, to different individuals, sometimes to Pedro Blanco, who was for a certain time an agent of Pedro Martinez." Then here he says, "We never sent goods or vessels to Pedro Blanco." "In answer to Question 5474, it is said by Mr. Macaulay, 'I stated, that it appears that it is a regular thing sending vessels to him, that is to Mr. Zulueta; if they come to England to him he sends them to Cadiz, and they get out again to the Havannah and come again into the trade. My answer was intended to describe only the course of that particular transaction, and not to apply to any other case.' I never received a single vessel from the coast of Africa at any time, nor any body for us." "Then that statement is entirely untrue?—Totally, from beginning to end; we never did so; and nobody for us, and nobody to our knowledge, or with our connivance; I deny it in the most distinct manner. In answer to Question 5487, Mr. Macaulay is asked, 'Have you any thing further to say with regard to the connexion of Zulueta with the slave trade?' The answer is, 'I would refer to his connexion with the Gollupchik, which was lately captured. In that case it appeared that the vessel went out direct to the Gallinas from London.' That is the same vessel as the Augusta, which I have already explained; it formerly bore the name of Gollupchik." Then the Chairman says, "Have you been concerned in the purchase of vessels frequently for Pedro Martinez or Pedro Blanco?—We have sometimes bought such vessels here as we could resell at the Havannah, such as the Arrogante, which we have bought." "Upon orders?—Partly on orders, and sometimes on our own account on speculation." "For what particular trade were they calculated when they reached the Havannah?—I think for the same trade which they were calculated for when they were sold here." "For the conveyance of merchandise?" The answer is, "As well as anything else. They were sold here publicly." There is no doubt that vessels which are fitted for carrying goods may also be adapted for carrying slaves. Then Mr. *Forster* asks the question, "If it was legal for them to be sold here, you considered that it was legal for you to buy them?—I never had any doubt of the legality of buying here, or of selling them again afterwards." "Mr. *Wood*. But the questions appertaining to the carrying on of the slave trade do not confine themselves within strictly legal grounds, but they have other more important considerations attaching to them?—As to that point there may be a difference of opinion; I would be very sorry indeed, for the sake of catching the approval of other persons, to make a disclaimer of any particular set of opinions whatever; but I believe the only point with which the Committee have to do, is the legal point. As to the moral point, it seems to me, that I am to judge of that; upon that point, I think I have stated quite enough, having stated distinctly that I never had any connexion, nor derived any profit from the slave trade whatever."

There are then several questions: in answer to which he states, "That he never had any thing to do with slave transactions." Those I leave to my learned friend to read. Then question 10451 is, "Had you ever employed Jennings before?—Jennings had had charge of vessels before, chartered by Martinez, and hence the connexion between Martinez and Jennings. There are some captains in all trades that make a great deal of difficulty about every thing, and others that do not; of course merchants like to deal with those that do not, more than those that do." Then the Chairman says: "It would appear from Question 5087, that your name is supposed to have been mentioned in a Parliamentary Paper as connected with a slave trade transaction. Will you refer to page 38, in Class B, Paper of 1839 and 1840, which is the place referred to in the answer, and see if there is any trace of your name in that transaction?—I do not find my own name there; I only find an allusion at the bottom to the name of Pedro Martinez, but in a manner in no way connected with me, and stating a circumstance which I never knew. In Question 7965*, it is stated, 'The Augusta had touched at Cadiz on her way out from England?'—The answer is, 'Yes, and landed part of her cargo at Cadiz, although it was consigned to be delivered at Gallinas.' Now Captain Hill, who has given this answer, must have known why she touched at Cadiz, and why she discharged part of her cargo; for it must be in the log-book of the vessel. It was because she was nearly wrecked in her passage; she put into Cadiz in distress; and there she landed a part of her cargo, which was tobacco which was rotten, and sold for the benefit of the underwriters. Now that has not been stated here; but I think Captain Hill must have known it, because it is in the log-book of the vessel which he took." "And the log-book he must have read?—I should think so; because if he has not done that he has done nothing. All I mean to say is, that it is an *ex parte* statement." "It was not intended when she left England that she should put into Cadiz?—Most certainly not; all the facts of the case show that she went there because she was obliged. I have not seen the log-book, but it must be there; because in the log-book the captain is bound to enter those things, and whoever captured the vessel must have seen the log-book of course. In answer to Question 7967*, it is said, 'Messrs. Zulueta must be aware that it is contrary to law to act as agents, or otherwise, for the shipment of goods that are to be employed in the slave trade; they were bound to do nothing illegal; they are merchants residing in England, and they must conform themselves to the laws of England, and they cannot by the laws of England plead ignorance of those laws.' Now I and my partners are British subjects, and therefore we are bound by the law, and we must obey the law; and I say that to endeavour to elude the law is criminal in my estimation of things. In the answer to Question 7970*, it is stated, 'I have endeavoured to be particular in making it appear that this vessel was chartered to a place where there were no constituted authorities.' I think that in the Gallinas there are constituted authorities. It is the first time that I ever heard that it is illegal for any merchant to ship goods for any places without ascertaining beforehand whether there are constituted authorities there. I believe that if they like to send goods to any place they may do it; and as to the fact of there being constituted authorities in the place or not, I do not see what that has to do with the question; besides, there have been such things as treaties made with persons at the Gallinas, so that there must be some constituted authorities there. But I do not know why I should be called upon to know whether there are constituted authorities at the port or not. Then it is stated, in answer to Question 7971*, 'As far as I am able to give my own opinion, I believe that Messrs. Zulueta were perfectly criminal; at least they had a knowledge of what they were doing. I think I am borne out in that by the secrecy they have endeavoured to pursue in putting in a false owner.'" Then in answer to that observation Mr. Zulueta says, "I have answered all that before: I state again, that all the secrecy and mystery of the thing lies in supposing other things different from what appear. Then it is said, 'In fact there can be no want of evidence to show that Messrs. Zulueta had for a length of time been agents to slave dealers.' Mr. Blanco and Mr. Martinez may have been engaged, as I have stated, in slave operations; and I have stated that we conducted their general business here."

Mr. *Forster* then asks: "Is not Pedro Blanco a partner in a commercial house at the Havannah, who are general merchants?—Yes, I have stated that before."

"Captain *Fitzroy*.] Have you ever discounted any bill drawn by Pedro Blanco on Pedro Martinez & Co. for goods delivered for them on the African coast at the Gallinas?—I have accepted bills drawn by Pedro Blanco and others from the Gallinas upon our house, and paid them to the order of several houses in Sierra Leone and houses in London. I have paid them in money that I had in my hands resulting from the general transactions of business which I have explained. But discounting would be this, if I had paid those acceptances before they were due, and received some consideration for them; that I never did, but I might have done it in the case of these bills." "Were those bills negotiated through your hands in payment of goods delivered at the Gallinas?—No; they were drawn generally with the advice attached to them, saying, I have drawn a thousand pounds upon you for account of Blanco and Carvalho, or Blanco & Co., at the Havannah.

"Mr. *Wood*.] By whose orders were you desired to honour it; was it by the order of Pedro Blanco at the Gallinas?—No; by the house at the Havannah, or by the house at Cadiz; sometimes the one and sometimes the other. Blanco had a house some time ago in Malaga, as a general merchant, occupied in shipping the fruits of the country and oil to the United States, &c. &c. In answer to Question 7961*, the following is stated:—'In one of these letters, dated Cadiz, 30th of November, 1840, is a paragraph to the following effect:—In a letter, dated London, the 21st instant, which I have just received from Messrs. Zulueta & Co., merchants in London, I had the pleasure of receiving a bill drawn by you on them for 250*l*., which I this day place to their credit, waiting your advice of the same.' There is here certainly a mistranslation of some kind, because it says that this man receives a bill upon us, and credits it to us, which is, of course, contradictory in the very terms of it; because, if the bill was remitted to this man upon us, he would have debited it to us, and not credited it."—I believe it is perfectly consistent when the letter is produced.—"But altogether there is some confusion about it; I suppose arising from the mistranslation of the documents, because the fact is this, the bill is one of the bills I have already mentioned, drawn from the Gallinas upon ourselves, to the order of a third party. It is a bill drawn at the Gallinas upon ourselves, on account of the credit, and therefore it could never have been received by the person in Cadiz." That would be explained by a former answer, in which he says, he had sometimes sent bills of lading on which he had accepted a bill drawn from him on the Gallinas, and sent it to the house at Cadiz. He would have just said, This is a bill drawn upon me from Gallinas; I have accepted the bill, and placed it to your credit.

Question 10459 is: "Can you give the Committee any information upon this: 'The other letters,' nine of them, 'were all on slave business: not a word of any innocent trade, but the whole directing how slaves were to be shipped on board various vessels.' How do you account for this vessel carrying letters upon slave business?—I account for it in this way. First of all, it is impossible for us to answer here what letters will be put on board a vessel at Cadiz; but there is very seldom any communication between Cadiz and the Gallinas; whatever letters there were must have gone by such random occasions as arose. As to the fact that whoever wrote those letters is engaged in the slave trade, the letters will speak for themselves."

"*Chairman*.] Those letters were not prepared in the expectation of the arrival of this vessel, because this vessel was not destined to that port, and was only driven there by stress of weather?—Most certainly. I will add one circumstance in proof of that. The vessel was supposed to have been lost, from the circumstance of a boat having been found upon the coast with the name of T. Jennings upon it, and it was supposed that it was a boat belonging to the vessel; it was, in fact, a boat from the vessel, but the vessel had not been lost; therefore the vessel was quite unexpected in Cadiz by every soul. It went there from stress of weather and nothing more. Then it is said in answer to Question 7972*, 'I think the papers are quite conclusive to the mind of any man that Zulueta was cognizant of what he was doing; but as far as it is an illegal transaction, it is not for me to judge; but the Judge of the Vice-Admiralty Court of Sierra Leone did think it illegal, and condemned the vessel; and moreover, the man who is put forward as captain and owner did not defend the vessel on her trial.' Now, as to the statement of his being a false owner, I have already stated that he was not. But then, again, with regard to the other part of the business, the man did not defend it, because he was prevented from defending it."

With respect to the first part of that answer—it is stated that she put into Cadiz from stress of weather—the evidence I shall lay before you is, that when she received injury from the weather (and there is no doubt there was a storm), she was within two days sail of Cork, and 18 or 19 days from Cadiz. The crew actually resisted; they did not mutiny, but they opposed going to Cadiz; and it was only on his making the arrangement that those persons should be discharged at Cadiz, that they consented to go on. My version, therefore, of the affair is, that she put into Cadiz, not from stress of weather, but from other reasons. Ultimately she got there, and there were certain letters put on board there when she was fortunate enough to get there, addressed to Martinez & Co., who were engaged in this transaction, who, according to appearance, were actually charterers of the vessel for Zulueta & Co., who gave directions where those goods that were on board were to go.

It appears that there was an objection to answer the question at the moment, on whom the bills were drawn, and it was deferred to the following day. On the next day he appeared again, when the Chairman says, "The Committee understand that you have some further observations to make upon the evidence which has been given with reference to your house?" The answer is, "With reference to the destination of the Augusta, from Liverpool to Gallinas, and the fact of its having put into Cadiz unforeseen, and unpremeditated altogether, in consequence of stress of weather, I omitted to mention a circumstance which will put the thing beyond doubt, and it is this: an insurance was made at Lloyd's from Liverpool to the Gallinas, and it is well known that, of course, we should have forfeited the insurance by going to any other port, except from the peril of the sea; and the British consul at Cadiz is well aware of the circumstance, because he is Lloyd's agent there; and therefore he had to interfere in the whole proceeding; without his sanction nothing could have been done. We have called upon the underwriters upon that account, and it has been paid, and which would not have been paid without its being proved. I stated yesterday that the transactions of my house with Pedro Martinez & Co. of the Havannah, with Blanco & Carvalho of the Havannah, and with Pedro Martinez of Cadiz, had amounted in the 20 years to 100,000*l.* I was afraid of over rating the amount, but on reference to the books of the house, I find that our transactions with them in 20 years have amounted to 400,000*l.*, out of which the 22,000*l.* that was mentioned is the whole amount of goods that have been shipped by their orders for the coast of Africa." No doubt, gentlemen, that is a very serious answer when you have this fact as coming within general knowledge: it was stated that beyond doubt they dealt in slaves, and that the whole amount of exports from Africa, as arising out of transactions to the amount of 400,000*l.* is stated to be 22,000*l.*; and that amount of goods from Africa would, no doubt, be in repayment for the same transactions. "Can you state how much of the 22,000*l.* has accrued within any given period; is it distributed equally over the whole 20 years, or has it grown up in the last four or five years?— In the last few years it has decreased, but otherwise it is spread over the whole number of years. In such a length of time it forms to our minds a mere speck. In the last six months our transactions with the house of Pedro Martinez of Cadiz amount to already 30,000*l.*, and with Pedro Martinez of the Havannah, to nearly the same amount. With the house of Pedro Blanco & Co. of the Havannah, the amount has been 15,000*l.* for what has passed in the last six months, and with the houses generally at Cuba, throughout the island, it amounts to 100,000*l.* altogether, arising entirely from cargoes of sugar, and from tobacco, and remittance of bills from there in carrying on banking operations, upon which they draw again, which are negotiated in the Havannah and sent to houses in London to cash, and remittances of drafts on the Spanish treasury at the Havannah, and bills of lading of specie and bullion, and such things from Mexico. I state these things only to show the nature of our trade, and I have been particular, because as these are large amounts I wish to show what they arise from. Another fact escaped my attention yesterday, and it is this, that Don Pedro Martinez is owner of several large vessels of 300 tons and 400 tons, which are in the trade of sugar, tobacco, and such things, with us, in England and with Cadiz." I believe the cargo on board the Augusta was worth about 5,000*l.*; I do not know whether this may be considered as part of this or not; you will judge whether they are to be attributed or not to Captain Jennings. Then he says, he has bought other vessels:—"There was the Star, Captain Jennings. That vessel was sent from here to the Gallinas, precisely the same as the Augusta has been sent. She delivered her cargo; she went from thence to Cape Coast, I believe, and from there to Madeira; she received a cargo of wheat; she came back to Spain, and she was sold at Liverpool to a third party, not Martinez, or any body connected with him; in fact, she was sold for very little. The object of that vessel was just the same as the Augusta, to maintain a legal trade with Gallinas; that is within my own knowledge."

"Mr. *Aldam*.] What is the description of legal trade that was carried on?—Sending out goods to be sold at those places, and to go to other ports, not to carry any cargo from there to the Havannah." "There has been a good deal of evidence, in which it has been stated that no legal trade is carried on with Gallinas?—I could not say what trade there is at the Gallinas of a legal nature; but I know that those vessels would have taken nothing, if there was nothing legal to take, from that place to the Havannah, or to any other place; I am aware that my answers upon this point must be deficient, because I am really very ignorant of the trade of the West Coast of Africa." "Do you suppose that the vessels would be used to carry on a legal trade?—Most certainly I do; because persons find it worth while to send goods there constantly. The Committee will observe, that what the application of the goods is afterwards I cannot say, but I speak of the fact of the vessels having gone there with the intention of returning to the Havannah to bring a cargo of some description here, to pay a freight, and then to go again with the same kind of goods to Africa."

"*Chairman*.] You have stated before, that you have cleared out for the Gallinas from Liverpool?—Yes." "In carrying on operations of that kind, should you have ever thought it necessary to exercise any disguise as to what part of Africa you were clearing out for?—Not at all." "You did not imagine, that in being the instrument of sending lawful goods to any part of Africa you were doing any thing which required concealment?—Nothing at all of the kind; and the proof of that is, that in the bills of entry in Liverpool any body could see our names as consignees of the vessel, and see entries made in our own names of every thing."

Gentlemen, no doubt this is most important, and if this had been—it is for you to say whether it was—but if it had been a legal trade, would it not have appeared in the ship's papers that this had been shipped by Messrs. Zulueta the charterers, and consigned to Mr. Martinez? In all this statement it is said, that it is beyond all question that this was not a transaction which ought to be concealed, for that their name would not have appeared in the cockets, the bill of lading, and every thing connected with it. Now, the fact is, that their name does not appear, for it only appears as shipped by Thomas Jennings. Now, Thomas Jennings is the captain; he makes a contract with Zulueta; he is not the person who ships the things; but in all the ship's papers, and every thing connected with them, it all appears as shipped by Jennings, and their name is not introduced from beginning to end. "Is not there a document, officially published daily in London and at Liverpool, stating the daily entries at the Custom-house of all goods shipped, with the description of the goods, and the name of the port and of the shipper?—Yes, there is."

I am not aware of any such; but there is none with Mr. Zulueta's name as the shipper on this vessel. "Is not this printed from time to time in the public papers?—It is in general circulation; there is hardly any merchant in Liverpool or in London who is not possessed of one. The Liverpool entries are reprinted in London, Liverpool being such an important place of business. The bill printed in London contains also Liverpool, Hull, and Bristol." "So that every such transaction is perfectly notorious to every one?—Notorious to every one who chooses to read the public papers. There is another thing which escaped me till I came into the room this morning. As I have been in the business from my childhood, I know every thing that is going on an it. The Arrogante, after we sold her at the Havannah, was sent to Vera Cruz with a cargo of Spanish paper, spirits, raisins, &c., such as is sent for the South American trade, for the purpose of breaking the blockade of Vera Cruz, which she did break and went in. It was asked in Question 7147, whether the Augusta was equipped for the slave trade the second time; the answer was, 'She was not.' I wish to state, that before any goods were put on board of her, it was our express wish and order that every thing in her that was fit for that trade should be taken down, and the vessel put in the same condition as any other merchant vessel; and we should not have loaded any thing in her if that had not been done." Beyond all question: she could not have gone out of the port of Liverpool if that had not been done; if she had been fitted up as a slave trader, she would have been seized before she went out of the port of Liverpool. "It is stated in the evidence that the Augusta was consigned to three notorious slave dealers; now we had never in our lives heard of the name of any one of the parties to whom she was consigned." That is a most extraordinary thing. You will see how that is, if the letters are put in. Here are persons shipping to the Gallinas for two years; there are five persons there who are slave dealers, and nothing else; the prisoner has consigned goods there for twenty years, and yet he has never known the names of three of them as slave dealers. There is a difficulty in that answer, because he does not remember their names before he sent goods to them. He is asked, "You mean that the first time you heard their names was when the order to ship those goods was given to you?—Yes, and the circumstance of three consignees is a regular thing with distant consignments, such as South America and Africa. There is such an uncertainty attending the residence of parties in those places, that we invariably put a second and a third consignee in addition, in case the first should not be in the way." Then Mr. *Forster* says, "Some bills were referred to in your former evidence drawn by Mr. Pedro Blanco upon your house; have you any objection to put those bills before the Committee?—Not any. And I ought to state now, as I have been looking at the bills more closely, that they are not all drawn to the orders of Sierra Leone houses, but to the orders of other Spaniards, and those people endorsed them to the Sierra

Leone houses. This does not alter the case materially, but for the sake of accuracy I mention it." "You will put them in for the inspection of the Committee?—Certainly.—(*The same were delivered in.*)" Then it is said, "You only hesitated in giving the names yesterday from motives of delicacy, not from any motive of concealment?—Yes, I do not wish to withhold any thing; but I am indisposed to introduce any name. I have no wish to conceal any thing whatever. I have been consulting with my partners upon this subject, and I have a request to make to the Committee. Our position is one which is certainly an unpleasant one. I think that what I have stated will have proved to the satisfaction of the Committee that we have not in any way intended to elude the law." Then there is a suggestion that it is not necessary I should state to you, that if there is any difficulty a new Act of Parliament should pass.

Gentlemen, I have read to you, I believe, every word of the statement of Mr. Zulueta which is material to the question. I wished to read it, because I wish that there should not be the slightest possible ground for stating that I conceal any thing which he had stated in his own favour. You are perfectly aware, that where you put in the statement of any person against him, you take it all; you examine into the truth of that which is said in his own favour, and the truth of that which makes against him; you examine the correctness or incorrectness of the whole from this. It will be for you to say, how far you are satisfied that he had the means of knowing, and did know, that Pedro Martinez was a slave trader, dealing in slaves at the Gallinas. If you gather from this that he knew it, then the next question you will have to decide will be,—Was this vessel going to the Gallinas for the purpose of supplying the dealers with goods, the materials for carrying on their business, and the materials for the use of the slaves while in that situation? for there is no doubt that that will be an offence within this Act of Parliament. You are to say, whether he did know it or not. The goods sent were partly iron pots used for boiling their rice while in barracoons. Then there are other goods fit for barter with reference to the exchange of slaves, that being, as far as any evidence can be laid before you, the only trade carried on at that place: you will say, whether they were intended to be used for that trade. The question is, Do you know of any other trade in the Gallinas but the slave trade? The prisoner did not know of any other trade; he did not pretend to know of any other. Gentlemen, undoubtedly you cannot look into the mind of any one; you must judge from the facts; and therefore one material question you will have to decide is, Was this trade carried on in the way in which a person would carry on a trade who knew it to be of such a nature—was it carried on *bonâ fide*, or with a most careful concealment of the name of Zulueta throughout the whole of this transaction? If you find there was concealment, you must undoubtedly, as far as you are able, ascertain whether there was a guilty knowledge. If a prisoner had been charged with receiving goods knowing them to be stolen, and it appeared that he had concealed them in the way in which an honest man would not, that is evidence; so if you are satisfied there was a course of concealment, and that the name of Jennings, the man who knew of the affair, was used to cover these goods, they being shipped in the name of Jennings; if you consider that in the fair ordinary course of trade that would be evidence of fraud, then you will consider whether that is not proof that they were sent for the purpose of slave trading. That is the question to which you must turn your attention. I will lay the evidence before you: I have opened a part of the evidence, it will be a question whether any more will be laid before you; if no more is laid before you, you must take the evidence which will be before you, and consider whether the goods being sent to these persons engaged in the slave trade, with the concealment, is not evidence of the intention of sending them. If the other evidence is laid before you, you will take the whole, under the direction of the learned Judge, into your consideration.

Gentlemen, there is one observation I ought to make before I close. My learned friend has thrown out the question, Who is the prosecutor in this case? It is quite immaterial, in point of law, who is the prosecutor; the question is, What is the evidence against the defendant? But you will not for a moment understand that the prosecutor wishes to conceal himself or his name. The name of the prosecutor is the attorney in the case, Sir George Stephen; he is the son of a gentleman whose name has been known as long as any attempt has existed in this country, as one deeply interested in the attempt to overthrow the slave trade, and cause its suppression; and he is the nephew of a man to whom undoubtedly I should say is due very great praise, it would be hardly too much to say the greatest praise, in removing the stain which rested upon this country—I mean Mr. Wilberforce. Sir George Stephen has no fear or apprehension upon the subject; he has felt it to be necessary and proper in his judgment, and the judgment of those with whom he is connected and with whom he has acted, that some person should stand forward to bear all the responsibility which rested upon any individual in bringing a case of this kind before you for your consideration. He has no objection to bear that responsibility; he has performed his duty in this respect. But that is quite immaterial to the question in this case, which is simply this,—Is the prisoner at the bar guilty or not guilty of that with which he is charged in this indictment? And I mention the name of Sir George Stephen, because he does not wish to shrink from the responsibility which rests upon him. You will attend only to the evidence, and upon the evidence you will give your verdict of guilty or not guilty. I am sure, if the prisoner is innocent, you will give that verdict with great satisfaction; but if he is guilty, you will not shrink from that important duty which rests upon you in giving a verdict—a verdict of the utmost importance to those human beings for whose protection you are now sitting. If he is innocent, no feeling of that description will influence you in giving a feather's weight to the prosecution; on the other hand, if you feel that he is guilty, you will not shrink from saying so by your verdict.

EVIDENCE FOR THE PROSECUTION.

Captain *Henry Worsley Hill*, R.N. sworn. Examined by Mr. Serjeant *Talfourd*.

Q. You were formerly the commander of a ship called the Saracen?—*A.* Yes, I commanded her on the coast of Africa.

From what time to what time? Did you command the Saracen on the 1st of October, 1837?—I commanded her from October, 1837, to June, 1841.

What was the general nature of the service you were engaged upon?—The protection of British commerce, and the prevention of the slave trade.

Mr. Justice *Maule*. What was the Saracen?—She was a man-of-war, a brig.

A king's ship?—Yes.

Mr. Serjeant *Talfourd*. Did you become acquainted in the course of that service with the river Gallinas?—Yes.

How far is the river Gallinas from Sierra Leone?—For large vessels navigating it is necessary to go round a large tract of shoals, which makes it 150 or 200 miles; but there is a nearer navigation for smaller ships and boats. It depends so much upon the draught of water of the vessel you are navigating.

Is there any town on the river Gallinas?—On the river Gallinas there are several small towns.

What is the nature of the population there?—The population of the Gallinas consists of the inhabitants, negroes, they are all blacks; and the European population are chiefly Spaniards.

Mr. *Kelly*. The European population is principally Spaniards?—Yes, chiefly so.

Mr. Serjeant *Talfourd*. At the time you first became acquainted with the river Gallinas, were there any barracoons there?—Yes.

How many barracoons were there?—

Mr. Justice *Maule*. When was this he is now speaking of?

Mr. Serjeant *Talfourd*. When was it?—The river Gallinas was part of my station in December, 1838; in fact, it was upon my station from December, 1838, till May, 1841; and I was constantly at Gallinas during that period.

Mr. Justice *Maule*. When were you first at Gallinas?—I called there before that in 1837, but I did not land there.

Did you see if there were any barracoons there then?—I did not land there. I know there were barracoons from hearsay; and I know the slave trade was extensively carried on.

Mr. *Kelly*. Do not tell us any thing you know from hearsay.

Mr. Serjeant *Talfourd*. You did afterwards land there, and became acquainted with the establishments there?—

Mr. Justice *Maule*. Is it merely to ascertain the fact of the existence of barracoons there?

Mr. Serjeant *Talfourd*. No; they are destroyed now. They were destroyed by Captain Denman?—It was in consequence of arrangements made by Captain Denman. I was there when they were destroyed. I was there, and saw the whole slave establishments; there were six or seven of them.

When you first knew the Gallinas, were there slave establishments there?—I was merely cruizing off there to prevent the slave trade. The slave vessels took their cargoes from there, as I have every reason to believe.

Mr. *Kelly*. Have the kindness to confine yourself to what you know.

Mr. Justice *Maule*. You have been ashore there?—Yes.

What did you see there?—The first time I was on shore there and saw the barracoons was in November, 1840—

Mr. *Kelly*. There is no doubt of the fact of barracoons being there, and that they were destroyed.

—I was cruizing off there for two years for the purpose of preventing the slave trade; but I did not land to see them till 1840, and that was in November.

Mr. Serjeant *Talfourd*. At that time how many slave establishments were there at the Gallinas?—

Mr. *Kelly*. Do you know it of your own knowledge? Let Captain Hill distinguish between what he saw and knows to be the fact, and what he has heard.

Mr. Justice *Maule*. Barracoons seem now to be changed into slave establishments. Do you make any point of that?

Mr. *Kelly*. No, my Lord, I do not; it means the same thing.

Mr. Justice *Maule*. Are these barracoons for the slaves?

Mr. Serjeant *Talfourd*. Are the barracoons used for the purpose of warehousing the slaves?—They are for confining the slaves before they are exported.

Is this a plan made by yourself? (*handing a paper to the Witness.*)—Yes, it is made from my recollection of the river; it has never been surveyed. I made it from my recollection of the spot.

Does it give a representation of the river Gallinas and the barracoons upon it?—Yes it does, to the best of my ability. Those places which are marked black are where the barracoons were, which were destroyed in consequence of Captain Denman and myself going into them and giving directions for that purpose.

It represents them as they were before they were destroyed?—Yes.

Just mention them one after the other, and whose they were.

Mr. *Kelly*. I do not know how my learned friend intends to show that this is evidence.

Mr. Serjeant *Talfourd*. That will be for your cross-examination.

Mr. *Kelly*. I do not wish to charge my Lord's notes with a quantity of matter that is not evidence. How can this gentleman tell these were the properties of particular parties? How can he say, upon his oath, that these are the properties of particular parties?

Mr. Serjeant *Talfourd*. Do you know who the parties were who were the owners of these barracoons?—The first place we landed at was Angeline's, called Dombocoro; to the best of my belief it was his. I may go into a house and not know who is the owner; but that it was Angeline's I understood from himself.

Mr. *Kelly*. This I must object to. If my learned friend thinks it necessary to address any question to Captain Hill as to facts that took place, from which your Lordship or the Jury may infer that any particular individual was the owner of any particular place or places, I cannot object to it; but when it is sought to be given in evidence against Mr. Zulueta, who was never at the place in his life, and never saw any of the parties, and something is to be built upon the reputation that existed as to the property of these individuals, I submit to your Lordships that direct evidence should be given of the fact; and I must object to the question, what was generally understood as to the ownership of these barracoons. Any thing he saw, from which an inference may fairly be drawn, I cannot object to; but I do object to any thing he prefaces, by saying, "I understood so and so."

Mr. Serjeant *Talfourd*. The mode of ascertaining who is the owner of any establishment, is by going there and seeing who is taken to be the owner.

Mr. Justice *Wightman*. I understood that Captain Hill had gone in there and seen some person there?—No; I learned at Dombocoro.

Mr. *Kelly*. That is not evidence.

Mr. Justice *Maule*. If you wish to show that A. B. is the owner of any house, you must show it by specific evidence; but there is no point here as to parties being the owners. One is called Señor Antonio's, and another by another name. I do not see why any dispute should be made about it. If you wish to charge the prisoner with the specific fact of a particular party being the owner of a building or piece of ground, it must be proved by legitimate evidence.

Mr. *Kelly*. I wish to deal fairly by my learned friend, and to save time, which is the object of us all. My learned friend, in his opening speech, stated that certain parties were notorious slave dealers: now what may be notorious to any gentleman who hears all the tittle-tattle that may be spoken at the place is one thing, but what was known to the prisoner is another thing. The notoriety there is not evidence against the prisoner. The question will arise, if the fact is proved, whether it was known to Mr. Zulueta in this country? Let us have the fact there, and not what was known there?

Mr. Serjeant *Talfourd*. How many barracoons were there at this time?—I had better explain that the barracoons are extensive buildings of themselves; and the buildings, necessary for the parties to live in to attend upon the slaves, are numerous. At Dombocoro there may be fifty or sixty houses, storehouses, and places for the people to live in who look after the slaves. Tiendo covers a very large space of ground.

Mr. Justice *Maule*. I may take it that each barracoon is a slave building, and that there are storehouses for stores?—Yes; the barracoons themselves are like large barns to keep the slaves in, and they contain five or six hundred slaves sometimes.

Mr. Serjeant *Talfourd*. Are there any other buildings but the barracoons and the houses for the attendants?—At Dombocoro there are none other. At Tiendo there is a town just adjoining it: the slave establishment is towards the point. At Jaiera I saw nothing but the slave establishments. At Carmatiendo there is a large slave establishment, and the reputed owner is—

Mr. *Kelly*. Never mind the reputed owner.

Mr. Justice *Maule*. Any body might prove that an island was called Juan Fernandez without proving that he was seized of it in fee.

Mr. Serjeant *Talfourd*. Is there any thing but a slave establishment there?—No, I saw nothing else: and the same at Camasuro; and I saw the same at Paisley: and at one or two of the islands there were some small slave establishments likewise.

Do you know of any other trade or commerce which is carried on there but the slave trade?—None other; and I think I was in the whole of the slave establishments I have mentioned. I went over the whole of them before they were destroyed, and saw no signs of any trade but the slave trade.

Having been cruizing off there for some years, should you have known it if there had been any other commerce carried on but the slave trade?—

Mr. *Kelly*. I object to that question, it is asking the witness to come to a conclusion, from being on the coast of Africa, that he had become acquainted with the whole of the commerce. I am quite sure that the last answer of the witness cannot be correct.

Mr. Serjeant *Talfourd*. I submit to your Lordships that my learned friend cannot be correct in stating that the witness is not correct.

Mr. *Kelly*. I will prove it.

Mr. Justice *Maule*. I have taken down the substance of what he has been saying, and it is this: He mentions five or six places where there are barracoons with the appurtenances; and "except at one or two, where native towns are near, I saw no sign of any other trade but the slave trade." You were cruizing off there to watch the trade?—Yes.

Did you know of any trade but the slave trade?—No, the native king told me there was no other.

Mr. *Clarkson*. Never mind what the native king told you.

Mr. Justice *Maule*. We cannot even take the word of a king, so extreme is our repugnance to hearsay evidence.

Mr. Serjeant *Talfourd*. Do you know a merchant there of the name of Ignatio Rolo?—He was on board the Saracen for some two or three days. Captain Denman had taken a slave vessel—

Do you know of your own knowledge what his occupation was there?—I never saw him buy a slave, nor did I see him sell one; but as far as knowing the course of trade, I should say he was a slave dealer, and solely and only a slave dealer; but I never saw him buy one. Jaiera was his slave establishment, and there was no sign of any thing but the slave trade.

And there he resided himself?—I never saw him there. I understood from him that he did: in the first instance he denied it.

Mr. *Kelly*. Do not tell us what he denied. I must once for all take his Lordship's opinion whether this course of evidence can be persisted in. I am extremely sorry to consume time, but it is essentially necessary for the interests of justice that the prisoner should be protected from answers of this kind. It seems that Captain Hill thinks it his duty, instead of answering the question put to him, to state any thing that occurs to his own mind.

Mr. Justice *Maule*. I cannot say that he seems to give answers quite connected with the subject; but he is not so well acquainted with what we exclude in evidence as you are.

Mr. *Kelly*. I only wish once for all, if he would be good enough to understand, that he is not to repeat what he heard; what he saw no one can object to; what conversations he had with other people can form no ground of charge against a party not upon the spot. —I was speaking of a conversation I had with Ignatio Rolo himself, he acknowledged to me he lived there.

Mr. Justice *Maule*. We cannot admit that.

Mr. *Kelly*. I am not blaming Captain Hill, but I am only reminding him of his duty as a witness not to repeat whatever he heard.

Mr. Justice *Maule*. He has not stated whatever he learnt from any party: if you push that to the extreme point, how is a witness to be allowed to say that he was examined in Court by Mr. Kelly?

Mr. *Kelly*. I do not push it to that extent.

Mr. Justice *Maule*. Did you see Ignatio Rolo in any occupation—No; the way I saw him was this, Captain Denman had seized a slave vessel, and he had sent it up in charge of a prize officer and crew.

Mr. *Kelly*. If I cannot induce Captain Hill to confine himself merely to answering the questions, I must object. It is singular that when your Lordship puts a question, and Captain Hill has answered it, he goes on to enter into a story about Captain Denman and a slave vessel. I object to that; we cannot go into evidence of what Captain Denman had done about a slave vessel; all he knows is mere rumour.

Mr. Serjeant *Talfourd*. When was it you first saw Ignatio Rolo?—I myself landed there in the month of November, a day or two previous to our going into the river Gallinas, in order to make some arrangements with the chiefs, owing to the interruption that had been offered to us.

Was there any establishment there called by his name?—None; but Jaiera was the name of the establishment.

Did you ever see him there?—No.

Mr. Justice *Maule*. You saw him somewhere?—Yes, he came on board a slave vessel, and was there detained by the prize officer.

What is Ignatio Rolo?—To the best of my belief he is a Spaniard; an European, to the best of my knowledge. I never saw him in Spain.

Mr. Serjeant *Talfourd*. Do you know a person named Don José Alvarez there?—I was not personally acquainted with him; I only knew him by name.

Did you know a merchant named Don Ximenes?—I saw him at Sierra Leone; and I learnt from him—

Mr. Justice *Maule*. Are you going to prove that the river Gallinas was a slave trading place?

Mr. Serjeant *Talfourd*. Yes, my Lord.

Mr. Justice *Maule*. There is enough evidence of that.

Foreman of the Jury. We are quite satisfied of that.

Mr. *Kelly*. There is no doubt that where there are barracoons, there is slave dealing; but whether these individuals were slave dealers I do not know. Let that be proved in evidence.

Mr. Serjeant *Talfourd*. Did you fall in at any time with a vessel called the Golupchik?—Yes.

When was that?—I fell in with her several times, and chased her; and ultimately captured her in April 1839.

Under what colours was the Golupchik then sailing?—Russian.

Who was it had the command of her?—It was Thomas Bernardos.

Of what nation was the crew composed?—They were Spaniards principally; there might be a few Portuguese.

Was there any thing in the fitting up of that vessel, which enabled you to judge in what trade she was engaged?—She was fitted up for the slave trade.

Have you any doubt of it?—No.

What was the nature of the fittings up?—I have the report of the Mixed Commission Court, which would be the best evidence.

Mr. *Kelly*. No, it would not.

Mr. Serjeant *Talfourd*. What were the fittings up, which to your eyes indicated her as a slave vessel?—She had more water-casks than are necessary for an ordinary trading vessel.

What is the size of them?—They are large vessels; they are called leagers.

They are called leagers?—Yes; but any vessel may have a leager; but she had a larger quantity than any ordinary merchant vessel, and that is one of the articles prohibited to be used by our treaties with foreign powers.

What else did you observe?—She had a sliding caboose to hold a very large copper; that is another of the prohibited articles. She had also gratings covered over with temporary planks; and a few other trifling things, quite sufficient, according to our treaties with foreign powers, to authorise me to seize her as a vessel fully equipped for the slave trade, had she been under the Spanish flag. I seized her, believing her to be a Spanish vessel, though under the Russian flag.

The crew were principally Spaniards?—Yes; and it did not appear that she had been in a Russian port for two years.

What did you do with the vessel?—I sent her to Sierra Leone, and tried to prosecute her in the Mixed Commission Court as a Spanish vessel; but she was not received into that Court, being under the Russian flag, and with Russian papers. I afterwards determined to send her to England, that the Court of Admiralty might dispose of her, as I felt satisfied she could not be a Russian vessel.

Mr. Justice *Maule*. You sent her to England to be condemned?—Yes, and before that I obtained from Bernardos—

Mr. *Kelly*. You are not asked what you obtained from Bernardos.

Mr. Serjeant *Talfourd*. Did Bernardos go in her?—Yes. I tried her a second time in the Mixed Commission Court.

We cannot enter into that. Did you afterwards see the same vessel again under another name?—Yes.

When was that?—In February 1841.

Where was she at the time?—Close to the Gallinas; at anchor at Gallinas: she anchored as I went on board.

Mr. Justice *Maule*. Under what name?—The Augusta; and under the English flag.

Mr. Serjeant *Talfourd*. Are you quite certain it was the same vessel you had captured before?—Yes, quite certain.

Who did you find in command of the vessel at that time?—A man of the name of Jennings.

In consequence of any suspicions you entertained, did you make application to him for the ship's papers?—I asked for the ship's papers directly I went on board—

Mr. *Kelly*. I must object to any thing that passed between the witness and Captain Jennings; the fact I do not object to.

Mr. Justice *Maule*. You do not object to the fact of his asking for and getting the papers?

Mr. *Kelly*. No; but it must be the fact alone. I never interpose when the Captain states facts.

Mr. Justice *Maule*. Did you ask for the ship's papers?—

Mr. *Kelly*. To that I have no objection, and I do not object to the question of my learned friend; but it is the only way I have of warning Captain Hill not to give us other people's statements.

Mr. Serjeant *Talfourd*. Did you obtain the papers in the first instance?—Yes; on going on board it is my duty to demand them, and I received them on board.

Were there any other papers subsequently given to you by Jennings, or did you receive them all at once?—I received other papers afterwards; I received the ship's papers in the first instance.

Mr. *Kelly*. Confine your answer to the question.

—It is necessary to explain.

Mr. *Kelly*. No, not at all.

Mr. Serjeant *Talfourd*. You received some papers in the first instance?—Yes; the vessel's papers on demand. I had demanded them, and on being refused by Captain Jennings to answer a question which he was bound to answer to the commander of a British man-of-war, I insisted upon its being answered, and said I should detain the vessel till it was; and that question was to whom did the vessel—

Mr. *Kelly*. Here I must interpose; and unless Captain Hill is to be the sole judge of what is to be admissible evidence, I ask your Lordship to interpose, or to hear me and dispose of my objection. I cannot complain of my learned friend; he puts nothing but perfectly regular questions. Captain Jennings is not my client here.

Mr. Justice *Maule*. You gave back the ship's papers to Captain Jennings, and afterwards you insisted upon having these papers, or having some more?—I insisted upon having the question answered to whom the vessel was consigned.

Mr. Serjeant *Bompas*. He has a right to ask that; that is a question which the captain is bound to demand of him, to whom he is consigned.

Mr. *Kelly*. I am quite well aware that in your Lordship's hands I am quite safe; and if Captain Jennings had committed a murder on this occasion, it would not upon your Lordship's minds produce any influence; but it is impossible to tell, knowing that Jennings was the captain of the vessel, and that the prisoner at the bar may have had some hand in the fitting it up, what influence it may have upon the minds of the Jury if we are to have conversations or recognitions, supposing there to have been any made by Captain Jennings; and all this done in the absence of Mr. Zulueta, who had no knowledge of it or control over it. If I at all understand it to be your Lordship's impression, that any thing said or done by Captain Jennings is evidence, having made the objection I have nothing further to submit to your Lordships; but I do conceive, that nothing done by Captain Jennings long after the vessel sailed, and long after the offence, if any, was committed, is admissible. I do feel it my duty to ask, whether evidence is to be received of what was said and done by Captain Jennings months after the departure of the vessel from this country?

Mr. Justice *Maule*. I do not entertain either of those two opinions. You do not put two cases which exhaust all other possible cases, but you say if I am of opinion that every thing said and done by Captain Jennings is evidence, you say no more; you say nothing. But I do not think that the thing is evidence, because Captain Jennings says it; nor do I think we can say, that nothing that Captain Jennings said can be evidence in the course of the trial. But with respect to what we have to decide, it is not whether there is such a large and general rule as that, but whether this question falls within any rule that excludes it. I think it does; I think what Captain Jennings said on that occasion is not admissible in evidence. If Captain Hill demands some other papers from him, that fact may be given in evidence.

Mr. Serjeant *Talfourd*. Did you afterwards receive some other papers from Captain Jennings on board?—Yes, I received a packet.

Mr. Serjeant *Talfourd*. Is the clerk here from the Court of Admiralty?

Mr. *Kelly*. I take for granted that the papers to be produced in Court are the papers given to this gentleman by Captain Jennings.

Mr. Serjeant *Bompas*. Yes, they have been produced before; we shall want them in a moment.

Mr. Serjeant *Talfourd*. What steps did you take upon receiving these papers?—I took the papers on board my own vessel on purpose to read them. It was towards the close of the evening I received them, and I sent an order on board the Saracen that an officer and a certain number of men should be sent to me, and I entrusted that officer with the charge of the vessel.

Did you, in consequence of the view you took afterwards, detain the vessel?—Yes, I detained the vessel.

She was afterwards taken, I believe, to Sierra Leone?—Yes.

Did you prosecute her there?—

Mr. *Kelly*. I must object to all this—

Mr. Serjeant *Talfourd*. I thought that that might be taken as a fact; the evidence of Mr. Zulueta before the Committee is in evidence; and there it is stated that the vessel was condemned, because Captain Jennings had no funds to defend her: I thought I might take that as a fact.

Mr. *Kelly*. No, nothing of the kind; I object to any evidence of the proceedings in Sierra Leone respecting this vessel. Mr. Zulueta, as it appears by what is in evidence, namely, his own statement before the Committee of the House of Commons, was the agent of Messrs. Martinez & Co. for the purchase of this vessel, and afterwards the shipment of the goods, but was no party at all to any proceeding, judicial or otherwise, which took place in Sierra Leone. Now judicial proceedings, in which there is a judicial sentence, are no doubt evidence, and may be very important evidence against the parties to those proceedings; but I apprehend as that was a proceeding to which Mr. Zulueta was no party, they are not evidence against him here.

Mr. Serjeant *Talfourd*. We need not argue that; I only put the question in order to trace the vessel.

Mr. Justice *Maule*. At present he says the vessel was sent to Sierra Leone; that was all, I believe?

Mr. *Kelly*. No, he was going on to talk about the proceedings in Sierra Leone.

Mr. Serjeant *Talfourd*. There were some proceedings there?—She was condemned in the Vice-Admiralty Court there.

Was she sent to England afterwards?—I have seen nothing of her since.

Cross-examined by Mr. *Kelly*.

Though you were for some two or three years cruizing upon the coast of Africa, it was not till November 1840 you landed at Gallinas—I landed upon the island there for half an hour previous to that time.

With that exception, I believe you had not landed there before that?—No.

You have spoken of slave establishments; are there not villages or towns, whatever names are given to them up the river?—It is necessary to mention—

You will greatly oblige me if you will answer the question. Is it the fact, that there are several towns and villages up the river?—It is necessary for me to explain. If you know nothing of the river Gallinas that question may imply more than I can answer. The river Gallinas extends some distance into the interior as I believe: I have been up it ten or a dozen miles, and I know that there is the native village of Mera, another of Tardia, and another of Tinda.

That is exactly what I am asking.

Mr. Justice *Maule*. It is a very harmless statement.

Mr. *Kelly*. I was going to ask him how far he had gone up the river?—At least twelve miles.

As far as you have gone, there were towns?—There were villages.

Was the river navigable further up?—Do you mean further than I went?

Yes.—I cannot say; I should think not from the appearance of it, except by canoes.

It is navigable for canoes, so that the population of the place can pass further up?—I cannot say.

Did you ever see canoes higher up?—I could not see them.

If you were ten miles up, you can say if you saw canoes beyond that distance?—I did not see any. I think from the appearance of the river as high as I went, it is navigable for canoes; but I never saw any there.

You were upon this coast for the protection of British commerce and the prevention of the slave trade?—Yes.

Did not that British commerce consist among other things of the exportation of the merchandise of Britain to various places on the coast of Africa?—Certainly.

Do you not know that British merchandises, sometimes in British vessels, and at other times in other vessels, were exported to a very considerable extent to various parts of the coast of Africa?—Certainly, I do.

Now with respect to the Gallinas, do I understand you to say that no British merchandises were exported there, except for the purposes of the slave trade?—Any British merchandise exported there from the Gallinas?

No, I said imported into the Gallinas.—That question was not asked me.

Do you not know that British merchandise to a considerable extent was from time to time exported to the Gallinas in a lawful manner?—I have known English vessels arrive at the Gallinas and part with a little of their cargo; but I never knew an instance before the Augusta of a vessel arriving at the Gallinas consigned to deliver her cargo there.

I ask you, whether you have known of various British vessels, containing British merchandise, arriving there for a lawful purpose?—I have known one or two English vessels dispose of a part of their cargoes there; but I doubt its being for a legal purpose, because I am satisfied there is no export from the Gallinas but slaves, and therefore I do not think it could be lawful.

You say you have known them land part of their cargo there?—I have known them sell part of it.

And you gave as your reason for doubting whether it was for a lawful purpose, because you are not aware of any merchandise that is exported from there in return?—I said I should doubt whether it was lawful, because there was no produce in exchange for it.

Have you never known an instance of ivory and palm-oil being exported from Gallinas?—Never, and I believe it never was during the time I was there.

I am asking your experience; I will come to your belief presently. You say you doubt whether British merchandise has ever been landed there for lawful purposes; is that so?—I have given my reason for doubting it.

Is it so, that you doubt whether it was ever landed for any purpose?—I am speaking of the time I was there.

I am asking you about your own experience; of course that must be while you were there. You say you have never known any British produce landed that you did not doubt the legality of its purpose; is that so?—Yes; because there was no produce to be lawful given in exchange; no produce that I met with.

Allow me to ask you, was there any thing illegal in the landing of British produce for the use of the native chiefs, or the inhabitants of those towns and villages you speak of?—You are asking me my opinion?

Yes; you say you doubt the legality of it?—

Mr. Justice *Maule*. That is a question of law.

—That is a question I cannot presume to answer.

Mr. *Kelly*. As the gentleman has given me his doubts, I wished to know the reason for them.—I have seized this vessel, because I conceived her freight to be illegal.

Do you remember a vessel called the Gil Blas?—I have seen her.

Did she not land goods at the Gallinas?—Yes: if she is the vessel I mean, she was commanded by a man of the name of Serjeant, and he landed some goods there; he gave me to understand so.

Was the Gil Blas there at the time your vessel was there?—Yes.

And you did not think it necessary to seize the Gil Blas?—No.

Do you know for whom any goods were landed?—I am only speaking from what I understood from him when I learned it. I do not know to whom he delivered them; but he gave me to understand he sold them to Pedro Blanco; but I was not present. I am only speaking to my belief.

Did this man, about that time, make you any present?—Serjeant brought out from Pedro Blanco a dozen fowls and a sheep for me, which I was very glad of. I had never seen Pedro Blanco in my life. I had had no fresh provisions for some time, and I was very glad to accept the fowls and the sheep, which he told me had come from Marseilles in a vessel which had taken some slaves. The sheep I gave to the Judge of the Mixed Commission Court.

How long was the Gil Blas off there?—I do not know, perhaps a day.

Tell me the name of any other vessel that was out there landing goods, which you did not seize?—I do not remember any.

Were you there at the time the Star was there?—I do not remember the name. I do not recollect seeing her. I am sorry I have not the boarding-book here, or I could tell you.

Do you remember the Laburnum?—No.

The Milford?—No.

Do you not know that the Milford landed a large quantity of goods at the Gallinas?—Not to my knowledge.

Or the Sublime?—Not that I know of.

How long were you so near to the river Gallinas, or within it, as to be able to know from your own observation what quantity of goods, if any, was landed?—My cruizing ground was extensive. I was a good deal at the Gallinas, because it was a notorious slave place, but I had many other places to visit.

You are not answering my question. I ask you how long you were within the river, or within sight of it, so as to know what quantity of goods were landed?—It was part of my cruizing ground; sometimes I would be there for two or three days at anchor, then I would be away a month or two, and then back again for two or three months; sometimes I was continually there.

Can you give me any idea of the population upon these banks of the river with which you were acquainted? You say you went twelve miles up; what was the extent of the whole population?—I can only answer from guess. I should say, at Tiendo, the population might be eight or nine hundred; at Tardia, one or two hundred; at Mena, seven or eight hundred. There is another native town, which I do not know the name of, further down the river; but it is not thickly populated by any means.

You say you were stationed upon the coast of Africa for the protection of British commerce: as far as your experience goes, was not that British commerce to the coast of Africa exceedingly serviceable to the natives?—That depends upon what way it is employed. If it is to be employed in the slave trade, it is doubtful whether it is serviceable.

I am not asking you a speculative question of that description: you were there for the protection of British commerce, and it is a plain question. I ask you, in your judgment, founded upon your experience, was British commerce serviceable to the natives upon the coast of Africa?—Are you taking the whole of the coast of Africa, or confining it to the Gallinas?

I am confining it to the parts you are acquainted with?—That was all the coast of Africa, from Portendique round to Madagascar; if you are taking in all that, undoubtedly British commerce must be a great benefit to Africa.

Let me ask you another question, and that I may not take you by surprise, I may tell you that I am taking it from the book in which you gave your evidence; I ask you, from your experience upon the coast of Africa, whether, in many places, a lawful trade was not carried on to a considerable extent by some persons, who likewise carried on the slave trade?—By the same persons, or in the same places?

I say the same persons?—I have not seen the persons trading, and I cannot tell.

Though you have not seen them trading, you may be able to answer the question?—I do not hesitate in telling you, that in many places on the coast of Africa, the same trade was carried on both for slaves and in exchange for the produce of the country, but at the Gallinas I do not think there was any trade of that kind.

In many places, the same trade was carried on in the lawful trade and the slave trade by the same persons?—Yes; Iam speaking of hearsay; but I am as confident it was not so at the Gallinas, as one can be confident from having been at the place.

The experience which leads you to think it has not been so at Gallinas is from your own knowledge, being on the spot?—I have already stated I have been a great deal there, and during that time I saw no other trade, nor the sign of any other trade, than the slave trade.

We are here dealing with a gentleman who was never at the Gallinas, and I am asking you a question founded upon your experience: you say you believe no lawful trade was carried on there, as there was at other places; I ask you, whether the knowledge you have acquired, which leads you to suppose that European trade was carried on, was derived from your own knowledge of the persons?—Yes.

Allow me to ask you, are the officers of the navy in your own distinguished situation entitled to share in the value of the vessels which they seize, and which happily for them are condemned?—Yes they are; certainly.

To what extent: suppose you were to seize a vessel and cargo of the value of 10,000*l.*, what would be your own share?—I should imagine the vessel in question—

I want to know, if you seize a ship and cargo of the value of 10,000*l.*, 5000*l.* each, what is the share, if that vessel is condemned for being engaged in the slave trade, that the commanding officer seizing it is entitled to?—You must tell me the port she is to be condemned in; it makes a considerable difference; if it is in the Mixed Commission Court, that makes a very considerable difference, or if it is in the Vice-Admiralty Court.

Take it as being condemned in the Vice-Admiralty Court?—Half the proceeds go to the Crown, and the other half to the captors, after all the expenses are paid.

You say half goes to the Crown, if condemned in the Vice-Admiralty Court?—This vessel—

I am not asking you about any particular vessel.—It depends upon the different Acts under which she is condemned.

Forget for a moment this vessel the Augusta, if you can, and suppose a vessel under British colours is seized in the African seas by an officer in your own situation, and is condemned in the English Vice-Admiralty Court for a breach of the English law, how is the value divided?—Half goes to the Crown, and the other half, after the expenses are paid, is divided amongst the captors; the admiral gets one-sixteenth, and the captain one-eighth of the remainder.

Suppose she is condemned by the Mixed Commission Court?—I believe it is nearly the same in the Mixed Commission Court; but half goes to the nation under whose flag she is sailing.

The Mixed Commission Court is a court composed of commissioners of two nations, or various nations, and who have to determine the cases of foreign vessels not British, Spanish for instance?—Yes; I think that is the division after the nation under whose flag she is sailing; but under the Act that was passed authorising us to seize Portuguese vessels, and to prosecute them in the Vice-Admiralty Court, I do not know how the proceeds were divided.

It is a Mixed Commission Court which decides upon the Spanish or Portuguese ships; and the British Vice-Admiralty Court decide upon a vessel under the British flag?—Yes.

Are not Spanish vessels prohibited from being navigated by British captains? Did you ever see a vessel under the Spanish flag navigated by a British captain?—I never recollect seeing one.

Now, as to the vessel in question, the Augusta; you say when she bore the name of the Gollupchik, she was in every respect fitted up for the slave trade?—Not in every respect; I do not think she had a slave-deck laid.

I correct myself: she was in many respects fitted up for the slave trade?—Yes.

And that led you to seize her?—Yes.

When she came to England, and was claimed by the Russian authorities, do you know whether they succeeded in their claim?—I know nothing of her; I sent her to England.

You do not know whether she remained in English hands, or was delivered up to the Russian government?—I was on the coast of Africa at the time. I have received nothing from the Vice-Admiralty Court in respect of her.

To a certain extent, to the extent to which you have described her, she was, when you seized her under Russian colours, fitted up for a slave vessel?—Yes.

When she bore her name of the Augusta, and was in the hands of Captain Jennings, was she then fitted up for the slave trade?—Not in my opinion; and I did not seize her for that, but for her freight: at least I saw nothing; I do not know what might be under her cargo.

I did not ask you what you did not see; it is the very thing I have been objecting to a hundred times over: I ask you what you did see. You have said two or three times that you were three years upon this coast; to what extent of coast did your cruizing extend?—From December, 1838, until April or May, 1841. The Gallinas was within my station in the first instance. I had charge of the station under Admiral Palmer. Then there was another officer appointed.

I do not wish to go into the whole history of your service; but have the goodness to confine yourself to the question: over what extent of coast did the whole performance of your duties extend?—It depended upon the nature of the orders I received.

Was it altogether 1,000 miles of coast or 500 miles, from 1837, when you began, till 1841? Was the whole extent of coast, over which at various periods your service extended, 1,000 miles?—From October, 1837, till December, 1838, I was on the coast at different periods from Sierra Leone as far as Madagascar: but from December, 1838, until I left the coast of Africa in June, 1841, I was confined to the coast between Cape Palmas, Portendique, and the Cape de Verd Islands: from December, 1838, till June, 1841—

What extent of coast is that?—

Mr. Justice *Maule*. How many degrees of latitude is it?

—It is about 1,000 miles I should say.

Mr. *Kelly*. During that period you acquired some experience, I presume, in the nature of the British commerce carried on upon the coast of Africa: let me ask you, whether the sort of articles of British commerce, exported to Africa during that period, were not gunpowder, muskets, tobacco, brandy, and cotton goods?—Oh, yes.

And iron articles?—I do not think it is possible to distinguish the articles intended for the slave trade, from the articles intended for legal commerce.

Mr. Justice *Maule*. The articles sent in both instances are welcome to the African consumers?—Yes; I am speaking of the West Coast of Africa; I cannot speak to other parts of the coast; I do not think it is possible to distinguish them.

What people want in Africa is determined by that which they receive, and whether they pay for it in coin or in produce only, the same thing would be welcome?—Yes.

Mr. Justice *Maule*. Just as if you were to ask, why do people give bank notes in England for guineas or sovereigns: it is just what they want.

Mr. *Kelly*. With regard to these articles you have mentioned, when exported to various parts of Africa, is the return made sometimes in doubloons or money, and sometimes in ivory, dye-wood, palm oil, and other commodities produced there?—If you will let me answer the question in my own way, I can do it more satisfactorily. Where goods are landed, and doubloons are obtained in exchange, the doubloons come from the Spaniards, and I never knew a Spaniard engaged in any trade upon the coast of Africa but the slave trade: when you get produce in exchange, it is more likely you get that from the natives.

Do you mean to say, that the Spaniards who trade upon the coast of Africa do not give produce for the merchandise that goes there; I am not speaking merely of the Gallinas?—I think I know of but one, and I do not know whether he is a Spaniard or not. I can mention his name, it is Carrote; I think he exported palm oil as well as slaves; but he told me he was an agent to Pedro Blanco.

Do not tell us what he told you: what I ask you is, whether a return is not sometimes made in ivory and palm oil, and dye-woods?—The question calls for an answer which I cannot give in a satisfactory manner.

You do not do justice to your own understanding.—I wish to give you every information.

You never saw any of the house of Zulueta & Co. in the course of your travels on the coast of Africa?—Never to the best of my recollection.

Do you know any of them?—No: I saw Mr. Zulueta before the Committee of the Privy Council for the first time.

Re-examined by Mr. Serjeant Talfourd.

You have been asked if you saw any slave fittings when you seized the Augusta; did you take up any of the cargo?—No, I did not; I went into the hold.

Do you know whether the slave fittings were what could be taken to pieces and stowed away?—The hatches were grated when I first seized her. When I seized her the second time she had new hatches and no gratings at all. I saw nothing to induce me to believe she had slave fittings when I seized her as the Augusta, though I had heard that.

Mr. Justice *Maule*. The learned Serjeant is asking you not what you heard, but what you looked for; you searched to see if there were slave fittings?—Yes; so far as going down into the hold. I did not disturb the cargo; I do not know what was in her.

You did not find any leagers?—No.

Are you able to say whether she was or was not fitted for the slave trade?—If she was equipped for it I should have seized her at once; but she was not.

You saw enough of her to see that she was not equipped for the slave trade?—Certainly; she had not slave equipments, leagers, hatches with open gratings, or irons, or coppers, or any of those things.

Mr. Serjeant *Talfourd.* How long were you on board the vessel?—The first day a couple of hours, and the next day about the same time. I was on board her three or four times.

Can they get the equipments after they come into port when they discharge their cargo?—Yes, in many places they can; I can give you an instance of an American vessel—

Can the fittings be obtained there after the discharge of a vessel like the Augusta?—

Mr. *Kelly.* Where?

Mr. Serjeant *Talfourd.* At the place where the cargo is discharged.—The only way in which I can answer that question is this; if an agent at Gallinas expects a slave vessel to come out without equipments, he may take care to procure them from other vessels, and may have them perfectly ready: I can give an instance of that—

Mr. *Kelly.* Never mind that.

Mr. Serjeant *Talfourd.* How long would it take to put on board slave equipments in a vessel of the size of the Augusta?—A very short time: they may send out the water-casks filled with water in two or three canoes; and if they do not choose to lay down a slave deck, they put mats upon the casks, and it is done in a very short time. They may embark 500 slaves in a couple of hours or upwards and be off.

Foreman of the Jury. One of my brother jurors wishes to ask this question of the witness through your Lordship: when he went on board the Augusta, whether he found any thing on board her to warrant her being supposed to be fitted out as a slave vessel?

Mr. Justice *Maule.* He says he did not; that has been pursued for some time; and now in answer to questions put to him, the gentleman was saying, though she was not fitted out in that way, that her goods might be landed, and slaves might be put on board, in a few hours.—I can say—

Mr. *Kelly.* I object to these speeches: I object to this gentleman, who thinks because he has seized this vessel that if any thing falls from the Jury, or from one of her Majesty's judges, that he may begin making a speech. There has been a great deal said that is not evidence: that every body must feel; but it is impossible to stop him, although a gentleman as respectable as himself is under trial.

Mr. Serjeant *Talfourd.* You have been asked about the share which the captain has in the capture of a vessel of this description; do you accurately know what share you would have under the circumstances?—Yes; what I have stated is the share: half the proceeds go to the Crown, and after the admiral has had his share, the remaining half is divided.

What would be your share of this vessel the Augusta?—I believe the proceeds amounted to about 3,800*l.*; one-half goes to the Crown, and there are the expenses of the appeal to the Judicial Committee of the Privy Council, which are not paid.

Have you got any thing?—No, not a sixpence.

Do the expenses swallow up?—

Mr. Justice *Maule.* 1,900*l.* is the half; the captain gets one-eighth of fifteen-sixteenths?—There are several hundred pounds to come out of it for the Privy Council appeal, that has not been paid yet.—

Mr. *Clarkson.* You must not say any thing, unless you are asked a question.

Mr. *Kelly.* I shall let him talk on till he is tired after what I have said.

Mr. *John Brown* sworn. Examined by Mr. *Payne.*

Do you come from the Admiralty Court?—Yes.

Do you produce any documents?—Yes, I do.

Mr. Serjeant *Talfourd.* The first document we want is the letter of the 20th August, 1840, from Zulueta & Co. to Captain Jennings?—Will you allow me to hand you a schedule of the different documents; they are numbered according to that. (*The Witness handed in the same.*)

Mr. *Payne.* Nos. 14 and 17 are what we want. (*The Witness handed in two papers; one being a letter, dated 20th August, 1840.*)

Mr. Serjeant *Talfourd* (*to* Captain *Hill.*) Look at this letter and see if it is one of the letters you found on board the Augusta? (*handing the same to the Witness.*)—Yes, that is one; there is my handwriting upon it.

(*To* Captain *Hill.*) Look at this also (*handing another paper to him*), the signature appears to be cut off, and say if it is in the same state as when you found it?—Yes, it is in the same state as when I found it on board the Augusta; the signature was then cut out.

Mr. Serjeant *Talfourd* (*to* Mr. *Brown.*) Now produce the charter-party, Nos. 11 and 12. (*The Witness produced the same.*)

(*To* Captain *Hill.*) Just look at these two papers (*handing them to the Witness*), and see if they are two of the papers which were found on board?—Yes, they are.

Mr. *Kelly* (*to* Captain *Hill.*) You have looked at these three or four papers, and you say they are the papers you found on board the vessel?—They are papers given to me by the master: I did not find them by searching.

Were they given to you on board the vessel?—Yes, by the master.

Did you put any mark upon them?—Yes, you will see a mark on the back; that is what I looked at in the first instance when they were handed to me.

Is this it? (*pointing to a mark on the paper.*)—It is a pretty large number upon the paper: that is my handwriting.

Mr. <u>Abrao De Pinna</u> sworn. Examined by Mr. Payne.

Will you look at this letter, and tell me if you know the handwriting of the postscript at the end? (*handing a paper to the Witness.*)

Mr. *Kelly.* What is the date of it?—24th of September, 1840.

Mr. *Payne.* Whose handwriting is that postscript?—I presume it to be Mr. Zulueta's.

Do you believe it to be?—Yes.

Mr. *Kelly.* Which of them?—The father.

Mr. *Payne.* Do you believe it to be his writing?—Yes.

Mr. Justice *Maule.* You say the father; is that the prisoner?

Mr. Serjeant *Bompas.* No, the father of the prisoner.

Mr. *Payne.* Look at that (*handing another paper to the Witness*), and tell me if you know the handwriting; that is, the 20th of August?—It looks like the handwriting of Zulueta the son.

Mr. Justice *Maule.* What is the date?

Mr. *Payne.* The 20th of August, 1840. Just look at this memorandum on the charter-party; look at the signature to that charter-party: do you know the handwriting of that document?—I suppose that one to be the signature of Mr. Zulueta the son.

Do you believe it to be so?—Yes; the other I do not know.

(The Letters and the Charter-party were handed in.)

Mr. *Payne.* Do you know the handwriting of the body of that first letter of which I showed you the postscript?—I did not pay sufficient attention to it. With your leave I will look again. (*It was again handed to the Witness.*) I do not know it.

Cross-examined by Mr. *Kelly.*

I believe you are the notary to the Spanish consul in this city?—I am.

Have you known the house of Zulueta for any length of time?—For some years.

During that time has the prisoner Pedro de Zulueta, like the rest of his firm, maintained a high character for integrity and propriety of conduct?—The highest, the very highest character; and unimpeachable to the best of my knowledge.

To the best of your knowledge, from their character and the character of their dealings, do you believe them to be wilfully capable of violating the law?—

Mr. Serjeant *Bompas.* No, I object to that question.

Mr. *Kelly.* Has their character been that of violators of the law, or the reverse?—As far as my knowledge goes, I should say that it was perfectly impossible that the house of Zulueta & Co. should be violators of the law.

Have you ever had any transactions in business with that house?—Yes.

Do you know that they act as agents for various houses in Spain, the Havannah, and other places?—Yes.

Do you know that they have for a great many years carried on business to a great extent indeed?—Yes, I do.

Perhaps you may happen to know that vessels under the Spanish flag cannot be commanded by English captains?—

Mr. *Payne.* Do you know any thing about it?

Mr. *Kelly.* Do you know that?—My impression is, that that is the case.

How long have you been a notary?—I have been admitted about twenty years.

Are you a native of Spain?—A native of this country.

Where did you acquire your knowledge of the Spanish language?—In this country.

Have you had a good deal to do with the commercial and maritime affairs of Spain?—Yes, very largely; my connexion is almost exclusively Spanish.

In your experience, have you ever known a Spanish vessel, or a vessel under the Spanish flag, commanded by an English captain?—Never.

Re-examined by Mr. Serjeant Bompas.

Who are the partners in the firm of Zulueta, do you know?—The father Don Pedro Antonio Zulueta, and the son Don Pedro Gonzalez Zulueta. I do not know that I can go any further; I do not know that there is another partner.

Mr. *Kelly.* There is another son Moriarte?—I do not know that he is a partner; I believe he is.

Mr. Serjeant *Bompas.* Besides being a notary, do you carry on the business of a merchant at all?—No, not in the least.

How do you become possessed with your knowledge?—In my notarial capacity I have often had to prepare bills of sale of ships, and various documents connected with shipping, and that is the only way I obtain my information.

Mr. Serjeant *Bompas.* We will read these documents; the one signed by the prisoner at the bar first of all.

Mr. *Kelly.* Take them one at a time; they stand under very different circumstances. Let me look at it. (*It was handed to Mr. Kelly.*)

The same was then read, dated London, the 20th of August, 1840, signed "Zulueta &. Co.," and directed "Captain Jennings," Portsmouth.

"Sir,—In reply to your favour of yesterday, we have to say that we cannot exceed 500*l.* for the vessel in question, such as described in your letter, namely, that excepting the sails, the other differences are trifling from the inventory. If you cannot therefore succeed at those limits, we must give up the purchase, and you will please act accordingly."

Mr. Serjeant *Bompas.* We propose now to read the one in which there is a postscript from the father.

Mr. *Kelly.* I feel that this letter is no evidence against the prisoner at the bar. It is a letter written in a handwriting not proved; the signature does not appear at all; but the postscript was in the handwriting of the prisoner's father. I need hardly say that that is no evidence against the prisoner; but I have not the slightest objection to their reading it. I only add these few words, that because I consent to this being read, it is not to be taken that other documents, if there are any others under different circumstances, are admitted.

The following Letter was read:—

["London, 26th September, 1840," the signature cut off, addressed Captain Thomas Jennings, Portsmouth.

"Dear Sir,—We have received your letter of yesterday, whereby observe that the sum we have remitted you will not be sufficient to cover all the expenses to clear the ship. We much regret you have omitted mentioning the sum you require, which prevents our remitting you the same by this very post, thus causing a new delay in leaving that port, so contrary to our wishes; you will therefore write to us to-morrow, that we may receive your reply on Monday morning, informing us of the amount necessary to finish paying all your accounts and expenses, to remit you the same by Monday's night post, in order that you maybe able to sail for Liverpool on Tuesday or Wednesday at the furthest. You must not omit stating the amount required; and waiting your reply, we remain, very truly, dear Sir, your obedient servants."

Postscript. "According our Liverpool house notice, you will go there to the Salt-house Dock."

Mr. Serjeant *Bompas*. Now put in the charter-party, and the paper referred to in it.

Mr. *Kelly*. Put in one at a time; you cannot read two documents at a time.

[The same was handed in, dated London, 19th October, 1840, signed Thomas Jennings; for Pedro Martinez & Co., of Havannah, Zulueta & Company.

Mr. *Kelly*. All these documents appear in the printed Appendix, which it would be convenient to hand up to your Lordship.

Mr. Justice *Maule*. Is that the joint Appendix on the appeal to the Privy Council?

Mr. *Kelly*. Yes.

Mr. *Clarkson*. The number of the document is 11, on page 5.

The same was read as follows:—

"It is this day mutually agreed between Mr. Thomas Jennings, master and owner of the good ship or vessel called the Augusta, of the burthen of   tons, or thereabouts, now lying at the port of Liverpool, and Messrs. Pedro Martinez & Co., of Havannah, merchants: that the said ship being tight, staunch, and strong, and every way fitted for the voyage, shall with all convenient speed load from the factors of the said Messrs. Pedro Martinez

& Co. a cargo of legal goods, which the said merchants bind themselves to ship, not exceeding what she can reasonably stow and carry over and above her tackle, apparel, provisions, and furniture; and being so loaded, shall therewith proceed to Gallinas, on the coast of Africa, or so near thereunto as she may safely get and deliver the same; after which she may be sent on any legal voyages between the West Indies, England, Africa, or the United States, according to the directions of the charterers' agents (restraint of princes and rulers, the act of God, the Queen's enemies, fire, and all and every other dangers and accidents of the seas, rivers, and navigation, of whatever nature and kind soever during the said voyage, always excepted.) The freight to be paid on unloading and right delivery of the cargo, at the rate of 100*l.* sterling per calendar month that the ship may be so employed, commencing with this present month; all port charges and pilotages being paid by the charterers; and   days on demurrage, over and above the said laying days, at   pounds per day. Penalty for non-performance of this agreement 500*l.* The necessary cash for ship's disbursements to be furnished to the captain free of commission: the charterers to be at liberty of closing this engagement at the end of any voyage performed under it, on settling the freight due to the vessel; the captain being indebted to the charterers in certain sums, as per acknowledgment elsewhere, the freights earned by the vessel to be held as general lien for such sums, and in any settlement for such freights, the said advances to be deducted from the vessel's earnings."

Mr. Serjeant *Bompas.* The next document is the acknowledgment—

Mr. *Kelly.* I do not understand how this addition to the charter-party is evidence.

Mr. Justice *Maule.* It is at the top of page 6?

Mr. *Kelly.* It is a memorandum: you propose to read this?

Mr. Serjeant *Bompas.* Yes.

Mr. *Kelly.* I do not see the importance of it; but I do not see how it is evidence.

Mr. Justice *Maule.* Do you object to it?

Mr. *Kelly.* Yes, my Lord. I will not say any thing of the purpose for which it is offered in evidence, or the object of it. The charter-party is signed by the prisoner at the bar himself, on behalf of the house, as agents for the house of Martinez; but with regard to this document, which my learned friend calls a "memorandum of charter-party," it is the sheet of paper in my hand, signed "Thomas Jennings," and signed by nobody else: it is not shown to be in the handwriting of the prisoner, nor ever to have been in his hands, nor that he had any thing to do with it: it is a paper signed by Captain Jennings, and found by Captain Hill on board the vessel, or delivered to him by Captain

Jennings on board the vessel. What evidence is that against the prisoner at the bar? I do not know what the paper is worth; but I do not know how your Lordships can admit it. It may be a document treasonable in its nature, or it may have been written the day before it was delivered to Captain Hill.

Mr. Justice *Maule*. There is some doubt about this: our opinion is, that in the present stage of the case this document is not admissible. There is certainly a reference in the charter-party to the captain being indebted to the charterers in a certain sum, acknowledged elsewhere, the freights being held as a lien against those debts. This charter-party is dated London, 19th of October; the paper proposed to be put in evidence is dated the 21st of October, so that it may not have been in existence at the time when the first paper was signed; it is therefore hardly to be referred to as a document mentioned in the charter-party. Whether something may arise to make the custody of Mr. Jennings evidence against Mr. Zulueta, is a question not now necessary to be decided: but the question is, whether in the present stage of the cause this is admissible. There is a reference certainly to an acknowledgment elsewhere. The proper and natural custody of that acknowledgment would be either the house of Zulueta & Co., or Pedro Martinez & Co.; it is an acknowledgment of a debt to them, and it is found in the custody of the debtor; it is proved by the signature of Zulueta & Co., and they or their principals are the parties who would have the custody of it; they may produce it if they wish to repel any inference which may arise from it, but at present we think it not admissible in evidence.

Mr. Serjeant *Bompas*. We call for that paper mentioned at the end of the memorandum; we have given you notice to produce it.

Mr. *Kelly*. If you mean to call for any paper, just put in your notice, so that we may see what document it is.

William George White sworn. Examined by Mr. Serjeant *Bompas*.

Just take that in your hand. (*Handing a paper to the Witness.*) Are you a clerk to Sir George Stephen?—I was employed by him.

Did you serve a copy of that notice upon any body, and upon whom?—Yes, I did serve a copy of it.

Upon whom?—Upon Messrs. Zulueta and Messrs. Lawford & Co., and Mr. Jennings, or left it at the office: I either served it on the parties, or left it at the office.

Cross-examined by Mr. *Kelly*.

There was a question put to you, which my learned friend did not give you time to answer; are you a clerk to Sir George Stephen?—No.

How came you to be employed in this matter?—I happened to be in his office, and he asked me to serve it.

What are you?—A clerk in a wine-merchant's counting-house.

When did you serve this?—Will you allow me to look at it again? By all means. (*It was again handed to the Witness.*)—I served one copy on the 20th on Messrs. Zulueta & Co.

The 20th of this month?—Yes, and the 21st on Messrs. Lawford & Co., and on the 23rd upon Thomas Jennings: it was not signed or dated.

You have not answered the question; I wanted to know when you served that paper, of which that is a copy, either upon Mr. Zulueta, or Messrs. Lawfords, his solicitors?—On the 20th of October on Messrs. Zulueta & Co.: the copy was without any date or signature.

Who gave you it to serve?—I had it from Sir George Stephen.

Did he tell you why it was without any signature at all?—No.

He desired you to go and serve it?—Yes.

Now I perceive that that one has a signature; when did you serve upon either Messrs. Zulueta & Co., or Messrs. Lawford & Co., a notice with a signature?—Upon the 26th of October I served all three with a copy.

That was yesterday; what time was it?—I think that Mr. Jennings was about—

I am not asking you about Mr. Jennings; but upon my client, Pedro de Zulueta, or Messrs. Lawford, what time did you serve it upon them?—About five o'clock I served it.

Upon whom?—Not upon Mr. Zulueta himself.

Upon the solicitors?—No; not upon the solicitors themselves.

I am speaking of the one with a date and a signature; when did you serve either Mr. Zulueta or his solicitors?—The 26th.

Was that yesterday? Does your recollection enable you to say?—

Mr. Justice *Maule*. It was either yesterday, or yesterday twelve months, or two years ago?—It was the 26th of October, 1843.

Mr. *Kelly*. Will you tell me at what hour you served it?—Upon whom?

Upon either Messrs. Lawford & Co. or Messrs. Zulueta. First, did you serve it upon either? Leave out Captain Jennings. Did you serve a copy of that paper, signed and dated, upon either Mr. Zulueta or Messrs. Lawford?—No; I did not.

You only served it upon Captain Jennings?—Yes; that is all.

Mr. Justice *Maule*. As far as the signed paper goes, there was no service upon Mr. Zulueta?

Mr. *Kelly*. No.

Mr. Justice *Maule*. He did serve something upon them which was not signed.

Mr. *Clarkson*. Nor dated.

Mr. Justice *Maule*. Let us look at it; it may be a very good notice, though not signed. (*It was handed to his Lordship*).

Mr. *Kelly*. I am not going to raise any objection to it; but I shall make some observations upon it.

Mr. Serjeant *Bompas*. The name was in the instrument, though it was not signed by Sir George Stephen?—Yes.

Mr. *Kelly*. Was that so?—Yes.

When did you serve a copy besides that?—I served a second copy of it at the general office of Zulueta & Co., and you will find the words "General Office," written upon it.

Mr. *Kelly*. Now just refer to your notice, to produce any document you propose to call for?

Mr. Serjeant *Bompas*. When you say you left it without date and signature, was it served in this way, the blank day of blank, with Sir George Stephen's name upon the back of it?—Yes.

Mr. Justice *Maule*. The non-signature of a notice to produce is not worth inquiry; a dot to an *i*, or a cross to a *t*, would be equally available.

Mr. *Kelly*. It is my learned friend who renews the subject. I ask him to point out the document.

(*The Notice to produce was read, specifying among other documents, the additional memorandum of Charter-party, &c.*)

Mr. *Kelly*. I have no such document. I do not know of its existence.

Mr. Justice *Maule*. You call for the document referred to at the end of the memorandum of charter-party?

Mr. Serjeant *Bompas*. Yes.

Mr. *Kelly*. No, my Lord, they call for it by a particular description; it may be that document; but according to that description, as far as I know or am instructed, we have not got it. The document referred to in the terms of the charter-party is supposed to be an acknowledgment of the debt from Captain Jennings to Martinez and Co.; that might be in the possession of Messrs. Zulueta—

Mr. Justice *Maule*. It would be in the possession of Zulueta & Co., or Martinez & Co.?

Mr. *Kelly*. Yes, my Lord; if in the possession of Martinez, of course I have not got it.

Mr. Justice *Maule*. You call for the additional memorandum of charter-party of the 21st of October 1840?

Mr. Serjeant *Bompas*. Yes, or the 19th of October.

Mr. William Thomas sworn. Examined by Mr. Serjeant Bompas.

Are you a clerk in the bank of Messrs. Glyn, Mills, & Co.?—Yes.

Are they the bankers of the prisoner Mr. Zulueta?—Yes, they are.

Did you pay any sum of money of 650*l.* for him upon his account, in August 1840? (*The Witness referred to a book*).—On the 29th of August.

Was there a cheque?—A cheque or bill; I cannot say which.

Mr. *Kelly*. I presume that is kept by yourself, and in your handwriting?—Yes.

Mr. Serjeant *Bompas*. You return the cheques?—Yes, we do.

Mr. Serjeant *Bompas*. We have given them notice to produce any cheque of that date.

Mr. *Kelly*. Now, what is it you call for?

Mr. Serjeant *Bompas*. For that cheque for 650*l.*

Mr. *Kelly*. Does it purport to be a cheque signed by the defendant?—I cannot tell that, it might be a bill made payable upon our house on their account.

Mr. *Kelly*. I am quite prepared to produce any document in the handwriting of the prisoner at the bar, which is in his possession; but as to any document that may bear the signature, or be in the handwriting of any other member of the firm, that I shall not produce unless that member of the firm is made a witness to show the circumstances accompanying the document; unless it passed through the hands of the prisoner. If you prove any cheque in the handwriting of the prisoner, I will produce it if I have it, and if not, I shall not object to secondary evidence of it.

Mr. Serjeant *Bompas*. You say that that is in your writing, have you any book by which you can ascertain whether it was paid through a cheque or bill?—No, certainly not.

None whatever?—No; I could not tell whether it was a cheque or a bill. I cannot tell which; there is no book in our house that will tell us that.

On whose account was it paid?—

Mr. *Kelly*. I object to that: I do not want all the payments made by this witness; we are upon the question if you can give secondary evidence of the cheque.

Mr. Serjeant *Bompas*. I am going to see on whose account it was paid.

Mr. *Kelly*. I object to any evidence of bankers paying a sum of money on account of the firm, or on account of any other person, unless the document is in the handwriting of the prisoner at the bar, or the payment proved to have been made to his orders. What is to prevent, by the order of the partner in Spain, of which he never heard, this person being charged with felony?

Mr. Serjeant *Bompas*. I submit that the evidence is sufficient; here is an express statement in the printed evidence.

Mr. Justice *Maule*. It is not in evidence yet.

Mr. *Kelly*. I consider it in evidence; my learned friend may refer to any part of that book; I consider that that is in evidence now.

Mr. Justice *Maule*. Very well.

Mr. Serjeant *Bompas*. He first states he managed all the business. In answer to Question 10432 he was speaking about the transactions with Africa, he was examined about the Augusta, and Mr. Kidd, he says, "My father knew there was such a man upon the coast, but I did not know even that, though I have managed all this business."

Mr. *Kelly*. That relates to a business upon which another insinuation was made, and which has no more to do with it than this.

Mr. Serjeant *Bompas*. My learned friend assumes that this has no relation to it; he is quite mistaken in that. The question is, what is the meaning of the term, "this business," it is not the business of the man of the name of Kidd; he says he never heard of him; but the question is, whether it is not the business of the Augusta and the trade with Africa; he says he manages all that business. I submit, if he takes upon himself to say he managed "all this business"—

Mr. Justice *Maule*. What are the words?

Mr. Serjeant *Bompas.* "All this business."

Mr. Justice *Maule.* I think the fair inference is, that the Mr. Zulueta, who came before the Committee, was the person who knew best about the matter suggested against them relating to the Augusta, and he came to speak to the matter of the Augusta, either solely or among other things; if so, "this business" must mean that.

Mr. *Kelly.* No, not if your Lordship looks at the context; he comes forward voluntarily, understanding there were charges against his house, not because he knew more about it than any body else, for he knew the least about it, but because he spoke English best. There is nothing from which you can infer in this evidence that Pedro Zulueta knew all that had passed through the house.

Mr. Justice *Maule.* It is not very satisfactory to select a man who can speak English, but did not know much about the matter.

Mr. *Kelly.* I mention that in answer to your Lordship's observation, "that he knew most about the matter."

Mr. Justice *Maule.* The Committee must have taken that to be the fact.

Mr. *Kelly.* If your Lordship thinks it must fairly be supposed to refer to that matter, then the question is whether that makes it evidence; I will call your Lordship's attention to what he says: The *Chairman* asks him, "Is there any other part of the evidence which has been given that you wish to observe upon?—It is asked here in question 5086, 'Who was he?' The answer is, 'The name is mentioned in the Parliamentary Papers as being connected with the purchase of a slave vessel, Mr. Kidd; and it is mentioned in connexion with that of Mr. Zulueta, of London.'" There was some former transaction of the purchase of a slave vessel, in which Mr. Kidd was a party. He goes on to say, "Now, as to Mr. Kidd, the very first thing I ever knew or ever heard of his name, was to see it here. I never heard of his name at all. I never had a letter from him or through him, or knew any thing of the man whatever. That is with regard to myself. With regard to my partners, I can say the same; I have been making inquiries about it. My father knew there was such a man upon the coast, but I did not know even that, though I have managed all this business." What business can that relate to, but the business in which Mr. Kidd's name was mentioned, which was the purchase of a slave vessel?

Mr. Justice *Maule.* I should think not: his father knew there was such a man upon the coast; "I did not know that, although I had that management of the business" which would lead me to know all the men on the coast, that is to say, all the coast business; that is the way I understand it, I confess.

Mr. *Kelly.* I cannot conceive that it is so; but it is for your Lordships to decide. Supposing that it is, I do not know how that makes this entry in the book evidence. Your Lordships will look at the next question: He is asked, "You have no connexion with Mr. Kidd in any way?—No; nor any knowledge of him." Then he goes on with the same business; he was never alluding to the principal business, that of the Augusta.

Mr. Serjeant *Talfourd.* You will find he gives there an account of the whole transaction. Mr. *Forster* says, "You advanced the money to Captain Jennings for the purchase of a vessel; Jennings transferring the vessel to you as a security for the amount so advanced?—That is just the description of operation, which is a very general one in business."

Mr. Serjeant *Bompas* (*to* Mr. *Thomas.*) Whose handwriting is that?—The handwriting of a Mr. Daniel, in our office.

Mr. *Kelly.* I submit that this relates to the business of Mr. Kidd.

Mr. Justice *Maule.* It struck me otherwise; but at the same time you seem so extremely satisfied with your own view, and my view is just as it struck me, that you stagger me by your positiveness.

Mr. *Kelly.* I should not like your Lordship or the Jury to be misled as to the amount of interference by this gentleman in the business. Suppose it is so, that he had the management of the fitting out of the Augusta, how does that make evidence of an entry in the banker's book of the payment of a sum of money? He cannot say to whom he paid it, or on whose account? How can that make it evidence upon a charge of felony? I do not know the nature of it, but I am quite sure it is quite consistent with Pedro Zulueta, having done all he has admitted to have done before the Committee, that he never heard of that payment.

Mr. Justice *Maule.* In whose handwriting is the signature to the charter-party?

Mr. *Kelly.* It is the signature of the prisoner that has been read.

Mr. Justice *Maule.* I do not think you are in a situation to put in this evidence. This witness paid across the counter to somebody, upon something which they produced, a sum of money, and the thing then produced you call for.

Mr. Serjeant *Bompas.* We call for the document upon which it was paid, and we are going to take another step to show that the money so paid was applied to this vessel. Your Lordship has got the statement that they advanced the money for the purchase of the vessel.

Mr. *Kelly.* There is no doubt that the house of Zulueta & Co., on account of Martinez & Co., paid for this ship. My learned friend says he calls for that document. He calls for a document he has not shown to be in existence. Let him prove the existence of the cheque; and then the question arises, whether secondary evidence is admissible.

Mr. Serjeant *Bompas*. Can you say whether it was paid through a cheque or draft?—No, it is impossible.

Mr. Justice *Maule*. He says it was paid through an acceptance upon their house, or upon a cheque upon their house; that it was something purporting to come from Zulueta & Co., but that does not bind the prisoner; that cheque so purporting to come from Zulueta & Co. was sent back to Zulueta &, Co., and notice was given for the production of it?

Mr. *Kelly*. Yes, my Lord, notice has been given to produce the cheque or draft; that does not mean a bill of exchange accepted at Cadiz, where they had a house, or at Liverpool, where they have another house.

Mr. Serjeant *Bompas*. Cheque or draft would apply to a bill.

Mr. Justice *Maule*. If it refers sufficiently to the contents of it.

Mr. *Kelly*. Read the words of the notice, and we will see.

Mr. Serjeant *Talfourd*. "And also a certain draft or cheque," &c. (*Reading the terms of the notice.*)

Mr. *Kelly*. I make two objections to this evidence; the first is, that no such cheque is proved to be in existence; and secondly, if there were, such cheque is not proved to have been in the handwriting of the prisoner at the bar, and therefore it is not admissible. I ought to add, as the notice to produce has been referred to, and is now upon the table, that the notice calls upon the prisoner, Mr. Zulueta, to produce all the books, documents, and accounts of his house, between certain dates, at all relating to the transaction in question; and all letters written, and copies of letters written by this house, or any body for them in relation to this matter. My Lord, every document there mentioned is here in Court, and in two minutes ready to be put upon the table.

Mr. Serjeant *Bompas*. To try you, I call for the paper referred to in the charter-party.

Mr. *Kelly*. The greater part are in Spanish, and the prisoner at the bar can distinguish them, but the clerks who kept these books, the corresponding clerk, and the clerk in whose handwriting they are, are ready to speak to any thing my learned friend may call for from the beginning to the end.

Mr. Serjeant *Bompas*. I call for that letter referred to in the charter-party.

Mr. *Kelly*. Put the documents upon the table.

Mr. Serjeant *Bompas*. You need not go through that performance. Will you produce the receipt mentioned in the charter-party?

Mr. *Kelly*. I have said I have it not.

Mr. Serjeant *Bompas*. There is a letter mentioned here: "We have received your letter of yesterday." Will you produce that? Captain Jenning's letter of the 25th of September, 1840?

Mr. *Kelly*. Certainly.

Mr. Serjeant *Talford*. Mr. Jenning's letter is in English.

Mr. *Kelly*. Yes; I know that.

The same was produced and read, as follows:—

"Portsmouth, 25th September, 1840, Messrs. Zulueta & Co.:— Gentlemen, I am in the receipt of your favour of the 24th instant, and beg leave to acknowledge the favour you have conferred on the house of Messrs. Grant, Gillan, and Medley, and have acknowledged the same to the parties mentioned; at the same time beg leave to mention this port is different from many ports in England for men, and we have to give the month's advance under favour in consequence of the many vessels of war wanting men, so that I have agreed with the men as I consider you will deem necessary; and from the heavy charges of the different tradesmen, and all other expenses I formerly mentioned, I do not consider the sum you have remitted sufficient to clear this port: under such circumstances, you will please to favour me with your advice by return of post, who I shall draw upon for the remaining balance, and hoping my accounts, when seen, may meet your approbation, I remain, your obedient humble servant, THOMAS JENNINGS."

Mr. Serjeant *Bompas*. This is in answer to that.

Mr. Justice *Maule*. The letter of the 26th of September is the answer:—

"We have received your letter of yesterday, whereby observe that the sum we have remitted you will not be sufficient to cover all the expenses to clear the ship. We much regret you have omitted mentioning the sum you require, which prevents our remitting you the same by this very post, thus causing a new delay in leaving that port, so contrary to our wishes. You will therefore write to us to-morrow, that we may receive your reply on Monday morning, informing us of the amount necessary to finish paying all your accounts and expenses, to remit you the same by Monday's night post, in order that you may be able to sail for Liverpool on Tuesday or Wednesday at the furthest. You must not omit stating the amount required, and waiting your reply, we remain, very truly."

Mr. Serjeant *Bompas*. That is the directing him to go to Liverpool.

(*To Mr. Thomas.*) On the 29th of August; have you a memorandum of the notes you paid on that day?—Yes.

The numbers of the notes?—Yes I have.

Mr. *Kelly*. While we were discussing this point, my learned friend called for something else, which I now produce; I do not know that your Lordships decided it. I had objected to the entry in the banker's book being given in evidence against Mr. Zulueta, unless it was proved that that entry was in some way or other made known to him.

Mr. Serjeant *Bompas*. I am going to show that certain notes were paid to some person or other, and paid for this vessel; and these letters are evidence to show that he was the owner of the vessel.

Mr. Justice *Wightman*. There is a certain document taken to the bank, and notes paid for it.

Mr. *Kelly*. Then I object upon this ground. This is an indictment against Pedro Zulueta. I have not the least objection, that where documents are in existence, and members of the firm are connected with them, that they should be called to explain them; but I do object to any thing being given in evidence, done under the order of another person, unless it is proved to have come home to the knowledge of the prisoner. There is no proof that that entry ever came home to the prisoner, that he ever saw the notes, or that it was by any order signed by him or known to be his signature that these notes were paid, and therefore I object to its being any evidence against him. One can suppose a case like this. It is entirely unlike a mercantile transaction, where notice to one is notice to all the firm. If an action was brought against any one, a document affecting mercantile matters, the act of one partner is the act of all; and where it is a civil action or liability, the act done by the father would be evidence against the son, his partner, and that, though the son was not in England at the time, but was in Spain, and had no notice of the proceedings. Now let us try that: here is a transaction respecting the payment of bank-notes, and if, because it is supposed to be done by the house of Zulueta, it is evidence against this particular member of the firm, without any proof that it was done by him, it would be equally evidence against a member of the firm who was in Spain during the whole of the time; and it might have pleased Sir George Stephen to have selected him as a subject of prosecution; he might have been indicted for equipping this vessel and the other acts charged in the indictment; and if an act done by one member of the firm is evidence against another, it would be evidence against him. I apprehend that, supposing this payment of money to have any thing to do with this transaction, which I apprehend does not appear, unless it is proved it was done with the defendant's knowledge or by his order, it is no evidence against him; and no act done by another member of the firm is any evidence against him. There is no proof that he saw these notes, or gave any order; and under these circumstances, upon this criminal charge, I submit it is not evidence against him.

Mr. Serjeant *Bompas*. I am aware of the necessity of the accuracy of the evidence to convict a party on a criminal charge; but I apprehend there is abundant evidence to establish that the notes given were the notes paid for the purchase of the vessel. It is not a case where you have no evidence of Mr. Zulueta having taken a share in the purchase of the vessel; you have evidence of his control over the purchase in his lending the money for the purchase, and that he interfered in the purchase of the vessel. You have also a letter written by him to Captain Jennings in respect of it, and I am going to show that Captain Jennings was present when this sum was paid for the purchase. I am going to trace it to two individuals, Bernardos and Jennings, and I am going to show that these notes were for the purchase of this vessel, and that the prisoner at the bar interferes with the vessel afterwards, as if he was acting as interested in it. I have put in two letters, one from the captain communicating to him as owner, giving an account of the transactions, and asking upon whom he is to draw for the amount required. The letter from Mr. Zulueta states that he will pay all the disbursements; he regrets the captain did not give him the amount, and requests him to go to the Salthouse Dock. In addition to the control over the actual purchase, he states that the money was paid for the purchase, he exercises a control over it, and directs the amount. Then you have the previous letter of Captain Jennings, and you have in these two letters a distinct act of ownership over the vessel, directing where she is to go, and distinctly exercising dominion over her. The question undoubtedly is, whether Captain Jennings was nominally appointed as master, he not being substantially the owner, and whether Mr. Zulueta did not from the beginning to the end transact the business of the vessel. That is for the Jury. I show he exercised control over it, and I show that this money was delivered to a person, and paid in purchase of the vessel. I submit it is quite clear that I am entitled to show that it was paid by these bankers.

Mr. Serjeant *Talfourd*. I submit that there is another ground on which this evidence is admissible. Pedro Zulueta, the prisoner, has undertaken to give an account of the transaction, and the account given in substance in the evidence is this:—That his house was authorised by Martinez & Co. to advance a certain sum out of the funds in their hands for the purchase of this vessel; that that sum was lent in advance to Captain Jennings by Martinez; that Captain Jennings became the purchaser, and was *bonâ fide* the owner of the vessel; that is not the precise evidence, but the substance. We propose to show that that account is not true; that the price of the vessel was not 500*l*.; the extent to which they were authorised to advance, but 650*l*. That that 650*l*. was a sum paid in some sort; that it is debited to the account of Martinez & Co.; that that sum was advanced out of the funds at a time when it was impossible that they could have had any communication with Martinez & Co., at the Havannah, to advance beyond the sum of 500*l*., which was stated to be the sum. Having taken that account, as given in the evidence, we are entitled to show that, in giving this account, the prisoner gave a false account as to a part of the transaction.

Mr. *Kelly*. If it is competent to my learned friend to give evidence of the falsehood of any statement made before the Committee, I challenge them to show the falsehood of any one statement made, with all the facilities I have given them with the books and documents of the house. But that is not the question: the question is, whether, because Mr. Zulueta has given certain evidence before a Committee of the House of Commons, in which he has stated his participation to a certain extent in the transaction in question, and in which he has stated the general effect of the transaction, any act done by any other member of the firm, or any one connected with the house, is to be made evidence against him. I apprehend, upon the plainest and clearest principles in the law of evidence, it is not; and in order to illustrate my argument I will merely put this case: Mr. Zulueta states, before the Committee of the House of Commons, and truly states, that his house, for a house at Cadiz, negotiated the purchase of this vessel, and the shipment of these goods. As far as that statement goes, for better or worse, it is evidence against him. But my learned friend says, therefore whatever was done by any other member of the firm, as a part of the transaction, is evidence against him. Let me suppose that the prisoner at the bar, having, by a letter read in evidence, authorised the purchase of the vessel; and, in addition to that, which is not yet in evidence, but may be had, directed that his correspondents, in Liverpool should ship goods for a certain place on board the vessel. Having been charged with the knowledge of the secret object and destination of the vessel, suppose his partner, unknown to him, had given some secret instructions to disregard the charter-party—Whatever orders my son, or my house, may have given you, take all these goods to the Gallinas, or any other slave dealing port, and barter them for two hundred slaves— and yet, upon the argument of my learned friend, that would be evidence here. My learned friend says, the prisoner has admitted he negotiated the transaction; and, therefore, any thing done by any member of the firm is evidence against him; that any thing done by any member of the firm, or any thing done by any body connected with the firm, would be a part of the transaction. To say that any thing done, which may be a felonious act, for aught I know, and though in relation to this transaction, not in my knowledge, to make that evidence against him, would be to indict one man for a felony committed by another, because he was a partner of that other, and because that house was concerned in the transaction out of which the felony arose.

(The Judges conferred together.)

Mr. Justice *Maule* (*to* Mr. *Thomas*). I think you stated, that the order upon which the money was paid on the 29th of August, was returned to Zulueta & Co.?—Yes, it was.

When was it returned?—We have no particular periods; but when the pass-book is called for, the vouchers are in the pocket of the book.

There was a pass-book between you and Zulueta & Co.?—Yes.

In that pass-book were all the payments entered?—Yes.

And this amongst the rest?—Yes; but I would not state whether it was a draft, or a bill at twelve months date.

It would state the account upon which it was paid?—Yes.

And you would with that send back the draft or order upon which it was paid?—Yes.

When was that done?—I cannot say when the book was called for: it might be upon the following day, or in the course of a fortnight or so.

It would be in the course of a fortnight?—It might be so, I cannot say: there are parties who do not call for their book in a year, or not at all.

Zulueta & Co. do not call for their book for a year?—No, I do not say that; they would have it frequently.

Did you return it with the vouchers in the pocket of the book?—Yes.

Did you do that frequently?—Yes.

When was the payment made?—The 29th of August, 1840.

You said the book was returned to them frequently?—Yes, I imagine so, that they would call for it: they call for it, or send for it.

When it is called for, it is put into the hand of the caller, and sent away?—Yes.

About how frequently?—It depends upon circumstances; some persons send frequently.

Do, for God's sake, put out of your mind all other customers of your principals, but Messrs. Zulueta?—It is not my department, and I really do not know how frequently they send.

I have taken it that they had it returned frequently?—I imagine so; I think so.

That is, you think so, from knowing it?—No; from the general custom of merchants of their standing.

What you do know is this: that the payment is entered in the book; that the course is to return the book: whether it has ever been returned you do not know?—No, I do not; of my own knowledge, I do not: I believe so.

I thought it might probably appear that Messrs. Zulueta & Co. had this cheque.

Mr. Serjeant *Bompas*. Are either of your principals here?—I am not aware of it.

Not in obedience to the subpœna?—I am not aware of it.

Mr. Justice *Maule*. You had better postpone it till to-morrow; you will be able to get at it by that time?—It is not in my department.

Mr. Serjeant Bompas. What is the name of the person in whose department it is?—In that of the receipt-clerks.

Give me the name?—Mr. Hayburn.

Mr. Justice *Maule*. As this extreme rigour of proof is insisted upon, you may have twenty clerks?—I have no doubt that Messrs. Zulueta had the book away frequently; but I do not know it myself.

Mr. Justice *Maule*. Suppose we had an earthquake every three years, one would say that was frequently. If a man got a dinner only once a week, one would not say that that was frequently. It depends upon what it is?—I do not know how often it was.

Do you mean once in ten years, or what?—Almost daily.

Mr. Justice *Maule*. I think now, assuming that Mr. Kelly does not raise any question as to the fact of the pass-book going back with the vouchers, it being now taken that the draft whatever it was, or order, upon which this money was paid, having been returned to Zulueta & Co. before the notice to produce was given to the prisoner, that notice naming the cheque or order mentioning the date and mentioning the sum, and it containing the subsequent clause, "all other papers, &c., relating to this matter," supposing instead of being a cheque or draft it was an acceptance for a sum made payable at their bankers, the subsequent part of the notice to produce is to be drawn in aid of the previous part, and that taking the two parts together it amounts to a reasonable notice to the prisoner to produce the paper, if in his power, even if it was an acceptance and not a cheque or draft. Then the question comes to this, whether the document here is admissible in evidence against the prisoner. The prisoner is a member of the firm in England, not absent in Spain as he might be, but he is in England attending to this matter; and notice having been given by the bankers of Messrs. Zulueta by the return of the vouchers that they had paid such a sum of money upon such an account, that that amounts to a statement to each of the partners of Zulueta & Co., and it is reasonable to suppose that they were acquainted with the statement in the pass-book and that document, and that they amount together to this, that it is the same as if you could show this gentleman had said to Zulueta & Co., on such a day I paid to such a person such an amount for your house: and we think the witness may be interrogated as to the account upon which he paid this money.

Mr. Serjeant *Bompas*. On whose account did you pay that 650*l.*?—Zulueta & Co.

On what day?—On the 29th of August, 1840.

What were the numbers of the notes?—47,194, dated the 9th of March, 1840, 100*l.*; 41,674, the same date and amount; 48,204, 9th March, 100*l.*; 36,020, 25th of May, 1840, Liverpool Branch Bank of England, 100*l.*; 46,243, 9th March, 100*l.*; 38,288, 9th March, 1840, 100*l.*; 1,364, 50*l.*, August the 8th, 1840.

Mr. *Emanuel Emanuel* sworn. Examined by Mr. Serjeant *Bompas*.

I believe you reside at Portsmouth?—Yes.

Did you know a vessel called the Gollupchik?—Yes.

Was she sold by auction, or in any way?—Yes, by auction.

Were you the purchaser?—I purchased her for a friend.

What amount did you give for her?—600*l.*

And there were the auction expenses?—And the auction expenses.

Did you afterwards sell the vessel?—Yes.

To whom did you sell her?—I sold her to two parties who came together to purchase her.

Do you know their names?—Captain Bernardos and Captain Jennings.

What was the day of the month?—That I cannot tell you exactly.

Was it in August 1840, about that time?—I could tell you; I think it was in June.

Just tell me, if you can by any means?—I can tell you by the day I received the money, which was the same day I sold her.

Have you any memorandum made by yourself?—No, by my clerk, of the number of the notes.

Did you see the entry the day it was made?—Yes.

Mr. *Kelly*. That is not in your own handwriting; when was it made?—The same day as the letter was posted.

Mr. Serjeant *Bompas*. What was the day?—It was sold in September last.

Did you keep a memorandum of the numbers of the notes you received?— Yes, that is the only memorandum that was kept.

Tell me the numbers of the notes?—The numbers, as they are entered here, are single 100*l.* notes, J. B., March the 9th, 1840; J. B., 48,204; J. B., 47,194, same date, 100*l.*; J. B., 46,243, 9th March, 1840, 100*l.*; J. B., 41,674, same date, 100*l.*; J. G., 36,020, May 25, 1840, 100*l.*; J. G., 38,288, May the 9th, 1840, 100*l.*; then there was a note for 50*l.*, No. 1,364, 8th August, 1840; making a total of 650*l.*

Were there any papers or documents you received or delivered in respect of the vessel?—I received no documents; she was sold by public auction.

Did you give any?—No, I only gave an order to the ship-keeper to deliver her up.

Have you got that letter?—No, it was not a business transaction, it was merely for a friend.

Had you the bill of lading, or any thing?—No.

Cross-examined by Mr. Kelly.

Who originally sold her?—She was advertised to be sold by auction, at the Exchange Rooms, by Mr. Robinson.

Do you know who he was?—An auctioneer at Portsmouth.

Mr. Serjeant *Bompas*. To whom did you pay the money for your purchase?— The money was originally paid by a cheque from the party by whom she was purchased, who attended the sale himself to bid for her; that cheque by some accident was not presented at the place where it ought to be; it came back to me and I paid it myself.

Mr. Justice *Maule*. You paid the auctioneer?—I paid the bankers myself finding there was a mistake, and it was immediately repaid to me.

That cheque was given to somebody?—To the auctioneer; not that cheque of mine, but the cheque of the party who purchased her.

Mr. Serjeant *Bompas.* I am now going to offer in evidence the papers of the vessel, the cockets that were on board the vessel. I am going to call for those, as my learned friend wishes me to call for one thing at a time.

Mr. *John Brown* called again. Examined by Mr. Serjeant *Talfourd.*

Have you the cockets there?—Yes, I have.

There are seven of them; No. 5 is the document we want. (*The Witness produced the same.*)

Mr. Serjeant *Bompas.* These are the cockets; they are not objected to; they are in page 30 of the book.

Mr. Serjeant *Talfourd* (*to* Captain *Hill*). Were those found on board the vessel, and delivered to you?—Yes.

They were delivered to you by Captain Jennings?—Yes.

Mr. *Kelly.* Do you propose to read all these documents?

Mr. Serjeant *Bompas.* No. There is one entry made of plate-glass, upon which a drawback is to be obtained by the person who ships it; all the rest are in the same form. Now, No. 7. (*Mr. Brown hands that in.*) Now, the bill of lading: hand that to Captain Hill.

Mr. *Kelly.* There is no occasion to trouble Captain Hill. I do not know how it is important, but I do not see how it is admissible; it is not in his handwriting, nor contains his name; it is found in the vessel early in 1841, many months after he sails. How is that evidence against the prisoner? The charge is, that the prisoner at the bar did equip and use the vessel for the purposes of the slave trade; that the prisoner at the bar shipped goods on board the vessel for the purposes of the slave trade. I need not refer to the letters in evidence or any other document; but here is a document purporting to be a bill of lading, not bearing the signature of the prisoner or any of the firm, nor seen by any of them, but found many months afterwards on board the vessel: how can that be evidence against him? Is that the only document found? There may be treasonable papers found there, and how can they be evidence against Mr. Zulueta, unless it is proved it was done by his orders.

Mr. Justice *Maule.* I suppose the object of the evidence is to show that there was no mention in these papers of Mr. Zulueta having any thing to do with it?

Mr. Serjeant *Bompas.* I ought to say there is the name of Zulueta and Co., the Spanish house at Cadiz.

Mr. Justice *Maule.* There is nothing found on board the vessel to indicate any concern that the Zuluetas in London had in freighting the ship or shipping the goods. I suppose it must be taken for granted, unless it is shown on the part of the prisoner that Mr. Zulueta's name was in the document, that it was not his.

Mr. *Kelly*. The prosecutor is to make out his case that the prisoner at the bar equipped the vessel for the slave trade.

Mr. Serjeant *Bompas*. Employed it for that purpose.

Mr. Justice *Maule* (*to* Captain *Hill.*) Did you find any document mentioning the house of Zulueta in London?—None, but the papers before the Court.

And none of those mentioned any house in London?—The letter read is the only one.

Mr. Serjeant *Bompas*. We now produce certain letters found in the ship, not the ship's papers. There is one in which the name was cut out, the letter authorising Captain Jennings to purchase the vessel; except that in, there is nothing to show they had any interest, or that they shipped the goods.

Mr. Justice *Maule*. These are all the papers found on board?

Mr. Serjeant *Bompas*. Now we are going to offer certain other letters.

Mr. Justice *Maule* (*to* Captain *Hill.*) Are these all the papers you could get?—Yes, these are all I could get.

Mr. Serjeant *Bompas*. I am going to offer the letters objected to in my address; we are going to show letters giving directions.

Mr. *Kelly*. My learned friend should not state the contents of the letters.

Mr. Serjeant *Bompas*. I have stated nothing injurious to the prisoner, only enough to call the attention of the Judges to them. I am going to prove the handwriting of them.

Mr. *Kelly*. The evidence at present is, that Captain Hill found on board the vessel, or that the master delivered to him, certain papers, those you now produce; you say nothing about the contents, but you are going to prove the handwriting?

Mr. Serjeant *Bompas*. Yes.

> (*Mr. Brown produced certain other papers, which were handed in.*)

Mr. *Brown*. That packet contains nine enclosures.

  Mr. *Sebastian Gonzalez Martinez* sworn. Examined by Mr. Serjeant *Talfourd*.

Do you know Pedro de Martinez, of Cadiz?—No.

Have you had any correspondence with him?—Never.

You are not acquainted with his writing?—Not at all.

Where have you lived; at Hampstead?—Yes, at Hampstead.

What is the name of your house at Hampstead; has it a name?—Yes, it has.

What is it?—Bellasise Park.

Cross-examined by Mr. Clarkson.

Do you know the gentleman in this dock?—Yes, I do; I have known him since he was a child.

What character has he borne in this city for integrity and good conduct?—Most excellent; he has been a good son, a good father, and a good husband, and a most honourable merchant.

Mr. Serjeant *Bompas*. I thought we should have been able to prove the handwriting. These letters are addressed to the correspondent to whom the vessel was consigned, giving directions in respect of the vessel, and there are instructions as to what is to be done with the cargo. Your Lordships will probably look at them; there is no actual signature.

Mr. Justice *Maule*. I have heard enough of them.

Mr. Serjeant *Bompas*. They are in Spanish; there is no name signed to them at all; there is the letter M, and there are directions in respect of the cargo which is on board. Now I apprehend we have two things to prove, and to give in evidence to your Lordships and to the Jury; the one is, what was the object of the vessel, what was to be done with her cargo, what was the object of her freight? There is the captain found on board, who delivers up the ship's papers, and among others the directions to the consignees as to what is to be done with the cargo, and general instructions.

Mr. *Kelly*. I have three times heard my learned friend make an assertion to your Lordship, which I beg leave to deny. I am certain my learned friend is speaking under instructions false in themselves. He has never read the letters; I have. They have been before another Court in a proceeding to which this gentleman was no party, and I undertake to say they do not refer to the disposal of this cargo or this vessel in any way; and it is cruel in the extreme that such statements should be made in the hearing of the Jury, which they will never forget; and that those statements will remain when your Lordship rejects them, as you will do. I have read them all, from the beginning to the end; they were before the Privy Council, and I say they do not relate to it.

Mr. Serjeant *Bompas*. I have read them from the beginning to the end; I do not put my judgment against Mr. Kelly's; but he asserts that they do not, and I assert that they do: whatever is in these letters I have carefully abstained from stating it in any way which shall injure the prisoner at the bar.

Mr. Justice *Maule*. Mr. Serjeant Bompas does not state that they contain any direction to employ the goods in slave trading.

Mr. *Kelly*. I deny that they contain any direction to employ the goods in any way.

Mr. Justice *Maule*. It is rather favourable to the voyage that there should be a document so produceable and regular, as instructions to the persons interested in the cargo: where there was nothing to conceal, persons would have those instructions.

Mr. Serjeant *Bompas*. When we come to matters of assertion, I yield to my learned friend; but when we come to the examination of documents, and to decide whether they are evidence, then we look at the evidence. It is absolutely necessary, if they are directions, that your Lordships should look at them to ascertain whether they are so or not, and in that way I should not have the slightest objection to submit them to the Court: they are at page 7; and there is one document I will call your attention to, in which there is a distinct direction as to what is to be done with the cargo on board; as far as that is necessary these are directions, or, as your Lordship says, there are none.

(A printed copy of the Letters was handed to their Lordships.)

Mr. Serjeant *Bompas*. If your Lordships look at the general direction, you will find it in page 7, "I have to request," down to the words "so very precious."

Mr. Justice *Maule*. Does that refer to any mention of the Augusta before that?

Mr. *Kelly*. Not at all; it refers to the vessel Urraca.

Mr. Serjeant *Bompas*. The vessel first in question was the Urraca, not the Augusta.

(Their Lordships referred to the printed Letter.)

Mr. Serjeant *Bompas*. If your Lordships will look at the bottom of page 38, you will see a paragraph beginning "From my preceding communication."

Mr. Justice *Wightman*. He dispatched that ship?

Mr. Serjeant *Bompas*. Yes.

Mr. Justice *Maule*. Are there any other letters to the consignee relating to this ship, unless these do?

Mr. *Kelly*. I hope your Lordships will not take that for granted upon my learned friend's statement: there are a great variety of documents, of the existence of which the prosecutors are perfectly aware; they have given no notice to produce them, and they would lay the matter open before the Jury.

Mr. Serjeant *Bompas*. I hope your Lordships will not give the least credit to these statements of Mr. Kelly; they deserve no credit.

Mr. Justice *Maule*. There are documents, Mr. Kelly says, which we shall see in due time.

Mr. Serjeant *Bompas*. There are papers here, and we wish every one to be put in, no doubt. The form in which we put it is this: that if a letter is directed to consignees giving directions, that is evidence of what is to be done with the cargo, they are directions in respect of it; and the question whether Captain Jennings was the owner of this vessel, or whether it was used as a cover under his directions, is a question for the Jury. That Messrs. Zulueta, on behalf apparently of Martinez, entered into a contract of charter-party with him there is no doubt, according to the statement and admissions in this examination; and they also ship these goods on board the ship of Captain Jennings: they were shipped for the consignee; they were the agents. What was to be done with those goods? The only way that can be ascertained, is by the actual order to the consignees in respect of them.

The second question will be how far Mr. Zulueta was implicated in it, and that will be shown by the conduct pursued, and the concealment he practised; but the question is, what was the object of it? What was to be done? If we see he employs this vessel to accomplish a particular object, we say it was for that purpose. My learned friend says, how can you give in evidence any thing that took place after the vessel left England? How can you say that it was employed for that purpose, except by something done in England? Suppose I show that these goods were ordered by an individual to be used for the purpose of the slave trade, and suppose I can show they were so used, that is, after they were sent. But I am to show by the conduct of Mr. Zulueta that that was the object. They are two separate things; how am I to show that was the object? I show the bill of lading by which they were consigned to certain persons; I show a letter directing those persons how to apply them. Suppose there is no signature to any one of these letters, does that prevent their being given in evidence? You must expect there will be concealment, if there is an illegal voyage; but if these are the orders upon which they are to proceed, how is it to be said that that is not the object of the voyage? I must show what was the object: how is it possible to show that? It is only by showing the orders given in that respect; there is no other way of showing that that was the purpose, except showing something after the vessel left. My learned friend has said many times, how can Mr. Zulueta be affected by any thing that took place after the vessel left England. Suppose a vessel was sent from England for the express purpose of receiving slaves, and did receive slaves; if I can affect him, I must show that it was done afterwards; if it was for slave transactions, I can only show by the directions and orders given to the parties to whom they were consigned what was to be done with them. They were shipped in the name of Captain Jennings by Mr. Zulueta: but what is to be done? If Captain Jennings was the agent of Messrs. Zulueta, the fact of ordering these things to be done would be evidence against Mr. Zulueta. It would be for the Jury to say whether Captain Jennings was employed, or was the real owner of the vessel; whether the owner or the captain. If we could show written orders to dispose of the goods, how could that be done but by putting in the document? If I could show Captain Jennings's coming to the Gallinas, and stating he must apply these things in a particular way, can he turn round and say I have no instructions? Yes, these are your instructions; and no concealment in the case of a crime can prevent them being given in evidence, because, in that case, the captain is safe in taking out papers not giving general instructions as to the whole of the cargo: but if there is concealment, if a party hides himself, and acts in another name, and you find that vessel with certain documents on board giving directions what is to be done with the cargo, is it to be said that those documents are not receivable in evidence in respect of that cargo? If it is so, it is not possible to give evidence against any one who does not go to Africa to do it. It is nothing to show they sent out a vessel with that object. First, I show that in fact the directions were to send them for the purposes of the slave trade, and I show next that it was so used. If you show it was not so used, if you cut off the latter part, if you say the directions were on board to be so used, I submit it is evidence when the captain gives up the directions to the consignees as to how they are to treat these goods; and therefore, my Lord, I say it is no answer to say they are not signed. If I do not show by Mr. Zulueta's conduct that he had some guilty knowledge—

Mr. *Kelly.* I do not take the objection that they are not signed.

Mr. Serjeant *Bompas.* I do not show that they are signed by Mr. Zulueta, which he says is necessary: in point of fact, I say it is immaterial, because, if a person whom Mr. Zulueta never heard of, had given directions in respect of these goods, that they were to be used for the purpose of slave dealing, he having shipped them, the only question is, did he ship them for that purpose? How do you show that? By his conduct. That he did employ the vessel is proved: he chartered it, and that is the only purpose. I submit that the only way is to show the directions at the time which they were to receive; I submit that the directions are evidence; and the last question is, whether Mr. Zulueta did it with that object.

Mr. Serjeant *Talfourd*. In this prosecution there are two propositions which the prosecutors are bound to establish; the first is, that this vessel was employed for an illegal purpose; and, secondly, that Zulueta was conscious of it at the time he entered into this contract. Those two propositions are separate and distinct. It is true you cannot establish the second without the first; but it does not follow that you cannot give all the evidence to establish the first without interfering with the second. You must establish the felony, before you show the receipt of the goods. There the object and purpose for which the vessel was fitted out are part of the transaction, and must be shown by legitimate means. It is said by my learned friend, that if Mr. Zulueta was guilty of the offence, he was guilty of it at the time he dispatched the vessel from this country; but it does not follow that all the evidence is to be confined to this country. No one can suppose that, if a vessel is fitted up with these leagers and other fittings, it was not intended to be used on deck in some other than legitimate trade; and, whether she was driven in by stress of weather or not, if she was turned into a slave trader, is it to be said that instructions what was to be done with her, whether they consisted in writing, in words, or acts, are not evidence? I grant it does not establish the guilt of the prisoner, but it is a step to it; and if we are excluded showing the nature of the directions to the consignee of the vessel, who must be known to the prisoner, we are prevented from showing any painting or any alteration done after the ship left this country. They are not evidence as the history of any other slaving transaction, or any other history or confession; they are not for that purpose evidence against the prisoner; but they are evidence against the prisoner in so far as they are acts done in respect of the dispatch of the cargo, and the employment of the vessel.

Mr. Justice *Maule*. I do not think it is necessary to trouble Mr. Kelly. It seems to me that Mr. Serjeant Talfourd is quite right in saying there are two things to be proved: one, the body of the offence, the slave trading, or the intention to do it, the taking the voyage; and the other is the participation and knowledge of the prisoner in it; and I think it quite true, that it might well be that the first matter might be established, and established completely, quite consistently with the innocence of the prisoner, and yet, notwithstanding, that these papers might be admissible in evidence upon this trial. There is no rule that requires, that in order that a matter may be given in evidence upon a trial between parties, that the evidence should be such as in itself is sufficient to prove the case; if so, all other evidence would be excluded. I admit it is quite competent to the prosecutor to prove, though he has not fixed the knowledge of the prisoner, any fact constituting any suspicion, or a plausibility. I think he might do that: but here the objection is not so much to the subject of proof, slave trading, as the medium of proof—the document seeking to establish it—this being a document not at all traced to the prisoner, nor any body in privity with him; it is merely found on board the vessel, and is not a document that can be read against him. It is not a statement accompanying any act done, it is found on board the vessel, found by some one who may be an agent or accomplice of the prisoner, and handed to Captain Hill. I think the mere circumstance of handing it to Captain Hill does not remove the objection of want of privity between the prisoner and the paper: I think it cannot be given in evidence. If the vessel sailed without any instructions, no doubt it is a very strong circumstance against the honesty and legal purpose of the voyage: if she is in a latitude, where slave trading is carried on, it affords an observation against the legality of the voyage.

Mr. Justice *Wightman.* I am of the same opinion: I think the document is not admissible, for the reasons stated by my brother Maule.

Mr. Serjeant *Bompas* not objecting, the prisoner was admitted to bail, and left the dock.

[*Adjourned.*

SECOND DAY.
SATURDAY, 28TH OCTOBER, 1843.

The names of the Jury were called over.—All present.

The Defendant took his place within the Bar.

The Witnesses on both sides, except those to character, were directed to withdraw.

(*Joseph Bankes was called, but was not in attendance.*)

William Thomas Onion sworn. Examined by Mr. Serjeant *Bompas.*

Do you reside at Portsmouth?—I do.

Did you know a vessel called first the Gollupchik, afterwards the Augusta?—I did.

Did you know a Captain Jennings?—I did.

Did you know his mate also?—Mr. Mottley.

In consequence of your knowing one or both of them, were you occasionally on board the vessel?—I was on board sometimes, almost the whole time.

Were you ever applied to to sail in the vessel?—Not directly.

Was any application made to you to join the vessel going any where?—An observation was made, but not a direct application.

You say you were on board; did you see the captain when he received any letters?—Yes; I generally saw him receive letters.

What is your occupation at Portsmouth?—A teacher of navigation.

Were you employed to teach anybody in that vessel?—I was giving Mr. Mottley instructions.

Mr. Justice *Maule*. What is the name of the gentleman?

Mr. Serjeant *Bompas*. Motley: M-o-t-l-e-y.—No; M-o-t-t-l-e-y.

You say you saw the captain receive letters; did you see him do any thing with any part of the letters?—He generally used to cut the name out.

Mr. *Kelly*. I must object to this. What can we have to do with all this? Here is a witness, of whom we never heard till to-day, to speak to what Captain Jennings has done with certain letters he received. How can that be made evidence against Mr. Zulueta, the prisoner at the bar? Any thing, which Mr. Zulueta authorised the captain to do, which he directed, or which he sanctioned after it was done, is evidence against him; but on what conceivable principle are the minds of the Jury to be perplexed and overloaded by circumstances taking place, which occurred in his absence, over which he had no control, and of which he had no knowledge till he hears it three years and a half afterwards?

Mr. Justice *Maule*. I do not know, at present, how it can be made evidence.

Mr. Serjeant *Bompas*. I do not know how it can be said that nothing is evidence against a person, unless he is present at the time. I conceive this is evidence on the same ground, as if the captain bought slaves with money sent by Mr. Zulueta for the express purpose of buying slaves, it would be evidence against him. The question is, whether from Mr. Zulueta's conduct, it is not evident that he sent this vessel for slave trading; that must appear from all the facts: but here we have the confirmation, that there is one of Mr. Zulueta's letters actually found on board the vessel with the name cut out. We shall prove also another letter, which the captain received. There is all that practice of secrecy, which shows at the time the vessel had been purchased by Mr. Zulueta, when Mr. Jennings was acting as captain of that vessel. We are to show the nature of the transactions of that vessel, and of the prisoner. One thing is, that there was a universal concealment. Supposing we could distinctly show that Jennings was going to the Gallinas for the purpose of dealing in slaves, then we might show, by Mr. Zulueta's conduct, that he knew that was the object of the voyage; but in order to show what was the intention, we must show what passed; and if we cannot show the conduct of the captain on board that vessel, at the time he is the captain of that vessel, which we say there is evidence that Mr. Zulueta purchased; if we cannot account for that letter which is produced, in Mr. Zulueta's handwriting, with the name cut out, and give evidence when it was cut out, and how it was cut out, it appears to me excluding us from a means of giving evidence of the facts. If this be not evidence, it is utterly impossible to prove any combination for the purpose of dealing in slaves, unless the prisoner charged says so himself, or is present when they say it. If they employ agents, and he is only one of the parties, I must show the acts of the parties: but here is a letter from on board the vessel, with the name cut out. I am showing that this person received letters while he was at Portsmouth from Zulueta, and that he cut out the name of the person writing those letters. I submit to your Lordship that that is evidence.

Mr. Justice *Maule*. We think the evidence is not admissible. It is very true, that you might prove slave trading by the captain of the vessel, although you did not show the prisoner to have been present at the time; but it does not follow that every thing which tends to show slave trading, and which would be admissible against the captain of the vessel, would be admissible against Zulueta. I do not think that follows with respect to the evidence now offered. In my opinion it does not necessarily tend to prove slave trading; it amounts to an admission on the part of the captain, that the letter he had received was from a correspondent, whom he desired to conceal; it amounts therefore to no more, if so much, as if Captain Jennings had said to this witness—This is a letter from a person from whom I am desirous of concealing that I have received letters. I think this is not evidence.

Mr. Serjeant *Bompas*. You say you were on board that vessel frequently, giving instructions to Mottley, and occasionally with the captain; did you see any thing on board that vessel in a bag at any time?—I saw some deck-screws; I found them.

Mr. Justice *Maule*. You say you saw them; do you mean that you found many, or only a few?—It was one bundle, wrapped up in canvas.

A bundle of deck-screws, wrapped up in canvas?—Yes.

How many?—About twenty, or two-and-twenty.

Mr. Serjeant *Bompas*. Will you explain what you mean by deck-screws?—Screws that are formed for placing a temporary deck for slaves, to go through the deck, and fasten to a beam to ship a deck.

To screw it on, and then take out the screws and move the deck?—Yes.

Mr. Justice *Maule*. Whereabouts did you find these?

Mr. Serjeant *Bompas*. Where did you find them?—In a secret place at the back of the cupboard.

Mr. Justice *Maule*. The cupboard; in what place?—In the cabin of the ship.

Mr. Serjeant *Bompas*. How came you to be looking there?—A boy, in putting the soup-tureen into the cupboard, happened to put it too far, and the tureen fell over; he told me—

Mr. *Kelly*. Tell us what you saw, not what he told you?—Consequently I got over and recovered the tureen, and I said, "Here is a store—"

Mr. Serjeant *Bompas*. Never mind what you said, but what you saw: you got up, and recovered the tureen?—Yes; and in searching about, I found these.

Did you do anything with them, or leave them there?—I put them on the table, and Mr. Mottley opened them.

What was done with them then?—They were put into a cabin abaft by the boy.

About what time was this, as near as you can tell?—About the middle of September, 1840.

Did you see any thing else in the cabin at all?—I have seen some shackles amongst the ballast.

Mr. Justice *Maule*. How many?—Oh, I do not know; it was mixed with the ballast, and one thing and another.

Have you been at sea yourself?—Some years.

How long have you left the sea?—About four years.

Did you see any false tops, any covers for the tops of cabins?—False tops, yes; all the bed places were false tops.

Just tell us what you mean by false tops?—A vacancy between the deck and the lining.

Was there any opening to them?—Yes.

Just describe it?—About four inches I suppose, so as to enable any thing to be stowed away there.

When it was stowed away, was it possible to be seen to be stowed away, or concealed?—No; it was concealed.

Mr. Justice *Maule*. All the bed places you say were with false tops?—What they call lined, between the deck and the lining, leaves a vacancy.

Mr Serjeant *Bompas*. Was there any thing to open or shut? Will you describe how anything could be put in?—A piece of, I do not know what you call it, a piece of furniture came over the facing.

Do you know what is the moulding?—A kind of moulding, and there was this vacancy.

To any body who came into that cabin and saw that, was that perceivable?—Not at all.

Cross-examined by Mr. Kelly.

What are you now by business or trade?—A teacher of navigation.

Were these articles, of which you have spoken, articles calculated for the carrying on the slave trade?—I presume so.

Will you allow me to ask in what way you have acquired your knowledge of what is fit for the slave trade, and what is not?—A representation of Mr. Mottley himself, who was on the slave trade on the coast for years.

It was by the representation of Mottley, who was on the coast for years, you acquired this knowledge?—Yes, that was the way.

That leads you to suppose that these were calculated for the use of the slave trade?—Yes.

Did you know that the Gollupchik had been sent to England to be sold by reason of its having been fitted up for the slave trade?—I heard so.

Was it not perfectly notorious through Portsmouth?—I believe she was not condemned, but it was said so.

You are a teacher of navigation; do you know whether before a vessel clears out from a British port for the coast of Africa, she is not examined by a Custom-house officer, to see whether there are any articles used for the slave trade?—I believe she is.

These articles you saw were at Portsmouth, before the vessel went to Liverpool, where she received her cargo?—Yes.

Do you live at Portsmouth?—I do.

Joseph Bankes, the elder, sworn. Examined by Mr. Serjeant *Talfourd*.

Do you live at Portsmouth?—Yes.

What business do you there carry on?—A cooper.

Do you remember the Gollupchik being at Portsmouth in the year 1840?—Very well.

While she was there did you go on board her?—Yes.

Were you employed to do any thing on board that vessel with the water casks?—Yes.

The leagers?—Yes; large casks for leagers; double leagers.

About what size were the casks?—There were different sizes; but those casks we are now speaking about would contain nearly a thousand gallons each.

How many were there?—About a dozen.

Were they entire on board when you first went on board the vessel?—Yes.

Where were they?—They were on one side the kelson, full of water.

Who was in command of the vessel at that time?—A person of the name of Mottley, apparently to me assumed the command.

Did you see Jennings there?—Yes.

Do you know a man called Bernardos?—No, I do not.

Did you receive any directions, I do not ask what they were, to do any thing with the casks?—

Mr. *Kelly*. I do not understand here, how this is evidence against Mr. Zulueta. The cause has lasted quite long enough, without our having all the directions given by all persons.

Mr. Serjeant *Talfourd*. My question was simply: Did you receive any directions from any person? I put that, and was putting it in the most unexceptionable manner.

Mr. *Kelly*. I will not object; go on.

—I received directions at my own shop, from a person calling himself Mr. Jennings.

Mr. Serjeant *Talfourd*. Did you, in consequence of any directions you received, go on board the vessel?—He took me on board the vessel the same day, in the shipwright's boat.

In pursuance of any directions you received, did you do any thing?—I numbered each cask, beginning at 1, 2, 3, and completing each.

Each stave?—Yes; and then took the heads off the staves, put them on the inside of the staves, put them up together, and formed them into stacks.

Mr. Justice *Maule*. When you went on board, you found some staves and heads of casks?—I found the casks.

Mr. Serjeant *Talfourd*. He found the casks, and took them to pieces.

Mr. Justice *Maule*. You found the casks in the state of casks?—Yes, they were stowed in the hold of the vessel, full of water.

How many casks?—I think of the larger kind there were about twelve.

Mr. Serjeant *Talfourd*. About how many smaller ones?—I should say there were about fifty of the smaller kind.

Mr. Justice *Maule*. What did you do with the large casks?—Razed the staves of the large casks. I numbered each stave, stave by stave, till I had completed the circle of thirty or forty staves.

Did you mark them with chalk, or what?—I razed them with a proper razing iron.

Razing is scratching a mark?—Yes.

What did you do with them?—Took the hoops from them and put them together, and put them in close packs as we do sugar-casks.

You emptied the water?—Yes, emptied the water and took the casks to pieces.

You put the parts of the casks together as correctly as you could, to enable them to be put together again?—Yes.

Mr. Serjeant *Talfourd*. Where did you leave them?—I left them stowed in the ballast, after the ballast had been taken out and limbers cleared out of the bottom of the vessel and stowed them on the top of the ballast in packs.

Mr. Justice *Maule*. Each cask in a pack?—Yes, in a separate pack.

Mr. Serjeant *Talfourd*. Did you do any thing with the smaller ones?—Yes, some of them, and others I repaired for water for the voyage for the present crew.

Mr. Justice *Maule*. You did the same with some of the smaller ones, and repaired others for water for the crew?—Yes, just so.

Mr. Serjeant *Talfourd*. How long did it take you to do this?—About three weeks; from the 8th of September to the 19th we were positively engaged entirely in that work.

Did you see any thing else that attracted your attention, while you were engaged on board the vessel?—Yes.

What was it?—In two of the smaller casks, which we came to in the tier, our attention was attracted by a noise in the cask; it proved to be a quantity of what we call shackles when I was in the West India trade: we did not count them, but there might be from one to two hundred pair.

They were in the cask?—Yes.

Can you tell how many there were?—We did not count them, but I should consider from the weight and height of the cask, there were nearly two hundred pair.

Was any thing done with those while you were there?—Not that I saw.

Then they were left in the place where you found them?—Yes, they had been in the vessel before.

Mr. Justice *Maule*. What did you do with that cask?—We restowed it again.

Did you take that cask to pieces?—No.

How could you see the shackles?—Because we took the head out.

Did you put the head in again, or leave it so?—I left it so; but I believe my son did the remainder.

You do not know whether it was done or not?—No.

Cross-examined by Mr. *Clarkson*.

This was in September, between the 8th and 19th; you were eleven days about this?—That was the time that we were specially engaged on the large casks.

Was it necessary to hammer them to separate them?—Of course, we took all the hoops off.

That makes a good deal of noise?—Sometimes it does.

Had you any person to help you?—I had my own son, and the ship's crew at times, at any time I wanted to get the large casks out of the hold.

How long was this after the vessel had been sold, and these casks in her, by public auction, as a condemned slaver?—I did not know she had been sold; I heard of it.

When did you hear of it?—Some time before, in August, I heard it.

Did you go to the sale?—No.

Do you recollect the vessel leaving Portsmouth?—Yes; that was two or three days after.

She left in ballast for Liverpool; did she not?—They said she was going to Liverpool.

Perhaps there was a doubt about that; did any persons come on board her to see her?—I did not see any persons particular; there were comers and goers, such as persons who do come on board to vessels, such as watermen, and men coming on board wanting to go out as men in the vessel.

Any body else that you remember?—Not that I know of.

Just describe: the hold of the vessel had been fitted with these large leagers which you speak of?—Yes.

Those you took down, where did you put them?—We stowed them on the top of the ballast, in the wings, any where, where there appeared to be room.

What was the ballast of the vessel?—Iron ballast.

Where do you say you saw the shackles, which you assume to be a hundred or two hundred in number?—On the starboard side.

That is where you left them?—Yes.

Did they form part of the vessel's ballast?—I should say not.

What was the ballast?—The ballast was pigs of iron, such as are used on such occasions.

Have the kindness to tell me, whether or not you left those shackles on the top of the ballast?—I left them in the hold, on the starboard side.

On the top of the ballast?—Yes.

Were there any persons on board the vessel at the time you went away?— Yes, the ship's company.

Any body else?—Not that I know of, except two shipwrights.

Were they two Portsmouth shipwrights?—I believe they were.

What were their names?—Case the elder, and Case the younger.

Are they here to-day?—No, they are not.

Had they been working on board the vessel?—Previous to me, and after I left her also.

Do you recollect the names of any other persons who bad been working on board her?—No, I know there were two others; but I do not know their names.

What were they?—Scrapers, and caulkers, and so on.

Portsmouth men?—I believe so.

Who called upon you to come here and be a witness?—The King's solicitor, Mr. Greetham.

When?—Last Thursday.

Was that the first time you ever heard of being called here?—Oh, dear no; I had heard of it being talked about before.

Was that the first time you were called upon to attend?—Yes, positively to attend.

Did you communicate to Mr. Greetham that there were shipwrights, whose names you knew, working on the vessel, both before you were on board and afterwards?—No, I never mentioned it to any person.

You were never taken before any magistrate on this subject, were you?—No.

So that the party accused had no opportunity of knowing that you, or any person who comes with you, were about to attend?—No.

Mr. Justice *Maule*. I do not think it is convenient to put speeches, containing inferences to be derived from the evidence: it was the old practice, I am well aware, when speeches could not be made, and a very fair one then.

Mr. *Clarkson*. You have stated to the Jury what you saw of the vessel when she was at Portsmouth; can you give any account of what was on board her when she was at Liverpool, and whether there was any thing of the nature you have described?—No, for I never went to Liverpool.

Joseph Bankes, junior, sworn. Examined by Mr. *Payne*.

Are you the son of the last witness?—Yes.

Did you assist your father at Portsmouth on board the Augusta?—Yes.

Mr. *Kelly*. Is it only to confirm the other witness? I do not dispute that.

Mr. Serjeant *Bompas*. I thought the intention of the cross-examination was to break in upon that witness.

Mr. *Kelly*. Certainly not; you misunderstood it, then.

Mr. *Clarkson*. You may stand down, Sir.

Henry George Moon sworn. Examined by Mr. *Payne*.

Are you clerk to Mr. Vandenburg, the Russian consul at Portsmouth?—I am clerk to him, but he is not the Russian consul.

Do you remember the arrival of the Gollupchik at Portsmouth?—I do.

On the day of her arrival, did you go on board her?—I went on board with Mr. Vandenburg.

Do you remember the day of her arrival?—I think it was the 10th of June, 1839.

Who was the captain of the vessel at that time?—Thomas Bernardos described himself as captain.

Did he act as captain?—The vessel was under the charge of an officer of Her Majesty's customs at the time; I forget the officer's name.

Did you receive any letter from Bernardos to put into the post?—I took a letter on shore, addressed to Messrs. Zulueta & Co.

What did you do with it?—I put it into the post.

From whom did you get it?—From Captain Bernardos.

Mr. *Payne*. Here it is; "A Letter addressed by the said Thomas Bernardos, addressed to Messrs. Zulueta; posted at Portsmouth, the 10th day of June, 1839." We call for that.

Mr. Justice *Maule*. Was that the same day you got the letter?—Yes, the same day.

Cross-examined by Mr. Kelly.

You saw nothing of the vessel, I presume, when she sailed on the voyage?—Her voyage out, do you mean?

Yes, when she sailed from Liverpool?—No, certainly not.

Mr. Justice *Maule*. Of course not.

Mr. *Kelly*. You know that ultimately this vessel was given up to the Russian government?—Yes, I do.

Thomas James Clark sworn. Examined by Mr. Serjeant Bompas.

How old are you?—Nineteen.

Are you a sailor?—Yes.

How long have you been a sailor?—Several years.

Did you sail on board the Augusta?—Yes.

Where did you enter on board?—At Portsmouth harbour.

Where did you enter for?—To go to Liverpool, at first.

At that time you entered only to go to Liverpool?—That was all.

Did you continue on board?—Yes.

You went from Liverpool in the vessel?—Yes.

Where were the sailors hired generally, at Liverpool or Portsmouth?—At Portsmouth some were hired.

And afterwards went on with the vessel, as you did?—Yes.

How many men were on board about, I do not wish to know exactly, when you sailed from Liverpool?—About twenty-one or twenty-two.

What was your occupation on board the ship?—I was shipped as a boy, a cabin-boy.

Had you any thing to do with the loading of the vessel, or not?—I was acting as a cabin-boy.

You had nothing to do with the loading of the vessel?—No.

Do you remember any storm arising after you had left?—Yes; after we left Liverpool we had a very heavy gale of wind, which lasted some time.

How shortly was that after you sailed?—I do not know; it might have been several days.

Do you remember about how far you were from Cork or Falmouth?—Not a very great distance.

Do you remember whether the wind was fair for going to Cork or Falmouth?—Yes; it was a fair wind back, if the skipper had been disposed to run back.

Did anything take place in the ship about going back?—Yes, there was a great disturbance with the crew; they said the vessel was not safe to go to where the skipper sailed to.

Where was she going to?—The coast of Africa: he said he would not go back, that he should lose his crew if he put back.

Mr. *Kelly*. They said it was not safe to go to the coast of Africa?—Yes.

Mr. Serjeant *Bompas*. Where did he sail for at last?—Sailed to Spain.

Was the wind fair for Spain, or not?—I do not know.

How many days were you before you got to Spain?—We were some time before we got to Spain.

Can you tell whether it was a fortnight or three weeks, or between the two?—I dare say it was a fortnight, or more.

You know the port in Spain; Cadiz, was not it?—Yes.

Were any of the men discharged at Cadiz?—Yes, the best part of them.

Do you know whether that was arranged before they went to Cadiz, at the time of the storm?—It was all the captain's misconduct.

What was?—Their leaving of us.

How long did you remain at Cadiz?—We remained there, I do not know exactly the time, a month, or it might be two months.

Was any of the cargo discharged at Cadiz?—Yes; the best part of it was moved out of her into small vessels.

There was some tobacco that was damaged, was there not?—Yes.

Did some part remain?—I do not know.

You acted as cabin-boy, we understand?—Yes.

Cross-examined by Mr. Kelly.

You were on board this vessel at Portsmouth?—Yes.

Do you recollect a number of large water-casks, and a good many small ones, that there were on board the vessel at Portsmouth?—Yes.

That Bankes and his son were working at for some time?—Yes.

You sailed with them on board from Portsmouth to Liverpool?—Yes.

Were not they sent out at Liverpool, and sold to Mr. Toplis, the agent, who shipped the goods?—I know very well they were put on shore.

And the vessel sailed without them?—I am not very sure whether they were put on board again.

Did you ever see them again?—No.

Were there not some iron bolts and screws, which had been on board the vessel formerly, made up and thrown overboard while the vessel remained at Portsmouth?—No, not to my recollection.

You do not know any thing of that kind?—No.

Re-examined by Mr. Serjeant *Bompas*.

Do you remember any thing about the quantity of water that was actually on board; had they much or little water?—When they sailed from Liverpool they had a great quantity of water.

Were the water-casks carried all the way or not?—We had several great puncheons on deck at the time of the storm; we knocked one or two of the heads in to help the vessel; one or two of the casks went overboard.

You had been at sea before?—Yes.

Had you a less or a greater quantity of water?—

Mr. *Kelly*. How often had he sailed, and had he been on the coast of Africa?

Mr. Serjeant *Bompas*. How often had you been at sea before?—I had been to North America before.

You had never been to Africa before?—No.

You do not know what is usual on the coast of Africa?—No.

The Honourable Captain *Denman*, R. N. sworn. Examined by Mr. Serjeant *Talfourd*.

Were you commanding on the African coast at any time?—I was commanding on a district of the African coast.

Did that embrace the river Gallinas?—The river Gallinas was within the district.

How long, while you were on that coast, were you acquainted with that river?—I was myself constantly in sight of the river for a period of eight or ten months.

Had you also, besides the period you were opposite that river, other opportunities of observing what was going on there?—Whenever I was not there myself, I left a vessel to watch the place and report to me what occurred.

We have heard there were some slave factories, barracoons there?—There were no less than six slave factories on the shore.

According to your observation, what was the trade carried on there?—There was no trade whatever but the slave trade; exclusively the slave trade.

You did not yourself know the proprietors of the barracoons?—I did not know any of them personally.

Did you ever see any of them in their warehouses?—No, except one.

Who was that?—I believe it was Martinez, but I am not certain: the name we knew him by was Pedro Fernandos.

Mr. *Kelly*. You will state what you do know?—The name we knew him by was Domingo Fernandos.

Mr. Serjeant *Talfourd*. Did you know Ignatio Rolo?—Yes, I have seen him at Gallinas.

What did he do at the Gallinas?—He was landing from the Saracen when I saw him.

That was the vessel commanded by Captain Hill?—Yes.

Did you ever see him on any of those factories?—I never saw him, except at the factory at which he landed.

Did he land at the factory?—He was landed in a man-of-war's boat.

Cross-examined by Mr. Kelly.

Had you means, while in the river Gallinas from time to time, of ascertaining how many towns or villages there were as far up the river as you went?—There were, to my knowledge, some three or four or five towns on different branches of the river.

How high up did you go yourself?—I went up about ten or twelve miles, I suppose.

You say that as far as your knowledge extends there was no other trade there but the slave trade?—My positive knowledge is that there was nothing but the slave trade there.

Do you mean to represent that you knew all the ships containing British merchandise consigned to that place, and what became of the merchandise which was landed by the ships? Have you no doubt that you knew enough of what took place at that place, to be aware what became of the merchandise landed from every ship?—The question involves two or three points; I must answer in the first place, that every vessel that landed cargoes there I knew of.

During what period?—During a period of ten months most particularly.

What ten months was that?—From the month of March or the month of April, 1840, until the month of February 1841.

Have you never heard of a ship, called the Supply, landing merchandise there to the value of between 13,000*l.* and 14,000*l.*?—Not during that period. I beg not to be misunderstood; I do not deny that vessels have landed cargoes there to a large amount, but I say the slave trade is the exclusive business there: there is no produce.

That is inference, perhaps, hardly warranted by your premises: is there any thing in the nature of the case to prevent the importing merchandise for consumption by the natives on the spot, and is it not consumed by the natives?—I say no produce is exported.

Mr. Justice *Maule*. The question is, what was done with the merchandise; was it given in exchange?—There were two articles of import, which are the one eaten, and the other used by the slave traders to buy slaves.

Mr. *Kelly*. What I understood you to say was, that you are not aware that there is any produce exported; but I ask whether articles are not imported to be consumed by the natives?—I do not mean to say a few hundred weight or a ton is not exported, but nothing to be called produce or exports.

You do not say there are not a few hundreds of tons?—I say not a hundred weight.

That was the case during the ten months you were there?—I have known the Gallinas since 1835. I was in charge of that station during two years; during that time I was ten months stationed at Gallinas, and had reports from the place.

When you say there is no trade carried on there but the slave trade, do you exclude from your observation the shipments of goods from England landed there and sold for money? for consumption there, sold for money?—If you put that question again, I shall understand it.

I wish to ask you, as you state that there is nothing but the slave trade carried on, that there are no exports, whether the trade may not consist of landing goods and selling them for money, as well as purchasing goods there, and carrying them away?—Just so.

Do you mean to exclude or include the fact of merchandise being landed there, and purchased there, and paid for in money, so that a stranger carrying it there, and selling it and receiving his money, would be doing what of course was perfectly lawful?—My answer is, that a person landing his goods there would not be able to procure a return, but that all the goods would go for the purchase of slaves, and nothing else: that is my reason for saying nothing but the slave trade is carried on there.

I will call them all slave traders, if you please. Do you mean to say a man may not purchase a quantity of goods which he may barter for slaves; may he not sell a part of them also to the natives?—The natives have no means of paying for them, except by the exchange for slaves: there is no produce.

As regards the shippers from this country; supposing that a man were to ship, not as agent, but on his own account, a cargo from this country, receiving money for what he exported, do you mean to say there would be any slave trading in that?—I should say not of necessity.

Mr. Justice *Maule*. Suppose he comes away in ballast, if such a transaction happens?—I have never known of such a case; there was no English trade during the time I was there.

Mr. *Kelly*. Do you mean that no English vessels went there?—Oh, yes; English vessels passed and had some little proceedings; the Augusta, for instance, was a vessel I always suspected.

Whatever took place at that place, the Gallinas, for some years before you do not know?—I know from the statement of the natives that there was no trade.

I ask you, do you know of a vessel, called the Supply, having landed and disposed of merchandise at the Gallinas to the amount of 13,000*l.* or 14,000*l.*?—There was no such vessel there during the two years I was there; certainly not during the ten months.

This is a place to which trading of the nature to which I have referred may have taken place at a time previous to the time you mention?—The trade of the nature I describe has taken place since 1835.

I will give you the dates; I will mention the year 1837; do you know of a vessel called the Milford, having landed and disposed of goods to the amount of 6,000*l.* or 7,000*l.* at the Gallinas?—No, I was not there at the time; but that does not alter the case, for the slave trade existed there.

I do not ask you as to the existence of the slave trade, but whether there has not been lawful commerce and ships coming away in ballast?—I know that 800 tons of goods were landed during the time I was there, and that none of the vessels went away except with money or goods, and except when they were consigned for cargoes from the Havannah, which was the case in nine cases out of ten.

According to your experience some vessels do carry commodities to a great extent, and receive payment in actual money and sail away?—Yes, those are exceptions, but such cases do occur.

Others would go and carry their goods there and receive slaves?—No, that is not the system. The freight of the vessel is consigned from the Havannah to a slave factor, Rolo, for instance, at Gallinas; she sails again in ballast, the freight is all paid to Havannah; that is the general rule.

From what, according to your sense of the word "slave trade," do you make out that that vessel was at all engaged in the slave trade?—I do not say that vessel is of necessity engaged in the slave trade, for I do not think it is of necessity that persons know what they are about, but I say that the consequence of it is the slave trade.

You mean that those merchants and mercantile persons are carrying on the slave trade?—Precisely so.

A person living any where else, and exporting produce there, might very well export it and get his money for it, without at all knowing to what purpose that should be applied?—Certainly, that is very possible.

With respect to this place, called the Gallinas, I am quite sure that you have given the account of the place as you believe it to exist; had you not a hand in destroying the factories there, which is the subject of one or two actions against you at this moment?—There are actions brought against me for the destruction of slave factories.

When did the event take place? I do not ask whether you had any thing to do with it of course, but when did the event take place?—About November, 1840.

Has your experience led you to various other parts of the coast of Africa, where the slave trade is carried on?—Yes.

Are not there certain parts of the coast where there is a lawful trade as well as an unlawful trade?—In almost all places, the Gallinas is the exception.

Is your knowledge, that the Gallinas is the exception, obtained from your personal presence on the spot?—It is obtained from my personal presence on the spot.

So that any person, in England or elsewhere, might export commodities to half a dozen places along the coast of Africa, and might as well export there without knowledge as any other place?—With the distinction that there is no other trade carried on there.

How is a merchant carrying on business in this country, receiving an order for 5,000*l.* worth of goods from the Gallinas, to know that the Gallinas is an exception to other places?—I think if he does not know any thing of the character of the parties, he may be ignorant of the use to which they are applied.

You mean the character of the party to whom the goods are to be sent?—Yes.

What would the character of the person, to whom the goods were sent, have to do with the fact how the person in this country is to know that the Gallinas is the exception, and that the goods are not going there to fair persons as well as to other persons?—If he knows the person to whom the goods are shipped at Gallinas, I should suppose he would know there was nothing but slave trading carried on.

That is, if he knew as well as you who have been on the spot; are there not many persons who carry on the slave trade, who also carry on a very extensive lawful trade?—Undoubtedly.

Then how is a gentleman in England or America, who exports his merchandise on those orders, to know the use to which they are to be applied?—If he knows any thing of Gallinas, he will know the object to which they are applied.

If he does not know?—If he does not know any thing of Gallinas, he is not necessarily guilty of doing any thing which is wrong.

When a vessel is under the English flag, and manned by English sailors, is there not a far greater facility as to search, and as to fair trial and condemnation, than if it is a foreign vessel?—Yes, when there is suspicion of the slave trade; it depends upon some of the treaties.

Is there any thing at all to restrict or prevent your searching every vessel under the English flag, commanded by an English captain, and manned by an English crew?—Nothing at all, if we suspect.

You do it without opposition?—Yes.

When a vessel is seized which is English, it goes without any delay before an English tribunal?—Yes.

When it is a foreign vessel, does not it go before a Mixed Commission?—It depends upon the nature of the treaty; under some of the treaties it would go to the tribunal before a Mixed Commission.

A French vessel would go before a French tribunal?—Yes.

A Spanish before a mixed tribunal?—Yes.

And a Portuguese?—Yes.

When was it you first sailed for the coast of Africa?—I left England in February, 1840.

Did you before that know the Gallinas?—Yes, I knew it in 1835.

You had been there in 1835?—Yes.

You went there first in 1835, in the discharge of your professional duties? Before that time were you aware there was such a place?—No, I knew nothing about the coast of Africa.

You did not know that the Gallinas was a place where slaves were more or less dealt in than any other place?—I had no reason to know any thing about it till I went there.

Re-examined by Mr. Serjeant Talfourd.

Nor the trade any where else I presume?—No.

How many merchants are there at the Gallinas to whom goods might be consigned?—I believe they are all agents; there are no actual merchants.

How many people are there?—There are twenty or thirty Europeans altogether.

Were there persons to whom goods would be consigned, except those in slave factories?—There was not another white man.

Have the natives, in any of those villages, any means of paying for British produce?—They have no means of paying but by slaves; the country does not produce any produce.

You have been asked, whether a merchant here may not ship to the coast of Africa without knowing the nature of the trade there; do you think a merchant who had exported for twenty years could be ignorant?—It is impossible he could fail to know the nature of the trade.

Mr. <i>Kelly</i>. My Lord, my learned friend has called for a letter, which the witness says was put in the post on the 10th of June, 1839.

Mr. Justice <i>Maule</i>. I thought it was 1840.

Mr. <i>Kelly</i>. No, 1839, four years ago. The letter has been most carefully looked for, and is not in existence. A few days ago, Mr. Lawford looked carefully for it, with the assistance of some of Mr. Zulueta's people, and they are utterly unable to find it. I shall not consider him a witness, if my learned friend wishes to examine Mr. Lawford as to that matter, he may. The effect of it has been stated. If he wishes to ask those persons who are aware whether such a letter had existence, and whether it is not lost, I will produce them, in order to afford him the opportunity of putting the question.

Lieutenant Colonel <i>Edward Nichol</i> sworn. Examined by Mr. Serjeant <i>Bompas</i>.

Have you become acquainted with the coast of Africa?—A long time.

How long?—Since the year 1822.

Had you any official employment upon that coast?—I was governor of the Isle of Ascension, and afterwards of Fernando Po, five years at each place.

In that situation, was it your duty to attend to the coast in other parts besides Fernando Po and the other place where you were immediately governor, and to make a report upon it?—It was.

Did you receive reports from the officers of the navy, or others, with respect to the various parts of the coast?—I have received reports from upwards of 200 officers of the navy, and masters of merchant ships on different parts of the coast, and have sent a small schooner attached to my command at Fernando Po, to make reports of the different slave trading stations and what was going on there.

Did you know the river Gallinas?—Yes.

Have you been there yourself?—I have.

For what period has it been within your observation?—Since 1822; I visited it in 1822, in His Majesty's ship Victor.

Up to what time?—We did not stay long; we were chasing a slaver off the port.

How long had you occasion to know that place?—From that time to 1834; from 1822 to 1834; I left the coast in December, 1834; I have had continual communication with it since.

During that time what was the trade carried on at the Gallinas?—The slave trade.

Was there any produce exported from the Gallinas at all?—Not a particle that ever came to my knowledge, or under my observation, or from the information I have received.

Was the country round the Gallinas a country producing that which was fit for export or usually exported?—Nothing but stones and trees, hardly what would subsist the people living there.

Did you know of the existence of slave establishments there?—As notoriously as that this Court is here.

You have seen them yourself?—Yes, certainly, and had reports from the officers I sent there.

Were you there more than once?—No.

Did you know any persons residing there? Did you know Pedro Blanco?—I knew him from reports; they kept out of my sight, they did not come near me.

Was it part of your duty to suppress the slave trade as much as possible?—That is the duty of every British officer.

It is necessary I should ask you whether it was part of your duty?—Certainly. I had no authority to seize slave ships though, but to give information to His Majesty's squadron; and I believe I did that to some good amount.

It was your duty to obtain information of what was going on along the coast, and to communicate it to the naval officers, to enable them to seize the vessels?—Certainly.

What was about the distance of your station from the Gallinas?—About 1500 miles I should say, except when I have been running down the coast. Fernando Po is a long way from the Gallinas.

But you have been running down the coast and obtaining reports?—Yes, both by myself and my officers.

Had you the means of ascertaining the way in which the slave trade was carried on?—I had.

What was the course; was it by barter or money?—You cannot get slaves for money. I never saw a slave got for money. They cannot be got without British manufactured goods supplied by the merchants.

They get British manufactured goods and barter them for slaves?—That is the general course of dealing for slaves.

They are brought from the interior of Africa to places where the trade is carried on?—Just so.

Are the slaves brought to the Gallinas for the purpose of being bartered for the goods there?—It is the most notorious and infamous slave port on the coast of Africa. There is a continual drain of slaves from all parts of the country to it; there is nothing going on there but the slave trade, any man sending goods there must know that.

Mr. *Kelly.* I do not know why we are to listen to these speeches, or even to this evidence. Unless something of this, so well known to this gentleman so constantly visiting that spot, had been communicated to the prisoner at the bar before the transaction in question, I am at a loss to know how he can be affected by it. I dare say there are many persons in this Court, whose geographical knowledge may have extended as far as the Gallinas, who never heard of such a thing until they heard it upon this occasion; and I do not know how notoriety to people on the spot can be evidence against the defendant, who has never been on that spot, and never had any communication of any kind with any person on the spot.

Mr. Serjeant *Bompas*. I hardly know how many objections are to be raised; to show the nature of the trade I must call these witnesses.

Mr. *Kelly*. I have no question to ask you.

Mr. *John Brown* called again. Examined by Mr. *Payne*.

Will you produce enclosure No. 18? (*The same was produced*).

(*To* Captain *Hill*). Will you look at that, and state whose handwriting you believe it to be?—I believe this handwriting to be Bernardos's, but I did not see him write it; I have some writing I saw him write in my possession.

From the knowledge you have acquired, seeing him write, do you believe it to be his writing?—Yes.

Have you had that paper in your possession before?—This is one of the papers I found on board the vessel when I seized her.

Mr. *James Brodie* sworn. Examined by Mr. Serjeant *Bompas*.

I believe you come from the Post Office?—Yes.

You have been accustomed to see the post-mark on letters?—I have.

Have the goodness to look at that, and tell me whether that is the post-mark, and the date of it?—It is.

What is the date?—The 23rd of September, 1840, as far as I can judge.

Mr. *Kelly*. This is the letter about which we have already had a discussion?

Mr. Serjeant *Bompas*. I am not aware of any discussion about it at present.

Mr. *Kelly*. Are you about to offer it in evidence?

Mr. Serjeant *Bompas*. Yes.

Mr. *Kelly*. Then I object to it; I do not understand the principle on which it is offered. This is a letter which Captain Hill proves to be in the writing of Bernardos, written to Captain Jennings, and dated September, 1840. That is sought to be given in evidence against the defendant. There is no proof that he ever saw or heard of the letter in the whole course of his life.

Mr. Serjeant *Bompas*. Your Lordship will find the letter No. 18.

Mr. *Kelly*. It is a letter, I understand, which is printed at page 35, in the Appendix to the Appeal Case, at the top of that page.

Mr. Serjeant *Bompas*. It is a letter written by one of the parties to the other of the parties who were engaged in paying the money for this vessel, which was received from the prisoner at the bar. It is a letter from Bernardos, your Lordship will see, describing the voyage.

Mr. *Kelly*. You had better not speak of the contents of the letter; it is before their Lordships, and for the purpose of deciding the point of law, my Lord may look at the letter. I cannot help complaining of the course taken, which is not correct or usual. My learned friend takes the opportunity of stating, in the hearing of the Jury, something of the contents of that letter, which is before your Lordships, and of which your Lordships may possess yourselves while we are discussing whether the contents of it are to be stated in Court at all. If your Lordships hold it admissible, it will then be read; but, for the present, you may read it yourselves, and hear the argument upon it.

Mr. Serjeant *Bompas*. I cannot argue, without referring to the contents in some degree. I am quite sure that I am in your Lordships' judgment, that in referring to the contents of the letters, I have abstained from using one single expression which could have an effect until your Lordships decide. I have not made use of a word which can justify the slightest possible degree of observation of my learned friend's in the fair argument on the admissibility of the letters; I have gone only as far as was necessary for the purpose. As far as I have referred to their contents, I am quite sure your Lordships will be of opinion I have governed myself by the most careful attention not to say any thing which was unnecessary. It is important to ascertain where the vessel was to go. This is the person who paid the notes received from Mr. Zulueta for this vessel. I ask your Lordship whether that is not evidence of his being an agent of Zulueta in respect of this vessel. He writes to him upon his arrival in this vessel; he is employed to pay for this vessel, to purchase it; there is a communication from the one to the other of these two persons, so employed to purchase this vessel, in respect of the vessel and the trade—I say no further than that—and also giving instructions. I ask your Lordship if it is not open to me to prove where the vessel was to go to, having shown the communications which took place between the parties in respect of her going. This contains the actual instructions. The same rule exists as to evidence in criminal proceedings as applies to evidence in civil cases. The question has been before the House of Lords as to instructions given by one party to the other, and the judgment was set aside on that very point of instructions.

Mr. Justice *Maule*. I do not know what case you refer to.

Mr. Serjeant *Bompas.* There was one case as to Chambers's bankruptcy, where the directions were considered a fact, and as such given in evidence in order to show that there were directions given. We know that it is necessary to have a certain quantity of water provided for the men going on that trade. This letter does not refer to supply of water, and therefore I use that simply as an illustration. Can it be said, that if a person employed to engage in a certain trade, employed by the person upon his trial to purchase a certain vessel, going to a certain place for a certain object, gives instructions in respect of what is necessary for the trade carried on at that place, that is not matter to be given in evidence on the trial? The object of that is to ascertain for what purpose she went there. I apprehend I have clearly connected these two persons and the prisoner. Supposing I could give this distinct evidence, that the prisoner knew of it, would not that be admissible? Do I not give evidence for the Jury to determine whether he was cognizant of these transactions? Is not that part of the case for the Jury to determine, whether by his conduct it is evident he did know what took place? I apprehend this is a part of the proceedings between two persons, both of whom have been employed by the prisoner; they proceed onwards with the knowledge of the prisoner in the prosecution of that voyage, which was ultimately accomplished, or would have been accomplished, if she had not been taken. This is one part of that proceeding, and it is for the Jury to say whether there was, on the part of the prisoner, a guilty knowledge of the proceeding or not. If there was not, there will be an acquittal of the prisoner. If there was that which amounts to a guilty knowledge of what took place, I apprehend it is impossible to exclude this which is evidence, and which may be important evidence, in showing that there was a guilty knowledge. This letter is found passing from one to the other; is proved to be posted while she was at Portsmouth in preparing for the voyage, and is found afterwards on board. But we prove the period of its transmission by the post-mark.

Mr. Justice *Maule.* I don't think this is evidence. I am the more satisfied in excluding it, that I do not think it of the smallest importance; it does not prove any thing which is very material but what is already in proof.

Mr. Serjeant *Bompas.* That, my Lord, is the case on the part of the Crown.

Mr. *Kelly.* My learned friend having stated that this is his case, I feel it my duty to take your Lordship's opinion whether there is any evidence to go to the Jury in support of this charge; and I will, in doing so, call your Lordship's attention to what the charge is on the indictment, and in respect of the Act of Parliament, to which my learned friend has hardly alluded. The indictment charges the defendant with having employed (there are several words used, but I take the more general words), with having employed a vessel to accomplish a certain object, that object being trading and dealing in slaves. That the defendant was a party to the purchase of a vessel there is no doubt.

The great question here is, whether there is any evidence at all, notwithstanding the great length of time this case has occupied, whether there is any evidence at all that the defendant, Mr. Pedro de Zulueta, had any intention of employing that vessel, or those goods, for the purpose of the vessel or the goods being used in the dealing in slaves. Now, where is the evidence? I reject, as your Lordship will, all that was mere matter of observation on the part of my learned friend. The evidence against Mr. Pedro de Zulueta consists in this—that he wrote a letter on, I think, the 20th of August, by which he authorised Jennings to give a certain sum of money for the vessel; the vessel was afterwards purchased, and the defendant puts the name of his firm to the charter-party of that vessel—the charter-party, by which Jennings having become the purchaser of the vessel, charters the vessel to the foreign house of Martinez & Co., for which the house of Zulueta & Co. were agents—Martinez & Co. thus become the charterers of the vessel, Jennings, on certain terms contained in that instrument, being the captain of the vessel.

It is said, also, that the defendant dispatched the vessel; that he shipped goods on board the vessel. My Lord, with regard to the whole of the rest of the case, as to his using, employing, equipping, or dispatching; as to his shipping the goods by the vessel; as to his interfering in any way in respect of the vessel or the cargo, that depends entirely upon his own evidence before the Committee of the House of Commons. That is evidence against him; that evidence I need not go into at length; that evidence, taken together and stated shortly, is this:—I am a member of the firm of Zulueta & Co.; that firm, including myself, did purchase this vessel, did cause it to be dispatched in the way stated, did cause certain goods to be shipped on board the vessel. We acted as agents for Martinez & Co., the goods being consigned to correspondents of Martinez and Co., named by Martinez & Co.; but as to the purpose for which that was done, as to the vessel itself, or any goods on board that vessel, being used for the purposes of the slave trade, I declare, though I admit that my house did dispatch the vessel, and did ship the goods, we had no idea or any suspicion that the vessel or goods could be intended for any illegal purpose whatever. That is the whole of the evidence, with this addition, that three gentlemen have been called, whose public duties have for some years past led them to the coast of Africa, and among other places to the Gallinas, who have stated that which has come within their personal observation—the place itself, and the dealings carried on at the place, having been familiar to them for a considerable time past. They state that they knew very well that it was a slave trading place. There is no evidence that the defendant, the prisoner at the bar, ever was at the Gallinas in his life; on the contrary, the evidence is the other way. There is no evidence that the defendant ever gave any instructions or authority, directly or indirectly, to Jennings, or to any other person, to use the vessel or to use the goods for the purposes of the slave trade, or for any other illegal purpose. There is no evidence that any communication was ever made by the house of Martinez & Co., or any other house, to the defendant, Pedro de Zulueta, that the vessel or goods were to be employed in the slave trade, or that any such illegal object was in contemplation.

Now, my Lord, what is the effect of the statute? The statute declares that slave trading, of a particular description, shall be illegal. The statute proclaims it a felony in any British subject to employ or equip a vessel, or to ship goods, for the purposes of the slave trade. That it may be taken on the admission of the prisoner himself, by his evidence before the Committee of the House of Commons, though there is no other evidence, that he did employ the vessel, and that he was concerned in the shipping of goods, I admit; but where is the evidence that he did those acts, or that he participated in those acts, for the purpose of those goods, or that ship, being employed in the slave trade? If this be so, if your Lordships hold that it is evidence to go to the Jury, that because a mercantile house in this city executes the order of a foreign correspondent, and sends out a ship with certain goods, which may be lawfully shipped, but which it is possible may be improperly employed, that therefore it is to be taken that they were to be unlawfully employed, and that therefore there is evidence to go to the Jury that he dispatched the vessel, and shipped the goods, in order that they might be unlawfully employed, I do not see how any mercantile house in this kingdom can trade in ships or goods, or execute any order, at the instance of any house in any part of the world, where either from that house personally dealing in the slave trade, or having communication with parts of the coast of Africa, it is possible that the ship, or the goods, may be applied to the unlawful purposes of the slave trade. If, without any proof of the party having used the ship, or the goods, for the purposes of the slave trade, without any document under his hand alluding to the slave trade, where all that is done is perfectly lawful, because it is possible that other persons, to whom he may have consigned his goods, may apply the ship, or the commodities, to the uses and purposes of the slave trade, that is to be held to be a case for the Jury that they were so intended, I do not know how any trade can be carried on. I submit, therefore, that here there is no evidence to go to the Jury of Mr. Pedro de Zulueta, the prisoner at the bar, having used this ship, or having shipped these goods, for the purpose of their being employed for the slave trade. I can easily conceive that a case might have been made out. The prosecutors seem to have been aware that communications had taken place between Messrs. Martinez & Co. and the house of Zulueta & Co., and they have called for the production of letters. I can easily imagine that a case might have been made out, inasmuch as Mr. Zulueta has stated that he purchased this ship by order of Martinez. But the prosecutor is bound to make out that case: he is not to raise a suspicion, and then to call upon the prisoner to clear himself from it: he must prove his case. He might call for any letters that had taken place between Martinez and the prisoner at the bar; for any communications between the prisoner at the bar and the captain of the vessel. If they had been produced, he might have established from them that something had been proved that established this offence. Then there might have been a case to go to the Jury; but the case here is one in which the prosecutor alleges, that Pedro de Zulueta himself employed the vessel, and shipped these goods, for the purpose of their being employed in the slave trade. The question is, the slave trade being prohibited by law, whether he is concerned in the intent and design of their being so to be used; whether there is any evidence that he knew of the slave, trade being carried on there; whether there is any evidence that he knew that these goods would be employed, or might be employed, for the purposes of the slave trade. I submit there is no case calling upon him, I will not say for an answer, but even for observation; I submit that it would be extremely unsafe where the prosecutor has the means of proving if there has been a guilty knowledge on the part of the defendant, if it is the fact that the intent of the proceeding is something illegal, and where the prosecutor might prove it by direct evidence, that he should content himself with proving that a ship was dispatched which might be used for the purposes of this trade, leaving it to the defendant to prove the negative of that, and to give in evidence all the documents which may have taken place, merely proving that it is possible that the ship the defendant dispatched might be so employed. I submit to your Lordships that is a dangerous doctrine, that it is contrary to the practice of the Court, and that there is no case in which the charge would not apply equally to every merchant in the kingdom who exported goods which might, after they left this country, be applied to an illegal purpose.

(The learned Judges consulted together.)

Mr. Justice *Maule*. Mr. Kelly, you may go to the Jury.

Mr. *Kelly*. My Lord, after what has fallen from your Lordships, of course I shall not hesitate to address the Jury upon the evidence which has been offered by my learned friend. There are one or two points, however, to which I would call your Lordship's attention, and bring the terms of the statute under the attention of the Court; which, I apprehend, will be fatal to the prosecution, without troubling the Jury with observations which may extend to a considerable length of time, and which I shall feel it my duty to bring before the Court.

Mr. Justice *Maule*. Do you mean something in arrest of judgment?

Mr. *Kelly*. No, my Lord; on the effect of the evidence.

Mr. Justice *Maule*. I cannot think it is at all right that the question whether the case should go to the Jury should be twice put.

Mr. *Kelly*. No, my Lord. I say, supposing even that the charge is well made, that it is not an offence within the Act of Parliament.

Mr. Justice *Maule*. It comes to the same thing; I cannot see what you mean to say to the Court, except that the indictment is bad. That you state you do not propose to say?

Mr. *Kelly*. It is not that which I first contended.

Mr. Justice *Maule*. You did not propose to say that, and you now propose to say that the indictment is bad?

Mr. *Kelly*. My Lord, there is one point on which I do contend that the indictment is bad, though that is not the point to which I would call your Lordship's attention. I was first about to submit to your Lordship, that the offence charged upon the evidence is not a felony within the Act of Parliament.

Mr. Justice *Maule*. That it does not support the indictment?

Mr. *Kelly*. Yes.

Mr. Justice *Maule*. It appears to me that that is exactly what you have been saying before.

Mr. *Kelly*. No, my Lord, the point is altogether and totally different.

Mr. Justice *Maule*. It may be a different reason, but it is the same point.

Mr. *Kelly*. I am sure your Lordship will see that it is different, when I come to explain.

Mr. Justice *Maule*. It is going for a nonsuit?

Mr. *Kelly*. Yes, it is in effect, my Lord; but if the Court will indulge me with a few moments of time, they will see that the Court is under a mistake, and that the point is most grave and proper for the consideration of the Court, and totally apart and distinct from that I have already submitted.

Mr. Justice *Maule*. All I want is that you should explain. Sometimes, when gentlemen are moving for a new trial, they are asked whether they move for a new trial on the point of misdirection, or the verdict being against evidence; I do not say it is imperative they should state distinctly, sometimes a gentleman might not feel prepared to state that?

Mr. *Kelly*. I will answer your Lordship's question in as few words as I can. The point I make is this:—The charge is, that of fitting out a vessel to accomplish the object of trading in slaves, or slave trading at Gallinas, which I submit was not an illegal object: that supposing for a moment the facts were to convince the Jury that the defendant had fitted out this vessel, in order that Pedro Martinez & Co., or any other persons, might trade in slaves at Gallinas, that is not a felony within this Act of Parliament.

Mr. Justice *Maule*. Do you mean to say, that proof would not support the indictment; or, that supporting the indictment, it would not amount to felony? One of those things it must be.

Mr. *Kelly*. I say both: it would not support the indictment, and it would not amount to felony.

Mr. Justice *Maule*. Inasmuch as you say it would not support the indictment, that is going on the very ground you have gone on before, only giving another reason. If you do not see that—if you tell me you do not think it—I will hear you.

Mr. *Kelly*. I beg to state with the most perfect sincerity, I do not feel that.

Mr. Justice *Maule*. You mean to insist that the indictment is not supported, having previously insisted that the indictment was not supported?

Mr. *Kelly*. Yes; but on a totally different ground.

Mr. Justice *Maule*. I do not say you are not entitled, not on the same ground to say that the indictment is not supported, but you are not entitled to say that the indictment is not supported twice over; that you cannot put forward one set of reasons, and when they are overruled, put forward another set of reasons; for if you could, in case they were overruled, you might then put a third.

Mr. *Kelly*. If I had had the slightest idea that it would be deemed inconvenient that I should submit one point for your Lordship's consideration, and ask for a decision on one before I proceeded to the other, I should have submitted both; I have only to ask your Lordship's pardon for the course I have taken.

Mr. Justice *Maule*. I am quite sure that you must see that where there are several grounds for making that motion, it is desirable that they should be all stated in the outset, for otherwise they might split into separate motions. The universal course is, that all the grounds should be stated, and the unity of the object preserved; and the Court yields with apparent reluctance to a different course. The object you now have is to induce the Court to rule that there is no evidence to go to the Jury. That, you have before submitted; you say you have a different reason, but that different reason does not raise a ground for the Court hearing the application repeated. I only regret you did not take the course which the Court thinks the best. If you insist upon it, I shall feel bound for the convenience of the Court, not to allow an old and very able counsel to do that which would not be fair in ordinary cases; but if you say you have made some slip or omission I will hear you.

Mr. *Kelly.* That is really so. If your Lordship will pardon me one moment, I will take what course your Lordship thinks most convenient for practice.

Mr. Justice *Maule.* You omitted something?

Mr. *Kelly.* Yes, my Lord; I will state what is quite unconnected with the objection I have taken. This indictment charges the prisoner with having equipped a vessel, and shipped goods, in order to accomplish an object, that object being the exercising of the slave trade, and it is framed upon the Act of Parliament of the 5th of George IV, chapter 113. Now, my Lord, by the 2nd section of that Act of Parliament, slave trading by certain persons, and under certain circumstances, is declared to be unlawful. By the 10th section of the Act, it is enacted that if any person shall among others, equip a vessel, or ship goods, in order to accomplish any of the objects theretofore declared to be unlawful, he shall be guilty of a felony. That is the felony charged in this indictment, namely, that the prisoner at the bar equipped a vessel, and shipped goods, in order to accomplish one of the objects declared to be unlawful, namely, that of trading in slaves. Now, the point is this: the charge, supposing it substantiated by evidence, is this—that the prisoner at the bar equipped this vessel, and shipped these goods, in order that they might be used in the slave trade, in order to accomplish the object of trading in slaves at Gallinas, in Africa. The Gallinas is not a British settlement, and is not a British colony, and therefore that species of trading is not declared unlawful by that Act of Parliament; the trading declared by that Act of Parliament to be unlawful must be a trading by British subjects. The trading, in order to be unlawful within the meaning of this Act of Parliament, must be a trading by British subjects; and moreover, at the time when this offence is supposed to have been committed, it must have been a trading at some colony either in Great Britain, or some colony or settlement belonging to Great Britain. That will appear from another Act of Parliament, passed to remedy the defect under the former Act of Parliament; your Lordships will see, that by the 2nd section of the Act of Parliament, the terms are general.

Mr. Justice *Wightman.* What Act are you upon Mr. Kelly?

Mr. *Kelly.* I am now on the 5th of George IV. By clause 2, it is provided, "that it shall not be lawful (except in such special cases as are hereinafter mentioned) for any persons to deal or trade in, purchase, sell, or barter, or transfer, or to contract for the dealing or trading in, purchase, sale, barter, or transfer of slaves, or persons intended to be dealt with as slaves," and to do a variety of other acts which are by that section declared to be unlawful. Now, my Lord, though the words are general, "that it shall not be lawful for any persons to deal or trade in slaves," the legal effect of them is, that it shall not be lawful for British subjects to deal in slaves; and your Lordship will see by the subsequent Act of Parliament it also means, that it shall not be lawful for British subjects to deal in slaves, either in Great Britain, or in the settlements or colonies of Great Britain, and that that Act of Parliament did not extend to the trading in slaves in foreign states.

Let us take the two points of the proposition. First of all, this manner of trading in slaves by foreigners becomes material in this view: I presume, from the opening and the evidence, it was intended that this ship and these goods should be taken to Gallinas, and there used by the consignees of the vessel and the goods, either by bartering the goods for the purchase of slaves, or selling the goods and with the produce buying slaves. It is not material to consider now how far that is within the Act of Parliament, but the object, which I presume is the unlawful object with which the prisoner at the bar is charged with having dispatched this ship, is the object that the consignees or some other persons at Gallinas should trade in slaves by means of the ship or the goods. I submit that is not a trading in slaves within the 2nd section of the Act of Parliament, that though the words are general, it does not apply to aliens as the consignees of goods, which Martinez were, but to British consignees of goods, which in the Act of Parliament makes the act criminal. If the act be committed abroad, it is not an offence within the Act. A trading in slaves abroad by Rolo, by Martinez, or any persons whose names we have heard mentioned, would not be criminal within the Act of Parliament. The object of the charge is the trading at Gallinas. Now, the trading in slaves any where abroad by an alien is not an offence within this statute.

In order to illustrate this, let me suppose that the vessel had reached the Gallinas, that the consignees of the vessel had employed it for the transport of slaves, and had taken the goods and bartered them for a quantity of slaves, that would not have been illegal within this Act of Parliament. It would undoubtedly have been illegal for any British subject to have done so within any British colony, for this Act is binding on all British subjects throughout the British dominions, but it would not have been illegal for Martinez or any foreigner to deal in slaves in that place; and therefore, supposing it were proved that the prisoner at the bar had dispatched this vessel, that Martinez or Rolo might deal in slaves in foreign parts, that is not one of the objects to which this statute applies, for it applies only to British subjects, and not to foreigners.

My Lords, I need not cite authorities, they are numerous. There is one which is precisely to the point, The King *v.* Depardo; that is perfectly conclusive upon that subject: that is in 1st Taunton, in which a Chinese sailor who had enlisted, or rather had become a seaman on board one of His Majesty's ships, committed manslaughter in the Chinese seas, and the question was, whether he was amenable. The great point argued by the late Lord Tenterden and Mr.

Burrough was, whether that offence, committed by an alien, was within the Act of Parliament. The prisoner having been convicted, he was afterwards pardoned, on the ground that an Act of Parliament, declaring any particular act to be a felony, such act, if committed abroad by an alien, was not within the Act of Parliament, an alien not being within a British Act of Parliament: so I apprehend no position to be clearer than that a trading in slaves at Gallinas by Rolo, or Martinez, or any person to whom it can be imputed to the prisoner that he intended this ship and goods to be consigned, the trading in slaves by any alien there, would not have been unlawful within this Act of Parliament. If it would, the consequence would have been that a foreigner, Rolo or Martinez for instance, who might be lawfully, according to the laws of their own country or the laws of that place, trading in slaves, might, by engaging in that trade in slaves in the course of this very transaction at the Gallinas, have afterwards been prosecuted here, and convicted here; whereas nothing can be clearer than that these laws against the slave trade can only make the act an offence when it is done by British subjects, who alone are the objects of a British Act of Parliament: therefore I submit that the object being established, supposing the case sought to be established to be so established that Mr. Zulueta dispatched this vessel to enable Martinez to deal in slaves, that is not an object declared unlawful by this statute, for that would have been a trading by aliens who are not within this statute, and the shipping of goods to accomplish that is not within it.

But, my Lord, I go further; I have the case of Depardo, in Russell on Crime, it is not at so much length as in the report in Taunton. The marginal note is, "A manslaughter committed in China by an alien enemy, who had been a prisoner at war, and was then acting as a mariner on board an English merchant ship, on an Englishman, cannot be tried here under a commission issued in pursuance of the statutes 33 Hen. VIII, cap. 23, and 43 Geo. III, cap. 113, sec. 6. 1 Taunton 26." The principle is perfectly clear, that a person afterwards coming to the country, is not to be treated as if he had previously been a subject of the country; so I say here, that the trading in slaves at Gallinas, or any where abroad by a Russian or a Pole, or any other alien, would not have been within this Act of Parliament at all; it would not therefore be an illegal object within this statute, and the dispatch of goods or a ship to accomplish that object would be no felony.

But, my Lord, the case is rendered perfectly clear by the highest authority, namely, the authority of the Legislature itself, by means of another Act of Parliament, the 6th and 7th of Vict. cap. 98. This Act of Parliament shows that the case is stronger than I have put; and it shows that until the passing of this last Act of Parliament, which took place in the present year, 1843, it was not illegal, within the statute of the 5th of Geo. IV, even for British subjects to trade in slaves, except within the British dominions. The object of this Act of Parliament is to extend the provisions of the 5th of Geo. IV, so as to make it, from some day mentioned in the Act, criminal in British subjects to trade in slaves in any part of the world, in foreign states as well as in the British dominions.

Your Lordship will find this Act recites the 5th of Geo. IV, and recites the second section, to which I have called your Lordship's attention; "whereby it is enacted (among other things) that it shall not be lawful (except in such special cases as are hereinafter mentioned) for any persons to deal or trade in, purchase, sell, barter, or transfer, or to contract for the dealing or trading in, purchase, sale, barter, or transfer of slaves, or persons intended to be dealt with as slaves," and so on. Then it recites all the different acts which are declared unlawful by the 5th of Geo. IV, and then it proceeds: "And whereas it is expedient, that from and after the commencement of this Act, the provisions of the said Act hereinbefore recited shall be deemed to apply to, and extend to render unlawful, and to prohibit the several acts, matters, and things therein mentioned, when committed by British subjects in foreign countries and settlements not belonging to the British Crown, in like manner and to all intents and purposes as if the same were done or committed by such persons within the British dominions, colonies, or settlements, and it is expedient that further provisions should be made for the more effectual suppression of the slave trade, and of certain practices tending to promote and encourage it; Be it therefore enacted by the Queen's Most Excellent Majesty, by and with the advice and consent of the Lords Spiritual and Temporal and Commons, in this present Parliament assembled, and by the authority of the same, that all the provisions of the said consolidated Slave Trade Act, hereinbefore recited, and of this present Act, shall, from and after the coming into operation of this Act, be deemed to extend and apply to British subjects wheresoever residing or being, and whether within the dominions of the British Crown, or of any foreign country," and so forth: so that your Lordship sees this Act of Parliament clearly shows this, that before the passing of this Act, though it was declared to be unlawful to trade in slaves, the Act meant that it should be unlawful only for British subjects to trade in slaves any where within British settlements or colonies, and that it required the aid of another Act of Parliament to make it unlawful (not for aliens—for as to them it still is not unlawful—but to make it unlawful) even for British subjects to trade in slaves, or do the other acts referred to in this statute. The state of the law was, that aliens might trade in slaves in foreign parts without contravening that Act of Parliament, and that British subjects might trade in slaves in foreign parts without contravening that Act of Parliament. By the Act of the 6th & 7th of Vict. the provisions of the Act of Geo. IV are extended to the case of British subjects: it leaves the case of aliens as it was before, and it makes it unlawful for British subjects to deal in slaves, in the Gallinas for instance—so that your Lordship sees the objection presents itself in this way—this is an indictment for a felony, the felony being the dispatching a ship for the accomplishment of an illegal object, that being the slave trading at the Gallinas; but at the time when this Act passed, it was not illegal for foreigners to trade in slaves at Gallinas. If it is not illegal now, it was not then illegal for British subjects to trade in slaves in foreign countries. The present Act of Parliament renders it illegal for British subjects to trade in slaves in the Gallinas, or any other foreign country; but it was to come into operation only on the passing of the Act in 1843. My learned friend reminds me that it does not come into operation until the 1st of November: but that is quite immaterial; it has no retrospective operation; it was not in operation in 1840 or 1841, when it is stated that this felony was committed by the prisoner.

Before I sit down, I would also take your Lordship's opinion whether there is any offence proved within the city of London. Your Lordship observes this is not a trial under a section contained under one of the Acts of Parliament, providing that any offence against the statute may be laid in Middlesex. The indictment is not at all framed on that section of the Act of Parliament; it is framed on the common law, except so far as it is governed by the Central Criminal Court, and the venue is laid in London. It must be proved, therefore, that a felony was committed in London. The felony, said to have been committed, is the equipping, dispatching, using, and employing the ship, as charged in one set of counts; and the shipping the goods, as charged in another set of counts. Now, the dispatching the ship was at Portsmouth, and afterwards at Liverpool. It was dispatched at Portsmouth, went to Liverpool, was there loaded and then dispatched, and there all the goods were shipped. So that your Lordship sees the equipping, the using, the dispatching the vessel, any thing that could be done with the illegal object of dealing in slaves, must have been done at Liverpool. Neither the vessel, nor the goods, as far as appears, were ever in London. I submit to your Lordship, on that ground, there is no offence committed in London. Another objection which arises on the indictment I do not trouble your Lordship with, for it will apply in future, if necessary.

Mr. Justice *Maule*. Are there any others?

Mr. *Kelly*. No, my Lord.

Mr. Justice *Maule*. I think there is no ground for the second point on the Act of Parliament of 6 & 7 Vict., cap. 98, as affording a construction to the Act of 5th Geo. IV, cap. 113. The suggestion is, that this Act amounts to a Parliamentary declaration, that the Act of the 5th of Geo. IV, cap. 113, does not prohibit Englishmen engaging in slave trading abroad. I should be very sorry to put a construction upon that Act, which would involve so great an absurdity to it, as would be created by its being supposed to be laid down that that which was declared to be illegal in Great Britain, and Ireland, and the Isle of Man, and also in the East Indies, and West India Islands, is not at all prohibited on the coast of Africa, which is the construction sought to be put upon this Act of Parliament. I cannot help thinking the Legislature have expressed the intention of prohibiting English subjects trading in slaves on the coast of Africa; and if that be so, the construction which Mr. Kelly insists ought to be derived from the statute of Victoria is not the true construction, or one which ought to prevail. With respect to the other objection, we think there is evidence to go to the Jury of Mr. Zulueta's acts in London.

Mr. Serjeant *Bompas*. May I call your Lordship's attention to the 50th section: "And be it further enacted, That all offences committed against this Act may be inquired of, tried, determined, and dealt with, as if the same had been respectively committed within the body of the county of Middlesex." If it is within the jurisdiction of the Central Criminal Court, the venue is perfectly immaterial, if it is within the venue of the Court.

Mr. Justice *Maule*. I apprehend, that if a prisoner is indicted for a felony in Essex, within the limits of this Court, he will be tried here.

Mr. *Bodkin*. In a case in this Court where the venue stated merely the jurisdiction of the Central Criminal Court, the Court of Queen's Bench held that indictment bad, because it was impossible to say from what county the Jury were to be called.

Mr. Justice *Wightman*. There the indictment had been tried in Middlesex, being removed from the Central Criminal Court. It was removed by *certiorari* and tried in Middlesex, and it was said there was no direction on the record to try it in Middlesex.

Mr. Justice *Maule*. But Mr. Bodkin says, if it is a London case, there ought to be a London Jury; if in Essex, an Essex Jury.

Mr. *Bodkin*. The Court of Queen's Bench held the locality to be material.

Mr. Justice *Wightman*. Not generally. I have stated how it became material there, and why it is not material here. The case was removed by certiorari, and therefore it became material.

Mr. *Kelly*. As this is the first trial under this Act of Parliament, your Lordship will probably consider it proper to reserve the point whether this trading is within the Act.

Mr. Justice *Maule*. The point has been very fully and ably argued, and I think the Court has given it sufficient consideration. We have no doubt about it; we do not consider it a point on which there is any doubt.

Mr. *Kelly*. Perhaps the Jury will retire for a few moments before I begin my address.

Mr. Justice *Maule*. For a few moments, not to exceed a quarter of an hour.

[*The Jury retired, and after a short time returned into Court.*

Mr. *Kelly*. May it please your Lordships.

Gentlemen of the Jury,—Their Lordships having determined that this case is fit to be submitted to your consideration, I now proceed to discharge the very anxious, the painfully anxious, duty imposed upon me in consequence, of addressing you on behalf of the prisoner.

Gentlemen, *I should ill discharge that duty if I hesitated one moment to denounce this prosecution as one of the most unconscientious prosecutions that ever any individual has dared to bring forward in an English court of justice.*

Gentlemen, pardon me if I should express myself in any part of this case with any undue warmth; attribute it to the anxiety I must naturally feel, when I know that all the interests in life, the happiness here—I had almost said hereafter—of the young man at the bar, whose defence is committed to my charge, depend upon your verdict upon this transaction, upon which I, and I only on his behalf, have to address you.

He is a young man, now I believe only seven or eight-and-twenty; he is a foreigner, born in Spain of a Spanish family; he and his ancestors are of that country and not of this, and he has become a member of the mercantile house of which his father is the head. He has, during the latter years of his life, been resident in England, and has from time to time bestowed some attention upon the business of the counting-house and the commercial concerns in which the firm were engaged, and he has participated but as a member of the firm in the ordinary course of business in this transaction, which is, indeed, a very small transaction among many very great and important ones passing through that house; and now, to his consternation, and to his unspeakable astonishment—he, a young man of spotless character—he, who one of the witnesses for the prosecution has already described to you upon his oath as a good son, a good brother, a good father, a good husband, and as an honourable member of society—he finds himself charged here with a felony, and that upon evidence such as I shall have in detail to call your attention to. He is charged with a felony upon which, if from want of ability or from want of caution in his advocate he was to be convicted, he must be transported for fourteen years as a felon, and forfeit his property, and forfeit his character, and be ruined for life.

Gentlemen, this is the case before you, and I do ask in the outset, is this a prosecution which ought to be brought forward? Mr. Serjeant Bompas, whose duty it was to state the case to you, having opened that case—how, I shall have to remind you when I call your attention to something which in the opening fell from my learned friend—having opened his case fully and in detail in a speech of some two or three hours, after he has sat down thinks it necessary to rise again and tell you that Sir George Stephen is the prosecutor in this case.

Gentlemen, you have already heard from one of their Lordships, and you know it is a matter of history, that the British government has long exercised its energies and its mighty powers in putting down and preventing the odious slave trade: you know that the powers of the government have been wielded for many, many years past with that view, by those who are sincerely, from the bottom of their hearts, determined by every lawful means to put down that trade; you know that the whole conduct of this honourable and innocent young man has been under the consideration of the former government and the present government. The late Colonial Secretary, Lord John Russell, whose duty it would have been to have protected his own character, and that of Great Britain, by this prosecution, if any offence had been committed, was a member of the Committee, and inquired minutely and distinctly into the transaction; Lord Stanley, also, the present Colonial Secretary, was a member of the Committee. Both governments were regularly and fully acquainted with all the transactions in question, and those governments, whose duty, as my learned friend has told you, it was to do every thing they might to put down the slave trade, so far from feeling it a case for prosecution, the Committee themselves, and the present and the former governments, have fully acquitted this young man, and the house to which he belonged, of any guilty participation in this transaction, as I trust you will to-day acquit him by your verdict. The government of 1840 and the government of 1842, the past and the present government, fully acquainted with all the circumstances, have thought it proper, so far from dreaming that any guilt could be imputed to this young man, to agree to a Report of a totally different character. And a society, called "The Anti-Slavery Society," existing in this very town, failing to take up the prosecution, you have this very singular fact, that Sir George Stephen, though he put his name upon the back of the indictment, dare not put himself in the box for me to cross-examine. You have Sir George Stephen failing to sign his name to the notices, and you have at last the tardy and reluctant acknowledgment of his counsel that he is the prosecutor. I ask you, gentlemen, to recollect this: Lord John Russell and Lord Stanley were both of them members of the Committee; both were present when this matter was inquired into; before whom Captain Hill was examined, before whom Captain Denman was examined, and before whom another gentleman, Colonel Nichol, was likewise examined. That Committee put forth the large volume which I hold in my hand, and before them this young man voluntarily came, and was examined as to every part of this transaction;

aye, and as to the conduct, and character, and dealings of his house, from the time it was first established. And do you believe, if this had been a proper subject for prosecution, that the members, the leading members of a government, the government of a kingdom which has spent twenty millions of the public money to put an end to the slave trade—do you think, if they had felt that this was a proper subject for prosecution, that it would have been left to Sir George Stephen to come forward with his own money, and with his own means—for what purposes I cannot conceive, they must be left to his own feelings, and I do not envy him his feelings—to be the prosecutor of an indictment, which, if it succeeds, must for ever crush and ruin a young man, with respect to whom I shall demonstrate there exists but at most that species of suspicion, which ought never to be cherished against one whose character is, as I shall prove this young man's character at the bar to be, above all sort of suspicion—that suspicion, which, if it does exist, may be a fit reason for inquiry, but ought no more to be the ground for a prosecution for felony than it ought to be the ground for a conviction without any inquiry at all.

Gentlemen, what is the charge brought forward? Pedro de Zulueta, the young gentleman for whom I appear before you, is, I believe, the eldest son of his father: his father, now advanced in years, is the head of the house. He is a gentleman, who has filled the very highest offices in his own country, and who has been, I believe, at one time, the President of the Cortes in Spain, an office analogous to that of Speaker of the House of Commons in this country, and was member for the city of Cadiz as long as his commercial concerns required him to remain and discharge the duties of that situation. He is a gentleman, who has now reached a very advanced age without a shadow of imputation upon his character; who has been engaged during the whole of his life in commercial transactions of the largest and most important nature and extent, and who not only himself, but his father and grandfather before him, who for seventy years carried on an extensive trade in Spain, and at a time when not only Spain, but I grieve to say our own country, Britain, was engaged through her colonies in extensive slave trading, abstained from ever dealing or turning to their own account the value of a copper farthing in that trade; who, so far from that, when from some bankrupt estate some slaves became the property of the father, he immediately gave them their freedom—a number of slaves passed to him as a part of a bankrupt estate, as they might do at that time, he immediately manumitted them, and gave them their freedom—he it is, who having mainly conducted this transaction, he finds it in vain to look back to a long life, spent in honour, honesty, and integrity, a life spent in deeds of charity and kindness—he finds it in vain to look to the character of his house never before assailed by the breath of suspicion—he finds his own son indicted in this country—a country, under the protection of the laws of which he is living, and to which he has brought his commerce, and in which he and those belonging to him are spending the large fortunes they have gained in their trade; he finds, under the laws of this country, his son is indicted as a felon, for having signed his name to one or two documents—and I will prove to you that is all he has done in the course of a transaction which passed through their house as commission agents for the house of Martinez & Co., at the Havannah—and I will convince you, when I refer to the evidence before you, *evidence which has been, I must say, most unfairly adduced, which has been perverted and brought before you in a way which I cannot commend*, I will show you upon the evidence that that is all that can be charged upon this young man—that in the course of a transaction which passed through the house in which he is now a principal, but only since he has been of age has he been a member at all to entitle him to sign documents—he signed a letter, perfectly innocent in itself, and a charter-party, a regular mercantile transaction, the profit of which to the house was of the most trumpery amount—he did those two acts, in the absence of his father, the house here conducting the business for their agents—and for that he is brought to the bar of the Central Criminal Court, and you are asked to pass against him a verdict of guilty, fixing upon him the crime of felony, and all the dreadful consequences of that guilt, which by this indictment he is liable to.

Gentlemen, *I must say, that a proceeding of this kind does no honour to those great and zealous efforts made for the total extinction of the slave trade by Britain and British means.* If those, who sincerely desire to see that trade effaced, as we all trust in God it soon will be, from the surface of the earth; if they desire to see their efforts succeed, and if they desire to aid the great exertions of Britain for the destruction of the slave trade, let them not treat as felons those merchants in Great Britain or elsewhere, who may, without having any reason to suspect they are illegal, carry on trading concerns with the coast of Africa; let them try, by their cruizers, to stop the slave vessels and liberate the slaves on board; let them exert themselves to put an end to the slave trade wherever their arms or their efforts can be carried; but let them remember, it is not by force of arms it will be abolished—it is by civilisation, and the arts and commerce, the basis of civilisation, it alone can be put an end to. If you would lead to the total destruction of that trade, let it be indeed by vigilance, let it be by all the great efforts made by our ships abroad and our councils at home; but, above all things, seek to introduce commerce—for where there is commerce, there must in time be civilisation, intelligence, and moral improvement, and education, and progress in the arts, which are calculated to raise the character of any country—wherever there is commerce, there must be commercial people, there must be educated people, there must be persons to carry on the government, there must be courts of justice established, and persons to administer the law—that commerce will increase, and will lead to civilisation, and we can introduce all that is good in this world, and promote all the best objects in life—and then the slave trade will cease, not by force, but by civilisation. And I will show you, when I go through the evidence, if you will fairly consider it altogether in the way in which it ought to be brought before you, and in which it ought to be presented to your minds, I undertake to satisfy you that these gentlemen are not capable, and that there is no ground for imputing it to them, of lending their assistance to that odious traffic; and I say, that no Englishman, nor English house, has done more to prevent and destroy it than the house of Zulueta & Co., both in Spain and in this country.

Now, Gentlemen, let us see what the charge is. The charge is this:—That the prisoner at the bar employed and dispatched a vessel, and shipped certain goods, in order that the goods and vessel might be employed in the slave trade. Gentlemen, I wish that my learned friend, Mr. Serjeant Bompas, had been more explicit in his opening address. I think it would have been but fair if he had stated distinctly what he alleged to be the object of the party prosecuted. To say he has the general object of engaging in the slave trade is speaking most vaguely. Does he mean that the prisoner has dispatched this vessel, intending that slaves should be taken on board the vessel? Does he mean, that Pedro de Zulueta engaged in shipping the goods, in order that the goods might be bartered against slaves? or, does he mean, that he shipped the goods, in order that the goods might be sold for money, and with that money that slaves might be bought? Gentlemen, whatever might be the object, I think I shall satisfy you that Mr. Zulueta was perfectly innocent; that he had no such object, that he had no such intention, that he had no such idea: but it is hard for him, that in a matter so much affecting his happiness I should have to grope my way in the dark to find out what the charge is, and that while I am exhausting my strength and your patience in finding out the charge, it may turn out that something more was in the mind of the prosecutor, or in the mind of the person who framed the indictment, merely because Mr. Serjeant Bompas, acting under the instructions of Sir George Stephen, has not properly defined what he imputed to Mr. Zulueta. It is very easy to say to a British merchant, who purchases and ships for another house a quantity of goods, and sends them on board a vessel consigned to the coast of Africa, it is easy to say to him, upon some part of the coast of Africa the slave trade is carried on, and you, in some way or other, intended to promote it; it is easy to say that may be, but it seems to me, it ought to have been fully and distinctly alleged what was the object they meant to impute to him— whether it was to do that which my learned friend has thought fit to accuse him of.

But, let us see what the charge is. I must assume it to be this—that, in some way or other, Mr. Zulueta knew, that when he, as a member of the firm, took some part in dispatching the vessel, or in shipping the goods, that the vessel, or the goods, or both, were to be employed in the slave trade—by whom employed, whether by Messrs. Martinez & Co., at Cadiz, or the consignees, Rolo & Co., or Captain Jennings himself, my learned friend has found it to be convenient to withhold even from you—therefore, what the precise charge is I am seeking to find out, but I am utterly unable to ascertain. It may be, that they contend that the object was that Martinez & Co., who are supposed to have some agents at the Gallinas, intended to convert the goods directly into slaves, or into money to buy slaves; it may be, that the consignees of the goods are the parties to do that; it may be, as he says, that Captain Jennings was a slave trader on his own account, and that he was to do it: which of the three it is I do not know; but whichever it is—though it would make considerable difference in the legal form, because sending goods to be converted into money is no offence, though that money may be converted into slaves, although sending goods may be an offence—but I am not entering into that, for though there is a distinction in law, I make none in fact—I entirely, on behalf of the prisoner, disclaim the slightest notion or idea of giving the slightest countenance or aid, directly or indirectly, to the slave trade, in any shape or form that any man can suggest; and I say it would be a most uncharitable wresting and perverting of facts, which may be capable of two constructions from their ordinary and fair effect, to say that they throw a shade of suspicion upon any part of the conduct of the prisoner.

Gentlemen, I pray you to consider the real nature of the transaction, as it is to be collected from that to which my learned friend has been obliged to refer—and he could not make out his case without it—from that statement made by Mr. Zulueta himself voluntarily before the Committee. It is this, that this young man, born in Spain, but having from the high station of his father had a most excellent education, being of amiable character and intelligent, thought he might be of use to the house in England—there is a house in Cadiz, but the house we have to deal with is that in England—he comes here, becomes a member of the firm, and remains here; he speaks English a great deal better than his father, and in the transactions requiring more of speaking English he took a more prominent part: but the correspondence and the evidence in the case shows, that the orders given in the commercial transactions are entirely in the handwriting of the father almost; and it is a mere accident that the name of the son is put to documents not prepared by him, as I will show you he puts his signature to them in the ordinary course of business in the house. The house of Zulueta & Co. has transactions with most parts of the world, but is most largely engaged with Spain, and the Havannah, and several other places. With regard to Africa, the house has nothing to do with it—and I pray your attention to this point, I implore your attention to it, or you may misunderstand the evidence given by Captain Hill and Captain Denman—they had no more—Zulueta & Co., had no more to do with the trade to the coast of Africa than I have, or any of you I was going to say, I hope, you have, but if none of you, had. But it so happened, that trading to the amount of three or four hundred thousand pounds in the course of three or four years, or more largely still, with this house of Martinez & Co., that Martinez & Co., whose business was carried on at the Havannah and Cadiz, also had some dealings with various parts of the coast of Africa, amongst others at the Gallinas; and out of transactions to the amount of 200,000*l.* or 400,000*l.*, there are transactions to the amount of 18,000*l.* or 20,000*l.* in ten years or more—call it twenty years—I believe it is ten years— to the amount of about 18,000*l.* or 20,000*l.*, which consisted in this—not a trade to Africa, but this kind of dealing—Martinez & Co., who trade to the Havannah, to which Zulueta & Co. trade, also were in the habit of consigning cargoes of sugar, and other produce, from the Havannah to England; and having some dealings with the coast of Africa, they have upon some five or six occasions desired the house of Zulueta & Co., who live in England and carry on their business here, to furnish them with this trifling amount of British manufactures, and send them on board any vessel they may buy or engage for the purpose, to such part of the coast of Africa as they may direct. The house of Zulueta & Co. carrying on business here, from the immense extent of their transactions having a house at Liverpool, upon receiving an order to ship goods to the amount of a few hundred pounds, they order the goods through their Liverpool house, the great emporium of manufactures in that part of England, and they put them on board any ship directed by Martinez & Co.; they ship the goods in any shape or way as they may direct; and from the time the goods are shipped, they know no more of them, and have no more to do with the subsequent disposition of them, than any one of you I am addressing. It turns out, for so Captains Hill and Denman who have been upon the coast say, that the Gallinas has no produce to return for goods; they say that there is nothing but the slave trade there; that though the goods may be unshipped and landed, there is no return produce: but Messrs. Zulueta & Co., who had no trade with the Gallinas, who I will show you upon the evidence never until this transaction heard the name of any one of the three parties to whom this cargo was consigned, they sent the goods to the Gallinas as they would have done to the Havannah or to Gambia, to Madagascar or the East or West Indies, and troubled themselves no more about it as soon as the goods are shipped: because it is suggested that some parties concerned in these slave trading establishments may make an iniquitous use of these goods in the slave trade, they are to be told that this young man—(not attacking his father, whose ancient name and character for honour and integrity would protect him)—has committed a crime; they seize upon this unhappy young man; they say, because your house have sent goods to that place, ordered by your correspondents, you shall be seized as a felon and tried for a felony.

Now let us look at the evidence. I will take the evidence as it was given, and consider the evidence apart from the statement: take my statement as nothing, and take my learned friend's statement as nothing; let us see what the case is, divested of speeches and speech-making, and those reasonings which I will show you have no application to the conduct of Mr. Zulueta.

There is the house of Zulueta & Co. many years established in England, they have correspondents abroad, the house of Martinez & Co. at Cadiz—and this young man writes a letter, in these terms, dated the 20th August, 1840: "In reply to your favour of yesterday, we have to say that we cannot exceed 500*l.* for the vessel in question, such as described in your letter, namely, that excepting the sails the other differences are trifling from the inventory; if you cannot therefore succeed at those limits, we must give up the purchase, and you will please act accordingly;" then it is addressed to Captain Jennings, Portsmouth. What is stated concerning that letter is true, that it is not written by this young man at all. I do not know whether the original letter was handed in, but you shall see it: my learned friend says, it was proved that it was written altogether by this young man himself to the captain.

Mr. Justice *Maule*. It was proved so in this way, "I believe it to be the writing of Pedro Zulueta."

Mr. *Kelly*. Whether it was so or not it is quite immaterial, I need not say that the contents are perfectly innocent. It is clear, that before this time the house had employed Captain Jennings to treat for the purchase of this vessel. There was some demur about the price. This letter was written, in order, if possible, that the vessel might be obtained for the sum of 500*l.*; and in the way in which people bargain they tell them, that if they will not take that sum they will not buy it at all. That letter is written by Mr. Zulueta: I need not say that there is no felony in the member of a firm like Zulueta & Co. authorising Captain Jennings, or any other man, to offer 500*l.* for a vessel. Here the evidence with regard to the young man I am defending is a blank: it does not appear he interfered directly or indirectly in any way, or knew what was going on; but it appears that the vessel was ultimately purchased at that sum, dispatched to Liverpool, and the goods were loaded on board the vessel; and then the charter-party was made out, to which I will now call your attention, and which was signed by the prisoner Mr. Zulueta. Now you will see how my observations apply: it is in the usual form; it is printed, and the blanks, as you will see, are filled up, not in the handwriting of the prisoner nor any member of the firm, but in the ordinary course of business by the clerk whose duty it is to prepare the charter-parties; and it is signed, because it had to be signed. Mr. Pedro Zulueta was in the counting-house, and his father was out upon some other business, and Pedro Zulueta signed, "for Martinez & Co., of Havannah, Zulueta & Co." These are the two papers in the handwriting of the prisoner—a letter to Captain Jennings, saying, offer 500*l.*, if they will not take that no more will be given, and the charter-party by which the vessel is chartered from Captain Jennings to Martinez & Co., the house of Zulueta acting as agents, not buying the ship, not entering into the transaction as on their own account, but acting as agents for Messrs. Martinez—that is a paper partly written and partly printed, and the name is subscribed "for Martinez & Co., Havannah, Zulueta & Co." Those are the only two documents in the handwriting of the prisoner: his evidence I will refer to more particularly by and bye. The evidence shows what I never denied, that the house of which he is a member are civilly responsible for all the house may do. That his house effected the purchase of a vessel at the time—that it was desirable that Captain Jennings should be the captain (and I will give you a reason for that presently)—and that the house caused goods to be shipped in it at Liverpool—and that from that time they heard no more of it, is not denied. It is perfectly clear, if the case rested there, it was merely this—that the house of Zulueta & Co., as agents for Martinez & Co., purchased the ship for Jennings, and that the purchaser made Martinez & Co. the mortgagees of the ship, so as to put them in possession of the property, but to leave Captain Jennings nominally the proprietor and captain; and then they shipped for their principals a quantity of merchandise, regularly passing through the Custom-house on board the vessel, and consigned to the coast of Africa. It is perfectly clear no sort of imputation can be thrown upon any one concerned in that transaction.

But, Gentlemen, let us see what are the circumstances upon which the prosecutor calls upon you to infer, not only that Zulueta & Co., and particularly the prisoner at the bar, purchased this vessel, and dispatched this vessel, and loaded the goods on board it, but that he did it not merely knowing, but for the very purpose, in the language of the indictment, "to accomplish the object of using them in the slave trade." What is the evidence upon which they call upon you to infer that? First of all they do this, and *I do pray your attention to this part of the case, because it is a point affecting, and vitally affecting, the safety of every manufacturer, every merchant, nay every tradesman in this country,* who happens to deal in any goods, however lawful, but which may be shipped to the coast of Africa; they say this, you, young man, Pedro Zulueta, a member of this firm, you knew that these goods in this ship were to be used for the slave trade, and you dispatch the ship and goods that they may be used in the slave trade. Why, have you ever admitted you knew it? No, I have denied it, and have offered to deny it upon oath.—Have we proved you ever gave any secret instructions they should be used for that purpose? We give you notice that we call for your instructions, but before the Court and Jury we dare not call for them.—Did you receive any information from Martinez & Co. that they might be used for that purpose? No. We give you notice to produce all the letters from Martinez & Co., and his counsel comes forward and says—*Here is every document, here is every account, every scrap of paper at all relating to this transaction,*[15] and I offer you the oaths of every body in the counting-house, without examining them myself, that this is all that can be found. No, says the prosecutor, it suits us better to charge you with a felony, and call for documents which might or might not support the charge; but when you have got them here we will not read them before the Jury, we will not lay them before the Jury, but we will do this—in order that Sir George Stephen, sitting near Mr. Serjeant Bompas and instructing him *from his own grossly perverted views of the facts and the truth, to misrepresent and to colour almost every material document* to be given in evidence in the cause, in order to give them a reply, they say "you may produce them." That is what they do. This, then, is a case in which they say we will call for your instructions to the captain, because we say, although there was nothing in your handwriting found in the vessel, except this innocent letter offering 500*l*. for the purchase of the ship, and the charter-party signed by the house, there were some secret instructions. We call for all the letters, we will not use one, but we leave you to prove there were none such. We say, you were informed by Martinez & Co. that they were to be so used, and we give you notice to produce the letters; we will not call for them, we leave it to you: and if we were to read twenty different letters, all the letters from Martinez & Co. to Zulueta & Co., you would have from Mr. Serjeant Bompas, with Sir George Stephen behind him suggesting—Oh, there were secret instructions behind! How do we know there was not a letter behind, which contained secret instructions? That is the way that a case for felony is to be conducted; and therefore I beseech you not to look at what my learned friend urges upon you, but look at the facts. The facts are, that this young man offered 500*l*. for the vessel, and that this young man signed the charter-party, and those facts he admitted before the Committee of the House of Commons; he admitted that this ancient and honourable house, without a stain upon its character, purchase the ship, and charter the ship, and ship the goods, as the agents of Martinez & Co., to the coast of Africa. Then, when they have to prove the guilty knowledge that this was done for the purpose of these goods being used in the slave trade, after going through this farce of calling for papers they dare not use, they say this—We cannot prove that this young man ever thought, or wrote, or sent, about the slave trade; we cannot prove he ever said a single word to Captain Jennings that he was to use the ship or goods in the slave trade; we cannot prove that their correspondents ever wrote or said a word to them upon the subject; but I will tell you what we will do, he was never at the Gallinas, but Captain Denman was at the Gallinas, Captain Hill was at the Gallinas, Colonel Nichol was at the Gallinas, and we will prove by them that the slave trade is carried on to a considerable extent there; we will prove through them, that there are such persons there as Rolo, Alvarez, and Ximenes; and we will prove that those three persons are notorious slave dealers; and we trust that the Jury will say, here are goods sent to the coast of Africa—and it is true, because goods are constantly sent there, British produce to the amount of millions is sent there, and forms a great part of our commerce, but it is sent to that part of the coast where these three honourable gentlemen will say that nothing but the slave trade is carried on—and it will then lie upon him to show that they were not intended to be so used.

[15] Pointing to a mass of books and papers on the table.

Now, Gentlemen, if Mr. Zulueta had known as much of the Gallinas as Captain Denman does, who has been cruizing about there since 1835, or as much as Captain Hill knows, who has been upon that coast for several years past, or as much as Colonel Nichol, who has been there twenty years; if he had ever been there or lived there to see the kind of commerce carried on, and to know that there is no lawful commerce at all, but that there is the slave trade only, I should say that you put a man living in England in a very peculiar situation, to which I will call your attention in a moment, but it would raise the question in your minds, whether he might not suspect that these goods might be sold for money, and the money applied in the purchase of slaves, or the slave trade be promoted by the transaction. But, Gentlemen, I beseech you to remember this; they have not proved this, and the contrary appears, that this young man—and I speak of the father as well—that neither he nor his father were ever on the coast of Africa. "Oh, but" says my learned friend, Mr. Serjeant Talfourd, in a question put on re-examination to Captain Denman, "could a person who had traded for twenty years to the Gallinas be ignorant that nothing but the slave trade was carried on there?" If it was so, if he had thought so, it is not by his inferences—whose honourable zeal in putting down the slave trade has carried him so far as to make him a defendant in two or three actions, which may come on to be tried in this country—however honourable his motives and feelings (and I admire the zeal he feels upon the subject, political as well as private zeal)—it is not what he knows which is to determine whether Mr. Zulueta is to be convicted of felony. But it is not that to which I was about to call your attention. If my learned friend, Mr. Serjeant Talfourd had reflected when he used that expression in the question he put, "Do you think that a person trading twenty years there could be ignorant of the nature of the trade carried on?"—he would have seen it was wholly inapplicable to the case of Messrs. Zulueta & Co. In the first place, this young man has not been a third part of twenty years in the house; in the next place, the house has not traded to the extent of 20s. to the Gallinas, they have never had any communication with it. Mr. Serjeant Bompas opened among many other things which he has left unproved, that he would show that was untrue, and that he had had dealings with them. If that was so, it would have been easy to do it; but they find he never had any dealing with the place; he had no letter or bill from the place, or any article or thing of any sort or kind from any person there, which could convey to his mind whether it was a slave trading place, or a place where a great deal of commerce was lawfully carried on—nothing of the kind. I pray your attention to what it is my learned friend has founded this observation upon. All that Zulueta & Co. have done, as you will see by the evidence before you, is, that they have received directions from their foreign correspondents to ship goods to the Gallinas, and have put those goods on board a vessel, and then dispatched that vessel, and shipped those goods for the Gallinas; and from that time forth they have heard no more of them. Now, I beg to ask you, their correspondence taking place with Martinez &. Co. at the Havannah or Cadiz, but having no correspondence with the Gallinas, unless their curiosity led them, as it did me this morning to look at the map or globe to find the place—and they looked in vain, unless they looked at a pretty large map, to see whether it was a river, or an island, or city, or what place it was—how should they know any thing about it? I agree we did not want Captain Denman's evidence, for that they had shipped goods for twenty years, and traded there in the ordinary sense of the word, if they had had correspondents there and dealt on their own account with them, and sent them goods from time to time, and had goods in return, or written letters to them, and had letters in return, they might through them have obtained some information of the nature of the business carried on there. But, it is no such thing. What this young man said in his evidence before the Committee turns out to be true; if it had not been so, they had abundant means to contradict that evidence: and Sir George Stephen, whose zeal spares no expense, no effort, would have satisfied you that they had written letters to the Gallinas, and had sent goods there. All that appears is, that from time to time—the transactions being really a drop of water in the ocean of their great mercantile dealings—they have out of 400,000*l.* in ten or twenty years shipped goods to the amount of 22,000*l.*, which have gone to the Gallinas. But how should they have known it was for the purposes of the slave trade? Suppose any one of you were a dealer in muskets (for they are some of the goods shipped on board this vessel) and that a person in Spain writes to you, saying, I want a thousand muskets for a place called Gallinas, on the coast of Africa—would you dream, if you prepared the muskets and sold them, and made out the proper papers and dispatched them according to the order—would you dream, that you were committing a felony? That is what it comes to.

Just see how the case stands—Captain Denman knows, and Captain Hill knows very well, that shipments to the Gallinas may be something suspicious, because they say, as far as their experience goes, there is no lawful trade there, and that they are all slave traders there; but how is any body in this kingdom who has never been there, and never corresponded with the place, to know that?

What is the next fact? *Captain Hill proves—though it was with the greatest reluctance he ever gave an answer in favour of this young man whom he is endeavouring to send to*

Botany Bay—at last, he let out by accident that there are places, on the coast of Africa, to which British produce in large quantities is sent, where the trade is perfectly proper, and where goods lawfully are sent and disposed of; and that at many of those places there are persons, who trade largely, and to a very great extent in British produce, who also deal in slaves.

Here, again, I beseech you to turn your attention to the facts and forget the statement. You may be manufacturers of guns or gunpowder, or commission-agents living in the country, who for the purpose of shipment purchase those goods; in either case a party comes and says, I want a thousand muskets and two tons of gunpowder to be shipped to a certain place on the coast of Africa. I ask you—are you first to consult the map to ascertain the place, and having ascertained where it is, are you to go to somebody you may hear of—Captain Hill or Captain Denman—and inquire, whether they have been upon the coast of Africa, and can tell you the character of the trade carried on there? Are you next, the person being a Spaniard or Portuguese, to inquire whether they ever deal in slaves, and if you find they do, are you to say, I will execute no order you give me? *That would annihilate two-thirds of the commerce of Great Britain, and would prevent the most useful transactions of commerce which can occur upon the coast of Africa.* It is, therefore, I say, in a charge of this momentous character, it is not to be determined upon suspicion. You are not to hang or transport a man upon vague suspicion; you must show that the crime has been committed; you must have before you direct evidence to prove that he must have known—not that he might have known—by inquiry, if it had been duly answered, and in the mean time the orders would be lost—not that he might have learnt, or that the result of the inquiry might be that the goods might by possibility be unlawfully employed—you must have direct evidence that they were shipped for that purpose. The statute does not say, that every one who ships goods to a slave colony shall be guilty of slave dealing; the Act does not say, that whoever ships goods to a place where the slave trade is principally carried on shall be guilty of slave dealing; the Act does not say, that any body who shall ship goods without taking care that they shall not be employed in slave dealing shall be guilty of felony; the Act does not say, that any one who ships goods which may be employed in the slave trade shall be guilty of felony—God forbid that it should say that!—but the Act says, if a man ships goods for that object, if he ships goods with the intent—which as far as in him lies he seeks to carry into effect, that they may be used in the slave trade—that is a felony. Where, in God's name, is there a particle or scintilla of evidence to that effect here? Where Captain Denman tells you it is a well-known slave trading colony, and that he knew it before he went there? Did you know it? I apprehend, if my learned friend knew it before he was instructed in this case, he knows geography, as he does every thing else, much better than I do. My learned friend says, you are not to shut your eyes to what you are doing. No; I agree if a man commits a crime, or does a mischief, he is not to shut his eyes to the consequences of it. I deny, once for all—and I appeal to the learned Judges whether I am not correctly stating the effect of the law—whether a man, who has no intention to do an unlawful act in the shipment of goods, is bound to make any inquiry as to what is to be done with goods, which, in obedience to the orders of a foreign correspondent, he ships to any place on the face of the earth. He is not bound to make inquiries; if he was, it would throw impediments in the way of commerce more injurious than the slave trade itself in any part of the world. Again, they speak of Messrs. Martinez being slave traders, and they speak of the admission that appears upon the evidence of Mr. Zulueta, that he knew that Martinez & Co. had been engaged in the slave trade. I will show you, when I come to refer to this evidence, which is all-important in this case, that there is nothing of the kind—he speaks of the knowledge he had; he gave his evidence in 1842, and you will find, when you look on a little further, he had learnt it since the transactions in 1840.

Now, suppose he did know it—suppose a commission-agent knows that a foreign correspondent of his house is extensively engaged in the slave trade—he knows, at the same time, he is extensively engaged in a lawful trade in sugar, tobacco, and other commodities—I ask you, whether if that foreign correspondent, by letter, desires him to freight a ship with a quantity of goods, and he does so, he is to be treated as a felon? whether, because a trader in both ways—a trader lawful and unlawful—may use his goods unlawfully, and the shipper knows it and cannot prevent it, he is to be treated as a felon or wrong doer? I deny it: if it were so, the first mercantile houses in the country would consist of none but felons. It would be in vain to suggest houses—though one rose before my mind, whose extent of transactions is equalled only by the honour and integrity of their character, that house trading largely as it does with the Havannah and the Brazils, where all the extensive merchants are slave dealers, that house must sacrifice two-thirds of its trade—and all that loss must accrue to Great Britain, because that trade may enable those who carry it on to carry on also a trade in slaves. It is quite intelligible, that that was the very object of the inquiry before the Committee, where Mr. Zulueta, Captain Hill, and Captain Denman, and a score of other persons were examined before the Colonial Secretaries under both governments, and some of the most practical men of the present day—it was for the purpose of determining and reporting to the House, whether it would be desirable to extend the criminal law of the country, and prohibit the trade altogether with places where the slave trade was carried on, or with persons notoriously carrying it on. Nobody ever dreamt, but Sir George Stephen, that it was illegal to trade with a slave dealing place, or a notorious slave dealer; it is only illegal where you know the trade you carry on is to promote the slave trade, and you know that to be the object. That was one of the objects of the Committee, to ascertain whether it was desirable to prevent the trading with slave dealers, or slave trading places. I may not regularly refer to their opinion; but they made a Report in 1842, and no law is passed at all affecting transactions of that nature—the only Act is that, which, for another purpose, I called my Lord's attention to, and which made that illegal, not illegal before, namely, the trading by British subjects in foreign ports—not making it criminal to trade with slave traders or slave trading places. Then let us see the result. You are called upon, where the shipment is innocent, and the employment of the ship is innocent, you are called upon to destroy this man, because he has put his name to one or two innocent documents, and because they say it was so notoriously a slave trading place that he must have known that they were to be so used. My answer is in a single sentence—he knew nothing of the kind; they have not proved it; they have proved that Captain Hill, and Captain Denman, and others, conversant with the spot, knew it; they have not proved that Mr. Zulueta knew it—the evidence is entirely a blank upon the subject. If he thought of it at all, and I think that a man is bound to inquire about the matter, he would probably think this—there are a great number of houses in the city of London executing large commissions for the African trade, and a great deal of British commerce goes to the coast of Africa is lawfully disposed of, and promotes the civilisation of Africa; and I have every right to suppose that this goes for a lawful purpose; if that is not so, it must be shown to be for an unlawful purpose. If that is not fair in the mouth of Mr. Zulueta's house, it is not fair in the mouth of any firm trading in that way with the coast of Africa; and unless it had been shown that Mr. Zulueta himself was personally informed of, or knew, the character of this place, what is proved by Captain Denman or Captain Hill has nothing to do with the question—so much for that part of the proof, from which you are called upon to infer that the prisoner shipped these goods to accomplish this wicked object, because it is proved the slave trade was carried on there.

Now, Gentlemen, let me say one word more of Captain Denman: he does not show, in the correct sense of the words, that the slave trade is extensively carried on there; he may be right in saying there is no produce there; but is there no mode of receiving goods and selling them for money, though no goods are exported? There are various towns or villages, one of nine hundred inhabitants, and others of various numbers, and native chiefs also; there are also Europeans, principally Spaniards—I should like to know, whether the native chiefs, and the Spanish population, and the nine hundred, the population of Tiendo, do not lawfully, for pieces of money or doubloons, buy British produce lawfully? It may be said, that they can only get this money by the slave trade; that is, by having previously dealt in slaves; but where is that to stop? If you are to trace the money from hand to hand, in order to ascertain whether, since a bank note was made or stamped, or the money coined, it has not been the medium of some illegal transaction, there is an end to all commerce. It may be, that these men, Rolo and Pedro Blanco, may have sold a thousand slaves for dollars, and may have paid a debt to Rolo, and with that Rolo may have paid somebody else, who may have bought the goods of Mr. Zulueta—I wish to know, whether Mr. Zulueta for that is to be accused of dealing in slaves, or shipping goods to dealers in slaves? There is nothing of the kind, as far as regards that part of the evidence, relating to the character of the place, or as relating to the character of the parties there. My answer to that is, that, however well known to Captain Denman and Captain Hill, it was unknown to Pedro de Zulueta; that he neither knew the place nor the persons, but that there was such a place to which his house had, without a suspicion, shipped considerable quantities of goods for their foreign correspondents—and it would be hard and cruel to say, that because other people possess a knowledge that he does not, he is to be charged as a felon—because he did not know what other parties, who had passed the latter part of their lives upon the spot, knew.

But, Gentlemen, a great deal has been said upon the mode in which this was to be carried into effect; and they say, because this vessel was bought really by Martinez & Co., and with their money—but Captain Jennings was made the captain, and Captain Jennings was made the apparent owner; therefore, that is a mark of suspicion, that is a concealment, that is putting a false colour upon the transaction—and therefore you are to infer that the transaction was with some guilty intent with respect to the slave trade. Upon that, in the first instance, I would say, this is not an indictment against Mr. Zulueta for putting an English captain on board a foreign ship, and treating it as an English ship—such a proceeding is not, that I am aware of, contrary to the law at all; and it can only be important in this case, if the nature of the transaction is such as necessarily to lead you to infer that the object of the transaction was connected with the slave trade.

Now, let me try that in all its parts; let us see if there is any thing in the mode in which the transaction was carried into effect, which ought fairly to lead a Jury to infer that the object in sending the vessel to Africa was that it should be engaged in the slave trade. First, as to the English captain—I had some difficulty in getting the facts out—it is always desirable, when the Jury have some experience in the matter, for the ends of justice—I hope you may be some of you familiar with Spanish maritime transactions: but we have the notary of the Spanish consulate, before whom charter-parties and other maritime documents come, and we have had the judgment of a naval officer upon the spot, and their evidence goes to show, that by the maritime laws of Spain, a Spanish vessel cannot be commanded by an English captain. Then, if Messrs. Martinez & Co. wished to ship these goods to the coast of Africa from England, and they wished at the same time to employ Captain Jennings as the captain, how are they to do it, except by giving an English name to the vessel, putting it under English colours, and making Captain Jennings the apparent owner? And, Gentlemen, is that to be wondered at? Is the character of a British sailor so low, that there is any thing upon which you are to suspect a man of felony, because one of his foreign correspondents prefers that a vessel he is going to freight to Africa should be commanded by an Englishman and not a Spaniard? You will find, from the evidence, that Captain Jennings had been more than once employed by Martinez & Co.—there is no doubt he is a man of considerable experience; he is a man of considerable courage, as all English sailors are—and explained in that way, what more natural than that Martinez & Co., hearing he was in England, should wish that a man they could trust should be employed in bringing out a cargo of goods to Africa, or wherever it was? Therefore it was he would employ Captain Jennings. How was he to do it? If the vessel was their own, it must sail under the Spanish flag, it would be a Spanish vessel, and could not be commanded by an English captain; so, to obtain that object, they employed Captain Jennings, whom they thought a trustworthy person—and in order to employ him, he is obliged to make the vessel appear an English vessel, and make him appear as the owner of the vessel—and this arrangement is accordingly made. And, Gentlemen, let me observe, though it was not given in evidence—but I will not stand upon technical points, I am dealing with the character of a house as high as any in Britain; I believe their Lordships, after some argument, excluded the bill of lading, in which the name of Captain Jennings appeared as the shipper—I do not know how it is—suppose he appeared—

Mr. Justice *Maule*. He appeared so in the cockets.

Mr. *Kelly*. I do most earnestly hope that some of you have sufficient experience of the mode in which business is conducted, with respect to ships, to know, that this is not an unusual circumstance. Just consider the object of the voyage: these goods were to be taken to the Gallinas, and they were consigned to those persons whose names you have heard. You have heard that slave trading is carried on there, as it is along the whole coast—that is known to Martinez & Co.—they have a great deal of trade there, and no doubt they would know it; they would know very well that the seas swarmed with British cruizers, for the purpose of interrupting and preventing the slave trade—what more natural? If their correspondents should happen not to be upon the spot at the time the goods arrived, so that they could not be delivered, or that there should be a blockade, and the ship could not enter with the goods shipped by Martinez & Co., the captain must sail back to England or to Cadiz, and get authority from Martinez to alter the destination of the goods; if, on the contrary, they were shipped in the name of Captain Jennings, if he found a blockade, or the correspondents of Messrs. Martinez were not there, or there was any opposition to his communications with the shore, he would have the complete disposal of the goods; he might take them to other parts of the coast of Africa, or any other part of the world, or deal with them as he pleased—and the whole mystery is explained. Every body, who knows any thing of these commercial transactions, knows that a supercargo is sent out with goods, and the shipment is most frequently in the name of the supercargo; and it is for that reason, that in case when the goods arrive at the place to which they are consigned, if there is any difficulty, or any thing which requires the control or disposition of the owner, the supercargo is the party to act, and he can only do that when the shipment is in his name. Here there is a supercargo, or somebody they had confidence in, Captain Jennings, and accordingly the shipment is made in the name of Jennings, in order, in a case of difficulty, that he may exercise a control over the goods. And so far from there being any thing illegal in it, so far from there being any thing unusual in the transaction—because Captain Jennings was made the master, the apparent owner of the vessel, and the person in whose name the goods were shipped—it is the constant custom. If Messrs. Martinez wished to send these goods to the coast of Africa, and if, by reason of any blockade, it would be necessary to give them another destination, they wished to have the benefit of an English captain, Captain Jennings—and by taking the course they did, of making out the charter-party from Captain Jennings to Martinez & Co., and at the same time shipping the goods in his own name, retaining a share of the superintendence as the real owner throughout the voyage, they accomplished that. To tell me, because that is done, which is a matter of constant custom, the good sense of which strikes one at the first sight—for my learned friend to rise and say, this is a concealment, and you are to condemn this young man to transportation—is perfectly monstrous. But I will tell you what the prosecutor ought to have done—and what I should have expected from the experience of my learned friend, who has called Sir George Stephen the public prosecutor—if he meant to say, that a charter-party in this form was an illegal and unmercantile act, he ought to have called persons engaged in the trade, parties engaged in shipments of the same description, or any other foreign trade, to prove that this was an illegal, and consequently an unusual transaction. He has left that in blank. I make the same observation as to the nature of the trade: how is it—when you are called upon here to denounce this young man as a felon, because it is supposed that slave trading was carried on at this place, the Gallinas, and that any body engaged in trade to that part of the world must have known that slave trading was carried on there—how is it, that out of the scores, to say the least, of highly respectable, intelligent, and experienced merchants, carrying on trade in this city, not one is called before you—not a merchant, not a shipper, not an individual is called to speak to any part of this transaction? You are to take Mr. Serjeant Bompas's statement for every thing—whatever Sir George Stephen instructs him to say in this case, unless you have experience in it yourself, you are to take every thing as proof. I say it became the public prosecutor to call merchants, acquainted with the coast of Africa, to give a fair mercantile character to the transaction; they have not done so; and I protest against the doctrine, that any man is to be treated as guilty, and denounced as tainted with crime, not upon any proof that the character of the transaction is contrary to mercantile usage, but upon the statement of counsel, unsupported by evidence, and more particularly where that evidence is so completely within the power of the prosecutor.

Gentlemen, let me make another observation upon this point—I fear that the length to which this case has been drawn may weary you, and my address more so than any other part of the case; but, for mercy's sake, consider—

Foreman of the Jury. We are quite glad to hear all you have to say.

Mr. *Kelly.* I thank you, Gentlemen. What would be my feelings, if any thing adverse was to happen to this young man, from my omitting to say what occurred to me as important? It is said by Mr. Serjeant Bompas, but not proved, that this was done under concealment: they have not called man or boy from Liverpool to prove that any part of the transaction was unusual. I appeal to any man, who knows any thing of the nature of shipments, whether it is possible that this cargo could have been shipped without clerks and shipping agents being employed, and without the cargo and ship undergoing the inspection of the Custom-house officers. All that has been done, and my learned friend and Sir George Stephen know that that has been done; and I believe, in his opening speech, he alluded to evidence from Liverpool; but not one witness has been called. You will see the effect of that in another part of the transaction to which I have not arrived; but when Mr. Serjeant Bompas tells you, that the employment of Mr. Jennings, as captain and owner, and shipping the goods in his own name, was done for the purpose of concealment, I say it is idle; and it is an insult to the understanding of any man to say there was any concealment. Messrs. Zulueta employ Captain Jennings—he employs other people—you heard that that was the mode in which the business was conducted—the Russian consul and Mr. Emanuel are not Zulueta & Co.—it appears that the transaction could not have been conducted but by the house of Zulueta—and yet my learned friend contents himself by saying, that this was secretly done, though he has not called one witness to prove it.

Gentlemen, I was upon the point, that the employment of Captain Jennings, and the making it appear that Captain Jennings was the owner, was a circumstance of concealment. If it was, I have told you the reasons humbly occurring to my own mind for thinking it was not; but suppose it was concealed—concealment, which would facilitate the carrying on the slave trade. Now, Gentlemen, I pray your attention to this question—Was the putting this ship under British colours, and under the command of a British captain, calculated at all to enable it to carry on the slave trade? That is the question. If it was, I clearly admit—though God forbid a man should be convicted upon it!—that it is a circumstance that may require some consideration in your minds; but if I demonstrate to you, that for all the objects of the slave trade, the employment of a British captain, and the employment of British colours, was fatal to it, and rendered discovery, and forfeiture, and punishment, almost inevitable, what becomes of the statement that all this was done clandestinely to facilitate the slave trade? Recollect the account of the trade given by Captain Denman. If it be a foreign vessel, a Portuguese or Spanish, which engages in the slave trade, there are very great impediments and very great difficulties in interrupting it, in searching and in bringing the transaction to light, or the perpetrators to justice, investigating the matter judicially, and finally causing the vessel and goods to be condemned. Our newspapers are filled with discussions about the right of search. Whereas, Captain Denman could, without a moment's pause, without any obstruction, enter upon any English vessel, and seize the English captain, and search the vessel from top to bottom—while, in an American vessel, and many other vessels, he might be met by obstruction, and it might be the cause of a war. It is true, under some treaties, it may be done; but it is not so as to Russia, because this vessel ultimately, according to my learned friend, defeated justice, and was given up to the Russian government. Where a vessel, therefore, is under foreign colours, there are many difficulties in searching, and if suspicious circumstances appear, in bringing the vessel, if I may so speak, to justice. What does Captain Denman say? "If it is an American vessel, I could not search at all unless by main force, at the peril of a war; if a Russian, it is the same thing; if a Spanish or French vessel, then, under the treaty, a search may take place." But, remember the mode of searching: if he saw an English vessel, the English captain would feel that of necessity he must, unless he meant to be condemned, tender his vessel, and all in it, to the investigation of a British naval officer; and if the vessel has any thing suspicious about it, you may prosecute it in the British Vice-Admiralty Court, in any of the colonies throughout the world; and, if condemned, as it may be, by British law, by British officers of justice; whereas, if it be a Spanish or Russian vessel, or a Portuguese, or of any other country, there are all sorts of difficulties and formalities before a search can take place; and if any thing suspicious is found, even Captain Hill, with all his furious zeal, would pause before he seized a foreign vessel. Again, supposing there are suspicious appearances, and the officer determines to try the question, it is tried not in the British Vice Admiralty Court—not in any British court at all—but before a Mixed Commission, composed of British, Spanish, and, perhaps, the subjects of other nations, surrounded with all these difficulties, and, I grieve to say, all that corruption which taints the administration of justice in almost every other country but this.

Now, Mr. Serjeant Bompas says—Sacrifice this young man, and condemn him as a felon. Why? Because, the more easily to carry on the slave trade, he fitted out a vessel—not as a Spaniard, with a Spanish crew and Spanish colours, but with English colours, an English captain, and an English crew, which Captain Denman, Captain Hill, or any other captain might search and condemn. Now, I am the humble and inefficient advocate of this young man, and the matter may occur to my mind erroneously; I may take an erroneous view, from the zeal I feel in the case, in presenting it before you, in the terms in which his innocence will ultimately appear; but, unless I grievously deceive myself, that argument admits of no answer, as Captain Denman said there are difficulties in the one case and none in the other—a trial by a British Court in the one case, and a Mixed Commission in the other; that there are great impediments where it is a foreign vessel, and none in the other. And has the prosecutor a right to call upon you to come to a conclusion that this young man is guilty of felony, because he fitted out a vessel with English colours, and an English captain, the more easily to carry on the slave trade? You will have to answer that question, if you think the slave trade could be more easily carried on by an English captain and an English crew. You have heard of the mutiny before they reached Cadiz; if you think an English crew were used, and English colours hoisted, the more safely to carry on the trade, it must be for some reason that does not occur to my mind, and I trust in God it will not occur to yours.

Now, Gentlemen, we come to the next point. They say—Though true it is, that this vessel was not employed in the slave trade, there is the most direct evidence that the man who fitted out the vessel meant to employ it in the slave trade, and really employed it with that object. If you cannot show the orders given by him to the captain so to employ it, the next thing would be to show it was so employed. If this ship had sailed from England to the Gallinas and discharged its cargo, and had taken in a number of slaves; or if it had bartered its cargo against a number of slaves; if that had been done, unless you can show it was done by Mr. Zulueta's orders, he is not responsible: you may challenge the captain, and you might say, whether Mr. Zulueta intended it or not, it was so used: but there is no such evidence. Captain Hill, with his zeal to discharge his duty and to prevent slave trading, took time by the forelock, and seized the vessel in the hands of the captain before it reached the shore, and you have therefore no means of drawing inferences of what was intended by what was done. But they endeavour to make up for that in this way: they say, we will show that the vessel was originally built for the slave trade; and we will show that, while it was in the hands of Mr. Zulueta, or while Captain Jennings had it under his hands, it had fittings added, or articles furnished, calculated to assist in the slave trade. And I must say, upon this part of the case, it grieves me to refer to the mode in which it has been conducted in terms of reprobation; *but I should ill discharge my duty if I did not say, that the mode in which the evidence was laid before you was unworthy the high reputation and the honourable character of my learned friend.* I pray you to remember what it is has been proved upon this occasion. He calls a witness from Portsmouth, or two or three; and, as Mr. Clarkson, and my other learned friend, obtained from them on cross-examination they had been lately subpœnaed, the prisoner could not be prepared by any possibility for their testimony; and what do they prove? They prove, that on board this vessel, while Captain Jennings was in command of it, they had seen, I do not know how many, water-casks for slave trading; that they had seen shackles and bolts, and all the muniments necessary to carry on the slave trade. Now, I ask you, is that fair? Is that just? The prisoner is charged, not with having thrown away those things, and destroyed them, and fitted up a vessel, which, for aught he knew, might be used in the slave trade, or might be for perfectly lawful purposes; but he is charged with having dispatched it from Liverpool for the purposes of the slave trade; and, in order to prove that, the prosecutor thinks it right to give in evidence what was done at Portsmouth with these shackles and water-casks which were on board the vessel, and there he leaves the case. I cannot trust myself to speak of that mode of giving evidence. Gentlemen, the way in which they ought to have convinced you there was any thing on board this vessel calculated to carry on the trade, was to show the condition of the vessel at the time she left the port of Liverpool. There all the control of the house of Zulueta & Co. finished; the charter-party was made out, the goods were put on board, and the ship, on the 8th of November, 1840, sailed from Liverpool; then, if this young man is a felon, the felony was completed. What was the condition of the ship then? Had it then the water-casks for the nourishment of the slaves? Had it shackles and other instruments of torture, or for the conveyance of the slaves from one part of the world to the other? Gentlemen, that was the time; that was the place to show it: and it could not be by inadvertence it was omitted. Why, Captain Hill, their witness, who would not drop a single syllable, who could not bring himself to say any thing favourable to this young man (not from any improper motive, he will not understand me to say), that even Captain Hill was obliged to say—"When I seized the vessel, where the slave trade was to be carried on, it was not fitted up for the slave trade;" and one of you gentlemen of the Jury—and from the bottom of my heart I thanked you—put the question in another form through my Lord, and the answer was—"No; at the time the vessel was seized it was not fitted up for the slave trade." So that you have this fact, that when it left Liverpool it was not fitted up for the slave trade, and had not the means on board to be so fitted up, and when on the coast of Africa it was not so fitted up; but, from their own witnesses knowing that, they call other witnesses to raise a suspicion in your minds that it was secretly prepared for the slave trade, because there were water-casks and shackles on board. And remember the evidence of the cabin-boy: they had the choice of the whole crew, and no one can say that the crew would be favourable to Mr. Zulueta, the owner, or his house; they were discharged as mutineers: they had their choice of the whole crew, and no expense, and no exertions have been spared, and yet they dare not call one of the crew to say what Captain Jennings stated, or what his object was; they called the cabin-boy, who says, "I know nothing of the loading of the vessel."

There is a person to be tried for a felony in fitting out a vessel perfectly lawfully, but for the slave trade, and they seek to show that it was fitted up for the slave trade: they do not show it at the only time it was material to show it, but they seek to ruin and destroy this unfortunate young man, by giving evidence of its state at Portsmouth, when we have from this boy the damning fact for the integrity of their case, that though the water-vessels were changed in their form, which was to make you think that they were sent in a disguised form, they were put on shore at Liverpool, and not put back again. If there had been an inch or a scrap of old iron, or a nail, the ship was in the possession of Captain Hill, and those who acted under him, as long as he thought fit to keep it. It was put into the Vice-Admiralty Court; it was open to the witnesses for the prosecution: I have no doubt they searched it from end to end, and from top to bottom, and every crevice and cranny, and in no place was a scrap of rusty iron found applicable to the slave trade; and yet you are to be told by Mr. Serjeant Bompas, that he will prove it was adapted for the slave trade, when his own instructions had already told him that they gave a false appearance to the case, and the true appearance of the case was entirely left out of consideration. However, Gentlemen, I thank God, whatever may be the consequence, and however terrible to my own feelings as counsel for the prisoner, I had no hand—God forbid!—in such a prosecution.

Gentlemen, it is not only in the mode and to the extent I have pointed out to you, that the evidence has been sought to be perverted—and if there had been a case, and facts to be proved from the condition of the vessel, it is only from the evidence they have submitted to you that it can appear—Captain Hill seized the vessel and cargo; he had the full control of it; every species of information, every scrap of paper on board is in their power, and every thing that could be given in evidence before you has been brought before you.

Gentlemen, I must observe that I am not counsel for Captain Jennings. Captain Jennings, for aught I know, though he is an Englishman, and there is no charge against him, may have been in collusion with Martinez & Co. I am not responsible for his acts. I thought there had been some refusal to give up the papers, but Captain Hill negatived that altogether; he did not say there was any opposition; the vessel did not sail away from him, on the contrary, it sailed up to him. I do not know how that was. He asked for papers and they were given up to him—he made some request which was refused, but as to the running away, or concealment, nothing of the kind was practised; but you have here a felon, in the situation of a partner in the house of Zulueta & Co., trading to the amount of millions, trading with the house of Martinez & Co. to an immense amount in sugar and tobacco, and all sorts of goods passing between Britain and its Colonies, and a little trading upon commission in the last fifteen years, in which the commission put into the pocket of Zulueta & Co., would not pay a day's salary to their clerks in their office, and you have a charge of felony for what this young man has done as it appears in the evidence to which I have called your attention. To talk of its being a concealment to use an English captain and an English vessel, when it would have insured a prosecution—when it would have insured discovery—when it would have insured punishment—is absurd. They say, here was something in the nature of the vessel, and to enable you to arrive at the same conclusion they prove her condition at Portsmouth, which was altered before the voyage was embarked upon, and they do not prove the condition of the vessel at the only time important for you to inquire into.

Gentlemen, Captain Hill said it would be very easy when the vessel arrived at Gallinas to get the fittings up there; that it would be easy for the factor there, when he expected the vessel, to get them ready. No doubt it would be very easy for a man to get a gun, and load it with powder and ball, and so shoot the Queen. But, good God! are we in cases of felony not to look for evidence, not to look for facts, but to suppose a felony, because it is physically possible that somebody may do something to put this ship into a condition that may be unlawful? So I might say of Captain Hill, that when he went with one of Her Majesty's ships upon the coast, he was disposed to assist in the slave trade instead of destroying it; he might have harboured the slaves in his vessel, or turned it into a slave establishment, or any thing else. But we are dealing with something more than the life of this young man. You are not to look at what a man 4000 miles off did, but what this man did. What he has done he is responsible for, and he is ready to answer here—he is ready to answer at a higher tribunal; but, in the name of that Judge before whom we must all stand, I implore you, do not visit him with suppositions of what other men might have done, instead of what he is proved to have done in this transaction.

Gentlemen, the evidence in the cause would have gone no further than I have stated but from the circumstance—a most extraordinary one, and unprecedented as far as my experience goes in criminal cases—of a great body of evidence being produced, that being neither more nor less than the voluntary, unsought, and unasked testimony of the criminal himself in his evidence given before the Committee of the House of Commons; and it is that to which I have finally to call your attention. I have stated to you, that the house of Zulueta & Co. had enjoyed the highest reputation from the time of their establishment, nearly seventy years ago, until the year 1842. That Committee was appointed, and is declared to have been assembled for the purpose of inquiring into the mode in which the slave trade at various places on the coast of Africa was effected by British commerce and by the employment of British capital. It was suggested, and perhaps truly suggested, that from various British houses, dealing largely in British manufactures, and exporting them as principals, or as agents to the order of Spanish houses, or Portuguese houses, or American houses, particularly in the states of South America—that by reason of those exports, commerce was introduced, and great sums of money procured, which money, being employed in the slave trade, thereby British capital and commerce tended to support the slave trade. The object of the Committee was to determine to what extent this particular allegation was true, and if true, whether it could be remedied by any alteration in the law. It is not necessary to notice the result of their deliberations; but it is important to observe, that upon the Committee were two most zealous men, Lord Stanley and Lord John Russell, neither of whom could have seen enough in the conduct of this young man to justify his prosecution. And this Committee seem to have thought whatever evil might arise in fostering or in facilitating the slave trade, directly or indirectly, by British capital and commerce, that they would too fatally interfere with the commerce and civilization of the Africans themselves, from which, and not the force of arms, the destruction of slavery must ensue, if further restrictions were placed upon general commerce of the country; and no further restrictions have been placed. But in the course of the investigation before this Committee, and at a very late period of their sittings, because it is after this part of this *immense volume*[16] had been given the house of Zulueta & Co. learnt that some evidence had been given *ex parte* and in their absence, which they thought threw some reflection upon the honour and integrity of their house. They felt their honour involved, and they felt themselves entirely innocent of the charge—they felt that the house of Zulueta & Co., both here and abroad, so far from assisting in the slave trade, had cautiously desisted from it, and made great sacrifices, even when both nations were engaged in it; and one of their firm came forward to give such explanation as he thought necessary to clear the house, if possible, from the imputation cast upon it— not because he knew more of it than any other member of the firm, that will appear from the evidence; but, because he spoke English more fluently than his father, he came forward and gave the evidence which is before you. And, Gentlemen, but for that evidence the whole case would have been, that the house of Zulueta & Co. shipped these goods and dispatched this vessel, and in the course of their proceedings this letter and charter-party were signed by the prisoner at the bar. But they say, what is wanting, that evidence will complete, and out of his own mouth they can clearly show he has betrayed himself into a most awful predicament—that when he went before this Committee voluntarily, he has admitted himself to be a felon. But, thank God, that is for you to judge of. It is for you, a Jury of British men, not dealing with a fellow-countryman, but where you would be more tender than with any of your own countrymen—it is you, and I thank God for it, who are to decide whether this young man has admitted himself to be a felon: if he has, he must be punished for it; but he has given a fair statement from beginning to end, and if there was any thing false, the prosecutor could prove it false by the clearest evidence; and I can, with that confidence with which I should appeal to Heaven for truth and justice, appeal to you for a verdict of acquittal of the prisoner.

[16] Pointing to a large folio volume in his hand, "Parliamentary Report on the West Coast of Africa," from which Mr. Kelly read the quotations contained in the subsequent parts of his speech.

Gentlemen, he appears before the Committee upon the 22nd of July, 1842, and the Chairman says to him, "You have seen some statements that have been made to this Committee upon the subject of a transaction in which your house was engaged; have you any observations to offer upon it?—I received from the Clerk of the Committee a letter." He accounts for having heard of it, and then says, "I would beg, first of all, to refer to the letter which I had the honour to address to the Chairman." That letter ought to have been brought before you—it is not—we have it not, and have no control over it. The prosecutor could have produced it, because, with the permission of the House, by which he has produced this evidence, he might have produced that letter, or had a copy of it. He says, "My reason for wishing to be examined before this Committee was, that the statements contained in the evidence which I have mentioned are all of them more or less incorrect, some of them totally so. I will begin by stating what has been the nature of our, I will not say trade, for we have not had a trade ourselves, but of our connexion with the shipment of goods to the coast of Africa." I pray your attention to this—it is not, as my learned friend Mr. Serjeant Talfourd seems to assume in a question put to Captain Denman, it is not that this house has ever traded, in the proper sense of the word, to the coast of Africa; they never send goods there on their own account, and they never received goods from there; they never had any transaction or correspondence with any person at the Gallinas, or any where else upon the coast of Africa; all their transactions were confined to the execution of foreign orders from the Havannah, and other parts of the world; all that they did being to dispatch the vessels and ship the goods; and from the moment of shipping the goods in England, from that moment their interference entirely ceased. He says, "I will begin by stating what has been the nature of our, I will not say trade, for we have not had a trade ourselves, but of our connexion with the shipment of goods to the coast of Africa. We have been established as merchants for upwards of 70 years in Spain, for nearly 20 years in this country, and we have had connexions to a large extent in Spain, and in the Havannah, and in South America, and in several other places; among them we have had connexions, or commercial intercourse, with the house of Pedro Martinez & Co. of the Havannah, and with Blanco and Cavallo of Havannah. With them we have carried on a regular business in consignments of sugars and of cochineal, which they have made to us." I pray you to put this case—Suppose the house of Zulueta & Co. received a consignment of cochineal and sugars from the house of Martinez, the value of the consignment being 5,000*l*, they convert it into money, and they have that 5,000*l.* at the disposal of Martinez & Co.; suppose any one of the gentlemen, who are doing me the honour of attending to me, had money of Martinez by him, say 10,000*l.*, the house of Martinez, instead of drawing it out, order it to be invested in English goods; suppose they write and say, we have received your account sales of sugars and cochineal, we find we are credited for 10,000*l.*, and we request you to ship the undermentioned goods by the Augusta, Captain Jennings, for the Gallinas, or any other place on the coast of Africa, and they set one against the other—would you hesitate in doing it? would you dream you were committing a felony? It is not that this is an only transaction (I do not know whether that would affect the case)—there is a trading for twenty years—it is a little more than ten years that they have had transactions of that kind, and have shipped goods to, they did not know who—they have never heard of the goods being seized, or the vessels seized, or what became of the money, whether invested in the slave trading, or any other traffic—all they know is, that they have received the consignments of cochineal or sugars, that they have sold them, and hold 5,000*l.* or 10,000*l.* in their hands—they are ordered this day to pay part of the money by accepting bills, and the next day they are ordered to send the remainder of the money they owe, in brandy, tobacco, or iron, to be shipped to the Gallinas, or any where else, and they act upon it—whether the goods are sold for slaves, whether they are used, whether they are sold for money, and the money spent in the purchase of other merchandise or in the support of the families of those who have received them, to them is indifferent—they have shipped the goods, they have debited the account, and there the matter ends, that is perfectly clear. He says, "With them we have carried on a regular business in consignments of sugars and of cochineal, which they have made to us; and in specie received by the packets from Mexico and other places. We have several times acted for them here in this country, buying raw cotton for instance at Liverpool, and re-selling it very largely; that has been principally with Pedro Martinez & Co." "They are general merchants?—They are general merchants, and their transactions with us have been of that nature. As general merchants, we have bought stock here for them rather largely; and, in the course of those transactions, we have received orders from Don Pedro Martinez & Co., of the Havannah, and from Don Pedro Martinez, of Cadiz, to ship goods to the coast of Africa." It must be doubtless so that they received the order one day to remit money, and the next to remit goods to the coast of Africa. If they were slave traders, you have no right to assume that they knew it; it is not proved that they knew it; and if Martinez & Co. were notorious slave dealers, if they are also much larger traders in cochineal and sugars, what right had they to suppose, if, instead of the money they owe, they are to ship merchandise, what right have they to suppose that they will deal unlawfully with this commodity? It is a case to which the law never pointed, and it would go to the destruction of commerce if any man was bound to pause or make any inquiry at all before he shipped. He is then asked, "Have you received orders from Pedro Martinez for shipments for the coast of Africa?—Yes; in the course of business we have received orders to ship goods upon the funds in our hands belonging to them; and we have shipped the goods described in the letter, and sent the bills of lading to Pedro Martinez; but beyond that we have never had any returns from the coast of Africa."

This is the whole case; it is a full defence to this prosecution, and disposes of the offence it is supposed this young man was committing. And further, he says, "Nor any control of any kind from the moment the cargoes left the ports of this country." Now here again, if this is false, it might be proved. They have given us notice to produce the accounts, and all letters that have passed between Martinez and Zulueta & Co.; they might have shown that this was false, that they had dealt in some other way, and that they had some interest in the final event of the shipment: they have not proved any thing of the kind. I say they have proved the contrary, and *I will never in my person establish so fatal a precedent as to recognise the notion that any man upon his trial for a felony is to prove himself innocent before evidence is given to prove him guilty.*

He is then asked, "You have had no interest in the result of the venture?— No, nor any notice, nor any acquaintance, nor any correspondence with any one upon the coast; we have never had any kind of knowledge, either subsequently or previously, of the shipments, except the mere fact of buying the goods and shipping them." "Your whole interest was a commission upon the transaction?—Entirely. The extent of those transactions has been so limited in the course of nearly twenty years that we have been in this country, that the amount of the invoices that we have sent out has been something like 20,000*l.* or 22,000*l.* in the course of all that time. That is one part of the operations we have performed. The other operations are the acceptance of bills drawn by people on the coast; among them Pedro Blanco when he was there, upon ourselves, on account of Blanco & Cavallo, of Havannah, upon funds which Blanco & Cavallo had in our hands: for instance, the people at the Havannah, or in Spain, open a credit with us, and we accept the bills of the parties on that credit with us, just the same as we should do with any other correspondent in any other part." "You would have funds in your hands, arising from some commercial transactions between you and the Havannah merchant, or the Cadiz merchant; and Pedro Blanco, upon the coast of Africa, would draw upon the credit of those funds, being authorised by the Cadiz or the Havannah merchant?—Yes; and if Pedro Blanco had drawn 5*s.* beyond that, we should have protested, and in some instances we have protested." This shews they had nothing to do with the owner of the property abroad. They had received consignments, and had accounted for the sums of money, and they either accept bills or consign goods; if bills are drawn beyond the amount due, they protest them, and if they are asked to consign goods beyond that amount, they refuse to do so. "With regard to the vessel alluded to in this Report, the Augusta, our part in that concern has been simply that which appears from one of the letters: that is to say"—

Now here again, Gentlemen, I must refer you to the mode in which this prosecution has been carried on.

In this evidence before the Committee, the prisoner now at the bar refers to one of the letters received by the house from Martinez & Co.: I must say where the counsel for the prosecution availed themselves of this evidence before the Committee, as evidence against the prisoner upon the charge of felony, I think they were bound to make evidence of every document he referred to in it, as explanatory of the evidence he gave.

I speak this subject to the correction of their Lordships; and I know that their Lordships will overrule and correct what I say, if I am wrong, and therefore I say it with the more confidence, because I know it will not be controverted; I say, that in a prosecution for a felony, or any other crime, if the counsel for the prosecution give in evidence a statement made by a prisoner, charged with a crime which refers to a document, he ought—

Mr. Serjeant *Bompas.* I understood this was the letter about the 500*l.*; that and all the other letters are in the Appendix, and to be found there: they are deposited, every one.

Mr. *Kelly.* We will try my learned friend's accuracy by looking at what it was. He says, "With regard to the vessel alluded to in this Report, the Augusta, our part in that concern has been simply that which appears from one of the letters: that is to say, Pedro Martinez, of Cadiz, had made choice of Jennings to buy the vessel, and lent him money to buy the vessel; because Pedro Martinez wanted him to have a vessel in the trade, for the purpose of taking his goods to their destination." He says that the object of Pedro Martinez was, that Captain Jennings should buy the vessel, and that it should be conducted in the way he states. That may appear in a letter—how could it appear but in a letter from Martinez & Co. to Zulueta, containing their instructions? That letter my learned friend should have called for—he has given notice to produce it, and he ought to have called for it and made it a part of the examination, as if the witness had produced and read the letter, and it had not been set out in the evidence. He then says, "I have now described the three kinds of operations in which we have been concerned, and our knowledge of all of them terminated with the execution of the orders of our correspondents. We had nothing more to do than to follow the orders of the purchaser in shipping the goods. With regard to the purchase of the vessel by Jennings; Jennings is a man—" Here is a solution of every thing called concealment. "Jennings is a man who has been employed some time by Martinez; he has served Martinez as a chartered captain, and Martinez, having been satisfied with his services, agreed to lend him that money on the security of the vessel, provided it did not exceed a certain amount." Now the next question is put by Mr. Forster, the member for Berwick. Mr. Forster all the world knows, and I hope you know, is very extensively concerned in the African trade; he is a man as perfectly conversant with this subject as any man in Britain; and I cannot help making the same observation as to him which I did as to Lord Stanley and Lord John Russell, I cannot help thinking, if there had been any thing dishonourable in the character of the trade and to the character of a British merchant, instead of bringing out the true colour of the transaction, as you will see he did, he would have done every thing to hold it up to reprobation. He learns from the witness the nature of the transaction as to the purchase of the vessel, that Captain Jennings had been engaged in similar transactions; he catches at it in a moment, and puts it in a few words—"You advanced the money to Captain Jennings for the purchase of the vessel, Jennings transferring the vessel to you as a security for the money so advanced?—That is just the description of operation, which is a very general one in business." If the counsel for the prosecution says it is not the ordinary course of business, why does he not call Mr. Forster, or any other gentleman in the trade, to show that it is not correct, and that it is not a usual transaction? He has attempted no such thing; the evidence is a blank; you have only the evidence of this young man. I do not pretend to say that because this gentleman has given a long statement, in which he has vindicated his house from the statement made against them, that you are bound to believe all he says; but I do appeal to you whether, if what he says could be proved false by the prosecutors, they would not have done so? They have proved nothing false. He is speaking of an ordinary transaction of commerce before some of the first commercial men in Britain: there was a check upon his evidence which would have restrained him, if wicked enough to tell a lie, which would have prevented him saying what was not true. I say that the character of the Committee is a guarantee of the correctness of his statement, speaking of it as the ordinary course of trade.

The Chairman then says, "What is the object of such an operation?—I know very little, or almost next to nothing, of the operations in those parts of the world." Is that true or untrue? That is the very essence of the case, as I submit to you: he has been only six or seven years in the business; they have only in the last ten years had seven or eight transactions, and in the last six or seven years they may have two or three. He says, "I know very little, or almost next to nothing, of the operations in those parts of the world." Why, are you to suppose that he, by intuition or by magic, was to know all that Captain Hill, Captain Denman, and Colonel Nichol knew in twenty-five years of constant observation? Mr. Serjeant Bompas asks you to believe he knew every thing as well as any body living upon the spot. Then he speaks of the object of the transaction, which I will not weary you in repeating.

Then he is asked, "What advantage would there be in Mr. Jennings taking the articles rather as the owner than as captain under Martinez; was not he commander of the vessel as well as owner of the vessel?—Yes." "He is made the owner, instead of being captain?—He is the owner as well as the captain of the vessel; he stands indebted to Martinez, and gives a bottomry bond for the vessel." Then he goes on to illustrate what he says.

Then Mr. *Forster* says, "You acted in this transaction merely as agent in the usual manner, as you would have acted for any house in any part of the world?—Exactly; if Martinez had told me, 'You have got 500*l.* in your hands, pay that to Captain Jennings,' I should have known nothing more of the transaction; I should have paid the money. But Martinez did not wish to go beyond a certain amount; and he says, 'You exercise control, do not allow the man to pay more than 500*l.* for the vessel.'" "But beyond the purchase of the vessel and the shipment of the goods, the other arrangements and the subsequent transactions were entirely between Jennings and Martinez & Co.?—Most assuredly; except with the order of Martinez, I do not know how we could have done any thing with him in any way."

Gentlemen, that reminds me of this fact: my learned friend has sought to give in evidence certain papers, which were found in the year 1841 on board this vessel, and which it is now perfectly manifest were put on board that vessel in Cadiz long after she had sailed from Liverpool; I objected to that evidence. Gentlemen, I will not go over again what I said at the time: I certainly did think, considering that these letters were in print and before my Lords, that the only object of the discussion was to have a legal opinion of my Lords whether these letters were admissible in evidence. My learned friend could have argued the point without referring to the contents of the letters, and so filling your minds with the contents of those letters, which, as they were rejected, ought not to have been submitted to you; for any one, knowing how the human mind is constituted, must feel that in the mind of one or two out of the twelve the effect might have been to draw your attention to something foreign to the matter; and I objected and complained of Mr. Serjeant Bompas for referring to the letters. My Lords held that they were not evidence, but my learned friend seemed to be pressing upon you their contents in opposition to the opinion of my Lord. I will remind you that these letters were written by Martinez & Co., and put on board this vessel at Cadiz months after the vessel had sailed from England. Mr. Zulueta had never heard of these proceedings; and whether he is guilty or innocent, all that is charged against him had been committed months before these letters were in existence, and therefore to attempt to use what Martinez had said or written, against the prisoner, was only calculated to raise a prejudice injurious to the administration of justice. You may easily imagine that Martinez may be, for aught I know, a man who, besides dealing to the extent of a million a year in sugars and other things, does deal to some extent in slaves, and it is possible he may have written letters to his correspondents in Africa relating to the slave trade; and consider the wickedness of using these letters against Mr. Zulueta, who never saw the letters, and could not know any thing of them or their contents, or have any control over them. It was this sentence reminded me of that: he is asked, "But beyond the purchase of the vessel and the shipment of the goods, the other arrangements and the subsequent transactions were entirely between Jennings and Martinez & Co.?—Most assuredly; except with the order of Martinez, I do not know how we could have done any thing with him in any way." It therefore comes to this, whatever might have passed between Martinez and Captain Jennings, Captain Jennings may be responsible for, or Martinez; but Mr. Zulueta is wholly irresponsible: all that passed through his hands he is ready to account for and abide by, and stand to the consequences of it; but what took place between Captain Jennings and Martinez is wholly beyond his knowledge; and it is unjust and unreasonable that I, as his counsel, should for one moment permit it to be given in evidence if I could prevent it.

Then Sir *Thomas Acland* asks him, "Do you mean that you know that the Augusta was not engaged in any slaving transactions during the voyage upon which she left Liverpool?—Most assuredly not; in fact, my testimony is hardly required of that, because every thing proves that. When she was detained, it was never said that she was upon a slaving operation at all. Before she left this port, after she was bought, she was completely rendered useless for that purpose." Here again have they attempted to prove that the contrary was the fact, and that this answer was false? Remember that this is not said by this young man as if then upon his trial and defending himself against the charge of felony, and when he would have a strong temptation, if capable of falsehood, to say what was false to protect himself against the heavy punishment. All this is said freely. If any one of you were to hear to-morrow morning that another had said of you, you had been offered a bribe to give a particular verdict, you would go before the first tribunal and deny the statement, and request that it might be made public; that is all this young man has said, he is denying the accusation and submitting that what his accusers have said is untrue. If he was saying what was untrue, they could have shown it. He says, "After she was bought she was completely rendered useless for that purpose;" and it is proved that she was—for the leagers, the water-vessels, it was proved to you were rendered useless; and though my learned friend would not admit it, I proved that they were put ashore at Liverpool, and therefore this is every word of it true, and my learned friend has failed in proving it false.

The Chairman then says, "The charge is, that she was engaged in carrying goods to a person engaged in the slave trade; not that she was engaged in the slave trade herself?" Then he says, and here is a very important answer—"I most certainly say, that I do not know whether the person is so engaged or not." That is, the consignee of the vessel. The Chairman observes, "The charge is, that this vessel was sent to somebody engaged in the slave trade?" And what does he say?—"I do not know whether he is or not; I do not know any thing about him." Whether they could have proved the contrary as to Ximenes or Rolo, or all of them, I do not know. Then he goes on to say, "It seems to me that English captains and English subjects are not prohibited from borrowing money from Spaniards." There is no doubt of that; it is quite lawful. "She was bought with money lent by Pedro Martinez to Captain Jennings for the purpose."

Then Mr. *Wilson Patten* asked him, "You have stated that yours is an agency trade?—It is so; and in the multitude of business, any one can understand that 20,000*l.* in 15 or 20 years, can only be a mere trifle in the business of any merchant, without laying claim to a large business; and in following that business, we have executed shipping orders."

This is another repetition of the observation made before, that it was a shipping order in the transactions of their house, and that he had only executed the orders given by a foreign correspondent. Then he is asked, "To what part of the coast of Africa has that business been chiefly conducted?— I believe, almost exclusively to the Gallinas."

Then he goes on, and this is the part of the evidence upon which Mr. Serjeant Bompas relies—this is really the only part of this body of evidence given by this young man upon which the learned Serjeant relies in support of the prosecution—"Do you know the nature of the trade of Pedro Martinez at the Gallinas?—I know from general report, that Don Pedro Martinez himself is supposed to deal in slaves, and I believe it is so." "Is he known at the

Havannah as a dealer in slaves?—I do not know, but I believe so. I do not know why it should not be known at the Havannah, if it is known in other parts." From that my learned friend says he does know it. You must take the whole of the evidence together. He says his house "never had any thing to do with any slave transaction, nor does he know that any vessel that ever went from their house was engaged in slave transactions, but he had heard that Pedro Martinez was engaged in the slave trade;" but you have it from other parts of the case, that he was a large dealer in other transactions quite lawful.

Now this is a statement, not of what this young man knew at the time he participated more or less in the transaction now under your consideration— these transactions took place in 1840—this examination takes place in July 1842. He does not say, that at the time they sent the Augusta they knew that Pedro Martinez was engaged in the slave trade; he says, "I know it," speaking in the present tense, meaning "I now know it."

Now, Gentlemen, I beg your attention to a question I besought my learned friend to read, I besought in vain—I thank God I have now the means of reading it—

Mr. Serjeant *Bompas*. Yes, I did read it.

Mr. *Kelly*. "Have you reason to suppose that a large portion of the trade that they carry on at the Havannah is the slave trade?"—His answer is, "I had no reason to know any thing of the kind; I have known more of their transactions with the slave trade since these things have been mooted than I ever knew before; I have had more knowledge of these things lately than I ever had in my life before; and when I say, 'I,' I beg to state that I ought to state, 'we,' for all my partners are in the same situation."

Now, what does this come to? This gentleman tells you, that out of many hundred thousand pounds, a few trifling orders are sent to the coast of Africa; he is asked in 1842 if he knows of their correspondent being engaged in the slave trade, and he says he does only from common report; and in another part of the evidence, when his attention is more particularly called to it, he says, "I had no reason to know any thing of the kind; but since these transactions have been mooted I have known more of their connexion with the slave trade." What is the meaning of this? I do implore you to remember that we are here upon a grave crime, the effect of a conviction upon which would expose this young man to utter and irremediable ruin, and bring disgrace upon his family; he is called upon after a loose examination upon the subject to explain what he has in a long examination loosely admitted, that a man was a slave trader, and also that these goods were to be so used. Looking at it fairly, what is it?—I had no reason to know it four years ago; but since these matters have been discussed I have inquired more about it, and have found, from the evidence of Captain Denman, that an event took place there which made the Gallinas, and in the character of the trading there, a matter of as much notoriety as the battle of Waterloo, or any other great event.—It appears that this officer of Her Majesty's navy descended upon the coast and burnt every slave establishment upon the spot, and the consequence is, that reclamations have been made and actions have been brought; it was the subject of investigation before this Committee, and is the subject of proceedings in Courts of Justice, and the attention of every body has been called to it, and of course that brings to the mind of this young gentleman a great deal of knowledge of the character of the place, and those who have lived in it, more than he ever possessed before; and I put it to you, if this was a civil instead of a criminal case, and in which a man was to pay a sum of money, whether the fair inference is not, that, they shipped these goods without knowing that they were to be employed in the slave trade, that they did not know that Martinez was engaged in it till it became the subject of discussion; and I ask you, what is there to establish that it was so notorious that Martinez was a slave dealer, that Mr. Zulueta must have known that the goods were to be so employed? I ask you, why may not Mr. Zulueta, as much as any other merchant or manufacturer in the kingdom, who is asked to sell goods to go to the coast of Africa, why may he not, when there is an immense extent of lawful trade to that coast, have supposed that they were to be used in the lawful trade as in the unlawful trade, which it would be criminal in him to promote? I say that in a civil case, but in a criminal case, if there is a shadow of doubt upon your minds whether he is innocent or guilty—and in this I shall be sanctioned by my Lords the Judges—if doubt be left in your minds, when it was the duty of the prosecutor to remove that doubt, the prisoner must have your verdict. It is not because it is probable or possible that the goods might have been so employed—it is not because there is something doubtful in the transaction—you must be satisfied that he knew they were to be so employed, and that he shipped them with that object—and unless you are convinced of that, there is no case for a verdict of guilty. I say the whole question rests upon the notoriety of the place and the character of the parties, and upon that you find that this gentleman knew nothing at the time of these transactions either of the nature of the trade or the character of the persons there.

Then they talk about the ship, and so on. Then Mr. *Forster* says, "Your house had nothing to do with any letters that might be put on board the Augusta after she sailed from this country?—Nothing whatever." And that is the way that was perfectly disposed of, and so the Judges have held in rejecting the letters put on board after the vessel left the country. He says, "The Augusta was seized on the coast of Africa, on the charge of slave trading?—I believe that was the case." Then he is asked, "Have you reason to suppose that the whole of that large commerce is subservient to the carrying on of the slave trade by the house of Blanco and Martinez at the Havannah?—I do not know; I know that they have large transactions in general business. I know that a short time ago I got 40,000*l.* or 50,000*l.* of Spanish bonds in the market for Martinez. I know that he is a large speculator in Spanish bonds and in securities of state." Then he names the house for whom that was done. Then he goes on, "Have you been employed by the house at the Havannah to ship manufactured goods from this country to Havannah, suitable for the African trade?—We have sometimes shipped goods to the Havannah of the same kind as those that were in the 'Augusta;' cotton goods and other things of that sort." Would that make it felony if you shipped goods to the Havannah, if the persons there used them in the slave trade? Where is it to stop? It is essential that it should be so understood by juries, as well as mercantile men; there must be some clear and distinct rule. Men are not, while carrying on their fair and mercantile transactions, to be treading on the verge of transportation every moment of their lives, which they would be if they deal in these goods which are sent in these ships, and may be so employed or engaged.

Then he is asked, "Have you been employed by the house at the Havannah to ship manufactured goods from this country to Havannah, suitable for the African trade?—We have sometimes shipped goods to the Havannah of the same kind as those that were in the 'Augusta;' cotton goods, and other things of that sort." "Have you sent any goods of that description since you first began to send goods out direct to the coast of Africa?—They have been mixed; I cannot draw a distinction between the two destinations; some have gone to the Havannah, some to the Gallinas." Then he is asked, "How long have you conducted the trade upon the coast of Africa?—As I said before, I do not think we have conducted any trade on the coast of Africa, either legal or illegal." He persists in maintaining, as I do on his behalf, that his transactions were closed at Liverpool; he knows nothing more about it. Then he is asked, "How long have you acted as agents for Martinez, on the coast of Africa?—As long as we have had any connexions with Martinez; it is part and parcel of other operations; that is to say, in the multitude of other operations that have intervened we have shipped goods as I have said." And it would be a strange thing if these gentlemen, for the sake of putting into their pockets an inconsiderable sum of money by this purchase—I am afraid to calculate it, for fear I should fall into an error—were to put themselves in jeopardy of an indictment for a felony, and transportation for fourteen years. If they have done so, it must be from some strange ignorance. To suppose they would do so for that which would not pay their clerks' salary for a day, when they have stood so far above suspicion, is absolutely incredible and impossible.

Then he is asked, "Have you ever received consignments from them, or on their behalf, of palm oil, gold dust, or ivory, from the coast of Africa?"—He says, "Never; we never have received any thing from the coast of Africa whatever. With regard to all these transactions, it will perhaps appear strange to the Committee that I should not know more of the coast of Africa, having shipped things there; but if we had shipped to the amount of 100,000*l.* to the coast of Africa, or carried on any considerable trade there, we should certainly have known more about the coast of Africa; but in transactions of a very large amount, an invoice occasionally of about 2,000*l.* or 3,000*l.* of goods was a thing that we sent as a matter of course, and did not trouble our heads about, especially as the remuneration we got was a mere trifle, not of itself worth pursuing, if it had not been for the general business we had?"

Now you see, Gentlemen, this in one respect confirms what I do not intend to dispute, the testimony of these naval gentlemen that there are not shipments from this colony; but the question is not whether that is the fact, or what information it conveyed to them, or what information it conveyed to Mr. Zulueta; he says, "We never received any produce from that country but that would not show that there were no produce. "Our shipments were in discharge of former liabilities; we had received sugars and sold them, and we were called upon to make shipments to the coast of Africa, and we do so; and the nature of the transaction is such that we could not have any return;" and therefore he says, "if our transactions had been larger, we should have known a great deal more of this trade than we do. We had a sum of money, the proceeds of sugar and other articles, and we sent a small shipment to Africa debiting the house with that shipment; that being all we knew, and our transactions closing the moment the ship left Liverpool, how can we know any more of it? We know no more, and that accounts for our ignorance."

Then he is asked about another vessel in which the name of Mr. Kidd was introduced—that is quite unimportant. He is asked, "You have no connexion with Mr. Kidd in any way?—No, nor any knowledge of him." He then says something to which I should call your attention. Something had been said by another witness, "Zulueta, the gentleman in London to whom the vessel was sent, and who sold her again to her former Spanish owner, is a name well known on the coast in connexion with the slave trade." That is what somebody had said before the Committee, which he came before the Committee voluntarily to contradict; he says, "Now, what is known on the coast I really cannot pretend to say; but I believe that not many persons can say that which I can say, that neither myself, nor my father, nor my grandfather, nor any body in our firm, has ever had any kind of interest of any sort, or derived any emolument or connexion from the slave trade." Gentlemen, would to Heaven that every gentleman in a mercantile house could say the same I But this gentleman is challenging contradiction, he is speaking in the presence of those conversant with the trade, and in the presence of the Secretaries of State he is laying himself open to contradiction, and he says openly, knowing it will be published to the world, and knowing he may be denounced as a man guilty of gross falsehood if it is untrue, he says, "Neither myself, nor my father, nor grandfather, ever made one shilling by the slave trade:" and yet this young man is to be selected out of the firm and made the victim in respect of the Augusta, and that upon this statement, as my learned friend reminds me; that he who comes before the Committee and challenges disproof—he says, "I challenge any one to say that I was ever engaged in the slave trade—" that that is to be made evidence and offered in a British Court before a British Jury. Now see what follows, and I believe it is not a vain boast, it is not a mere statement—he says, "My father had at one time an interest in a bankrupt's estate at the Havannah, upon which he was a creditor. There were some slaves on the estate, and they formed part of the property assignable to the creditors, and my father got the slaves assigned to him; because the other gentlemen and the creditors were not of the same opinion." That is, because the other people did not think there was any thing wrong in the slave trade. "He got them assigned to him, and made them free; and that is all the connexion we have ever had with any slaves in the world. I do not know how far that may be considered irrelevant to the point, but I state it because we are here mentioned three or four times as connected with slave dealers, as a name well known in connexion with the slave trade. That sort of statement—" Well indeed may he say so, and I say on his behalf, "that sort of statement is rather a difficult thing to deal with." It is indeed, Gentlemen. When I hear my learned friend say, that because he sent out a vessel with an English captain, and because at Portsmouth there are some shackles, and because Captain Hill and Captain Denman knew this was a slave trading colony, therefore you are to convict him; I say, "it is a very difficult thing to deal with." That is what he said before the Committee; this has been published fifteen months, and before the public; the prosecutor has had it fifteen months—has he contradicted any one letter in it? He says, "My father, and my grandfather, and my house, never had any connexion with the slave trade; except that he took some slaves, because he wished to make them free, under a bankrupt's estate, and he made them free, that is the only connexion we ever had with the slave trade in the world." That is his evidence, and I beg you to contrast it with the other evidence of my learned friend and the doubtful inferences he has suggested.

Then he is asked, "If it is meant to insinuate by these observations that you ever had any other connexion with the slave trade, than being the shipping agent of goods which were sent to a man who was a dealer in slaves, you entirely deny it?" He says, "I assure the Committee, that although I have a general notion as to what interest Blanco and Martinez have in slaves, yet, if I was put upon my oath to make any particular statement, I really could not, because I do not know it. Of course I believe it; but my personal knowledge amounts only to that which the knowledge of what we read in a newspaper amounts to." It is quite evident what he means—I know nothing of their being slave traders: since these matters have been under consideration I have read the newspapers, and I see enough to lead me to suppose that they deal in slaves. But he does not say he had that knowledge in 1840, when these transactions took place. Then he is asked, "There was nothing upon the face of the transactions which you had with those parties which spoke of a connexion with traffic in slaves?—Nothing whatever. It is well known, that, fifty years ago, it was in the ordinary course of business in Cadiz"—There is another point inviting attention and contradiction.—He says, "It is well known, that, fifty years ago, it was in the ordinary course of business in Cadiz to insure operations in slave trading." So it was at that time: slave trading, in all its branches, and of the worst character, was perfectly legal both in Spain, and I grieve to say, also in England, or English colonies. And he goes on to say, "My house at that time were underwriters, and it was notorious that a policy of that kind would never enter the doors of our house; and nobody would come to offer such a thing to us upon any terms. It is notorious, both here and in Spain, that we set our faces distinctly against having any interest of any kind in the slave trade."

Now, Gentlemen, is it not grievous, is it not cruel, that this young man, almost just entering life, belonging to a family, belonging to a house, which can say this with truth, that while the slave trade was deemed lawful by the British law and universally practised throughout Spain and the Spanish colonies, and recognized in all its forms, "My house would not execute a policy for slaves?" Is it not cruel, that the youngest partner at the very outset of life is to have his character blasted and held up as a felon, because it is said he had done something to assist that trade?

Then he is asked, "It is further stated, 'It appears, that it is a regular thing sending vessels to him, that is to Mr. Zulueta; if they come to England to him, he sends them to Cadiz, and they get out again to the Havannah and come again into the trade.' Have you any observation to make upon that?— It is all untrue, the whole of it; I have never received a vessel from those gentlemen; there has been nothing of the kind." He denies it; it might have been proved, and it has not been proved. "Have you any thing further to state upon the subject?"—Then he states a number of other matters, which as nothing has been said upon them I do not comment upon. Then he says, at the end of the last answer, "'My answer was intended to describe only the course of that particular transaction and not to apply to any other case.' I never received a single vessel from the coast of Africa at any time, nor any body for us."

Then Mr. *Forster* says, "Then that statement is entirely untrue?—Totally, from beginning to end; we never did so, and nobody for us; and nobody to our knowledge, or with our connivance; I deny it in the most distinct manner. In answer to Question 5487, Mr. Macaulay is asked, 'Have you any thing further to say with regard to the connexion of Zulueta with the slave trade?' The answer is, 'I would refer to his connexion with the Gollupchik, which was lately captured. In that case it appeared that the vessel went out direct to the Gallinas from London.'—That is the same vessel as the Augusta, which I have already explained; it formerly bore the name of Gollupchik."

Then he is asked about some other matters, but as they have not been made the subject of evidence here I will not comment upon them. He speaks upon the moral point, and he enters into a very lengthened statement in which he says, "I am not here to discuss the moral propriety or impropriety of the slave trade; I have my own opinions upon it, and if I thought it was a justifiable trade I should not shrink from expressing it." That is the result of a long statement: and, in answer to a very comprehensive question of Sir Thomas Acland, "You have stated in your letter, that your principle is, that of 'not wishing to derive profit or advantage from the sufferings of humanity, whether avoidable or unavoidable,' and you have acted upon that principle?"—He says, "That is the principle upon which we have acted." Then there is a great deal about the nature of various other transactions.

Then we come to something that appears upon another point—a point made a distinct matter, and which I very much rejoice is the last one to which I shall have to refer, and that not requiring any large consumption of your time. Among other reasons urged upon you as tending to the conclusion that this ship, was dispatched for the purposes of the slave trade was this by Mr. Serjeant Bompas, that the vessel in the course of the voyage unnecessarily put into Cadiz, as if there was some previous concert or arrangement that the vessel though dispatched nominally for the Gallinas should go to Cadiz, and that there some one or other should afford them facilities for carrying on the slave trade. Upon that I have some observations to make. First, one does not see how that was to be better promoted by touching at Cadiz than if she had proceeded direct to the Gallinas, and for this reason, if it had been found when she arrived on the coast of Africa that she had taken on board any materials to facilitate the carrying on the slave trade, that would be something to draw an inference from; but no such thing appears. Why she should have touched there to facilitate the carrying on the slave trade I do not understand, and still less do I understand why it is to be imputed to Mr. Zulueta that a vessel to all outward appearance cleared for the Gallinas, that it was intended she should touch at Cadiz; and I pray you to answer the question to yourselves, you cannot answer it to me, if it was intended for the purpose of good or evil she should touch there, why conceal it? Why not give out "with liberty to touch at Cadiz," if any suspicion attached to the transaction?

Foreman of the Jury. Did we not understand that the English sailors were landed at Cadiz, and took in Spanish sailors there?

Mr. *Kelly.* No, some English sailors were discharged; but there is nothing about the Spanish sailors being taken in: there is nothing about that—some English sailors, two or three of them, did go on shore, but it was not in any way connected with Mr. Zulueta, or to which he could be a party. You understand, when they had sailed from England some of the sailors rebelled and mutinied; the captain, like a clear-sighted man, said, if I go to Cork these men will all leave me; I will not do that, but as it is necessary to go somewhere, I will go to Cadiz. It was not the result of any previous concert. They say it was intended before he left that he should stop there. If it had been intended I do not see why it should not have been stated in the charter-party, it would not have had a more suspicious appearance that the vessel should touch there than go to the Gallinas direct, the suspicion of the slave trade was the mention of the Gallinas. Captain Denman, who knew the place, might draw his suspicious inference from the mention of the Gallinas, but nobody would suspect it from Cadiz. It was from some mutiny of the men, added to the stress of weather, the master would not go to Cork, he went to Cadiz: it was an event arising from something in the course of the voyage, and not from any thing that occurred before the vessel left England, and it was when the vessel left England that the participation of Mr. Zulueta in the whole transaction ceased; but if it were of any importance for the purpose of the prosecution, you should have had it distinctly explained to you what took place on board the vessel, what the nature of the bad weather was which should have made it desirable to go to Falmouth or to Cork: why do they not produce the log? they have the ship's papers.

Mr. Serjeant *Bompas.* My learned friend says he has not it.

Mr. *Kelly.* How did they get the papers from the Admiralty? The log is on board the vessel; some of the crew were on board; none of them were produced but the cabin-boy, who knew nothing; it was more convenient to bring a boy who knew nothing, than men who should enlighten you upon the object. But whether it was for a good or bad purpose that Captain Jennings went to Cadiz, what had Mr. Zulueta to do with it? To make it of any importance, the prosecutor should have proved that Mr. Zulueta had contrived, for some purpose or other, that he should touch at Cadiz. Nothing of the kind is proved upon the subject; all that is said upon the subject is what Mr. Zulueta says. Now what is it that he says? The Chairman says, "It would appear from Question 5087, that your name is supposed to have been mentioned in a Parliamentary Paper, as connected with a slave trade transaction. Will you refer to page 38, in Class B. Paper of 1839 and 1840, which is the place referred to in the answer, and see if there is any trace of your name in that transaction?—I do not find my own name there; I only find an allusion at the bottom to the name of Pedro Martinez, but in a manner in no way connected with me, and stating a circumstance which I never knew. In Question 7965*, it is stated, 'The Augusta had touched at Cadiz on her way out from England?' The answer is, 'Yes, and landed part of her cargo at Cadiz, although it was consigned to be delivered at Gallinas.' Now Captain Hill, who has given this answer, must have known why she touched at Cadiz, and why she discharged part of her cargo, for it must be in the log-book of the vessel. It was because she was nearly wrecked in her passage; she put into Cadiz in distress, and there she landed a part of her cargo, which was tobacco which was rotten, and sold for the benefit of the underwriters. Now that has not been stated here, but I think Captain Hill must have known it, because it is in the log-book of the vessel which he took."

Now Captain Hill has said the same thing here to-day—the purpose of going to Cadiz was by some previous contrivance, for some purpose of Mr. Zulueta. The log would have shown the state of the weather registered from day to day during the passage of the vessel, and the rebellious part of the crew would have no desire to give Mr. Zulueta much benefit by their evidence.

Mr. Serjeant *Bompas*. It is not fair for Mr. Kelly to state that: the log would not be evidence against Mr. Zulueta. After you had decided against four documents, I would not offer a fifth.

Mr. *Kelly*. I have to thank my learned friend for this very singular instance of his forbearance; if the log, as it regards this transaction, was not evidence against me, and I do not say it would be, I cannot understand how letters written by other persons found in the vessel could be evidence against me;— but let us waste no more time upon that subject; if the log would not be evidence, he might have called some or the crew; he has only called the cabin-boy; there is no evidence to show the state of the weather; and you are called upon in a case like this to suppose that there was some previous contrivance by which the Captain was to touch at Cadiz.

Then he says, in answer to another question, and the question is directly put to him by Sir Thomas Acland, "It was not intended when she left England, that she should put into Cadiz?—Most certainly not; all the facts of the case show that she went there because she was obliged. I have not seen the log-book, but it must be there; because in the log-book the captain is bound to enter those things, and whoever captured the vessel must have seen the log-book of course. In answer to Question 7967*, it is said, 'Messrs. Zulueta must be aware that it is contrary to law to act as agents or otherwise for the shipment of goods that are to be employed in the slave trade; they were bound to do nothing illegal; they are merchants residing in England, and they must conform themselves to the laws of England, and they cannot by the laws of England plead ignorance of those laws.' Now I and my partners are British subjects, and therefore we are bound by the law, and we must obey the law; and I say that to endeavour to elude the law is criminal in my estimation of things. In the answer to Question 7970*, it is stated, 'I have endeavoured to be particular in making it appear that this vessel was chartered to a place where there were no constituted authorities.' I think that in the Gallinas there are constituted authorities. It is the first time that I ever heard that it is illegal for any merchant to ship goods for any places without ascertaining beforehand whether there are constituted authorities there." Then, at the end of his examination, he is asked, "You have given the Committee the names of the parties drawing the bills, and on whose account they were drawn, and you speak of their being drawn in favour of Sierra Leone houses; have you any objection to furnish the names of the houses in whose favour they were drawn?—I say that I have no objection, except that I should not like to introduce names unnecessarily; but the bills are in my hands, and any gentleman can look at them who chooses; they are at the disposal of any body who likes to look at them." He says, in another part of the evidence which refers to the documents, "I do not like in this transaction to mention names; any gentleman may see at my counting-house documents to verify what I state." Gentlemen, I am reminded that it will appear that he put in the bills themselves in order to verify the statement; they were produced before the Committee, it is written down in express terms—"The witness produced the bills;" so that you see, when he makes a statement of what were his transactions, he verifies it by the documents, and produces them to the Committee.

Then, the next day, he states a fact which is perfectly conclusive as to this matter at Cadiz. He is asked, "The Committee understand that you have some further observations to make upon the evidence which has been given with reference to your house?—With reference to the destination of the Augusta, from Liverpool to Gallinas, and the fact of its having put into Cadiz unforeseen and unpremeditated altogether, in consequence of stress of weather, I omitted to mention a circumstance which will put the thing beyond doubt, and it is this: an insurance was made at Lloyd's, from Liverpool to the Gallinas, and it is well known that, of course, we should have forfeited the insurance by going to any other port except from the peril of the sea, and the British consul at Cadiz is well aware of the circumstance, because he is Lloyd's agent there; and therefore he had to interfere in the whole proceeding; without his sanction nothing could have been done. We have called upon the underwriters upon that account, and it has been paid, and which would not have been paid without its being proved. I stated yesterday that the transactions of my house with Pedro Martinez & Co. of the Havannah, with Blanco and Carvalho of the Havannah, and with Pedro Martinez of Cadiz, had amounted in the twenty years to 100,000*l.*, I was afraid of overrating the amount; but on reference to the books of the house, I find that our transactions with them in twenty years have amounted to 400,000*l.*, out of which the 22,000*l.* that was mentioned is the whole amount of goods that have been shipped by their orders for the coast of Africa."

Now observe what he here states: he says, I am charged with having known, before this vessel quitted England, that she was to go to Cadiz, and that it was for some unlawful and improper purpose. He says—Not only do I deny that I knew it (I say not only is there no proof that he knew it, but he gives this convincing evidence), he says, before the vessel sailed I effected an insurance upon the ship and goods, and by that policy of insurance there was no provision for going to Cadiz. I need not observe that by the law, if a vessel deviates from the course stipulated in the policy, unless it is matter of compulsion and stress of weather, the policy is forfeited—here it is clear that there was a policy effected, under which the vessel was in no condition to touch at Cadiz—the policy would be forfeited; and yet it is supposed that this old established house, having effected this policy, into which they might have introduced the going to Cadiz, contrived that this deviation should take place, under which, if a loss had happened, they could not have recovered a shilling. It is perfectly clear, whether by accident or design, with which we have nothing to do—I think it was by accident—it is perfectly clear, that Zulueta & Co. knew nothing of it; and if a loss had happened, they could not have enforced it.

Now there are one or two more lines, and one or two only, with which I have to trouble you in this evidence. The witness is asked as to the former transactions of his house upon the coast of Africa: he is asked, "Have you bought other vessels for him (Martinez) than those which have been employed in the slave trade?—Yes, decidedly so; there was the *Star*, Captain Jennings." You remember, I think, Captain Denman said there was no lawful trade carried on at the Gallinas—the question is, how far Mr. Zulueta knew that, and I asked him if he had heard of the Star; he said "No." See what Mr. Zulueta says, "There was the Star, Captain Jennings. That vessel was sent from here to the Gallinas, precisely the same as the Augusta has been sent. She delivered her cargo; she went from thence to Cape Coast, I believe, and from there to Madeira; she received a cargo of wheat; she came back to Spain, and she was sold at Liverpool to a third party, not Martinez, or any body connected with him; in fact, she was sold for very little. The object of that vessel was just the same as the Augusta, to maintain a legal trade with Gallinas; that is within my own knowledge."

Now I do think—I should rather say I venture to submit to you—that it appears to me, that this answer which might clearly have been contradicted, because there are specific facts stated which could have been contradicted if untrue—this answer, if true, is perfectly decisive of this case. What is it? Gentlemen, this is the nature of the transaction: he says—My house has had other transactions of the same description with the coast of Africa; we sent out the Star to this very place, the Gallinas. And the question is, whether Messrs. Zulueta & Co. had any reason to know that this was an illegal trade. If the goods had to their knowledge been bartered for slaves, if the Star had brought an illegal cargo, and if she had been seized and condemned for slave trading, then they might begin to suspect—Here is one vessel we have sent to the Gallinas for Martinez & Co. seized, we must consider before we send any more. But here was a case in which they had sent in a ship, commanded by Captain Jennings, a cargo of the same description—the transaction had been legally completed without any thing partaking of an illegal character— the ship had taken a cargo of wine and gone to some other part of the world, and then returned to England and been sold at Liverpool. Then I pray of you—and nothing can be safer than to ask you—to put yourselves for a moment in the situation of the party charged with this offence. Suppose that you had been charged with putting on board a ship a quantity of merchandise for the Gallinas—the question is, if you would have any reason to suspect there was any thing illegal in it? If you had the year before, when these British cruizers were in the seas, sent a cargo of the same goods for the same house to the same place, and the transaction had been legally completed, and if you had heard that the ship had carried a cargo of goods to Madeira, would not you say, I have done one transaction of this kind, I know nothing illegal in it, and I may enter into another of the same description? And that it was so here, you have the evidence that the Star had been there, a case in all forms of this transaction, and never impugned in the slightest degree. The present transaction of the Augusta is of the same character, and yet you are asked to believe that Zulueta & Co. knew that this last transaction was altogether unlawful and to encourage the slave trade, when they had completed a former transaction without any suspicion of any thing illegal in it.

Then he is asked some questions about the nature of the trade, and he says, "I could not say what trade there is at the Gallinas of a legal nature, but I know that those vessels would have taken nothing if there was nothing legal to take, from that place to the Havannah, or to any other place; I am aware that my answers upon this point must be deficient, because I am really very ignorant of the trade of the West Coast of Africa." You are called upon to believe that this is all false, that he knew all about it; and he says—"At this period I am ignorant of it:" and it is not because a man is ignorant that he is to be impeached. He is asked, "Do you suppose that the vessels would be used to carry on a legal trade?—Most certainly I do; because persons find it worth while to send goods there constantly. The Committee will observe, that what the application of the goods is afterwards I cannot say, but I speak of the fact of the vessels having gone there with the intention of returning to the Havannah to bring a cargo of some description here, to pay a freight, and then to go again with the same kind of goods to Africa." Then he is asked about Liverpool; and the Chairman says, "You have stated before, that you have cleared out for the Gallinas from Liverpool?—Yes." "In carrying on operations of that kind, should you have ever thought it necessary to exercise any disguise as to what part of Africa you were clearing out for?—Not at all." Nor did he. "You did not imagine, that in being the instrument of sending lawful goods to any part of Africa you were doing any thing which required concealment?—Nothing at all of the kind; and the proof of that is, that in the bills of entry in Liverpool any body could see our names as consignees of the vessel, and see entries made in our names of every thing."

Now here again is a matter in which the prosecutors might, if they had thought proper, have contradicted this gentleman, and overset the foundation of his case. He says—"True it is that the goods may have been shipped in the name of Captain Jennings, but the whole of the transactions were conducted by our house, and the name of our house appeared in all the documents in Liverpool." It is impossible there should have been any concealment: they might have produced the documents, or official copies of them, from Liverpool, and have shown that the shipment was not in the name of Zulueta & Co., and have contradicted him; they have produced no one document, and you are bound to suppose that it is true; and if it was so done—and there is no doubt of it, though Captain Jennings's name may have been mentioned as the shipper, what becomes of the charge of secrecy, or any thing clandestine? It fades away before you, and vanishes before the truth, as it now appears.

Then he is asked, "Is not there a document officially published daily in London and at Liverpool, stating the daily entries at the Custom-house of all goods shipped, with the description of the goods, and the name of the port and of the shipper?—Yes, there is." "Is not this printed from time to time in the public papers?"—There were on the Committee people connected with Liverpool, and knew every thing about the trade, or they could not have put these questions.—"It is in general circulation; there is hardly any merchant in Liverpool or in London who is not possessed of one. The Liverpool entries are reprinted in London, Liverpool being such an important place of business. The bill printed in London contains also Liverpool, Hull, and Bristol." Then he is asked, "So that every such transaction is perfectly notorious to every one?—Notorious to every one who chooses to read the public papers. There is another thing which escaped me, till I came into the room this morning. As I have been in the business from my childhood, I know every thing that is going on in it." Then he speaks of the Arrogante, but as that has not been made the subject of evidence, I do not trouble you with it. Then he was asked, "whether the Augusta was equipped for the slave trade the second time; the answer was 'She was not.' I wish to state, that before any goods were put on board of her"—he states, that an order was given, which we have evidence was obeyed—"it was our express wish and order that every thing in her that was fit for that trade should be taken down and the vessel put in the same condition as any other merchant vessel; and we should not have loaded any thing in her if that had not been done. It is stated in the evidence that the Augusta was consigned to three notorious slave dealers; now we had never in our lives heard of the name of any one of the parties to whom she was consigned."

Now, Gentlemen, what becomes then of the evidence you had from either of the honourable officers called before you to prove that they, who almost lived upon the coast of Africa, knew that these parties were notorious slave dealers? and yet you are called upon to infer that Mr. Zulueta, who had never been there in his life, knew it himself, notwithstanding this account which he gave when not charged with felony. If he gave it now you might suspect it, but it was a voluntary statement; he need not have gone voluntarily to tell a series of falsehoods, he might have left it uncontradicted; but he is asked with reference to the persons to whom these vessels were consigned, Alvarez, Rolo, and Nimenes, and he says, "neither he, nor any of his house, ever heard of the names before." If it were otherwise it could be proved, and it is not proved. His evidence is used against him, and it is surely but fair to use it as far as it goes for him. You have this young man freely coming forward and stating that, as to these parties to whom the goods were consigned, "I knew very little about it, and as to these people I never heard of any one of them." Then, what becomes of the effect of the evidence of Captain Denman and others, which no doubt they have given truly, as to the nature of the slave trade? This gentleman never having been there and knowing nothing about it, how can you fix this dreadful charge of guilt upon him upon evidence which leaves him entirely untouched upon this important part of the case, and untouched by this part of the evidence given by himself?

There is a good deal more said in the course of the evidence which I do not feel it right to read. I know you must be wearied as I am myself by the exertions it has been my duty to make, and therefore I do not go over the rest of the evidence. The effect of the whole is, that as to these goods having been shipped, and this vessel consigned to the coast of Africa under the circumstances you have heard mentioned, the part that was taken in it by Mr. Zulueta, the prisoner, was but a small part, but as far as it went it was perfectly legal. The question remaining is, whether he participated in the transaction with the object, that is in order to accomplish the object, of the slave trade.

That is the question to be submitted to you. The whole evidence shortly stated is, that Captain Denman and others familiar with the spot knew that the slave trade was carried on there to a very great extent, but the evidence does not show that this unfortunate gentleman, the prisoner, knew any thing of the place or the persons by whom it was carried on, that is a matter of speculation, and the only mode in which the case could be completed so as to induce you to find a verdict of guilty is, by bringing before you the evidence he himself gave upon the subject.

Gentlemen, take that evidence as it is; I am sure you will consider it fairly—consider it altogether; consider that if it had been false in its material parts, it could have been contradicted, and if it be true, as you have every reason to believe it is, what does it prove? It proves that these gentlemen, in trading with Spain and Portugal, and Africa and the Brazils, must trade with persons more or less engaged in the slave trade, and it proves his own solemn declaration, that in this transaction, as in every other in which the house was ever engaged, neither he, nor as far as he knows, his father or grandfather, ever had any participation, direct or indirect, to the most minute particular in this nefarious trade. He does not confine himself to a mere denial; he states facts, and points to other facts as far as concerns his father and the early history of the house; he details the taking of slaves under a bankrupt estate, and liberating them at a time when there were not the same opinions upon the subject which happily exist; he points to those facts as in confirmation of his solemn declaration, that as far as his own knowledge goes, that neither himself, nor to his belief his father, nor his family, nor any member of the house were directly or indirectly concerned in the trade, but endeavoured earnestly, and heartily endeavoured, to discountenance it.

Gentlemen, such is the case before you, and I have only to say in conclusion, not only do these facts appear in evidence before you, but I shall call before you a body of witnesses to the character of this gentleman; I shall call before you some of the most honourable and eminent men in the City of London in all branches of commerce, who have known this gentleman in trade, and in every way; and they will all tell you, Gentlemen, that to their experience and knowledge, according to the language in which they may express themselves, what was told you by one witness in the box before you, that this young man was a good son, a good brother, a good father, and a good and honourable member of society, incapable of wilfully evading or violating the law. Such is the character he has hitherto sustained, such is the character I shall sustain before you, and when I have called those witnesses to establish that character, rare indeed for a man so young, I shall then with confidence, under the Judge's directions, leave this case in your hands, knowing well that when all that is dear in life, and all that which is more dear than life, his honour, is resting upon your verdict; *it will not be upon vague suspicions, not upon doubts, but upon what does not exist here, clear and direct and positive proof of guilt, that you will convict him of that offence, of which he is incapable from his heart's core.*

I shall sit down confidently awaiting your verdict of Not Guilty, which will restore this young man to that high and honourable station, and to that happiness which he has hitherto worthily enjoyed.

EVIDENCE FOR THE PRISONER.

Mr. *James Cook*, sworn. Examined by Mr. *Bodkin*.

Do you reside in London?—Yes.

Are you a colonial-broker?—I am a colonial-broker under the firm of Truman and Cooke.

How long have you known the prisoner at the bar?—From ten to fifteen years.

What character has he borne during the time you have known him?—A very high character: I consider Mr. Zulueta to be one of the most honourable men in the City of London. It falls to my lot to be acquainted with a very large circle of the mercantile community. I am in close connexion with most of the large houses—Messrs. Baring, Messrs. Rothschilds, and houses of that stamp—and if I were put in a position to make any exception as to honour and integrity among the houses I have named, including Mr. Zulueta, the young man at the bar, I should put my finger upon him as the exception, as the most honourable and most straightforward man I ever knew.

Is that the mode in which you have heard him spoken of among mercantile men?—I believe I may say, without exception, it is generally understood to be so.

[*Adjourned.*

THIRD DAY.
MONDAY, 30TH OCTOBER, 1843.

The names of the Jury were called over.—All present.

The Defendant took his place within the Bar.

Alderman Sir *John Pirie*, Bart., sworn. Examined by Mr. *Bodkin*.

I believe you are extensively connected with trade and shipping in the City of London?—Yes.

Do you know the house of Zulueta & Co.?—Perfectly.

And the defendant, who we understand is one of the firm?—I believe so.

How long have you been acquainted with him?—I should think about twelve years.

What character during that time has he borne among those who have known him for veracity and honour as a British merchant?—I have always considered him as one of the most respectable merchants in the City of London; a gentleman very unlikely to give encouragement to this nefarious trade.

Anselmo de Arroyave, Esq., sworn. Examined by Mr. *Clarkson*.

I believe you live in Tavistock Square?—Yes.

Are you a merchant of this City?—Yes.

Extensively engaged in business?—Yes.

Do you know the gentleman who stands behind you, Mr. Pedro de Zulueta?—Yes.

How long have you been acquainted with his firm?—With his firm I have been acquainted about thirty-two years—the firm in Spain.

How long have you known the gentleman who stands at the bar?—I should think about twelve years.

What character has the house, and himself a member of it, borne for the honourable nature of their transactions, their integrity, and their compliance with the laws of this country?—I always heard that they were men of the most correct principle in all dealings; his father and grandfather always bore the best character.

Mr. Justice *Maule*. I understand the gentleman to give him a very high character; I cannot hear the expressions.

Mr. *Clarkson*. Is there a house, in your judgment, in the City of London, which bears a higher character for principle and honour than the house of Zulueta?—It stands second to none.

Thomas Hallifax, Esq. sworn. Examined by Mr. *Clarkson*.

Are you a banker of the firm of Glyn, Mills, & Co.?—I am.

How long have you known the gentleman who stands before you?—The firm have been known to our house, I believe, eighteen or nineteen years; I cannot say the precise time I became acquainted with Mr. Zulueta, but I should say from ten to fifteen years.

Have you had an opportunity of knowing during that time the reputation he bore in the City of London for the honour and integrity of his dealings and conduct?—I believe him to bear the highest possible character; I believe him to be a man of the highest honour, and the most amiable disposition. I have known him as connected with his eminent firm in the City, and also in private, and I have great pleasure in giving to the best of my knowledge the high character he has borne from his amiability and irreproachable conduct.

Samson Ricardo, Esq., sworn. Examined by Mr. *Clarkson*.

Are you a merchant of the City of London?—I am a member of the Stock Exchange.

Are you acquainted with Mr. Pedro de Zulueta?—Very well.

You know the house and the whole of the members?—Yes, perfectly.

Have you had transactions with them?—Yes.

What has been the character and reputation of the gentleman in the dock for honour and integrity in his personal conduct and his mercantile dealings?— The highest possible, and most straightforward: he is quite incapable of engaging in any transactions of a questionable nature.

The Honourable Baron *Lionel de Rothschild*, sworn. Examined by Mr. *Clarkson*.

Are you acquainted with the gentleman who stands in the dock?—Yes.

How long have you known him?—I have known him the best part of twenty years.

What character has he borne for honour and humanity as a man of business?—Most highly honourable as respects personal character, and as respects his firm the best and most straightforward.

Is he a man of humane disposition?—I should think perfectly so, incapable of being connected in any way with the offence charged.

Manuel Gregorio de Isasi, sworn. Examined by Mr. *Clarkson*.

Are you a merchant of this City?—Yes.

Where do you carry on your business?—In Water Lane.

Are you concerned in shipping at all?—No.

What is the business in which you are engaged?—A wine-merchant.

Are you acquainted with Mr. Pedro de Zulueta?—From his childhood.

Did you go to school with him?—Yes.

You knew him before he came to this country?—Yes, quite well, at Cadiz.

You are yourself from Cadiz?—Yes.

Have you had an opportunity of forming an opinion of the character he bears and deserves for integrity and honour, and his feelings of humanity in his personal character?—The highest, and his family at Cadiz. I should say that in every relation of life it is so.

     José Maria Barrero, sworn. Examined by Mr. *Clarkson.*

You are at the head of the consulate of this country from Spain?—I am.

Are you acquainted with Mr. Pedro de Zulueta?—Yes.

Have you known him long and well?—About twenty years.

That is very much the greater part of his life I suppose?—Yes.

What has been his conduct and character in the City of London?—The highest possible.

Are you acquainted with him in his relations in private life, as well as his conduct as a merchant?—Yes.

Have you had an opportunity of knowing whether his character and conduct in private life have been altogether unexceptionable?—Yes.

     Charles Tottie, Esq., sworn. Examined by Mr. *Clarkson.*

Are you a merchant in this country?—Yes.

Are you also at the head of the consulate of Spain?—I am consul for Sweden and Norway.

Do you know Mr. Zulueta and his firm?—Yes.

What have you to say to his Lordship and the Jury respecting his character for integrity and humanity?—I have known Mr. Pedro de Zulueta for upwards of fourteen or sixteen years, and I always considered him of the highest character, and a truly Christian man. His cousins and my sons went to school together.

What has been his character for humanity and veracity?—Oh, very high.

Dr. *Neil Arnott*, sworn. Examined by Mr. *Clarkson*.

Your name is Neil Arnot?—Yes.

You are a physician?—Yes.

Do you know the gentleman who stands by your side?—I have known him from his youth as physician to the family.

Have you had an opportunity of forming a judgment with relation to the character he has borne for honour and integrity as an individual and as a merchant?—From the many opportunities I have had of conversing with him, and knowing him in the character of a physician to his family, I have had an opportunity; also, as physician to most of the Spanish ambassadors; and I have known him as a countryman of theirs.

What character has he borne?—His father spared nothing on his education; it was the best this country could afford.

Is he a man of veracity and humanity?—In all the relations of life, kindred, friendship, and acquaintance, I consider him as standing very high.

Has he always borne the character of a humane, upright, Christian man?—As much as possible.

Charles Dodd, Esq., sworn.

I believe you are a solicitor?—I am.

Where do you live?—In Billiter Street, my house of business.

Are you acquainted with Pedro de Zulueta the prisoner?—I am.

I believe you have known him from his youth?—I have known him for twelve or fourteen years most intimately. I have the highest possible opinion of his honour and his integrity, and his moral and religious character. I have considered it a great blessing that my sons formed a strict intimacy with him, believing him as incapable of committing an offence against the law as it is possible for a man to be.

Christobal de Murrieta, sworn. Examined by Mr. *Clarkson*.

Are you of the firm of Aguirre Solarte and Murrieta, merchants of London?—Yes.

Do you know the gentleman who stands in the dock?—Yes.

How long have you known him?—About eighteen years.

What is the reputation which he has borne for honour, veracity, uprightness of conduct, and humanity, during the whole of the time you have known him?—The highest in both ways.

You mean the highest in all ways?—Yes.

Mr. *Charles Dodd*, Jun., sworn. Examined by Mr. *Clarkson*.

You are the son of the gentleman who has been just examined?—I am.

Have you formerly been at school with the prisoner at the bar?—No, I have not been at school with him; I have known him since the year 1831.

What opinion have you formed as to his character for honour, veracity, and integrity of conduct?—I do not believe a more honourable man exists. I have felt the greatest pleasure in his acquaintance since when I first left school; and when I was forming those acquaintances which would conduct me through life, there is no man whose society I regretted losing more than Pedro de Zulueta's when he left Camberwell.

Hugh Sandeman, Esq., sworn. Examined by Mr. *Clarkson*.

Are you a stock-broker in this City?—Yes.

Do you know Mr. Zulueta?—Yes, perfectly well, for sixteen years.

What opinion have you formed of him during that time?—Of the very highest description, and in all my intercourse with houses in the Royal Exchange, I have never found but the same opinion was expressed by all of him as a private individual, and as a member.

Has his moral and religious character been perfectly unexceptionable—Perfectly so.

William Gibbs, Esq., sworn. Examined by Mr. *Clarkson*.

Are you of the firm of Anthony Gibbs & Son of this City?—I am.

Do you know the house of Zulueta & Co.?—Perfectly well.

And every one of its members?—Perfectly well.

Have you had an opportunity of ascertaining the reputation which Mr. Pedro Zulueta has enjoyed in the City; whether it is an unexceptionable character, morally as well as religiously speaking?—I consider him as entitled to the highest honourable character. I have always heard him so described.

Have his transactions been to your knowledge of that character?—Perfectly; all marked with integrity and honourable conduct.

Timothy Bevington, Esq., solemnly affirmed. Examined by Mr. *Clarkson*.

Are you a member of the Society of Friends?—I am.

The Society has expended much money and labour to put down the traffic to which reference has been made in the course of this trial?—Yes.

Do you know Mr. Pedro Zulueta?—Yes.

How long have you known him?—The last ten years.

What character has he borne during that time?—Excellent.

Do you know the house of which he is a member?—Very well; they have been my next door neighbours for many years.

Regard being had to the nature of the charge against him, what can you say as to his general character for uprightness and honour?—I have been perfectly satisfied in all the transactions I have had with him.

Have you always heard him spoken of as a man of humane and honourable conduct and feelings?—Perfectly so.

William Tindal, Esq., solemnly affirmed. Examined by Mr. *Clarkson*.

You are a member of the Society of Friends?—I am of that persuasion.

Are you a ship-owner of the City of London?—I am.

Do you know Mr. Pedro de Zulueta?—I know him well.

How long have you known him?—I have known the elder Mr. Zulueta for fifty years; the younger one ever since he came over.

During that time have you had opportunities of ascertaining the general character and reputation he has borne in all the relations of life?—Yes.

What can you say to his Lordship and the Jury in those respects?—He has been a very exemplary character, both as a merchant and in moral character in every way.

Do you know a house in the City of London which stands higher than that house?—There is not one; and also they have the same reputation in Cadiz.

For humanity and integrity?—Yes, for humanity and integrity, and in every way as merchants.

Samuel Jones Loyd, Esq., sworn. Examined by Mr. *Clarkson*.

You are a banker in the City of London?—I am.

Do you know the house of Zulueta & Co., of which this gentleman is a partner?—I have no personal knowledge of the gentleman, but I know the house by character.

What character did the house bear in the City of London for general honour?—They have a very high reputation in every respect as mercantile men.

Frederick Huth, Esq., sworn. Examined by Mr. *Bodkin*.

Are you a merchant in the City of London?—I am.

I believe you are one of the Directors of the Bank of England?—My son is.

How long have you known the house of Zulueta & Co.?—For the period of forty years. I have known them forty years.

Are you acquainted with the member of the firm who is unfortunately where he is now?—Perfectly so.

How long have you known him?—For twelve years.

As to individual character, how can you speak of him during the time you have known him with regard to integrity and humanity?—I cannot better describe him than that I know of no man in the City of London or any where else, a merchant, of whom I should give a higher character.

Have you ever heard a suggestion against his character as an individual, or against his regularity as a merchant?—Nothing whatever.

Abraham Mocatta, Esq., sworn. Examined by Mr. *Bodkin*.

Are you one of the firm of Mocatta and Goldsmid?—I am.

You are bullion dealers in the City of London I believe?—Bullion merchants.

How long have you known Mr. Pedro de Zulueta?—I have known him about sixteen years.

Have you also known the firm of which he is a member?—Yes, I have known them for that time or longer.

Have you any knowledge of their transactions in the City, the reputation they bear?—I have always understood them to bear the highest character that I have known as gentlemen of character. I have known the gentleman as a neighbour of mine for several years. He was in the habit of visiting our family, and we have the highest opinion of him; he was considered particularly humane and considerate of the wants of others.

Edwin Gower, Esq., sworn. Examined by Mr. *Bodkin*.

Are you of the firm of Gower & Co.?—I am.

Merchants in this City?—Yes.

How long have you known Mr. Zulueta.—I have known him ever since he has been connected with the City of London, he and his senior.

And his family I suppose before him?—Yes.

What reputation has he enjoyed during the time you have known him, and his family, and the house as a mercantile firm?—I should say, as our connexions and theirs are very similar, we have almost daily more or less intercourse with him, and I never heard the most distant rumour against his character; I believe it to be quite unimpeachable: and the house, as a house of business, stands as high as any house in the City of London.

George Rougemont, Esq., sworn. Examined by Mr. *Bodkin.*

Are you a merchant in the City?—I am.

How long have you known Mr. Pedro de Zulueta?—I have known the house for a great number of years, and always heard it spoken of in the highest terms. Mr. Pedro de Zulueta I have been acquainted with and visited him perhaps six or eight years, and I have had frequent opportunities of seeing his conduct as a son, as a husband, as a father, and as a neighbour, and have always found it in the highest degree unexceptionable in every respect. I consider him an amiable and kind-hearted man, and quite incapable of any thing of the kind laid to his charge.

Joseph Sadler, Esq., sworn. Examined by Mr. *Bodkin.*

Are you a merchant?—I am.

In the City of London?—Yes, Sadler, Harris, & Co. is my firm.

How long have you known Mr. Pedro de Zulueta?—I have known him ten or twelve years.

What character has he appeared to bear as a man of integrity and humanity?—The very first character; I should say he is the last man I have known that I consider would be guilty of that which is charged.

F. I. Vanzeller, Esq., sworn. Examined by Mr. *Clarkson.*

You are the Portuguese consul I believe?—I am.

Do you know the house of Zulueta & Co.?—I have known it well.

Do you know Mr. Pedro de Zulueta?—I have known Mr. Pedro de Zulueta for ten years.

What character can you give of him, as a general character, to the Jury for humanity, integrity, and good conduct of every description?—The very highest character possible.

Is that the reputation which the house of which he is a member has borne in the city of London?—Certainly.

SUMMING UP.

Mr. Justice *Maule*. Gentlemen of the Jury—Pedro de Zulueta is indicted for an offence against an Act of Parliament made for the prevention of the slave trade, for employing a vessel for the purpose of accomplishing objects declared to be illegal by that Act; that is to say, dealing in slaves, and also having loaded goods on board a vessel for that purpose.

Now, although this case has occupied a very considerable portion of time, I do not think it will be necessary for me to add much to it in the observations I shall think it necessary to make to you with respect to the evidence. It is not very long, and the points to which it goes are not very numerous—I mean the evidence on the substance of the charge. The case occupied about fifteen hours on Friday and Saturday, but the evidence did not occupy much above four hours. It will not be necessary for me to occupy much time in observations upon it, and I should think it will not be necessary for me to read over the evidence.

The offence, as I have told you, is put in these two shapes—the employing a vessel, and the loading goods for a purpose prohibited by the statute; that is, for the purpose of dealing in slaves. The charge is not, it does not necessarily import, nor is it necessary to support it, that it should be proved that the ship in question, the Augusta, was intended to be used for the conveyance of slaves from the coast of Africa. If there was a slave adventure—if there was an adventure of which the object was that slaves should be brought from the coast of Africa, that there should be slave trading there, and if this vessel was dispatched and employed for the purpose of accomplishing that object, although it was intended to accomplish that object otherwise than by bringing home the slaves in that vessel, that is within the Act of Parliament. So, if the goods were loaded for the purpose of accomplishing the slave trade—whether it was intended to bring back the slaves in the vessel in question, or that they should be brought away in some other vessel, or whether that was a matter left undecided at the commencement of the adventure, and to be determined according as matters might turn out to be convenient for the accomplishment of it—in any of these cases the crime charged in this indictment would be committed, the allegations in the indictment would be supported, and the prohibition of the

Act of Parliament would be violated. The Act would have been very imperfect indeed, if it had prohibited slave trading and had not prevented any dealing of that description, except where the same vessel was to bring home the slaves; if, at all events, it went out for the purpose of carrying goods which were to be bartered for them. From one of the witnesses, who, in the course of his public duty was conversant with what takes place on this slave coast of Africa, we hear that it frequently happens that the slaves are got away by a different vessel from that which carries out the goods which formed the fund for their purchase. That is the nature of the offence.

Gentlemen, I do not think there will be any great difficulty in some of the preliminary questions you will have to decide upon this occasion. One is, whether the prisoner at the bar did at all dispatch, did at all employ this vessel, the Augusta, or did at all load any goods on board; because, though a person may employ a vessel and load goods—he may do that quite innocently—the fact, that he employed a vessel and loaded goods, is by no means conclusive of his guilt till you go further and show that he did it for the illegal purpose charged in the indictment. If it had not been shown that the prisoner at the bar did employ the vessel, or load the goods, the inquiry would have been stopped; for the purpose never could have been brought in question, and there would have been an end, or rather there would have been no beginning of this enquiry: but with respect to that branch of the case, there appears to have been no doubt made on the part of the prisoner that he did employ this vessel. He says he did it as the agent of Pedro Martinez & Co., and that he did it without knowing what the purpose was for which the vessel was employed, or whether it was employed in the slave trade; and that he did load the goods on board the ship—and there appears to be to the value of a good many thousand pounds, a considerable cargo (the value I get only from the cockets), a considerable quantity of goods. The vessel undoubtedly was dispatched with the knowledge of the prisoner and through his agency to carry goods to the coast of Africa. So much does not seem to be a matter in dispute.

Then the matters in dispute are two—one, whether this vessel was dispatched for the purpose of slave trading at all; if it was not, there is an end of all question. If it appears that there was no slave trading, or intention of slave trading, no person is guilty of the violation of the law charged in this indictment. There is no offence on the part of any one, if a slave adventure was not contemplated by the persons engaged in this transaction. Unless you decide that question in the affirmative, that is to say, unless you think there was such an adventure, there is no case made at all against the prisoner at the bar. It has been contended, and strenuously—not in a separate form, but mixed up with the other point in the case to which I will next draw your attention—it has been contended on the part of the prisoner, that there was no slave adventure, that the ship Augusta went to the Gallinas loaded in this way not for the purpose of dealing in slaves, or for any unlawful purpose, but that she went either for some lawful purpose, or else without any purpose of dealing at all: you will say whether there could be any such possibility. It has been contended that at any rate the ship did not go for the purpose of slave trading. If you are of opinion there was no slave trading contemplated, that that was not the object of the voyage, there is an end of that question; but, supposing you should think there was slave dealing intended, and the vessel went out for the purpose of slave dealing, then there is another important question—and that is the object of the evidence to character— whether, supposing there was a slave trading intended, the prisoner was cognizant of it?

It appears from the evidence, that the Gallinas is a place described by some witnesses of great experience—two captains in the navy, and Colonel Nichol, who was the governor of a district in the neighbourhood, whose employment was mainly to watch the slave coast of which the Gallinas forms a part, and to contribute to the putting down the slave trade—that the Gallinas is a place of slave trading, and of no other trade at all. It seems that the Gallinas is a river navigable for vessels of some size about twelve miles, that there were some barracoons for slaves which were destroyed by Captain Denman— destroyed, as it is alleged, by Captain Denman some time ago—there being about six establishments called barracoons, which seem to be very large buildings in which five or six hundred negroes may be confined, and are confined when brought from the country till they can be exported in vessels carrying on this trade. These barracoons have, by way of appendages to them, store-houses for the various stores that may be wanted for those negroes, and also some places of residence for the Europeans, who appear to be some thirty in number, who live there; there is nobody else living there, except that there are two or three negro villages or towns, not places of any trade, but inhabited by those uncivilised savages. The country produces nothing, and exports nothing but slaves—that is the description of the place given by that gentleman. It is said, and I think with great probability, that the Gallinas is not generally known as a slave trading place, in fact, it seems very little known at all; it seems to be a place where any other description of felons may resort to concert their schemes and hide their stolen goods, and which, of course, they do not make public, and which is not likely to be known by honest and true people. Except those employed as police or otherwise in aid of justice, as these captains were, of course it would not be spoken of at all. There might be slave traders in London knowing it very well, but they would be perfectly silent probably, and hardly mention it by name even in speaking one to another. It is very probable, therefore, that the place was not very well known; that when these persons spoke of the Gallinas, they might say the Gallinas on the coast of Africa; and a person might be very conversant with the geography of Africa in an honest way, who had not been active in putting down the slave trade, and yet might not know where it was, except that it was on the coast of Africa. It is important to show not only that it is on the coast of Africa, but that it is itself a slave trading place; and that fact appears to be very evident from the case on the part of the prosecution. Probably those honest persons, those honestly dealing persons who know best about it, are those who have been called upon by their public duty to ascertain it. Such persons have been called, and they give it this character and description, and they state that it is distinguished from other parts of the coast of Africa; for on other parts of that coast it is said slaves are sold as one article of export, but that other things, such as palm oil—I believe that is the principle thing—and ivory, and wood, and other things, are sold in immense quantities on the coast of Africa; but that that is not the case at the Gallinas. They might be carrying out goods to other parts of Africa, intending to bring home palm-oil or slaves, as might be most profitable; they might intend to bring home an honest commodity, and not have to do with this dishonest and perilous commodity; but it appears difficult to conceive what a person carrying a cargo of goods to the Gallinas could intend to do with it, unless he intended to have those goods employed in the slave trade. The prisoner might say they were to be employed by others in the slave trade; that would be plain and simple: it is wrong, but it is a plain and simple account of that which was intended to be done. It is a place, as it appears, without any trade; and if there be an obvious plain interest in a person carrying goods to that place, it appears to me that it may be taken that they were for the purpose of the slave trade. If that be the plain and obvious inference, it appears to me that might be the inference very properly drawn by Colonel Nichol, that this was a slave adventure, unless the contrary were proved.

It is possible that this might be an adventure, not slave trading; if so, nothing can be more simple than to prove it; Martinez & Co. might prove that it is an honest adventure. If it was a dishonest adventure, it could not be expected that Martinez & Co. should be called to give evidence at all; but if it were an innocent adventure it would be very easy for them to be called. It is true that persons are to be convicted, not by evidence they did not produce, but by evidence produced against them; not on suspicion, but on conviction; but where such evidence is offered of the trade being slave trading, as is offered here, namely, that the vessel was loaded with goods, that a cargo of goods was dispatched to a place where slave trading is the only known object for which vessels ever go, a slave mart and nothing but a slave mart, you have a case, though it is an answerable case; but if the answer, which if it exist could be easily given, is not given, it may very fairly be inferred that the vessel was proceeding on a slaving voyage, a voyage either for the purpose of bringing home slaves, or of landing those goods for the purchase of slaves. That, Gentlemen, is the first question you have to consider. You will say whether, considering the nature of this charge, and considering that the vessel is chartered to go from this place to the Gallinas, that being the place and the only place mentioned in the charter-party for the outward voyage, she might have been subsequently employed in voyages to the West Indies or Madeira, at the discretion of the charterers; but it will be for you to say whether, in your judgment, in your opinion, on this occasion the vessel did not sail for the purpose of her being employed, or the goods on board her being employed, for the trading in slaves. If you are not satisfied of that, it will be your duty to give a verdict of not guilty. You need not trouble yourselves to go further, but the prisoner must be acquitted.

Gentlemen, I have not read over to you the evidence which establishes these facts I have mentioned to you, namely, that the vessel was chartered. You have heard the charter-party, and you have heard what Mr. Zulueta says in his evidence, that he did dispatch the vessel, and that the house were the agents in sending the vessel abroad, and in putting the goods on board; and you have heard the remainder of the evidence. I suppose I need not read the evidence which the captains gave at such great length.

Foreman of the Jury. No, my Lord.

Mr. Justice *Maule.* These are facts not disputed, except that it is disputed that the vessel went out for the purpose of slave trading—that is an inference to be drawn or not from the evidence.

Then the next question, and an important question is, whether the prisoner at the bar, Pedro de Zulueta, is a person who was cognizant of that fact. It certainly is a very grave and serious charge, and one of a very highly penal nature. It is, however, a trade, which till a recent period was lawful for persons in this country, and many persons of very good character certainly did engage in that trade, and a great number of persons justified it. I suppose those same persons would now say it is not to be engaged in, because it is a prohibited thing—it is a regulation of trade enforced by very severe penalties made by this country—but that the dealing in slaves is in itself a lawful, right, good, and proper thing, which ought not to be prohibited. Those persons would now consider slave trading as a thing prohibited only by positive regulation. There is no one who does not at once perceive that practical distinction between them. There is no person who, in point of feeling and opinion, does not perceive the difference there is between a thing which is prohibited by positive law, and that kind of thing, against which, if there were no law at all against it, the plain natural sense and conscience of mankind would revolt. This trading in slaves, in the opinion of a great many persons, is itself an abomination, a thing which ought to be considered with the greatest horror, whether prohibited or not; but those who think it was right when it was not prohibited, probably do not think it so very bad if it be committed now, since it has been prohibited by law, only that it is to be avoided on account of the penalty to which it subjects the individuals engaged in it.

This has some bearing on the question of how far considerations of character would have weight with respect to such an offence; but it is necessary undoubtedly on the part of the prosecution that there should be a case made of knowledge on the part of the prisoner, of the purpose for which this adventure was meant. Now, with respect to that, it is taken partly from what he says before the Committee of the House of Commons, and partly what is given in evidence here, that the house of Zulueta & Co., (of which the prisoner appears to be an active member, and with the whole proceedings of which in this matter he appears certainly according to the statement he himself made to the Committee of the House of Commons to have been quite conversant)—and it is admitted that the house of Zulueta were the doers in this country of whatever was done with respect to this vessel, the Augusta—the Augusta had been called the Gollupchik, had been captured as a slaving vessel, and she was then fitted up with the apparatus fitted to that traffic; she was brought to this country and proceeded against, and ultimately sold, whether sold under a condemnation which turned out effectual or not does not distinctly appear. Some one has said that the Russian Government claimed her, and she was given up to the Russian Government. It appears, however, that she was sold at Portsmouth; I think she was sold to Mr. Emanuel, or some person for whom he acted, for 600*l*., and the expenses, which were about 30*l*. Then she was bought with money furnished by Zulueta & Co., the amount being 650*l*.—it does not exactly appear by whom—according to the testimony one would say, bought by Jennings, who was employed as captain on the voyage in question, a letter having been previously written by the prisoner's house, stating to Jennings that they could not give more than 500*l*., but it appears that ultimately 660*l*. was paid for her. On the occasion on which that money was paid, the witness says, "I sold her to Jennings and Bernardos; Bernardos came with Jennings—they came together and paid the money." Now, probably you must not take that quite to the letter. This was a ship sold, not by means of a written instrument as the subject of a British registry, but as any other British chattel might be sold, such and such a bale of goods, merely by agreement altogether verbally, that one should have the goods and the other the money, the article being handed over when it was so sold. All that the seller cares for is, that he shall have his money. Whether there are one or a dozen persons present he may very properly, as a matter of business, leave it to them whether one or all of them is to pay the money. The witness who is called, Mr. Emanuel, seems to have thought that Bernardos and the other bought the vessel; but it seems, according to the charter-party, that the other party, Jennings, is the only purchaser. According to a representation I think made at the bar by Mr.

Kelly, the real purchasers were Pedro Martinez & Co., who wanted Jennings for some purpose to appear as colourable owner, and wanted Jennings to command the vessel. An Englishman could not by the laws of Spain command a Spanish owned vessel, and Jennings therefore, if he was to command her, should be apparently made the owner of her, and that is the reason suggested why Jennings was made the owner (if he was the owner) by the desire of Pedro Martinez & Co.

At the end of the charter-party there is a recital, that whereas the owner, Jennings, is indebted to the charterer in a certain sum of money, as appears by an acknowledgment elsewhere, he consents that the earnings of the vessel shall be a lien for the money. Now that refers you see to another document, which other document, if we had it, would throw some light upon the transaction, but it is not called for or produced. The circumstance of Jennings being the commander, and made owner for the purpose of being the commander in apparent consistency with the law of Spain, may account for that which has been put very powerfully on the part of the prisoner as having been inexplicable on the supposition that any slave trade was intended; for, they say, if the slave trade was intended, why not have a Spanish captain; because then, though perhaps within the terms of the treaties there might be a power of search on the part of British cruizers, no power was given by foreigners which was not watched by those who gave that power, and such power might be exceeded by those who exercised it, who were not lawyers or special pleaders; and it is said it would be much more convenient in case of search to have that difficulty thrown in the way than the total absence of all difficulty which exists when a ship professes to be British owned. But if Jennings was an adventurer, if he were, as suggested, a very clever and intelligent person, and very conversant with every thing to be done on this occasion, a competent master of the vessel, supposing the slave trade to be intended, a thing which requires qualities one is sorry to see exercised so ill— a great deal of courage, sagacity, and presence of mind, and an unscrupulous readiness to employ them for the commission of this felony, not to be found in every body—a man of such a description would be the paramount object of a slave trader, whose aim would be, whoever the owner may be, to elude all search, so to manage the thing as that the cruizers of any country shall not stop him. Probably, if the adventure succeeds, it must succeed by such means; so that one sees a perfectly good reason why, consistently with this being a slave trading voyage, it may have been English owned.

The sale is negotiated in the first instance by Zulueta & Co.; they say they do it for Martinez. The vessel was bought by Bernardos or Jennings. I do not know whether I called your attention to that, that Bernardos was the man who commanded the vessel on an undoubted slave voyage when she was seized and brought into Portsmouth. Whether Pedro Martinez or the captain bought the ship, or however it was bought, that transaction appears to have been managed by Zulueta & Co., and through the intervention of Jennings.

Then there comes the transaction of chartering. The vessel was chartered subject to this proviso at the end of it, and the charter-party is negotiated entirely by Zulueta. Whatever Pedro Martinez & Co., supposing there were such persons (and it may be taken that there were such persons, though the evidence of there being such persons is, that Mr. Zulueta says so in his evidence before the Committee of the House of Commons, and it is a fact the negative of which could easily have been proved, but it has not been proved); you may fairly assume, therefore, that there are such persons as Pedro Martinez & Co., for that observation of the learned counsel for the prisoner on the statement of Mr. Zulueta before the Committee is as far as it applies to that particular part of the evidence well founded, namely, that if it were not true the contrary might be proved; but that is not true in the generality to which Mr. Kelly applied it, for there might be a great many statements in that evidence before the Committee of the House of Commons which were not true, but which the prosecutor would not be allowed to prove were not true—I mean those not connected with this particular transaction. There are many things stated in that evidence, which I apprehend, if false, the prosecutor would not be entitled to prove the falsehood of; but I apprehend that does not apply to the existence of Pedro Martinez & Co. But they appear to have existed and to have employed as their agents in this country Pedro Zulueta & Co., and whatever is done in this country by Pedro Martinez is done by Pedro Zulueta & Co. just as much as if they had done it themselves; they knew as much about the matter as the parties themselves; they negotiated this charter-party, and they dispatched the vessel and put on board all the goods. The goods appear by the cockets to have been entered in the name of Captain Jennings; I do not know that that is a circumstance of any suspicion; it is not proved to be out of the way, and I do not see any good reason for suspecting the integrity of the transaction arising out of that particular circumstance. It seems to me, therefore, that Zulueta & Co. do stand in a very different situation from that put a considerable number of times to you by the learned counsel for the prisoner, namely, the situation of a person who is simply the manufacturer or dealer in goods, and who has those goods ordered, such a weight of gunpowder, and who inquiring, "Where shall I send it?" is answered, "Send it on board the Augusta, now lying at Liverpool." It would be a strong thing from that circumstance to infer that a person sending that gunpowder had any thing to do with slave trading: but that appears not to be the nature of this transaction. In regard to there being a slave trading, all that is done, is done by Zulueta & Co. It is not merely that they had goods sent on board the ship, but they chose the number of the goods to be sent on board the ship—goods which they had bought, for which they had negotiated, and they made out such charter-party, and that charter-party provides that the ship shall proceed to Gallinas, on the coast of Africa.

Gentlemen, that is I think pretty nearly all the evidence that there is in the case. You have the evidence of the captains on the subject. If you think that this was a slaving voyage, you will consider the conduct of Zulueta & Co. in buying, and chartering, and loading it, and dispatching it. Now, Zulueta & Co. are shown to be merchants with very extensive connexions and concerns, and the prisoner particularly is a person of great knowledge and education, and generally speaking one would say that as merchants, though that is a matter for you to consider, I do not know that I can put it higher than this, that they are persons of great skill and great experience. The prisoner had the whole management and direction of the voyage to a particular place to carry goods to that place, that being a place not without suspicion; the vessel itself also being a vessel which had been used for the slave trade, though it might be innocently used afterwards; but, still your attention has been directed to that circumstance, and it has been particularly directed to the circumstance that every thing applicable to slave apparatus was ordered to be removed before the vessel was dispatched. That would be a thing of course to be done, whether the vessel was going on a slave expedition or not, for as has been suggested, the officers of Government always examine a vessel, particularly on going to the coast of Africa. With a view to this, I should think it would be quite a matter of course, even if the vessel was intended to be sent to promote the slave trade, that she should not go out with shackles or leagers, or any thing of that kind on board, for if they are on board, the vessel would be at the mercy of any Custom-house officer; it would be quite advertising the adventure. And there being found these shackles and these leagers on board the vessel at Portsmouth, and their being so dealt with, I do not think at all helps on the case for the prosecution, for the vessel undoubtedly had been a slave vessel, it had been fitted up with these things, and would naturally have them on board her, and as naturally, whether she was intended to be sent out on a slave expedition or not, these things would be taken from on board her; and you find that they were taken from on board. The fact of their having been on board, when the schoolmaster and the cooper saw them on board, does not appear to me to be any thing against her, for she had been a slave vessel. On the other hand, the circumstance of their being taken out and landed before she sailed on her voyage does not appear to be any thing for her, for both these circumstances would have taken place whether the voyage was an innocent or a guilty voyage; those circumstances, in my opinion, have no bearing on the question. Whether the vessel was intended to be engaged in slave trading or not, that is a point I have already put to you in considering whether the voyage was a slave voyage, or for the accomplishment of the slave trade. I did not before advert to the circumstance of these things being on board, and I mention it now only, as it has a sort of colourable look, to show why it is I do not lay any stress upon it.

I was observing that though people in general might not be well aware of this trade being intended to be carried on, yet persons not extremely simple, but skilful people, may be fairly taken to know what the object is with which a voyage is undertaken when they themselves are the agents, supplying, chartering, loading, and dispatching a ship for the voyage. It may be that the object may be concealed from them, or that they may not know that this voyage to the Gallinas was a slaving expedition. A simple person, who knew nothing about these matters and had not some special acquaintance with the trade, might know nothing at all about it, they might not know the nature of the trade carried on at this place. The mention of Gallinas on the coast of Africa would not convey to the mind of an ordinary person that it was to a mere den where this traffic and nothing else was carried on; but this vessel is sent to the Gallinas by these gentlemen, who are very skilful persons, who negotiate the whole transaction. Now, it may very generally be taken that people know what they are about, unless they can show there was some particular concealment, some hinderance to their knowing to this extent that this was a place connected with the slave trade, and so exclusively engaged in the slave trade as it really seems to be; but, supposing that a case is made which requires an answer, if it is shown that there was a slave trade, and that a person did employ a vessel in that business, and did load it for that business, that certainly is a case raising some degree of presumption against the person who has been engaged, and one would be very glad if the case were of a description in which it had been met by a decisive answer in point of fact.

It is said on the part of the prisoner, first, that this was not a slaving voyage. Now, if it had been a slaving voyage—it is possible that there might be a case, which unless fairly answered would lead to the presumption that that was the object—in which an answer might exist, but where it would be impossible for the prisoner to get it, you would feel a difficulty in acting on such a case; but in the present case, supposing that this was not a slaving expedition, the answer exists, and the answer might be given with the greatest ease. There appears to me no reason why it should not be given. The house of Martinez & Co. have a house at Cadiz, and a house at the Havannah, and if they did not send this vessel for the purpose of the slave trade, and they were quite innocent in this matter, any one of them or their clerks might with the greatest ease be called. There is no deficiency of funds here, and it would put an end to all question if they could say, "This was not for the slave trade; these goods were to be employed for—and then they might fill up the blank, I do not know how, but by some words expressing an innocent purpose, and that would be a full answer; but there is an absence of all answer that bears on the question whether there was slave trading intended or not.

Now, supposing you should be of opinion that there was no slave trading intended, there is an end of the case. I think you may perhaps be of opinion this vessel was intended for slave trading. Supposing you are of that opinion, then you come to that which is the anxious and important question, namely, whether the prisoner was cognizant of that fact. It is alleged that the prisoner is not the exclusive manager of the concerns of the house; it is not very likely he should be; he appears to have been fully cognizant of this particular matter; and, supposing that considering the exclusive part taken by these gentlemen in this transaction of dispatching the vessel, supposing you should think that a case requiring an answer, then you will consider whether it should not have an answer, if one exists. Now, it appears that the prisoner is not exclusively cognizant of all the transactions of this house. There are two other partners; there are—though it is not in evidence, but it may be presumed that there are—clerks and persons employed in the house of Zulueta, all or any of whom might have been called. It is alleged that the profit on this transaction would be extremely small. I do not think that the petty gain of this one transaction is the matter, for it appears that Pedro Martinez & Co. do a great deal of business, and it is possible that whenever persons have a large and valuable business to conduct, there is some small portion that the correspondent and agent would willingly get rid of if he could; but he is not allowed to pick and choose, but he must take the whole. That is one of the grounds they put; the other is as to character.

Now, inasmuch as there are two other partners, and it is probable there might be some other persons in the concern, there arises this consideration. It is true, supposing that there were a case made, but that the prisoner was innocent of it, that he could not call Martinez & Co. on that supposition as he might on the supposition of there being no slave trading, for Martinez & Co. would not be innocent persons, and they would not be willing to come into this country and say, "We carried on the slave trading, but it was disguised from our correspondent Zulueta & Co." If you think there is a case requiring an answer, the question then is, would there have been any difficulty in the prisoner calling his two partners and others conversant with the business of the firm, and proving that Zulueta & Co. knew nothing at all about this, that they had not the least suspicion, that Martinez & Co. never communicated the fact to them, and that the illegal purpose was utterly unknown to them, for some reasons which the prisoner cannot give, but which his partners could? It would be extremely desirable they should do it, if the defence existed in point of fact.

Supposing the case made to require an answer, there are two modes of answering a charge. The one is, that of calling a great number of persons to prove that it was unlikely, from the high character of the firm, that they should engage in such a transaction; that is one. Another mode, is calling three or four persons, who if he were guilty must know it, and who will prove that he was not. The former of these modes has been adopted on this occasion. You have, however, the case before you. I do not think it necessary to go any further into the evidence, having, I conceive, stated the effect of it sufficiently. If you are satisfied that there was a slave trading, you will consider whether Zulueta, the prisoner, was cognizant of it, and shipped these goods, and dispatched the ship for the purpose of accomplishing the object of slave trading; and then, in considering that, you will consider the observations, as far as they are entitled to attention, and the evidence of the very high character of the prisoner—a character I should say very strong indeed, and almost conclusive, supposing the case were one that did not admit of an answer in point of fact. If he has the means of showing that he did not do that with which he is charged, and he only says, I will prove that I am extremely unlikely to do it; I do not say how far you should give weight to that sort of evidence. You ought to be well satisfied of a fact of this sort, before you find him guilty of such a charge as this.

Foreman of the Jury. We beg to retire, my Lord.

A Juryman. May we find on any particular count?

Mr. Justice *Maule.* You will consider the charge as that of employing a vessel, or loading goods on board, for the purpose of accomplishing the slave trade. The great question is, the knowledge and intention of the prisoner. If the thing was done with his knowledge and intention, and it was for the purpose of slave trading, there is no doubt that he bought and dispatched the ship, and loaded the goods. I do not see why you should trouble yourselves with any particular count.

[*The Jury withdrew at Twenty Minutes before Twelve, and returned into Court at Ten Minutes after One, finding a verdict of* "NOT GUILTY."

Mr. Serjeant *Bompas.* My Lord, there is another indictment against the prisoner for a misdemeanour. It appears to me that it involves necessarily the very same question, and therefore, as far as I can judge of it, and of course with the authority of the prosecutor, I feel that it would be wrong to put the prisoner again on his trial for that offence. It seems to me that it will depend upon the same evidence, and I cannot but conclude that the Jury will come to the same conclusion. I will take the opportunity of saying one word. Observations having been made with respect to myself when the former case was going on, when I could not interfere, I can merely say, that with regard to myself, the prosecutor, and of every person connected with the prosecution, there was no possible fact or document which I could have admitted, which could have done the prisoner the slightest benefit.

Mr. Justice *Maule*. That observation was made in Mr. Kelly's address.

Mr. Serjeant *Bompas*. It was impossible we could have any view but that the Jury should have the whole before them, and we rejoice in the result.

Mr. *Kelly*. With regard to what has fallen from my learned friend, Mr. Serjeant Bompas, I am greatly obliged to my learned friend for making that observation to his Lordship. As far as respects that part of what has fallen from my learned friend, which respected the other indictment, it will be desirable in the course of the present session—I do not say to-day or to-morrow—but in the course of the present session, to empannel a Jury, and that the prisoner, Mr. Zulueta, should be acquitted in respect of that indictment. With regard to the other observation which has fallen from my learned friend, I beg to assure him, which I do with the utmost possible sincerity, that I never intended to say any thing which could be construed in the slightest degree as disrespectful to him. There is no gentleman at the bar less deserving of any disrespectful observation than my learned friend.

Mr. Serjeant *Bompas*. Your observations were made in public, and therefore I felt it necessary to say what I did. Your Lordship will order the expenses to be paid?

Mr. Justice *Maule*. Certainly: I think that it was a very proper case for inquiry. The most convenient course will be just to swear the Jury in the second case, and take a verdict.

Mr. Serjeant *Bompas*. If the Jury have no objection.

The Jury were sworn to try the Indictment for Conspiracy.

(The Jury were charged with the Prisoner in the usual way.)

Mr. Serjeant *Bompas*. Gentlemen, you have heard what I stated to the learned Judges. The case has been already before you, and I am quite satisfied with your decision; you will, therefore, find the prisoner Not Guilty.

*The Jury immediately pronounced the Prisoner "*NOT GUILTY.*"*

Milton Keynes UK
Ingram Content Group UK Ltd.
UKHW040834071024
449371UK00007B/793